DATE DUE

THE BABYLONIAN GILGAMESH EPIC

THE BABYLONIAN GILGAMESH EPIC

INTRODUCTION, CRITICAL EDITION AND CUNEIFORM TEXTS

Volume II

A. R. George

OXFORD
UNIVERSITY PRESS

OXFORD
UNIVERSITY PRESS

Great Clarendon Street, Oxford OX2 6DP

Oxford University Press is a department of the University of Oxford.
It furthers the University's objective of excellence in research, scholarship,
and education by publishing worldwide in

Oxford New York

Auckland Bangkok Buenos Aires Cape Town Chennai
Dar es Salaam Delhi Hong Kong Istanbul Karachi Kolkata
Kuala Lumpur Madrid Melbourne Mexico City Mumbai Nairobi
São Paulo Shanghai Taipei Tokyo Toronto

Oxford is a registered trade mark of Oxford University Press
in the UK and certain other countries

Published in the United States
by Oxford University Press Inc., New York

First published 2003

British Library Cataloguing in Publication Data
Data available

Library of Congress Cataloging in Publication Data
Data available

ISBN 0–19–927842–3
Set ISBN 0–19–814922–0

3 5 7 9 10 8 6 4

Typeset by SNP Best-set Typesetter Ltd., Hong Kong
Printed in Great Britain
on acid-free paper by
Antony Rowe Ltd.,
Chippenham, Wiltshire

CONTENTS

VOLUME II

12

Bilgames and the Netherworld 172–End

The text of the Sumerian poem of Bilgames and the Netherworld (BN), known in ancient times as u_4.ri.a u_4.sù.rá.ri.a, 'In those days, in those far-off days', has been presented in a variorum edition by Aaron Shaffer.[1] Nearly forty years have elapsed since then, and further publications have advanced our knowledge of the composition considerably. The cuneiform text of Shaffer's MS Q, Ni 9744, was published in *ISET* II pl. 53, while copies of MSS g, r, t and U 16878 appeared as *UET* VI nos. 55–8. The Jena source, MS V, has been supplemented by new joins.[2] Additional manuscripts in Istanbul, London and Baghdad have become available in cuneiform over the years: *ISET* I pl. 199 Ni 9847, *ISET* II pl. 51 Ni 9626, *CT* 58 no. 54 and Cavigneaux, *Uruk* (AUWE 23) no. 98. The two tablets from Mê-Turan announced in 1993[3] have since been published alongside editions of *UET* VI nos. 59 and 60 from Ur;[4] the latter is a manuscript that continues the poem after the place where it ends in the scribal traditions of Nippur and Mê-Turan.[5] Further pieces from Nippur have been identified in Philadelphia, Chicago and Baghdad, especially during the cataloguing of the 3N-T collections from Area TA.[6] Two fragments cut down from a single tablet of unknown provenance are now in the Schøyen Collection awaiting definitive publication (Fig. 15).[7] A tablet from Isin is also still to be published, as are further pieces from Ur.[8]

That this composition was some sort of counterpart to Tablet XII of the Standard Babylonian epic was first seen by C. J. Gadd in publishing Shaffer's MS r.[9] In due course, as the Sumerian poem became better known through the efforts of Samuel Noah Kramer and others, the history of the text became clearer. The latter half of Bilgames and the

[1] A. Shaffer, 'Sumerian Sources of Tablet XII of the Epic of Gilgameš', PhD thesis (Pennsylvania, 1963), distributed by University Microfilms, Ann Arbor (63-7085). On the text in general see further the relevant section of Ch. 1 above.

[2] Wilcke, *Kollationen*, pp. 19–21.

[3] A. Cavigneaux and F. Al-Rawi, 'New Sumerian literary texts from Tell Haddad (ancient Meturan): a first survey', *Iraq* 55 (1993), pp. 93–5.

[4] Eid., 'La fin de Gilgameš, Enkidu et les Enfers d'après les manuscrits d'Ur et de Meturan', *Iraq* 62 (2000), pp. 1–19.

[5] First revealed as such by Tournay and Shaffer, *L'épopée de Gilgameš*, pp. 272–4.

[6] See J. W. Heimerdinger, *Sumerian Literary Fragments from Nippur* (Philadelphia, 1979), p. 25. Previously unpublished tablets in the University Museum, Philadelphia, are quoted here by permission of Professors S. Tinney and E. Leichty, curators of the Babylonian Section.

[7] I am grateful to M. Civil for allowing full quotation of them here, and to Mr M. Schøyen for permission to reproduce my photographs of them.

[8] See C. B. F. Walker and C. Wilcke, 'Preliminary report of the inscriptions', *Isin* II, p. 92, D 1: IB 930.

[9] C. J. Gadd, 'The Epic of Gilgameš, Tablet XII', *RA* 30 (1933), pp. 127–43.

FIG. 15. The two fragments of BN MS rr, rr_2 = SC 3361 (*top*) and rr_1 = SC 2887 (*bottom*). SC 3361: height 5.7 cm, breadth 9.0 cm, thickness 2.5 cm; SC 2887: height 11.2 cm, breadth 8.4 cm, thickness 2.5 cm.

Netherworld had been translated into Akkadian prose and attached in that form to the Standard Babylonian epic as Tablet XII.[10]

To facilitate comparison between the Sumerian poem and the Akkadian translation edited in the preceding chapter, the relevant part of the former (ll. 172–end) is given here in synoptic style, with the text of all manuscripts given in full for each line (Nippur sources first) and the Akkadian interpolated in transcription as if in a regular bilingual text. The sigla used for the Sumerian sources follow the series established by Shaffer (A–FF) and supplemented by Attinger (GG–kk),[11] with capital letters for Nippur manuscripts and lower case for tablets from Ur and other sites. Manuscripts not previously given sigla follow in sequence (ll–iii).

All sources for ll. 172 ff. currently known to me in Philadelphia (MSS H, W, Y, Z, AA, CC, DD, EE, FF, SS–UU, CCC–EEE), London (MSS r, t, kk, ll, mm, nn) and Oslo (MS rr) have been studied at first hand. The results of these collations are incorporated in the transliterations given below.[12] Most changes to the previously available text are minor, but substantive new readings have been obtained in ll. 204, 228–9, 260, 266, 271, d 2, e 2, k 3, o 2, q and s 1. MS rr offers significant new knowledge of ll. 250–3 and provides for the first time the Sumerian original (p) of the Akkadian line SB XII 150.

MANUSCRIPTS

MS	Number	Disposal of lines	Publication of cuneiform text
Nippur			
A	N 1452	1–27, 52–74	Shaffer, 'Sumerian Sources', pl. 1
B	CBS 14068	1–25, 26–58	Chiera, *SEM* no. 21; photograph Kramer, *Sumerian Mythology*, pl. 8 (obv. only)
C	3N-T 381	1–14, 23–33	Shaffer, 'Sumerian Sources', pl. 2
	+909y (A/33276)	7–16	unpublished
D	3N-T 903, 132	1–10, 36–45	Shaffer, 'Sumerian Sources', pl. 3
E	Ni 4507	1–18, 46–64	Kramer in Shaffer, 'Sumerian Sources', pl. 4; *ISET* II 52
F	Ni 4249	1–23, 63–75, b–e	Kramer, *SLTN* no. 5
H	CBS 15150 + 19950 + UM 29-13-438 + N 3280 + 3474 + 3634[13]	11–26, 62–86, 98–112, 127–49, 177–92, 196–225, 231–68, a–e, q–t	Shaffer, 'Sumerian Sources', pls. 5–6; photograph Kramer, *From the Tablets of Sumer*, p. 140, fig. 69 (CBS 19950 only)

[10] The literary history is given above, in Ch. 1.

[11] P. Attinger, *Eléments de linguistique sumérienne* (Fribourg and Göttingen, 1993), p. 37.

[12] Collation of the Ur MSS of ll. 1–171 produced only one significant result: l. 137: on MS r (*UET* VI 56 obv. 10) traces are visible of ⌜50 ma.na⌝.àm. I have not used MS XX.

[13] As kindly confirmed by Kevin Danti, this is the full number of the assemblage copied by Shaffer as MS H and catalogued by Gerardi, *A Bibliography of the Tablet Collections of the University Museum*, p. 188.

MS	Number	Disposal of lines	Publication of cuneiform text
I	3N-T 557	13–25, 26–39	Shaffer, 'Sumerian Sources', pl. 3
J	3N-T 905, 198	13–23	Shaffer, 'Sumerian Sources', pl. 2
K	Ni 2513	40–7, 63–74	Chiera, *SRT* no. 39
L	CBS 13121 +N 3137	65–81, 100–18	Radau, *HAV* no. 12 unpublished
M	HS 1445	75–104	Bernhardt, *TuM* NF III no. 13
N	Ni 4354	106–15, 141–7	Kramer in Shaffer, 'Sumerian Sources', pl. 4; *ISET* II 54
O	CBS 9869	105–50	Chiera, *SEM* no. 22
P	3N-T 124	125–69	Shaffer, 'Sumerian Sources', pls. 7–8
Q	Ni 9744	126–31, ii unplaced	Kramer in Shaffer, 'Sumerian Sources', pl. 4; *ISET* II 53
S	Ni 2270	135–59	Langdon, *BE* XXXI no. 55
U	3N-T 905, 190 +907, 262	138–42, 151–5	Shaffer, 'Sumerian Sources', pl. 10 unpublished
V	HS 1482 +2502 + 2612	173–81, 204–24, 249–52, 262–8, a–g, i–k, q–r, t	Bernhardt, *TuM* NF III no. 14 (HS 1482 only); Wilcke, *Kollationen*, p. 21
W	CBS 10400	176–85, 237–9	Shaffer, 'Sumerian Sources', pl. 10
[X]			
Y	UM 29-16-463 +N 2696 + 3162	183–97, 226–38	Shaffer, 'Sumerian Sources', pl. 10 (without N 2696)
Z	UM 29-16-58	188–221	Kramer, *From the Tablets of Sumer*, fig. 70; id., *History Begins at Sumer*, p. 259, fig. 19
AA	UM 29-15-993	199–214, 225–32	Shaffer, 'Sumerian Sources', pl. 9
BB	Ni 2378	228–47, 252–65	Langdon, *BE* XXXI no. 35
CC	N 1470	253–8, ii traces	Shaffer, 'Sumerian Sources', pl. 11
DD	CBS 13116 +15360	255–68, a–e, i–k, o, q–t, u	Radau, *HAV* no. 11 (13116 only)
EE	3N-T 927, 527	256–62	Shaffer, 'Sumerian Sources', pl. 11
FF	UM 29-13-536	259–68, b	Shaffer, 'Sumerian Sources', pl. 11
GG	Ni 4585	234–48	Çığ/Kızılyay, *ISET* I 149 ((+) JJ)
HH	Ni 9847	136–41, 177–82	Çığ/Kızılyay, *ISET* I 199
JJ	Ni 9626	231–42	Kramer, *ISET* II 51 ((+) GG)
SS	UM 29-15-847	i, k, o, q–r, t	unpublished
TT	N 4507	230–9	unpublished

MS	Number	Disposal of lines	Publication of cuneiform text
UU	3N-T 902, 66	222–9 // 231–7, rev. unplaced	unpublished
VV	3N-T 902, 95	114–20	unpublished
WW	3N-T 903, 124	15–22, 45–52	unpublished
XX	N 1867	225–9, 236–44	unpublished
YY	N 3311	127–35	unpublished
ZZ	N 4209	14–26	unpublished
AAA	3N-T 906, 228	3 ll. then 95–101, 119–23	unpublished
BBB	3N-T 908, 292	15–21 or //	unpublished
CCC	3N-T 908, 302	159–68, 207–15	unpublished
DDD	3N-T 918, 443	277–8, a–d	unpublished
EEE	3N-T 923, 498	195–8 (or 217–20?)	unpublished
FFF	3N-T 923, 500	34–9 // 77–82 etc.[14]	unpublished
GGG	UM 29-16-740	?–13, 40–5	unpublished
HHH	3N-T 496	15–31?	unpublished
Sippar			
kk_1	BM 54325+54900	13–22, 31–4	Geller, *CT* 58 no. 54
kk_2	BM 99876	4–12	Geller, *CT* 58 no. 54
Ur			
g	U RRx44	1–30, 31–62	Gadd, *UET* VI no. 55
r	U 9364	128–63, 164–201	Gadd, *RA* 30 (1933), pp. 128–9; *UET* VI no. 56
t	U 16874	136–49, 150–66	Gadd, *UET* VI no. 57
ll	U 16878	f, h–i, l–n, q–r, t, v–y	Gadd, *UET* VI no. 58
mm	U unnumbered	f, j–m, o, q–r, t	Gadd, *UET* VI no. 59
nn	U 17900L	traces, 1′–17′	Gadd, *UET* VI no. 60 (rev. only)
iii etc.	U 5635 etc.		forthcoming in *UET* VI/3
Isin			
ii	IB 930	57–63, 84–98	unpublished
Uruk			
oo	W 17259ad	70–81	Falkenstein in Cavigneaux, *Uruk* no. 98

[14] Rev. unplaced: 1′: . . . k]i.ág [. . . , 2′: . . .].àm mu.10.[. . . , 3′: . . .].un.dab_5 ⌜unug^{ki}⌝[. . . , 4′: . . .]x. šè im.[. . .

MS	Number	Disposal of lines	Publication of cuneiform text
Mê-Turan			
pp	H 154	212–28, 257–68, a	Cavigneaux, *Iraq* 62 (2000), pp. 10–11
qq	H 157	255–68, c–i, k, r, t	Cavigneaux, *Iraq* 62 (2000), pp. 14–17
Unknown provenance			
rr$_1$	SC 2887	249–68, a	Fig. 15
rr$_2$	SC 3361	237–48, f, i, k–t	Fig. 15
ID	Inanna's Descent to the Netherworld		

Composite editions

1938 S. N. Kramer, *Gilgamesh and the Ḫuluppu-Tree. A Reconstructed Sumerian Text* (AS 10): MSS B, K, L, O, r, S only; L lacking N 3137

1963 A. Shaffer, 'Sumerian Sources': MSS A–FF only; V lacking HS 2502 + 2612, Y lacking N 2696, DD lacking 15360

2000 J. A. Black et al., The Electronic Text Corpus of Sumerian Literature (www-etcsl.orient.ox.ac.uk) Text 1.8.1.4: lacking ii, oo, rr, TT and CBS 15360 of DD

TRANSLITERATION

172	V	i 1′	^{giš}E.⌜KID?.ma.mu é nagar.ra⌝.k[a . . . .d]a.gál.àm
	r	45	u$_4$.ba ^{giš}ellag.mu é nagar.ra.ka nu.uš.ma.da.gál.la
		XII 1	*ūma pukku ina bīt naggāri lū ēz[ib]*
173	V	i 2′	dam nagar.ra ama.ugu.mu.gá / nu.uš.ma.da.gál.la.àm
	r	46	dam nagar.ra ama.ugu.gá.gin$_7$ nu.uš.ma.da.gál.la
		XII 2	*[aššat naggāri ša kī umm]i ālittīya lū [ēzib]*
174	V	i 3′	dumu nagar.ra nin$_9$.bàn.da.mu.gin$_7$ nu.uš.ma.da.gál.la.àm
	r	47	dumu nagar.ra nin$_9$.bàn.da.mu nu.uš.ma.da.gál.la
		XII 3	*m[ārat naggāri ša kī a]ḫatī[ya ṣ]eḫerti lū [ēzib]*
175	V	i 4′	^{giš}ellag.[m]u kur.šè mu.da.šub a.ba.a ma.ra.ab.e$_{11}$.dè
	r	48	^{giš}ellag.mu kur.ta a.ba im.ta.e$_{11}$.dè
		XII 4	*ūma pu[kku] ana erṣeti imq[utannī(ma)]*
176	V	i 5′	^{giš}E.KID.ma.mu ganzir.šè mu.da.šub / a.ba.a ma.ra.ab.e$_{11}$.dè
	W	iii 1′	[. . . . . . .] ganzir.t[a . . . .]
	r	49	^{giš}E.KÌD.ma.mu gànzir.ta a.ba im.ta.e$_{11}$.dè
		XII 5	*mikkê ana erṣeti i[mqutannī(ma)]*
177	H	iv 1′	[en.ki.dùg.e ^{d}]⌜bil.ga.mes inim mu⌝.[ni.ib.gi$_4$.gi$_4$]
		XII 6	*[E]nkidu Gilgāmeš i[ppalšu]*
	V	i 6′	ìr.da.ni en.ki.dùg.e inim mu.un.ni.ib.gi$_4$.gi$_4$
	W	iii 2′	[. . .] en.ki.dùg.ra K[A . . . .]

	HH	rev. 1′	[. . . . .].⌜e inim⌝ [. . . . . . .]
	r	50	ìr.da.ni en.ki.dùg.e gù mu.un.na.dé.e
178	H	iv 2′	lugal.m[u èr] e.ne ba.še$_8$.še$_8$ š[à. . . . .]
	V	i 7′	lugal.mu èr e.ne ba.še$_8$.en šà.ḫul a.na.aš mu.e.dím
	W	iii 3′	[. . . . è]r e.ne ba.še$_8$.š[e$_8$ . . . .]
	HH	rev. 2′	[. . . . . . .n]e ba.še$_8$.š[e$_8$ . . . .]
	r	51	lugal.mu èr e.ne ba.še$_x$(ŠEŠ$_4$).še$_x$(ŠEŠ$_4$) šà.zu a.na.aš ḫul ba.gig
		XII 7	*bēlī minâ tabki libbaka* [*lemun*]
179	H	iv 3′	^{giš}ellag.zu ku[r].ta gá.e ga.mu.r[a. . . . . . .]
	V	i 8′	⌜u$_4$.da ^{giš}⌝ellag.zu kur.ta gá.e ga.mu.ra.ab.e$_{11}$.dè
	W	iii 4′	[. .d]a ^{giš}ellag.zu kur.ta gá.e ga.[. . . . . .]
	HH	rev. 3′	[. . . . .].ta gá.[. . . . .]
	r	52	u$_4$.da ^{giš}ellag.zu kur.ta gá.e ḫu.mu.ra.ab.è.dè
		XII 8	*ūma pukku ultu erṣeti anāku uš*[*ellâkka*]
180	H	iv 4′	^{giš}E.KID.ma.z[u] ganzir.ta gá.e ga.[. . . . . . .]
	V	i 9′	⌜^{giš}E.KID⌝.ma.zu ganzir.ta / [gá].⌜e⌝ ga.mu.ra.ab.e$_{11}$.dè
	W	iii 5′	^{giš}E.KID.ma.zu IGI.ZA.ta gá.e ga.[. . . . .]
	HH	rev. 4′	[. . . . . ga]nzir.ta [. . . . .]
	r	53	^{giš}E.KÌD.ma.zu gànzir.ta gá.e ḫu.mu.ra.a[b.e$_{11}$.d]è
		XII 9	*mikkê ultu erṣeti anāku uše*[*llâkka*]
181	H	iv 5′	^{d}bìl.ga.me[s.(e)] en.ki.dùg.e inim mu.[na.ni.ib.gi$_4$.gi$_4$]
	V	i 10′	[. . .g]a.mes en x x x x x
	W	iii 6′	bìl.ga.mes.e en.[k]i.dùg.ra in[im . . . .]
	HH	rev. 5′	[. . .].mes en.ki.[. . . . .]
	r	om.	
		XII 10	*Gilgāmeš Enkidu* [*ippalšu*]
182	H	iv 6′	tukum.bi u$_4$.[da kur.š]è mu.ni.in.e[$_{11}$.dè]
	W	iii 7′	u$_4$.da kur.ra mu.un.e$_{11}$.[. .]
	HH	rev. 6′	[. . .b]i u$_4$.da kur.[. . . . .]
	r	54	tukum.bi u$_4$.da kur.šè im.e.a.e[$_{11}$.d]è
		XII 11	*šumma ana erṣeti* [*turrad*]
183	H	iv 7′	na ga.ri n[a. . . . . . .]
	W	iii 8′	na ga.ri na.ri.mu [. . .]
	Y	obv. 1	[. . .] na.ri.mu ḫé.dab$_5$
		XII 12	*ana ašírtīya* [*lū tašaddad*]
184	H	iv 8′	inim ga.ra.ab.d[ug$_4$ . . . .]
	W	iii 9′	inim ga.ra.ab.⟨. . .⟩ géšt[u. . . .]
	Y	obv. 2	[. . . g]a.r[a].ab.dug$_4$ inim.mu.šè géštu.zu

One source transposes ll. 183–4:

184	r	55	inim ga.ra.dug$_4$ inim.m[u ḫé].dab$_5$
183	r	56	na ga.e.ri na.[ri].mu ḫé.dab$_5$

185	H	iv 9′	túg.dan$_4$.dan$_4$.na.[. . . . .]
	W	iii 10′	túg.dan$_4$.na.zu [. . . . .]
	Y	obv. 3	túg.dan$_4$.dan$_4$.na.zu na.an.mu$_4$.mu$_4$.un
	r	57	túg.dán.dán.na.⸢zu⸣ [na].an.mu$_4$.mu$_4$
		XII 13	*ṣubāta zakâ [lā taltabbiš]*
186	H	iv 10′	gir$_5$.gin$_7$ gis[kim . . . .]
	W	iii 11′	illegible traces
	Y	obv. 4	gir$_5$.gin$_7$ giskim na.an.ni.⸢ib⸣.è.eš
	r	58	gir$_5$.gin$_7$ giskim [na].an.⸢è⸣.[d]è.eš
		XII 14	*kīma ubārātāma u'add[ûka]*
187	H	iv 11′	ì dùg.ga bur.[. . . . .]
	Y	obv. 5	ì dùg.ga bur.ra na.an.šeš$_4$.šeš$_4$.en
	r	59	ì [dùg].ga bur.ra na.an.šeš$_4$.šeš$_4$
		XII 15	*šaman pūri ṭāba lā tappaššiš*
188	H	iv 12′	ir.si.im.bi.[. . . . .]
	Y	obv. 6	ir.si.im.bi.šè nam.mu.e.nigin.ne.eš
	Z	1	[ir].si.bi.šè n[a]m.mu.nigin.ne.[eš]
	r	60	ir.sim.zu.šè ba.e.dè.[n]igin.ne.eš
		XII 16	*ana irīšīšu ipaḫḫurūka*
189	H	iv 13′	^{giš}illar kur.r[a . . . .]
	Y	obv. 7	^{giš}illar kur.ra nam.mu.e.⸢sìg⸣.ge
	Z	2	$^{⸢giš⸣}$illar kur.ra [nam].mu.un.sìg.ge
	r	61	^{giš}illar kur.ra nam.m[u].e.sìg.ge
		XII 17	*tilpāna ana erṣeti lā tanassuk*
190	H	iv 14′	lú ^{giš}ill[ar . . . .]
	Y	obv. 8	lú ^{giš}illar ra.a nam.mu.e.[n]igin.ne.eš
	Z	3	lú ^{giš}illar ra.[a na]m.mu.nigin.ne.eš
	r	62	lú ^{giš}illar ra.a ba.e.dè.⸢nigin.ne⸣.eš
		XII 18	*ša ina tilpāni maḫṣū ilammûka*
191	H	iv 15′	^{giš}ma.nu [. . . . .]
	Y	obv. 9	^{giš}ma.nu šu.za ⸢nam⸣.ba.e.gá.gá.an
	Z	4	$^{⸢giš⸣}$ma.nu šu.[za na]m.mu.ni.in.gar
	r	63	^{giš}⸢ma⸣.nu šu.za nam.mu.un.gá.gá
		XII 19	*šabbiṭu ana qātīka lā tanašši*
192	H	iv 16′	gidim ba.[. . . . . . .]
	Y	obv. 10	gidim ba.e.[d]è.[u]r$_4$.re.eš
	Z	5	gidim [. . .d]è.ur$_4$.re.eš
	r	64	gid[im ba].e.dè.ur$_4$.re.en
		XII 20	*eṭemmū i'arrurūka*
193	H	iv 17′	[^{kuš}]⸢e⸣.s[ír . . . .]
	Y	obv. 11	$^{⸢kuš}$e.sír gìr⸣.zu [n]am.mu.e.si.ge
	Z	6	$^{kuš⸢}$e.sír⸣ [. . .] nam mu.ni.in.si

	r	65	^{kuš}⌜e⌝.sír gìr.za nam.mu.un.si.ga
		XII 21	*šēnī ina šēpīka lā tašên*
194	Y	obv. 12	[. .(dun$_5$).d]un$_5$ [na]m.mu.un.gá.gá.an
	Z	7	kur.ra [x (x)] nam.[m]u.un.gá.gá
	r	66	kur.⌜kur?⌝.ra gù nam.mu.un.gá.gá
		XII 22	*rigmu ina erṣeti lā tašakkan*
195	Y	obv. 13	[. . .á]g.gá.zu [ne] na.an.su.ub.bé.en
	Z	8	dam ki.ág.zu ne na.an.su.ub.bé
	EEE	1	[d]am ki.ág.a.ni ne na.an.su.ub.[bé]
	r	67	dam ki.ág.zu ne na.an.su.ub.bé
		XII 23	*aššatka ša tarammu lā tanaššiq*
196	Y	obv. 14	[. . . .gi]g.ga.zu [níg nam.m]u.ra.ra.a[n]
	Z	9	dam ḫul.gig.ga.zu [níg] nam.mu.ra.ra.an
	r	68	dam ḫul.gig.ga.zu níg nam.mu.un.ra.ra
		XII 24	*aššatka ša tazerru lā tamaḫḫaṣ*
197	Y	obv. 15	[. . . .].zu ne n[a.a]n.s[u. . .]
	Z	10	dumu k[i].ág.zu n[e n]a.an.su.ub.bé
	r	69	dumu ki.ág.zu ne na.an.su.ub.bé
		XII 25	*mārāka ša tarammu lā tanaššiq*
198	Y	obv. 16	[. . . . .gi]g.ga.zu níg nam.⌜mu⌝.[. . .]
	Z	11	⌜dumu⌝ ḫul.gig.ga.zu níg nam.mu.ra.ra.an
	r	70	dumu ḫul.gig.ga.zu níg nam.mu.un.ra.ra
		XII 26	*mārāka ša tazerru lā tamaḫḫaṣ*

Two sources give ll. 196–8 in different orders:

198	H	iv 20′	dumu ḫul.[gig. . . . .]
197	H	iv 21′	dumu ki.ág.[. . . . .]
196	H	iv 22′	dam ḫul.g[ig. . . . .]
197	EEE	2	[du]mu ki.ág.a.ni ne na.an.su.ub.[bé]
196	EEE	3	[dam ḫu]l.⌜gig⌝.ga.a.ni níg nam.mu.u[n.ra.ra]
198	EEE	4	[dumu ḫul.gig.ga.a].⌜ni⌝ níg nam.mu.[un.ra.ra]
199	H	iv 23′	i.^{d}utu kur.[. . . . .]
	Y	obv. 17	[. . .ku]r.ra nam.ba.⌜e⌝.[. . .]
	Z	12	i.^{d}utu kur.ra ba.⌜e⌝.dab$_5$.bé.e[n]
	AA	obv. 1	[. .]utu kur.ra ba.e.dab$_5$.bé
	r	71	i.^{d}utu kur.ra ba.e.dab$_5$.bé
		XII 27	*tazzimtu erṣeti iṣabbatka*
200	H	iv 24′	ì.ná.a.r[a . . . .]
	Y	obv. 18	[. .].⌜a⌝.ra ì.n[á. . .]
	Z	13	ì.ná.a.ra ì.ná.a.ra

	AA	obv. 2	[ì.n]á.a.ra ì.ná.a.ra
	r	72	⸢ì⸣.ná.a.ra ì.ná.a.ra
		XII 28a	*ša ṣallat ša ṣallat*
201	H	iv 25′	ama ^{d}ni[n. . . . .]
	Y	obv. 19	[. . .].⸢a⸣.zu [ì].n[á. . .]
	Z	14	ama ^{d}nin.⸢a.zu ì⸣.ná.a.ra
	AA	obv. 3	[am]a ^{d}nin.a.zu ì.ná.a.ra
	r	73	ama ^{d}nin.a.zu ì.ná.a.ra
		XII 28b	*ummu Ninazu ša ṣallat*
	ID	301	^{d}ereš.ki.gal.la.ke$_4$ ì.ná.ná.ra.àm (// ID 258)[15]
202	H	iv 26′	mur kù.g[a. .] t[úg . . .]
	Y	obv. 20	[. . . .].ni túg [. . .]
	Z	15	mur kù.ga.na túg nu.um.dul
	AA	om.	
		XII 29	*būdāša ellētu ṣubātu ul kuttumā*
	ID	232	mur kù.ga.ni gada nu.un.búr (// ID 259)
203	H	iv 27′	g[aba k]ù.[. .] gada [. . .]
	Y	obv. 21	[. . . . .].ni [. . . . . . .]
	Z	16	gaba kù.ga.na ⸢gada.nu.um⸣.búr
	AA	obv. 4	[gab]a kù.ga.ni gada nu.un.búr
		XII 30	*irassa kī pūr šappāti lā šaddat*
	ID	233	gaba.ni bur.šagan.gin$_7$ (*var.* .na) nu.un.gíd (// ID 260)
204	HZ	om.	
	V	ii 1′	[. . . . .].gi[n$_7$? . . .]
	Y	obv. 22	[. . . . .]x.TU.gin$_7$ [. . . .]
	AA	obv. 5	[šu.si.ni ^{urudu}]lul.bi.⸢gin$_7$⸣ an.da.gál
	ID	234	šu!.si.ni ^{urudu}lul.bi.gin$_7$ an.da.gál[16]
	ID	261	⸢šu⸣.si.ni ^{urudu}lul.bi.gin$_7$ àm.da.gál[17]
205	HZ	om.	
	V	ii 2′	[. . . . . . ^{sa}]^{r}.gin$_7$ ì.[. . .]
	AA	obv. 6	[. . . . . . . .g]in$_7$ ì.gur$_5$.gur$_5$
	ID	235	sí[g].ni ga.raš^{sar}.gin$_7$ sag.gá.na mu.un.ur$_4$.ur$_4$[18]
	ID	262	síg.ni ga.raš^{sar}.gin$_7$ sag.[. . . . . .].ur$_4$.re[19]
206	H	iv 28′	e[n.ki.dùg? ini]m lugal.la.na.aš [. . . . .]
	V	ii 3′	[. . . . .]x x lugal.ka⸢šu⸣ nu.um.BU(su$_{13}$?).bé[20]

[15] W. Sladek, 'Inanna's Descent to the Netherworld', PhD thesis (Baltimore, 1974), pp. 132 and 135. Cf. B. Alster, *Acta Sum* 5 (1983), pp. 1–2.

[16] Ibid., p. 1 and fn. 2.

[17] *UET* VI 10 obv. 3a // Sladek, 'Inanna's Descent', p. 285, N 983, 4′. Cf. S. N. Kramer, *PAPS* 124 (1980), p. 303; Alster, *Acta Sum* 5, p. 2.

[18] Ibid.

[19] *UET* VI 10 obv. 3b // Sladek, 'Inanna's Descent', p. 285, N 983, 5′. Cf. Kramer, *PAPS* 124, p. 303; Alster, *Acta Sum* 5, p. 2.

[20] Not nu.um.gíd.i.

	Z	om.	
	AA	obv. 7	[. . . . . . . lug]al.⸢la.na⸣.šè šu nu.um.ma.B[U.X]
		XII 31–2	*[Enkidu ana erṣeti] urrad / [ana aširti Gilgāme]š ul išdud*
207	H	iv 29′	t[úg dan$_4$.da]n$_4$.na.ni im.ma.a[n. .]
	V	ii 4′	túg dan$_4$.dan$_4$.na.ni im.ma.an.mu$_4$
	Z	17	[túg da]n$_4$.dan$_4$.na.ni [. . . . .]
	AA	obv. 8	[. . . . .] ⸢im.ma⸣.an.mu$_4$
	CCC	rev. 1′	túg d[an$_4$. . . . .]
		XII 33	*ṣ[ubāta zakâ] ittalbiš*
208	H	iv 30′	g[ir$_5$.gi]n$_7$ giskim im.ma.an.n[e. .]
	V	ii 5′	gir$_5$.gin$_7$ giskim im.ma.an.ne.eš
	Z	18	[. . .gi]n$_7$ giskim i[m. . . . .]
	AA	obv. 9	[. . . . . .m]a.an.ne.eš
	CCC	rev. 2′	gir$_5$.g[in$_7$ . . . .]
		XII 34	*kīma ub[ārūma] u'addûšu*
209	H	iv 31′	[. .].ga bur.ra im.ma.an.š[eš$_4$]
	V	ii 6′	ì dùg.ga bur.ra im.ma.an.šeš$_4$
	Z	19	[. .].ga $^{\text{na}_4}$bur.ra im.ma.⸢an.šeš$_4$⸣
	AA	obv. 10	[. . . . .].ma.an.šeš$_4$
	CCC	rev. 3′	ì dùg.g[a . . . .]
		XII 35	*šaman pūri ṭ[āba] ittapšiš*
210	H	iv 32′	[. .].im.bi.šè im.ma.nigin.ne.[.]
	V	ii 7′	ir.si.im.[bi.š]è gú im.ma.gar.re.eš
	Z	20	⸢ir⸣.si.im.bi.šè im.ma.an.nigin.ne.eš
	AA	obv. 11	[. . . . . . i]m.ma.da$_5$.gar.re.eš
	CCC	rev. 4′	ir.si.[. . . . .]
		XII 36	*ana irīš[īšu] iptaḫrūšu*
211	H	iv 33′	[^{giš}ill]ar kur.ra im.ma.ni.in.sìg.[ge]
	V	ii 8′	^{giš}illar kur.ra [i]m.ma.ni.in.⸢sìg⸣.[ge]
	Z	21	^{giš}illar kur.ra im.ma.an.sìg.ge
	AA	obv. 12	[. . . . . . i]m.ma.ni.in.sìg!
	CCC	rev. 5′	^{giš}illa[r . . . .]
		XII 37–7a	*tilpāna a[na erṣeti] issukma / eṭemmū ētarrū*
212	H	iv 34′	[lú ^{gi}]^{š}illar ra im.ma.nigin.ne.e[š]
	V	ii 9′	lú ^{giš}illar ra.a im.ma.an.nigin.ne.eš
	Z	22	lú ^{giš}illar ra.a im.ma.an.nigin.ne.eš
	AA	obv. 13	[. . . . . . i]m.ma.nigin.⸢ne⸣
	CCC	rev. 6′	lú ^{giš}[. . . . .]
	pp	obv. 1	[. . . . . . i]m.⸢ma.nigin⸣.ne.eš
		XII 38	*ša ina tilpāni [maḫṣū] iltamûšu*
213	H	iv 35′	[. . .n]u šu.na im.ma.ni.in.⸢gar⸣
	V	ii 10′	^{giš}ma.nu šu.na im.ma.ni.in.gar
	Z	23	^{giš}ma.nu šu.na im.ma.ni.in.gar

	AA	obv. 14	[. . . . . . i]m.ma.ni.i[n. .]
	CCC	rev. 7′	^{giš}má.[. . . . .]
	pp	obv. 2a	[. . . . .].ma.an.íl
		XII 39	*šabbiṭa ina qāt*[*īšu i*]*ššīma*
214	H	iv 36′	[. .] ba.e.da.ur$_4$.re.eš
	V	ii 11′	gidim ba.an.da.ur$_4$.re.eš
	Z	24	gidim mu.un.dè.ur$_4$.re.eš
	AA	obv. 15	[. . . . . . .ur]$_4$.⌈re⌉.e[š]
	CCC	rev. 8′	gidim [. . . . .]
	pp	obv. 2b	gidim mu.un.da.e.re
		XII 40	[*eṭemmū ē*]*tarrū*
215	H	iv 37′	[. .s]ír gìr.na im.ma.an.si
	V	ii 12′	^{kuš}e.sír gìr.na im.ma.ni.in.si
	Z	25	^{kuš}e.sír gìr.na im.ma.ni.in.si
	CCC	rev. 9′	[^{ku}]^{š}⌈e⌉.s[ír . . . .]
	pp	obv. 3	[. . . . .] im.ma.ni.⌈in⌉.gar
		XII 41	*šēnī ana* [*šēpīšu išēn* (or *ištēn*)]
216	H	iv 38′	[. . .].du$_6$.un im.ma.ni.⌈in⌉.[.]
	V	ii 13′	kur.ra tu$_{13}$.tu$_{13}$ im.ma.ni.in.gar?
	Z	26	kur.ra du$_6$.du$_6$ im.ma.ni.in.gar
	pp	obv. 4	[x x x]x.bi (or [d]u$_7$?) im.⌈ma⌉.gá.gá
		XII 42	*rigma* [*ina erṣeti ištakan* (or *iškun*)]
217	H	iv 39′	[. . . .á]g.gá.ni im.ma.an.su.u[b]
	V	ii 14′	dam ki.ág.gá.ni ne im.ma.an.s[u.ub]
	Z	27	dam ki.ág.gá.ni ne im.ma.an.su.ub
	pp	obv. 5	[x x x n]e im.ma.ni.su.[u]b
		XII 43	*aššass*[*u ša irammu ittašiq*]
218	H	iv 40′	[. . ḫu]l.gig.ga.ni níg im.ma.ni.in.[ra]
	V	ii 15′	dam ḫul.gig.ga.ni níg im.ma.ni.[.]
	Z	28	dam ḫul.gig.ga.ni níg im.ma.ni.in.ra
	pp	obv. 6	[. .] ⌈ḫul⌉.[gig.g]a.⌈a.ni⌉ im.ma.ni.ib.ra
		XII 44	*ašš*[*assu ša*] *izerr*[*u imtaḫaṣ*]
219	H	iv 41′	[. . .].ág.gá.ni im.ma.ni.i[n. . .]
	V	ii 16′	dumu ki.ág.gá.ni ne im.m[a. . . .]
	Z	29	dumu ki.ág.ni ne im.ma.an.⟨su⟩.ub {x}
	pp	obv. 7	[. .] ki.ág.[. . . i]m.ma.n[i.s]u.u[b]
		XII 45	*m*[*ārāšu š*]*a irammu i*[*ttašiq*]
220	H	iv 42′	[. . ḫu]l.gig.ga.ni níg im.ma.ni.[. .]
	V	ii 17′	dumu ḫul.gig.ga.ni im.m[a. . .]
	Y	rev. 1′	[. . . . . . .] ní[g . . . .]
	Z	30	dumu ḫul.gig.ga.ni níg im.ma.ni.in.ra
	pp	obv. 8	[du]mu ḫul.⌈gig.ga.a⌉.ni [. . .n]i.ib.r[a]
		XII 46	*mār*[*āšu š*]*a izerru imt*[*aḫaṣ*]

221	H	iv 43′	[i].^{d}utu kur.re im.ma.an.[.]
	V	ii 18′	i.^{d}utu kur.ra im.m[a. . .]
	Y	rev. 2′	[. . . .r]a⸢im⸣.m[a. . .]
	Z	31	i.^{d}utu kur.ra im.ma.an.dab$_{5}$
	pp	obv. 9	i.^{d}utu.bi kur.ra ba.e.dab.⸢bé⸣
		XII 47	*tazzimti erṣeti iṣṣabassu*
		XII 48	*ša ṣallat [ša ṣa]llat ummu Ninazu ša ṣall[at]*
		XII 49	*būdā[ša e]llēti ṣubāta ul kuttumā*
		XII 50	*irass[a k]īma pūr šikkati ul šaddat*

MS pp has the following text at this point:

221a	pp	obv. 10	u$_{4}$ ḫul.gál.da en.na⸢u$_{4}$⸣imin.[n]a.šè
221b	pp	obv. 11	šubur.ra.a.ni ^{d}en.ki.dùg {ra} kur.ta nu.mu.un.è.dè
		XII 51	*inūš[ūma E]nkīdu ultu erṣeti ana e[lât]u ⟨ul īlâ* (or *ūṣâ*)⟩
221c	pp	obv. 12	lugal.e i.lu mu.un.na.bé é[r gi]g še$_{x}$(A.IGI).še$_{x}$(A.IGI)
221d	pp	obv. 13	⸢šubur šà.ga⸣.a.mu tab.ba gi.n[a.m]u a[d.g]i$_{4}$.⸢gi$_{4}$⸣.a.⸢mu⸣kur.ra i[m?.ma.an.dab$_{5}$]
221e	pp	obv. 14	nam.tar nu.dab á.sàg nu.d[ab] ku[r].r[a i]m.ma.a[n.dab$_{5}$]
		XII 52	*Namt[ar ul iṣba]ssu Asakku ul iṣbassu erṣetu [iṣbass]u*
221f	pp	obv. 15	^{d}udug ^{d}nè.eri$_{11}$.gal sag [(x)]x⸢nu.dab⸣kur.ra⸢im⸣.m[a.an.d]ab$_{5}$
		XII 53	*rāb[iṣ Nergal l]ā pādû ul iṣbassu erṣetu [iṣbass]u*
221g	pp	obv. 16	⸢ki⸣n[am].x mè nu.un.šub⸢kur.ra⸣i[m].m[a.a]b.dab$_{5}$
		XII 54	*ašar t[āḫāz z]ikarī ul imqut erṣetu i[ṣbass]u*

Other sources have a single line only:

222	H	iv 44′	[u]r.sag ^{d}bìl.ga.mes dumu ^{d}nin.[sún.na.ke$_{4}$]
	V	ii 19′	ur.sag ^{d}bil$_{4}$.ga.m[es . . . .]
	Y	rev. 3′	[. . .]bìl.ga.mes dumu ^{d}n[in. . . . . .]
	UU	obv. 1	[. . . . .] x [. . . . .]
		XII 55	*inūš[ūma šar]ru mār Ninsun ana ardīšu Enkīdu ibakki*
223	H	iv 45′	[é].kur.re é ^{d}en.líl.lá.šè gìr.[ni aš mu.un.gub]
	V	ii 20′	⸢é.kur⸣.[(re)] é ^{d}en.líl.l[á. . . . .]
	Y	rev. 4′	[. . . .]⸢é⸣^{d}en.líl.lá.šè gìr.ni [. . . . . .]
	UU	obv. 2	[. . . . .].šè gìr.n[i . . .].gub
	pp	obv. 17	é.kur.ra⸢é⸣[^{d}en].⸢líl.lá⸣.[a.š]è gìr.⸢ni⸣aš mu.⸢un⸣.gub
		XII 56	*ana E[kur b]īt Ellil ēdiššīšu ittalak*
224	HUU	om.	
	V	ii 21′	[igi ^{d}en.líl.l]á.šè é[r im.ma.še$_{8}$.še$_{8}$]
	Y	rev. 5′	[. . . .].lá.šè ér im.m[a. . .]
	pp	obv. 18	igi ^{d}mu.ul.líl.lá.šè KA x x x ma? x ba?.gub
225	H	iv 46′–7′	[a.a ^{d}e]n.líl ^{giš}ellag.mu kur.ta [mu.da.an.šub] / [^{giš}]⸢E.KID⸣.m[a.mu . . . .]

	Y	rev. 6′	[. . . . . .]ellag.mu kur.šè mu.d[a. . . . .]
	AA	rev. 1′	[. . . . . gan]zir.[ta/šè mu.da.an.šub]
	UU	obv. 3–4	[. . . . .] kur.šè mu.da.an.šub / [. . . . . .] ⌜kur⌝.šè mu.da.an.šub
	pp	obv. 19–20	^{giš}LAGAB.A.mu ⌜kur.ta⌝ [mu.u]n.[da].⌜šub⌝ / ^{giš}E.KÌD.a.mu KUR.ZA KUR.ZI.da mu.⌜un.da⌝.[šu]b
		XII 57–8	*abu [Elli]l ūma pukku ana erṣeti imqutannīma / mikkê ana erṣeti imqutannīma*
226	Y	rev. 7′	[en.ki.dùg e]$_{11}$.dè ì.g[i$_{4}$ . . . .]
	AA	rev. 2′	[. . . . . ì.g]i$_{4}$ kur.r[e im.ma.an.dab]
	UU	obv. 5	[. . . . . .g]i$_{4}$ kur.re im.ma.an.da[b$_{5}$]
	pp	obv. 21	^{d}en.ki.dùg è.dè ⌜e$_{11}$?.dè⌝
		XII 59	*Enkīdu ša ana šūlîš[unu ūrdu? erṣetu iṣbassu]*

MS pp alone has the following line:

226a	pp	obv. 22	[šubur š]à.⌜ga⌝.a.mu tab.ba gi.na.a.mu ad.[g]i$_{4}$.gi$_{4}$.a.m[u kur.ra] ⌜im.ma.an.dab$_{5}$?⌝
227	Y	rev. 8′	[nam.tar nu.un.d]ab$_{5}$ á.sàg nu.un.[. . . . .]
	AA	rev. 3′	[. . . . . nu.m]u.un.dab$_{5}$ kur.[re im].ma.an.dab$_{5}$
	UU	obv. 6	[. . . . .] nu.un.dab$_{5}$ kur.re im.ma.an.da[b$_{5}$]
	pp	obv. 23	[. . . . .] ⌜á⌝.sàg nu.dab kur.r[a . . . .]
		XII 60	*Namtar ul iṣbassu Asakku ul iṣbassu erṣetu iṣbassu*
228	Y	rev. 9′	[. . ^{d}]nè.eri$_{11}$.gal sag ⌜šu.nu.ba nu.un⌝.dab$_{5}$ kur.⌜re im.ma⌝.[. .]
	pp	obv. 24	[. . . . .] x x x ⌜nu.dab$_{5}$ kur⌝.[. . . . . . .]
		XII 61	*rābiṣ Nergal lā pādû ul iṣbassu erṣetu iṣbassu*
229	Y	rev. 10′	ki nam.nita.a.ke$_{4}$ mè.a nu.un.šub kur.re im.ma.an.dab$_{5}$
		XII 62	*ašar tāḫāz zikarī ul imqut erṣetu iṣbassu*

Three sources transpose ll. 228–9:

229	AA	rev. 4′	[. . . . . n]u.un.šub kur.re im.ma.an.dab$_{5}$
	BB	obv. 1	nam.nita.a.ke$_{4}$ mè.a nu.šub kur.r[e . . . .]
	UU	obv. 7	[. . . . .] nu.un.dab$_{5}$(*sic*) kur.re im.ma.an.dab$_{5}$
228	AA	rev. 5′	[. . . . .] ⌜sag šu.nu.ba⌝ nu.mu.un.d[ab$_{5}$] / [. .] im.ma.an.dab$_{5}$
	BB	obv. 2–3	^{d}udug ^{d}nè.eri$_{11}$.gal sag šu.nu.[. . . . .] / kur.re im.ma.an.[.]
	UU	obv. 8	[. . . . . . . .ga]l? sag šu.nu.⟨ba/du$_{7}$ nu.mu⟩.un.⟨dab$_{5}$ kur.re⟩ im.ma.an.dab$_{5}$
230	H	v 1′	[. . . . in]im?.[. . . . .]
	Y	rev. 11′	a.a ^{d}en.líl inim.bi nu.mu.e.dè.gub eridu^{ki}.šè ga.gen
	AA	rev. 6′	[. . . . ini]m.bi nu.mu.dè.gub nibru(*sic*)^{ki} ba.gen
	TT	1′	[. ^{d}e]n.lí[l] ⌜inim.bi nu⌝.mu.u[n. . . . .]
	BB	obv. 4	a.a ^{d}en.líl inim.⌜bi nu.mu.dè.gub⌝ eridu^{ki}.šè ba.gen
		XII 63	*abu Ellil amāta ul īpulšu*
		XII 64	*[ana Uri bīt Sîn (ēdiššīšu)] ittallak*
		XII 65	*abu Sîn ūma pukku ana erṣeti imqutanni*
		XII 66	*mikkê [ana erṣeti] imqutanni*

		XII 67	*Enkīdu ša ana šūlêš[unu ūrd]u? erṣetu iṣbassu*
		XII 68	*Namtar ul iṣbassu Asak[ku] ul iṣ[bas]su erṣetu iṣbassu*
		XII 69	*rābiṣ Nergal lā pād[û ul iṣbass]u erṣetu iṣbassu*
		XII 70	*ašar [tāḫāz zikarī u]l imqut erṣetu iṣbassu*
		XII 71	*a[bu Sîn amāta ul īpulšu]*
231	H	v 2′	[. . . . .].ke$_4$ gìr.ni aš⸢mu⸣.un.gu[b]
	Y	rev. 12′	eridu^{ki} é ^{d}⸢en.ki⸣.ga.šè gìr.ni aš mu.un.gub
	AABB	om.	
	JJ	1′	[. . . . .].⸢ki.ga⸣.šè g[ìr. . . . .]
	TT	2′	[. .] ⸢é ^{d}en⸣.ki.ga.⸢šè⸣ gì[r. . . . .]
		XII 72	*a[na Eridu bīt Ea ittallak]*
232	HBBJJTT om.		
	Y	rev. 13′	igi ^{d}en.ki.g[a.š]è ér im.ma.še$_8$.še$_8$
	AA	rev. 7′	[.] ⸢^{d}⸣en.ki.ga.šè ér im.ma.še$_8$.še$_8$
233	H	v 3′–4′	[. . . . .].mu kur.ta mu.da.šub / [. .].ma.mu ganzir.ta mu.da.šub
	Y	rev. 14′	a.a ^{d}en.ki ^{giš}⸢ellag⸣.mu kur.šè mu.da.an.šub ^{giš}E.KID.ma.mu ganzir.šè mu.da.an.šub
	BB	obv. 5–6	a.a ^{d}en.ki ^{giš}ellag.mu kur.šè mu.da.an.šub / ^{giš}E.KID.⸢ma⸣.m[u . . .š]è mu.da.an.šub
	JJ	2′–3′	[. . . . . ku]r.šè mu.da.a[n. .] / [. .].ma.mu ganzir.šè m[u.da.an.š]ub
	TT	3′–4′	[. . .] ^{giš}ellag.mu kur.šè mu.⸢da⸣.[. . . . .] / ganzir.[. . . . .]
		XII 73–4	*a[bu Ea ūma pukku ana erṣeti imqutannī(ma)] / mek[kê ana erṣeti imqutannī(ma)]*
234	H	v 5′	[. . . . e]$_{11}$.dè ì.gi$_4$.en kur.re im.ma.an.dab$_5$
	Y	rev. 15′	en.ki.dùg e$_{11}$.dè.dè ì.gi$_4$.in kur.re im.ma.an.dab$_5$
	BB	obv. 7	[en].ki.dùg e$_{11}$.dè [ì].gi$_4$ kur.re im.ma.an.dab$_5$
	GG	1′	[. . . .] e[$_{11}$. . . . .]
	JJ	4′	[. . . . . e]$_{11}$.dè ì.gi$_4$ kur.r[e . . . .].an.dab$_5$
	TT	5′	[. . . .] e$_{11}$.dè.dè ì.gi$_4$.i[n . . . .]
		XII 75	*Enkid[u ša ana šūlîšunu ūrdu? erṣetu iṣbassu]*
235	H	v 6′	[. . . . . . .da]b$_5$ á.sàg nu.mu.un.dab$_5$ kur.re im.ma.an.dab$_5$
	Y	rev. 16′	nam.tar nu.un.dab$_5$ á.sàg nu.un.dab$_5$ kur.re im.ma.a[n.d]ab$_5$
	BB	obv. 8	[nam.t]ar nu.un.dab$_5$ á.sàg nu.un.dab$_5$ kur.re im.ma.an.dab$_5$
	GG	2′	[. . . . .m]u.un.dab$_5$ [. . . . .]
	JJ	5′	[. . . . .] á.sàg nu.mu.un.[. . . . .m]a.an.dab$_5$
	TT	6′	[. . .] nu.mu.un.dab$_5$ á.sàg nu.mu.u[n. . . . .]
		XII 76	*Namtar u[l iṣbassu Asakku ul iṣbassu erṣetu iṣbassu]*
236	Y	rev. 17′	^{d}udug ^{d}nè.eri$_{11}$.gal sag šu x x.⸢un⸣.dab$_5$ kur.re im.ma.an.dab$_5$
	TT	7′	[. .] ^{d}nè.eri$_{11}$.gal sag šu.nu.du$_7$ nu.mu.[. . . . .]
		XII 77	*rābiṣ Nergal lā pādû [ul iṣbassu erṣetu iṣbassu]*

237	Y	rev. 18′	ki nam.nita.a.ke$_4$⸢mè⸣.a [. . . . ku]r.re im.ma.an.dab$_5$
	TT	8′	[. . .].nita.ke$_4$ mè.a nu.un.šub kur.[. . . . .]
	rr$_2$	i′ 1′	traces
		XII 78	*ašar tāḫāz zik[arī ul imqut erṣetu iṣbassu]*

Five sources transpose ll. 236–7:

237	H	v 7′	[. . . . .] mè nu.un.šub kur.re im.ma.an.dab$_5$
	BB	obv. 9	⟨ki⟩ nam.nita.ke$_4$ mè nu.un.šub kur.re im.ma.an.dab$_5$
	GG	3′	[. . . . .ni]ta.ke$_4$ mè [. . . . .]
	JJ	6′	[. . . . .] nu.un.šub kur.re [. . . .da]b$_5$
236	H	v 8′–9′	[^{d}]⸢udug ^{d}⸣[nè].⸢eri$_{11}$⸣.⟨gal⟩? sag šu.nu.du$_7$ nu.mu.un.dab$_5$ / kur.r[e i]m.ma.an.dab$_5$
	W	iv 1′–2′	[. . . . . .da]b$_5$ / [. . . . . . .a]n.dab$_5$
	BB	obv. 10–11	^{d}udug ^{d}nè.eri$_{11}$.gal sag šu.[nu] x x[. . . . . .] / kur.re im.ma.an.dab$_5$
	GG	4′–5′	[^{d}udu]g ^{d}nè.e[ri$_{11}$. . . . . . .] / [nu.m]u.un.dab k[ur. . . . .]
	JJ	7′–8′	[. . . .].GAR.gal.la sag [. . .] / [. . . . . . kur].re im.ma.a[n.dab$_5$]
238	H	v 10′	a.a ^{d}en.ki inim.[bi] ba.⸢e⸣.dè.gub
	W	iv 3′	[. . . . . .gu]b
	Y	rev. 19′	⸢a⸣.a ^{d}en.ki i[nim. . .].⸢e⸣.dè.gub
	BB	obv. 12	a.a ^{d}en.ki inim.bi ba.e.dè.⸢gub⸣
	GG	6′	[. .^{d}e]n.ki inim.b[i . . . . .]
	JJ	9′	[. . . . . . . .b]i ba!.e.d[è. .]
	TT	9′	[. . .].⸢ki?⸣.ke$_4$ inim.bi ba.⸢e⸣.[. .]
	rr$_2$	i′ 2′	a.a ^{d}en.ki inim.[. . . . . .]
		XII 79	*abu Ea i[na? . . . .]*
239	H	v 11′	ur.sag šul ^{d}utu.ra dumu [. .]x.e⸢tu⸣.da gù mu.na.dé.e
	W	iv 4′	[. . . . .].⸢e⸣
	BB	obv. 13	ur.sag šul ^{d}utu dumu ^{d}nin.gal.e tu.da gù [. . . . . . .]
	GG	7′	[. .sa]g šul ^{d}utu.r[a . . . .]
	JJ	10′	[. . . . . .r]a dumu ^{d}ni[n. . . . .]
	TT	10′	[. . . . .]x gù m[u. . . . .]
	rr$_2$	i′ 3′	ur.sag šul⸢^{d}⸣[. . . . .]
		XII 80	*ana qarrādi e[ṭli Šamaš iqabbi]*
		XII 81	*qarrādu eṭlu Š[amaš mār Ningal . . .]*
240	H	v 12′	ì.ne.šè ab.làl kur.ra gá[l u]m.ma.an.tag$_4$
	W	iv 5′	[. . . . . .ta]g$_4$
	BB	obv. 14	ì.ne.[š]è ab.làl kur.re gál ù.bí.in.tag$_4$
	JJ	11′	[. . . . . . . k]ur.ra gál⸢ù⸣.[. . .]
	GG	8′	[ì.n]e.šè ab.làl [. . . . .]
	rr$_2$	i′ 4′	ne.šè ab.l[àl . . . .]
		XII 82	*lūman takkap [erṣeti tepette]*
241	H	v 13′	šubur.a.ni kur.ta e$_{11}$.d[è.m]u.na.ab
	BB	obv. 15	[. .].a.ni kur.ta e$_{11}$.dè.mu.na.ab
	JJ	12′	[. . . . . . . e]$_{11}$.dè.[. . .]

	GG	9′	[. . .r]a.ni kur.ta [. . . . . .]
	rr$_2$	i′ 5′	šubur.a.ni kur.ta [. . . . . .]
		XII 83	*utukku ša En[kīdu kī zaqīqi ultu erṣeti tušellâ]*

MS rr has the following extra line:

241a	rr$_2$	i′ 6′	ur.sag šul ^{d}ut[u dumu ^{d}nin.gal.e tu.da?]
		XII 84	*ana qibīt [Ea . . . . . .]*
		XII 85	*qarrādu eṭlu Šamaš mār Nin[gal* x x]x
242	H	v 14′	ab.làl kur.ra gál im.m[a.a]n.tag$_4$
	BB	obv. 16	ab.làl kur.re gál mu.na.ab.tag$_4$
	JJ	13′	[. . . . .].m[a. . .]
	GG	10′	[ab.l]àl kur.ra gá[l . . . . .]
	rr$_2$	i′ 7′	ab.làl kur.r[a . . . .]
		XII 86	*{lūman} takkap erṣeti iptēma*
243	H	v 15′	si.si.ig.ni.ta šubur.a.ni kur.t[a mu.u]n.⌜da⌝.ra.ab.e$_{11}$.dè
	BB	obv. 17	[si].si.ig.ni.⌜ta šubur⌝.a.ni kur.ta mu.ni.in.e$_{11}$
	GG	11′	[. . .i]g.ni.ta šu[bur. . . . .]
	rr$_2$	i′ 8′	šubur.a.ni ^{d}en.k[i.dùg . . . .]
		XII 87	*utukku ša Enkīdu kī zaqīqi ultu erṣeti uštēlâ*
244	H	v 16′	gú.ni gú.da mu.ni.in.⌜lá⌝ n[e m]u.un.su.ub.bé
	BB	obv. 18	[. . g]ú.da mu.ni.lá ne mu.un.su.[. .]
	GG	12′	[. .n]i gú.da mu.ni.i[n. . . . .]
	rr$_2$	I′ 9′	gú.ni.da gú.[. . . . .]
		XII 88	*innedrūma uttaššaqū*
245	H	v 17′	èn.tar.re im.kú[š].ù.[n]e
	BB	obv. 19	[. . . r]e im.mi.in.kúš.ù.ne [Ø?]
	GG	13′	[. . .ta]r.re im.[. . . . .]
	rr$_2$	i′ 10′	èn.tar.re [. . . . . . .]
		XII 89	*imtallikū ištanallū*
246	H	v 18′	á.ág.gá kur.ra igi [b]í.in.d[uḫ.à]m?
	BB	obv. 20	[. . .g]á kur.re igi bí.duḫ [Ø?]
	GG	14′	[. . .g]á kur.r[a . . . .]
		XII 90–1	*qibâ ibrī qibâ ibrī / ûrti erṣeti ša tāmuru qibâ*
247	H	v 19′	nu.uš.ma.ab.bé.en ku.⌜li⌝.mu nu.uš.⌜ma⌝.[ab.b]é.en
	BB	obv. 21	[. . .m]a.a[b.bé].⌜en ku⌝.li.mu n[u. . . . .]
	GG	15′	[. . . . .a]b.[bé.e]n k[u. . . . .]
		XII 92	*ul aqabbâkku ibrī ul aqabbâkku*

One source transposes ll. 246–7:

247	rr$_2$	i′ 11′	nu.uš.ma.ab.bé.[. . . . .]
246	rr$_2$	i′ 12′	á.ág.gá [. . . . .]
248	H	v 20′	tukum.bi á.ág.gá kur.ra mu.ra.ab.[bé.en]
	GG	16′	[. . .] ⌜á?⌝.á[g. . . . .]

	rr$_2$	i′ 13′	trace
		XII 93	*šumma ûrti erṣeti ša āmuru aqabbīka*
249	H	v 21′	[za].e tuš.a ér gá.⸢e⸣ ga.tuš ga.é[r]
	V	iii 1′	za.[. . . . .]
	rr$_1$	i′ 1′	x[. . . . .]
		XII 94–5	[*att*]*a tišab biki* / [*anāk*]*u lūšibma lubki*
250	H	v 22′	[giš? š]u bí.in.tag.[g]a šà.zu ba.e.ḫúl
	V	iii 2′	x[. . . . .]
	rr$_1$	i′ 2′	UŠ.UŠ [. . . . .]
		XII 96	[*ibrī*? *iš*]*ara*? *ša talputūma libbaka iḫdû*
251	H	v 23′	[x x (x x) mu.u]n.ši.du.un bí.in.dug$_4$
	V	iii 3′	U[Š?. . . . .]
	rr$_1$	i′ 3′	UŠ giš.ùr.[gin$_7$? . . . .]
252	H	v 24′	[x x x sumun].⸢a⸣.gin$_7$ uḫ bí.in.t[ag]
	V	iii 4′	g[al$_4$? . . . .]
	BB	rev. 1′	[. . . . . . . .gi]n$_7$ uḫ [b]í.in.[.]
	CC	iii′ 1′	[. . . . . . .].⸢gin$_7$⸣ [. . . . . . .]
	rr$_1$	i′ 4′	gal$_4$.la tuba(ME) [. . . . .] / [. . . . .]
		XII 97	[x x *kī lub*]*ārī*? *labiri kalmatu ikkal*
253	H	v 25′	[. . . ki].in.dar.gin$_7$ saḫar.ra ab.[s]i
	BB	rev. 2′	[. . . . .].dar.ra.gin$_7$ saḫar.ra a.ab.si
	CC	iii′ 2′	[. . . . . .d]ar?.ra.gin$_7$ saḫar.r[a . .]
	rr$_1$	i′ 5′	gal$_4$.la ki.in.[. . . . .]
		XII 98	[*ibrī*? *ūru*? *ša ta*]*lputūma libbaka iḫdû*
		XII 99	[*kī nigiṣ erṣet*]*i eperī mali*
254	H	v 26′	en.e u$_8$ bí.in.dug$_4$ saḫar.⸢ra ba⸣.[da].an.dúr
	BB	rev. 3′	[. . . b]í.in.dug$_4$ saḫar.ra ba.da.an.dúr
	CC	iii′ 3′	[. .] ⸢u$_8$⸣ bí.in.dug$_4$ saḫar.r[a . . . . .]
	rr$_1$	i′ 6′	en.e bil$_4$.[ga.mes . . . .]
		XII 100	[*bēlu ū'a*] *iqbīma* [*ina e*]*pri ittapalsiḫ*
		XII 101	[*Gilgāmeš ū'a*] *iqbīma* [*ina epr*]*i ittapalsiḫ*

MS rr alone has the following extra line:

254a	rr$_1$	i′ 7′	nu.uš.ma.ab.[bé.en ku.li.mu nu.uš.ma.ab.bé.en]
255	H	v 27′–8′	lú dumu.ni diš.àm igi bí.duḫ.àm [igi bí].⸢duḫ⸣.àm / a.na.gin$_7$ an.ak
	BB	rev. 4′	[. . . .].diš.àm igi bí.duḫ.a igi bí.duḫ.a a.na.g[in$_7$ an].⸢ak⸣
	CC	iii′ 4′	[. .dum]u.ni diš.àm igi bí.duḫ.àm igi b[í. . . . .]
	DD	obv. 1	[. . . . . à]m igi bí.duḫ.àm igi bí.duḫ.àm ⸢a.na.gin$_7$ an⸣.ak
	qq	obv. 1–2	[. . . . . b]í.duḫ.a / [a.na.gin$_7$] ⸢ì⸣.gál
	rr$_1$	i′ 8′	lú dumu.ni diš.àm [. . . . .]
		XII 102	[*ša mārūšu ištēnma tāmur*]*u ātamar*

256	H	v 29′	^{giš}gag é.gar$_8$.a.na ab.⸢rú.a gig⸣.ga i.i
	BB	rev. 5′	[. .] é.gar$_8$ rú.a gig.ga⸢i⸣.[i]
	CC	iii′ 5′	^{giš}gag gar$_8$.ra.an.na ab.rú.a gig.g[a . .]
	DD	obv. 2	[. . . . .].an.na ab.rú.a gig.ga [i].i
	EE	1	[. . . . . a]b.rú.a gig.ga i.i
	qq	obv. 3	[. . . . .] gig.ga {x} i
	rr$_1$	i′ 9′	^{giš}gag é.gar$_8$.r[a. . . . .]
		XII 103	[*sikkatu ina igarīšu ret*]*âtma* [*marṣiš ina m*]*uḫḫi ibakki*
257	H	v 30′–1′	lú dumu.ni min.àm igi bí.duḫ.àm igi bí.duḫ.àm / a.na.gin$_7$.na.an.ak
	BB	rev. 6′	⸢lú!⸣ dumu.ni min.àm igi bí.duḫ.a igi bí.duḫ.a a.na.⸢gin$_7$⸣ a[n.ak]
	CC	iii′ 6′	lú dumu.ni min.àm igi bí.duḫ.àm igi bí.d[uḫ . . . .]
	DD	obv. 3a	[. . .].ni min.àm igi bí duḫ.àm 〈. . .〉
	EE	2	[. . .].⸢ni min!?⸣.àm igi bi.duḫ.àm a.n[a. . . . . .]
	pp	rev. 1′–2′	[. .dum]u.ne min.à[m . . . . . . / a.na.gi]n$_7$ [ì.gál]
	qq	obv. 4–5	[. . . . . ig]i bí.duḫ.a / [a.na.gin$_7$] ì.gál
	rr$_1$	i′ 10′	lú dumu.ni min.à[m . . . .]
		XII 104	[*ša mārūšu šināma tāmur ā*]*tamar*
258	H	v 32′	sig$_4$ min.a al.tuš ninda al.gu$_7$.e
	BB	rev. 7′	sig$_4$.a al.tuš ninda al.g[u$_7$.e]
	CC	iii′ 7′	sig$_4$ min.àm a.ab.tuš ninda al.g[u$_7$.e]
	DD	obv. 3b	sig$_4$ min.àm [. .].⸢tuš ninda al⸣.gu$_7$.e
	EE	3	[. . . . . nind]a al.KA.e
	pp	rev. 3′	[x x]x a.⸢ab.tuš⸣
	qq	obv. 6	[. . . . .] ab.tuš
	rr$_1$	i′ 11′	sig$_4$ min ab.tuš [. . . . . .]
		XII 105	[*ina šitta libnāti ašibma*] *akalu ikkal*
259	H	v 33′	lú dumu.ni eš$_5$.àm igi bí.duḫ.àm igi bí.duḫ.àm a.na.gin$_7$ an.ak
	BB	rev. 8′	lú dumu.ni eš$_5$.àm igi bí.duḫ.a igi bí.duḫ.a a.na.[gin$_7$] an.ak
	DD	obv. 4a	[. . dum]u.ni eš$_5$.àm igi bí.duḫ.àm 〈. . .〉
	EE	4	[. . . . .].àm igi bí.duḫ.àm a.[. . . . .]
	FF	1′	[. .] ⸢dumu⸣.[. . . . . à]m igi b[í. . . . .]
	pp	rev. 4′–5′	[. . . . .n]e? eš$_5$.⸢àm⸣ igi bí.in.⸢duḫ⸣ / [. . . .] ⸢ì⸣.gál
	qq	obv. 7–8	[. . . . .] igi bí.duḫ.a / [a.na.gin$_7$] ì.gál
	rr$_1$	i′ 12′	lú [dum]u.ni eš$_5$.à[m . . . .]
		XII 106	[*ša mārūšu šalāšatma tāmur*] *ātamar*
260	H	v 34′	^{kuš}ùmmu dag.si.ke$_4$ a al.na$_8$.na$_8$
	BB	rev. 9′	[^{kuš}ùm]mu dag.si.k[e$_4$ a] ì.na$_8$!.⸢na$_8$⸣
	DD	obv. 4b	^{kuš}ùm[m]u ⸢dag⸣.si.[. . .].⸢na$_8$⸣.na$_8$
	EE	5	[. . . . .] ⸢a⸣ ì.na$_8$.[. .]
	FF	2′	[^{ku}]^{š}ùmm[u da]g.si a a[l. . .]
	pp	rev. 6′	[. . . . .] x [. . . . .n]a$_8$.n[a$_8$]
	qq	obv. 9	[. . . . .] a mu.na$_8$.na$_8$
	rr$_1$	i′ 13′	^{kuš}ùmmu dag.s[i. . . . .]
		XII 107	[*ina nādi ša dakšî*] *mê išatti*

261	H	v 35′	lú dumu.ni limmu$_5$.àm igi bí.duḫ.àm igi bí.duḫ.àm a.na.gin$_7$ an.ak
	BB	r. 10′–11′	lú dumu.ni limmu$_5$.àm igi bí.duḫ.a igi bí.duḫ.a / a.na.gin$_7$! na.an.⸢ak⸣
	DD	obv. 5a	[.] dumu.ni limmu$_5$.àm igi bí.duḫ.àm ⟨. . .⟩
	EE	6	[. . . . . du]ḫ.àm igi bí.duḫ.à[m . . . .]
	FF	3′	[. d]umu.ni limmu$_5$.à[m] igi bí.in.[. . . . .]
	pp	rev. 7′–8′	[. . . . . i]n.⸢du$_{11}$⸣/ [. . . . . ì].gál
	qq	obv. 10	[. . . . .] igi bí.duḫ.a / ⸢a⸣.na.gi[n$_7$] ì.[gá]l
	rr$_1$	i′ 14′	lú dumu.ni limmu$_5$.àm i[gi . . . .]
		XII 108	*[ša mārūšu erbetma tāmu]ru ātamar*
262	H	v 36′	lú anše.limmu$_5$.lá.gin$_7$ šà.ga.ni al.ḫúl
	V	iii 14′	⸢lú anše⸣.limmu$_5$.lá.⸢gin$_7$ šà.ga⸣.n[i . . .]
	BB	rev. 12′	[. . anš]e.limmu$_5$.lá.gin$_7$ š[à.g]a.ni al.⸢ḫúl⸣
	DD	obv. 5b	l[ú . . . .lim]mu$_5$.lá.gin$_7$ šà.⸢ga.ni al⸣.ḫúl
	EE	7	[. . . . . .n]i [. .]
	FF	4′	[. .] anše.limmu$_5$.[l]á.gin$_7$ šà.g[a. . . .]
	pp	rev. 9′	[. . . . . .n]i al.dùg!(KAM)
	qq	obv. 12	[l]ú an[še x x] ⸢šà.ga.a.ni⸣ a[l. . .]
	rr$_1$	i′ 15′	lú anše.limmu$_5$.lá.gin$_7$ [. . . . .]
		XII 109	*[kī ša imēr ṣind]âti libbašu ḫadi*
263	H	v 37′	lú dumu.ni iá.àm igi bí.duḫ.àm igi bí.duḫ.àm a.na.gin$_7$ an.ak
	V	iii 15′	lú dumu.ni iá.àm igi bí.[duḫ].a ⟨. . .⟩
	BB	r. 13′–14′	lú dumu.ni iá.àm igi bí.duḫ.a igi bí.duḫ.a / a.na.gin$_7$ an.ak
	DD	obv. 6	⸢lú⸣ dumu.ni iá.àm igi b[í.duḫ].a ⟨. . .⟩
	EE	8	traces
	FF	5′	[. .d]umu.ni iá.àm igi bí.in.duḫ.àm [. . . . .]
	pp	r. 10′–11′	[. . . . . .d]u$_{11}$ / [. . . . . .]
	qq	o. 13–14	[. . . . . . . .à]m igi bí.duḫ.⸢a⸣/⸢a⸣.[na.gin$_7$] ì.[gál]
	rr$_1$	i′ 16′	lú dumu.ni iá.àm igi [. . . . .]
		XII 110	*[ša mārūšu ḫanšatma t]āmuru ātamar*
264	H	v 38′–9′	dub.sar ša$_6$.ga.gin$_7$ á.ni gál bí.in.tag$_4$ é.gal si.s[á.bi] / {U} ba.an.ku$_4$.k[u$_4$]
	V	iii 16′	dub.sar ša$_6$.ga.gin$_7$ á.ni gál bí.t[ag$_4$ . . . .]
	BB	rev. 15′–16′	[. . . š]a$_6$.ga.gin$_7$ á.ni gál bí.in.tag$_4$ / é.gal si.sá.bi ba.an.ku$_4$.ku$_4$
	DD	obv. 7	dub.sar ša$_6$.ga.gin$_7$ á.⸢ni gál bí⸣.[. . . .g]al si.sá.bi ba.an.ku$_4$.ku$_4$
	FF	6′–7′	[. .].sar ⸢ša$_6$.ga.gin$_7$⸣ á.ni gál bí.t[ag$_4$ . . . . . .] / ba.an.ku$_4$.[ku$_4$]
	pp	rev. 12′	[. . . . . .ta]g$_4$ é.gal s[i. . . . .]
	qq	obv. 15	dub.sar ⸢sa$_6$⸣.g[a.gi]n$_7$ ⸢á⸣.ni gál bí.in.t[ag$_4$ ⟨. . .⟩]
	rr$_1$	i′ 17′	dub.sar ša$_6$.ga.[. . . . .]
		XII 111–12	*[kī ṭupšarr]i damqi issu petât / [išariš] ana ēkalli irrub*
265	H	v 40′	lú dumu.ni àš.àm igi bí.duḫ.àm igi bí.⸢duḫ⸣.àm a.na.gin$_7$ a[n. . . .]
	V	iii 17′	lú dumu.ni àš.àm igi bí.d[uḫ.àm ⟨. . . .⟩]
	BB	r. 17′–18′	lú dumu.ni àš.àm igi bí.duḫ.àm igi bí.duḫ.àm / a.na.gin$_7$ an.ak
	DD	obv. 8a	lú dumu.ni àš.à[m . . . .]
	FF	8′	[. .dum]u.ni àš.àm igi bí.in.duḫ.àm igi bí.[. . . . .]

	pp	r. 13′–14′	[. . . . .] ⌜igi bí⌝.in.d[u$_{11}$] / [. . . .] ì.gál
	qq	o. 16–17	[l]ú dumu.ne àš.à[m igi bí.duḫ.a] / [a.na.gi]n$_7$ ⌜ì⌝.[gál]
	rr$_1$	i′ 18′	lú dumu.ni àš.àm ig[i . . . .]
		XII 113	*[ša mārūšu šeššetma t]āmuru ātamar*
266	H	v 41′	lú ^{giš}apin lá.gin$_7$ šà.ga.ni al.dù[g]
	V	iii 18′	lú ^{giš}X.AB lá.gin$_7$ šà.ga.ni ì.ḫ[úl]
	DD	obv. 8b	[. . . . . .gi]n$_7$ šà.ga.ni al.dùg
	FF	9′	[. .^{g}]^{iš}apin lá.a.gin$_7$ šà.ga.ni al.[.]
	pp	rev. 15′	[. . . . . .g]a.a.ni ⌜al⌝.dùg
	qq	obv. 18	[.]apin íl.la.gin$_7$ šà.g[a. . . .]
	rr$_1$	i′ 19′	lú apin.lá.gin$_7$ [. . . . . . .]
267	H	v 42′	lú dumu.ni imin.àm igi bí.duḫ.àm igi bí.duḫ.àm a.na.gin$_7$ ⌜an⌝.a[k]
	V	iii 19′	lú dumu.ni imin.àm igi bí.duḫ.àm ⟨. . .⟩
	DD	obv. 9	lú ⌜dumu.ni⌝ imin.àm [. .].duḫ.a x x x ⟨. . .⟩
	FF	10′	[. .du]mu.ni imin.àm igi bí.in.duḫ.àm igi b[í. . . . .]
	pp	rev. 16′–17′	[. . . . . .à]m igi [b]í.in.du$_{11}$ / [. . . .] ì.gál
	qq	obv. 19–20	[lú dumu.n]e imin.àm [igi bí.duḫ.a] / [a.na.gin$_7$] [ì.gál]
	rr$_1$	i′ 20′	lú dumu.ni imin.àm [. . . . .]
268	F	vi 1	[. . . . .].⌜tuk⌝
	H	v 43′	dub.ús dingir.re.e.ne.ke$_4$ ^{giš}gu.za íb.tuš di.da giš ba.t[uk]
	V	iii 20′	dub.ús dingir.re.e.ne.ke$_4$ ^{giš}gu.za íb!.⟨tuš⟩ di.da giš ba.tuk
	DD	obv. 10	dub.ús ⌜dingir⌝.re.e.ne.ke$_4$ ^{giš}gu.z[a] ⌜i⌝.íb.[. . d]i.da giš ba.an.tuk
	FF	11′	[. . . d]ingir.re.e.ne.ka ^{giš}gu.za i.í[b . . . .]
	pp	rev. 18′	[. . . . . . .].⌜e⌝.ne ^{giš}gu.za íb.tuš d[i.d]a giš ba.an.t[uk]
	qq	obv. 21	[. . . . .]x.⌜re.ne⌝ [. . . . .]
	rr$_1$	i′ 21′	dub.ús dingir.re.e.n[e . . . .]

From here onwards the manuscripts disagree as to the number and order of the remaining lines. In order to avoid an artificial line count I have assigned to each group of questions and replies a letter instead of line numbers and organized them roughly by theme. First are childless people (a–e), then those that have been disfigured (f–k), those that have sinned against parents and gods (l–n), those that are denied funerary rituals (o–q), those that have a comfortable afterlife (r–s) and those whose ghosts are not to be found in the Netherworld but roam the world above (t):

a 1	H	vi 20′–1′	[lú ibila? nu].tuku / [igi bí.duḫ.àm igi bí.duḫ.à]m a.na.gin$_7$ an.ak
	V	iii 21′	lú ibila nu.tuku igi bí.duḫ.àm
	DD	obv. 19	lú i[bil]a nu.tuku igi bí.[. .]
	DDD	1′	[. . .] ⌜nu.tuku⌝ i[gi . . . .]
	pp	r. 19′–20′	[. . . . . .tuk]u igi bí.in.du$_{11}$ / [a.na.gin$_7$] ì.gál
	rr$_1$	i′ 22′	lú ibila nu.tuku igi [. . . . .]
a 2	H	vi 22′	[sig$_4$ GIŠ.KID.ra.gin$_7$ ninda a]l.gu$_7$.e
	V	iii 22′	sig$_4$ GIŠ.KID.ra.gin$_7$ ninda al.gu$_7$.e
	DD	obv. 20	sig$_4$ G[IŠ.KID.r]a.gin$_7$ ⌜ninda? ì⌝.g[u$_7$.e]
	DDD	2′	[. . . .KI]D.ra.gin$_7$ [. . . . . . .]

	pp	rev. 21′	[. . . . .] ninda ì.gu$_7$.e
	rr$_1$	i′ 23′	⸢sig$_4$ GIŠ.KID.ra⸣.[. . . . .]
b 1	F	vi 2	[. . . . . a]n.⸢ak⸣
	H	v 44′–5′	tiru.e igi bí.duḫ.àm igi bí.duḫ.à[m] / a.na.gin$_7$ an.[ak]
	V	iii 23′	tiru.e igi bí.duḫ.àm
	DD	obv. 11	tiru.⸢e⸣ [i]gi b[í. .].àm
	FF	12′	[. .].⸢e⸣ igi bí.in.duḫ.a igi bí.duḫ.àm ⸢a⸣.[. . . . .]
	DDD	3′	[. .].⸢e⸣ igi bí.⸢duḫ⸣.à[m . . . .]
b 2	F	vi 3	[. . . . .].⸢ús⸣
	H	v 46′	pa a.la.la ḫur.ra.gin$_7$ ub.dug$_4$.ga.a a[b. .]
	V	iii 24′	pa a.la.la ḫur.ra.gin$_7$ ub.dug$_4$.ga ab.ús
	DD	obv. 12	pa a.la.[l]a ḫu.r[u.g]in$_7$ ub.du[g$_4$. . .]x[21]
	DDD	4′	[. . .].la ḫur.ra.gin$_7$ [. . . . . . .]
		XII 118–19	*kī šurinni damqi tub[qa] a[ḫi]z? / kī . . . . . .* [. . .]x
c 1	F	vi 4	[. . . . .].ak
	H	v 47′–8′	munus ù.nu.tu igi bí.duḫ.àm igi bí.d[uḫ.àm] / a.na.gin$_7$ an.a[k]
	V	iii 25′	⸢munus nu⸣.ù.tu igi bí.duḫ.àm
	DD	obv. 13	géme⸢ù⸣.[nu].t[u] igi b[í. .].a
	DDD	5′	[. . . . . .t]u igi bí.duḫ.àm [. . . . .]
	qq	rev. 1–2	munus nu.ù.t[u] igi b[í.duḫ.a] / a.na.gi[n$_7$] ì.[gá]l
c 2	F	vi 5	[. . . . .] x x ⸢lú nu.mu.un.ḫúl⸣.e
	H	v 49′	[^{du}]^{g}zal.líl.da.gin$_7$ ti.na ì.gurud [x (x) x] / lú nu.mu.un.ḫ[úl.e]
	V	iii 26′	^{dug}za.líl.⸢da.gin$_7$⸣ [t]i.na ab.gurud lú nu.mu.ḫúl.e
	DD	obv. 14	^{dug}zal.l[íl. . .] ti.na ì.[. . . . . . .ḫú]l?.e
	DDD	6′	[. . .l]íl.⸢da⸣.gin$_7$ ti.na a[b. . . . .]
	qq	rev. 3	DUG ⸢SAḪAR? x.ga?⸣ ti.la in.šub lú n[a.me? igi? nu].ši.lá.e
d 1	F	vi 6	[. . . . .].⸢um⸣.si.ge / [. . . . . .à]m a.na.gin$_7$ an.ak
	H	v 50′	[. . .t]ur úr dam.na.ka túg n[u.ub.si.ge / igi bí].duḫ.àm igi bí.duḫ.àm ⸢a⸣.[na.gin$_7$ an.ak]
	V	iii 29′	guruš.tur úr dam.na.ka t[úg nu.s]i.ge igi bí.duḫ.àm
	DD	obv. 15	guruš.tur ú[r. . .n]a.ka túg nu.si.g[e? . . . . .]
	DDD	7′	[. . . ú]r ⸢dam⸣.ma.na túg [. . .] / igi bí.duḫ.[. . . . .]
	qq	rev. 4–5	guruš tur ⸢úr dam⸣.na.ke$_4$ túg nu.si.ga igi [bí].duḫ.a a.na.gin$_7$ ì.gál
d 2	F	vi 7	[. . . . .] x x x x x x
	H	v 51′–2′	[. . . .] šu im.mi.in.d[u$_7$. . . . .] / [ér im.mi.i]n.š[e$_8$.še$_8$]
	V	iii 30′–1′	[éš.šu.a]k (or ⸢a⸣?) šu im.mi.du$_7$.du$_7$ [ugu éš.šu.(a).a]k.ba / [ér mi.in.š]e$_8$.⸢še$_8$⸣
	DD	obv. 16	éš.šu.⸢a!(GAR)⸣ [. .i]m.mi.du$_7$ ugu éš.šu.a[k?.ba . . . . .]
	DDD	8′	[. . . . .].⸢mi⸣.[. . . . .]
	qq	rev. 6	gi.šu.ak.a šu mi.⸢ni.du$_8$⸣ u[g]u gi.šu.ak.a gig i (= e 2!)

21 x = ⸢GÁ⸣ or similar.

e 1	F	vi 8	[. . . . .].um.si.ge / [. . . . . .du]h̬.àm a.na.gin$_7$ an.⌈ak⌉
	H	v 53′	trace
	V	iii 27′	ki.sik[il ú]r d[am. . . tú]g nu!.si.ge igi bí.duh̬.àm
	DD	obv. 17	ki.sikil [úr] dam.na.ka túg nu.si.ge i[gi . . . .]
	qq	rev. 7–8	ki.sikil tur úr dam.na.ke$_4$ ^{giš}dála nu.du$_{10}$ igi bí.duh̬.⌈a⌉ / a.na.gin$_7$ ì.gál
e 2	F	vi 9	[. . . . .] x x x x x x
	V	iii 28′	gi.šu.ak šu im.[. . . ug]u gi.šu.ak ér mi.in.še$_8$.še$_8$
	DD	obv. 18	gi.šu.a.[ak š]u i[m.m]i.du$_7$ ugu gi.šu.a [. . . . . .]
	qq	rev. 9	éš eš$_5$.tab.ba šu im.mi.du$_8$ ⌈ugu eš$_5$!.tab⌉.ba.a gig.ga i (cf. d 2!)
f 1	V	iv 6′	lú ùr šub.ba i[gi bí].duh̬.àm
	ll	obv. 1	lú ùr.ta šub.ba igi b[í.duh̬.àm] / igi i.ni.⌈in⌉.duh̬.à[m a.na.gin$_7$ an.ak]
	mm	obv. 4	[l]ú ùr!.ta[22] šub.ba igi bí.duh̬ / a.na.gin$_7$ ì.gál
	qq	r. 13–14	lú ùr šub.ba igi bí.duh̬.a / a.na.gin$_7$ ì.gál
	rr$_2$	ii′ 9′	lú ùr.ta šub.ba igi bí.in.duh̬.a igi ì.d[uh̬.a] a.na.gin$_7$ ì.gál
f 2	V	iv 7′	[gìr].pad.rá.ni š[u.gibil nu].ub.bé.eš
	ll	obv. 2	gìr.pad.rá.ni šu.gibil nu.u[b.b]é.[eš]
	mm	obv. 5	[gu$_4$].gin$_7$ al.šub úh̬ im.da.ab.⌈gu$_7$⌉
	qq	rev. 15	gìr.pad.a.⌈ni šu.gibil?⌉ 〈. . .〉
	rr$_2$	ii′ 10′	[.].pad.rá.ni šu.gibil nu.ub.di?
g 1	V	iv 4′	[l]ú ur.mah̬.e gu$_7$.a [igi b]í.duh̬.àm
	qq	o. 34–5	lú [u]r.e gu$_7$.a ⌈igi bí.duh̬.a⌉ / a.na.gin$_7$ ì.[gál]
g 2	V	iv 5′	[a] šu.mu a gìr.mu g[ig.ga.b]i im.me
	qq	obv. 36	á š[u.m]u á gìr.mu ⌈á?⌉ [. . .]
h 1	ll	obv. 3	lú ^{d}iškur.ra ⌈gìr.bal⌉ mu.ni.in.[ra].ra / igi bí.duh̬.àm igi i.ni.duh̬.àm a.na.[gin$_7$ an.ak]
	qq	r. 10–11	lú ^{d}iškur bulug$_5$.gá igi bí.duh̬.a / a.na.gin$_7$ ì.gál
h 2	ll	obv. 4	gu$_4$.gin$_7$ al.dúb uh̬ im.da.gu$_7$.[e]
	qq	rev. 12	gu$_4$.gin$_7$ im.gurum mur im.da.ab.gu$_7$.⌈e⌉
i 1	V	iv 8′	[lú.sah̬a]r.šub.ba igi b[í.d]uh̬.àm
	DD	rev. 3′	lú.sah̬ar.[šub.ba igi bí.duh̬.àm]
	ll	obv. 5	lú.sah̬ar.šub.ba igi bí.duh̬.àm igi i.ni.⌈duh̬.àm⌉ / a.na.gin$_7$ an.⌈ak⌉
	qq	rev. 17	lú sah̬ar šub.ba igi bí.duh̬.a a.⌈na.gin$_7$ ì⌉.[gál]
i 2	V	iv 9′	[gu$_4$.gim] al.dúb uh̬ im.d[a.g]u$_7$.⌈e⌉
	DD	rev. 4′	gu$_4$.gin$_7$ a[l.dú]b uh̬ im.da.gu$_7$?.e
	SS	obv. 1′	[gu$_4$.gin$_7$ al.dúb uh̬ i]m.d[a].g[u$_7$.e]
	ll	obv. 6–7	ú.[ni al.b]ar a.ni al.bar ú.bu al.gu$_7$.e / a.bu al.na$_8$.na$_8$ / uru.bar.ra.a al.tuš

22 *PSD* A/3, p. 196, reads ama.ta, but the other sources are unequivocal.

	qq	rev. 18–19	a al.bar.ra ú al.bar.ra / udug di in.⸢duḫ⸣ bar.bi.a im.tuš
	rr_1	ii′ 1′–2′	ú.ni al.bar a.ni ú šeš al.gu$_7$.e / a šeš al.na$_8$.na$_8$ uru^{ki}.bar.ra al.tuš
j 1	V	iv 1′	[. . .].b[a? . . . .]
	DD	rev. 1′	⸢lú⸣.[. . . . . igi bí.duḫ.àm]
j 2	V	iv 2′–3′	[ú.n]i a[l.bar a.ni al.bar ú.bu al.gu$_7$.e] / a.b[u a]l.n[a$_8$].na$_8$
	DD	rev. 2′	ú.ni a[l.bar a.ni al.bar ú.bu al.gu$_7$.e a.bu al.na$_8$.na$_8$]
	mm	rev. 1′–3′	[ú.ni al.bar a].ni [al.bar] / [ú.bu] al.[gu$_7$.e] / a.[bu al.na$_8$.na$_8$]
k 1	V	iv 15′	[lú ^{giš}má].NI ra ⸢igi bí.duḫ.àm⸣
	DD	rev. 9′	lú ^{giš}má.GAG ra ù.ni.in.šú.šú igi b[í!?.in.duḫ.àm]
	SS	o. 9′–10′	[lú ^{giš}má.GAG ra igi bí.duḫ.à]m igi bí.duḫ.àm / [a.n]a.gin$_7$ an.ak
	mm	obv. 1	[lú] ^{giš}má.GAG ra igi bí.[duḫ] / a.na.gin$_7$ ì.g[ál]
	qq	o. 37–8	lú má.GAG igi [bí.duḫ.a] / a.na.gin$_7$ ì.[gál]
		XII 144	*ša ina tarkulli maḫṣu tāmur ā[tamar]*
k 2	V	iv 16′	[á.š]e ama.gá lú mu.na.ab.[bé?]
	DD	rev. 10′	á.še ama.mu ⸢lú ḫé?⸣.na.ab.[bé]
	SS	rev. 1	[á.še ama.m]u.ra lú ḫé.en.na.a[b.bé?]
	mm	obv. 2	⸢á⸣.šè ama.mu lú ḫé.en.na.ab.⸢bé⸣ / ti bu.ra.ni a ⟨. . .⟩
	qq	obv. 39	á.šè ama.mu lú mu.na.bé ^{giš}kak.e dù.d[ù? . . .]
		XII 145a	*lūman ana ummī[šu u] ab[īš]u*
k 3	V	iv 17′	[^{gi}]^{š}má+GAG bu.ra a mu.⸢dè?⸣.eb?.bé.[x x]
	DD	rev. 11′	^{giš}má.GAG bu.ra.ba.a a ⸢ḫé⸣.x x[x x] x x
	SS	rev. 2	[^{giš}má.GAG b]u.ra.ni a ḫé.em.mi.ib.x x
		XII 145b	*ina nasīḫ sikkat[i itt]analla[k]*
k 4	V	iv 18′–19′	[giš] sag.du pad.pad.rá.ni / NÍG mu.ni.ib.gu.ul.e
	DD	rev. 12′	giš sag.du ninda.pad.pad.rá DA?.gá NÍG ḫé.⸢da⸣.[ab.gu].ul?.e
	SS	rev. 3–4	[giš sag.d]u ninda.pad.pad.da.ni / [x] ḫé.bí.ib.gu.ul.e
	mm	obv. 3	[gi]š sag.du ninda.pad.pad.rá.[n]i / A bí.ib.gul.la.[Ø?].a
	qq	obv. 40	níg.gu$_7$.e ⸢sag.du⸣ ninda bad.bad.dè NÍG gul.gul [. . .]

One source transposes ll. k 3–4:

k 4	rr_2	ii′ 2′	[giš sa]g.du.AŠ ninda.pad.pad.rá.ni NÍG ḫé.eb.gul.e
k 3	rr_2	ii′ 3′	[^{gi}]^{š}má.GAG bu.ra.ni a ḫé.mu.na.dé.e
l 1	ll	obv. 8	lú in[i]m ama.a.a.na.ke$_4$ ní nu.te.gá.dam / igi bí.duḫ.àm ⸢igi i⸣.ni.duḫ.àm a.na.gin$_7$ an.ak
	mm	o. 10–11	[lú inim] a.a.na ù ama!.na / [ní n]u.⸢te.gá.dam⸣ igi bí.duḫ / [a.na.gin$_7$] ì.gál
	rr_1	ii′ 3′–4′	lú inim ama.a.a.na.ka ní nu.te.gá.e.dam / igi bí.duḫ.a igi ì.duḫ.a a.na.gin$_7$ ì.gál
l 2	ll	obv. 9	a IM.mu a giš.re.[e]n.na mu.nag.ge$_4$ nu.na.gul.e
	mm	obv. 12	[. . . . .]x x x[x]
	rr_1	om.	

m 1	ll	obv. 10	lú áš ama.a.a.na.ke$_4$ sá bí.du[g$_4$.g]a / igi bí.duḫ.àm igi i.ni.duḫ.àm ⸢a.na⸣.[gin$_7$ a]n.ak
	mm	obv. 6–7	[lú á]š! ama.na.ke$_4$ / sá bí.in.dug$_4$.ga / [igi b]í.duḫ a.na.gin$_7$ ì.gá[l]
	rr$_1$	ii′ 5′–6′	lú áš ama.a.a.na.ka sag bi.sal.la / igi bí.duḫ.a igi ì.duḫ.a a.na.gin$_7$ ì.gál
m 2	ll	obv. 11	ibila ba.da.kar gidim.ma.ni šu al.[dag.d]ag.ge
	mm	obv. 8–9	[ibil]a ba.an.da.kar / [gidim.a.n]i! ⸢šu al⸣.GÁ.GÁ$^{x-x}$.ke$_4$
	rr$_1$	om.	
n 1	ll	obv. 12	lú mu.dingir.r[a.na] sag bí.in.[sal].la / igi bí.du[ḫ.àm igi] ⸢i⸣.ni.duḫ.à[m a.n]a.gin$_7$ ⟨an⟩.ak
	rr$_1$	ii′ 7′	[l]ú mu dingir.ra.ni sag bi.sal.la igi bí.duḫ.àm / igi ì.duḫ.a a.na.gin$_7$ ì.gál
n 2	ll	obv. 13	gidim.ma.ni ⸢ú⸣ [. . . . . . . a]l.[. .]
	rr$_1$	ii′ 8′	[gi]dim.a.ni ú šeš al.gu$_7$.e a šeš al.na$_8$.na$_8$
o 1	DD	rev. 5′	lú mè.[a] šub.ba igi bí.i[n.duḫ.àm]
	SS	obv. 2′–3′	[lú mè.a šub.ba] igi bí.d[uḫ.àm] / [igi bí.duḫ.àm] a.na.gin$_7$ a[n.ak]
	mm	rev. 4′–5′	[lú mè.a] šub.ba igi bí.[duḫ] / a.na.gin$_7$ [ì.gál]
	rr$_2$	ii′ 4′	lú mè.a šub.ba igi bí.duḫ.a igi ì.duḫ a.na.gin$_7$ ì.gál
		XII 148	*ša ina tāḫāzi dēku tāmur āta[mar]*
o 2	DD	rev. 6′	ad!(KI).ama.ni sag.[du.(ni) nu?].⸢mu⸣.un.dab$_5$ dam.a.ni ér ì.še$_8$.š[e$_8$]
	SS	obv. 4′	[. . . . . da]m.a.ni é[r ì.še$_8$.še$_8$] ninda al.⸢gu$_7$⸣.[e]
	mm	rev. 6′–7′	[ad.ama.ni] sag.du nu.dab.⸢dab⸣.[bé.n]e / dam.a.ni ér ba.ni.še$_8$.še$_8$
	rr$_2$	ii′ 5′	[a]d.ama.ni sag.du.ni nu.un.dab$_5$ dam.a.ni ugu.ni / ér gig mu.un.še$_8$.še$_8$
		XII 149	*abūšu u ummašu rēssu našû u aššassu ina muḫḫiš[u ibakk]â[šu]*
p 1	rr$_2$	ii′ 6′	[lú] ad$_6$.da.ni edin.na an.ná ⟨. . .⟩
		XII 150	*ša šalamtašu ina ṣēri nadât tāmur ātamar*
p 2	rr$_2$	om.	
		XII 151	*eṭemmašu ina erṣeti ul ṣalil*
q 1	H	vi 17′–18′	[gidim lú níg.sè.ke nu.tuku i]gi bí.duḫ.à[m] / [igi bí.duḫ.àm a.na.gin$_7$ an].ak
	V	iv 10′	[gidim lú ní]g.sè.ke nu.tuku igi bí.[duḫ.àm]
	DD	rev. 7′	gidim lú níg.⸢sè.ke⸣ nu.tuku igi bí.in.[duḫ.àm]
	SS	obv. 5′–6′	[gidim lú níg.s]è.⸢ke nu.tuku⸣ igi ⸢bí.duḫ.àm⸣ / [igi bí.d]uḫ.à[m a.n]a.⸢gin$_7$⸣ a.an.a.ak
	ll	obv. 14	gidim lú níg.sè.ke [nu].tuku [igi bí.du]ḫ.àm / igi i.ni.duḫ.àm [a.n]a.gin$_7$ an.a[k]
	mm	r. 12′–14′	[gidim lú níg].ki.sì.ga nu.tuku / [igi b]í.duḫ / [a.na.gin$_7$] ì.gál
	rr$_1$	ii′ 9′	[gi]dim lú níg.sè nu.tuk.a igi bí.duḫ.a igi ì.duḫ.a / a.na.gin$_7$ ì.gál
		XII 152	*ša eṭemmašu pāqida lā īšû tāmur ātamar*

q 2	H	vi 19′	[šu.su.ub.bé ninda.pad.pad.rá x sila] šub.ba ì.gu$_7$.e
	V	iv 11′–12′	[šu.su.ub.bé nind]a.pad.pad.rá PA.a⸢sila⸣ [šub.ba] / [ì].g[u$_7$.e]
	DD	rev. 8′	šu.su.ub.bé⸢ninda.pad.pad.rá PA.a?⸣ sila šub.ba ì.g[u$_7$.e]
	SS	obv. 7′–8′	[šu.su.ub.b]é ninda.pad.pad.rá / [x sila šub].ba ì.gu$_7$.e
	ll	obv. 15	[š]u.su.ub.bé útul.a ninda.p[ad.pad].rá PA sila šub.ba / ì.gu$_7$.e
	mm	r. 15′–16′	[šu.su.ub.bé] ninda.pad!(NINDA).pad.rá.a.ni / [x sila šu]b.ba ì.gu$_7$.⸢e⸣
	rr$_1$	ii′ 10′	[šu.s]u.ub.bé útul.a ninda.pad.pad.rá.ni PA sila šub.ba ì.gu$_7$./e
		XII 153	*šukkulāt diqāri kusīpāt akali ša ina sūqi nadâ ikkal*
r 1	H	vi 26′–7′	[n]ìgin.gar.tur.tur mu ní.[ba] nu.zu / [igi b]í.duḫ.àm igi bí.duḫ.àm [a.na.gin$_7$ an.a]k
	V	iv 20′–1′	[nì]gin.gar tur.tur mu ní.ba nu.zu / igi bí.duḫ.àm
	DD	rev. 13′	nìgin.gar.tur.tur mu⸢ní.ba nu.zu⸣ [. . .].duḫ.a
	SS	rev. 5–6	[nìgin.gar].tur.tur mu ní.ba nu.zu / [igi bí.du]ḫ.àm igi bí.duḫ.àm a.⸢na⸣.gin$_7$ an.ak
	ll	rev. 1–2	[nìgin.gar.tur.tur] mu ní.ba nu.zu igi bí.duḫ.àm / [i]gi ì.ni.duḫ.àm a.na.gin$_7$ an.ak
	mm	r. 17′–18′	[nìgin].gar.ra tur.t[ur mu n]í.bi nu.zu / [igi bí.duḫ] / a.na.g[in$_7$ ì.gál]
	qq	rev. 20–1	nìgin mu nu.⸢sa$_4$⸣.àm igi bí.duḫ.a / a.na.gin$_7$ ì.gál
	rr$_1$	ii′ 11′	[nì]gin.gar tur.tur mu ní.bi nu.zu igi bí.duḫ.àm / igi ì.duḫ.a a.na.gin$_7$ ì.gál
r 2	H	vi 28′–9′	[^{giš}]banšur kù.sig$_{17}$ kù.babbar là[l ì].⸢nun.ta⸣ / e.ne im.di.⸢e⸣.ne
	V	iv 22′–3′	[^{g}]^{iš}banšur kù.sig$_{17}$ kù.babbar làl ì.nun.ta / e.ne im.di.e.ne
	DD	rev. 14′	^{giš}banšur kù.s[ig$_{17}$ k]ù.babbar làl ì.nun.⸢ta e⸣.[ne im.di.e.n]e
	SS	rev. 7–8	[^{giš}banšur kù.si]g$_{17}$ kù.babbar.ra làl ì.[n]un.na / [e.n]e im.di.[e.n]e
	ll	rev. 3	⸢^{giš}bugin kù.sig$_{17}$ kù⸣.babbar làl ì.nun.na / e.ne im.da.e.ne
	mm	rev. 19′	⸢^{giš}⸣bugin k[ù.sig$_{17}$ kù.babbar làl ì.nun.na e.ne im.di.e.ne]
	qq	rev. 22	^{giš}⸢banšur kù⸣.[sig$_{17}$ kù.babbar x x x]x e.ne [. . .]
	rr$_1$	ii′ 12′	[^{gi}]^{š}bugin kù.sig$_{17}$ kù.babbar.ra làl ì.nun e.ne im.di./e.ne
s 1	H	vi 23′–4′	[lú . . . .].e / [igi] ⸢bí.duḫ.àm igi⸣ [bí.duḫ.à]m a.na.gin$_7$ an.ak
	DD	rev. 15′	lú ug$_7$.⸢a dingir.ra⸣.na ì.ug$_7$.⸢e igi bí⸣.[in.duḫ].⸢a⸣
	rr$_2$	ii′ 7′	[l]ú ug$_7$ dingir.ra.ni mu.un.ug$_5$.ga igi bí.duḫ.a
		XII 146	*ša mūti ilīšu [imūtu t]āmur ātamar*
s 2	H	vi 25′	[ki.^{gi}]^{š}ná dingir.re.e.ne al.ná
	DD	rev. 16′	ki.^{giš}ná [dingir.r]e.⸢e⸣.na⸢al?⸣.[n]á
	rr$_2$	ii′ 8′	[^{gi}]^{š}ná dingir.re.e.ne.ke$_4$ ì.ná a.girin⸢mu.un⸣.na$_8$.na$_8$
		XII 147	*ina mayyāl [il]ī ṣalilma mê zakûti išatti*
t 1	H	vi 30′–1′	[lú] izi.lá igi bí.duḫ.[à]m / [ig]i nu.mu.dè.duḫ.⸢àm⸣
	V	iv 24′–5′	lú izi.lá igi bí.duḫ.àm / igi nu.un.ni.duḫ.àm
	DD	rev. 17′	lú izi.lá i[gi bí.i]n.duḫ.a igi⸢nu.mu⸣.[ni.du]ḫ.a
	SS	rev. 9–10	[lú izi.lá ig]i bí.duḫ.à[m igi] / [nu.m]u.ni.duḫ.[àm]
	ll	rev. 4	lú izi.lá igi bí.duḫ.àm igi nu.mu.⸢na⸣.[d]uḫ.à[m]

	mm	r. 20′–1a′	[l]ú izi.b[il.lá igi bí.duḫ] / igi ⟨nu.mu.ni.duḫ⟩
	qq	rev. 23	lú izi b[il.l]á igi ⌜nu.bí⌝.d[uḫ.a]
	rr$_1$	ii′ 13′	[l]ú izi bil.lá igi bí.duḫ.a igi ì.duḫ.a a.na.gin$_7$ / ì.gál

One source has two extra lines at this point:

t 1a	qq	rev. 24	a.na.aš.àm k[u.l]i.a.mu nu.bí.in.tar [(. . .)]
t 1b	qq	rev. 25	èn.bi in.ta[r] ku.li.a.mu
t 2	H	vi 32′	[gidim.m]a.ni nu.gál i.bí.ni an.n[a? b]a.e.e$_{11}$
	V	iv 26′–7′	gidim.a.ni nu.gál / i.bí.ta an.na ⌜e$_{11}$.dè⌝
	DD	rev. 18′	gidim.m[a.ni nu.gál] ⌜i.bí.ni an⌝.[na ba.e.e$_{11}$]
	SS	rev. 11	[gidim.a.ni nu.gál i].bí.n[i an.na ba.e.e$_{11}$]
	ll	rev. 5	i.bí.ni an.na ba.a.e$_{11}$.àm / gidim.a.ni ki.a nu.ub.tuš
	mm	rev. 21b′	⟨i⟩.bí ⌜ni an⌝.[na e$_{11}$?]
	qq	rev. 26	[g]idim.a.⌜ni kur.ta⌝ [x] x x e?.bí⌝.da an.e ba.e
	rr$_1$	ii′ 14′	[gidi]m.a.ni ki.in.gub.a nu.gál i.bí.ni an.na ba. : / è

MSS HVSSmmqqrr end the list of shades at this point but MS DD offers a catch-line to a continuation:

u 1	DD	rev. 19′	⌜lú? x igi⌝ [bí.in.du]ḫ.a

MS ll adds more:

v 1	ll	rev. 6–7	lú dingir lul.lul.sè.k[e] nam.érim ba.an.kud / igi bí.duḫ.àm igi i.[ni.du]ḫ.àm a.na.gin$_7$ an.ak
v 2	ll	rev. 8	ki.a.nag sag kur.r[a.ke$_4$ x (x) x]x.ra.aḫ? / nag.a ⌜i⌝.[n]ag.e
w 1	ll	r. 9–10	dumu gír.su ki a.n[ir?.k]e$_4$? a.a.na ù ama.na / igi bí.duḫ.àm [igi] ⌜i⌝.ni.duḫ.àm a.na.gin$_7$ [an.ak]
w 2	ll	rev. 11	igi lú.diš.ta.àm li.im dumu mar.dú.me.⌜eš⌝ / gidim.a.ni šu la.ba.an.ta.ra.ra gaba nu.ši.dub.⌜bu⌝
w 3	ll	rev. 12	dumu mar.dú^{ki}.a ki.a.nag sag kur.ra.ke$_4$ / igi.ba bí.íb.dab$_5$.bé.en
x 1	ll	rev. 13	dumu ki.en.gi ki.uri.ke$_4$ igi bí.duḫ.àm / igi i.ni.duḫ.àm a.na.gin$_7$ an.⌜ak⌝
x 2	ll	rev. 14	a ki.lul.la a lù.a bí.íb.nag.me.eš
y 1	ll	rev. 15	a.a.mu ù ama.mu me.a sig$_7$.[me.e]š / igi bí.duḫ.àm igi i.ni.duḫ.à[m a.na.gin$_7$ an.ak]
y 2	ll	rev. 16	[min.na].a.ne.ne.ne a ki.lu[l.la a lù.a] / bí.[í]b.n[ag.(me.eš)]

The end of the composition as it was known at Ur is presented on MS nn:

1′	nn	rev. 1′	[unug^{ki}.šè?] ⌜im.mi.gi$_4$⌝.g[i$_4$.ne]
2′	nn	rev. 2′	[u]ru.bi im.mi.gi$_4$.gi$_4$.n[e]
3′	nn	rev. 3′	[^{g}]$^{iš!}$šu.kár á.kár.ra.ke$_4$ *pa-a-šu* á.gíd.[da] / da.da.ra.šè mi.ni.in.k[u$_4$]
4′	nn	rev. 4′	é.gal.la.na ḫúl.ḫ[úl].la mi.ni.in.gar
5′	nn	rev. 5′	guruš ki.sikil unug!^{ki}.ga sag.tuku bu[r.š]úm.ma kul.[aba^{ki}]
6′	nn	rev. 6′	alam.bi igi mu.un.bar.bar.re.ne / im.ma.ḫúl.ḫúl.la
7′	nn	rev. 7′	^{d}utu agrun.na.ta è.a / sag mu.un.na.⟨íl⟩ {mi.ni.in.ág}
8′	nn	rev. 8′	á.bi mu.un.da.an.ág
9′	nn	rev. 9′	a.a.mu ù ama.mu a.si.⌜ig.ga nag.zé⌝.en

10′	nn	rev. 10′	u$_4$ nu.mu.un.da.sa$_9$ àm.da.dirig / àga.bi in.ši.TAG.ne
11′	nn	rev. 11′	^{d}bìl.ga.mes.e ki.ḫul.a ba.an.šub
12′	nn	rev. 12′	u$_4$ 9.kam ki.ḫul.a ba.an.šub
13′	nn	rev. 13′	gur[uš] ki.sikil unug^{ki}.ga sag!.tuku [b]ur.šu.ma k[u]l.aba^{ki} / ér ba.še$_8$.še$_8$
14′	nn	rev. 14′	bí.in.dug$_4$.ga.gin$_7$.nam
15′	nn	rev. 15′	dumu gír.su^{ki}.a zag bí.in.tag
16′	nn	rev. 16′	a.a.mu ù ama.mu a.si.ig.ga nag.zé.en

At Mê-Turan a different ending was current, following on from t 2:

1″	qq	rev. 27	⌜šà⌝ ba.sàg ⌜mu.ra⌝.a.⌜ni⌝ ba.ug$_7$
2″	qq	rev. 28	lugal.⌜e⌝ nam.ti.⌜la ì.kin⌝.[kin]
3″	qq	rev. 29	en.e kur l[ú t]i.la.šè ⌜géštug.a⌝.[ni] ⌜na.an⌝.gub

Doxologies and colophons:

H	vi 33′	[. . . . .] zà.mí	
V	iv 28′	2 *šu-ši* 52?	
nn	rev. 17′	ur.sag ^{d}bìl.ga.mes dumu ^{d}nin.sún.ka / zà.mí.zu dùg.ga.àm	
qq	rev. 30	[x] x [x x] x [(x)] ⌜ù?⌝ mu.bi im.gíd.da	
rr$_1$	ii′ 15–16	[x x] dingir-*še-me* / [x x x]	3,20,1

Unplaced lines:

F	vi 10	[. . . . . .du]ḫ.⌜àm⌝ a.na.gin$_7$ an.ak
F	vi 11	[. . . . .]x.la
F	vi 12	[. . . . .].àm a.na.gin$_7$ an.ak
F	vi 13	[. . . . .].um.x[(x)]
F	vi 14	[. . . . .] trace
H	vi 1′	[. . . . .].íb?
H	vi 2′	[. . . . .]x
H	vi 3′	[. . . . .].e
H	vi 4′	[. . . . .].x.e
H	vi 5′–6′	[. . . . .].duḫ.àm / [a.na.gin$_7$ an].ak
H	vi 7′	[. . . . .].ma?
H	vi 8′	[. . . . .]x.ni
H	vi 9′	[. . . . . .n]á
H	vi 10′–11′	[. . . . . .duḫ].àm / [a.na.gin$_7$ an.a]k
V	iv 13′	[. . . . .]x.a igi b[í.duḫ.àm]
V	iv 14′	[. . . . . .] x[. . . . . .] x[. . . . . .]
DD	obv. 21	x[. . . . . igi] ⌜bí⌝.d[uḫ.àm]
UU	rev. 1′	[. . . . .] traces
UU	rev. 2′	[. . . . . .du]ḫ.àm igi bí.duḫ.àm
UU	rev. 3′	[. . . . .] x
mm	r. 8′–10′	[x x x]x.na x.na / [x x x].ma igi bí.duḫ / a.na.gin$_7$ ì.gál
mm	rev. 11′	[x x x]x.ta šu.ta im.x.ki

nn	obv.	mostly illegible; traces of igi bí.duḫ at the ends of several lines
qq	obv. 25[23]	[. . .] x [x x]x [. . . . .]
qq	obv. 26–7	[. . .] x [. . .] i[gi bí.duḫ.a] / [a.na.gin$_7$] ì.[gál]
qq	obv. 30	[x x x]x a na$_8$.⸢na$_8$⸣
qq	obv. 31–2	[x x x].àm igi bí.duḫ.a / [a.na.gi]n$_7$ ì.gál
qq	obv. 33	[x x]x uḫ!(ḪUR) im.da.ab.gu$_7$.e
qq	r. 15b–16	x x.ni di? in.duḫ.a igi b[í.duḫ.a] / a.na.gin$_7$ ⸢ì⸣.[gál]

TRANSLATION OF THE SUMERIAN TEXT

172 'On that day, if only my ball had stayed for me in the carpenter's house!
173 O carpenter's wife, like a mother to me! If only it had stayed there!
174 O carpenter's daughter, like a little sister to me! If only it had stayed there!
175 My ball has fallen down to the Netherworld, who will bring it up for me?
176 My mallet has fallen down to Ganzir, who will bring it up for me?'[24]
177 His servant Enkidu answered:[25]
178 'My lord, why are you weeping? Wherefore are you sick at heart?
179 This day[26] I myself will bring your ball up for you from the Netherworld,
180 I myself will [bring] your mallet up for you from Ganzir!'
181 Bilgames [answered] Enkidu:[27]
182 'If[28] this day you are going down to the Netherworld,
183 I will give you instructions, you should take in my instructions,
184 I will tell you a word, give ear to my word![29]
185 Do not dress in your clean garment,
186 they would surely take it as the sign of a stranger!
187 Do not anoint yourself with sweet oil from the flask,
188 at the scent of it[30] they will surely surround you!
189 Do not hurl a throwstick in the Netherworld,
190 those struck by the throwstick will surely surround you!
191 Do not hold a cornel rod in your hand,

[23] Cavigneaux's transliteration makes the line count higher by 2, supposing the lacuna that intervenes in the middle of MS qq obv. to account for 'six lignes perdues?' (*Iraq* 62, p. 12). However, the copy and photograph clearly do not allow so many (*Iraq* 62, pp. 14–15).

[24] So MS V; MS r (and probably W) hold a shorter version of the 2 lines: 'Who will bring my ball up from the Netherworld? Who will bring my mallet up from Ganzir?'

[25] So MS V; MSS H and HH: '[Enkidu] answered Bilgames'; MS r: 'his servant Enkidu called to him'.

[26] So MSS VWr; MS H omits 'this day'.

[27] So MSS HVWHH; MS r omits the line.

[28] So MSS HrHH; MS W omits 'if'.

[29] So MSS HWY; MS r transposes ll. 183–4.

[30] So MSS HYZ; MS r: 'you'.

192 the shades will tremble before you!
193 Do not wear sandals on your feet,
194 you will surely make [the Netherworld] shake![31]
195 Do not kiss the wife you loved,
196 do not strike the wife you hated,
197 do not kiss the son you loved,
198 do not strike the son you hated,[32]
199 the outcry of the Netherworld will seize you!
200 To the one who lies, the one who lies,
201 to the Mother of Ninazu who lies—
202 no garment covers her shining shoulders,[33]
203 no linen is spread over her shining breast,
204 her finger (nails) she wields like a *rake*,
205 she wrenches [her hair] out like [leeks.]'[34]
206 Enkidu paid no attention to the [word] of his master:[35]
207 he dressed in his clean garment,
208 they took it as the sign of a stranger!
209 He anointed himself in sweet oil from the flask,
210 at the scent of it they surrounded him![36]
211 He hurled a throwstick in the Netherworld,
212 those struck by the throwstick surrounded him!
213 He held[37] a cornel rod in his hand,
214 the shades did tremble before him!
215 He wore[38] sandals on his feet,
216 he made[39] the Netherworld shake!
217 He kissed the wife he loved,
218 he struck the wife he hated,
219 he kissed the son he loved,
220 he struck the son he hated,
221 the outcry of the Netherworld seized him!
221a From (that) evil day to the seventh day thence,
221b his servant Enkidu came not forth from the Netherworld.
221c The king uttered a wail, weeping bitter tears:

[31] So MS Y; MSS Zr: 'Do not make a noise in the Netherworld!'
[32] Ll. 195–8 are so given in MSS YZr. MS H orders them [195], 198, 197, 196; MS EEE has 195, 197, 196, 198.
[33] So MSS HYZ; MS AA omits the line.
[34] Ll. 204–5 in MSS SVYAA only; MSS HZ omit both.
[35] So MSS HVAA; MS Z omits the line.
[36] So MSS HZ; MSS VAA: 'they gathered about him'.
[37] So MSS HVZ; MS pp: 'carried'
[38] So MSS HVZ; MS pp: 'put'.
[39] So MSS HVZ; MS pp: 'making'.

221d 'My favourite servant, [my] steadfast companion, the one who counselled me—the Netherworld [seized him!]
221e Namtar did not seize him, Azag did not seize him, the Netherworld [seized him!]
221f The sheriff of Nergal that [releases no] man did not seize him, the Netherworld seized him!
221g He did not fall in battle, at the place of *manly endeavour*, the Netherworld seized him!'[40]
222 The warrior Bilgames, son of Ninsun,
223 made his way alone to Ekur, the house of Enlil,
224 before Enlil he [wept:][41]
225 '[O Father] Enlil, my ball fell into the Netherworld, my mallet fell into Ganzir,[42]
226 Enkidu *went* to bring it up, the Netherworld [seized] him![43]
226a My favourite [servant,] my steadfast companion, the one who counselled me—[the Netherworld] seized him![44]
227 [Namtar did not] seize him, Azag did not seize him, the Netherworld seized him!
228 The sheriff of Nergal that releases no man did not seize him, the Netherworld seized him!
229 He did not fall in battle, at the place of manly endeavour, the Netherworld seized him!'[45]
230 Father Enlil did not help him in this matter. He went to Eridu.[46]
231 He made his way alone to Eridu, the house of Enki,[47]
232 before Enki he wept:[48]
233 'O Father Enki, my ball fell into the Netherworld, my mallet fell into Ganzir,
234 Enkidu *went* to bring it up, the Netherworld seized him!
234a [My favourite servant, my steadfast companion, the one who counselled me—the Netherworld seized him!]
235 Namtar did not seize him, Azag did not seize him, the Netherworld seized him!
236 The sheriff of Nergal that releases no man did not seize him, the Netherworld seized him!
237 He did not fall in battle, at the place of manly endeavour, the Netherworld seized him!'[49]
238 Father Enki helped him in this matter,
239 he spoke to Young Hero Utu, the son born of Ningal:

[40] Ll. 221a–g in MS pp only.
[41] So MSS VY; MS pp: 'before Mullil he. . . '; MSS HUU omit the line.
[42] So MSS AApp; MS UU: 'the Netherworld'.
[43] So MSS YAAUU; MS pp, corruptly: 'Enkidu, to go out, to bring (it) up'.
[44] This line in MS pp only.
[45] MSS AABBUU transpose ll. 228 and 229; in l. 229 MS UU erroneously reads 'seize' for 'fall'.
[46] So MS BB; MS AA, erroneously: 'Nippur'. MS Y, corruptly: 'I will go to Nippur.'
[47] So MSS HYJJTT; MSS AABB omit the line.
[48] So MSS YAA; MSS HBBJJTT omit the line.
[49] MSS HBBGGJJ transpose ll. 236 and 237.

240 'Now, when you make an opening in the Netherworld,
241 bring his servant up to him from the Netherworld!'
241a Young Hero Utu, [the son born of Ningal,][50]
242 he made an opening in the Netherworld,
243 by means of his phantom he brought his servant up to him from the Netherworld.[51]
244 He hugged him tight and kissed him,
245 in asking and answering they made themselves weary:
246 'Did you see the way things are ordered in the Netherworld?
247 If only you would tell me, my friend, if only [you would tell] me!'[52]
248 'If I am to [tell] you the way things are ordered in the Netherworld,
249 O sit you down and weep!' 'Then I will sit and weep!'
250 'The one who handled (your) *penis* (so) you were glad at heart,
251 (and) you said, "I am going to [. . . *like*] a roof-beam,"
252 (her) vulva is infested with vermin like an [old] cloak,
253 (her) vulva is filled with dust like a crack in the ground.'
254 'Ah, woe!' said the lord, and sat down in the dust.
254a 'If only [you] would [tell] me, [my friend, if only you would tell me!]'[53]
255 'Did you see the man with one son?' 'I saw him.'[54] 'How does he fare?'[55]
256 'For the peg set in his wall bitterly he laments.'
257 'Did you see the man with two sons?' 'I saw him.' 'How does he fare?'
258 'Seated on two bricks[56] he eats a bread-round.'
259 'Did you see the man with three sons?' 'I saw him.' 'How does he fare?'
260 'He drinks water from the waterskin (slung) on the saddle.'
261 'Did you see the man with four sons?' 'I saw him.' 'How does he fare?'
262 'Like a man with a team of four donkeys his heart rejoices.'[57]
263 'Did you see the man with five sons?' 'I saw him.' 'How does he fare?'
264 'Like a fine scribe his hand is deft[58] and he enters the palace with ease.'
265 'Did you see the man with six sons?' 'I saw him.' 'How does he fare?'
266 'Like a man with plough in harness his heart is content.'[59]
267 'Did you see the man with seven sons?' 'I saw him.' 'How does he fare?'
268 'Among the junior deities he sits on a throne and listens to the proceedings.'
a 1 'Did you see the man with no heir?' 'I saw him.' 'How does he fare?'
a 2 'He eats a bread-round like a *kiln-fired* brick.'

[50] This line in MS rr only.
[51] So MSS HBBGG; MS rr probably read: 'his servant Enkidu [he brought up to him from the Netherworld]'.
[52] MS rr transposes ll. 246 and 247.
[53] This line in MS rr only.
[54] Some sources always include Enkidu's response, others sometimes, and still others always omit it.
[55] So Nippur MSS passim; MSS mmppqqrr passim: 'How is he?'
[56] So MSS HCCDDrr; MS BB: 'a brick'; MSS ppqq: 'He is seated [on. . .]', omitting 'he eats a bread-round'.
[57] So MSS HVBBDD; MS pp: 'his [heart] is content'.
[58] Lit. 'his arm is open'.
[59] So MSS HDDpp; MS V: 'his heart rejoices'.

b 1 'Did you see the palace *eunuch*?' 'I saw him.' 'How does he fare?'
b 2 'Like a useless *alala*-stick he is propped in a corner.'
c 1 'Did you see the woman[60] who had not given birth?' 'I saw her.' 'How does she fare?'
c 2 'Like a *defective* pot she is discarded with force, no man takes pleasure in her.'[61]
d 1 'Did you see the young man who had not bared the lap of his wife?' 'I saw him.' 'How does he fare?'
d 2 'He is finishing a hand-worked rope, he weeps over that hand-worked rope.'[62]
e 1 'Did you see the young woman who had not bared[63] the lap of her husband?' 'I saw her.' 'How does she fare?'
e 2 'She is finishing a hand-worked reed mat, she weeps over the hand-worked reed mat.'[64]
f 1 'Did you see the person who fell from a roof?' 'I saw him.' 'How does he fare?'
f 2 'They cannot repair his bones.'[65]
g 1 'Did you see the man eaten by a lion? How does he [fare?]'
g 2 'Bitterly he cries, "O my hand! O my foot!"'
h 1 'Did you see the man whom Iškur struck down in an inundation?'[66] 'I saw him.' 'How does he fare?'
h 2 'He twitches like an ox as the vermin consume him.'[67]
i 1 'Did you see the leper?' 'I saw him.' 'How does he fare?'
i 2 'His grass is set apart, his water is set apart, he eats uprooted grass, he drinks *waste* water, he lives outside the city.'[68]
j 1 '[Did you see] the [. . . ' 'I saw him.' 'How does he fare?]'
j 2 'His grass is [set apart,] his [water is set apart,] he [eats uprooted grass,] he drinks *waste* water.'
k 1 'Did you see the man struck by a mooring-pole?'[69] '[I saw him.]' 'How does he fare?'
k 2 'Whether a man says for him, "O my mother!", or pours a libation of water whenever a mooring-pole is pulled out,
k 3 a wooden "head" (is) his daily food ration, he destroys the. . .'[70]

[60] So MSS HVqq; MS DD, erroneously: 'slavegirl'.
[61] So MSS FHVDD; MS qq: '[no] man gives her [*a glance*]'.
[62] So MSS HVDD; MS qq: 'He holds a hand-worked reed mat, bitterly weeping over the hand-worked reed mat' (cf. e 2).
[63] So MSS FVDD; MS qq: 'undone the pin of'.
[64] So MSS VDD; MS qq: 'She holds a triple-ply cord, bitterly weeping over the triple-ply cord'.
[65] So MSS Vllqqrr; MS mm: 'He twitches (šub for dúb!) like an ox as the vermin consume him'.
[66] So MS ll; MS qq: 'the man whom Iškur *swamped*'.
[67] So MS ll; MS qq, corruptly: 'He kneels like an ox eating fodder.'
[68] So MS ll; MSS VDDSS: 'He twitches [like an ox] as the vermin consume him.' MS qq: 'Water that is set apart, grass that is set apart, . . . he lives outside'; MS rr: 'His grass is set apart, his water ⟨is set apart⟩, he eats bitter grass, he drinks bitter water, he lives outside the city.'
[69] So MSS VSSmmqq; MS DD adds: 'after *it was dropped*'.
[70] MS rr transposes ll. k 2 and k 3.

l 1 'Did you see the man who did not respect the word of his mother and father?' 'I saw him.' 'How does he fare?'

l 2 'He drinks water *measured* in a scale, he never gets enough.'[71]

m 1 'Did you see the man afflicted by[72] the curse of his mother and father?' 'I saw him.' 'How does he fare?'

m 2 'He is deprived of an heir, his ghost still roams.'[71]

n 1 'Did you see the man who *made light of* the name of his god?' 'I saw him.' 'How does he fare?'

n 2 'His ghost eats bitter bread, drinks bitter water.'

o 1 'Did [you see] the man fallen in battle?' '[I saw him.]' 'How does he [fare?]'

o 2 'His father and mother could not hold his head,[73] his wife weeps.'[74]

p 1 'Did you see [the one] whose body lies out in the plain?' '[I saw him.' 'How does he fare?]'

p 2 '[His ghost is not at rest in the Netherworld.]'

q 1 'Did you see the shade of him who has no one to make funerary offerings?' 'I saw him.' 'How does he fare?'

q 2 'He eats scrapings[75] (as) bread rations,[76] *a stick* tossed away in the street.'

r 1 'Did you see the little stillborn babies, who knew not names of their own?'[77] 'I saw them.' 'How do they fare?'

r 2 'They play amid syrup and ghee at tables[78] of silver and gold.'

s 1 'Did you see the man who died a natural death?'[79] '[I saw him.' 'How does he fare?]'

s 2 'He lies drinking clean water on the bed of the gods.'[80]

t 1 'Did you see the man who was burnt to death?' 'I did not see him.[81]

t 1a Why, my friend, did you not *spare* [. . . ?]'

t 1b 'I asked that question, my friend.'[82]

t 2 'His ghost is not there,[83] his smoke went up to the heavens.'

The version of the poem known at Nippur ended abruptly here. MS D adds as catch-line:

u 1 'Did you see the . . . man?' [. . .]

u 2 [. . . . .]

[71] So MSS llmm; MS rr omits the line.

[72] So MSS llmm; MS rr: 'who *made light of*'.

[73] Or, 'could not do him honour'. One source, MS DD, may not have included the negative particle.

[74] So MSS DDSSmm; MS rr: 'weeps bitterly'; MS SS adds: 'he eats bread'.

[75] So MSS DDSSmm; MSS llrr add: 'from the pot'.

[76] So MSS VDDSSll; MSS mmrr: 'his bread rations'.

[77] So MSS HVDDSSllmmrr; MS qq: 'who were not given names'.

[78] So MSS HVDDSSqq; MSS llmmrr: 'troughs'.

[79] Lit. 'the death his god'.

[80] So MS rr; MSS HDDmm omit 'drinking clean water'.

[81] So MSS HVDDSSllqq; MS rr: 'I saw him.' 'How does he fare?'

[82] These two lines in MS qq only.

[83] So MSS HVDDSS; MS ll: 'His ghost does not dwell in the Netherworld.' MS qq: 'His ghost [is not] in the Underworld.' MS rr: 'His ghost has no *place* (there).'

MS ll, from Ur, adds:

v 1 'Did you see the one who cheated a god and swore an oath?' 'I saw him.' 'How does he fare?'

v 2 'At the places where libations of water are offered at the top of the Netherworld, he drinks . . .'

w 1 'Did you see the citizen of Girsu at the place *of sighs* of his father and mother?' 'I saw him.' 'How does [he fare?]'

w 2 'Facing each man there are one thousand Amorites, his shade cannot push them off with his hands, he cannot charge them down with his chest.

w 3 In the place where the libations of water are offered at the top of the Netherworld, the Amorite takes *first place*.'

x 1 'Did you see the sons of Sumer and Akkad?' 'I saw them.' 'How do they fare?'

x 2 'They drink water from the place of a massacre, dirty water.'

y 1 'Did you see where my father and mother dwell?' 'I saw them.' '[How do they fare?]'

y 2 '[The two] of them drink water from the place of a massacre, [dirty water.]'

MS nn, also from Ur, concludes the text thus:

1′ He sent them back to [*Uruk*,]
2′ he sent them back to their city.
3′ Gear and equipment, hatchet and spear he put [away] in the *store*,
4′ he made merry in his palace.
5′ The young men and women of Uruk, the old men and women of Kullab,
6′ looking upon those statues, they rejoiced.
7′ He lifted his head as Utu was coming forth from his chamber,
8′ he issued instructions:
9′ 'O my father and my mother, drink clear water!'
10′ The day was not half gone by, . . . , they were . . .
11′ Bilgames performed the mourning rites,
12′ for nine days he performed the mourning rites.
13′ The young men and women of Uruk, the old men and women of Kullab wept.
14′ And it was just as he had said,
15′ the citizen(s) of Girsu 'touched the edge':
16′ 'O my father and my mother, drink clear water!'

Another ending adds three lines that link the text with the beginning of Bilgames and Huwawa A (MS qq, from Mê-Turan):

1″ The heart was stricken, his mind despaired.
2″ The king searched for life,
3″ the lord to the Living One's land[84] did turn [his] mind.

Doxology (MS nn):

O warrior Bilgames, son of Ninsun, sweet is your praise!

[84] Or 'mountain'.

13

Critical and Philological Notes on the Standard Babylonian Epic

TABLET I

1–6. Soon after Thompson's edition of 1930 A. Schott wrote: 'die Anfangszeilen des GE [Gilgameš-Epos] können leider immer noch nicht vervollständigt werden, ohne daß man reichlichen Gebrauch von der Phantasie machte' (*ZA* 42 (1934), p. 93). Much fantasy has indeed been brought to bear on the text's incipit, for the situation has changed only very recently, with the discovery of Rm 956, a new piece of MS d. This fragment demonstrates that for the past century, ever since Haupt's copy identified the first line preserved on MS B_3 as SB I 1, readers of the epic have been telescoping into one couplet what is in fact two parallel couplets. The new piece also provides the ends of the the first four lines. However, the beginnings of ll. 2 // 4, 5 and 6 are still open to restoration, as is the end of l. 5. In discussing these lines, as elsewhere in this commentary in comparable situations, I have thought it useful to collect for comparison the many and different restorations of earlier editors and the more recent translators, insofar as they have not been refuted by the discoveries of the intervening years. Though some ideas put forward for these opening lines are more attractive than others, there is often little to choose between them. It also remains eminently possible in each case that none of them is right. The recovery of the end of l. 1 is a case in point, for none of the many suggestions had come close to *išdī māti*, and we are reminded how perilous it is to restore all but the most predictable lines of this poem. In many lines, here and elsewhere, I thus prefer to leave open the question of restoration.

1 // 3. The incipit of the Standard Babylonian epic, *ša naqba/ī īmuru*, is known from the many colophons which refer to the text under this title (Tablet I: MSS [B]F, Tablet V: MS aa, Tablet VI: MSS AOa, Tablet VIII: MS R, Tablet IX: MS D, Tablet X: MS K, Tablet XI: MS C, Tablet XII: MS G). Note that contra the transliteration of C. Wilcke, *ZA* 67 (1977), p. 202, the colophon of MS F_4, his Kol_g, reads *i-mu-ra* éš.g[àr, not *i-mu-ra lu-*[, and is thus not at odds with the text given here.

On *naqbu* see Chapter 10, the introduction to Tablet I. The phrase *išdī māti* is well attested in the meaning 'stability of the land', especially in the expression *išdī māti kunnu*, 'to keep the land stable' (used by e.g. Hammurapi: D. Frayne, *RIME* 4, pp. 334–5, 12–15 // 13–16: suḫuš ma.da . . . ma.ni.in.ge_4.en // SUḪUŠ KALAM . . . *ú-ki-in-nam*). Its use as an epithet without *kânu* or another such verb is found in the description of things in the divine sphere (gods, goddesses and temples), but it is not a phrase that describes kings, so here it qualifies *naqbu* rather than Gilgameš. A line with identical structure, in which the verb of a relative clause is sandwiched between its object and an epithet that modifies its object, is SB VII 136: *ša . . . kurunna išqûka simat šarrūti.*

2 // 4. The variety of restorations proposed for the beginning of the line is considerable. Thompson, ignoring the case ending, opted for *kul-la-t*]*i*, followed by Böhl (cf. also Heidel, Speiser, Tigay, *Evolution*, p. 261, Dalley, Kovacs, Pettinato, Shaffer, *Sumerian Sources*, p. 20, Parpola, *SAA Gilg.*). Oppenheim suggested [*ta-ma-a*]-*ti*, 'the seas' (*Or* NS 17 (1948), p. 17; also von Soden, *ZA* 53, p. 221, Reclam², Labat, Jacobsen, *Studies Moran*, p. 246, fn. 22). Other ideas are [*ru-qe*]-*ti*, 'die Ferne' (von Soden, *ZA* 72, p. 162, Reclam⁴) and [*šá kib-ra-a-t*]*i*, 'the world regions' (Wilcke, *ZA* 67, p. 201; cf. Bottéro's '[la terre en]tière(?)'). At the end of the line only Wilcke and Parpola had suggested *ḫassu*. It should be noted that in l. 4 MS F does not leave enough room after *īdû* for *kalāma ḫassu*; presumably the repetition was not fully spelled out on this tablet.

5. The older commentators, in particular, were sensibly very reluctant to restore in this line. Viable modern suggestions for the first word are: Böhl, [*puzrāt*]*imma*; Wilcke, [*šá* x (x)-R]I?-*ma*; Tigay [*ib-r*]*i*?-*ma*; Parpola, [*i-ḫi-i*]*ṭ-ma*. The last word, now *pa*-x-x, might be *pa-r*[*ak-ki*]. This is reminiscent of the omen apodosis that probably records Gilgameš's dominion over *šarrānī āšibūt parakkī* (l. 8 of the collection of omens quoted in Chapter 3, the sub-section on omens mentioning Gilgameš), but until the beginning of the line is recovered it is probably unsafe to persevere.

6. With this line the reader reaches safer ground. I restore after *CAD* N/2, p. 160, though others have read the first word [*šug-m*]*ur* (Wilcke etc.) and [*ra*]-*áš* (Böhl etc.). At the end of the line there is only room for two signs at most following *i* (see MS F_3), which discounts *i*-[*šim-šu* ᵈ*A-nu*] (von Soden, *ZA* 72, p. 162, Reclam⁴). Böhl and others restored *i*-[*du-ú*], Parpola *i*-[*ḫu-uz*]. The latter fits better the metrical requirement at the line end of a stressed penultimate syllable.

7. The orthography *ip-tu* for *ipte* is no sin in a Late Babylonian manuscript such as MS d. Indifference to the nature of final vowels already occurs in manuscripts of Gilgameš from Kuyunjik and Aššur, though less frequently. See the list of culprits assembled in Chapter 9, the section on Spelling conventions sub (t).

8. On the significance of this line see the introduction to Tablet I in Chapter 10.

9. The expression *urḫa rūqta*/*rūqata alāku*/*rapādu* is a stock phrase in SB Gilgameš, occurring on its own in SB I 9, II 262 // III 24–5, III 47–8, IX 54, X 64 // 141 // 241, and also as part of a standard couplet (for which see SB 120–1 and commentary).

10. The conventional restoration at the beginning of this line, since Thompson's edition at least, has been [*iḫ-ru*]-*uṣ*, supposedly meaning 'he engraved' (e.g., *CAD* Ḫ, p. 94; *AHw*, p. 324; Böhl, Wilcke, *ZA* 67, p. 202; C. B. F. Walker, *JCS* 33 (1981), p. 194; Tigay, *Evolution*, p. 262; Parpola, *SAA Gilg.*), even though *ḫarāṣu*, 'to cut off, in', is not used in such a meaning elsewhere. In fact, Haupt annotated the broken sign in his copy (*Nimrodepos*, p. 1) as either *kin* or *ḫub*, with no suggestion of *uṣ*. To my eyes the traces are even less ambiguous, certainly of *kin* or *ṭàr*. The shape of the fragment (B_3) also discounts [*iḫru*]*ṣ*, for it indicates that only one sign can be missing before these traces, and only a short one, at that. Compare each of the immediately preceding lines, where only a single sign, or parts of a single sign, are missing: [*nap*], [*ni*], [*u*]*b* and [*ur*], the last three absolutely secure (note also that since the fragment is from near the top left corner of a typical Gilgameš library tablet, the margin will not be vertical, but slightly inclined along the tablet's bevelled edge, allowing more slightly space for, e.g., [*nap*] in l. 4, than for [x] in the present line). This consideration rules out as too long the obvious [*ú-k*]*in*, and we are left only with [*šá-k*]*in*. I take this as an active stative, the first of many in SB Gilgameš.

11. Thompson's reading of the first word as *u-še-piš* was taken from BM 34916, since published separately in Pinches's copy (*CT* 46 17) and now joined and recopied by I. L. Finkel as MS h. As

the new copy reveals, Thompson's reading was erroneous in every particular, though this lapse is fully explained by the bizarre orthography. Consideration of the space available on MS B_3 should have indicated that [*ú-še-pí*]*š* was impossible, however: there is only room there for [*up-pí*]*š*. The use of the II/1 stem for construction work is not common, but note, in an inscription of Aššur-rîm-nišēšu, *dūru ša . . . ab-ba-ia ú-up-pi-šu-ni*, 'the wall that . . . my predecessors built' (A. K. Grayson, *RIMA* 1, p. 101, 5–8). *CAD* E, p. 232, explains the use of the II/1 stem in this passage as marking plurality of subject, a point which cannot be made in our line; perhaps the building of a city wall, which would best be begun in several places at once, was in itself an intensive activity.

The designation of Uruk as *supūru*, 'sheepfold', which almost everywhere in the SB text replaces the OB epic's *ribītum*, is also found in *Šurpu* II 168 and the poetic narrative K 3200 (Thompson, *Gilgamish*, pl. 59, 11, 13). The epithet alludes to the common notion of the ruler protecting his people as a shepherd does his flock. The image of the city with its wall encompassing the human flock like the fence of a sheepfold is also found in the ceremonial name of the wall of Borsippa, Ṭāb(i)-supūršu, 'Its sheepfold is pleasant' (for references see George, *BiOr* 53 (1996), 365–6).

12. On the temple E-anna in the Gilgameš epic see Chapter 5, the introduction to the Pennsylvania tablet. The epithet it bears here also occurs in the Great Prayer to Ištar, King, *STC* II pl. 77, 28: *a-ḫu-lap-ki be-let* é.an.na *qud-du-šú šu-tùm-mu el-lu* // *KUB* XXXVII 36, 25′: [. . . *bēlat*(gašan)[*a*]][*i* d]*a-a-ak-ki qú-ud-du-š*[*i* . . .], ed. E. Reiner and H. G. Güterbock, *JCS* 21 (1967), p. 260; on the reading of the temple name é.an.na as *ayakku* see most recently P.-A. Beaulieu, *NABU* 2002/36.

13. The reading of the last word of the line continues to cause difficulty, with the traces on MS F_3 very difficult to read. In his earlier copy of this fragment (*Nimrodepos* no. 1f) Haupt saw a sign beginning with two horizontals, the lower preceding the upper, but later thought he saw more (no. 43, like *t*[*u*] or *l*[*i*]). Despite this, most commentators have opted for *ni-ip-ḫ*[*u-šu*] or *né-eb-ḫ*[*u-šu*] (from E. Ebeling, *AfO* 8 (1932–3), p. 226, to J. N. Postgate, *NABU* 1998/30). I agree with Haupt's first impression. The new copy of MS h confirms the possibility of only one sign after *ni-ib*, and a short one at that. Since the sign on F_3 is not *ḫu*, *ḫa* or *ḫi*, all readings that use *nipḫu*, *nēbeḫu*, *nebḫu*, etc., are discounted. An added difficulty is the ambiguity of *qû*, which can mean 'thread, string, cord', and 'copper, bronze'. The last word either qualifies *qê*, 'like a *q.* of *n.*', or is a predicate, 'whose *n.* is like a *q.*' or 'who is *n.* like a *q.*'.

One possibility is suggested by Kovacs's rendering 'which gleams like *copper*(?)', namely that *ni-ib-š*[*u*] derives from the root √*nb'* > *nebû*, 'to shine'. In that case the phrase *kīma qê n.* would literally mean 'whose gleaming is like *q.*', i.e. the wall gleams red like copper. An argument against this is that before a possessive suffix one would expect a trisyllable in triptotic declension (GAG^3 §65h), whether the form is parsed as the infinitive (*nebûšu*) or as a previously unattested noun **nību* (*nībūšu*). As is well known, the construct state of nouns of the type **pars*, **pirs* and **purs* deriving from finally weak roots can be monosyllabic (e.g. *bīš*, *mār*) as well as bisyllabic (e.g. *bīši*, *māri*). However, a search of such nouns reveals almost no cases of a possessive suffix attached to a monosyllabic base. In the dictionary articles on nouns from finally weak roots that display monosyllabic stems (*bīru* III, IV, *bīšu* II, *būnu* II, *būšu* I, *dīku* II, *dīlu*, *dīšu* II, *ḫīpu*, *ḫīṭu*, *ḫūdu*, *kīlu*, *kīsu* III, *kīṣu* II, *kūṣu*, *līqu* II, *māru*, *mīlu*, *mīnu* II, *mīru* II, *mīsu* I, *mīšu*, *mīṭu*, *mūšu*, *nību* I, *nīdu*, *nīqu*, *nīšu* I, *pānu* I, *pīdu* I, *pītu* I, *pūṣu*, *qēmu*, *qību*, *qītu*, *rību* II, *rīdu* I, *sību*, *sīḫu* I, *ṣēlu*, *ṣīpu* I, *ṣūmu*, *šīqu* I, *šīsu*, *šūqu* I, *tību*, *ṭēḫu*, *ṭību*, *ṭīmu*, *ṭīpu*, *ṭīru* IV and *zūku* I), the only such cases I can find among the dozens of regular, triptotic forms that hold to the paradigm *mārūšu*, *mārāšu*, *mārīšu* are three: (a) s.v. *ḫūdu*, the reading *mullāt ḫu-ud-ka* in the Tukultī-Ninurta Epic iv b 19 (*CAD* H, p. 224); (b) s.v. *nību*, the LB PN *Ṭāb-ni-ib-šu* (*VAS* V 49, 24, as analysed by *CAD* N/2, pp. 205 and 248); and (c) s.v. *zēru*, one spelling *ze-er-šu* in OB Susa (*MDP* XXII 70, 1). However, these are all treacherous witnesses, for different reasons. Case (a) is now discredited (read *mul-tar-ḫu-ut-ka*). In case (b) the derivation of the second element of the name is not *nību* but *nipšu*, 'Sweet is the (newborn's) smell (or breath)' (with *AHw*, p. 792). The remaining case (c) is the lapse of a single foreign scribe; set against the many attestations of *zērūšu* and *zērāšu*, it is not enough to overturn a grammatical rule. Transcriptions such as *mār-ka* and *mār-šu* (e.g. even *GAG*³ §§15e, 135g, 138k) remain ungrammatical, accordingly, and in the line under comment a reading **nībšu*, 'its gleam', is ruled out.

For help in this problem one may ask what is the conventional imagery attached to walls. It is a cliché that walls are 'high as a mountain', but this figure does not fit *kīma qê*. As already noted in George, *NABU* 1991/101, in Lugalbanda Epic II the wall of Uruk is compared with the drawstring of a bird snare stretched out over the plain (ll. 305, 371: bàd unug^{ki}.ga gu mušen.na.gim edin.na ḫé.ni.lá.lá), and in an inscription of Nabopolassar the wall of Babylon is described as 'a mighty cincture' (F. N. H. Al-Rawi, *Iraq* 47 (1985), p. 10, ii 41: *e-bi-iḫ dan-num*, see *NABU* 1991/19, 3; against this interpretation see W. Farber, *NABU* 1991/72; cf. also H. Vanstiphout, *NABU* 1991/103). These passages bear witness to an image of the city wall as a cord or belt. In the light of this it seems more probable that *kīma qê* in the present line means 'like a cord' not 'like copper'. As the text stands, I can suggest no better than *qê nipši*. The word *nipšu* appears to signify one of the strands that are the result of pulling apart (*napāšu*) a tuft of wool (*itqu*), and thus a stage in the process of turning raw wool into woollen thread. As such a *nipšu* can be twined (*karāku*) around *materia medica* for insertion into the nostril as a remedy for nosebleeds (S. Parpola, *SAA* X 321 rev. 8, 14), and used to bind (*rakāsu*) hands (*BBR* 60 obv. 20′, ed. B. Menzel, *Tempel* II 51; divination ritual). The image is not wholly convincing, however, and it remains possible that the text is corrupt. Emendation to ⟨*in*⟩-*né-ep-š*[*u*] yields tolerable sense ('which is constructed to be like a cord'), but is rather neutral.

14. The form *samītašu* is literary for *samīt-su*; see further Chapter 9, the section on Language and style sub (i). The suffixed *-šá* for *-šú* in both Babylonian manuscripts contrasts with the previous line but is otherwise unremarkable in such late copies.

15. Most translators take ^{giš}kun$_4$ as 'threshold' or 'doorsill', i.e. *askuppatu*, and it could be so, for the determinative has no significance. However, if the line is to be taken as conveying the idea of feeling the wall's ancient threshold, the verb *ṣabātu* presents a difficulty, for it means 'take hold of' rather than simply 'touch'. There may have been paving slabs that one could grip in the hand, of course, but I agree with Tournay and Shaffer ('prends donc l'escalier') that what is meant is not the threshold of a city gate but a stairway on the wall, which the reader is invited to climb so that he can go up on to it (l. 16: *elīma*). The idiom *simmilta ṣabātu*, 'to take the stairs' (cf. *ḫarrāna*, *urḫa ṣabātu*), is also known from an inscription of Esarhaddon (Borger, *Esarh.*, p. 58, v 12): *pe-tan bir-ki ša iṣ-ba-tu si-im-me-lat šadî*(kur)^{i} *ru-qu-u-ti*, 'those who ran fast and took to the slopes of distant mountains'. Though E-anna is situated in the middle of Uruk, the topography of the town is such that there are stretches of city wall that take one nearer to the temple area (l. 16: *qitrub ana E-anna*).

17. The line is slightly long as it stands; perhaps *amēlu* is a late intrusion.

18–23. These lines are repeated in SB XI 323–8, addressed to Ur-šanabi at the end of Gilgameš's wanderings, where the second imperative is correctly given as *i-tal-lak*. For their exegesis see Chapter 10, on Tablet XI.

21. By older standards MS h's *uš-šú-šú* displays the wrong case, but this is unremarkable in a LB copy; in the parallel line the two Kuyunjik manuscripts have, as one would expect, *uš-ši-šú* (SB XI 326). The seven *muntalkū* are presumably none other than the Seven Sages (*apkallu*) who in Babylonian mythology instructed mankind in the arts of civilization (see E. Reiner, *Or* NS 30

(1961), pp. 1–11; J. J. A. van Dijk, *UVB* 18, pp. 44 ff. = van Dijk and Mayer, *Rēš-Heiligtum* no. 89; Berossus: B. R. Foster, *Or* NS 43 (1974), p. 347). Here they are a byword for hoary antiquity.

22–3. As I. L. Finkel, the copyist of MS h, first noticed, the new variant in l. 22 for *pitir*, the number 1800, demonstrates that *pitru* here has nothing to do with the word for uncultivated land but is simply the term for one half of a *šāru* (šár = 3600 or, in the sexagesimal system, 1,0,0). According to the metrological table appended to the E-sagil Tablet, as a linear-based surface measure the *šāru* is 1080 *ikû*, equivalent to 108 kor in the capacity-based system (*TCL* VI 32, 5, ed. George, *Topog. Texts*, p. 118). In Kassite and early NB metrology, which in measuring land customarily employed a large cubit, 1 *ikû* was the equivalent of about 0.81 hectare, and the area of Uruk as roughly given here, 3.5 *šāru*, would convert to 3,062 hectares, or a little over thirty square kilometres. Even using the smaller cubit standard, so that 1 *ikû* was the equivalent of about 0.36 hectare, 3.5 *šāru* converts to 1,360 hectares. Neither figure is remotely close to the actual area enclosed by the walls of Uruk, which is about five square kilometres (see A. von Haller, *UVB* 7, p. 44). The exaggeration is not out of place, of course, in a text such as the Gilgameš epic. The question remains, if 1 *šāru* = 1,080 (or 18,0) *ikû*, of what unit is it the 3,600-fold multiple? The arithmetic produces 30 *mušaru* (0,18 *ikû*), but such an area is not known as a unit in itself. There may be another explanation: according to M. A. Powell the largest unit in the linear-based system of surface measure is the *būru* (Sum. bùr), but 'sixty bur is called šar, a word normally meaning 60^2; 3600 bur is šargal, which normally means 60^3. This suggests that both the regular number words and the terms for 60 bur and its multiples are named after counters (tokens), perhaps šar, "ball", šargal, "big ball"' (*RLA* VII, pp. 480–1).

The clay-pit, *essû*, is what is left after people excavate material for brick-making, mud-plastering, flooring and other purposes that require coarse clay (see, most famously, the apocryphal tradition of Sargon's excavation of earth from the *essû*'s of Babylon: Grayson, *Chronicles*, p. 153, 18). In a country where groundwater is high, such holes very naturally fill with water, and this explains why in lexical texts *essû* is, in equation with Sumerian words for pond or cistern (pú, túl), associated with *būrtu*, itself a pit more often than not full of water (see *CAD* I/J, p. 204; other words that are roughly synonymous are *miḫṣu* and *šatpu*). In l. 23 the word *tamšīḫu* is new. Curiously, the verb *mašāḫu*, 'to measure', is not yet attested in the II/1 stem, from which *tamšīḫu* should take its meaning. The lack of syntactical relation in this line is noteworthy.

24. On *tupšennu*, 'tablet-box', and the similarity of this line to the incipit of the legend of Narām-Sîn, *tup-šen-na pi-te-e-ma* in both OB and SB versions, see C. B. F. Walker, *JCS* 33 (1981), pp. 192–3. The restoration of *pitēma* in our passage is, however, more likely with *bābu*, the box's lid, in l. 26.

25. For the first word (MS **g** only) Wiseman offered '?[*pe-te-*]*e*' (*Iraq* 37 (1974), p. 163), but this can be discounted as too unconventional a spelling. The trace does not appear to allow the obvious restoration [*pu-ṭu*]*r* (Parpola, *SAA Gilg.*). As restored here the verb uses the II/1 stem because of the plural object.

27. The scribe of MS h, *si-taš-ši*, evidently found *šitassi* a tongue-twister.

28. The phrase *atalluku kalu marṣāti* is a standard expression in Gilgameš: see OB VA + BM ii 3′; SB VII 251; X 55–6 // 132–3 // 232–3.

29. The phrase *šanu'udu bēl gatti*, literally 'valorous lord of bodily form', has no implication of lordly status but is an example of *bēlu* with reference to one especially well endowed with a particular attribute, in this case a fine manly figure. Comparable phrases in the area of physical excellence are *bēl birki*, 'runner', and *bēl emūqī*, 'strong man'.

31. The use of the present *illak* in this and the following line is a mark of the habitual past, the first of many such presents in the narrative (note especially ll. 63–93, describing Gilgameš's

tyranny, and ll. 110–12, describing Enkidu's behaviour in the wild). On this and other nuances of the present tense in Babylonian narrative poetry see now M. P. Streck's meticulous study, '*ittašab ibakki* "weinend setze er sich": *iparras* für die Vergangenheit in der akkadischen Epik', *Or* NS 64 (1995), pp. 33–91. Streck offers many different means of translation of such verbs, for example, 'stets ging er' for *illak* in the present couplet and 'immer verängstigt wurden' for *ūtaddar* in the narrative of Gilgameš's tyranny (SB I 67). He cites both as examples of 'generell-iterative Sachverhalte der Vergangenheit', one of many divisions of usage he distinguishes for the Akkadian present (op. cit., p. 40). In my translation I have often felt it unnecessary to use such precise phrasing. In poetic contexts in English the present and imperfect tenses and the participles adequately convey many of the nuances Streck identifies. On other occasions, where there is repetition, there are sound literary reasons for using present forms in translation (see the commentary on SB I 175–7).

32. The enclitic *-ma* cannot here coordinate *illak* with the following clause, for this line logically forms a couplet with the preceding. It is instead an example of the rarer usage in which it brings the nuance 'likewise' to the verbal predicate (*GAG*[3] §12a: 'gleichfalls'). On non-coordinative *-ma* see further below, on SB I 117–18.

33. Though a river bank is not usualy symbolic of protection in literature, compare its use in personal names, e.g. Ilī-kibrī, lit. 'My god is my bank', and Kibrī-Dagān, 'My bank is Dagān' (a selection of references is given in *CAD* K, p. 335; from OAkk to OA and OB, especially Mari). There *kibru* is best rendered 'refuge'; the imagery is drawn from riverine navigation, in which the bank offers safe haven in a storm or other difficulty. The juxtaposition of the protective river bank in this line and the destructive flood-wave in the next makes for a highly effective contrast.

35–6. Since there is also a word *rīmu* meaning 'one beloved' there may be intentional ambiguity in the expression *rīm Lugalbanda*. The meaning 'wild bull' takes obvious preference, however, since the prevailing imagery of the couplet is bovine. The goddess Ninsun's name, 'Lady Wild-Cow', is here very explicitly rendered in Akkadian. The compound Rīmat-Ninsun, standard in the SB epic, goes back to the Pennsylvania tablet's *rīmtum ša supūri(m) Ninsunna* (OB II 236–7). The variant ^{d}*nin-sún-an-na* (MS h) for ^{d}*nin-sún-(na)* is of the same order as ^{d}*dam-ki-an-na* for Damkina, which is common in late texts.

37. The word order *šīḫu Gilgāmeš* may be an example of inversion for emphasis; see Chapter 9, the section on Language and style sub (i).

39. For Gilgameš and wells see Chapter 3, the sub-section on Digging wells.

40. On *ayabba*, often Ocean in a mythological sense, see A. Malamat, *Mari and the Early Israelite Experience* (London, 1989), pp. 108–12. The phrase *ayabba tâmatu rapaštu* also occurs in exorcistic literature, where it is something of a cliché (e.g. *Šurpu* V–VI 190, VIII 84, *Maqlû* VI 100; further references in *CAD* A/1, p. 221). The word written *ta-ma-ti(m)* is most probably singular, literary for *tâmti*, as often in *Enūma eliš*. For the extra vowel see above, on l. 14.

42. The relentless succession of active participles in ll. 38–44 means *ka-šid* cannot here be an active stative. The resulting phrase is *kāšid dannussu*, in which a construct state is followed, exceptionally, by an adverbial accusative. Lexically this can be compared with Sennacherib's report that his warriors 'captured through their sheer force' the cities of the king of Elam: *ik-šu-du dan-nu-su-un* (Luckenbill, *OIP* 2, p. 75, 96–7). As for the grammar, note the common phrase *šar pāna* and its variant *šar maḫra*, 'king of bygone times', in which the construct state is qualified by an adverb. A more elaborate example of this syntactical peculiarity is displayed in an epithet of Aššurnaṣirpal II: *ka-šid ultu*(ta) *e-ber-ta-an* ^{id}ḫal.ḫal *a-di* ^{kur}*lab-na-na u tâmti*(a.ab.ba) *rabīti*(gal)^{ti}, 'who conquered from the River Tigris to Mount Lebanon and the Great Sea' (Grayson, *RIMA* 2, p. 306, 4–6); see *GAG*[3] §148b.

43. The LB manuscript confirms the reading of MS **g** proposed by W. G. Lambert, 'Gilg. I i 41', *RA* 73 (1979), p. 89.

45–6. As the text of Nimrud MS **g** stands, the verbs of both lines of this couplet are plural, which is ungrammatical after *mannu*, or subjunctive, with the relative pronoun omitted by mistake (there is no space to restore [*man-nu šá*] in MS **g**). In the LB MS h there is no problem in l. 45, where *ištannan* is indicative singular, but in l. 46, unless one construes *kī* as a subordinating conjunction, *iqabbû* is also plural or subjunctive for no reason. The solution is that the text is indeed defective, *ša* having dropped out after *mannu*. This is proved by an inscription of Esarhaddon that adapts l. 45 in its correct form (Borger, *Esarh.*, p. 58, v 21–2): *man-nu šá it-ti-ia iš-šá-an-na-nu a-na šarru-u-ti*, 'who is there that can be compared with me in kingly status?' MS h's *ištannan* probably arose from a scribe's desire to adjust the grammar of l. 45 in the absence of the relative pronoun, a correction that was not prosecuted into l. 46.

47. The new copy of MS **g** confirms that the penultimate word is *na-bu* (i.e. *nabi*), not *šu*!-*pu* (Wilcke). On vocalic endings in NA manuscripts that are erroneous by earlier standards, see Chapter 9, the section on spelling sub (i–t).

48. The line reappears in SB IX 51, which has nominative *šittāšu*, as MS h does here.

52. In the passage which gives Gilgameš's vital statistics it is reasonable to presume that the description begins with the hero's height, which will be *lāna* in this line. This word is the conventional term for the height of a human being (cf. OB II 184, and slave sales, *passim*), though there is uncertainty as to whether it refers to a person's full height or to his height to the shoulder (see M. A. Powell, *RLA* VII, p. 473). Unfortunately the edge of MS **g** has been damaged, so that the only witnesses to the text that follows *lāna* are the photograph and Wiseman's copy, from which the traces on my copy are drawn. Wiseman had no knowledge of MS h's *la-a-nu*, so missed the word *lāna* and read *na-ba-lu ú* [. . . Since both photograph and copy indicate that the two signs between *l*]*a-na* and *ú* are very damaged, there must be a suspicion that this is a measurement in cubits, i.e. ⌜10 + x⌝ *ammat*(kùš), a figure, incidentally, which bears comparison with eleven cubits in the Hittite version (*Chicago Hittite Dictionary* P, p. 65).

56. In the standard (OB) system of metrology, the unit *nikkassu* is three cubits, about 1.5 m, though in NB and LB it became 3.5 cubits (Powell, *RLA* VII, p. 471). The *nindanu*, 'rod', is twelve cubits (later fourteen), so, as the text stands, the hero's feet were half as long as his legs. Evidently the text is corrupt.

57. The expression *birīt purīdi*, literally 'between the legs', can also mean the area of the upper thigh or groin (= *šapūlu* in commentaries on *Šumma ālu* and *Sakikku*: see *CAD* Š/1, p. 492), but the reference here is certainly to the other end of the leg. A similar idiom occurs in bilingual liturgical texts: dùg.bad.(rá).zu a.ba ba.ra.šub.bu = *ina pi-it pu-ri-di-ka man-nu ip-pa-ra-áš-šid*, 'when you open your stride who can escape?' (IV R^2 26 no. 4, 41–2; *BRM* IV 8, 23; Böllenrücher, *Nergal*, p. 32, 40). Six cubits as the measure of Gilgameš's stride is equal to the length of leg, which is about right. The use of different wording to express the same thing, 6 *ammat* as against *mišil nindan*, looks like a stylistic device ('elegant variation'). The measurement of Gilgameš's stride, at least, is double the conventional norm of Babylonia, where the *purīdu*, 'pace', was a unit of length equivalent to three cubits, i.e. a man's longest stride (see Powell, *RLA* VII, p. 476; H. Hunger, *Uruk* I 102, 11: [2 *pu-r*]*i-du qa-nu-u* : 4 *pu-r*[*i-du nindan*], '[2] strides = 1 reed, 4 strides [=1 rod]').

58. The word *ašarittu* is not previously known in reference to part of the body. Tournay and Shaffer plausibly suggest that this is the thumb, restoring *šá* [*u-ba-na*]-*te-šú*.

60. The restoration follows l. 107, where the same verse describes Enkidu. The image alludes to the 'hairy' ear of ripe barley. Nissaba, the goddess of grain, had hair of barley tied thick in sheaves,

according to Gudea, Cyl. A iv 24 // v 21: sag.gá è ki.karadin mu.ak, 'sprouting on her head, sheaves were arranged'. It remains uncertain whether in the 'god description texts' *LKA* 72 rev. 10: [X.N]AGA *qim-mat-su*, and *KAR* 307 obv. 1: [. . .].NAGA *qim-mat-su*, one should restore (^{d})nissaba(ŠE.NAGA) = *nissabu qimmassu*, 'the hair of his head is barley', or ^{giš}šinig(GAD.NAGA) = *bīnu qimmassu*, 'the hair of his head is tamarisk' (*nissabu*: B. Landsberger, *WO* 1 (1950), p. 363, fn. 18; *CAD* N, p. 273; Q, p. 253; *bīnu*: *TuL*, pp. 31 and 47; Livingstone, *Mystical Works*, p. 94; id., *Court Poetry*, pp. 98–9). Livingstone states a preference for *bīnu* on grounds of the space available for restoration in *LKA* 72 (see *Mystical Works*, pp. 98–9), but there is little to choose between [ŠE.N]AGA (or [^{d}N]AGA) and [GAD.N]AGA. Note also, in a syncretistic hymn which equates parts of Ninurta's body with other gods (*KAR* 102, 10): *qim-mat-ka* ^{d}[. . .], 'the hair of your head is the god(dess) [Nissaba(?)]'.

61. The sign before IGI on MS d_1 can hardly be anything but AŠ, but a reading [*ina*] ⸢*pān*⸣ *a-ḫi-šú*, 'in the presence of his brother', is most unlikely. Even if elsewhere on this MS *ina* is written *i-na*, it is difficult to escape *ina ši'āḫīšu*. Tournay and Shaffer preferred to avoid *ina* by restoring [*itti š*]*i-a-ḫi-šú*, but either way the infinitive appears to be an exceptional, petrified form, taken over from an OB version of the epic and not brought up to date. At the end of the line there may be room for more than just ⸢*la*⸣*-l*[*e-e-šú*].

64. The trace after *re*, as well as the gender of *šaqû*, rules out dual *rēšāšu*. An image very close to the one given in this line is to be found in the Gula Hymn of Bullussa-rabi, where Ningirsu is described as *re-du-ú ri-i-mu šá-qu-ú re-e-šú*, 'a wild bull giving chase, head held high' (W. G. Lambert, *Or* NS 36 (1967), p. 116, 29).

65 // 82. The line can be taken to read 'the onslaught of his weapons has no equal', and most translators are content to render it thus. If this makes awkward sense—can an infinitive have a rival?—then *tebû* can be understood as a locative with Gilgameš the subject of *īši*. In SB Gilgameš this is a desperate measure, however. The option preferred here is to split the line into two separate clauses. For *tebû kakkūšu*, 'his weapons are at the ready', cf. Erra I 45: *šu-nu ez-zu-ma te-bu-ú kak-ki-šú-un*, 'they were in a fury and so their weapons were ready for action'; and Sargon II: *ša a-na šum-qut na-ki-ri šu-ut-bu-u* ^{giš}*kakkī*(tukul)*-šú*, 'whose weapons are made ready to bring down the enemy' (Fuchs, *Sargon*, p. 62, 11–12). The enclitic *-ma*, here attached to the object not the verb, is probably not coordinative but serves instead to stress the complete absence of any rival; compare *mātam-ma* in l. 108, which reports another negative state.

66. Comparison with l. 83, alongside MS F's *pu-uk-ku* (hardly *pu-uk-ku-*[*šu*]), suggests that *pu-uk-ki-šú te-bu-ú* in the LB manuscript very likely derives from a misreading (or mishearing in auto-dictation) of *pu-uk-ki šu-ut-bu-ú* (cf. von Soden, *ZA* 53, p. 221; Tigay argues for the opposite). Analysis of *pukku* in this passage has not yielded a consensus. Some modern commentators take it as the II/1 infinitive *puqqu*, 'to attend, wait on' (following B. Landsberger, *WZKM* 56 (1960), p. 125, fn. 49), while others derive it from the *pukku* which is paired with *mekkû* in the Sumerian tale of Bilgames and the Netherworld and its translation, SB XII (for these playthings see the commentary below, on SB XII 1). Tigay goes so far as to state categorically that the word in SB I is not the noun *pukku* but the verb *puqqu*, and that the 'Akkadian epic preserved the motif of athletic competition in this episode, but, ironically, misunderstood the word pukku which stood at the center of that episode in the original [Sumerian text]' (*Evolution*, pp. 190–1). There is no proof whatsoever that either contention is so. Indeed, the word in the Kuyunjik manuscript is written *pu-uk-ku*, which in the conventional orthography of the period would be most unusual for *puqqu*, though not entirely without parallel.

If the word is *pukku* not *puqqu*, the question then is: how does it tie in with the arousal, mobilization or excitation (all are possibly with *tebû* and *šutbû*) of Gilgameš's companions? The two translators who take *pukku* as a ball differ on this point. Jacobsen renders the line 'the young men are called up, away from the puck (of their game)', commenting to the effect that they are called away from their play in order to perform corvée work (*Studies Moran*, p. 234, fn. 7). J. Klein translates 'on account of his ball (game) his companions are (constantly) aroused', and later 'his companions are aroused by his *pukku*' (*Jacobsen Mem. Vol*, pp. 196–9). Klein seems to me to be nearer the mark. The subject of the verb, *rū'ūšu*, is too specific to refer to the considerable body of men who would be called up for public service; those are *eṭlūtu*. These are not just the menfolk of Uruk in general but Gilgameš's close companions (cf. B. Foster, *Essays Pope*, p. 24). The *pukku* which keeps them in a state of perpetual activity is, *pars pro toto*, a symbol of engagement in athletic and sporting contests.

67 // 84. The present form *ú-ta-ad-da-ri* (for *ūtaddarū*, l. 67) looks superior to the new variant *uš-ta-dir* (for *uštādirū*, l. 84), for its tense agrees with the other verbs in this passage (*ugdaššar*, *umaššar*, *ikaddir*). The reading *ku-kit-ti* is assured from MS h, as first read by W. R. Mayer (*VAS* XXIV, p. 13). The word *kukittu* is rare and obscure, occurring outside this line only in lexical and omen texts. In omens it appears in the apodosis as a negative comment (e.g., *Izbu* VI 6: *ku-kit-tu ta-aš-ta-ad-da-*[*ad*], 'it is *k*., you must wait', i.e. put off any plans until later), and in the protasis as the designation of what must be an inauspicious part of the exta. Commentaries on these texts, collected in the dictionaries s.v., equate it with disagreement (*lā mitgurtu*), lack of prudence (*lā mitluku*) and behaviour inappropriate to one's position (*lā šattu*).

69 // 86. The adverb *šēriš*, which is attested here for the first time, perfectly describes the violence which attends Gilgameš's behaviour.

70. The broken sign begins like *la* or perhaps *in*. Since this is probably the same line as l. 88 (q.v.), l[ugal can be proposed as appropriate. The hero is also *Gilgāmeš šarru* in SB IX 53 // 130.

71. This line appears to be the same as l. 87, but the trace on MS d_1 before *šá* introduces an element of doubt. It is not a well-written *ma*, nor a good sipa: it looks more like *á*]*š*.

73–4. This couplet remains very poorly preserved. It appears to be narrative, describing how the women begin complaining to the gods. Their complaint is articulated in ll. 75–6, two lines that develop the theme of Gilgameš's misconduct narrated in ll. 67–72. Towards the end of l. 74 perhaps read *it*]*-tés-ḫi*, 'it (their complaint?) has become unruly'.

75. The traces that follow *mūdû* in MS x appear to be the remains of signs that have been partly erased.

78. There has been some discussion about the significance of the use here of the I/3 stem of *šemû*. For von Soden the stem conveys careful attention on behalf of the listener (cf. *AHw*, p. 1212, 'genau anhören'). For Oppenheim it denoted the eventual realization of the action (*Or* NS 17 (1948), p. 22, fn. 9). For Foster it is 'a device to represent speaking or perception over a great distance, especially between heaven and earth' (*Essays Pope*, p. 24, with reference also to SB I 248 and VII 133). The answer may lie in the use in this episode of the present tense for recurring action (see M. P. Streck, *Or* NS 64 (1995), p. 41). Each time the women complained, the goddesses listened to what they had to say. The complaint being regular and repeated, the iterative stem is suitable for the divine response. When, eventually, the narrative moves from circumstance to action, the I/1 preterite is used (l. 94, *issû*), followed by a succession of perfects. However, this explanation does not explain the use of the I/3 stem in *iltanassâššu* (SB IV 195 // VII 133), where repetition of Šamaš's interventions is intrinsically unlikely.

The verb requires a plural subject, but there is not enough space to accommodate a plural determinative on ${}^{d}15$. The lack of it may not be an oversight. The same phenomenon occurs in a LB manuscript of *Mīs pî* III: *ilī* (dingir)^{me} *u* ${}^{d}15$ (F. N. H. Al-Rawi and George, *Iraq* 57 (1995), p. 225, 6). There are many other occasions when apparently singular spellings of *ištaru*, 'goddess', are paired with plural *ilū*, 'gods', and thus seem also to stand for a plurality. The following passages amply illustrate this convention: dingir^{meš} *u* ^{d}*iš-tar* (Borger, *Esarh.*, p. 23, 9, with var. ^{d}*iš-tar*^{meš}, ^{d}MÙŠ^{meš}); *na-áš-par-ti* dingir^{meš} *u* ^{d}*iš-tar* (ibid., p. 45, 6); [DN?] *ba-nu-ú* dingir[^{me}]^{š} *mu-al-lid* ^{d}*iš-tar* (A. Livingstone, *Court Poetry* no. 1, 16: Aššurbanipal's Hymn to Aššur); *ma-ḫa-*[*z*]*i*/*zu* dingir.dingir *ù* ^{d}*iš-tar* (F. H. Weissbach, *Wadi Brisa*, B viii 41–2; *PBS* XV 79 iii 65; Nbk); ^{d}*sîn* . . . *bēl*(en) dingir^{meš} *ù* ^{d}*iš-tar* (*CT* 34 27, 42; Nbk); *ana* dingir^{meš} *ù* ^{d}*iš*$_{8}$*-t*[*ár*] *gi-na-a ú-sa-ap-pu-ú* (V *R* 63 i 6; Nbn). Plural *ilū* is also sometimes written with just dingir, as in *Ludlul* I 55 (*šarru šīr ilī*, 'the king, flesh of the gods', spelled variously dingir, dingir^{meš} and dingir.dingir). The reverse can also occur, i.e. dingir^{meš} for the singular (see below on SB II 36–7).

Other writings indicate that a formally masculine plural *ištarū* existed alongside *ištarātu*: *pa-laḫ* dingir^{meš} *ù* ^{d}*iš-ta-ri* (*TCL* III 115, ed. W. Mayer, *MDOG* 115 (1983), p. 78: Sargon II; Borger, *Esarh.*, p. 97, 35); ^{d}*í-gì-gì* ^{d}600 dingir^{meš} *u* ^{d}*iš-ta-ri* (E. Ebeling, *Or* NS 17 (1948), pl. 26 (follows p. 272), 9, ed. B. Pongratz-Leisten, *Ina Šulmi Īrub*, p. 244, rev. 9′; Exaltation of Nabû); ^{d}*í-gì-gì* ^{d}600 dingir^{meš} *u* ^{d}*iš-ta-ri* (Livingstone, *Court Poetry* no. 2, 30: Aššurbanipal's Acrostic Hymn to Marduk; cf. ^{d}*iš-tar*^{meš} in l. 36). Note also the existence of a plural form *ištarāni*, parallel with *ilāni* (*STT* 45, 9: ^{d}*iš-tar-ni*). On this evidence it would appear that the spellings ^{d}*iš-tar* and ^{d}*iš*$_{8}$*-tár* are, in effect, logographic, standing for *ištaru* and (by homophony?) *ištarū*, if not also for *ištarātu* and *ištarāni*. In a note on the second passage cited in the previous paragraph, Borger offered a slightly different solution, repeating the old view of F. Delitzsch: '*ištar*(*u*) kann auch kollektiv "Göttinnen" bedeuten' (*Esarh.*, p. 45). In his study on the 'Assyrian Tree of Life' S. Parpola has inferred the contrary from these spellings, that 'there was, in fact, only one, not several, "female" deities', all the goddesses being subsumed in Ištar's person (*JNES* 52 (1993), p. 187, fn. 97). Whichever is the correct interpretation, there seems no reason why the spelling ^{d}15 should not also be used in the same manner as ^{d}*iš-tar* and ^{d}*iš*$_{8}$*-tár*, for a plurality of goddesses.

79. The expression *bēl zikri* seems unavoidable in the light of the new source, MS x. The word *zikru* here is to be compared with its use in ll. 96 and 100, where it signifies an idea or initiative. The epithet *bēl zikri* is probably to be understood as a reference to the fact that the gods of heaven, in this period the Igigi, are those that can exercise initiative in the divine assembly, unlike the deities confined in the Netherworld. As such, they are perhaps under an obligation, once the complaint of the folk of Uruk has been reported to them, to do something to relieve the problem. Accordingly they bring the complaint to the attention of the highest powers.

80. This line ought to narrate the action taken by the gods of the previous line. Since ll. 81–91 are speech, addressed to a single person, in all probability to Anu (see below, on l. 93), some conventional expression of address is expected. The last word might just read ⸢*i*⸣*-šas-*⸢*su-šu*⸣, 'they (the gods) called out to him (Anu)', but for the moment the extant traces here and at the beginning of the line (where ^{d}*e*]*n-lí*[*l* is one possibility) defy certain decipherment.

81. For the stressed enclitic *-mā* in questions see *GAG*^{3} §123b.

84. The spelling *uš-ta-dir* is ambiguous. I take it as III/1 perfect, subject Gilgameš, but, given the variant *ūtaddarū* in l. 67, it may also be parsed as III/2 preterite, subject *eṭlūtu* (*dir* then renders a bisyllable). Neither tense goes well in a passage replete with verbs in the present.

88. Probably a repetition of l. 70. The restoration of *nišī rapšāti* is encouraged by the feminine plural possessive in the next line (for *rapšu*, 'numerous, teeming', see below, the commentary on SB VIII 9–10). Such a restoration makes a participle such as *muštēšir*, *mušallim* or *muttarri* likely in the missing middle of the line, unless we read barely *šar nišī rapšāti*.

93. The subject of this line must be singular. The speech made to the mother goddess in ll. 95–8 are certainly the words of Anu, since they are described in l. 100 as *zikru ša Anim*. The fact that there

is no line introducing Anu as the speaker of ll. 95–8 makes it very difficult to avoid restoring him here as the one who listens (*šemû* I/3, as in l. 78) to the preceding speech.

94. With this line, which also occurs in MB Nippur$_1$ (l. 5), compare OB Atram-ḫasīs I 192: *il-ta-am is-sú-ú i-ša-lu*, 'they summoned the goddess and asked her', and SB Anzû I 172: *is-su-nim-ma* ^{d}*be-let ilī*^{meš} *a-ḫat* [*ilī rabûti*], 'they summoned Bēlet-ilī, the sister of [the great gods]'; both lines follow a speech of Ea. The line of Gilgameš may be a conscious imitation of Atra-ḫasīs, for the context there is similar to the present passage: the mother goddess is summoned to solve by an act of creation, in that case of mankind in general, a crisis marked by the mutiny of the lower orders against their king, in that case the Igigi's revolt against Enlil (for a detailed comparison between the respective passages of the two texts see Tigay, *Evolution*, pp. 194–7). The background of Aruru's epithet 'great one' is that she is as ancient as the universe itself; see the note on MB Nippur$_1$ 1.

95. The restoration follows MB Nippur$_1$ 7. The line is almost identical to one in a SB account of the creation of mankind and the king: *at-ti-ma tab-ni-ma lullâ*^{a} *a-me-lu*, 'you it is that created man, (now fashion the king)' (W. R. Mayer, *Or* NS 56 (1987), p. 56, 32′).

96. The word *zikru* in this and other lines of the SB text (SB I 100, VIII 212) is taken by many (following Oppenheim, *Or* NS 17, p. 23; *CAD* Z, p. 116), to mean 'image, counterpart, replica', and the suffix to refer to Gilgameš: 'create his image!' Though this makes good sense, and provides *lū maḫir* (or *māḫir*) with an explicit subject, it is not without problems. The phrase *zikra banû* in the other passages of Gilgameš cited, and elsewhere too (*CT* 15 46 rev. 11: Descent of Ištar), simply means to make the word flesh, i.e. to convert an idea or spoken initiative into reality. If the phrase *bini zikiršu* is understood in this way, it should be translated 'make his idea a reality!' But whose idea? In l. 100 the *zikru* is identified as Anu's, and von Soden and others have translated the phrase accordingly (Reclam^2 etc.: 'was er befiehlt', Wilcke: 'was er (= Anu) sagt', Bottéro: 'ce qu'(Anu) te dictera'). They implicitly ascribe the speech of ll. 95–8, in which direct instructions are given to Aruru, to the unspecified plural subject of *issû* (l. 94), i.e. the gods in general. However, MB Nippur$_1$ reveals that one god only issues the command to Aruru (l. 6: *izzaqqarši*). Accordingly it is probable that Anu himself is speaking in this line, and therefore the third person referent of the possessive pronoun on *zikiršu* cannot be him, but must instead be whatever god it was who made the original suggestion. I suspect that this figure was Ea. It is one of Ea's characteristic functions to solve crises by suggesting the creation of new life-forms, as he does in Atra-ḫasīs and related texts, or by creating them himself, as in the Descent of Ištar. He alone among the gods has the imagination to conceive ingenious ideas of this kind. As I see it, then, in a divine assembly convened to debate the crisis, Ea made his customary intervention in suggesting how the problem could best be solved, Aruru was brought on and Anu (in MS n Enlil) issued her with instructions: 'convert Ea's idea into reality!' The question is: was the line still so understood when all reference to the god who had the initial idea had been edited out of the text?

That Ea was instrumental in the creation of Enkidu has already been proposed on other grounds by Bottéro, *L'épopée*, p. 69, fn. 1, who sees a reference to such an idea in the writing of his name in the SB text as 'Enki.dù: "Enki (l')a créé"' (so also S. Parpola, *SAA* IX, p. xciii; id., *CRRA* 43, p. 318). Dalley has drawn attention to an improbable play on *zikru* and *zik(a)ru*, 'man, male' (*Myths*, p. 126, 9).

97. As Ebeling noted, as well as *ma-ḫ*[*ir*] one may also read *ma-š*[*il*] (*AfO* 8, p. 226).

100. Cf. above, on l. 96. There is a parallel line in Anzû I 157: ^{d}*é-a uz-nu ib-ta-ni ina lìb-bi-šú*, where *uznu* seems to correspond to this line's *zikru*: 'Ea fashioned a clever idea(?) in his heart.' Kovacs proposes a play on *zikru ša Anim* and *kiṣru ša Anim*, the phrase that foretells Enkidu's coming in ll. 248 and 262. Dalley's suggestion that *zikru* alludes also to *sekru*, among 'cult personnel

of uncertain sexual affinities' (*Myths*, p. 126, 10), makes assumptions about the latter word which seem to be unfounded. The feminine adjective *sekretu*, 'closed off', refers to women who live in seclusion, whether as devotees of a deity or royal concubines in the harem. The masculine only occurs in logographic spellings of *sekretu* (^{f}zi.ik.ru.um etc.) and may have existed as a lexical abstraction only. Babylonian men did not find themselves cloistered, so far as I know, and even if a word *sekru* was recognizable as a counterpart of *sekretu*, it is doubtful that it could readily have conveyed the idea of a 'male concubine'.

102–3. These two lines are one of only two quotations from Gilgameš known from commentaries (the other is SB VI 69). They are quoted in a commentary on the prognostic and diagnostic text, *Sakikku* I, to illustrate the received wisdom that man is made from clay (George, *RA* 85 (1991), p. 146, 2 b 4′–5′: *ṭi-iṭ-ṭi ik-t*[*a-ri-iṣ it-ta-d*]*i i-na ṣēri*(edin) : *i-na ṣēri*(edin) ^{md}*en-ki-dù ib-ta-n*[*i qu-ra-du*]). For the phrase *ṭiṭṭa karāṣu* see W. R. Mayer, *Or* NS 56 (1987), p. 62.

104. Most commentators follow von Soden's emphasis of *qūltu* as the quiet of night (*ZA* 53, p. 222: '(Nacht)-Stille'; cf. Ebeling, *AfO* 8, p. 227). Others have avoided this reading by emending to *kul-*⟨*la*⟩*-ti*, with *CAD* K, p. 506 ('offspring of potter's clay'). I prefer not to emend, but I do not see why Enkidu should be the offspring of the quiet of night as against any other part of the day. For me the reference is instead to Enkidu's supernatural birth. He was not delivered into the world through the travail of a human mother: silence, not screams, attended his arrival on the earth. The apparent variant *mūtu*, 'death', for *qūltu* is a mechanical error based on the misreading of *qul* and needs no further exegesis. The phrase *kiṣir Ninurta* makes several allusions. First, *kiṣru* as a description of a person evokes in comparison personal names such as Kiṣir-DN, DN-kuṣuršu/-kuṣranni and DN-kāṣir. The dictionaries interpret this use of *kiṣru*, 'knot, bonding', and *kaṣāru*, 'to knot, tie together', as referring to the support or strengthening of the individual by a god: his form is bonded and consolidated into a something strong and lasting, like a wall of brick. As the champion of the gods and the epitome of the young hero, Ninurta is a god associated with successful feats of arms, particularly in single combat with a mighty rival (e.g. Anzû, Asakku). Enkidu, whose physical being has been given cohesion by Ninurta, will be the champion of the people of Uruk and will meet with Gilgameš in single combat. In *An* VII Ninurta is also for some reason especially associated with *qūltu*, 'silence' (*CT* 24 41, 65: ^{d}inšušinak = ^{d}*nin-urta šá qu-ul-ti*), a reference which places the phrases *ilitti qūlti* and *kiṣir Ninurta* in a nearly synonymous relation. The latter expression also anticipates the *kiṣru ša Anim* that symbolizes Enkidu in Gilgameš's dreams.

106. The variant for *uppuš* in MS h (hardly *nuppuṣ*) is mystifying. The form *pēretu*, literary for *pērtu*, occurs in the status rectus only here and in SB II 176; see further Chapter 9, the section on Language and style sub (i).

107. This line has already been used to describe Gilgameš (SB I 60).

108. Athough I retain the conventional interpretation that the use of *lā* in a main clause represents emphatic negation ('überhaupt nicht', *GAG*^{3} §122a), this is a line where it might have the force 'not yet', as suggested by M. Stol, *OB History*, p. 53, fn. 30 (referring to OB II 93).

The words *nišū*, 'people, family', and *mātu*, 'nation', denote the smaller and greater social groups from which the individual takes his identity. The variant 'god' or 'gods' for the former raises the question of whether they were held in any way to be synonymous. In some peripheral areas of Mesopotamia, notably Emar and Nuzi in the second millennium, the two concepts are closely connected in the context of the ancestor cults, for the household gods (*ilu*) are mentioned alongside family ancestors referred to as 'dead persons' (*mītu*) and 'ghosts' (*eṭemmu*). Some equate the three terms (see K. van der Toorn, 'Gods and ancestors in Emar and Nuzi', *ZA* 84 (1994), pp. 38–59); others do not (see W. T. Pitard, 'Care of the dead at Emar' and B. B. Schmidt, 'The gods and the dead of the domestic cult at Emar: a reassessment', both in M. W. Chavalas (ed.), *Emar*, pp. 123–40, 141–63). In Babylonia proper the evidence for deified ancestors is patchy. At least two deceased *entu*-priestesses of Ur were included by those in charge of the offerings among the minor gods of the moon god's sanctuary (see P. Weadock, *Iraq* 37 (1975), p. 104). This distinction was no doubt accorded them not because they were dead but because they had been, in some sense, the brides of Nanna-Suen (the use of the divine determinative by kings who had been 'husbands' of Inanna, from Šulgi to Rīm-Sîn I, and the presence of much the same kings in litanies of dead gods in later cultic laments such as *Edinnausagga* are exactly analogous). Many dead Mesopotamian kings were the object of special funerary cults, and though they did not usually attract the term *ilu* their statues were often venerated, bathed and provisioned in that context much as gods' statues were (for a résumé see W. W. Hallo, 'Royal ancestor worship in the biblical world', *Studies Talmon*, pp. 387–99). An example of *ilu* used in reference to deceased royal ancestors can be found in an inscription of Aššurbanipal which reports the king's restoration of funerary offerings to the ghosts of his predecessors: *a-na ili*(dingir) *u a-me-lu-tum ana mītūti*(ug$_7$)^{meš} *u balṭūti*(ti)^{meš} *ṭābta*(mun) *ēpuš*(dù)^{uš}, 'I did a favour to god and man, to the dead and the living' (T. G. Pinches, *Texts in the Babylonian Wedge-Writing*, p. 17, rev. 3, ed. Streck, *Asb.*, p. 250). Ordinary Babylonians made funerary offerings (*kispu*) to their immediate ancestors but there is as yet no evidence that these could be called 'gods' as they may have been in Nuzi and Emar (see M. Bayliss, 'The cult of dead kin in Assyria and Babylonia', *Iraq* 35 (1973), pp. 115–25; A. Tsukimoto, *Untersuchungen zur Totenpflege (kispum) im alten Mesopotamien*). However, some have suggested that *ilu* in personal names sometimes refers to the spirit of a deceased family member (Stamm, *Namengebung*, pp. 245, 284; *CAD* I/J, p. 102; Bayliss, *Iraq* 35, p. 117, fn. 19). This, and the question of the relationship of dead ancestors to personal gods and protective deities such as the *šēdu*, are topics that need further investigation. For this reason it is best for the moment to allow that the variants 'gods' and 'family' in this line may be arbitrary and unrelated.

109. For the reading of ^{d}GÌR as Šakkan see W. G. Lambert, 'The reading of the divine name Šakkan', *Or* NS 55 (1986), pp. 152–8. 'Clad in a garment like Šakkan's' means simply wearing only the hairy coat that Nature had given him, as did all the creatures of Šakkan, the lord of the animals.

110 // 175. The mention of Šakkan in the preceding line paves the way for gazelles in this line, for these animals are the typical beasts of Šakkan (cf. *CT* 29 46, 13: $^{šak-kan}$dingir.$^{ma-šá-ku}$máš, 'Šakkan = the god of gazelles').

111 // 176. The verb of this line used to be read *idappir*, supposedly the I/1 intransitive stem of *duppuru*, which in legal documents from Elam means 'to satisfy' (*CAD* D, p. 104; M, p. 384), or *iṭapper* (*AHw*, p. 1380, 'Deutung unsicher'). More recently W. L. Moran has suggested a verb *dab/pāru* (i/i), 'to push in, become aggressive' (*JCS* 33 (1981), p. 44, fn. 3). However, the spelling *i-te-ep-pir* used in the Late Babylonian sources in the parallel passages (SB I 176, MS x; 281, MS h) suggests instead, given that a present tense is expected, a verb *tepēru* I/1 or *epēru* I/2 (cf. already W. R. Mayer, *VAS* XXIV, p. 13). In MB Ur 28 the precative *lideppir* might be the same verb with a voiced first radical. Whatever its derivation, the meaning is determined by its use to describe animals thronging at a water-hole, as here, and a crowd gathering to stare at Enkidu (SB I 253 // I 281 // II 105). Elsewhere MS P replaces *iteppir* with *išatti*, 'he drinks' (ll. 176 and, probably, 172), which suggests an unimaginative editorial change made in the face of an obscure word.

112 // 177. The verb of this line is also an object of doubt. The old reading *i-ṭib* was emended to *i-ṭàb*, present to match the other verbs of the passage, by von Soden, *ZA* 53, p. 222. This revision failed to take account of MS F's *i-ṭi-bu* in SB I 173, parallel to this line. This spelling of preterite *iṭīb* can be explained as an example of CV-CV for C$\bar{V}$C; others in Kuyunjik manuscripts of SB

Gilgameš are listed in Chapter 9, the section on Spelling sub (g). A present ventive *iṭibbu* is theoretically possible—for ventives spelled with *-u* see Chapter 9, the section on Spelling sub (v)—but I know of no other examples of *ṭâbu* in the ventive. The derivation of the forms spelled *i-ṭib* and *i-ṭi-bu* from *ṭâbu* is now challenged by the Late Babylonian source's *i*-DI-*pi* in the parallel passage (l. 177, MS x). Mayer, *VAS* XXIV, p. 13, suggests a parsing from the known verb *edēpu*, 'to blow', but its sense argues against this. The spellings of MSS F and x suggest a middle weak verb, for trisyllabic orthographies, exhibiting final, 'overhanging' vowels, often spell forms of middle weak verbs in NA, NB and later orthography, as also other words that in earlier grammar would end with a syllable that was both long and closed. Apart from *ṭâbu* there are the verbs *dêpu* and *ṭâpu*, which have to do with weaving and are plainly also out of contention; **dâpu* and **ṭêpu* are unattested. This being so, the principal obstacle to the traditional parsing is the sign *pi* in MS x, for it cannot usually express the consonant /b/. Confusion between /b/ and /p/ can arise in LB spelling, however: note in this book SB V 294 *nak-bi* (MS dd) for *nakpu*. Consequently it is unwise to place too much weight on one LB manuscript. For the moment MS x's *i*-DI-*pi* should be considered, like MS F's *i*-DI-BU, to be a spelling of *iṭīb*.

114. Prepositional phrases involving *pūt* + water have often proved awkward for translators (e.g. B. R. Foster, *ANES* 14 (1982), p. 33: '(hither) edge'). A collection of the extant attestations suggests that such phrases mean no more than 'on/to the bank/shore of', 'beside' a river, sea, etc.; see e.g. SB Atra-ḫasīs V 71 (ed. George and Al-Rawi, *Iraq* 58 (1996), p. 182): *ana pu-ut nāri*(íd) *it-ta-šab*, 'he sat down beside (*not* facing) the river', replacing older *pu-ti-iš na-ri* (OB Atram-ḫasīs II iii 26; cf. Assyrian recension S v 32); in OAkk inscriptions of Sargon (Frayne, *RIME* 2, p. 28, 8 // 8–10): *a-dì-ma pu-ti ti-a-am-tim*, 'as far as the sea shore' // zag a.ab.ba.ka.šè, 'to the edge of the sea', and Narām-Sîn (ibid., p. 91, ii 12–13): *a-na pu-ti* buranun:íd, 'to the bank of the Euphrates', (ibid., p. 133, ii 9–11) *iš-tum-ma pu-ti* buranun:íd, 'from the bank of the Euphrates'; and, if correctly transcribed, in Assyrian royal inscriptions of Tukultī-Ninurta II (Grayson, *RIMA* 2, p. 175, 83): *ina šadî*(kur)^{i} *ša pūt*(sag) ^{id}*pu-rat-te*, 'in the mountains beside the Euphrates'; Aššurnaṣirpal II (ibid., p. 214, 29): *a-na pūt*(sag) ^{id}*pu-rat-te a-aṣ-bat*, 'I marched to the bank of the Euphrates', (ibid, p. 215, 40–1) ^{kur}*bi-su-ru ša pūt*(sag) ^{id}*pu-rat-te lu iṣ-bat*, 'he took to Mt Bisuru, which is beside the Euphrates'; and Shalmaneser III (Grayson, *RIMA* 3, p. 46, 21′): *a-na pūt*(sag) ^{id}*e-ni šá* ^{id}*idiqlat*(ḫal.ḫal) *a-šar mu-ṣa-ú šá mê*(a)^{meš} *a-lik*, 'I went to the edge of the source of the Tigris, the place where the waters flow forth'.

In the Assyrian inscriptions there is a noticeable contrast between *pūt* and *šiddi*: see e.g. in Aššurnaṣirpal II (Grayson, *RIMA* 2, p. 199, 77): *ši-di* ^{id}*ḫa-bur a-ṣa-bat*, 'I marched along the River Ḫabur', (ibid., p. 218, 84) *ši-di* ^{kur}*lab-na-na lu aṣ-bat*, 'I marched along the Lebanon range', (ibid., p. 219, 96) *ši-di* ^{id}*pu-rat-te a-na e-le-ni aṣbat*(dab)^{bat}, 'I marched upstream along the Euphrates'. In agreement with the respective meanings of *pūtu*, 'short side', and *šiddu*, 'long side', it seems that *pūt* is used when the subject encounters the river or sea as a short stretch, *šiddi* when the subject travels alongside it for a long stretch.

117. Some appear to take this line to describe the trapper going home with his haul of game; others leave ambiguity. However, the pronoun *šū* (no other restoration seems obvious) probably marks a change of subject, as elsewhere in SB Gilgameš (e.g. I 272, X 181; cf. *šī* in SB I 143 // 164). The translation in *CAD* B, p. 292, 'he (Enkidu) and his animals had intruded into his (the hunter's) region', agrees, but is too contrived to convince. Enkidu and his herd leave the water-hole and head for home, leaving the astonished trapper frozen in terror (so already Schott, *ZA* 42 (1934), p. 97). The idiom *bītum erēbu* is thus a simple metaphor.

117–18. These two lines serve to highlight the frequent use in poetry of enclitic *-ma* on verbs that have no obvious need of coordination. At the end of a couplet (as *īrum-ma*) enclitic *-ma* cannot normally serve for coordination, for a sentence very rarely extends over the boundary between couplets. At the end of a line containing a verb (as *iqūl-ma*) it is also questionable whether coordination is intended, for main clauses in different lines usually exhibit no syntactical dependence. There are exceptions, for example SB XI 207–8: *eninnāma ana kâša mannu ilī upaḫḫarakkum-ma / balāṭa ša tuba''û tuttâ atta*, where there is a consecutive relationship ('so that'). However, most lines, and especially couplets, display syntactical autonomy. There are many other instances of *-ma* where no coordination is probable: OB II 6 *ipzirūnim*(?)*-ma*, 64 *alkāti-ma*, 162 *qabi-ma*, 177 *īrub-ma*, 179 *izzizam-ma*, 197 *nadi-ma*, 212 *itbe-ma*, 227 *ikmis-ma*, OB III 106 *īde-ma*, 172 *īdil-ma*(?), 184 *lukšussu-ma*, 201 *išme-ma*, OB Schøyen$_2$ 11 *iṣbat-ma*, 13 etc. *izzaqqaram-ma*, 27 *īli-ma*, 58 *īdēšu-ma*, OB Nippur 11 *appalsam-ma*, OB Harmal$_1$ 1 *eli-ma*, OB Ishchali 11′ *nešakkan-ma*, 26′ *inēr-ma*, OB VA + BM i 12′ *attīlam-ma*, ii 4′ *illik-ma*, iii 21 *wašbāti-ma*, iii 22 *amrāti-ma*, iv 26 *liqe-ma*, MB Nippur$_1$ 2 [*ibni-m*]*a*, MB Ur 42 *išassâššum-ma*, MB Emar$_2$ i 24′, 28′, 32′ *tar'amī-ma*, i 32′ *ašbāti-ma*, MB Boğ$_2$ vi 11′ *išme-ma*, SB I 15 *ṣabat-ma*; I 32 *illak-ma*; I 140 // 162 *uru-ma* // 167 *ūru-ma*, I 178 *īmuršu-ma*, I 185 *epšīšu-ma* // 192 *īpussu-ma*, I 241 *irāmšu-ma*, I 247 *ibšûnim-ma*, I 268 // 291 *illakakkum-ma*, I 295 *limqutam-ma*, I 297 *lurši-ma*, II 61 [*nīl*]*ūnim-ma*, II 100 [*ittaziz-m*]*a*, II 113 *iṣṣabtū-ma* (cf. III 19 *iṣṣabtū-ma*, probably coordinated with *illakū*), II 223 etc. *išemme-ma*, II 267 *lūrubam-ma*, II 287 *itbû-ma*, II 300 *išme-ma*, III 32 *lūpuš-ma*, IV 26 *i''aldam-ma*, IV 40 *īli-ma*, IV 43 // 88 // 171 *īpušaššum-ma*, probably IV 90 // 173 *ušnīlšu-ma*, IV 107 [*ta''ald*]*am-ma*(?), IV 194 *išme-ma*, V 137 *idkâššum-ma*, V 175 *amrāta-ma*, V 190, 230, 246(?) *išme-ma*, V 295 *ēpuš-ma*, VI 5 *ītepram-ma*, VI 8 *qīšam-ma*, VI 48, 51, 53, 58, 64 *tarāmī-ma*, VI 75 *tašmî-ma*, VI 77 *tušēšibīšu-ma*, VI 94 *binnam-ma*, VI 113 *išme-ma*, VI 119 // 121 // 123 *ippete-ma*, VI 141 *iṣūdam-ma*, VI 142 *iṣbassu-ma*, VI 151 *īli-ma*, VI 154 *išme-ma*, VI 160 *issi-ma* var. *paḫrūnim-ma*, VI 180 *utūlū-ma* (MS Q), VII 140 and 141 *ušnālka-ma*, VII 149 *inūḫ*-[*ma*], VII 183 *iksi-ma*, VII 189 *labšā-ma*, VIII 59 *iktum-ma*, VIII 84–5 *ušnālka-ma*, VIII 215 *ušēṣâm-ma*, IX 141 // 144 etc. *inamdinšu-ma*, X 10 *inaṭṭalšum-ma*, X 70 // 147 // 247 *anellam-ma*, X 75 *idnim-ma* // 152 *idnam-ma*, X 172 *ikšudam-ma*, X 189 *illakam-ma*, X 320 *išīm-me*, XI 2 *anaṭṭalakkum-ma*, XI 15 *itma-ma*, XI 19 *tami-ma*, XI 22 *šime-ma*; XI 27 *šūli-ma*, XI 39 *izēranni-ma*, XI 78 *šupšuqū-ma*, XI 87 *iškunam-ma*, XI 98 *īlâm-ma*, XI 99 *irtammam-ma*, XI 119 *itūr-ma*, XI 122 *aqbi-ma*, XI 149 // 152 *i-pi-ra-am-ma*, XI 155 *īmur-ma*, XI 180 *īde-ma*, XI 199 *īlam-ma*, XI 205 *lū ašib-ma*, XI 210 *ašbu-ma*, XI 253 *bilšu-ma* // 262 *ūbilšu-ma*, XI 303 *īmur-ma*, XI 315 *inaššâm-ma*, XI 321 *ikšudūnim-ma*, XII 57 // 58 *imqutanni-ma*, XII 151 *ṣalil-ma* (MS q). All are verbs of clauses where the end of the clause coincides with the end of the line or a couplet and where coordination with the following line is thus either unlikely or unnecessary. Other explanations must be sought, for example, (a) limiting verb to subject 'Ea alone knows' (XI 180 *īde-ma*), (b) temporal 'then, finally' (VI 5 *ītepram-ma*, X 172 *ikšudam-ma*), (c) modal 'likewise' (I 32 *illak-ma*, probably also VI 48 etc. *tarāmī-ma*). When none of these explanations is adequate one admits defeat, with von Soden, who surrendered with the terse observation 'dicht. zT unklar' (*AHw*, p. 570). This is an inadequate response but reflects the current state of knowledge. Serious research is needed to elucidate the full role of *-ma* in poetry.

119. Restore perhaps [*le-mu-un*] or [*il-mi-in*].

120–1. This couplet is standard in SB Gilgameš, appearing also in SB X (9–10, 42–3, [49–50], 115–16, 122–3, 215–16, 222–3). For *urḫa rūqta/rūqata alāku/rapādu* on its own see also above, on SB I 9. In none of these passages is *urḫu* construed as masculine, consequently the spelling *ru-qu-ti* stands for fem. sing. *rūqti* (for the use of a CV-sign to express VC in Kuyunjik manuscripts of Gilgameš see Chapter 9, the section on Spelling sub a). The spelling *ru-qa-t*V observed in other passages is singular, with extra vowel for literary effect (see Chapter 9, the section on Language and style sub i).

122. This is the first example in SB Gilgameš of the longer of the common literary formulae for introducing direct speech. For the syntax see Chapter 5, the note on OB II 51–2.

123–33. Restorations not marked as questionable are restored from the repetition of this speech in ll. 150–60.

124–5 // 151–2. This is a stock couplet, recurring also in SB I 269–70, 292–3 and II 162–3. The second line is used on its own in SB I 137 and II 43. The simile introduces the concept of the '"lump" of Anu', i.e. 'solid matter of the sky', as a byword for one endowed with superhuman strength (cf. SB I 137, where it refers to Gilgameš). In Gilgameš's dream the '"lump" of Anu' is clearly a meteorite, and symbolic of Enkidu (see SB I 248). Meteorites, of course, were an important source of good-quality iron in the Bronze Age. The celestial origin of this rare metal is explicit in the Sumerian poem of Lugalbanda, where the hero's mighty axe is described in the following passage:

> urudu ḫa.zi.in.na.ni kù.bi an.na šu im.ma.an.ti
> gír úr.ra.ka.ni an.bar.sù.àm im.ma.da.ri
>
> Lugalbanda Epic I 358–9, text after H. L. J. Vanstiphout in J. Prosecký, *Intellectual Life of the Ancient Near East* (CRRA 43; Prague, 1998), p. 411
>
> He took up in his hand his axe—its metal was 'of heaven',
> he grasped his dagger (worn at) the thigh—it was of iron.

The term an.na here can hardly be tin, which is useless for an axe-head; rather, kù.bi an.na is a literary circumlocution for the next line's iron (following Vanstiphout, *CRRA* 43, p. 399). The equation of the '"lump" of Anu' with meteoric iron, so much stronger than bronze, explains its use in Gilgameš SB I as a symbol signifying great strength.

For *kiṣru* denoting a crude lump of unworked metal, note also *ki-ṣir par-zil-li*, 'a lump of iron', in broken context in the Fable of the Fox (Lambert, *BWL*, p. 204, A 5), which may well refer to meteoric iron in its raw condition (for *kiṣru* with other metals see *CAD* K, p. 441; note that the simile *kīma ki-iṣ-ri* there cited with reference to a meteor in an astrological report is now read *kīma di-pa-ri*: see *SAA* VIII 303 rev. 2). The usage *kiṣir Ani* is reminiscent of the coinage *kiṣir šadî* for the bedrock of mountains, and may be witness to the belief that the furthest heavens were made in part of hard, stony material (for the stony heavens see further Livingstone, *Mystical Works*, p. 86; Horowitz, *Cosmic Geography*, p. 263). Elsewhere Ištar is the *kiṣru* of the heavens (*BAM* 237 i 20′: *ki-ṣi-ru ša šamê*[e]), either because her planet was envisaged as a lump of celestial solid matter or, less pertinently, because she was sired by Anu.

127. The restoration is suggested by ll. 110 // 175.

129 // 156. Or, 'being afraid I do not go near him;' the hunter's fear may either be circumstantial to his inability to approach Enkidu or it may lead to it. On these alternative renderings of stative + *ma* followed by the present see Lambert, *BWL*, p. 309, the further references cited in *GAG*[3], §159a and, on this line, Streck, *Or* NS 64 (1995), p. 72.

131 // 158. There is not enough room for Thompson's *uš-[p]à[r-ri-ru]*. For *šunūlu*, 'to lay out, set' traps, cf. *sa-par-šá šu-par-ru-ru a-na a-a-bi šu-nu-⌈ul⌉-lu*, 'her net is spread out, laid ready for the

enemy' (R. C. Thompson, *AAA* 20 (1933), pl. 90, 9; Asb); *še-et* ⌈*damiqtim*^{tim}⌉ *tar-ṣa-at giš-*⌈*par-ru*⌉*-ka šu-*⟨*nu*⟩*-lu-*⌈*in*⌉*-ni*, 'the lucky net is stretched out, the snares are set for you' (*STT* 215 iii 18 // *CAD* N/1, p. 206; *Ḫulbazizi* incantation). The word *nuballu*, 'wing', is uniquely used in this line and its repetition (158); presumably it describes a net shaped like a wing (see further the discussion of E. von der Osten-Sacken, *MDOG* 123 (1991), pp. 140–1).

136. For *eli/elu ṣērīšu* see below, on l. 145.

138. The line is restored after l. 148, which realizes the old man's advice as narrative.

140–5. Restorations are taken from the parallel passage, ll. 162–6, where there is, however, no repetition of l. 141.

143 // 164. The enclitic *-ma* attached to the final word of a clause either stresses that word (cf. l. 65 above) or coordinates the two clauses. In this case I have assumed the latter. Clear examples in the Akkadian Gilgameš of coordinative *-ma* attached the last word of the clause where that word is not a verb are OB II 104 *īliṣ libbašu-ma pānūšu ittamrū*, 229 *ipšiḫ uzzašu-ma inē' irassu*, OB III 72 // 75 *ilmin libbašu-ma marṣiš*(?) *uštāniḫ*, MB Emar$_2$ i 27′ *izzaz ina* [*qišātim*]*-ma išassi kappī*, SB I 143 // 164 *šī lišḫuṭ lubūšīša-ma liptâ kuzubša*, II 60 [*uttapp*]*iṣ barbarī-ma l*[*abbī uktašši*]*d*, VI 155 *išluḫ imitti alêm-ma ana pānīša iddi*, VII 147 [*iltabbi*]*š mašak labbim-ma irappud ṣ*[*ēra*] (contrast VIII 91 *altabbiš-ma mašak l*[*abbi*(*m-ma*) *arap*]*pud ṣēra*), VIII 58 *ilput libbašu-ma ul inakkud mimmāma*, IX 43 *rašbat pulḫassunu-ma imrassunu mūtu*, IX 47 *iṣbat ṭēnšu-ma iqrub maḫaršun*, IX 83 // 140 etc. *šapât ekletum-ma ul ibašši nūru*, X 18 *ušaqqi zuqassu-ma ištak*[*anši*(?) *pānīšu*(?)], X 160 // 166 *erid* // *ūrid ana qištim-ma parīsī . . . iksa* // [*ikkissu*], XI 25 *muššir mešrâm-ma še'i napšāti* (parallel XI 26 *makkūra zēr-ma napišta bulliṭ*), XI 89 *erub ana libbi eleppim-ma piḫe bābka* // 94 *ērub ana libbi eleppim-ma apteḫi bābī*, XI 137 *apte nappašam-ma ṣētu imtaqut eli dūr appīya*, XI 155 *illik āribum-ma qarūra ša mê īmurma*, XI 173 *īmur eleppam-ma īteziz Ellil*, XI 200 *iṣbat qātīya-ma ultēlânni yâši*, XI 291 *šū ilqe šammam-ma iss*[*uḫa . . .*], XI 298 *lušākil šībam-ma šamma lultuk*, XI 304 *ūrid ana libbim-ma mê irammuk*. Whether such a location of the enclitic particle is determined by style, metre or some other consideration is a question that has yet to be studied.

145 // 166 // 187. As the line is conventionally translated it is the herd that is the subject of *irbû*, not Enkidu. If the conventional rendering is followed, this relative clause seems inconsequential and out of place: the point of the story is that a wild man grew up with the beasts, not the other way around. The animals in the herd were Enkidu's father and mother, and brought him up as part of it (*urabbû*: SB VIII 5).

I have translated the relative clause as a concessive, as elsewhere in the SB epic (I 200, VII 40). Concessive use of the relative pronoun is especially visible in royal inscriptions, where *ša* can introduce an adverbial dependent clause (lit. 'as to the fact that . . .') that highlights the contrast between the achievements of a king's predecessors and his own: *ša iš-tum da-ar ší-ki-ti ni-ši šar in šar-rí ma-na-ma ar-ma-nam*^{ki} *ù eb-la*^{ki} *la u-ša*$_{10}$*-al-pi*$_5$*-tu*, 'though from time immemorial, the creation of mankind, of all the kings no king whatsoever had destroyed Armānum and Ebla (Nergal gave them to Narām-Sîn)' (*UET* I 275 i 1–10, ed. Frayne, *RIME* 2, pp. 132); *ša iš-tu u*$_4$*-um ṣa-at a-lam ma-ri*^{ki} *ilum ib-nu-ú šarrum ma-ma-an wa-ši-ib ma-ri*^{ki} *ti-a-am-ta-am la ik-šu-du*, 'though from days of yore, when the god built Mari, no king at all who resided in Mari had reached the Mediterranean, (Yaḫdun-Līm went to the sea-shore)' (Frayne, *RIME* 4, p. 605, 34–7); *ša iš-tu u*$_4$*-um ṣi-a-tim iš-tu libitti* é.babbar *ib-ba-ni-ù in šàr maḫ-ra šarrum ma-am-ma-an* ^{d}*šamaš la im-gu-ru-ma dūr sippar*^{ki} *la i-pu-šu-šum-ma*, 'though from days of yore, since the brickwork of E-babbar was first created, of all the kings of old no king at all had done Šamaš's bidding and built for him the wall of Sippar (I, Samsu-iluna, moulded its brickwork)' (ibid., p. 377, 55–62). In OB letters *ša* can introduce clauses which in modern languages would be prefaced by a variety of conjunctions, concessive ('though

. . .') and concessive conditional ('even if . . .') among them (e.g., *AbB* XI 90, 27; 106, 32; 160, 23). Note also in a NB letter sent home by a man travelling abroad the reassurance *na-kut-ta-a la ta-re-šá-' šá ṭè-ma-a la ta-šá-ma-'*, 'Even though you hear no news of me, you must not start worrying about me!' (*CT* 22 6, 7–8). No doubt a thorough search would yield many more examples.

The expression *eli ṣērīšu* is often rendered 'on his steppe' or paraphrased as 'with him in the wild', but also 'sous sa tutelle' (Labat). I follow a private suggestion of A. Shaffer, that *eli ṣēri* in Gilgameš simply means 'in(to) the presence of' (see e.g. SB I 136, XI 6; cf. already Jacobsen, *Acta Or* 8 (1930), p. 67, fn. 2; also Bottéro: 'avec lui').

148. The preposition *ina* should perhaps be emended to *ana*.

161. This is the first instance of the less common formula used in SB Gilgameš to introduce direct speech, which employs only *izakkara*; on the use of the present tense in such formulae see Chapter 5, the note on OB II 1.

163. The spelling *bu-lam* for the nominative in a Kuyunjik tablet (MS P) is a notably aberrant orthography by the standards of earlier grammar. For comparable spellings see Ch. 9, the section on Spelling sub (j).

169. The word *adannu* usually signifies an appointed or prearranged time ('deadline'). Here it is evidently used with reference to an arranged point in space rather than time. The same usage may occur in the Anzû poem when the mother goddess enjoins her son Ningirsu to set out for battle with the enemy. Her instructions more obviously refer to location than time (SB Anzû II 1): *bi-šim ur-ḫa šuk-na a-dan-na*, 'fashion a path (to the mountain), determine a place to meet (Anzû in combat)' (in OB Anzû II 52 *šu-ku-un a-na-da-am* is an obvious error for *šukun adannam*).

170–1. The word *ušbu* remains a hapax legomenon. The suggestion that this means 'hiding-place' (*AHw*, p. 1441, 'Versteck') fits the context well enough, but since the preposition is *ana* not *ina* I have opted for a less concrete meaning, literally 'for their waiting'. The ventive on *ašābu* is very rare; *ittašbūni* (both MSS in l. 170, one MS in l. 171) may for that reason be corrupted by dittography from *iktaldūni* in l. 169.

172. In l. 176 MS P replaces *mašqâ iteppir* of the parallel line (l. 111) with *mašqâ išatti*, and the verb may thus once have been *iteppir* in this line also.

173. Note the orthography *nam-maš-⟨še⟩-e* (Kuyunjik MS P), apparently genitive or plural but expressing the nominative singular. On the verb see above, on XI 112 // 177.

174. Lit. 'his origin was the very uplands'; for *ilittu* meaning not so much 'offspring' or 'birth' as the stock from which one comes, see, with reference to the Sebettu, Erra I 24: *i-lit-ta-šú-nu a-ḫa-at-ma*, 'their origin was strange'. The phrase of the present line is also used of Enkidu in SB II 42, where it is replaced in some manuscripts with what is effectively an easier paraphrase, *alid ina šadî*, 'he was born in the hills'.

175–7. These lines repeat ll. 110–12. M. P. Streck analyses the repetition as circumstantial clauses, the original occurrence as 'generell-iterativ' clauses and adjusts his translations accordingly (*Or* NS 64 (1995), p. 62, fn. 119). Repetition is a literary device. The arrival of Enkidu here automatically invokes the description that accompanied his first appearance in the poem, as a kind of flashback. Such repetition is a feature of traditional narrative poetry and, in my view, it is best to keep the translation identical to highlight it.

178. The word *lullû* is typically used of man in the context of his creation (see Tigay, *Evolution*, p. 202). In SB X 318 the emphasis is on the mortality of man, appropriately enough, for in Babylonian theology it was essentially the mortality of the new being that distinguished it from its divine creators. Here, however, the emphasis is on the newly created as something untouched by civilization (cf. *CAD* Š/1, p. 71: 'the uncivilized man'; Bottéro: 'ébauche d'homme'). A. D. Kilmer's

suggestion that the word alludes to Enkidu's future role as sexual partner of Gilgameš (*Kraus AV*, p. 130: '*lullu*(*-amēlu*): pun on *lalû*/*lullû*') seems over-contrived.

180. The *kirimmu* is usually the folded arm which typically cradles a nursing baby. In l. 188 *kirimmu* is replaced with *dīdū*, usually translated 'loincloth' but perhaps an under-garment that covered more than just the lower trunk. The switch of words implies that *kirimmu* may also refer to a garment (cf. *CAD* D, p. 136). The undoing of the *kirimmu* would then mean the release of the over-garment behind which a babe in arms might be held for shelter and nursing. As well as releasing her grip on her garment, allowing it to fall, the prostitute's gesture opens her arms to prepare for embrace.

181 // 189. The phrase *ūra petû* is literally 'to open the vulva' and is taken literally by some, but it also means to bare the genital area (cf. *kuzba petû* in l. 164). Similarly *kuzba leqû* may mean to possess a woman sexually but also means to take in her charms, i.e. become physically attracted to her (see T. Jacobsen, *ANES* 5 (1973), pp. 207–8). Note in MS F the variant *ūrka* for *ūrki* (l. 181), unremarkable in a LB source but noteworthy in a Kuyunjik MS.

182 // 190. The prostitute's next act of seduction is described as *napīssu leqû*, literally 'to take in his breath (*or* smell)'. Some have understood this at face value or as indicating embrace, but Enkidu does not come that near Šamḫat until the next line. Others propose that *napīšu leqû* is parallel with *kuzba leqû* and that *napīšu* is a 'euphemism for virility' (*CAD* N/1, p. 305; cf. Speiser, 'welcome his ardour!', and similarly others). According to B. Landsberger's editorial footnote in Schott, *ZA* 42 (1934), p. 100, fn. 2, the phrase can mean 'ganz nahe an ihn herantreten'. With this in mind I follow a suggestion made privately by the late Thorkild Jacobsen, who very plausibly suggested that this is a trapper's language, 'to take his scent' (cf. already Dalley: 'take wind of him'). This would mean moving close enough to one's target to obtain a good shot: Šamḫat approaches Enkidu with a huntsman's caution, so as not to frighten him off.

183. Having advertised her wares the prostitute is to let Enkidu approach. Note that *ṭeḫû* commonly has the nuance of seeking sexual favours: the language is loaded. Curiously this line is never explicitly realized as narrative.

184 // 191. The phrase *lubūšī muṣṣû* recalls an idiom common in rituals, where *ṣubāta muṣṣû* refers to the spreading out of a piece of cloth as an adornment of the ritual area or object, if not as a precaution against dirt (typical is *LKA* 141 obv. 9: ^{giš}*kussâ*(gu.za) *tanaddi*(šub)^{di} *ṣubāt*(túg)^{há} *kitê*(gada) *ina muḫ-ḫi tu-ma-ṣa il bīti*(é) *ina muḫ-ḫi tušeššab*(dúr)^{ab}, 'you set up a chair, spread a linen cloth over it and sit the god of the house on it'; cf. J. S. Cooper, *ZA* 62 (1972), p. 72, 14; Mayer, *Gebetsbeschwörungen*, p. 523, 17; IV R^2 54 no. 2, 40; etc.). In the Descent of Ištar, ll. 42–60, *muṣṣû* means to remove an item of clothing, but elsewhere also to lay it out. The point here is not only that the prostitute takes off her garment but that she spreads it on the ground like a blanket and lies on it, a gesture which invites Enkidu to join her.

185 // 192. Nearly all modern translators take *lullâ* here as 'man', and *lullû amēlu* has just been used to describe Enkidu, in l. 178. Heidel held a different view, translating 'incita in eo libidinem(?), opus feminae' (cf. Grayson, *Papyrus and Tablet*, p. 142: 'show him lust, woman's art'). This idea is attractive, for in sex the traditional work of a woman, especially a prostitute, is to excite a man's desire. Perhaps the language is intentionally ambiguous: Enkidu is the *lullû* but also the prostitute is doing something *lullû*.

186. Here, and probably also in l. 193, the Babylonian source has the prostitute's *dādū* as the subject of *ḫabābu*. Given the nature of *ḫabābu*, as examined below, there is no determining whether the more original text is presented in the Kuyunjik sources or in the Babylonian manuscript, i.e. whether the line reports the instinctive reaction of Enkidu or the practised arts of the prostitute. When not rendered ad hoc *ḫabābu* is usually translated 'caress' or the like. *CAD*, s.v., distinguishes

between *ḫabābu* A, of noise (babbling of running water, chirping of birds, buzzing of flies, lowing of oxen, to which must be added the noise(!?) of lightning, *STT* 23, 12′: Anzû) and *ḫabābu* B, of motion involving sensuous physical contact (in lovemaking and of a snake sliding over someone). *AHw* takes them as one, meaning, in the context of lovemaking, 'to whisper' (cf. Reclam[4]; see further B. Groneberg, *RA* 80 (1986), pp. 189–90). Likewise I see no reason to separate *ḫabābu* into two verbs: movement, as well as sound, is characteristic of lovemaking. The ancient view is expressed by a line of the synonym list *Malku*, in which *ḫa-ba-bu* = *na-šá-qu*, 'to kiss' (III 8). This equation need not suggest exact synonymity, of course, but it confirms what is known from the present line and other passages, that *ḫabābu* can accompany sexual intercourse; note especially the sequence *ḫu-ub-bi-ban-ni . . . rit-ka-ban-ni* (Biggs, *Šaziga*, p. 31, 46–7), '*ḫ*. me, copulate with me!' in a potency incantation. Indeed, some have suggested that *ḫ*. can be a euphemism for coitus itself (T. Jacobsen, *Acta Or* 8 (1930), pp. 69–70, fn. 2; J. S. Cooper, *Finkelstein Mem. Vol.*, p. 43, fn. 22; etc.). However, the context indicates that *dādū ḫabābu* is, in this passage, the last stage of lovemaking before actual copulation (*reḫû* in l. 194).

It should be noted that the construction with *dādū* is unique. Elsewhere in Gilgameš the verb *ḫabābu* appears as Gilgameš's response in his dreams to the meteorite and axe that are symbolic of Enkidu (SB I 256, 267, 284, 289; cf. OB II 34). The construction used there also, with a personal subject, occurs in similar context in the goddess Anunnîtum's oracular promise to Zimrī-Līm, *a-na-ku e-li-ka a-ḫa-ab-bu-ub* (*ARM* X 8, 10–11), 'I will make love to you'. In these passages the expression *ḫabābu eli* means acting tenderly like a lover. In the present line, where the naked Šamḫat is lying down with the wild Enkidu on top of her, something more passionate is meant; the question is, what exactly is meant by *dādū*? This word seems to mean generally 'love', but it also denotes the object of love ('darling') and the physical realization of love ('lovemaking'). It comes also to be a euphemism for the lower abdomen, i.e. the genital region, in both female and male physiology (*AHw* s.v. 2; *CAD* s.v. *dādu* B 2). Use of the word therefore may convey the suggestive ambiguity that is characteristic of the language of flirtation and sex. The incipit of the love song *ḫi-i-pa-a-ku a-na da-di-ka* (*KAR* 158 rev. ii 11) means 'I am amorous at the thought of your love', but it also suggests 'I am amorous at the thought of your manhood' (for *ḫīpāku* see W. G. Lambert, *Or* NS 36 (1967), p. 132). In the same way the phrase used here, *dādū ḫabābu*, might refer both to general dalliance (the whispering of sweet nothings) and to the physical entwining of a reclining couple that is the prelude to coitus. Given Šamḫat's profession and Enkidu's animal nature we may be certain that in this line the latter is meant.

186–7. All the Kuyunjik manuscripts have transposed the lines of this couplet into an illogical sequence, as now proved by Late Babylonian MS x (cf. W. R. Mayer, *VAS* XXIV, p. 13).

188. Foster speculates that *kirimmu* in the parallel (l. 180) is replaced here by *dīdū* 'to prepare for a play on *dādu*' (*Essays Pope*, p. 24).

194. This line almost repeats a couplet of the Pennsylvania tablet, where, however, the period is probably 'seven days and seven nights' (OB II 48–50: *ūmī se*[*bet*] *u sebe mušī'ātim* / *En*[*kīdu t*]*ebīma Ša*[*mkata*]*m irḫi*). Twice elsewhere in the epic when the Old Babylonian text offers 'seven days and seven nights', we find 'six days and seven nights' in the late version: in the delaying of Enkidu's burial (OB VA + BM ii 8′: *sebet ūmim u sebe mušī'ātim* // SB X 58 // 135 // 235: 6 *urrī* [*u* 7 *mušâti*]), and in the duration of the Deluge (OB Atram-ḫasīs III iv 24: 7 u_4*-mi* 7 *mu-š*[*i-a-tim*] // SB XI 128 (MS T): 6 *urrī u* ⌜7⌝ *mušâti*). 'Six days and seven nights' is also the period of sleeplessness set Gilgameš by Ūta-napišti in SB XI 209, for which there is as yet no OB counterpart. The numerical sequence *n*, *n* + 1 is a well-known pattern in ancient Near Eastern poetry. For another example in Gilgameš see SB VI 18: *enzātūka takšî laḫrātūka tu'āmī līlidā*, where, exceptionally, the sequence is in reverse ('triplets . . . twins'). Elsewhere in Babylonian poetry and prose more conventional

examples occur, for example in an OB snake incantation: *ša ba-aš-mi ši-ši-it pí-šu se-bé-et li-ša-nu-šu* (*TIM* IX 65, 9 // 66, 17–19), 'the *bašmu*-viper's mouths are six, seven are its tongues'. Further examples in Mesopotamian and other ancient Near Eastern literatures have been collected by W. M. W. Roth, 'The numerical sequence x/x + 1 in the Old Testament', *Vetus Testamentum* 12 (1962), pp. 300–11 (see also M. L. West, *The East Face of Helicon*, pp. 259–61). In Babylonian literature the sequence six + seven was by some way the most popular of these numerical sequences. In Gilgameš the change from OB 'seven and seven' to SB 'six and seven' begins to look as if it was a conscious policy, perhaps reflecting a literary fashion.

Note the present of continuing action, *ireḫḫi*, in MSS Pn, which is at odds with the preterite *irḫi* offered by the Pennsylvania tablet as well as by MS B.

197. Most translators ignore the present tense of *irappud*. M. P. Streck translates 'liefen kopflos', counting it among a few other verbs in the literary corpus where he understands this tense to convey an 'iterative-plural' function, with the especial nuance that 'der Sachverhalt verläuft in verschiedene Richtungen' (*Or* NS 64 (1955), pp. 48–9). This nuance is not proven, for the examples Streck adduces can all be explained as presents of circumstance, as imperfects denoting action that continued for a time, or in other conventional ways. A less radical interpretation of *irappud* is that the tense denotes the result of *īmurāšū*, 'they saw . . . and as a result they ran'. However, I have understood it also to denote action that continues during the following lines, by analogy with the present in verbs that introduce direct speech (see Chapter 5, the note on OB II 1, and below on SB I 205).

199. For a history of the treatment of this difficult line see D. O. Edzard, *Or* NS 54 (1985), pp. 50–2. The verb *šuḫḫû* (so MSS Fn) has since been discussed at length by W. R. Mayer, *Or* NS 57 (1988), pp. 155–8. (see also A. Westenholz and U. Koch-Westenholz, *Studies Lambert*, p. 449, fn. 9). Very appropriately for the present context, it signifies defilement through illicit sexual congress. The variant *ultaḫḫit/ṭ* (MS B) does not produce notably better sense and is presumed a corruption. With Mayer and Westenholz I take *ullula* as the adjective, noting the semantic opposition which contrasts Enkidu's erstwhile innocence with his debasement. The result is a reversed adjectival phrase, with the adjective attracting special emphasis accordingly; for other examples of such reversal in Gilgameš see Chapter 9, the section on Language and style sub (iii–v). Others have taken *ullula* as a II/1 stative from *alālu*, to mean 'his body was bound', i.e. unable to move as freely as before, but this seems too contrived and disallows the parallelism in vocabulary noted by Westenholz, in which the sequence *ultaḫḫi–ullula–umtaṭṭi* in the narrative (SB I 199–201) fits the unambiguous *šuḫḫû* (SB var. *šaḫḫû*)*–ella–tušamṭînni* in Enkidu's reminiscence of it (MB Ur 38–40 and SB VII 129–31).

200. The word *birku* is literally 'knee' but often signifies the leg as an instrument of motion (see Chapter 5, OB Schøyen$_2$ 7 and note). For a comparable instance of *izuzzu* in the sense 'to stand still' see SB IV 250: [*ugammer*]*ū amātīšunu šunu izzizzū*, and the description of impossible marching conditions in Šittī-Marduk's *kudurru*: *ni-is-qu šá rabûti*(gal)^{meš} *sisî*(anše.kur.ra)^{meš} *it-ta-ši-iz-zu* (*BBSt* 6 i 20; Nbk I), 'the best of even the largest horses came to a halt'. The ventive on *alāku* is almost always to be rendered 'come, came', as is generally the case in Akkadian and demonstrated for this text in the recent study of H. Hirsch, 'Die Heimkehr des Gilgamesch', *Archivum Anatolicum* 3 (Bilgiç Mem. Vol.; Ankara, 1997), pp. 173–90. However, *illika* (var. *illaka*) in the present line looks like a rare exception to the rule, for the animals' motion clearly puts space between them and Enkidu. The alternative is to parse the verb as feminine plural. Though elsewhere in the SB epic *būlu* is construed as singular, note the apparent use of at least one feminine plural verb in a Mari letter: *bu-lum* [(. . .)] *a-na li-ib-bi na-we-em ša a-bi-ia li-*[*il-li-ka*?] *it-ti bu-lim ša a-bi-ia li-ku-la* (*ARM* II 45 rev. 9′–11′), 'let the herd [move] to my father's pasture so they can graze with my father's herd'. The

usage is perhaps born of analogy with comparable collective nouns that are genuine feminine plurals (*ṣēnū* 'flock', *sugullātu*, 'cattle').

201. Note the irregular orthography of *umtaṭṭi*, even in a Kuyunjik MS (F). The verb *mutaṭṭû* (II/1) can mean 'to be diminished' in speed as well as in strength. For the former nuance see a NA astrological report noting the slowing of Mars: ⌜*ina?*⌝ *ta-lu-ki-šú un-de-eṭ-ṭu* (Hunger, *SAA* VIII 312, 3), 'it was slowed in its course'. For the latter see the famous letter of Urad-Gula to Aššurbanipal, describing an unfruitful consultation with a prophet: *ma!-aḫ-ḫur ù di-ig-lu un-ta-aṭ-ṭi* (Parpola, *Studies Reiner*, p. 264=*SAA* X 294 rev. 32), 'he was contrary and weak of vision'. Both nuances apply to Enkidu.

202. Thompson's restoration of *i-ši-i*[*ḫ*, endorsed by von Soden (*ZA* 53, p. 222), is rejected here, since the space given over to the sign *ši* on the tablet (MS F) indicates that the sign that follows it starts a new word. We hold to Schott's *īši ṭ*[*é-ma* (*ZA* 42, p. 101), though with some reservation, since the typically OA–MA value *ṭé* is rarely used by NA scribes. Note that very little can be missing in the lacuna; *īši ḫ*[*i-is-sa-ta* would certainly be too long. Ebeling's *i-ši-i*[*m-me* (*AfO* 8, p. 226) is unsatisfactory for the same reason as Thompson's reading and, to my mind, also because it anticipates what has not yet happened.

203. The signs *i-tu-ra-ram-mu* were already clear to Haupt; Thompson's *i-tu-ur-ram-mu* is erroneous. However, I do not see how *ram-mu* can be a satisfactory form of *ramû* (so Parpola), and so take all five signs as one word. The enclitic *-ma* is here written *-mu*, as in SB X 81, also a Kuyunjik MS (cf. *AHw*, p. 664). This development is nothing to do with vowel harmony but is analogous with the displacement of /a/ by /u/ in the accusative singular of the noun. A similar trend can be observed in LB pronominal suffixes (*-ku* for *-ka*, *-šú* for *-šá*) and, less well documented, in verbal endings, including the ventive (on this see Chapter 9, the section on Spelling conventions).

204. The disagreement of the two Kuyunjik manuscripts over the gender of the pronominal suffix permits the alternative translations offered here. Both make sense. As he leaves the realm of the animals for good, Enkidu begins to treat Šamḫat in a less animal manner: he regards her face (*pānīša*) attentively and listens to her speech with new understanding (similarly Oppenheim, *Or* NS 17, p. 26). Alternatively one might comment that Šamḫat's observation in l. 207 might logically follow a prolonged gaze at his face (*pānīšu*). It is not impossible, however, that the masculine variant is an early attestation of LB orthographic practice noted in the commentary on the preceding line. In this analysis only the former interpretation is admissible.

205. The reading of the beginning of the line follows von Soden, *ZA* 53 (1959), p. 222. The verb *išemmâ* is present for the same reason *iqabbû* is: the action continues during the following direct speech (see Chapter 5, the note on OB II 1).

207. The restoration of *damqāta* is made from the parallel from Boğazköy, MB Boğ$_1$ Fragment a, 1. The variant in MS P is not, to my eyes, *tab-ba-ši* (so Thompson). This line and the following exhibit in slightly different form a couplet of the Pennsylvania tablet: *anaṭṭalka Enkīdu kīma ilim tabašši* / *ammīnim itti nammaštê tattanallak ṣēram* (OB II 53–5).

208. The line recurs as SB II 29.

209–10. There is no room on MS P for *lu-*⌜*ú*⌝*-ru-ka* (e.g., *CAD* A/2, p. 314); the broken sign is much shorter. Of the alternatives *lu-*[*u*]*t-ru-ka* and *lu-*[*t*]*ar-ru-ka* the latter is a better fit. The change from OB *lurdīka* (OB II 56) to SB *luttarrūka* is unexciting and the conversion of *Uruk ribītum* to *Uruk supūru* is routine, but the expansion of *mūšabi(m) ša Anim* (OB II 58) to *mūšab Anim u Ištar* is interesting; see Chapter 5, the introduction to the Pennsylvania tablet.

210a–b. This couplet, present only in the manuscript from LB Uruk, perhaps represents an expansion of the text known at Kuyunjik, with material taken from l. 217 (i.e. *quddušī*) as well as ll.

209–10. It should be noted, however, that the OB epic also spent two couplets on this theme (OB II 56–60); these are grounds for adopting an alternative position, that the Kuyunjik manuscripts preserve at this point a telescoped version of the text.

212. This line develops the image, first found in l. 64, of the bull dominating the herd by sheer physical presence and brute force.

213. Cf. the Pennsylvania tablet: *išme awāssa imtagar qabāša* (OB II 66).

214. Enkidu's *mūdû libbu* recurs in SB II 32, perhaps II 59, and, with a different allusion, II 240.

216. The orthography *šam-ḫat-ta* for *Šamḫat* is unusual in a Kuyunjik manuscript (MS P), but not unacceptable: see Chapter 9, the section on Spelling conventions sub (e). An alternative reading, *šam-ḫat ta-qé-re-en-ni* (as a command, 'you must invite me!'), is possible but less convincing.

217. This line repeats l. 210 but with the addition of a second adjective. Since double adjectives are very rare I assume *quddušu* qualifies *mūšabu* not *bītu*.

220. The spelling *lu-ug-ri-šum-ma* displays an ostensibly dative pronoun where an accusative is expected. There are alternative solutions: (a) orthographic: a syllable written closed can express an open syllable with a long or stressed vowel, *lugrīšú-ma* (see further Chapter 9, the section on Spelling conventions sub b); and (b) grammatical: the use of dative independent pronouns for accusative is a stylistic feature of SB that could transfer to suffixed pronouns by analogy. Other examples of *-šum* for accusative in the late epic are: SB I 265 *taššâš*(*tanši + am)*-šum-ma* // I 283 *aššâš-šum-ma* (both LB MS h), XI 197 *ušabri-šum-ma* (MSS CJ). Probably there is too much space on MS B, between *da-an* and the trace, to read *da-an-n*[*iš*] with Thompson, and such a reading is in any case unlikely on orthographic grounds. The traces at the end of the line (MS P) do not appear to allow *lu qab-lu* (von Soden, *ZA* 53, p. 222).

221. There does not seem to be room here for [*lu-uš-tar*]*-ri-iḫ* (cf. *CAD* Š/2, p. 39), and space is short even for [*lul-tar*]*-ri-iḫ*, but no better solution presents itself. Tournay and Shaffer offer '[*li-iṣ*]*-ri-iḫ* ou *lū ša-ri-iḫ*' (*L'épopée*, p. 58, fn. 62), but a verb in the first person is required. Parpola's [*lu-ṣar*]*-ri-iḫ* meets that need but employs an unexpected stem.

222. A restoration [*er-ru*]*-um-ma*, 'I will enter' (von Soden, op. cit.), is possible but bland; [*ana-ku*]*-um-ma*, emphatic, is a more plausible alternative (for *anāku-ma* spelled so at Kuyunjik see SB XI 123). The spelling *ši-ma-tú*, if correctly read, is taken as an example of a literary singular, *šīmatu*, as also in SB VII 102; cf. Chapter 9, the section on Language and style sub (i). An alternative parsing would be to take it as intending the plural accusative *šīmāti*, a scribal lapse easily paralleled.

224. The restoration of *nišū* provides a good antecedent for *līmurā*, though it produces a line that is perhaps something of a *non sequitur*. The spelling of the verb may not have to be taken at face value but, without the beginning of the next line also, the significance of the entire couplet remains to be discovered.

225. Foster's *u-kal-lim-ka* ^{d}*Gilgameš a-šar* . . . (*Essays Pope*, p. 29), unadorned by square brackets, relies on the parallel in l. 234, but the traces do not support it.

227. The word *nēbeḫu* is the conventional reading of ^{túg}íb.lá, but it does not provide the trochaic line ending required by the metre; perhaps read *ḫuṣannī*?

228. The trace after UD is more like T[E than M[I.

229. The line is restored after *AHw*, p. 959. More wordy restorations have been made (e.g. *a-šar* [*it-t*]*a-az-z*[*a-ma-ru pit*]*-nu a-lu-ú*: *CAD* A/1, p. 378), but the wide spacing of MS P, especially, makes a short line more probable.

232. The interpretation of this line has caused difficulty. Some ignore the gender of the verb and take the girls as subject: 'they drive the great ones from their couches' (Speiser). Von Soden

evidently restores differently: 'aufs Nachtlager sind gebreitet die großen *Decken*', i.e. *m*[*u-uṣ-ṣu-ú m*]*u-ṣu-ú* (Reclam[4]; cf. Kovacs). The space available on MS B will not admit this reading. Pettinato also has another verb in mind: 'i Grandi giacciono (con loro)'. If the verb is taken at face value the subject is masculine, however, either *rabûtu*, i.e. 'the great ones escape', using the rare meaning of *šūṣû* found in *Enūma eliš* (*CAD* A/2, p. 383), or impersonal for passive. For Foster 'the reference is to a well-known topos in Mesopotamian poetry wherein the "Great Ones" retiring for the night is used as an image for the silence and loneliness of the deep night' (*Essays Pope*, p. 29). The implication would be that night becomes day, but the image is not so common that it need be at issue here. Another possibility is that *rabû* here means 'old', as in the phrase *ṣeḫer rabi*; *rabû* may also have this meaning in OB II 117, SB II 287, 300. However that may be, the line certainly means that the merrymaking goes on all night.

233. The use in a relative clause of the third person with reference to the second is common in literature, particularly prayers.

234. The conventional way to take the final phrase of the line is as 'the happy-woe-man' (cf. *CAD* Ḫ, p. 24), and most recent translators follow (note, however, Pettinato's 'un uomo pieno di gioia'). The interpretation **ḫadi-ū'a amēla* is syntactically suspect and semantically unbalanced, coupling as it does an apparent stative (*ḫadi*) and an exclamation (*ū'a*) as a makeshift noun. It relies only on the orthography of MS P; B does not necessarily support it. I have thought it wise to abandon it in favour of the word *ḫaddi'u* (*ḫaddû*), which has the virtue at least of being a known word and one that is attested elsewhere in the epic, in SB X 265. There, significantly enough, Gilgameš uses *ḫaddû* of himself while reminiscing about the 'good old days' when life was fun, that is, the very time described here (see the commentary, ad loc.). MS P's *ḫa-di-'-ú-a* must therefore be explained as a spelling which preserves as variants two alternative accusative case endings, respectively NB and MB.

The discovery of *ḫaddi'u* in two lines of Gilgameš forces one to look again at the supposed attestations of the word *ḫaṭṭi'u*. This is a term which physiognomic omens use to denote someone whose temperament predisposes them to bad fortune or other troubles (Böck, *Morphoskopie*, pp. 265, 21: *ḫa-aṭ-ṭi-' la-a iš-šir*, 'he is a *ḫ*., he will not thrive'; 266, 24: *ḫa-ṭi-' ina* ^{giš}*kakkī*^{meš} *i-dàk*, 'he is a *ḫ*., he will die by the sword'; Kraus, *ZA* 43 (1936), p. 83, 3: DIŠ *libba ḫa-aṭ-ṭi-'-i ina-ziq*, 'if in temperament he is a *ḫ*., he will suffer'; cf. Böck, *Morphoskopie*, p. 140, 52: *šumma ḫa-ṭa-i aššat*-[*su* . . .], 'if he is a *ḫ*.(?), his wife [. . .]'). Since the spellings are ambiguous, some of these attestations may, in fact, belong to *ḫaddi'u*, the carefree seeker after pleasure, rather than *ḫaṭṭi'u*.

239. Nothing appears to be lost in the slender break between *ṣālilu* and *ša*: the latter introduces an unusual expression, but compare, e.g., *šāt urri*/*mūši*.

240. Sense insists that MS B's *še-ret-su* is an inferior variant born of a lack of understanding. To challenge Gilgameš is to dispute the will of the gods, specifically his particular patron, Šamaš (l. 241), and the ruling triad of Anu, Enlil and Ea (l. 242). With the couplet ll. 241–2 compare SB VII 78–81, which probably lists the same gods in the same order.

244. MS P's *i-na-ṭa-lu* is probably ventive; see further Chapter 9, the section on Spelling conventions sub (v).

245. The form *šunatum* is already found in the Pennsylvania tablet (OB II 1), OB Schøyen$_2$ 1 (where it is otherwise *šuttum*) and in MB Boğ$_3$ 3′. In the SB text the word recurs as a trisyllable in SB I 273a (MS h only), VI 181–2 and XI 197, but as *šuttu* in SB I 276, IV *passim*, VII *passim* (*šu-na-ta* in VII 165 is for *šunat*) and IX 13. A comparable example of this literary affectation in the SB epic is *rūqatu* for *rūqtu*; for this and other examples of such style in SB Gilgameš see Chapter 9, the section on Language and style sub (i).

246. Similar lines are SB VII 165: *mimmû ibrī šunat(a) aṭṭulu mušītīya* and *Ludlul* III 22 // 30: *ina šunat*(máš.gi$_6$) *aṭ-ṭu-lu mu-ši-t*[*i-ia*]. In the second of these *aṭṭulu mušītīya* is certainly a relative clause, in the former probably, and consequently I prefer to analyse the present line in the same way. If the verb written *attula* (MS B) and *attulu* (MS P) is taken instead as indicative it exhibits a ventive (as already in l. 244). In all three lines *mušītīya* is genitive and one must presume an idiomatic ellipsis of *ina*. For *mušītu* and other expressions of time with pronominal suffixes see now M. Stol, 'Suffixe bei Zeitangaben im Akkadischen', *WZKM* 86 (1996), pp. 413–24.

247. The word *ibšûnimma* is the rather neutral counterpart of the Pennsylvania tablet's probable *ipzirūnimma* (OB II 6).

248. SB *kiṣru ša Anim* replaces the uncertain phrase of the Pennsylvania tablet (OB II 7), and the verb is now iterative (though the significance of the I/3 stem here is uncertain). The *kiṣru ša Anim* is here clearly a meteorite, as entered in *CAD* K, p. 441; see further J. K. Bjorkman, *Meteors and Meteorites in the Ancient Near East* (Tempe, Ariz., 1973), pp. 115–17. The term refers to the very fabric of the sky, a material of proverbial strength (see above, on SB I 124–5).

249–50. This couplet is the same as the Pennsylvania tablet (OB II 8–9), but with OB *iktabit* making way for SB *dān*, and *unissūma* replaced by the iterative *ultablakkissūma*. In this passage and its parallels note the contrast between the plain *aššīšūma* and *taššīšūma*, used when the action is unsuccessful (ll. 249, 263), and the ventives *aššâššūma* and *taššâššūma*, which appear when the action leads to the successful delivery of the object to Ninsun (ll. 257, 265, 283).

251–5. These five lines expand the couplet OB II 10–11: *Uruk mātum paḫir elīšu* / *eṭlūtum unaššaqū šēpīšu*. The restorations are made from the parallels (SB I 279–82, II 103–7). For *i-tep-pir* see above, on l. 111. From the point of view of grammar, the simile 'like a little baby' can refer to object or subject (e.g. *CAD* L, p. 114: 'as if they were small children'). However, any parent knows that infants are not natural kissers of feet while adults commonly find babies' feet irresistible. The phrase obviously refers to the meteorite as the centre of a great fuss.

256. The restorations in this and the following lines are taken from Ninsun's reply and the second dream, though the actions are there given in a different order. For *ḫabābu* see above, on l. 186. This line has no place in the first dream as recounted in the Pennsylvania tablet, but appears only in the second dream (OB II 33–4: *arāmšūma kīma aššatim aḫabbub elšu*). It may be that here ll. 256 and 257 have been inadvertently transposed, for they appear in reverse order in ll. 283–4, and on three other occasions in the late text the line *arāmšūma kīma aššati elīšu aḫabbub* and its variants are paired with the line *u anāku ultamḫiraššu ittīka* and its variants (ll. 266–7, 284–5, 289–90). The verbs of the couplet thus formed vary in tense from manuscript to manuscript. I have given precedence to the most logical tense on each occasion, recording the variants in the footnotes.

257. The Pennsylvania tablet's *atbalaššu ana ṣērīki* (OB II 14) has turned into *attadīšu ina šaplīki*.

258. As with l. 256, this line is found in the Pennsylvania tablet only in the second dream (OB II 43: *aššum uštamaḫḫaru ittīka*). The making equal of Enkidu is achieved on his adoption by Ninsun as a brother for Gilgameš in SB III 127–8 (see already Cooper, *Finkelstein Mem. Vol.*, p. 40). For this reason I reject the translation of *šutamḫuru* in this passage as 'to compete' (e.g. *CAD* M/1, p. 70), noting also that the contest between Gilgameš and Enkidu was not arranged by Ninsun but by Anu (SB I 98), probably at Ea's suggestion (MB Nippur$_1$ 4).

259. Where MS h has *mārīšu* (as too MSS B and H in the parallel line, l. 286), MS P reads EN-*šá*. Neither *bēli-šá*, 'her lord', nor *ēni-šá*, 'her *en*-priest', makes sense in the context. Instead, MS P's spelling is an error arising from a confusion of Akkadian *māru*, 'son', with Aramaic *mara*', 'lord'. This and the opposite confusion, the use of the logogram for 'son' to signify 'lord' in a NA letter

(*SAA* I 220, 3: *a-na bēli*(DUMU)*-ia*), have been noted by Simo Parpola, 'Assyrians after Assyria', *Journal of Assyrian Academic Society* 12/II (2000), p. 12. This line and the following represent an expansion of the Pennsylvania tablet's shorter couplet: *ummi Gilgāmeš mūde'at kalāma / issaqqaram ana Gilgāmeš* (OB II 15–16). The same epithets are applied to Gilgameš's mother in SB III 17 and 117.

260. I do not agree with *CAD* R, p. 359, that *Rīmat-Ninsun* means 'Ninsun is a wild cow'. The endingless *rīmat* is an example of a name developing from the absolute state in the vocative, as with Bēl and Šamaš; as a name of Ninsun the phrase also occurs at SB I 287, II 167, III 35, III 100, III 116–17.

269. Note *e-mu-qí-šú* in the LB MS h, which may be a witness to a different tradition, rather than an example of crasis or a mistake.

272. MS h's *ušezzebka* now confirms MS B's iterative [*ušte*]*nezzebka* (von Soden, *ZA* 53, p. 222, suggested with reference to SB III 4).

273. The restoration of the Kuyunjik MS follows Landsberger, *RA* 62 (1968), p. 116, with reference to parallels later in the epic (SB IV 28–9, 109, SB VII 72–4, MB Megiddo obv. 10′–11′). Other suggestions for the broken word are [*ma-ag-r*]*at* and [*pa-áš-r*]*at* (von Soden). In view of the Pennsylvania tablet's *ittīlamma ītamar šanītam* (OB II 24), one should perhaps give precedence to the LB manuscript. There the spelling *šu-na-at-tú* is peculiar even by LB standards. Closing the second syllable in this way gives an irregular form but provides the required penultimate stress (*šunáttu*); is that really what the scribe intended?

274–5. This couplet develops the single line OB II 25: *itbe ītawwâm ana ummīšu*. The first line reappears as SB III 22.

276. The word *ippunnā*, a simple variation on *appu(n)nā*, is new. The LB MS h's *ummā* (instead of *ummī*) appears to represent an unusual intrusion of late dialect. The line is an expansion of the Pennsylvania tablet's *ummī ātamar šanītam* (OB II 26).

277. The beginning of the line is restored from OB II 27. Note the presence here of *Uruk ribītu*, as favoured by the OB tablets, against the stock SB phrase *Uruk supūru*.

279–85. These lines are repeated from the first dream, and, apart from l. 284 (= OB II 33–4), have no exact correspondence in the Pennsylvania tablet.

286–7. MS h's *ka-la-a* for *kalāma* is a spelling that is to be interpreted as *kalā'a*. For the late shift of intervocalic /m/ to /'/ see *GAG*[3] §31d.

295. It is unclear whether [*u*]*m-ma*, preserved only on the LB manuscript (MS o), is a writing for SB *ummī*, with indifferent final vowel, or, as in l. 276, the late dialect form *ummā*. As always, it is uncertain whether the spellings *ma-lik* and [*ma-l*]*i-ki* represent *māliku*, 'counsellor', or *malku*/*maliku*, 'prince'. According to the dictionaries Enlil can be either. The connection with Gilgameš's instinctive desire for counsel argues for the former. Enlil is *māliku* not so much because he gives advice but because he deliberates on it and thus comes to a decision that is well informed, judicious and correct. In this respect he is the divine prototype of the perfect mortal king, about whom the Tukultī-Ninurta Epic asserts (W. G. Lambert, *AfO* 18 (1957–8), p. 50, 18 // 10): *šu-ú-ma ṣa-lam* ^{d}*enlil*(idim) *da-ru-u še-e-mu pi-i nišī*(ùg)^{meš} *mi-lik māti*(kur), 'He himself is the eternal image of Enlil, who hears the people's voice, the nation's opinion.' The mortal king is in fact *māliku-amēlu*, 'the counsellor-man', the phrase coined for him in a mythological text which describes the separate creation of man and king (W. R. Mayer, *Or* NS 56 (1987), p. 56, 36′; cf. pp. 64–5). The ability of the perfect king to give careful thought to advice goes hand in hand with his ability to exercise dominion. Both are characteristic of Enlil, as we learn from the syncretistic god-list BM 47406 (*CT* 24 50) obv. 8: ^{d}*en-líl* = ^{d}*marduk*(amar.utu) *šá be-lu-tú u mit-lu-uk-tú*, 'Enlil

is Marduk of rulership and deliberation' (for this list see now S. Parpola, *Festschrift von Soden 1995*, pp. 398–9).

300. This line and the catch-line (SB II 1) are an inversion of OB II 45–6: *Enkīdu wašib maḫar ḫarimtim / urta"amū kilallun*, whence the restorations are taken.

TABLET II

1. The end of the line might very plausibly be restored [*it-taš*]-*qu*, 'they kissed each other', or another part of the same verb but the question must remain open for the time being. The material added to this line in Dalley's translation owes its presence there, at least in part, to a mistaken identification of what is actually a standard colophon of Aššurbanipal (see Colophons of the manuscripts, MS B).

28. Von Weiher read [ ] *šá* AN *nam* [, but it seemed to me that the line begins with *na* or *ina* UD. The parallels do not help. A vat (*namzītu*) is not an obvious *desideratum* here, though the spelling *na-an-zi-tú* is not without parallel. A more plausible reading would be *ina ūmi*(ud) *annî*, 'on this day', with the last word written as a kind of pseudo-logogram *an-nam*, but the sign after *an* is different from *nam* in vi 1 of the same MS (l. 247). For the moment it is best to reserve judgement.

29. The line is restored from SB I 208 (cf. the Pennsylvania tablet: OB II 54–5).

32. This line might be a repetition of SB I 214: *mūdû libbašu iše"â ibra*. However that may be, it may also recur as SB II 59.

34–5. The couplet is a reworking of the Pennsylvania tablet's *išḫuṭ libšam ištīnam ulabbissu / libšam šani'am šī ittalbaš* (OB II 69–72).

36–7. These two lines are restored from the almost identical couplet in the Pennsylvania tablet: *ṣabtat qāssu kīma ilim ireddēšu / ana gupri ša rē'îm ašar tarbāṣim* (OB II 73–6). The introduction of plural *ilī* for *ilim* may be simply an orthographic feature, but note that the same thing has happened in l. 110 (MS k). The writing dingir^{meš} for the singular is occasionally attested in the first millennium. Some examples are given in *CAD* I/J, p. 91; note also in l. 49 of the Theodicy singular *ili* (parallel *il-ti-i*, l. 51) spelled dingir, dingir.dingir and [dingir]^{meš}.

38. Cf. the Pennsylvania tablet: *ina ṣērīšu ipḫurū rē'û* (OB II 77).

39. As it stands on the tablets this curious line appears to comprise two prepositional phrases with no verb of any kind. Heidel found one by ignoring AŠ (which on the manuscript that was available to him is partly obscured by an erasure) and reading the remaining half line as *rammā nišūma*, 'the people whispered(?)' (*JNES* 11 (1952), p. 140–1). This was rejected by von Soden, *ZA* 53, p. 223, and rightly so, for the faithfulness of *ina ramānīšūma* to the tradition is now confirmed by MB Boğ$_1$ a 9: *i-na ra-ma-an*-DU-*uš*. One should assume that the beginning of the line is corrupt.

40–1. An older version of this couplet is *anāmi Gilgāmeš mašil padattam / lānam šapil eṣemtam pukkul* (OB II [80–2] // 183–5); l. 41 is probably repeated as SB II 164. The word *ši-i-ḫi*/*u* is stative *šīḫ* with a typical LB redundant final vowel (so already Heidel). At the end *ša*[*r-ḫu*] is accordingly for *šaruḫ*; *ša*[*r-raḫ*] is also possible.

42. The line exists in two versions (that of MS z is restored from SB I 174), but ultimately both go back to OB II [83–4] // 186–7: *mi*[*nde ša*] *iwwaldu ina šadîm* (cf. MB Boğ$_1$ Fragment a, 11). On *minde* see Chapter 5, the note on OB II 17.

43. This is a standard line much used in SB I (see the commentary above, on SB I 124–5).

44–5. This couplet develops the Pennsylvania tablet's *akalam iškunū maḫaršu* (OB II 87) by the addition of a parallel line.

46. The Pennsylvania tablet has *iptēqma inaṭṭal u ippallas* (OB II 88). Here the spelling *ip-te-gi* may signify that this word was no longer understood as *iptēq*, for though the 'overhanging' vowel would be unremarkable, the value *qì* is not typical of LB orthography outside the archaizing royal inscriptions. The translation nevertheless assumes in *ip-te-gi* a corruption of *iptēq*, for want of an alternative. A verb *pagû* or *pegû* appears in lexical texts (see *AHw*, p. 809), but its meaning is unknown. No verb *pâgu* or *pêgu* is known.

47–8. This couplet is freely restored in the spirit of the Pennsylvania tablet: *ul īde Enkīdu aklam ana akālim / šikaram ana šatêm lā lummud* (OB II 90–3).

50–1. This couplet presumably represents a variation on the harlot's encouraging words, as known from the Pennsylvania tablet and a fragment from Boğazköy (OB II 96–8; MB Boğ$_1$ a 15). Though *simat ilūti* and *simat šarrūti* might have been expected at the line ends, as in the Boğazköy piece (cf. also the parallels SB VI 27–8, VII 135–6), they do not fit. Instead the restorations are suggested by *šīmti māti(m)* in OB II 98.

52–3. The line of tablet ending in *ri* is so closely written that I have assumed it to contain two lines of poetry.

59. One may also read *nar-ba-šú-ma*, 'his greatness'.

60. The restorations are taken from OB II 115–16: *uttappiṣ barbarī labbī uktaššid*. The enclitic *-ma* could emphasize the object but more probably functions as a coordinative (for coordinative *-ma* attached to nouns see above, on SB I 143. The need for a trochaic ending indicates that MS k's 'overhanging' vowel is orthographic and without phonological or morphological significance.

61–2. This couplet offers only a slight variation on the Pennsylvania tablet: *ittīlū nāqidū rabû-tum / Enkīdu maṣṣaršunu awīlum ērum* (OB II 117–19). The stative *[nīl]ūnimma* is restored on grounds of space. The spelling na.gada-*sa-nu-ma* for **nāqid-šunu-ma* exhibits the occasional Neo-Assyrian preference for masculine plural pronouns with dissimilated vowels, as attested in the possessive suffixes *-šanu* and *-kanu* and the independent pronoun *šanu*. These variant forms seem always to occur in the presence of a suffixed particle, such as the enclitic *-ma* (as here) or subjunctive *-ni*. The present instance is a very rare case of a real Assyrian dialect form intruding in the text of a Kuyunjik manuscript of the SB epic. For others see Chapter 9, the section on Language and style sub (viii).

63. The beginning of the line is restored from OB II 120. As argued in the note on the OB text, the formula *ištēn eṭlu* marks the man in question as a new character, no doubt the wedding guest whose report of the customs of Uruk so shocks Enkidu. The difficult complex of signs É TA ME would therefore likely signify the house where the wedding ceremony was due to take place, i.e. *bīt emi*, and is presumed to be corrupt (von Soden, *ZA* 53, p. 222, suggested *ta-šib*, 'er sitzt').

ii 1′–2′. Though the context is not yet certain, dam in l. 2′ recalls the passage of the Pennsylvania tablet that describes the *ius primae noctis* (especially OB II 161); if so the the preceding line is very likely to be restored *šarru [ša Uruk supūri . . .]* (cf. OB II 154, 156).

100–2. These lines expand on a couplet of the Pennsylvania tablet: *ītakšamma ittaziz ina sūqim / iptaras alaktam ša Gilgāmeš* (OB II 200–3), but the sense of the interpolated line remains rather difficult to fathom. As von Soden noted, *ibēš* is not obviously meaningful; he suggested emending to *i-kaš-šad*, 'er erreicht' (*ZA* 53, pp. 222–3); Hecker's '*das Ausüben*' (*TUAT* III/4, p. 683) evidently takes *i-bi-eš* as an exceptional spelling of *epēš*.

103–7. These five lines repeat SB I 251–5 // 279–82.

109–10. This couplet is a slight rewording of the Pennsylvania tablet: *ana Gilgāmeš kīma ilim šakiššum meḫrum / ana Išḫara mayyālum nadīma* (OB II 194–7). In l. 109 there is no room for *[mu-*

ši]-*ti* [*na-di-ma*] (Thompson, Parpola); perhaps simply [*mu-ši*]-*ti*-[*šá*], with the verb held back until the next line. There the sources offer both *kīma ili* (MS X_2) and *kīma ilī* (MS k), but this may not be significant (see above on l. 36). The substition of *pūḫum* for *meḫrum* is discussed in Chapter 10, the introduction to Tablet II.

111. The line expands on OB II 215–16: *Enkīdu bābam iptarik ina šēpīšu.*

112. A literal translation of *šūrubi*, 'not allowing (them) to let Gilgameš enter', seems overcontrived. It appears that *šūrubu* here means little more than *erēbu*, as in OB omen apodoses, e.g. *YOS* X 22, 16: [lú]*nakrum*(kur)[*rum*] *ú-ši-re-ba-am-ma i-na* ⌈*li-bi ma*⌉-*ti-k*[*a*] *ša-la-tam ú-ši-iṣ-ṣe-e*, 'the enemy will invade and carry off plunder from your land' (further examples of III/1 stem for I/1 are given in *CAD* E, p. 273, 'to penetrate').

114. The Main-Street-of-the-Land is assumed to be a proper noun, as in the Pennsylvania tablet (OB II 214).

115. This line offers a variation on OB II 221–2 // 225–6: *sippam i'butū igārum irtut.* The emendation to *inūš* follows Ebeling, *AfO* 8, p. 227; Thompson's reading *i-tú-uš*, for perfect *ittūš*, is orthographically very unlikely.

162–3. This couplet is restored from earlier in the text (SB I 124–5 etc.). The spelling *ki*]-*ṣir* for *kiṣri* in l. 163 is an example of CVC for CCV, an occasional feature of NA orthography; to the examples collected by K. Deller, *Or* NS 31 (1962), p. 194, add the evidence collected in Chapter 9, the section on Spelling conventions sub (f). We have already encountered it without comment in LB manuscripts (SB I 270, 293, II 43).

164. As restored this is the same line as SB II 41.

167. The significance of the little horizontal wedge in the margin is unclear, unless it is a defective KÚR, marking a mistake (on this see below, on SB IX 172).

168–78. The speech of Ninsun survives, but also in fragmented state, in the Yale tablet (OB III 61–9). If we are to believe the marginal decimal markers on MS X_2, which fall at an interval of only nine lines apart (iv 1 and 10), one of the lines of tablet between ll. 170 and 180 contains two lines of poetry. None of the well-preserved lines seems at all cramped, so iv 1 is the best candidate and becomes ll. 170–1 in my reconstructed numeration.

168. After *mārī* perhaps [*ina bā*]*bi-š*[*ú* . . .]? Cf. l. 173 and OB III 61: *i-na ba*-[*bi-šu*?].

174. For the moment von Soden's emendation to *ú-nam*!-*ba* (*ZA* 53, p. 223; cf. [*un*]*amba šarpiš* in SB VIII 45) seems preferable to reading *ú-zi-zu* for *uzziz* (II/1 preterite). Though a failure to render geminated consonants in full is an occasional feature of MS X (l. 179: *uš-ta-dan*), the meaning of *uzziz* is not obviously appropriate to the context.

175. Restore [*kimta u sallata*], 'kith and kin'?

176. Loose-hanging hair is what Enkidu bore in his natural state. The phrase is also used of the demon Lamaštu, e.g.: *uš-šu-rat pe-ret-su* (Thureau-Dangin, *RA* 18 (1921), p. 166, 15). On *pēretu* for *pērtu* see Chapter 9, the section on Language and style sub (i).

179. The first word has also been read *uš-ta-kal* (Ebeling, *AfO* 8, p. 227) and *uš-ta-lap* (Tournay and Shaffer, p. 78, fn. 6), but neither seems compelling. With the restored line end compare SB XI 138.

180–7. Enkidu's misery and Gilgameš's compassionate response are given in much the same wording in the Yale tablet (OB III 71–82).

180. MS X displays Assyrian influence in both preserved words. The form *ēnāšu* is Assyrian dialect. The writing *i-mi-la-a* stands for *imlâ*, as is now clear from the repetition in l. 186. This type of spelling, V + CV for VC, is an occasional feature of NA orthography (see the examples collected by K. Deller, *Or* NS 31 (1962), p. 193).

183. At the beginning of this line Ebeling restored [*in-ned*]-*ru-ma* (*AfO* 8 (1932–3), p. 227), 'they embraced one another', for which there is just enough space, but other restorations are possible.

185. The spelling *a-mat* in the Kuyunjik tablet (MS X) for accusative singular *amāta* or *amātu* can be explained as (a) being an early indication in script of the loss of final vowels in the vernacular, (b) using a *rebus*-spelling, *a-mātu*(kur) or (c) exhibiting the principle that CVC signs can represent the bisyllable CVCV, not only where the two vowels are the same (well known in NA writing) but even where they differ. Spellings CVC for CV_1CV_2 are not remarkable in LB sources; other examples in Kuyunjik manuscripts of SB Gilgameš are collected in Chapter 9, the section on Spelling conventions sub (c). For examples in older Neo-Assyrian manuscripts see the introduction to Chapter 7.

186–7. Restored after ll. 180–1.

191. An older version of this line occurs in OB $Schøyen_2$ 64 // 67 // 76: *īrub adirtum ana libbīya.*

193. The writing of *pa-a-šá* for *pâšu* could be put down to typical LB indifference to the quality of a final vowel but for the fact that this particular spelling of the pronominal suffix is so infrequent that it must have been expressly avoided as an error. At a time when the feminine suffix *-ša* was very often written *-šú*, an example of the opposite may be an instance of hypercorrection. Alternatively, it is plain sloppiness, comparable with MS bb's *qibâniššimma* in l. 274.

213. Possibly *lu-u*[*k-kis*, 'let me cut' (Parpola).

217. Restored from the Yale tablet (OB III 129–30).

218a // 227 // 284 // 298. The spelling *šul-lu-mu* for the construct state *šullum* can be explained in one of two ways: (a) the writing preserves an OB literary construct state in *-u* or (b) it exhibits an unnecessary 'overhanging' vowel (CV for C?).

218b–29. This passage, which develops OB III 108–16 // 195–200, is repeated later in the tablet (SB II 275–86; cf. also 291–9). For recensional differences in the order of lines in both passages see Chapter 9, the section on Textual variants.

221 // [278] // 291. The late text retains the OB text's *rigmašu* (literary for *rigimšu*) in nearly all manuscripts.

222 // 279 // 292. The text retains the OB line, although the intermediate version of the text represented by Assyrian MS **y** offers the variant *siqiršu* ($\mathbf{y}_2$ obv. 12') for *napīssu.*

223 // 280 // 293. The reading *rimmat qišti*, already legible in MS X_2 (though badly abraded), is now confirmed by the additional evidence furnished by MS ee in l. 280. On the probable development of this line from the earlier *ana šūšiš bēr nummât qištum* see Chapter 5, the note on OB III 108.

224 // 281 // 295. MS k's *ur-rad*: the loss of subjunctive *-u* is unremarkable in a LB source; for *arādu* and forests see the OB version of this line, OB III 109 // 196 *mannu ša urradu ana libbīšu.*

225 // 282 // 297. For the point of this line see the note on its ancestor, OB III 134–5.

232–3. This couplet reworks the older *u atta* (*Enkīdu*) *kīma pasnāqi*(*m*) *taqabbi* / [*pīka ir*]*mâm tulemmin libbī* (OB III 156–7 // Assyrian MS $\mathbf{y}_1$ 7′ and 9′). It appears again as SB V 100–1; cf. SB IV 233.

234–5. Restored after the Yale tablet: *awīlūtumma manû ūmūša* / *mimma ša īteneppušu šārūma* (or *šarumma*? OB III 142–3). The second verb has changed from present to preterite. Assyrian MS $\mathbf{y}_1$ 2′ has a quite different version of the second line of this couplet (see Chapter 7).

236. The first three signs do not appear to yield *šāninka* and, in any case, the verb *ibaššâ* looks as if it requires a feminine plural subject.

237–9. Restored from the Yale tablet (OB III 151–3): *tawwaldamma*(!) *tarbi'a*(*m*) *ina ṣērim* / *išḫiṭkāma labbu*(*m*) *kalāma tīde* / *eṭlūtum iḫ-bu-tu maḫarka.* The intermediate text represented by

Assyrian MS $\mathbf{y}_1$ has the second and third of these lines, but separated by others (6′: *eṭlūtu iḫ-bu-tu₄* [*maḫarka*], 8′: [. . .] *kalāma tī*[*de*]). In l. 238 of the present passage the verb of the OB version has been replaced with a near homophone and its subject made plural: *išḫutūkāma labbī*. Consequently *tīde* is no longer entirely appropriate and its restoration is open to question. In l. 239 the late text represented by MS ee has retained *i'butū* (< the rare I/1 stem of *nābutu*; see George, *NABU* 1991/19.1), even preserving the /ḫ/ of the old spelling. However, the variant *iḫmuṭū* of MS e points to the interference of an uncomprehending editor, who at some time replaced *i'butū* with a common verb that sounded similar.

241–2. This couplet can be restored after OB III 161 and 163: [*alkam i*]*brī ana kiškattîm lumūḫa*(*m*) . . . [*iṣṣa*]*btūma ana kiškattî*(*m*) *imūḫū*, but it is by no means certain that the late text would favour the hapax legomenon *mâḫu* above other verbs of motion.

247. The first word is restored after the Yale tablet's *wašbū* (OB III 164). Note that OB *uštaddanū* (III/2) is replaced with *uštanamdanū* (III/2 lex.).

248. If *ni-ip-ti-qu* stands for the cohortative *ī niptiqu* (ventive in *-u*, as often in LB copies), it would appear that the narrative of the Yale tablet (OB III 165–70) has been replaced by speech (cf. von Weiher, *ZA* 62 (1972), pp. 225 and 228; Bottéro). For a clear example of a cohortative without *ī* see SB III 15: *nillik* (Kuyunjik MS). The alternative is to assume that the *ni* is an error and read the passage as narrative (with Hecker, *TUAT* III/4, p. 685).

250. For distributive *bilā* see Ch. 5, the note on OB III 166.

251. As the scribal annotations in ll. 251 and 254 indicate, the sole surviving source for the text of ll. 251 ff. was copied from a broken master copy. In this line the sign read as *i* could instead be the remains of an integer, i.e., '*x* [talents]', where *x* is a number between five and nine.

254. The surviving signs may be the remnants of narrative *iptiqūni*, 'they cast' (ventive, as in l. 248).

260. The annotation *x šumū šaḫṭū*, '*x* lines are skipped' (l. 260), is usually used where text is omitted as predictable (as in litanies), but it is unlikely that such would be the reason here. Given also the presence of the annotation *ḫepi* in the immediately preceding lines, I assume that the scribe has used it instead of *x šumū ḫepû*, '*x* lines are broken', which is the conventional way of expressing the loss of lines in a break (for *šaḫāṭu* as a technical scribal term for omitting lines, see W. R. Mayer, *Or* NS 59 (1990), pp. 32–3). From l. 254 on the damage was evidently so bad that the scribe could only report the number of lines missing. This is a particular shame, for these lines would have described the convening of the assembly, an episode which is also fragmentary in the Yale tablet (OB III 172–7). Though the scribal annotation follows *šimā'innu eṭlūtu* I assume that it summarizes the gap that precedes the line that begins so. There is otherwise no place to interpolate the convening of the assembly. Such a placement of the annotation is not illogical, for the missing end of this line is the last lacuna resulting from the break on the master copy in which the five lines fell. It is thus the only conveniently empty space suitable for annotation.

261. Cf. l. 273.

262–71. The lines are restored from the parallel passage SB III 24–34, where the line corresponding to l. 262 fills two lines of poetry. The present *allak* in the same line marks the result of *agdapuš*. The usage of *gapāšu* attested in this line finds a parallel in the older version of the poem of Anzû, where the occasion is also a warrior setting of for battle: *qì-it-ru-ud ta-ḫa-zi-im ig-da-pu-uš ša-di-iš* [*ig-gu-uš*], 'the hero of battle became bold, [he went off] to the mountain' (OB Anzû II 74), and again, [*qì-it-ru-ud ta-ḫa*]*-zi-im ig-da-pu-uš i-tu-ur a-na* [*ša-di-im*], '[the hero of] battle became bold, he went back to [the mountain]' (OB Anzû III 73). For *rūqatu* instead of *rūqtu* see Chapter 9, the section on Language and style sub (i).

271. For *alû rutaṣṣunu* see also SB I 229.

272. The verb is restored in the present tense because it introduces direct speech (see Chapter 5, the note on OB II 1). However, the last sign is indistinct. One might instead read *iš-*[*ta-kan ṭè-e*]*-ma*, 'he stated (his) opinion' (cf. SB III 120 *išakkana ṭēmu*).

274. One expects *qibâniššumma*!

275–85. See already SB II 218–29.

278–9. The first line of this couplet, which is written on one line of tablet in both extant manuscripts, one would expect to read *Ḫumbāba rigmašu abūbu*, as in the several parallels (OB III 110–12 // 197–8; SB II 221–2 // 291–2), but the traces do not quite fit.

287–90. These two couplets offer a slight variation on the Yale tablet: *šībūtum ša Uruk ribītim / siqra*(*m*) *uterrū ana Gilgāmeš / ṣeḫrētīma Gilgāmeš libbaka našīka / mimma ša tēteneppušu lā tīde* (OB III 189–92). Some of the changes also appear in the intermediate text represented by Assyrian MS **y**, which offers, however, further variants: [*itbûma mālik*]*ū rabûtu izzaqqurū* [*ana Gilgāmeš / ṣeḫrēta*] *bēlī libbaka* [*našīka /* (*u*) *mimma*] *ša taqabbû magir* [. . .] / (repetition) ($\mathbf{y}_2$ obv. 6′–10′). In l. 289 note the variation in the two LB manuscripts between the more archaic form *ṣeḫrēti* (MS bb) and the normal *ṣeḫrēta* (MS z). In addition MS z has added a phrase which overruns on to the end of the next line—where it is marked apart by repeated use of the *Trennungszeichen* (not, as sometimes read, BIR = giriš!)—and which can be confidently restored as [*ummaka*] *ūlidka* after SB V 145: *ṣeḫrēti Gilgāmeš ummaka ūlidka*. This extra phrase is thus a traditional variant, handed down as an alternative to *libbaka našīka*. The orthography *ta-ta-ú* (MS z) for *tātamû* is not an error (Heidel), but an example of the late development intervocalic /m/ > /w/ or /'/ (*GAG*[3] §31a, d). Compare further such LB spellings as *ka-la-a* for *kalā'a* < *kalāma* (SB I 286–7), *tu-ú-ru* for *tu'ru* or *tuwru* < *tumru* (SB V 104 and comm.), *šu-ú* for *šu'u* or *šuwu* < *šumu* (several attestations cited in *CAD* Š/3, p. 284), and also the evidence of the Graeco-Babylonian tablets, where intervocalic Akkadian /m/ is routinely transcribed as Greek υ (cf. M. J. Geller, *ZA* 73 (1983), p. 119; 87 (1997), p. 67; J. A. Black and S. Sherwin-White, *Iraq* 46 (1984), p. 136). Alternatively, the spelling *ta-ta-ú* may possess an older pedigree: note similar writings of the same verb in OB letters: *a-ta-ú* for *ātamu* (*TCL* XVIII 145, 12) and *ni-ta-ú* for *nītamu* (*YOS* II 19, 7).

291. If correctly read (in the absence of examples of IG and GI for comparison), the spelling *ri-gi-ma-šú* for *rigmašu* in MS z is an example of the use of a CV sign to express VC, common in LB writing as also in NA.

291–9. See already SB II 221–9, though the lines are this time given in a different order, perhaps to avoid monotony. I cannot reconcile the traces surviving on MS e vi 5′-6′ with ll. 294–5 or any other lines of this passage.

300–1. These lines develop a couplet of the Yale tablet: *išmēma Gilgāmeš siqir mālikīšu / ippalsamma iṣīḫ ana ibrīšu* (OB III 201–2). Less faithful to the OB text is the intermediate version of MS **y**: *Gilgāmeš annīta ina šamêšu / ussaḫir pānīšu ana i*[*brīšu*] */ iṣīḫ izzaqqara ana Enkīdu* ($\mathbf{y}_2$ obv. 16′–17′).

TABLET III

1–12. This speech, similar to that spoken by the elders of Uruk in the Yale tablet (OB III 249–71), is repeated later on as ll. 215–27. The correct restoration of l. 1 is now clear for the first time. Previously it had been assumed to be a line of narrative specifying the speakers and introducing the speech. Evidently that line must now be sought at the end of SB II.

2. The phrase *gimir emūqīka*, literally 'the totality of your might', is reminiscent of the lion loved by Ištar, who is *gāmir emūqi* (SB VI 51).

4–5. One is tempted to emend to ⟨*li*⟩-*iṣ-ṣur*, following l. 219 (MS c, LB) and also l. 9, but note that the forerunner of this couplet preserved on the Yale tablet also uses a combination of present and preterite: [*āli*]*k maḫra tappâ ušallim* / [*ša ī*]*nāšu šuwwurā pagaršu i*[*naṣṣar*?] (OB III 255–6). The use of the past tense leads me to assume that both sets of lines quote proverbial wisdom (see the commentary on the OB couplet).

10. Opinion is divided as to whether *ḫi-ra-a-ti* is the plural of *ḫirītu*, 'ditch', or of *ḫīrtu*, 'bride, (first) wife', or intentionally ambiguous (Dalley, p. 127, 26). In trying to make the line more meaningful, translations of *ḫirītu* as 'pitfall' (Speiser), 'grave' (Dalley), 'sepolcro' (Pettinato), 'chausse-trape' (Bottéro) obscure the fact that the usage of the word *ḫirītu* is limited in the extant documentation to channels of water, especially irrigation ditches and city moats. For me in any case *ana ṣēr* suggests motion towards, as against motion over (see the commentary on SB I 145), and for this reason too I favour the wives. The fact that Gilgameš was envisaged in the Sumerian story of Bilgameš and Ḫuwawa as unmarried and without the responsibilities of family (D. O. Edzard, *ZA* 81 (1991), p. 184, A 53: nita.sag.dili e.ne.gim aka, 'single men like him'), need not mean that he holds the same status in the Akkadian epic. The undeniable problem, however, is that an historical Babylonian would have one *ḫīrtu* only. Subsequent wives were not of the same status as the first. Gilgameš was an epic hero of fabled appetite: was he imagined to have had brides in large numbers? The sentiment expressed, that the king return safely home to his wives after a dangerous expedition, was no doubt a popular and topical one at the Babylonian court.

11. The spelling *pu-uḫ-r*]*i-in-ni-ma* (MS BB) for *puḫrīnīma* exhibits the convention of some first-millennium scribes that an open syllable with a long vowel can be denoted in writing by closing the syllable. Other examples in SB Gilgameš are listed in Chapter 9, the section on Spelling conventions sub (b). The elders are in the process of relinquishing temporarily their responsibility for counselling the king, so *nipqidakka* is an example of the 'performative' preterite (on this see further *GAG*³ §79b*). This usage is best known in the word *alsīka*, 'I hereby invoke you', at the beginning of SB prayers (*CAD* Š/2, p. 157). In SB Gilgameš it occurs also in SB III 28 *usappīki*, III 125 *ilqâ*, III 127 *elqâ*, VII 93 // MB Ur 4 *amḫurka*, XI 33 *amgur*.

12. The spelling *ta-pa-qid-da-na-ši* (MS M) exhibits a repeated consonant at the boundary between stem and affix; for this practice see Chapter 9, the section on Spelling sub (e).

15. Unless the scribe has inadvertently lost a sign, the form *nillik* must be a NB cohortative, for earlier *i nillik*. The temple name é.gal.maḫ, 'Exalted Palace', is given to sanctuaries of Gula (Ninsinna), most famously at Isin, but also at Babylon, Ur, Uruk and Aššur (see George, *House Most High*, p. 88). Ninsun occupies Gula's temple in Uruk by virtue of the syncretism which equated the divine couple Ninurta and Gula with Lugalbanda and Ninsun, as made explicit in the two-column Weidner god list (E. Weidner, *AfK* 2 (1924–5), p. 14, 17–18). This equation can be traced back to the early second millennium, for in an Old Babylonian copy of an *eršemma* Gula is explicitly invoked as (*CT* 42 7 iii 41, ed. Cohen, *Eršemma*, p. 102, 109) ù.tu.da {NI *sup ras.*} en ^{d}bil$_4$.ga.mes, 'the one who gave birth to the lord Bilgames'.

16. When preceding a noun the prepositional phrase is normally *ana maḫar* in OB and literary Babylonian. The variant *maḫri* offered in this line is rare. Other examples of genitive construct *maḫri* before a noun beginning with a consonant (i.e. where crasis is discounted) are rare, and more often than not comprise the second element of compounds: *Enūma eliš* I 149 // II 35 // III 39 *a-li-kut maḫ-ri* (III 97 *ma-ḫar*) *pa-an um-ma-ni*; Craig, *ABRT* I 55 i 5, ed. Livingstone, *Court Poetry* no. 4 i

6′: *a-li-kàt maḫ-ri šu-ut se-bet at-ḫe-e* (NA hymn); Langdon, *RA* 12 (1915), p. 191, 3: *a-lik maḫ-ri* ᵈ*sîn* (*ikrib*-prayer, NA copy); *KAR* 132 ii 12 (*RAcc*, p. 101): *ina maḫ-ri pa-ni-šú* (LB ritual). In first-millennium sources the variant may be orthographic only but, if genuinely morphemic, it can be explained as an example of the survival in literary style of the OAkk genitive construct (see Chapter 9, the section on Language and style sub ii). For other spellings like *šar-rat* (MS BB) for *šarrati* see also Chapter 9, the section on Spelling conventions sub (c).

17. These epithets have already appeared in SB I 259–60 // 286–7. On the spelling *mu-da-ti* (MS BB) for *mūdât* see Chapter 9, the section on Spelling conventions sub (g).

19–20. The sequence *iṣṣabtū . . . illakū* occurs also in MB Boğ$_2$ i 5′, where both verbs are ventive. I take the present *illakū* as an indication of a final clause; alternatively it can be circumstantial (M. P. Streck, *Or* NS 64 (1995), p. 61: 'während sie gingen'). The word *qātussun* (var. *qātussu*) is a variant of locative *qātuššun*, comparable with such forms as *kar-šu-us-sú-nu*, 'in their minds' (*Enūma eliš* I 111), *kak-ku-us-su*, 'with his weapon' (Anzû I 13), ᵈ*en-líl-us-su-nu*, 'before their supreme lord' (Anzû I 16), *šá-du-us-su*, 'to his mountain' (Anzû I 82 // 109 // 127 // 148), and *šip-ru-us-su*, 'for her work' (Bullussa-rabi's hymn to Gula: W. G. Lambert, *Or* NS 36 (1967), p. 118, 42). These variants, with *-ss-* instead of *-šš-*, perhaps arose by analogy with the ending *-ussu(m)* found in adverbs of time, especially in the late period (*ūmussu*, 'daily', *arḫussu*, 'monthly', OB *šanas-su(m)* > NB *šattussu*, 'yearly').

22. The restoration follows SB I 274: *itbēma īterub ana maḫar ištari ummīšu*. This line is thus revealed as part of the epic repertoire. It was not completely petrified, however, for MS M clearly differs in the preposition that precedes the common noun *ištaru*.

24–34. Cf. already SB II 262–71.

25. The trisyllabic spelling of *rūqta/i* as *ru-qa-t*V is the most common in SB Gilgameš, being also attested in SB III 48, IX 54, X 10, 116, 141 and 241; one also meets *ru-uq-ta/tum* (SB I 9) and *ru-qu-ti* (SB I 121, fem. sing., see ad loc.). The intrusion of a normally unwarranted epenthetic vowel is a mark of literary style. For other examples in SB Gilgameš see Chapter 9, the section on Language and style sub (i).

28. Note the additional word, *usappīki*, absent from the parallel SB II 265. Its tense is the 'performative' preterite (see above, on l. 11).

35–6. This couplet offers a very rare example in the Babylonian Gilgameš of what may be called enjambement—the continuation of a clause beyond the end of the verse—with the boundary of the poetic lines splitting the paired object *Gilgāmeš mārīša u Enkīdu*.

37. A similar line occurs in Nergal and Ereškigal: (*u*) *ši-i a-na* (*bīt*) *nar-ma-ki i-ru-um-ma* (*STT* 28 ii 45′ // iii 59′ // iv 5′ // iv 34′; Hunger, *Uruk* I 1 iv 14).

38. Another example of the use in combination of the two purificants, tamarisk and *tullal* (literally 'You-Make-Pure plant'), occurs in a ritual of the diviner: ᵍⁱˢ*bīna*(šinig) ᵘ*túl-lal ú-tal-lal*, 'he purifies himself with tamarisk and soapwort' (*BBR* no. 11 rev. i 6).

40. The adornment of Ninsun's breast was perhaps an ornamental stag (*lulīmu*). Such a thing, weighing 2.5 shekels, is listed in an OB dowry (*YOS* XII 157, 4).

42. The verb *i-pi-ra-ni* remains obscure, even though its subject is now recovered. Whether it can be the same verb as the enigmatic *i-pi-ra-am-ma* of SB XI 149 // 152 remains to be seen.

46. The line is over-long and may have once been two, perhaps divided so: *ammēni taškun ana mārīya Gilgāmeš / libba lā ṣālila tēmissu* (otherwise *CAD* Ṣ, p. 72, where the division is placed after *mārīya*). In doing without the second verb, MSS BB and aa leave the line with an unsatisfactory antepenultimate stress, *ṣālila*.

54. The phrase *mimma lemnu*, lit. 'something evil', is often translated as 'everything evil', but

there is no suggestion in the epic that Ḫumbaba is what such a rendering implies, the source of all evil in the land. In exorcistic and medical literature *mimma lemnu* refers not to a general abstract idea but to a very real being, though one that has to remain unspecified because its name and other particulars are unknown. A good illustration of this comes from an apotropaic ritual which rounds off a long list of identifiable malign powers with the catch-all phrases *lu mim-ma lemnu*(ḫul) [*ma-l*]*a bašû*(gal)*ᵘ* *lu mim-ma là ṭābu*(dùg.ga) *šá šuma*(mu) *là nabû*(sa_4)*ᵘ*, 'or any Evil Thing whatsoever that may exist, or any Bad Thing that has no name' (Wiggermann, *Protective Spirits*, p. 6, 9–10). Later on in the same text the unidentified malign influence is adjured to depart: *mim-ma lem-nu mim-ma là ṭābu*(dùg.ga) *šár bēr*(danna) *li-is-sa-a ma-ḫar-ku-un*, 'the Evil Thing, the Bad Thing shall depart a myriad leagues from your presence!' (ibid., p. 20, 306–7). This understanding of *mimma lemnu* fits Ḫumbaba well, for he is by reputation an Evil Thing of nature hostile to man but otherwise unknown because remote and untried. Since Ḫumbaba is assumed to be evil, Šamaš, the god of justice, is naturally seen to oppose him. For the spelling *ú-ḫal-laq* (MS BB), lacking the subjunctive *-u*, see Chapter 9, the section on Spelling conventions sub (c).

55. I follow Tournay and Shaffer, *L'épopée*, p. 102, fn. 17, in assuming that this line refers to the daytime journey of the sun across the sky, crossing the cosmic boundaries of heaven and earth. Instead of *itû* they restore the very rare word *itûtu*, 'circumference': 'les limites du ciel'. Other readings are possible.

56. For Aya as 'bride' see the references collected in *CAD* K, p. 81. On the spelling *kal-lat* for *kallatu* see Chapter 9, the section on Spelling conventions sub (c).

66. I assume *ruššâka* is an example of an adjective used as a noun. A derivation from the infinitive, 'your making red', seems less likely.

73. The restoration follows a couplet of a bilingual incantation to the Sun God:

izi.gar.zu.šè dug_4.ga ak dingir.gal.gal.e.ne
a-na nu-ri-ka ú-paq-qu ilū(dingir)^{meš} *rabûtu*(gal)^{meš}
^{d}a.nun.na.ke_4.e.ne gi.bar.ra sag.zu mu.un.i.du_8
^{d}*a-nun-na-ki gi-mir-šú-nu i-na-aṭ-ṭa-lu pa-ni-ka*
IV R^2 19 no. 2, 37–40

The great gods wait intent on your light,
all the Anunnaki gaze on your face.

74–5. Restored from ll. 56–7.

80–4. These five lines recur as SB III 130–4. The vocabulary of ll. 82 // 132 is reminiscent of statements in *EAE* XIV and ^{mul}*Apin* II of the seasonal changes in the lengths of day and night, e.g. *ūmū irrikū mūšū ikarrû* (see F. N. H. Al-Rawi and A. R. George, *AfO* 38–9 (1991–2), pp. 60–1). Line 83 is restored in the light of the common expression for travelling on foot, *purīdī petû*, 'to open one's stride'; see especially *Ludlul* IV 41, where *pe-ta-a pu-ri-du* is a metonym for all who go on two legs.

85. In its first and last words this line recalls the narrative statement OB $Schøyen_2$ 82: *nubattam iskipū inīlū*, though the traces do not allow the expected phrase *liskipū linīlū*.

88–92. The realization of this wish is SB V 137–41. The verb *īṭû* in l. 92 // V 141 may have been a variant of *iṭṭû*, 'they beat (Ḫumbaba's face)', for the Hittite paraphrase renders the narrative line as *nu-kan* [*ANA* ^{d}Ḫuwawa] IGI.ḪI.A-*wa* EGIR-*pa walḫi*[*sk*]*anzi*, 'und dem Ḫuwawa schlagen sie immer wieder die Augen zurück' (G. Wilhelm, *ZA* 78 (1988), p. 113). The list of winds in this passage is almost identical to that preserved on a lexical fragment from Emar:

im.u$_{18}$.lu : *š*[*u-ú-tu*]
im.si.sá : *il-*[*ta-nu*]
im.kur.ra : *ša-d*[*u-ú*]
im.mar.dú: *a-mur-*[*ru*]

---

zi-qu
zi-iq-zi-qu
[*š*]*a-pár-zi-qu*
[*d*]*a-al-ḫa-mu-na*
[im.*s*]*i-mu-ur-ru*

D. Arnaud, *Emar* VI/2, p. 423; cf. VI/4, p. 172, no. 576

Comparison suggests that im.ḫul can be read dalḫamun$_x$, but without further evidence I have transcribed it conventionally. MS y's *si-*GÍN*-ra* in l. 90 is clearly meant to be *si-mir-ra*.

The use of the winds in battle is a mythological device best known from the Creation Epic, where Marduk mobilizes eleven in his combat with Ti'āmat:

i-pu-uš-ma sa-pa-ra šul-mu-ú qer-biš ti-amat
er-bet-ti šá-a-ri uš-te-eṣ-bi-ta la a-ṣe-e mim-mi-šá
im.u$_{18}$.lu im.si.sá im.kur.ra im.mar.dú
i-du-uš sa-pa-ra uš-taq-ri-ba qí-iš-ti abi(ad)*-šú* ^{d}*a-nim*
ib-ni im-ḫul-la {im *lem-na*} *me-ḫa-a a-šam-šu-tum*
im.límmu.ba im.imin.bi im.sùḫ im.sá.a.nu.sá.a
ú-še-ṣa-am-ma šārī(im)^{meš} *šá ib-nu-ú se-bet-ti-šú-un*
qer-biš ti-amat šu-ud-lu-ḫu ti-bu-ú arki(egir)*-šú*

Enūma eliš IV 41–8

He made a net to enclose the inside of Ti'āmat,
he posted the four winds, so that no part of her would escape:
South Wind, North Wind, East Wind and West Wind,
the gift of Anu, his father, he placed hard by the net.
He created Tempest, Hurricane, Tornado,
the Four Winds, the Seven Winds, Chaos Wind and Indomitable Wind:
he let loose the seven winds he had created,
to stir up the inside of Ti'āmat they drew up behind him.

A comparable list of winds occurs in the Assyrian recension of Atra-ḫasīs, where the context is of Adad marshalling his forces for the coming storm:

šu-ú-tu il-ta-nu šadû(kur)^{ú} *a-mur-*[*ru*]
si-qu {siq?} *siq-si-qu me-ḫu-ú rādu*(IM × I(M] = agar$_x$)
im-ḫul-lu ad ma ḫu lu te-bu-ú šārū(im)^{m}[^{eš}]

W. G. Lambert and A. R. Millard, *Atra-ḫasīs*, pp. 122–4, rev. 6–8;
cf. Lambert, *JSS* 5 (1960), p. 121

Compare further the eight winds that are loosed against Ḫumbaba in the Hittite Gilgameš: IM.GAL ^{im}*EL-TA-NU* [^{im} . . . ^{im} . . .] ^{im}*ZI-IQ-ZI-QÚ* ^{im}*ŠU-RU-UP-PU-U* ^{im}*A-Š*[*A-AM-ŠU-TU*] ^{im}*AN-ḪUL-LU* (J. Friedrich, *ZA* 39 (1930), p. 12, 14–16; H. Otten, *Istanbuler Mitteilungen* 8 (1958), p. 116, 40–2).

Given the established sequence *šūtu–iltānu–šadû–amurru*, south–north–east–west, one is minded to consider *IM.GAL* in this list as standing for *šūtu*, 'south', and to restore the missing two winds accordingly (either IM.GAL is a corruption of the standard ^{im}ùlu(GÀL)^{lu} = *šūtu*, or it is related to *Erimḫuš* II 66: da.gal = *šu-ú-tu*). Many of the rare words for storm winds that occur in these passages are also collected in the synonym lists, for example *Malku* III 173–80: *zi-qi-qu, ma-ni-tum, me-ḫu-ú, še-ḫu-ú,* [*me*]*-er-ru, šá-par-ziq-qu, ziq-ziq-qu, im-ḫul-lum = šá-a-ru.*

93. I take ^{giš}tukul . . . *lik-šu-du* as an unremarkable LB spelling for *kakku . . . likšud*; alternatively one may read it as plural, *kakkū . . . likšudū.*

94. The verb *napāḫu*, 'to blow, rekindle', is commonly used to describe the rising of celestial bodies, especially the sun. The notion is that Šamaš's fires are rekindled each morning before he comes forth from the doors of heaven (see W. Heimpel, *JCS* 38 (1986), p. 142). A bilingual incantation from *Bīt rimki* takes the metaphor further, describing the sun god's rising much as if he were a householder starting the day:

én ^{d}utu an.úr.ra ḫi.i.ni.bu
  ^{d}*šamaš*(utu) *ina i-šid šamê*(an)^{e} *tap-pu-ḫa-am-ma*
^{giš}si.gar.kù an.na.ke$_4$ nam.ta.e.gál
  ši-gar šamê(an)^{e} *ellūti*(kù)^{meš} *tap-ti*
^{giš}ig an.na.ke$_4$ gál im.mi.in.tag$_4$
  da-lat šamê(an)^{e} *tap-ta-a*

IV R^2 20 no. 2, 1–6 and duplicates, cf. Langdon, *OECT* VI, p. 52

Incantation. O Šamaš, you rekindled (your fire) at the horizon,
you undid the pure bolt of heaven (Akk. the bolt of the pure heavens),
you opened the door of heaven.

96. The reference to mules is to the steeds that pull the sun's chariot through the sky. They are also known from a line of an incantation in *Bīt rimki*: *ta-(aṣ)-ṣa-an-da pa-re-ka* (var. gìr^{meš}) *šá šit-mu-ru la-sa-*[*ma*] (var. *a-la-kam*), 'you (Šamaš) have hitched up your mules, which are ardent for running' (cf. Laessøe, *Bit Rimki*, p. 57, 63).

97. The old break should perhaps be restored *mayyāl mūši.*

102–6. The force of *ul* in first position, remote from its verb, seems to be emphatic, as it is in SB X 304–6: *ul mamma mūtu immar / ul mamm*[*a ša mūti i*]*mmar pānīšu / ul mamma ša mūti rigmašu* [*išemme*]. While those clauses are emphatic statements, another occasion on which such syntax appears in SB Gilgameš is a rhetorical question (SB IV 213: *ul mārī ittaldū*). The problem of whether the present lines are statements or questions is resolved by ll. 105–6. These can hardly be interpreted as emphatic denials of Gilgameš's eventual function as a ruler of the shades in the Netherworld; they must be rhetorical questions.

102. Alternatively one might read ⟨*ina*⟩ *šamê izzaz*, 'will Gilgameš not stand with you in(!) the heavens?' Whichever decipherment is preferred, the point seems to be that Gilgameš will share the celestial role of the sun god. His association with Šamaš is well known for the Netherworld, where after death he will judge the dead in partnership with Šamaš. The two appear together or with the Anunnaki in a collection of incantations against ghosts (*KAR* 227 and duplicates; see Chapter 3, the sub-section on Gilgameš in exorcistic rituals). The prayer to Gilgameš from the same collection records that Šamaš himself made this arrangement: ^{d}*šamaš*(utu) *šip-ṭa u purussâ*(eš.bar) *qa-tuk-ka ip-qid*, 'Šamaš delegated to you verdict and decision' (quoted in full in Chapter 3). However, there is no unequivocal evidence in support of a celestial partnership, and the line's significance remains a puzzle.

103. By virtue of his *agû*, 'crown', the moon god is one of the traditional custodians of the symbols of kingship, as best articulated in the curses of Hammurapi's laws (Codex Ḫammurapi rev. xxvii 41–6): ^{d}*sîn*(EN.ZU) . . . *agâm*(aga) ^{giš}*kussi'am*(gu.za) *ša šar-ru-tim li-ṭe*$_{4}$*-er-šu*, 'May Sîn take from him the crown and throne of kingship!' Compare also the names of city gates in Babylon (*Tintir* V 72: ^{d}*sîn*(30) *mu-kin agê*(aga) *be-lu-ti-šú*, 'Sîn is the Establisher of his Lordly Crown') and Sennacherib's Nineveh (*CT* 26 32, 91 // R. C. Thompson, *Iraq* 7 (1940), p. 90, 28: ^{d}*nanna-ru na-ṣir* // *mu-kin agê*(aga) *be-lu-ti-ia*, 'The Moon is the Establisher (var. Protector) of my Lordly Crown'). The lack of agreement at the end of the line between the extant manuscripts can perhaps be resolved by positing an original ending *ḫaṭṭa u palâ*, 'sceptre and royal symbol.' These two items of regalia go together as a pair in an incantation to Enmešarra (Craig, *ABRT* II 13, 8): *na-din* ^{giš}*ḫaṭṭi*(gidru) *u palê*(bala). How exactly Gilgameš is to share the moon's regalia is not clear to me.

104. Perhaps one should emend to *ina apsî*. As deciphered, this line provides the first attestation of a verb *emēqu* (i/i), 'to be deep, profound, wise'. The meaning is evident from the well-known adjective *emqu*.

105–6. Irnini or Irnina is best known as an aspect of the warlike Ištar, as in Agušaya A (*VAS* X 214 vi 25) and a god list (*CT* 25 17 ii 11 // 44, Sm 1558, 5). The name is translated 'Victory' by T. Jacobsen, *Toward the Image of Tammuz*, p. 34. Elsewhere in Gilgameš Irnini is accredited with ownership of the Cedar Mountain, though there the name appears to refer to goddesses in general (SB V 6). In other lists there is a deity Irnina of chthonic character (*CT* 25 8 obv. 12; *KAV* 65 iii 8; E. Weidner, *AfK* 2 (1924–5), p. 73, 26), and that is certainly the point here, for in the next line is Ningišzida. For his role as the 'chamberlain' (*guzzalû*) of the Netherworld, and the mythology in which he figures, see now W. G. Lambert, *Studies Moran*, pp. 295–300.

117. Restored after l. 17, etc.

119. To my eyes the broken sign is not *n*[*a* (so Thompson).

120. This line offers another example of a problem noted earlier: we cannot determine whether *išakkana* is present tense to express a final clause or to introduce direct speech (or both); see Chapter 5, on OB II 1.

122. The word written *at-mu-ka* is difficult. It usually understood as the preterite or present of the verb *atmû*, though one would expect *ātam*(*m*)*ūka*, or the preterite of *tamû*, though one would expect *atmâka*. There is a marked lack of consensus as to what these parsings would mean in the context (<*atmû*: Oppenheim: 'I pronounce you'; Heidel: 'I have adopted(?) you', similarly Speiser; von Soden: 'sprach ich zu dir'; similarly Kovacs and Hecker; Labat: 'je te déclare (mien)'; Foster: 'I have bespoken you'; Lambert: 'I reflect upon you'; <*tamû*: Bottéro, 'je t'adjure', similarly Tournay and Shaffer; note also improbable *atmu*⟨*ḫ*⟩: Schott; unclear: Pettinato, 'ti ho esaminato e ti ho annoverato'). These difficulties of form and meaning lead me to reject both verbs, and to read *atmūka* as a regular form, from the noun *atmu* (cf. already Dalley, 'your offspring'). The clause is thus a nominal one.

The word *atmu*, 'hatchling, chick', is otherwise used of human young only by Shalmaneser I (Grayson, *RIMA* 1, p. 183, 42). The word is chosen carefully, for it vividly conveys the helpless plight of orphaned children when first taken into a temple's care and service. Perhaps it also highlights their parentless state, for elsewhere in the epic, when Ḫumbaba addresses Enkidu as someone 'who knew no father' or 'mother', he calls him an *atmu* (SB V 87–8).

123. For the plural of *ugbabtu* see OB Atram-ḫasīs III vii 6: *ú-ug-ba-ak-ka-ti*.

124. The exact nature of *indu*, lit. 'imposition', that is placed on Enkidu's neck to mark his new status is not clear. In Oppenheim's discussion of this episode he translated it as 'tag', referring to an object in the British Museum (*Or* NS 17 (1948), p. 34, fn. 1; also *CAD* I/J, p. 110). There are several such 'tags' extant. They are pierced ovoids of clay each bearing the names of an individual, the per-

son responsible for them and a date in the reign of Merodach-baladan II (catalogued by J. A. Brinkman, *Studies Oppenheim*, p. 43, 44.2.12–14). They may have been have been 'slave tags' worn around the neck (so M. A. Dandamaev, *Slavery in Babylonia*, p. 234), but this function is disputed (see Brinkman, *Studies Oppenheim*, pp. 37–8). The word *indu* fits nowhere in the known technical terminology for slave marking. We know from legal documents that the mark of a *širku* oblate of Ištar (as Bēlet-Uruk) in Neo-Babylonian Uruk was a star symbol (*kakkabtu*), which took the form of a brand mark (*arrātu*) on the hand (see the references collected in *CAD* Š/3, p. 106); on the marking of these and other temple slaves with branding irons (*šindu parzilli*) and other devices in the first millennium see Dandamaev, *Slavery*, pp. 488–9. Marking (zà šú) of slaves by branding, and perhaps also other means, was known in the third millennium but it was not common, nor do we know on what part of the slave's body the mark was imposed (see P. Steinkeller in *OIP* 104, p. 243; D. A. Foxvog, 'Sumerian brands and branding-irons', *ZA* 85 (1995), pp. 1–7). The classic slave mark of the second millennium was the style of hair called *abbuttu*. Judging from our passage, which serves as an aetiology of the ritual induction of oblates in Uruk, in earlier times some form of identification was displayed on the neck that denoted the oblate's status and obligation.

125–6. These lines can be taken as quoting the protocol by which foundlings were inducted into the temple personnel. Denoting as it does the act of induction, the verb *ilqâ* is certainly another example of the 'performative' preterite (see above, on SB III 11); *urabbâ* predicts the outcome of the induction and is present-future.

127. In MS M the reading of the sign *il* as *él* now seems inescapable. Other examples of writings of the first-person conjugation prefix /e/ with signs normally displaying /i/ are not uncommon; in this book SB III 127 *il-te-qé* (MS M) // *el-qa-a* (MS aa) is joined by XI 82 *i-ṣe-en-ši* (MS T) // *e-ṣe-en-ši* (MS J) and XI 314 *i-te-pu-uš* (MS C) // *e-te-pu-uš* (MSS Wj). MS aa's *elqâ* is a further example of the 'performative' preterite. This statement looks like a version of the very words spoken on adoption, for which the phrase used in OB legal documents is also *ana mārūtim leqûm* (see M. David, *Die Adoption im altbabylonischen Recht* (Leipzig, 1927), pp. 38 f.; M. deJ. Ellis, *JCS* 27 (1975), p. 142).

128. The verb *dummuqu* also occurs in the context of adoption in an OB manumission document from Sippar (*BE* VI/1 96, 1–7): [f]*su-ur-ra-tum . . . ša eriš-ti-*[d]*a-a nadīt*(lukur) [d]*šamaš*(utu) *um-ma-ša ú-da-am-mi-qú-ši-ma a-na ma-ru-ti-ša iš-ku-nu-ši* [*ù*] *eriš-ti-*[d]*a-a* . . . [*ú*]*-ul-li-il-ši*, 'Surratum, whom Erišti-Aya, the *nadītum* of Šamaš, her mother, had favoured with adoption (lit.: favoured and adopted): Erišti-Aya [also] redeemed her from slavery'. In the present line it is evidently Gilgameš who will show favour to his new brother; there is no hendiadys but the verb describes the expected behaviour of the adopting family towards the new member.

129. Parpola restores *e* [*ta-du*]*r*, 'do not fear!'

130–4. Restored after ll. 80–4.

135. Perhaps a repetition of SB III 5 // 219.

148. Perhaps [*ka*]*-bat-tuš-šú* or [*nu*]*-bat-tuš-šú*?

150. Or *ina* é.an.n[a (Parpola).

152. Or [*sa*]*-riq sur-qin-ni*, 'the one who scatters the incense offerings'.

166. This line compares with a line of the elders' blessing in the Yale tablet: [*liša*]*kšidka ernittaka Šamšu* (OB III 257).

167. This mention of Marduk, the god of Babylon, is unique in Gilgameš, in which the divine *dramatis personae* are predominantly drawn from the local pantheon of Uruk and the national pantheon of Sumer.

169. The first word can also be read *ku-ri-li*, 'sheaves' (<*kurullu*, see Landsberger, *RA* 62, p. 103, fn. 24).

173. This cannot be the catch-line for SB IV, appearing as it does on col. v of MS c. It is obviously too early for the narrative of the journey to begin, since the final valedictions are yet to be made, so one must assume that this line comprises instructions in direct speech and continues the episode in which Gilgameš and Enkidu are blessed for the journey. As such it would compare with the similarly detailed instructions of the elders in the Yale tablet (OB III 268–71).

202–5. Restored after ll. 51–4.

211. The line is related to OB Harmal$_2$ 17: *i niškun kakka ina bāb Ḫuwāwa.*

214. Note the alliteration that attends the kisses: *šakkanakkūšu unaššaqū šēpīšu.*

215–27. This speech is a repetition of ll. 1–12 (from which it is restored), with the addition of the single line 223. The burden of this incomplete line seems to be that Enkidu will guide Gilgameš safely through the mountains. In the Sumerian poems of Bilgames and Huwawa there is a comparable line: má.ùr.má.ùr ḫur.sag.gá.ke$_4$ ḫu.mu.ni.in.túm.túm.mu (A 45 and 60) // ḫé.mu.e.ni.túm.túm.mu.ne (B 50), 'let them lead you through the passes of the mountains'; for má.ùr so translated see A. Shaffer, *JAOS* 103 (1983), pp. 307–8, fn. 4; cf. perhaps *MSL* XIV, p. 386, *A* IV/4 129–30: $^{\text{ú-r}}$[^{u}ùr] = *ne-re-bu šá* x, *šá ki*-x[. . .]. In the Sumerian poem, however, this function is the duty of the seven constellations given to the hero by Utu.

TABLET IV

1–4 // 34–7 // [79–82] // 120–3 // 163–5. This passage has been studied by A. Shaffer, *Eretz Israel* 9 (1969), p. 159, B. Landsberger, *RA* 62 (1968), p. 99 (ll. a–d), and J. Klein and K. Abraham, *CRRA* 44/III, pp. 67–72, though necessarily without knowledge of its forerunner in OB Schøyen$_2$ 25–6, which confirms that the journey proceeded as a succession of three-day non-stop marches. One matter not fully discussed is the implications of the 'month and a half's march' that the heroes covered in each three-day period. According to the inscriptions of Esarhaddon, the normal day's march of the Assyrian army on a military expedition in hostile country was two *bēr* (R. Borger, *Esarh.*, p. 112, rev. 3 ff.; cf. Luckenbill, *OIP* 2, p. 74, 71). One *bēr* is one twelfth of a full day, or half a mean watch of four hours. As a measure of length it is the distance travelled in two hours, whether in the sky by the sun and stars (30°), or on earth by men (between 10 and 11 km: see M. Powell, *RLA* VII, p. 467). The standard march of four hours referred to by Esarhaddon represents a comfortable distance by comparison with the figures adduced for the OB itinerary known as the Road to Emar, which indicate that a party on a forced march could cover in one day up to 30 km as the crow flies (W. W. Hallo, *JCS* 18 (1964), p. 85), that is, about three *bēr*. The reason why the Assyrian army was evidently slower than the travellers of the OB text is presumably that it was encumbered by a heavier baggage train.

In our passage Gilgameš and Enkidu travel an heroic fifty *bēr* each day, which for ordinary mortals would have taken about 18 days. The notional journey of one month and a half in l. 4 is thus not the daily fifty *bēr* but presumably the distance covered by the third day (*ina šalši ūmi*), i.e. 150 *bēr*. So too in SB X 171, where the phrase *mālak arḫi u šapatti ina šalši ūmi* recurs in the context of Gilgameš's journey over the ocean with Ur-šanabi. According to von Soden (*Reclam*^{2}, p. 43, fn. 1), the distance covered in the three days roughly corresponds to the length of the conventional route from south Mesopotamia to Lebanon, and indeed, according to the evidence of the itinerary known as the Road to Emar the somewhat shorter journey to Ḫarran from Dūr-Apil-Sîn, one day out from Sippar, could be done in 35 days (Hallo, *JCS* 18, p. 85). However, one should not make too much of this, because as the text of SB IV stands it would seem that the distance of 150 *bēr* covered by the end of the third day was not the total distance of the journey from Uruk to the Cedar Forest, but only that covered before each dream episode. Von Soden avoided this problem by maintaining that 'für Sin-leqe-unnīni stellte Libanon nur ein Zwischenziel auf dem langen Marsch der Freunde [to the Cedar Forest] dar' (*Reclam*[4], p. 40, fn. 3), but the difficulty here is that, according to SB V (as well as OB Ishchali), the Cedar Forest was on Mt Lebanon. For this reason, too, kur *lab-na-nu* must be restored in all the parallels to the passage under comment.

To return to the discussion of distance and time, there are five dream episodes in the late version of the text, as reconstructed, so that in this account the journey took fifteen days. As Landsberger pointed out, there is a contradiction inherent in this, because the mention of Lebanon in l. 4 would seem to indicate that Gilgameš and Enkidu had already arrived at the Cedar Forest after three days' journey (*RA* 62, p. 102). To resolve this difficulty we have to assume that *ṭeḫû* here, and also in OB Schøyen$_2$ 26, means 'to draw *nearer*' (so already Renger in Oinas (ed.), *Heroic Epic and Saga*, p. 42). In the Hittite version of the epic the arrival at the Cedar Forest ostensibly occurred on the sixth day of the journey (H. Otten, *Istanbuler Mitteilungen* 8 (1958), p. 109), which would represent a simple doubling of this figure. However, the figure in question can be read [UD 1]6.KAM, i.e. after a journey of fifteen days, which would then agree with the SB text (E. Laroche, *RHA* 26 (1968), p. 126, Eg 4). However that may be, the late poet's enthusiasm for repetition and aggrandisement means that the account we have has left reality a long way behind and is, in effect, a fairy tale. As Landsberger wrote when reflecting on von Soden's attempt at reconciling the statistics of this passage with reality, 'je junger die Erzählungen von Gilgameš sind, desto mehr sie die Merkmale reiner Märchen tragen' (*RA* 62, p. 99, fn. 7).

4. To my eyes the place name on MS w is ⌜*lab-na-nu*⌝ not ⌜*lìb-na-nu*⌝ (collated against Lambert's copy). Late in this tablet, however, MS r has a clear *lìb-*[*na-nu*] (see l. 124). For this reason one would be tempted to read MS w's *lab-na-nu* as *lìb-na-nu*, were it not for the fact that other Babylonian attestations of the toponym, where unambiguous, unanimously report it as Labnānu (see M. Weippert, 'Libanon', *RLA* VI, pp. 644–5).

5–[6] // 38–9 // [83]–4 // 125–6 // 166–7. The second line of this couplet is not yet fully recovered; since it seems to mention water it may be narrative related to instructions like those given by the elders in the Yale tablet: *ina nubattīka ḫiri būrtam / lū kayyānū mû ellūtum ina nādīka / kaṣûtim mê ana Šamšim tanaqqi / ilka taḫassas Lugalbanda* (OB III 268–71). On Gilgameš and wells see Chapter 3, the section on Digging wells.

[7] // 40 // 85 // 127 // 168. This line is the late counterpart of OB Schøyen$_2$ 27: *īlīma Gilgāmeš ana ṣēr šadîm*.

[11] // [44] // 89 // [131] // 172. The reading [^{giš}]*dalat šarbilli* is based on Labat's 'un [abri (?) contre le] vent', and encouraged by the verb *retû*. I presume the shelter is a makeshift tent, and that this is the flap that goes over the entrance to keep out the weather. Others have supposed [*īt*]*iq* or [*iz*]*īq*, for both of which room is lacking, however. For *šarbillu*, 'stormwind', see *MSL* IV, p. 35, Emesal Voc. III 90: me.er.sig = mir.sig = *šar-bil-lu*, following *šāru* and *meḫû*, and *Malku* III 192: [*z*]*iq-ziq-qu* = MIN (i.e. *šār*) *bil-la* (von Weiher, *Uruk* III 120), among other winds.

[13] // [46] // 91 // [133] // 174. The three signs after *kīma* have usually been interpreted as 'mountain barley' (*še'šadê*, Assyrian orthography), but to my eyes the second sign seems more like ŠE than KUR. For *šēšû*, in Sumerian sa.(šu).ùr.ra, 'flat-laid net', a tool of the fowler, see *CAD* Š/3, p. 339 (despite the heading *ša šēšî* the entries in OB *Lu* clearly indicate that the genitive is *šēšê*). The verb described by this simile should mean 'he threw himself down flat', but no plausible restoration occurs to me.

[17] // [50] // 95 // [137] // [178]. For the syntax see Chapter 5, the note on OB II 1.

[20] // [53] // 98 // [140] // [181]. The spelling *e-ti-iq* is Assyrian. For examples of the 3rd sg. prefix *e-* and other marks of Assyrian influence in Kuyunjik manuscripts see Chapter 9, the section on Language and style sub (ix).

25. The conventional interpretation of *ki-i* NIM GI is 'like flies of the reed-bed', but given the lack of context this is still very uncertain.

26. It has not been noticed previously that this line and l. 107 are essentially the same. The line is related to OB IM 19, where it is clearly part of the narrative, introducing a speech by Enkidu: *waldam ṣērim mitlukam ile''i issaqqar*[*am*] *ana ibrī*[*šu*]. On account of *ni-le-'-*[x] in l. 107, one has to consider taking the late version of the line as direct speech, reading the first word [*t*]*a''aldamma*, and I have taken this option on that occasion, where the following line is fuller than it is here. But in the present line an antecedent subject is badly needed for *izakkara ana ibrīšu*, and for this reason I suppose that it was closer to the OB line, and restore *ile''i* not *nile''i*. The juxtaposition of Enkidu's illiterate origins and his cleverness in the interpretation of dreams (and in the OB text in advising a course of action) is an interesting poetical device. In this connection we may recall that dream interpretation, at least, is an intuitive art—in ancient Mesopotamia traditionally a female one—that needs no scholarly or courtly training.

27. The verb *šumḫuru* here and in the similar l. 108 means literally 'to make something acceptable'. The point must be that Gilgameš can only come to terms with the dreams that so bewilder him if their contents can be revealed as meaningful.

28. The line recurs as SB IV 109 and 155.

33. The phrase *amāt Šamaš damiqta* seems a little unlikely but is secure from the parallel SB IV 162.

102. Because of the need for penultimate stress it is better to parse *eklētum* as plural; accordingly, *ūṣâ* is no ventive.

105. Restoration from Parpola. Though separate from it, *nebūtu* agrees with *išātu* (so *CAD* N/2, p. 149), as is clearly the case in the forerunner of this line (OB Schøyen$_2$ 40: *šuppūtum ibteli išātum*). For other examples of remote adjectives in SB Gilgameš see Chapter 9, the section on Language and style sub (vi).

106. Comparison with OB Schøyen$_2$ 41 suggests that the first word should be restored as *nablū*. However, the SB line is not identical to the OB line, for they do not agree in the number of the verb in the second half of the line: OB Schøyen$_2$ 41: *itūru la'miš*, SB IV 106: *itūr ana tumrī*. For the moment one must assume that in the late version of the line the subject is not *nablū* but *išātu*, carried over from l. 105. I have restored accordingly.

107–9. See the notes on the parallel lines, IV 26–8.

124. The spelling ^{kur}*lib-*[*na-nu*] is unique for a text from Babylonia, where the mountain is usually rendered *Labnānu* (see above, on l. 4).

161. The LB spellings *ni-iz-za-za* (MS w) and *ni-iz-za-az-zu* (MS v) look ventive; for forms of *izuzzu* in the ventive see OB II 179 and the note thereon.

190–205. This passage has been studied by Landsberger, *RA* 62, pp. 105–7.

190. Landsberger restored this line as narrative, [*a-na pān Šamaš i*]*l-*⌈*la*⌉*-k*[*a di-ma-a-šu*], but this remains conjectural. More probably the line is direct speech.

191. The restoration of the beginning of this line and 193 rely on SB V 148: *per'umma ša libbi Uruk šarru Gilgāmeš*. If it is correct to restore thus Landsberger's reading *taq-bu-*[*ú*] at the end of the line looks less probable.

192. Note the ventive imperative of *izuzzu* (cf. l. 161 above).

194–5. As Landsberger noted (*RA* 62, p. 105), this couplet also occurs as SB VII 132–3: *Šamaš išmâ* (so also MS AA here) [*ziki*]*r pîšu* / *ultu ullānumma t*[*ukku ult*]*u šamê iltanassaššu*. The second verb is present before direct speech but the force of the *-tan-* infix is uncertain (see the commentary on SB I 78).

198. The seven cloaks are the seven terrible auras that Enlil bestowed on Ḫumbaba for his protection.

205. There is a temptation to compare this line with a passage of OB Harmal$_2$ in which Enkidu says, *miqitti meḫêmma* [*Ḫuwāwa* / *kīma*] *Adad išâ'am eli ṣērīni* (ll. 19–20), but while both contexts are so fragmentary it is best not to use this to justify restoration.

213. On *ul* in first position, separated from its verb, see the commentary on SB III 102–6. The word *e-tal-du* is taken as an Assyrianized spelling of *ittaldū* (see above, on l. 20). As such it makes a better active (I/1 perfect) than passive (IV/1 *itta'ladū*) *contra* Bottéro ('des enfants ont été mis au mo[nde]'). For *alādu* with an active masculine subject one need only cite *Enūma eliš* I 16: *ù* ^{d}*a-num tam-ši-la-šú ú-lid* ^{d}*nu-dím-mud*. Perhaps the point of the line was that Gilgameš fears he will die without heir.

215–16. The couplet is restored after OB Schøyen$_2$ 15–17: *inanna ibrī ša nillakūšum* / *ul šadûmmā nukkur mimma* / *inanna Ḫuwawa ša nillakūšum* / *ul šadûmmā nukkur mimma*. Cf. also OB Harmal$_1$ 10: [*il*]*um ibrī ša nillakūšum*.

230–48. This passage has been studied by Landsberger, *RA* 62, pp. 110–12. Not all his restorations have been adopted here.

231. The verb *i-man-g*[*i-ga* looks to my eyes a better fit than *i niš-m*[*uṭ* (*AHw*, p. 1155). The restoration of *idāya* is supported by *mangu ša idīka* in l. 242.

233. The line is restored after SB II 232 // V 100.

235. The traces do not support Tournay and Shaffer's [*ša a*]*-la-ki pat-tum* (*L'épopée*, p. 119, fn. 58).

238. Neither *itpēšu* nor *itguru* (ibid., p. 119, fn. 60) fits the traces.

239. Von Soden parses both *tal-tap-pit* here and *il-ta-pit* in SB X 175 from *šabāṭu*, 'to sweep' (*AHw*, p. 536). I follow Landsberger, op. cit., and *CAD* L, p. 89, in parsing instead from *lapātu*, assuming that the modified stems of this (a/u) verb can utilize (i/i) forms. Apart from these two instances, the incipit of an incantion in *Šurpu* exhibits a similar form (Tablet I rev. ii 5′): *at-ti ma-mit šá tal-tap-pi-tú*, 'You, O oath, who kept on touching!' That this also must be *lapātu* I/3 is accepted in *AHw*.

240. An *apillû* is some kind of marginal cultic figure according to an entry in a synonym list: *a-pi-lu-u* (var. *pil-pi-lu-u*) = *ku-lu-'u* (*CT* 18 5, K 4193 rev. 10 // *LTBA* II 1 vi 46).

241. The line is also known from OB Harmal$_2$ 5: *kīma lilissim liššapu rig*[*imka*]. Falling on the enemy with loud yells is a tactic also employed at SB X 97: *ina libbi qišti išeppu* [*rig*]*mu*.

242. The stock phrase *mangu u lu'tu* is common enough, but compare especially a narrative parallel to this line reproduced as a couplet in *Ludlul* II 77–8:

man-gu iṣ-bat i-di-ia	Stiffness seized my arms,
lu-'-tú im-ta-qut eli bir-ki-ia	feebleness has befallen my knees.

245–8. These lines appear to contain proverbial wisdom, some of it very similar to lines occurring earlier in the story (cf. OB III 255–6; SB III 4–5 // 218–19). Note the 'gnomic' preterites in l. 247.

TABLET V

1. The sixth sign on MS H is now more damaged than Haupt's and Thompson's copies show, but enough survives to vindicate them and to dispose of an alternative suggested reading, *i-na pa-at-tu qišti*, 'at the edge of the forest'. Compare *nap* in ll. 2–3 and *na* in l. 5. The analysis of *i-nap-pa-at-tu* as a 'Sandhi-Schreibung' for the same *ina pattu* (M. P. Streck, *Or* NS 64 (1995), p. 47, fn. 59) is open to the objection that such a spelling would not conform to the usual pattern. Sandhi is a term given in Sanskrit to a predictable change in the phonetic realization of a word made at the word boundary. In Assyriology the term 'Sandhi writing' has been used to describe those rare spellings that reflect a pronunciation in which one word is run into another, i.e. crasis. Sometimes this coupling involves elision, as when a word-final vowel that precedes a word beginning with a syllable normally written with a V or VC sign is lost, e.g. *is-sa-ḫi-iš*, etc., for *issi aḫîš*, *la-ma-ri* for *lā (w)âri* or *lā amāri* (see further *GAG*³ §17, 'Krasis'). More common are cases in which a word-final consonant in the same position is written as if opening the following word, e.g. *pu-zu-ra-mi-ip-te-(e)* for *puzzuram ipte* (OB Ishchali 38′ // OB IM obv. 18), *i-ni-li* for *in ilī* (elided from *ina ilī*). As well as fitting neither of these models, Streck's analysis of *i-nap-pa-at-tu* as a Sandhi writing should be tempered by the consideration that the preposition *ina* before a word beginning with *p* was not necessarily pronounced as a bisyllable. It was often *ip*, perhaps more often than we think. It could still be argued that *i-nap-pa-at-tu* is a peculiar kind of morpho-graphemic spelling for **ip-pattu*, but MS H does not otherwise exhibit bizarre orthography. Thus I agree with those who posit a verb *napātu*.

The spelling of *inappatū* with two Ts needs comment. Repetition of a consonant at the boundary between stem (or base) and affix is most typical of third-millennium orthography, being normal in Sumerian and also acceptable in Akkadian (typically when closed syllables written with CVC signs are resumed with a vocalic ending, e.g. *i-din-nam* = *iddin* + *am*). For literature on this phenomenon in texts from second- and first-millennium Mesopotamia see W. Mayer, *Or* NS 61 (1992), pp. 47–8 with fn. 34. At some point it became acceptable for such doubling to occur in resuming the consonant after a VC sign, exactly as here with *i-nap-pa-at-tu* and *i-na-pa-at-tu*. This development is already found in texts from the Late Bronze Age periphery (as noted by J. Huehnergard, *The Akkadian of Ugarit*, p. 49, and J. W. Durham, 'Studies in Boğazköy Akkadian', PhD thesis (Harvard, 1976), pp. 379–80), but in Mesopotamia it becomes more commonplace in the first millennium. The example with perhaps the highest profile is *i-ḫu-uz-zu* for *īḫuz* + *ū* in Aššurbanipal colophon d (Hunger, *Kolophone* no. 319, 5). In Gilgameš tablets from Kuyunjik note also the attestations listed in the section of Chapter 9 on Spelling (sub d and e). Examples in older Neo-Assyrian Gilgameš tablets are given in the introduction to Chapter 7, sub (s).

For von Soden such spellings marked a shift of stress (*GAG* §20g). Others view them as an orthographic phenomenon without significance for pronunciation (see I. J. Gelb, *BiOr* 12 (1955), p. 101; *GAG*³ §20g*). In Sumerian writing the practice of resuming final consonants at the morpheme boundary can be shown to be a matter of orthography only. Texts that use non-conventional syllabic spellings sometimes show elision of vowels before a consonant that is conventionally written double, thus showing it to be single nevertheless (e.g. in Ur-Nammu B, *SRT* 11, 68 ní bí.in.gùr.ru // *TCL* XV 38, 10 ni-ip-pi-ig-ru, ed. J. Klein, *Acta Sum* 11 (1989), pp. 44–56). Given the long history and wide spread of written Akkadian, however, it seems presumptuous to explain every analogous spelling in that language by reference to the conventions of the third millennium, when a variety of factors may have been at work.

4–5. Compare a version of this couplet in OB Harmal$_2$: *ša Ḫuwawa ittall*[*akū*] / *šakin kibsum šutēšur padānumma* (ll. 14–15).

6. The spelling *e-ma-ru* for *immarū* is Assyrian in its use of the prefix *e-* and in the non-marking of the gemination but, in the absence of vowel harmony, it is not actually an example of Assyrian dialect. For other examples in tablets of the SB text proper see Chapter 9, the section on Language and style sub (viii, ix).

The epithet of the Cedar Mountain given here is an expansion of the earlier *mūšabī ilī Enunnakkī* (OB IM 17–18) // *mūšab Enunnakkī* (OB Ishchali 38′). Given the clear parallelism in our line between *mūšab ilī* and *parak* ^{d}*ir-ni-ni*, I assume that the ^{d}*ir-ni-ni* stands not for the well-known aspect of Ištar (Irnina) but for goddesses in general; in other words, it is a variant on the common noun *ištarī*, which often appears paired with *ilī* in a formally masculine plural guise (on this see the commentary on SB I 78). It may be transcribed *irninnī*.

8. I take the spelling *ṭa-a-bu* for the stative *ṭāb* and not as the adjective (for extra vowels appended to closed syllables with long vowels see the section of Chapter 9 on Spelling, sub g). Otherwise one may translate as a single clause 'its shade so sweet was full of delight'.

9. The restorations are those of von Soden, *ZA* 53, p. 225.

11. Perhaps *ḫ*]*u-bal-la*, 'pit'.

74. Another version of this line can be found in MB Emar$_1$ iii 8′, q.v.

75. The word *taš-ka-a-ti*, so read by Landsberger, *RA* 62, p. 108, is taken to be a plural form of *takšû* (see *AHw*, p. 1309).

76 The 'three-ply rope' also occurs in the fragment, probably of proverbs, K 16804 (col. B 4: *áš-la šu-uš-lu-*[*šá*, cited *CAD* Š/3, p. 383). The Sumerian equivalent of the saying is éš.3.tab.ba lú nu.kud.dè, 'no man can snap a three-ply rope', a proverb which is embedded in similar context in the tale of Bilgames and Ḫuwawa A 107. Its equivalence to the well-known Hebrew proverb *whḥwṭ hmšlš l' bmhrh yntq*, 'a three-ply cord is not snapped in a hurry' (Ecclesiastes 4: 12, where the context is also of two prevailing over one), was first remarked by S. N. Kramer, *JCS* 1 (1947), p. 40, and established by A. Shaffer, *Eretz-Israel* 8 (1967), pp. 246–50, and again, in the light of the publication of MS u, *Eretz-Israel* 9 (1968), p. 160. Though in his edition of the Sumerian text D. O. Edzard persists in Kramer's reading túg.eš$_5$.tab.ba, 'einen dreifach zusammengefalteten Stoff' (*ZA* 81 (1991), p. 202, 107), the equation stands. Occasional confusion between éš and túg is to be expected in the work of learner scribes. In Proverb Collection 5 no. 56 the two signs occur as variants for the same reason (Alster, *Proverbs*, p. 403).

86. W. R. Mayer has proposed an alternative reading of the first two words, *ši-ri ku-lil-lu*, understanding the whole line as insulting: 'Fischmenschen-Brut, Gilgameš, dummer Kerl' (Deller, Mayer and Sommerfeld, *Or* NS 56 (1987), p. 210). In my view *šīr kulilli* (var. of *kulullû*), 'kinsman of a fish-man', is not a phrase that in Babylonian would convey abuse; as a creature of Ea the fish-man was a fabulous monster of apotropaic function in religious iconography (Wiggermann, *Protective Spirits*, pp. 182–3). The word *lillu* here has been cited as 'ein schönes Beispiel literarischer Ambiguität', on the grounds that as well as meaning 'fool' it alludes to the *lillu*-demon who fathered Gilgameš (Renger, *Studies Reiner*, p. 320). I am not convinced that the text gains from such ambiguity.

89. The spelling *a-qer-ru-bu-ka* could be for indicative *aqerrubka* (CV for VC) but can be otherwise explained as exhibiting a ventive in *-u*(*m*), on which see Chapter 9, the section on Spelling conventions sub (v).

90. The decipherment of the words that precede *ina karšīya* is a real problem. Previous translators have not been able to agree on whether the four signs *ul-tab-ba-a* represent two words or one. Most choose the verb *šebû*, 'to satisfy'. This is possible with *karšu* (see V *R* 9 ix 67, ed. Streck, *Asb*, p.

78: *ši-iz-bu la ú-šab-bu-u ka-ra-ši-šú-nu*, 'they could not sate their bellies with milk'), but *ina* would represent an unwanted intrusion. Other translations are no more compelling: Bottéro suggests 'l'âme épanouie(?)', Westenholz 'du betød ikke noget(?)'. It is difficult to parse what remains of the first half of the line as any form of *dâku*, 'to kill', though many have tried. Lambert suggests [*šá ta-a*]*d-da-ku-ka-a* (= *taddakkuka*) *ultabbâ* (<*tebû* III/II) *ina karšīya*, 'you who used to gambol about I put out of my mind' (personal communication). Until another manuscript sheds light on this line it seems best to leave the problematical words untranslated.

92. The emendation needs justification. Taking the line as it stands one might posit a word *gazz-izu* (or *gāzizu*), qualifying *nakri aḫî*, 'and you, yourself, like a hostile enemy with teeth bared'. The root of the verb in question seems to vary. The infinitive is usually *kazāzu*, *kaṣāṣu* or *gaṣāṣu* but note a form ostensibly from *gazāzu* in *Šumma ālu* XLV: DIŠ *šaḫû*(šaḫ)[meš] *šinnī*(zú)[meš]*-šú-nu i-gaz-za-zu*, 'if pigs gnash their teeth' (*CT* 38 45 obv. 14′). An objection is that *gazzizu* does not provide the stressed penultimate syllable required by the metre. In a manuscript where final vowels can safely be ignored, emendation to *ta-az-zi-zu*, for *tazziz*, cures this problem.

94. Others render *iṣṣur ṣarṣarī* as a mythical 'Schlangenvogel' or similar. I assume that the allusion is to the small birds that descend in large numbers on a dead animal to pick the carcass clean: by their number and voraciousness, if not also their noise, they could be said to resemble locusts or crickets (*ṣarṣaru*). Of the other birds mentioned, the vulture (*zību*) feeds on dead prey but the eagle (*arû*) generally does not, and thus is out of place. Perhaps the key lies in the participle *nā'iru*, 'snarling, vicious', which can be used on its own to denote a particular type of bird, as in *Hh* XVIII 193: Á.úš.gu.la[mušen] = *na-'-i-ru* (*MSL* VIII/2, p. 129) and perhaps *Nabnītu* III 157–9: Á.uz[mušen], NAM.zi[mušen], ugu.dù[mušen] = *na-ḫi-ru*[mušen] (*MSL* XVI, p. 65). In our line it may qualify *arû* and designate a particular kind of eagle-like raptor that will eat from a carcass.

96. The changing of Ḫumbaba's countenance implies that, confronted by the intruders, his expression turned hostile. The expression is used similarly in OB Agušaya: [*i*]*l-tum uz-zi-iz iš-nu-ú* [*pa*]*-nu-ša*, 'the goddess grew furious, her countenance changed' (*VAS* X 214 viii 26, ed. B. Groneberg, *RA* 75 (1981), p. 112).

97. The traces do not fully support the reading [*u*]*l-te-la-a k*[*i-i*] *ni-kaš-šad ana šá-a-šú* (A. Westenholz in von Weiher, *Uruk* III, p. 255).

98. The spelling *i-*⌈*pa-šá*⌉*-*[*ḫ*]*u*, if correctly read, is for indicative *ipaššaḫ*.

100–1. For this standard couplet see the commentary on SB II 232–3.

102. The second half of the line is perhaps reminiscent of OB Harmal$_1$ 16–17: *ninnemmidma išti'at neppeš* and OB Schøyen$_2$ 17: *tennemmidāma išti'at teppuš*. Here, however, a restoration [*ni*]*-pe-*[*eš*] is ruled out because in SB we expect *nippuš*.

103–5. The language is at least partly proverbial, with clear reference in ll. 103–4 to the work of the copper-founder. All three lines are characterized by the use of infinitives instead of finite parts of the verb. These may mark ll. 103–4 as direct quotations from procedural texts ('rituals'), for the infinitive can be used instead of the present of instruction in other practical texts, such as medical prescriptions (see *GAG*^{3} §150l*, on the 'heischenden Inf.'). However, this explanation will not work for l. 105, for it cannot be from such a context.

103. The conventional translation of *nappāḫu* as 'smith' does not do justice to the scale of his activities. As the etymology implies, the *nappāḫu* was a man who heated a furnace (note F. Joannès's translation 'fondeur' in 'Metalle und Metallurgie A. I. In Mesopotamien', *RLA* VIII, pp. 96–112, esp. 100). Before the Iron Age his work seems to have covered the whole range of copper-working: smelting ore, refining, alloying, casting in copper and bronze, and finishing rough castings by hammering. The *rāṭ nappāḫi* is dealt with in *Erimḫuš* II:

kúš.kúš	=	*ra-a-ṭ[u]m*	channel
šita.na	=	MIN *nu-ka-rib-[bi]*	date-cultivator's channel
kùš.kùš	=	MIN *nap-pa-[ḫi]*	coppersmith's channel
me.a	=	MIN *šá me-[e]*	channel for water, trough?

MSL XVII, p. 29, 53–6

Note also, in the context of copper-working vocabulary, *Diri* VI E 84: ku-ku-uš ^{urudu}kùš.kùš *ú-ru-du-ú-min-na-bi* = *ra-a-ṭu* (A. Goetze, *JAOS* 65 (1945), p. 225, 65). A *ra-aṭ siparri*(zabar), '*r.* of bronze', occurs in the context of bronze casting in a MA letter, *KAV* 205, 28 (ed. Freydank and Saporetti, *Bābu-aḫa-iddina*, pp. 34, 73). Goetze confidently identified kùš.kùš = *rāṭu* as an ingot mould: 'obviously another term for the furrows in front of the crucible [ama.tun = *agarinnu*]', with *agarinnu* already explained as the 'furrow in front of the crucible into which the molten metal flows, in which it hardens, and from which it is taken out in the form of ingots' (*JAOS* 65, p. 235). H. Limet translated the same lexical entry neutrally, as 'caniveau' (*Métal*, p. 276). The function of the *rāṭ nappāḫi* becomes clearer from the Sumerian literary contexts in which the phrases kùš.kùš.a sì.(sì) and kùš.kùš.a dè.dè are found in copper-founding contexts:

é.kur.ra ^{urudu}gí.dim (*var.* ^{urudu}ḫa.zi.in) gal.gal.bi kùš.kùš.a bí.in.sì.sì (var. i]n.dé.dé)
Of the Ekur, he poured (*var.* melted down) its great shovels (*var.* axes) into a *k*.

Curse of Akkade 128

alam.gim kùš.kùš.a dé.a.meš ì.[sì?.g]e.dè.en.dè.en
We are being [*poured out*] like figurines melted into a *k*.

Lamentation over the Destruction of Sumer and Ur 229

é.sikil é nam.tar.ra.ka alam.gim kùš.kùš.a sì.bí.ib
In the pure house, the house of destinies, pour (an item of bronze called a zabar.šu) into a *k*. like a figurine!

Sargon Legend 34, cf. 36 and 45

For dé, 'to melt down' see *Antagal* F 254 $^{de\text{-}e}$dè = *ṣa-a-du ša erî*, 'to melt, of copper' (*MSL* XVII, p. 219). These passages clearly show that kùš.kùš = *rāṭu* is a vessel for receiving molten copper and not, for example, the furnace's blowpipe. They have been discussed in detail by J. S. Cooper and W. Heimpel, 'The Sumerian Sargon legend', *JAOS* 103 (1983), pp. 81–2. Cooper identifies the kùš.kùš as a mould for casting objects generally. Heimpel follows Goetze's view that it is an ingot mould and sees the passages quoted as examples of recycling copper and bronze castings by melting them down into ingots. He adduces additional evidence that such ingots conformed to standards, but the passages he cites are open to other interpretations: the *rāṭu*s of copper, silver and gold in the OB list of coefficients, *MCT*, p. 134, 22–4, may be interpreted as metal vessels as well as standardized ingots, while the deified *rāṭu*s and *ḫiburnu* vats in the temple of Aššur were items of sacred brewing equipment and not necessarily standard measures; see Šalmaneser I's report of the refurbishment of the brewery, Grayson, *RIMA* 1, p. 192, 36.

Nevertheless, Goetze's original identification of the *rāṭ nappāḫi* remains tenable. Although the non-specific translation of kùš.kùš as a mould is repeated by Joannès, *RLA* VIII, p. 107, and by some translators of this line, it seems to me that if *rāṭu*, 'channel', describes a mould it does for reasons of shape rather than function. The word's use for a channel for the irrigation of date palms (see *Erimḫuš* II 54) and for the watering of sheep (OB Atram-ḫasīs III iv 20) suggests that the typical shape of a *rāṭu* was a shallow trough or ditch dug in the ground. Though open (one-sided) moulds for such things as spear and arrow-heads might conceivably be dubbed 'channels', a better case can be argued for Goetze's 'furrow'. Since Goetze's day many second-millennium bar ingots have come to light that seem from their triangular section and irregular aspect to have been rough-cast in small sand or clay channels as he described. Typically secondary castings from recycled copper, usually measuring 15–20 cm long and 2.5–3 cm wide, these ingots seem to be the readily portable working material of itinerant copper-smiths. For good examples from the Levant see W. G. Dever and M. Tadmor, 'A copper hoard of the Middle Bronze Age I', *IEJ* 26 (1976), pp. 163–9, from the Hebron hills; R. Maddin and T. Stech Wheeler, 'Metallurgical study of seven bar ingots', *IEJ* 26 (1976), pp. 170–3; more generally, J. F. Merkel and W. G. Dever, 'Metalworking technology at the end of the Early Bronze Age in the southern Levant', *Institute for Archaeo-Metallurgical Studies* 14 (1989), pp. 1–4. On casting in sand or clay in antiquity see P. R. S. Moorey, *Ancient Mesopotamian Materials and Industries* (Oxford, 1994), pp. 270–1, who makes the point that such moulds will not show in the archaeological record. The making of rough bar ingots in the *rāṭ nappāḫi* must have been a common sight in ancient Mesopotamia.

However, a dissenting view is expressed by J. Bottéro in his translation of the line under comment, namely that the *rāṭ nappāḫi* is not a mould, as such, but a channel down which molten metal flows on its way into a mould: 'la goulotte qui conduisait au moule (mot à mot: "la rigole du fondeur").' A technical term for such a channel is a 'runner', part of the 'gate-assembly' of a mould (for advice on the practicalities of ancient Near Eastern metal-casting I am indebted to John F. Merkel of the Institute of Archaeology, University College London). At their simplest, runners are hollow tubes that run from the outside of a closed mould into the cavity within. More complex channels (also known as pouring gates) are funnel-shaped and act as small reservoirs or basins to hold the molten metal as it sinks into the mould. Of whatever style, the runner is an integral part of the mould. The surplus metal that hardens in it, and in the 'riser' (the vent that lets the air out of a closed mould), is chiselled off the casting when cold.

The Sumerian evidence given above can accommodate the meaning 'runner' for kùš.kùš just as easily as it can 'mould'. As *rāṭu* seems also to mean 'tube' it might be an appropriate technical term for the runner. Study of the end of the line is needed to clarify which function is more appropriate, tube or ingot-mould. The second half of the line clearly refers to copper, *erû*, but the spelling *e-ra* is unsatisfactory and suggests that the text is corrupt. The word after *erâ* was not copied adequately by von Weiher and has been the subject of guesswork. It is the key to what happens to the copper in the *rāṭu*. The blank space left by the scribe between *e-ra* and *šá* very likely signifies a word division, which argues against an emendation such as *e-ra-a*! (*šá*) *ba-šá-*⌈*a*⌉. The simplest solution is to assume a missing *a* and read *e-ra-*⟨*a*⟩ *šá-ba-šá-*⌈*a*⌉, the significance of the lengthened final syllable being to mark a question. The well-attested phrase *epra šabāšu* means to scoop up dust from the ground; *erâ šabāšu* thus suits a situation in which copper ingots are moulded directly in channels in the floor and collected up when cool.

104. The theme of copper-working is expanded with two carefully balanced infinitive phrases. The first refers to bringing the crucible up to temperature by forcing air on to the coals; *tu-ú-ru* is a spelling of *tumru* (>*tu'ru* or *tuwru*?) that recurs in the commentary published by R. D. Biggs, *RA* 62 (1968), p. 54, 23. The equally time-consuming process described by the second infinitive phrase is less intelligible. The last word is written so small that I could not be sure whether it is *šá-lu-ú* or *me-lu-ú*. As a lengthy process following the heating of the crucible in the furnace, cooling comes to mind, whether it is the process of letting smelted copper cool in the crucible or allowing a casting to set in its mould; contra Bottéro's exegesis of these lines, which inverts ll. 103 and 104: 'le métal en

fusion, après avoir été chauffé (le durée de l'opération est définie par . . . *bêru* . . . , une "double-heure"), était laissé au repos dans le creuset ("refroidi"), puis versé dans la goulotte qui conduisait au moule (mot à mot: "la rigole du fondeur"): il n'était alors plus temps de l'arrêter' (Bottéro, *L'épopée*, p. 114, fn. 3), molten copper is not allowed to cool *before* being cast. A word written *šá-lu-ú*, at least, can be interpreted as known verbs, (a) the common *šalû* meaning 'to shoot' arrows and other weapons, 'to spray, splash' dust and liquids, and (b) the rare *šâlu* (with stressed final syllable again marking a question), meaning 'to plaster'. However, it escapes me how exactly either of these might relate to a stage in the copper-casting process that could last two hours. For techniques of working copper in the ancient Near East see further J. D. Muhly, 'Kupfer B. Archäologisch', *RLA* VI, pp. 348–64; idem, 'Metalle B. Archäologisch', *RLA* VIII, pp. 119–36, and literature there cited; Moorey, *Ancient Mesopotamian Materials and Industries*, pp. 242–78; K. Reiter, *Die Metalle im Alten Orient* (AOAT 249), pp. 204–5.

The function of this line and its neighbours in Enkidu's argument is a further problem. Enkidu has exhorted Gilgameš to act (l. 104). Why the mention of ingot-casting and lengthy processes in copper-founding at this point? I can only suppose that they form rhetorical questions for which l. 105, with its parallel syntax, gives an answer. In effect Enkidu tells Gilgameš, 'There's only one thing we have to do now' (102), asks 'Is the prize already there for the taking or does it require a lot more preparation?' (103–4), and answers, 'A task of mythical proportions calls for swift and sudden action!' (105).

132. With *imḫaṣ qaqqaramma* compare a phrase from the Sumerian account of Gilgameš's meeting with Huwawa, Bilgames and Huwawa A 136: šu ki.a bí.in.sè (*var.* ra), 'he placed (*var.* slapped) a hand on the ground' (ed. Edzard, *ZA* 81 (1991), p. 210).

133. On the analysis of *i-bi-iš-šú* as singular and ventive from *bêšu*, 'to go separate ways', see George, *ZA* 80 (1990), pp. 216–17.

137–43. These lines are the realization of Ninsun's prayer to Šamaš in SB III 88–93, q.v.

142. The present tense of the verbs dramatically convey Ḫumbaba's plight. Alternatively, they express consecutive meaning, 'so that he could not . . .' On *raḫāṣu*, 'to kick' of equids, and gìr—ra.ra, its Sumerian equivalent in this meaning, see the omen in which a donkey kicks an exorcist on his way to visit a patient (*Sakikku* I 26: DIŠ *imēru irḫiṣ*(ra)*-su*) and the ancient commentaries thereon (a: gìr ra.ra = *ra-ḫa-ṣu*; b: anše *ir-ḫi-is-su*; c: ra = *ra-ḫa-ṣi*, ra = *ma-ḫa-ṣi*), edited and discussed by George, *RA* 85 (1991), pp. 142, 148, 157–8). A meaning 'trample down' has also been suggested for *raḫāṣu* as an action characteristic of horses and donkeys in the context of damage to a standing crop (see B. Landsberger, *ZA* 43 (1936), p. 75 on Theodicy 60; id., *JNES* 8 (1949), p. 249, fn. 8). This nuance is confirmed by the lexical equation *Antagal* N ii 13′: gìr.PA$^{sa\text{-}ag}$GAN, 'to trample' = *ra-ḫa-ṣu šá* [*šēpi*] (*MSL* XVII, p. 240), where the Sumerian verb is a variant of the compound gìr.sag$_{11}$/sig$_{18}$(KIN)—dug$_4$/ak etc. (for which see J. S. Cooper, 'gìr-KIN "to stamp out, trample"', *RA* 66 (1972), pp. 81–3). A meaning 'trample, stamp' is not as appropriate in the present context, however, as 'kick', for understood thus, the combination here of *nakāpu* and *raḫāṣu* juxtaposes the modes of attack of bulls and horses respectively.

145. This is a standard line: see SB II 289 var. and commentary. Here it is not cautionary, as it was when used by the wise elders of Uruk in response to Gilgameš's youthful bravado, but flattery.

147. The customary reading is *Šamaš bēl*(umun) *šadî*. The sun god can be 'lord of the mountain' in liturgical texts (e.g. Cohen, *Lamentations*, p. 804, i 21: šul ^{d}utu ù.mu.un ḫur.sag.gá, OB; *SBH* 48 obv. 17: šul!(TIR) ^{d}[ut]u umun ḫur.sag.gá.ke$_4$, LB). I have reservations, however, because in the present context a logographic spelling umun = *bēlu* would be most unusual, though not without parallel. At the end, the traces do not support von Weiher's *t*[*at-b*]*i-e-ma*, though with regard to the first

sign the would-be collator is now handicapped by the disappearance of the middle of the three small fragments that are shown on the photograph (*Bagh. Mitt.* 11 (1980), pl. 15). A reading *t*[*as*?-*p*]*u*-⌜*un*⌝-*ma* was suggested privately by A. Westenholz. The line would then allude to the fact that, as described in ll. 133–4, Ḫumbaba's mountain now lies broken: 'by Šamaš's command also my mountain you levelled'. Something similar is preserved in OB Harmal$_2$ 44–5 but there, too, the text is damaged.

148. With this courtly line of greeting compare the similar wording of SB IV 191–3.

153. The spelling *taq-qa-ba-a* is presumed faulty, to represent *taqabbâ*.

154–5. An antecedent of this couplet is OB Harmal$_2$ 46–7: *lurabbi'akkum*(?) *erēnam šurmēnam supālam* / *šīḫūtim iṣṣī simātu ēkallim.*

177. Other translators see nothing wrong with *ina nēreb papalla qīštīya*, but the sense of the phrase is much improved if it is assumed that *nēreb* and *papalla* have become transposed. Enkidu's body, dangling low in the branches of a young tree at the forest's edge, would be a suitable warning for the next intruder. A comparable technique is still practised by British gamekeepers, who display the bodies of foxes and other predators at the boundary of game reserves in order to discourage the ingress of more of their kind.

178. This is a repetition of Ḫumbaba's earlier threat to Gilgameš (SB V 94).

182–4. These three lines are really a quatrain, but one that does not quite conform to the commonest pattern of repeated couplets, in which something, typically a name, is added to the first line of the couplet on its repetition (pattern *aba'b*; see K. Hecker, *Untersuchungen zur akkadischen Epik*, pp. 146–50). Possibly the appearance of Ḫumbaba's name in l. 182 as well as l. 184 is an inadvertent intrusion. However, there is at least one other example of unaltered repetition, after the pattern *abab*, in Nergal and Ereškigal (Hecker, *Untersuchungen*, pp. 148–9). Either way, the omission of *erēni* in l. 184 is a straightforward error.

183. Other translators take the penultimate word as an imperative, i.e. 'grind him, destroy him'. However, the spacing of the line on the tablet clearly reveals that the last word is *ḫulliq* not, for example, *ḫulliqšu*, which obliges one to take *ṭè-en-šú* as its object (= *ṭēmšu*). Since the verb *ṭênu* is never written with the sign *ṭè* but *ṭēmu* so often is, in the first millennium especially, the orthography corroborates this decipherment.

185–9. These lines are repeated as ll. 242–5, whence come some of the restorations.

229. Given the key word *êkâma*, one wonders whether this line might be related to OB Ishchali 15′: *ibrī iṣṣūram bārma êšam illakū watmūšu.*

254. With the traces compare MB Boğ$_1$ Fragment a, rev. 3′: *ē tāḫu*]*z aššata u lalêša* [*ē tešbe*?].

257. The spelling *ki-ib-ri* for *qēbirī* is already explained in *JNES* 52 (1993), p. 302, where I noted it as 'an unconventional spelling of *qé-bi-ri*: the same orthographic practice is well known in Neo-Assyrian (as first listed by Deller, *Or* NS 31 (1962), pp. 188 ff., "Schreibungen VK statt KV"), but has not yet been formally documented in NB and LB. For the idiom *qēbirī ay irši* in curses see further CAD Q, p. 202 (boundary stones and colophon).'

259. MS H's *a-qab-bak-kam-ma* refutes von Soden's statement that in the 'ninevitische Gilgamešepos' the 2nd masc. sg. dative suffix is always *-kum* before the enclitic *-ma* (*ZA* 40 (1931), p. 176); *-kamma* is a common vocalization in late grammar (ibid., fn. 2; *GAG*^{3} §42jk, n. 8).

262–5. These four lines are a reworking of a passage that appears in OB Ishchali 19′–23′: *išme Gilgāmeš siqir rā'êšu* / *ilqe ḫaṣṣinnam ina qātīšu* / *išlup namṣaram ina šibbīšu* / *Gilgāmeš inēr kišādam* / *Enkīdu ibiršu īpuš libba.* For variations on ll. 263–4 see the commentary ad loc. In l. 265 the first sign can hardly be ⌜*ù*⌝, and is ignored as an error. After Enkidu one might restore [*lìb-ba i*]-*bu-tu* or [*lìb-ba il*]-*pu-tu* as the counterpart of OB *libba īpuš*. Elliptical usage of *lapātu* in the meaning 'to use a blade' is attested in the common expression *puḫāda lapātu*, 'to sacrifice a lamb'. Note also, in OB legal documents, the clause *li-ša-an-šu i-la-ap-pa-at*, 'his tongue will be cut out' (*TIM* V 4, 19), as a variant for the standard penalty *lišānšu iššallap*, 'his tongue will be pulled out' (*TIM* V 21, 22 and *passim*). Whichever restoration is preferred, it is clear that here Enkidu cuts open Ḫumbaba's stomach and eviscerates him.

267. The spelling *i*-ŠUL-*lal* for *išallal* might be an error on mishearing dictation, but there is phonological evidence for a development /šal/ > /šul/, as already noted in *JNES* 52, p. 302: 'Rather than postulate a new value *šal*ₓ of ŠUL, perhaps we should understand the orthography *i-šul-lal* to represent a pronunciation *išollal*: compare also the variation in the first syllable of *šalḫû*/*šulḫû*, not only at Mari, where von Soden commented "in der Schreibung *šu-ul-ḫu-um* . . . hat vermutlich das l nach einem š dem Vokal gefärbt" (*JCS* 2 (1948), p. 295), but also in later Babylonian.'

268–9. As others have seen, the word *ṭuḫdu* makes an unlikely subject of *imqut*, so must be genitive after a preposition or, more likely, after a noun (or nouns) in the construct state. One possible candidate is 'rain', as in the literary fragment *SEM* 117 iii 15: ᵈ*adad*(iškur) *ú-ša-az-na-an el ni-ši ša-mu-ut ṭuḫ-di*, 'Adad causes a copious rain to fall on the people'.

290. The context is perhaps the size of the chippings of wood that fall to the ground with each swing of Gilgameš's axe, so a word for 'thickness' might be expected before *sunginnu* (*sumkinnu*). However, *tirku* means a 'blow' of a weapon or drum and the 'bruise' such a blow makes, and its significance here is obscure.

291. This line is a later version of OB Ishchali 39′: *Gilgāmeš iṣṣī ubattaq Enkīdu uḫarra urbazillī*, q.v.

293–4. An older version of this couplet survives in OB IM 22: *šuwwi'am erēnam šīḫam* / *ša muḫḫašu šamāyī šannu*. The imperative has become a statement of fact. In the light of the parallel the spelling *nak-pí* is clearly for *nakpu*.

295. Some take the word written *e-pu-uš* as preterite *ēpuš*, others as imperative *epuš*. Because the door is certainly Enkidu's work not Gilgameš's (see SB VII 46), an imperative would make for inconsistency of plot. In terms of syntax one might have expected an imperative clause to have been followed up with a precative one in l. 296, i.e. *lū ša ištēnma*. The preterite is clumsy, especially in the light of an old version of this line where the voluntative is used: *lūpuš daltam ša qana rupussa* (OB IM 23). For this reason I wonder whether *e-pu-uš* is corrupt.

296. Most translators are content that *ša ištēnma* means fashioned 'from a single piece'. A dissenting view, which reads *nindan ištēnma*, is exemplified by Bottéro's translation: 'les pivots: central, inférieur et d'en haut, soient chacun de six mètres'. Since the door itself was six *nindan* high (about thirty-six metres), it would not be well served by pivots that occupied an aggregate of only half that distance. The point is surely that the chosen tree was so huge that the pole and pivots on which the door turned could be made from a single, fittingly massive, piece of timber. In usual circumstances the pivot assembly was probably of tripartite construction. The technical terms of this assembly are dealt with in the same order by *Hh* V:

ᵍⁱˢsuku₅.ig	'door-pole'	=	*šu-ku-ú*	
ᵍⁱˢu₅.ig	'door-rider'	=	*ša-ga-am-mu*	
ᵍⁱˢu₄.sakar.ig	'door-crescent'	=	*sa-ḫi-ru*	'swivel'

MSL VI, p. 26, 252–4

These items are the pole on which the door-leaf turned and its end pieces, top and bottom: see further E. Speiser, *JCS* 2 (1948), pp. 225–7 (cf. Salonen, *Türen*, pp. 62, 66, 68). The top end of the pole appears to have been a knob, which held the door assembly upright in the door-frame or lintel; the bottom end acted as a load-bearing pivot, and needed to be rounded to fit snugly in the floor socket. However, I have rejected the translations 'ferrule' (Speiser on SB VII, *CAD*) and 'pivot-stone' (Kovacs, SB VII) for *sāḫiru* on the grounds that there is no evidence for it being made of any material other than wood, though, as Speiser notes, it may have been fitted with a metal shoe.

295–6. The line division is misplaced, for it should fall before *šukûša*. The verses are correctly rendered in the parallel SB VII 44–5.

297–8. The older text reads (OB IM 27–9): *ana bīti Ellil lībel Purattum / liḫdūma ummān Nippur / lirīssim Ellil*. Consequently it would appear that Kuyunjik MS H's *atmān* is a corruption of *ummān*. The correct word has nevertheless survived intact in the LB copying tradition represented by MS dd.

299. I assume that the opening of the line is corrupt. Tournay and Shaffer (p. 137: 'il recouvrirent le pont de branchages') evidently took *ḫar-mu* for *armū* and *am-mu* for *amu*, but this remains highly speculative.

302. The broken sign after ^{d}*ḫum-ba-ba* appeared to Haupt as *ab* but to Delitzsch as *r*[*a*] (Haupt, *Nimrodepos*, p. 26). Either way it rules out the restoration *ikkisamma* (or *ittaksamma*) *iqqelpâ* . . . that is suggested by Assyrian MS $\mathbf{y}_2$ obv. 22′.

TABLET VI

2. The variant of *unassis* offered by MS O_1 defies easy interpretation. Though *nussusu* also appears as *nuzzuzu*, and even *nuššušu*, *ú-na-zi*[*z-m*]*a* does not look a viable reading as the traces now stand, and nor quite does *ú-na-aš-*[*ši-i*]*s*, which in any case would be, as it were, a hybrid form. We are left with the solution presented in the apparatus, that the sign after *na* (which is perfectly clear, despite Haupt's annotation, *Nimrodepos*, p. 150) is an incomplete *s*[*i*, lacking the lower horizontal wedge.

6. The expression *īna/īnī našû*, meaning 'to look with desire' and so 'covet', also describes Ištar's lust for Išullānu (l. 67). It is now amply documented in *CAD* N/2, pp. 104–5. The classic example in Codex Ḫammurapi §25, where it describes the motive of a man looting a burning house. For a comparative study of the phrase in Akkadian and Hebrew see S. M. Paul, 'Euphemistically "speaking" and a covetous eye', *Hebrew Annual Review* 14 (1994), pp. 193–204.

9. This line is also found in MB Nergal and Ereškigal, where it is spoken by another goddess, the queen of the Netherworld (*EA* 357, 82: *at-ta lu mu-ti-ma a-na-ku lu áš-ša-at-ka*). S. Greengus has drawn attention to a third literary passage in which such words are spoken (*JAOS* 89 (1969), p. 516). In this text, an *Ardat lilî* incantation since republished, the words are spoken in the more conventional fashion, by a man to a female; the promise of lavish gifts also finds an echo in our passage:

> kù.sig$_{17}$ kù.babbar úr.zu ba.ni.in.si
> *kaspa ḫurāṣa su-un-ka ú-mal-lu*
> dam.mu ḫé.me.en gá.e dam.zu ḫé.a
> *at-ta lu-ú áš-šá-tú ana-ku lu-ú mu-ut-ka*
>
> S. Lackenbacher, *RA* 65 (1971), p. 126, 12–14
>
> I shall fill your lap with silver and gold!
> You be my wife, I will be your husband.

For the Sumerian counterpart to Ištar's proposal in Bilgames and the Bull of Heaven see Chapter 10, the introduction to this tablet.

10. The variant *lušeṣmidka* (MS Q) is Middle Babylonian.

11. The 'horns' of a chariot are the subject of a section of *Hh* V:

giš.si.dù.a.gigir	=	*qar-nu*
giš.dù.a.gigir	=	MIN
giš.ḫub.a.gigir	=	MIN
giš.á!(DA).šita$_4$.gigir	=	[*qar-nu*]

MSL VI, pp. 6–7, 25–7a

Salonen considered that these 'horns' were the looped rings through which the reins passed (*Landfahrzeuge*, pp. 93–4). Dalley suggests that they are the yoke terminals (p. 129, note 52). In this line they are in the dual, so there were two of them. The material *elmešu* can be a precious metal and in such usage is usually translated 'electrum', but it is also known to be a rare, semi-mythical stone and I have opted for that. This stone is known for its bright colour. Its identification as amber is most recently discussed by P. Kingsley, *JRAS* 1992, p. 342.

12. The *ūmu* (Sum. ud) or *ūmu rabû* (also *ugallu* and Sum. u$_4$.gal) is the lion-headed monster that pulls the chariots of the storm god Adad, the sun, the warriors Ninurta and Marduk and the warlike Ištar (see further Wiggermann, *Mesopotamian Protective Spirits*, pp. 169–72).

13. The rare word *sammūtu*, here plural, is perhaps cognate with Arabic *šamma*, 'smell at' (Lambert, personal communication).

14–15. Strictly speaking, a *sippu* is the angle formed where the brickwork of a wall gives way to the doorway. In temples the most important doorways were stepped back into the wall by means of several *sippu*s, the 'rabbeted' jambs that were a very distinctive feature of Mesopotamian religious architecture (see George, *Iraq* 57 (1995), pp. 181–2). Most previous translators have taken *arattû* as 'dais' (Heidel, Speiser) or 'throne' (=*šubtu*, *kussi nēmedi* in the synonym lists). Others have read the two words together, ⟨*i*⟩-*šip-pu arattû*, following *CAD* A/2 (p. 239: 'may the noble purification priests kiss your feet'; cf. earlier A. Schott, *ZA* 42 (1934), p. 120). This emendation fails to recommend itself: even if the adjective *arattû* could be used of priests, which would be unparalleled, it ought to be plural, *arattûtu*. Note that MB Emar$_2$ apparently has *kappu*, 'hand' (i 1′), for SB's *šēpu*, 'foot'.

16. The realization of this promise appears in a prayer that invokes Gilgameš as ruler and judge of the shades: *šarrū*(lugal)^{meš} *šakkanakkū*(GÌR.NÍTA)^{meš} *u rubû*(nun)^{meš} *maḫar*(igi)-*ka kam-su*, 'kings, governors and nobles are bowed down in your presence' (Haupt, *Nimrodepos* no. 53, 9, ed. Chapter 3 above, the section on Gilgameš in exorcistic rituals). The sequence *šarru kabtu* (*u*) *rubû* and its variants are literary clichés (e.g. IV *R*^{2} 55 no. 2, 4, 6, 10, 13: ritual to gain favour; *PBS* I/1 13, 37–8: hymn to Šamaš). The variation on this phrase in MS Q$_1$, *šarrū*^{meš} *bēlū*(en)^{meš} *u rubû*^{meš}, might be seen as a secondary development, in which idim = *kabtu* has been interpreted as BE = *bēlu*, for the use of BE for *bēlu* is characteristic of NA orthography (see S. Parpola, *Iraq* 34 (1972), p. 25). However, the slightly different version of this line in MB Emar$_2$ might already have *be*]-*lu-ú* (i 2′), so the variation between *kabtūtu* and *bēlū* may be old.

17. The word *liqtu* is something given to a superior, as in the OB extispicy prayer in which it refers to the diviner's offering to the sun god: ^{d}*šamaš*(utu) *na-ši-ku-um li-iq-tam lu-ú-qú-ut me-e sà-as-qí-im el-lu-tim*, 'O Šamaš, I am bearing to you (*našêkkum* < *naši'āk* + *kum*) a gift: pick up the pure drink of *sasqû*-water!' (*YOS* XI 22, 25, ed. A. Goetze, *JCS* 22 (1968–9), p. 26). The discovery of *liqtu* in this line settles the question of how to read *Malku* IV 231 (*LTBA* II 1 xiii 101): *liq-tú* = *biltum* with *AHw*, pp. 126, 555, against the emendation *ip*(!)-*tú* in *CAD* (B, p. 229; L, p. 207) and the

entry *ip-tum* : *bil-tum* in the commentary on the Babylonian Theodicy (Lambert, *BWL*, p. 80). Many previous commentators have been led astray by the only source which is complete for this line, MS $\mathbf{a}_1$, where the decipherment of NAR.NAR-*di* remains a problem. Von Soden ('die Lullubäer') evidently interpreted the signs as *lul-lub-di*, but serious emendation is still needed to yield *Lullubû*. A reference to one particular people is in any case unexpected, for the whole world will offer tribute. Dalley's 'verdure' interprets the signs 'very tentatively' as *lullumti* (p. 129, note 54), but the herb *lulumtu* is a specific plant, not found outside plant lists and medical texts, and unlikely to be used generically for vegetation in general. A development *mt* > *bd* is also improbable. It seems simplest to assume that NAR.NAR-*di* is corrupt.

18. The language of this line evokes a proverbial image: see Laḫar and Ašnan 8–9:

u_8.e sila_4 min.bi nu.ub.tu.ud	No ewe had given birth to its twins,
ùz.e máš eš_5.bi nu.ub.tu.ud	nor nanny-goat to its triplet kids.

B. Alster and H. Vanstiphout, *Acta Sum* 9 (1987), p. 14

Both passages are examples of the numerical sequence n, $n + 1$, though the sequence is reversed in our line. On this literary device in Gilgameš see further SB I 194 and commentary.

19. The reading in this line of dùr(ANŠE.NÍTA) as *mūru* has been doubted by *CAD* on the grounds that in this and other passages it signifies not a foal but a '(mature) male donkey' (*CAD* M/2, p. 230). I take the verb as ventive, *libā'a*, to satisfy the requirements of metre.

20. The plural determinative on *sīsû* (preserved only on MS **a**) is at odds with the verb it governs, *šaruḫ*, which is singular. The singular donkey and ox of adjacent lines suggest that the determinative is a corruption.

24–5. Compare MB Emar_2 i 7′–8′, where the verb is written *lu-um-ši*. Since the meaning of this is doubtful I am reluctant to restore it here. The solecistic use of the dative phrase *ana kâši/kâša* (etc.), where a direct object is expected, is found sporadically in SB. Other examples are *ana-ku ana ka-a-ši aṣ-bat-ki-ma*, 'I took hold of you' (Biggs, *Šaziga*, p. 77, 14: incantation); [*a-n*]*a ka-a-šá it-ta-nam-za-*[*ru-ka*] // *ana ka-a-šú . . . it-ta-na-za-ru-ka*, 'they will keep insulting you' (Lambert, *BWL*, p. 148, 68 // 34′: Dialogue of Pessimism); *a-na šá-šá-ma ter-r*[*a-*(*áš*)*-ši*], 'bring her back to me!' (*CT* 15 48, 21′: Ištar's Descent). These are unlikely to be cases of *ana* as *nota accusativi*, which is a late usage not expected in SB. Presumably the phrase is simply an irregularity deriving from the fact that in the dative *kâši*(*m*) often needs the preposition: the phrase *ana kâši* becomes a unit which can remain intact even when the pronoun is later used for the accusative and the preposition is thereby made redundant.

26. The words *kurummatī* and *bubūtī* are apparently reversed in MB Emar_2 i 9′.

27–8. These lines are restored with reference to Šamaš's words to Enkidu when reminding him of the advantages that meeting the prostitute had won him (SB VII 135–6): *ša ušākilūka akla simat ilūti* / *kurunna išqûka simat šarrūti*. An objection is that *tašaqânni* might have been expected. For *šaqû* with the ventive see the Lamaštu incantation *PBS* I/2 113, 17: *i-šaq-qa-a mê*(a)^{meš} *pu-uš-qí*!, 'She has (the newborn) drink amniotic fluid (lit. water of labour)'.

29. The only word remaining in this line is taken provisionally from *e'ēlu*, 'to bind (by agreement)'. Cf. Bottéro's '"Me faudra-t-il [. . .]?"'

30. The reading *lu-u uš-bu-uk* (*AHw*, p. 1441) does not seem plausible, for *ušbu*, otherwise known only from SB I 170, seems to be either the act of lying in wait for animals or a 'hide' where this is done. For examples of the voluntative written with *plene lu-u-* see SB XI 166 and 280.

32. Restoration after l. 24.

33. The restoration is owed to MB $Emar_2$ i 13′, where the word preceding *lā kāṣirat* may be *ḫalpû*, 'frost'. For *kaṣāru ša šurīpi*, 'to solidify, with reference to ice', in OB and SB see *CAD* K, p. 260.

34. The restoration goes back to von Soden, *OLZ* 50 (1955), 515. The *arkab/pinnu* door is glossed as *da-al-tum la qa-ti-tum*, 'incomplete door', in *Malku* II 172, which explains why it is not effective at keeping out draughts. There was one in E-sagil, the temple of Marduk at Babylon: see further George, *Topog. Texts*, pp. 404–5.

36. Foster has a partial restoration for the middle of this line, [x *mu*]*-ak-ki-lat*, and translates 'an elephant which [de]vours its own covering' (*Essays Pope*, p. 34; also Kovacs). I do not know what the textual justification for this reading is. In Oppenheim's view, the metaphor 'hardly refers to the elephant (and his cover) because this animal is very rarely mentioned in cuneiform texts, and especially because the other similes are all taken from the realm of daily life and its incidents' (*Or* NS 17 (1948), p. 36, fn. 4). Labat translates, seemingly ad hoc, 'un turban (?) [qui étouffe] celui qui en est couvert'. However, the signs *pi-i-ru* are clear and, in what was evidently a well-spaced line, are followed by a gap which marks the boundary of the word; until another word *pīru* (or *wīru*) is found the elephant remains. Wild elephants are known to have been hunted in parts of Syrian Mesopotamia until Neo-Assyrian times (cf. the allusion to the ivory trade in SB V 267). The translation and comment of Bottéro are worth repeating (*L'épopée*, p. 125 with fn. 1):

> 'Un éléphant [qui jette à bas] son harnachement:' il s'agit de la pièce de harnais qui permettait à un éléphant de transporter des passagers. Le trait est intéressant, sur le plan culturel, puisqu'il suppose connue par les Mésopotamiens la domestication de l'animal, propre à l'Inde, semble-t-il, d'ou l'on en aurait tiré l'image. Nous n'avons pas la moindre trace ni d'un pareil usage, ni d'un pareil animal, en Mésopotamie.

37. The spacing of the signs on MSS A (probably) and **a** (certainly) discounts a restoration [*qāt*] *nāšîša*, here and in the next line.

38. The participle conventionally restored in this line is *munakkisat* (R. Frankena in Garelli, *Gilg.*, p. 120), but note von Soden, *AHw*, p. 996 (*mu-*[*ra-as*]*-sa-at nāšîša*). Though MB $Emar_2$ i 16′ might have read *muna*[*kissat*], MS **a** seems not to, and I have followed von Soden.

39–40. These two lines represent an expansion, though perhaps not a very satisfactory one, of what was originally a single line (cf. MB $Emar_2$ i 17′: [*yaš*]*ubu mu'abbitu dūr abni*), where the point might be that in certain circumstances wood will overcome stone, despite its apparent disadvantage in hardness. However, the SB text explicitly informs us that the battering ram is active against the enemy's property. The lack of treachery in such a sentiment prompted Bottéro, *L'épopée*, p. 125, fn. 3, to translate the signs kur nu kúr ti as 'un pays non-ennemi', i.e. *māt là nukurti*(kúr)^{ti}. This is unconvincing, both because the orthography *māt nu-kúr-ti* is so standard it seems unlikely that it could also be read as the opposite, and because the phrase *māt lā nukurti* is never found. Instead the lines may allude not to Ištar's treachery but to her destructiveness: like a battering ram in action, the goddess is a blunt instrument, crude and violent. The expression *dūr abni ubbutu* also occurs in *Maqlû* II 141, describing the god of fire: ^{d}*gíra al-la-lu-u mu-ab-bit dūr*(bàd) *abni*(na_4), 'Mighty Girra, who destroys walls of stone' (from *KAR* 235, var. *iṣṣī*(giš)^{meš} *u abnī*(na_4)^{meš}, 'trees and stones'); and in Marduk's Address to the Demons (W. G. Lambert, *AfO* 17 (1954–6), p. 313, B 14): (*ana-ku* ^{d}*asal-lú-ḫi*) *šá bir-bir-ru-šú ub-ba-tu dūr*(bàd) *ab-ni*, 'I am Asalluḫi, whose fiery radiance destroys walls of stone'.

In MB $Emar_2$ i 17′ the gender of the battering ram is masculine, as indeed it is on the only other occasion known to me when it is qualified by an adjective ([^{giš}]*a-ši-bi dan-ni*: Lie, *Sar.*, p. 8, 63). However, in l. 40 MS $\mathbf{a}_2$ clearly reads *mu-ab-bi-t*[*a*-x], with probably no more than one sign missing before the margin (the line of poetry occupies two lines of tablet), and the restoration of the feminine participle is inescapable. Either this is an error or the word exhibits varying gender.

42. The form *ḫāmeraki* is literary for *ḫāmerki*; see further Chapter 9, the section on Language and style sub (i). Note the phonetic similarity between the second syllables of the two variants for the verb in this line, SB *ibūr* and MB Emar$_2$ *ilber* (i 19′).

43. The proposed restoration is tentative (A. Westenholz suggests [*ša šalmiš*]), but the verb *elû* is very suggestive. The point is that none of the lovers of the queen of heaven ever joined her there. If I am right, the language involves an untranslatable word-play between *allallu*, a type of bird which also appears in l. 48 as a former object of Ištar's desires, and the noun which is a synonym of 'warrior' (*Malku* I 27: *al-lal-lu* = *qar-ra-du*). The former meaning anticipates the story of the bird maimed by Ištar and the latter provides a human parallel with *ḫāmeru* in the first line of the couplet, and so introduces an implicit contrast between the capabilities of the bird and the man. The points made are thus twofold: by virtue of a broken wing, Ištar's *allallu*-bird cannot fly off to the sky; and unlike an *allallu*-bird, an *allallu*-man cannot go to heaven.

44. For *uppušu* used of calculation see the OB letter *LIH* 49, 12–15, ed. *AbB* II 47: *še-am* . . . *up-pí-ša-ma id-na*, 'work out (the amount of) barley . . . and hand it out'. With the idiom *minâti uppušu* cf. at Ugarit ^{d}*šamšī*^{ši} *mi-nu-ta e-pa-aš*, 'His Majesty will count (soldiers, i.e. review the parade)' (*PRU* IV, p. 192, 15–16). The restoration [*mi-na-t*]*a* is preferred to [*mi-nu-t*]*a* (or [*mi-ni-t*]*a*) because in late orthography 'overhanging' vowels on nouns in construct state are, more often than not, of the same quality as the vowel of the preceding syllable.

45. The phrase *ša būdimma* (or *pūdimma*) is uncertain and will probably remain so until the middle of the line is deciphered, but a little can be said. The section ll. 45–50 is the first of four, marked off by rulings, that recount the sticky ends to which Ištar's various lovers came (ll. 45–79). Each section exhibits an individual pattern of structure. Thus the second section comprises two couplets and a triplet, the third two triplets. The fourth section mixes couplets and triplets like the second. Given that the first section is, like the third, of six lines, it is realistic to expect it to comprise two triplets. The point of this analysis is to suggest that the section on the shepherd Dumuzi begins at l. 45 not l. 46. The term *ša būdimma*, which in the MB letter *PBS* I/2 79, 4, 8, 13, appears to be a professional title, thus ought to have some connection with him. As already seen by Dalley, who translates the phrase as 'he of the sheep (?)' (*Myths*, p. 78), the common link between *būdu* and Dumuzi is sheep. In fact sheep are not themselves *būdu* but one of the items suitable for a *būdu*, which in the OB period seems on the evidence available to be some kind of food-offering in the cult (note the lexical entry *MSL* VIII/1, p. 22, *Hh* XIII 163a: udu.ZAG$^{bu\text{-}du}$ḪA = *im-mer bu-du*; for further references see *CAD* B, p. 305; cf. *AHw*, s.v. *pūdu* II). A person denoted by the phrase *ša būdi* could reasonably be the official in charge of the collection, delivery or presentation of this *būdu*, or a person otherwise responsible for providing it. OB Lu does not know *ša būdim* but preserves an entry lú.bal = *be-el bu-di-im*, 'owner of *b*.' (*MSL* XII, p. 170, A 407), with probably the same meaning. However that may be, perhaps Dumuzi can properly be designated a *ša būdi* on account of the sheep regularly given by shepherds for sacrifice in honour of Ištar (cf. below, l. 60).

46. Dumuzi's epithet is a variant of that given in Ištar's Descent, *ḫa-mir ṣe-eḫ-ru-*[*ti-šá*] (*CT* 15 47 rev. 47 // 48, 22′) // *ṣu-uḫ*]*-re-ti-šá* (*KAR* 1 rev. 46).

47. Von Soden took *taltīmeššu* in this and the comparable lines (54–7) as examples of the I/2 stem of permanence, 'für immer bestimmen' (*AHw*, p. 1225). If this stem were current in such a meaning we would expect to encounter it much more often, given the nature of *šīmta šâmu*. A I/1 perfect is a perfectly good parsing. A damaged passage of a Middle Babylonian dialogue is reminiscent of the present line:

[. . . *ia*]-⌜*a*⌝?-*ši* *di-im-ma-tam mu-ši ù ur-ri*
[. . .] *bi-ták*!-*ka-a* *ta-aš-ti-mi*
[. . .] *na-an-gu-la* *at-ku-la ku-a-ši-im sa-ap-da*
[. . .] *la i-na-ad-di-nu-ši-na-ši* *ma-am-ma-an*

W. G. Lambert, *MIO* 12 (1966), pp. 48 f., pl. 4, 9–10

'[*You have established for*] *me* sobbing night and day,
[*to me*] you (fem. sg.) have allotted perpetual wailing.'
'[. . .] they (fem.) are distraught, in mourning, beating the breast for you (masc. sg.),
[. . .] that nobody gives to them (fem.).'

The first speaker has been lamenting the loss of his paramour. She seems to have withdrawn her favours, for he blames her for his unending grief. She replies that the women mourn him. The text ends with him describing the ruin of the shrine that witnessed their lovemaking. The context would seem to be the death of Dumuzi. The first speaker is Dumuzi, rejected by Ištar and held captive in the Netherworld. His interlocutor is Ištar, whose description of women in mourning refers to the ritual lamentation for the dead Tammuz. The ruined sanctuary is a symbol of their broken love.

48. The pairing of the *allallu*-bird with Dumuzi is no coincidence, for in *Hh* XVIII it is classified as a variety of the 'shepherd-bird':

sipa$^{\text{si-ba.mušen}}$	'shepherd-bird'	=	*re-é-a-um*	'shepherd'
sipa.tur^{mušen}	'lesser shepherd-bird'	=	*al-lal-lu*	
sipa.tir.ra^{mušen}	'wood shepherd-bird'	=	*kub-ši bar-mat*	'speckle-cap'

MSL VIII/2, p. 134, 239–41

The last of these fits well the description *bitrumu* here. The bird's familiar cry (l. 50) is proffered in *Hg* C to explain the second entry:

[sipa.tur^{mušen}] = [*al-la*]*l-lum* = *kap-pa ip-pu-uš* 'it makes a *kappa*-noise'

MSL VIII/2, p. 172, 18

A. Salonen equates the 'shepherd-bird' with the hoopoe (*Vögel*, p. 245), and although he identifies the *allallu*, or 'lesser shepherd-bird', with the Indian roller (ibid., p. 113, following Thompson), one is struck by the similarity of the hoopoe's eponymous cry with *kappī* and *kappa*. No other association of Ištar with this bird is known to me and presumably the myth of their liaison derives from its Sumerian name, which recalls the shepherd Dumuzi. Otherwise the bird of Dumuzi is a kind of pigeon or dove, as noted in a bird-call text (W. G. Lambert, *AnSt* 20 (1970), p. 114, 13): *a-mur-šá-nu*^{mušen} = *iṣ-ṣur* ^{d}dumu.zi *re-'-ú* [. . .]; cf. *wuršān* in modern Iraqi Arabic, J. A. Black and F. N. H. Al-Rawi, *ZA* 77 (1987), p. 125.

The enclitic -*ma* on the verb *tarāmī*, here and in ll. 51, 53, 58 and 64, is understood as emphatic by Foster, *Essays Pope*, p. 35: 'you even fell in love'. There may be other explanations; see the commentary on SB I 117–18.

49. The spelling *tal-te-bir* in MSS Q**a** is not solecistic use of a masculine form but an example of a CVC sign expressing CCV (-*bri*; see K. Deller, *Or* NS 31 (1962), p. 194). Examples in Kuyunjik tablets of Gilgameš are rare; see Chapter 9, the section on Spelling conventions sub (f).

50. I have taken the present tense of *izzaz* (var. *ašib*), and also of *uṭarradūšu* in l. 62, as present continuous, with reference to the habitual behaviour of *allallu*-birds and wolves, conditioned, as it

were, by their ancestors' encounter with Ištar. Both verbs can also be interpreted as indicating result in the past, referring to the individual cases of Ištar's lovers.

51. The variant *migir emūqī* in the Aššur MS does not yield good sense and is presumably corrupt. The lion is commonly associated with Ištar. The goddess can herself be personified as a lion (cf. her epithet *labbatu*, 'lioness'). She sometimes drives a team of seven (e.g. Bēlet-Uruk *ša ṣa-an-da-ti* 7 *la-ab-bu*: Messerschmidt, *MVAG* 1/I, p. 75, iii 14–15; cf. 31–33; Nbn; also *ṣa-lam* ^{d}*iš-tar šá nēša*(ur.maḫ) *ṣi-in-di-tum*: Meissner, *MVAG* 12/III, p. 16, 6–7; NB letter). The lion bears the epithet 'dog of Ištar' (ur.maḫ *kalab*(ur.gi$_7$) ^{d}*iš-tar*: R. Caplice, *Or* NS 34 (1965), p. 108, 6; Namburbi incantation). For a representation of Ištar holding a lion on a leash like a dog, see a NA seal impression drawn by Tessa Rickards in Black and Green, *Gods, Demons and Symbols of Ancient Mesopotamia* (p. 108 middle).

53. The epithet *na-'-id qab-li* is traditional for the horse, being also found in the fable of Ox and Horse (Lambert, *BWL*, pp. 177, 24; 180, 13). The phrase has been parsed as the adjective in the construct state and a genitive noun (e.g., *CAD* N/1, p. 66: *na'id qabli*). However, the variants *qab-l*]*a* and *qab-lum* in MSS **Qa** are accusative singular and speak for a stative phrase like *šaruḫ lasāma* (SB VI 20). The spelling *qab-li* (MSS AO), if to be taken seriously, is therefore for the accusative plural. The ambiguity of *na'id*, from *na'du* A or B, is felicitous, since fame and reliability are both feasible attributes of the battle-horse.

56. The horse's habit of muddying its water with its hooves was proverbial, being also remarked in Proverb Collection 5 no. 37, ed. Alster, *Proverbs*, p. 125: anše.kur.gim ì.⌜ḫur⌝.en ì.nag.zu, 'like the horse you paw as you drink'.

57. The identity of the divine Silili, presumably held to be the mythical ancestor of the horse, is still unknown. The name exhibits the well-known pattern of reduplicated second syllable common in the third and second millennia and is probably foreign, as one would expect given the northern origins of the horse. A name *Si*-NI-NI, which could be read *Si-lí-lí*, belongs to one of several persons listed as 'men of Šimaški' (lú.SU.me) in an Ur III document (see the discussion of I. J. Gelb, *Hurrians and Subarians*, pp. 100, 104, 108; for lú.SU, 'Šimaškian', see P. Steinkeller, 'On the identity of the toponym LÚ.SU(.A)', *JAOS* 108 (1988), pp. 197–202; M. Civil, *NABU* 1996/41). A connection with the goddess ^{d}*sí-li-li-tum*, the vizier of the Divine Rainbow (W. G. Lambert, *RLA* VII, p. 345), does not seem likely.

58. The variant for *nāqida utulla* in MS A_1, TA BU LA, can probably be put down to incompetent editorial work, via a spelling **ú-túl*(PÚ)*-la*. On the double consonant in the spelling *na-qid-da* (MS **a**), see Chapter 9, the section on Spelling conventions sub (e).

59. Von Soden's suggestion that *tumrī* is elliptical for *akal tumrī* or *kamān tumrī* (*AHw*, p. 1370) appears confirmed by the Emar version of SB *tumrī išpukakki*, which reads [*išpukū*]*nikki tumra* (MB Emar$_2$ i 34′). If it is maintained nevertheless that both versions are corrupt it has to be assumed that *akal* or *kamān* dropped out by mistake in a forerunner common to both versions. The variant verb in MS **a**, *šuppukakki* can be parsed as an active II/1 stative, but one wonders whether the scribe is using its consonants only (i.e. *šup* for *išp*). Comparable things can certainly happen in Assyrian tablets with CVC signs in non-initial position.

62. For the implications of the present tense of *uṭarradūšu* see the commentary above, on l. 50.

64. The name Išullānu seems to be a variant of the well-known Ur III and OB personal name Šullānu. The equation of Išullānu and Sumerian Šukalletuda, another gardener who fell foul of Inanna, has been observed in the entry šu.kal.e.tu.da = *šu-l*[*a-*(*a*)]*-nu-um* (*MSL* XIII, p. 118, OB *Nigga* bilingual 124; cf. W. W. Hallo, *RA* 74 (1970), p. 94). The word *šullānu* is a common noun, referring to a person with a physical defect of some sort. The personal name thus falls in to the

category of J. J. Stamm's 'Bezeichnungen nach Körperfehlern' (*Namengebung* §38.1). The omen texts report that the condition was, or could be, present from birth (*Šumma izbu* I 64; U. Jeyes, *OB Extispicy* no. 14, rev. 6′). According to *Šumma ālu* I, the presence of many such people in a city was a bad omen (*CT* 38 4, 71: *sapāḫ*(bir) [^{uru} *āli*], 'scattering [of the city]'). We learn that the condition was a defining characteristic of a person from an OB deed in which a house is described as *ṭēḫi*(da) *bīt*(é) *ib-ni-*^{d}*en-líl šu-la-nu-um* 'adjacent to the property of Ibni-Enlil, the *šullānu*' (*TIM* IV 22, 2). The exact nature of the defect suffered by a *šullānu* is uncertain. The usual suggestion is 'warty', from *šullu*, 'wart'. The ancient vocabularies equate the word with the equally obscure *še'ru* (*MSL* XII, p. 228, iii 31; *CT* 26 43 viii 14). This may or may not be the same *še'ru* that describes pig-like lips in physiognomic omens (*CAD* Š/2, s.v., translates *še'ru* as 'hairy' but 'fleshy' is also possible). More productive evidence is provided by an extract of three lines from a group vocabulary in one of the commentaries on *Sakikku* I 33: gig.til.la = *pe-su-ú*, 'dwarf', *šu-ú-lu*, *šu-ul-la-nu* (ed. George, *RA* 85 (1991), p. 150, 33 a). Note that the Sumerian equivalent of *šullānu* in bilingual *Nigga* is similarly a common noun associated with the physically defective. It can be masculine or feminine according to *MSL* XIII, p. 100, OB *Nigga* 158–9: šu.kal.le.tu.da, ^{f}šu.kal.le.tu.da. In OB Proto-*Lu* 539–43 (see now C. Wilcke in B. Hrouda, *Isin-Išān Baḥrīyāt* III, p. 100), it is listed between ba.za, 'dwarf', and ú.ḫúb, 'deaf' (see further Volk, *Inanna und Šukaletuda*, p. 171). The association with dwarfism and deafness suggests that the *šullānu* suffered a defect more severe than being afflicted with warts.

The significance of the name Išullānu in this episode has been discussed by J.-M. Durand, *RA* 73 (1979), p. 165, fn. 45. He compares Šukalletuda's epithet lú.tur, which he translates 'petit homme, serviteur', with the commentary on *Sakikku* I, where he understands all three Akkadian words to describe people of stunted growth. For this reason he suggests that '*Išullānu* pourrait être l'avatar de *TUR *šullânu*, comme si l'on disait le "nain Petit"'. An objection is that in literary Sumerian lú.tur means 'child, youngster' (e.g. Instructions of Šuruppak 107, Curse of Akkade 10, Nanna-Suen's Journey 320; see further Å. W. Sjöberg, *Mondgott*, pp. 161–2), and that is how it should be taken in Inanna and Šukalletuda, where the context is the gardener's conversation with his father (ll. 139, 177; cf. Volk, *Inanna und Šukaletuda*, p. 191). Nevertheless, the grouping of šu.kal.e.tu.da with ba.za and *šullānu* with *pessû* in the vocabularies remains suggestive. None of the ancient evidence contradicts the possibility that *šullānu* refers to people of stunted growth. The story narrated in the following lines is surely aetiological, like the five more briefly worded episodes that precede it, and thus will describe how the subject, by courtesy of Ištar, ended up in his present plight. Though the ultimate fate of Išullānu's counterpart, Šukalletuda, is still lost in a lacuna, there is some suspicion that his punishment involved a reduction in size (l. 254): šu.k[al.le].tu.da dili.ni im.a im.tur.tur.re, 'in the wind she makes Šukalletuda, him alone, small' (cf. J. Bottéro and S. N. Kramer, *Lorsque les dieux faisaient l'homme*, p. 268; Volk, *Inanna und Šukaletuda*, p. 205, is not certain that this is to be taken literally). If Durand's idea is right it would seem that the stories of Išullānu and Šukalletuda explained how dwarfs came to be so short. See further the commentary on *dallalu*, l. 76 below.

65. The variant for *šugurrâ* offered by the Aššur MS cannot be the synonym *tuḫalla*, as suggested by von Soden (*AHw*, p. 1366). Frankena's suggestion, that l. 65 is a repetition of l. 59, looks improbable too. Perhaps *šugrû* had a by-form *tug*(*a*)*rû*.

67. For the acquisitive nuance of the expression *īna našû* see the commentary above, on SB VI 6.

68. The unnecessary epenthetic vowel in *kiššūtaki* is a mark of literary style; see the section on language in Chapter 9. The feminine suffix on this word is very odd. Possibly Ištar is taunting the reluctant Išullānu as not man enough to take her. Otherwise *-ka* has turned to *-ki* by crasis in the presence of *ī nīkul* (so Abusch, *History of Religions* 26 (1986), p. 167, fn. 61). The orthography

na-kul for *nīkul* is remarkable in a manuscript from Aššur (**a**). A predilection for the vowel /a/ over /i/ is found in NA copies of literary texts from Sultantepe, e.g. MS **e** of Tablet VIII (from which similar spellings are collected in Chapter 7), but see also the commentary on *ḫurdatna* in the next line. Foster considered that 'the use of the "royal plural" seems to satirize the epithet "princess" applied to Ishtar throughout this episode' (*Essays Pope*, p. 35). However, the use of the plural in intimate amatory contexts is widespread, as shown by J. Goodnick Westenholz in her edition of an OB love song in which a woman voices similar explicit sexual advances (*Studies Reiner*, p. 417, citing also Sumerian parallels from the Inanna-Dumuzi literature). She suggests that the plural may imply shared enjoyment. On this subject see further Sefati, *Love Songs*, pp. 83–4, and S. M. Paul, 'The "plural of ecstasy" in Mesopotamian and biblical love poetry', *Studies Greenfield*, pp. 585–97.

68 ff. In a footnote to his translation Labat pointed out that *akālu* in Ištar's speech is repeated, with different nuance, in Išullānu's, and that *luput* is probably echoed in *elpētu*: 'I. feint de ne pas comprendre' (*Les religions*, p. 183, fn. 7; also Bottéro, *Lorsque les dieux*, p. 274).

69. This line is one of only two passages of Gilgameš quoted in the extant commentaries (the other is SB I 102–3). Illustrating the use of the rare word *ḫurdatu* in a compendium of treatments of women in labour (a copy survives as *BAM* 248 ii 30), a LB medical commentary from Nippur reads *qa-at-ka šu-ta-am-ṣa-am-ma lu-pu-ut ḫur-da-at-na* (M. Civil, *JNES* 33 (1974), p. 332, 41; cf. A. Cavigneaux, *Aula Or* 5 (1987), p. 255). This brings the number of variant forms of the first verb to three. I see *liš-te-ṣa-am-ma*, the least felicitous of the three, as the result of editorial misinterpretation of an erstwhile orthography *šú-tam-ṣa-am-ma*, though use of the sign *šú* in anything other than final position is exceedingly rare (according to Foster, collation by P. Machinist and C. B. F. Walker suggested that MS A actually reads *šú-te-ṣa-am-ma*, but *liš* and *šú* can look very alike in some Kuyunjik scripts and to my eyes *liš* remains preferable). The form *šutamṣâmma* preserved in the commentary is probably the original. Since the imperative takes a direct object here this will be a first attestation of the III/3 stem in the impt. (**šutaṣṣi*), not of the III/2 (impt. **šutēṣi*) exhibited in the awkward precative *lištēṣâmma*. Given Ištar's appetite for sex, the iterative stem can be seen as appropriate, though the Aššur MS uses the simple III/1 stem. Regarding *ḫurdatna*, von Soden attributes the 1st pl. poss. suffix *-na* to N/LB dialect (*GAG*[3] §42j–k, n. 9). Its appearance in an Aššur MS, as well as in the medical commentary, shows that the orthography *ḫur-da-at-na* entered the copying tradition quite early in the first millennium. Its presence alongside *nākul* in the previous line might be evidence for a provincial variant pronominal suffix and prefix, *na-* and *-na* for *ni-* and *-ni*. If so, Ištar appears to Išullānu as a country girl, using his kind of language.

Thorkild Jacobsen supposed that this line is an example of an ancient practice of the touching genitals in oath-swearing that he maintained is found in Sumerian texts and, in very special contexts, in Genesis: 'Ishtar demands it of Gilgamesh (*sic*!) as a binding acceptance of her offer of marriage' (Jacobsen, *Harps*, p. 168, fn. 2). It seems to me that Ištar's approach to the gardener Išullānu is impelled not by thoughts of marriage but by a simple desire for sexual gratification. The phrase *ḫurdatam lapātum* is standard sexual language. A similar invitation is issued in an OB love song: *bi-la-ma šu-me-li-ik lu-pi-it-ma ḫu-ur-da-at-ni*, 'put your left hand out and stroke our vulva' (J. Goodnick Westenholz, *Studies Reiner*, p. 422, i 13′). From an orgiastic OB cult song of Ištar comes the corresponding proposal from a male participant: *al-ki lu-la-ap-pi-it ḫur-da-at-ki*, 'come, let me stroke your vulva!' (W. von Soden, *Or* NS 60 (1991), p. 340, 11). Some have understood *qātu* in our line as a euphemism for penis, like Hebrew *yad* (for a history of the literature see Paul, *Studies Greenfield*, p. 593, fn. 30).

72. For Foster 'the archaic verb form [*tēpâ*] suggests a proverbial expression, here used perhaps with the obstinate recourse to clichés often thought characteristic of the peasant in literature'

(*Essays Pope*, p. 35). Alternatively, the 3rd fem. sg. prefix *ta-* might actually have been a provincial survival and so itself a device for marking Išullānu as a country bumpkin.

73. A. L. Oppenheim saw double meaning in the phrase *akal pīšāti u errēti* (*Or* NS 17 (1948), p. 37), and compared *errētu* with *erēru* (which he there translated 'to char, burn') and *arāru*, 'to curse'. The verb *erēru* and its adjective, *erru*, are now known to refer to the spoiling of grain in store (see *CAD* A/2, p. 238), and such grain will naturally make unpleasant bread. The first word provokes comparison with *bīšu*, 'smelly', which is used of other spoiled foodstuffs (dates, beer, garlic, fish: see the dictionaries).

75. The phrase *annâ qabâšu* and its variants *annâ qabā/qabê Ištar* (ll. 113 and 154) are hallmarks of SB Tablet VI. They appear in no other part of the epic and perhaps offer a hint that this narrative (or a forerunner of it) was composed independently. On reversed nouns and adjectives see Chapter 9, the section on Language and style sub (iii–v).

76. The word *dallalu* (or *dallālu*) is a hapax legomenon that has attracted several interpretations. *CAD* goes for 'frog' (D, p. 52) and 'toad' (M, p. 50), drawing attention to the river-dwelling animal *dālilu*. Thompson suggested 'spider' and Oppenheim ingeniously developed the image by reference to the spider-like water-wheel, at the centre of which he supposed it was Išullānu's fate to be trapped (*Or* NS 17, p. 37). Schott proposed 'mole' (*ZA* 42 (1934), p. 121). The aim of these translations was to provide the garden with a pest, just as earlier the shepherd's flock was provided with an enemy by its master's metamorphosis. A different train of thought led to 'scarecrow' (see Tournay and Shaffer, who are undecided: 'épouvantail/crapaud . . . araignée'). Von Soden, *AHw*, p. 154, prefers to associate the word with a root √*dll*, from which he derives a I/1 verbal adj. *dallu*, 'puny, stunted', and a **parras* stem adj. *dallalu*, 'very puny', or as a noun 'Verkümmerter', i.e. a person stunted in growth; note the equation tur.tur, 'tiny' = *dal-lu* in *CT* 11 36, 27 = *Diri* I 265. Westenholz accordingly translates 'dvaerg(?)' and, in view of our expectations of an aetiology of dwarfism (above, on l. 64), this is the view taken here.

78. Until the end of this line is recovered it is not possible to be sure of the syntax. The simplest analysis is to read *ēlû miḫḫi* and *ārid dalu*[. . .], i.e. active participles qualified by genitive nouns. The force is one of potentiality, as in a line of the Yale tablet, *mannu ibrī ēlû šamā'ī* (OB III 140), and a more literal rendering would be '(he is) not one who can go up to the *miḫḫu*, not one who can go down to the *dalu*[. . .]'; cf. Speiser: 'he cannot go up . . . nor can he come down . . .'; Foster: 'he can't get over a conduit or out of a bucket(?)'. Other translators take *e-lu-ú* and *a-rid* as finite verbs governed by *mi-iḫ-ḫa* and *da-lu*[. . .] respectively (see *CAD* D: 'the . . . does not come up, his water bucket does not descend'; *CAD* M similarly; *AHw*, p. 1550, s.v. *dalû*: '*ul arid* (ist unten) *da-l*[*u*!-*u*]'). However, the single attestation known to me of *arādu* in the stative appears to mean not 'in lowered position' but something like 'hanging vertically': DIŠ *awīlum*(lú) *ṣú-ba-at-su wa-ri-id* (F. Köcher and A. L. Oppenheim, *AfO* 18 (1957–8), p. 65, ii 6). The precise meaning of *mi-iḫ-ḫa* remains uncertain but, as has been observed before, the context is certainly irrigation. The word should be connected with the verb *maḫāḫu*, 'to soak, wet'. Though usually the process *maḫāḫu* describes the soaking of small items, such as mud and magic figurines, this verb is indeed now known in irrigation (see M. A. Powell, *Aula Or* 9 (1991), pp. 162–3). It describes the first of three activities performed by water-drawers ([lú]*dālû*) in an OB document (*TCL* I 174, 6; the other activities are *pašāru*, lit. 'loosening', and *šullušu*, 'going over a third time'). Oppenheim boldly claimed that '*miḫḫu* denotes the conduit which leads the water pouring from the buckets' of a water-wheel (*Or* NS 17, p. 37, fn. 4). Volk relates *miḫḫu* to another part of the irrigation engine. An obscure passage of Inanna and Šukalletuda reads (ll. 70–1 // 86–7) lag an.šè sìg.ge.da ki.šè tuš.ù.da / lag ki.šè sìg.ge.da an.šè è.dè.da, 'to thrust the clod into the sky, to seat it on the earth, to thrust the clod to the earth, to send it out into the sky'. Volk

supposes the context to be irrigation by shadoof, and identifies the 'clod' with a counterweight of mud fixed at other end of the pole from the bucket and the *miḫḫu* of our passage as the same (Volk, *Inanna und Šukaletuda*, pp. 57, fn. 158–9). This remains very speculative. The word *da-l*[*u*(-) . . .] is usually read as *dālu*, *dalû*, 'bucket' (with W. F. Albright, *RA* 16 (1919), p. 180), but until the end of the line is recovered it may be better to reserve judgement. Whatever the exact meaning of the line's technical vocabulary, it is apparent that the fate of Išullānu rendered him incapable of reaching the apparatus with which a gardener customarily irrigated his date palms.

82–3. This couplet is a variation on a standard literary cliché (see K. Hecker, *Untersuchungen zur akkadischen Epik*, pp. 178–9). Other examples are:

> *il-lik* ^{d}*šamaš*(utu) *i-na pa-an* (var. ^{d}*pap-sukkal ana* igi) ^{d}*sîn*(30) *abi*(ad)-*šú i-ba*[*k-ki*]
> *i-na pa-an* ^{d}*é-a šarri*(lugal) *il-la-ka di-ma-a-*[*šú*]
>
> *CT* 15 46 rev. 3–4: Descent of Ištar, var. from *KAR* 1 rev. 3
>
> Šamaš (*or* Papsukkal) went weeping before Sîn, his father,
> [his] tears flowing before King Ea.
>
> *il-lik tu-ul-tu ana pān*(igi) ^{d}*šamaš*(utu) *i-bak-ki*
> *ana pān*(igi) ^{d}*é-a il-la-ka di-ma-a-ša*
>
> *CT* 17 50, 7–8: Worm and Toothache
>
> The worm went weeping before Šamaš,
> its tears flowing before Ea.

Slightly different versions are:

> . . . *iš-ši re-ši-šú ana pān*(igi) ^{d}*šamaš*(utu) *i-bak-ki*
> *ana pān*(igi) *šá-ru-ri šá* ^{d}*šamaš*(utu) *illakū*(gin)^{ku} *di-ma-a-šú*
>
> Lambert, *BWL*, p. 200, 19–20: Fable of the Fox
>
> . . . He lifted up his head, weeping before Šamaš,
> his tears flowing before the rays of the sun.
>
> *iššì rēšīšu Enkīdu ana pān Šamaš inambi* (var. *ibakki*)
> *ana pān šarūrī ša Šamaš illakā dīmāšu*
>
> SB Gilgameš VII 91–2, var. from MB Ur 2–3
>
> Enkidu lifted up his head, lamenting (var. weeping) before Šamaš,
> his tears flowing before the rays of the sun.
>
> *ṣēru*(muš) *i-t*[*a-t*]*i-il-ma i-bak-ki*
> *a-na pa-an* ^{d}*šamaš*(utu) *i*[*l-la-ka di-ma-a-šu*]
>
> SB Etana II 59–60; cf. OB Etana I/C 36–7
>
> The snake lay weeping,
> [his tears flowing] before Šamaš.

85. For Frankena the Aššur MS's *in-din-na-a* represented a mistake for the Kuyunjik manuscripts' *undennâ* (<*umtannâ*), but if need be it can be taken as a legitimate variant, i.e. I/3 preterite (<*imtannâ*). Contra Foster, *Essays Pope*, p. 36, *undennâ* is a perfectly good MB form, exhibiting /nd/ and /e/ as in e.g. *un-de-ši-ir* < *umtaššir* (cf. *GAG*^{3} §31f; J. Aro, *StOr* 20 (1955), pp. 40–9); the change

from /a/ to /e/ in a closed syllable before /i/ remains valid even when the /i/ disappears through contraction (e.g. *limellâ* < **limalli'ā*).

89. The exclamation that opens Anu's speech is also found in OB Atram-ḫasīs III iv 5, where *a-bu-ma-an* expresses Nintu's grief at the effect of the deluge. Here *a-ba* may thus be an expression of a father's sympathy with an aggrieved daughter. However, it may also have a contrastive function ('but on the other hand'), as perhaps in the OB trial document Lutz, *UCP* IX/6, p. 381, 12 (A. Westenholz, private communication).

90–1. Like MS Q, MB Emar$_2$ apparently has a one-line version of this couplet: *u* [*Gilgāmeš errēt*]*īki pīš*[*ē*]*tīki ime*[*nnu*/*i*] (ii 3′–4′).

94. In common with most other recent translators I prefer *CAD*'s *bīnamma*, 'give me, please' (B, pp. 216–17, already in early NB), to von Soden's *binamma*, 'schaff mir' (for an Aramaic etymology of *bīna*, 'give me', see von Soden, *Or* NS 37 (1968), p. 269). The fiery bull of heaven was already present in heaven, as a constellation, when Ištar picked it as the perfect weapon with which to pursue her quarrel with Gilgameš.

95. As Frankena saw, the traces on MS **a** do not appear to allow simply *lu-nir i*[*n*]*a šub-ti-šú*. Nor do they allow *lu-nàr-r*[*i-iṭ* (or *riṭ*)] (*CAD* N/1, p. 349). If correctly read, the word *lu-nir-ru* is ventive; cf. Chapter 9, the section on Spelling conventions sub (v).

96. Note the Assyrian present *taddana* in MS **a**. The Kuyunjik MSS are not preserved at this point. The Assyrian form fails to provide a penultimate stress but so would Babylonian *tanaddina*. For other Assyrianisms in the SB text see Chapter 9, the section on Language and style sub (viii).

97. The object of Ištar's proposed strike is clearly the Netherworld, for by smashing it she expects to release the dead from the gates that keep them safely locked away below. Hence the emendation of MS Q to provide a rare synonym of *erṣetu*. The trace preserved after *adi* in MS Q and the space available after it suggest that this source had more than *adi šubtīšu*. It may be that, like the parallel passages of Ištar's Descent, it offered a variant text.

98. The traces present in MS Q$_3$ seem not to represent the second word. Possible readings are [*a-ša-ak-k*]*a-a*[*n*, an unlikely spelling in a Kuyunjik manuscript, and, with transposed words, [*a-šak-kan ana š*]*aplā*[*ti*(k]i.t[a)^{meš} *sa-pa-nam*? x x x x x].

100. The final vowel on the verb can be explained as an orthographic or a morphological phenomenon. If the former, it is to be disregarded as superfluous (CV for C, *ušam'ad*); for comparable spellings in Assyrian manuscripts see Chapter 9, the section on Spelling sub (w). If the latter, it is to be parsed as a ventive, on which see the same section sub (v).

104. The Aššur MS's variant *lupaḫḫir* is another Assyrian form (see l. 96) but not a good one, for it exhibits the wrong gender.

112. The spacing of the signs on the line suggests that very little is missing at the end of MS **a**; the independent pronoun that terminates the line in MS A was evidently not present at Aššur. I am uncertain about what verb √*n'x* is best restored in MS **a**. The verb *na'ādu* is construed with *ana*, but 'I will draw his attention to the bull's fury' is hardly compelling. Nor are derivations from *na'āru*, 'to roar', and *nê'u*, 'to turn aside'. The damaged verb must describe the means by which Ištar will avenge her humiliation. This has already been articulated as his death, *lunirru* in l. 95. The II/1 stem of the same verb is very rare but occurs in uncontracted Assyrian form in the version of SB VIII 22 from Sultantepe (MS **e**: *nu-na-er*). The rarity of the stem is not the only drawback, however. If one reads *ú-na-'-*[*ár-šú*] it must be assumed that the scribe has written *a-na* for *i-na*, 'I will slay [him] by means of the bull's fury'.

113. The construct state *qabā* (MS **a**, Aššur) is not current usage in Babylonia after the third millennium (see *GAG*^{3} §64i) but is good second-millennium Assyrian. In the parallel l. 154 the spelling

qa-bé-e in MS O bears witness to the Babylonian form of the word. I presume *qabā* represents a survival from an Assyrianizing manuscript of the late second millennium. In a manuscript from Aššur this is not so surprising. See also the commentary above, on SB VI 75.

118. There is no need to emend to the common formulation 7 ⟨*ina*⟩ *ammati*(1.kùš). The orthographic style *sebe*(7) *ammat*(1.kùš) is exactly paralleled in an inscription of Aššurbanipal (V *R* 1 i 46, ed. Streck, *Asb.*, p. 6: 5 *ammat*(1.kùš) *še'u*?(še-*am*) *iš-qu ina ab-sín-ni-šú*, 'barley grew five cubits tall in its furrows').

119. The circumlocution X-*šu ša* Y, meaning X of Y, first appears in Old Babylonian (see *GAG*³ §138j). It is another stylistic feature that is confined in the Gilgameš epic to SB Tablet VI, where it also appears in l. 132 and 134: *dunnašu ša alê*.

120. The spelling *im-ta-qu-tu*₄ represents *imtaqqutū*, which I would parse as a I/3 stem of serial action, (see *GAG*³ §91f): the men fell into the hole one by one. When an individual falls into a hole, as Enkidu does in l. 124, the I/3 stem is not used.

124. The spelling of the verb in MS **a** represents a mixed Babylonian-NA dialect form, *ittaqut* (see *GAG*³ §31g).

125. Repeated checking confirmed that the traces of *e-l*[*i*? are definitely so and cannot be read *iṣ-ṣ*[*a-bat*. The line as given in MS **a** was evidently rather shorter than the better-preserved variant of MS A. Although MS O is broken off too soon for us to be sure from its text whether it followed MS **a** rather than MS A, the spacing of the existing signs confirms it as a witness of the shorter line.

126. The traces on MS **a** do not allow a reading ⌈*ṣe-ri-šu*⌉.

127. The restoration favoured by recent translators is [*ka*]-*bu-us-su* [*id-di*] (or some such verb), which goes back to '[warf er] seinen Mist' (von Soden, *ZA* 53, p. 226); cf. 'he [flicked?] his excrement' (*CAD* K, p. 29). This is, however, too uncertain to become so established. If dung is wanted, [*ru*]-*bu-us-su* is also possible (Westenholz), but many other restorations might be put forward (e.g. [*il*]-*pu-us-su*, as Labat: 'le [frappa]', Hecker: 'traf er ihn').

131. The recovery of this line depends on MB Emar₁ iii 5′: [*kī*] *nippala kamrā*[*ti nišī*]. With *kamru* used of a crowd, compare the standard line *eṭlūtu uktammarū elīšu* (SB I 254, 282, II 106).

132. For the possessive construction used here see the commentary above, on l. 119.

133. It seems difficult to reconstruct the text in such a way that *alammadu* can be parsed as subjunctive. It is not clear whether the ending is superfluous or ventive (see above, on the verb in l. 100).

135. By comparison with l. 141 one expects the verb to be from *ṣâdu* (MS O) or *etēqu* (MS **a**); restore perhaps *e-t*[*e-né-et-tiq*], 'I shall keep passing'?

136–40. The restorations follow the parallel lines of narrative, 142–6.

137, 143. The last word is presumed to be the first recovered instance in Babylonian of the word entered in the dictionaries as *sīqu* (*AHw sīqu* II 'Oberschenkel, Schoß'; *CAD* S *sīqu* 'lap, thigh'), previously found only in Middle and Neo-Assyrian. Either there exists a doublet *sīqu* : *siqqu* or the Assyrian spellings, customarily defective, disguise the double consonant. Compare also *sāqu*, a paired body part cognate with Arabic *sāq*, 'leg below the knee', 'hock' (for drawing my attention to the Arabic word I am grateful to my colleague Muhammad Abdel Haleem). The root of these words is perhaps √*s'q* > Akk. *si'āqum*, 'to be narrow', the leg below the knee being narrower than above. The use of *sīqu*/*siqqu* and *sāqu* for 'lap' is analogous with the much more common use of *birku*, 'knee', in the same meaning.

138, 144. The last word is perhaps some part of *raḫāṣu*, 'to trample, stamp, kick'.

140, 146. The word *naplaku*, here clearly a part of the anatomy of the Bull of Heaven, is taken as a **napras* stem formation, which as a *nomen loci* indicates the place on the ox where the butcher places his knife in slaughtering the animal (*palāk*/*qu*). Because of the lexical entry restored as [gír.gud].⌈gaz⌉.zabar = *nap-la-qu* (var. *-ku*; *MSL* VII, p. 162, *Hh* XII 53), and the gloss *pat-ru šá* lú*ṭābiḫi*(gír.lá) in *Hg* (ibid., p. 172, d), the dictionaries have translated the word as 'butchering knife'. Though incontestable elsewhere, this is not a possible rendition in our context, where the knife is simply *patru*. The only other attestation of the word outside lexical texts can be interpreted either way: [*k*]*i-ma le-e šá ina nap-la-qu pal-qu i-ram-mu-um*, 'he bellows like a steer stuck with the butcher's knife *or* in the slaughter-spot' (W. von Soden, *ZA* 61 (1971), p. 52, 57: hymn to Nabû). It remains odd that Enkidu instructs Gilgameš to strike not at the 'slaughter-spot' itself, but between this point and the yoke of the horns.

147. The line is short and MS A combines it with the following one. The terseness is perhaps intentional, to indicate a pause at the start of a new episode or development in the narrative (cf. l. 168, and half-lines in formulae that introduce direct speech).

150. I consider a reading *aḫḫū*(šeš)meš less preferable: though in adopting Enkidu Ninsun made him Gilgameš's brother, nowhere in the Babylonian epic is the specific word *aḫu* used to describe their relationship. The orthography *áḫa-meš* is also found in A. Pohl, *Rechtsurkunden* I 3, 24 (house sale from Uruk, Nbk).

152. The idiom *ḫuppa* (var. *ḫuppī*) *šaḫāṭu*, 'to jump the *ḫuppu* (var. *ḫuppu*s)', is to be connected with *ḫuppa izuzzu*, which describes the stance of various deities in the 'Göttertypentext': see F. Köcher, *MIO* 1 (1953), pp. 64, 15 (Damu); 80, 22 (Niziqtu); 82, 35 (Tiruru). Damu is known as the object of mourning and the name of the demon Niziqtu, 'Grief, Anguish', speaks for itself. The causative stem appears in a bilingual lament to the mother goddess (C. Frank, *ZA* 40 (1931), p. 87, g–h; *CAD* Ḫ, p. 239): ká li.bi.ir.ra.ka ḫub.da.a[n].mu ga.an.gub // *ina ba-ab gal-le-e ḫu-up-pa lu-uš-*[*ziz*], 'at the gate of the *gallû* demon I will place (i.e. adopt?) the *ḫuppu* stance'. There, too, the context is mourning. Its inclusion among words for weeping, as one of several Akkadian equivalents of Sumerian ér (*MSL* XIV, p. 205, *A* I/1 141), confirms that *ḫuppu* is an attitude of mourning. In our passage Ištar is griefstricken for her bull. The bilingual lament suggests that this *ḫuppu* is connected with Sumerian ḫub. This word, also written ḫúb and ḫu.ub, is the nominal element in several compound verbs that denote running or galloping of four-legged animals, e.g., ḫúb—šú.šú of gazelles (*SBH* 50 a rev. 22–3: ḫúb mi.ni.íb.šú.[šú] // *il-ta-na-as-*[*su-ma*]) and wild donkeys (Šulgi A 72), ḫúb—sar.sar of mountain goats (Šulgi A 48). Demons also run in this manner: ḫu.ub mu.un.SAR.SAR.e.ne // *il-ta-na-as-su-mu* (*CT* 16 44, 98–9: incantation). Cf. further the lexical entry *MSL* IV, p. 28, Emesal Voc. III 15: ḫúb.zé = ḫub.duSAR = *la-sa-a-mu*, 'to run' (also XVII, pp. 154, *Antagal* III 115; 209, *Antagal* E i 10′). What these verbs have in common with Akkadian *ḫuppa šaḫāṭu* as a gesture of mourning is presumably a vigorous motion of the feet. A. D. Kilmer came to a similar conclusion in *Finkelstein Mem. Vol.*, p. 133: '*ḫuppu* = stamping of feet or running about (excitedly)'.

153. In the version of the line that includes it (MSS AO), the word written *al-lu-ú* is hardly the demonstrative *allû* (so *CAD* s.v.). An expression of grief at the bull's slaughter (cf. *AHw*, p. 37, 'wehe!'), though understandable in itself, would not be strong enough to provoke Enkidu's very violent and abusive reaction. What is needed is an exclamation that brings down a curse upon the object of Ištar's anger, i.e. Gilgameš, for doing what he has done. In this analysis the pronoun *ša* in MSS AO governs two relative clauses not one. Corroboration may come from the last word, which ought to be trisyllabic if it is not to upset the metrical requirement of penultimate stress. The spelling *id-duk* for subjunctive *iddūku* exhibits the principle that CVC signs can represent bisyllables, well known in NA writing.

154. MS A's *qa-bi* is a previously unnoticed construct state of an accusative infinitive of the **parīs* type (see *GAG*3 §87k; W. R. Mayer, *Or* NS 59 (1990), p. 452); see below, the discussion of *nasīḫ* in SB XII 145.

155. On MS **a** I do not see enough room for *iš-lu-u*[*ḫ*. The suggestion offered in the apparatus, *iš-lu-'*, supposes a variant (Assyrian?) form *šalā'u* for the verb *šalāḫu*, 'to tear off', perhaps by analogy with Bab. *salāḫu* : Ass. *salā'u*. An alternative analysis would derive it from the verb *šalû*, 'to hurl' (missiles), in which case the word would anticipate the action at the end of the line. The final verb is itself interesting, for the three extant MSS offer three different words, *iddi*, *issuk* and *iṣli*. MS O's *iṣli* is particularly striking, since the verb *ṣalā'u* is not found outside Assyrian; on Assyrianisms in the SB epic see Chapter 9, the section on Language and style sub (viii). The *imittu* (Sum. zag.dib) of a bull is the top portion of the leg, though whether the shoulder or the haunch seems unclear. Since it was a choice cut I assume it was from the rear leg. S. Parpola has suggested, on the basis of a supposed analogy with a bullfight that marked castration rites among the Galli of Anatolia, that the word is otherwise *imittu*, 'right hand', and 'clearly a "metaphor" for "penis"' (*SAA* IX, pp. xcvi–xcvii). It would certainly be more obviously an insult for Enkidu to toss the bull's penis at Ištar, and such an interpretation of *imittu* was first offered by George Smith in 1875, who intuitively translated the word as 'member' (*Assyrian Discoveries*, p. 174). However, the following line, in which Enkidu states a desire to do the same to the goddess, then becomes a problem, for he cannot castrate her. Though Ištar was bearded in some manifestations, in Uruk she was firmly of the female sex (on the gender of Ištar see W. Heimpel, *Syro-Mesopotamian Studies* 4/3 (1982), pp. 12–14; B. Groneberg, 'Die sumerisch-akkadische Inanna/Ištar: Hermaphroditos?', *WO* 17 (1986), pp. 25–46). However male she may have been elsewhere, the goddess of the Gilgameš epic is not likely to have had male genitals.

156. MS Q appears to start this line quite differently, though nothing is preserved beyond the first sign.

156–7. According to *GAG*[3] §152b.f, the force of *lū* and the preterite is either a matter of emphasis or one of wishful thinking ('hätte (tun) sollen'), both in the past (it also occurs in the hypothetical past, as in the Yale tablet, OB III 148: *šumma amtaqut šumī lū ušziz*, 'If I shall have fallen, I should have made my name'). The conventional rendering of *lū akšudki* in our line as a conditional is justified on the grounds of juxtaposition of clauses. A comparable passage is SB VII 47–55: *lū īde* . . . *lū aššī* . . . *lū ušarkiba*, etc., 'Had I known . . . , I would have picked up . . . , I would have shipped by raft . . .'

158. Uruk is 'the city of courtesans, prostitutes and harlots' in Erra IV 52 (*āl ke-ez-re-e-*[*ti*] *šam-ḫa-a-tú ù ḫa-ri-ma-*[*ti*]). For *kezertu*-women see Chapter 10, the introduction to SB Tablet I, on ll. 245 ff.

159. The spelling *iš-ku-nu* (MS **a**) is for *iškun* (CV for VC or C); on this orthographic feature in Assyrian manuscripts of Gilgameš see Chapter 9, the section on Spelling sub (a) and (w).

163. The problematical variant *šin-nu ú-ba-né-e* appears to be a corruption of an original *šin-nu-ú ma-né-e*, 'two minas each' (note the indecision of *AHw*, p. 1243: *š. manê*!, against p. 1302: 'je zwei Finger'; von Soden, *Reclam*[4], p. 60: '*zwei Zoll*'; cf. D. O. Edzard, 'Zahlen, Zählen und Messen im Gilgameš-Epos', in W. Gross et al. (eds.), *Texte, Methode und Grammatik*, pp. 62–3). However, while the meaning of *taḫbâtu* remains so uncertain it would be unwise to write the linear measurement off completely. The variant spellings *ta-ḫa-ba-tu-ši-na* (MS A) and *ta-aḫ-ba-tu-ši-na* (MS O) can be explained by reference to the principle in Neo-Assyrian writing that CV signs can stand for VC (see above on SB VI 159).

165. For Lugalbanda as the god of Gilgameš see OB III 271 and note.

168. The line is perhaps standard, for it occurs also in MB Bog$_2$ i 5: *iṣṣabtūni illakūni*, in the context of the heroes' march to the Cedar Forest. Note also the same verbs in sequence, but without the ventive suffixes, in SB III 19–20.

171. The variant *mu-ṭàp-pi-la* in MS O looks very out of place: in describing the people who

chorus the triumph of the returning heroes, it is obviously a variant inferior to the serving girls. Possibly it represents an intrusion of the same word from l. 177.

176–7. This couplet is poorly preserved but not beyond hope. The plural pronominal suffix on *uzzīni* demands a subject in the first person, which means that at least the first line is direct speech, and probably the second too. The vital question is: who is speaking? For von Soden, the end of l. 177 read *mu-ṭib l[ìb-bi] ul i-šu* (*ZA* 53, p. 227), and the line referred to Ištar's loss of prestige: she has no one in the street to please her. However, the traces visible before *ul* on MS A discount both *lib-b*]*i* and š]à.

TABLET VII

1. On the spelling *mi-in-na-ma* (MS Q) for *mīnâma* (or *mīnamma*) see Chapter 9, the section on Spelling conventions sub (b).

27. Haupt's copy of the traces suggests [*á*]*š-*⌜*šú ki-i*⌝ x[. . .], but the reading is not secure.

38. The conventional restoration is *kī* [*amēli*], 'like a man'.

39. This line begins Enkidu's speech. Some commentators view ll. 39–40 as narrative and l. 41 as the first line of direct speech. The absence there of any vocative makes such a reading less likely. Outside plant lists and two synonym lists (*Malku* II 159 // *CT* 18 4 iv 12: *ḫal-bu* = *qi-iš-tum*), the word *ḫalbu* only appears with reference to the forest of Lebanon, both elsewhere in the Gilgameš Epic (SB IV 197; note that the reference given in the dictionaries to *ḫal-bu* in the Yale tablet is a misreading of *wa-aš-bu* in OB III 101) and in the Divine Directory of Aššur (Menzel, *Tempel* II no. 64, 116: ᵈiškur (*šá*) *ḫal-bi*). In the latter text 'Adad of the Woodland' is presumably the Levantine storm god who resided on the Lebanon range, and who is known to Mesopotamian sources, including OB Gilgameš III, as Wēr (later Mēr). The trace of [*in*]*a* was seen by Haupt but not by Thompson. The presence of this preposition suggests an infinitive phrase, perhaps *ina lā ḫa-*[*sa-si-ki*], 'in your insentient state'.

40. The reading of the first word in this difficult line is open to other interpretations. Von Soden reads *ba-lat*, 'without' (*Reclam*⁴, p. 63; cf. *AHw*, p. 1546, s.v. *balûtu*), but this word is otherwise restricted to the Old and Neo-Assyrian dialects. Bottéro emends to obtain sense: '"Il n'y a pas de conscience ⟨en⟩ toi!" Le copiste a oublié un mot et employé, au lieu du pronom de la deuxième personne, celui de la troisième' (p. 136 with fn. 1). Parpola reads *ba-laṭ uz-ni-šá* (meaning?). Reading *bašât uznī* (sg.) Enkidu contrasts his own consciousness with the door's obvious lack of it. At the end perhaps restore *i-ba-áš-šu-*[*ki ka-a-ši*].

41. The phrase *ana* 20 *bēr* also occurs in SB XI 315. In both lines it may be an idiomatic expression for 'here, there and everywhere' (A. Westenholz). From this line (acc. sg. *i-ṣa-ki*) and l. 43 (nom. sg. *iṣ-ṣu-ki*) it appears that the singular noun *iṣu* or *iṣṣu* exhibits triptotic declension before possessive suffixes: *i*(*ṣ*)*ṣūki*, *i*(*ṣ*)*ṣāki*, *i*(*ṣ*)*ṣīki* (other examples in the dictionaries of this word with suffixed pronouns are not diagnostic, being genitive or plural). In this respect it follows the well-known pattern of three other bi-radical nouns, *aḫu*, *abu* and *emu* (see *GAG*³ §65h).

43. The verb *īšu* is unarguably singular, so the restoration offered by *CAD* A/1, p. 211: *iṣ-ṣu qí-*[*iš-ti*], 'the trees of the forest', is unconvincing. On *iṣu* or *iṣṣu* with pronominal suffixes see the note on l. 41. The use of *aḫû*, normally 'stranger, foreigner; enemy', to denote a rival is unparalleled but understandable.

44–5. See the parallel, SB V 295–6.

46. That the word after *elāniš* is from *retû*, the standard verb for hanging a door in a gateway, seems inescapable. I am unable to decipher the end of the line satisfactorily. Perhaps the text is a corruption of *artēki kâši*.

47. The restoration of *gimilki* is the suggestion of B. Landsberger (*RA* 62 (1968), p. 103, fn. 22).

48. The line is apparently given in the Kuyunjik MS as *u annû dumu*[*qki*], which is a little light for a poetic line. Though one does not usually prefer a Sultantepe reading to a Kuyunjik reading, probably the sign *ù* on MS L is a simple mistake for KIMIN, which would then stand for *lū īde dalat kī*.

53. The mythical Anzû bird was widely used as an apotropaic figure stationed at gates and elsewhere in temples. To the attestations cited in *CAD* A/2, p. 155, add Frayne, *RIME* 3/II, p. 135 (in E-meslam at Kutha; Šulgi), and George, *RA* 82 (1988), p. 144, 42′ (in E-sagil at Babylon; Nebuchadnezzar II) and p. 151; see also Wiggermann, *Protective Spirits*, p. 159. This function of Anzû incidentally explains how in the eponymous myth he came so easily by the opportunity to carry off his master's regalia from the temple of Enlil at Nippur.

58. The last word is unlikely to have been preterite *id*-[*di-n*]*a*, for that form fails to provide the usual penultimate stress. For examples of the perfect tense where assimilation of /dn/ to /nn/ is explicit in the spelling see SB XI 275: *ta-at-tan-na-áš-šum-ma* and 280: *at-tan-nak-kúm-ma*; here there is room for the morpho-graphemic spelling *it-ta-ad-na* only if the text continued on to the edge.

60. It is difficult to take this line as a factual statement: Enkidu knows that he is dying and will not be able to destroy his handiwork himself. The truth of this is confirmed by the curses of the next three lines, which anticipate the door's destruction by some future king. Accordingly I have taken the line as a rhetorical question. The unspoken, negative answer ('No, you cannot') leads directly to a statement of who can.

62. The god seems to be out of place here: human agents are expected to be the instrument of all these curses.

64. The verbs of the line fit the context of the destruction of a door as envisaged in l. 60 but the door cannot be the object here for, as I understand it, Enkidu is in Uruk and the door is in Nippur. What is wanted is some violent expression of frustration and despair. Probably he ripped off his clothing and cast it aside, exactly as Gilgameš does in SB VIII 64: *inassaḫ u inamdi damqūti*.

73. The conventional restoration is *šaptāka*, 'your lips' (Landsberger, *RA* 62, p. 119), but more may be missing.

75–6. The import of this couplet is that when a death occurs it is those who are left behind that are afflicted with pain. Already noted for its 'proverbial insight' (cf. H.-P. Müller, *ZA* 68 (1978), p. 247), the couplet is confirmed as a proverbial saying by use of the preterite. On the 'gnomic preterite' in such contexts see Chapter 5 above, the note on OB III 255–6. In l. 76 the conventional restoration is [*šu-ut*]-*tum*, but the identification of the line as a saying means it need have no immediate relationship with the context. The suggestion *mītu* is supported by the use of *ezēbu*, which often means 'to leave for posterity' (see *CAD* E, pp. 420–1). This is the exact verb for the context of the deceased and his legacy, being used with *mītu* in an OA letter in which the writers identify themselves as heirs (G. Eisser and J. Lewy, *MVAG* 33 no. 246, 5): *me-er-ú me-tim ni-nu a-bu-ni ṭup-pá-am e-zi-ib-ni-a-tí*, 'we are the sons of the deceased. Our father left us a tablet'.

78. The word written *i-lu-ka* (both MSS) is, as Landsberger observed, 'für *ilka* sehr hart' (*RA* 62, p. 122, fn. 90). However, recent translators all take this word exactly so, as the singular object of the following verb. In the context it is difficult to win any other decipherment except perhaps *ilīka*

(acc. pl.). The god of Enkidu is not so far identified explicitly, but Šamaš plays a special role in protecting the heroic pair on their adventures, pleads Enkidu's case before Anu, Enlil and Ea, and comforts him on his deathbed, so his restoration here seems very probable. The spelling *lu-us-ḫir* (MS **f**) is assumed to be for *lusḫur* (Landsberger); the use of a CVC sign with abnormal vowel is unsurprising in a tablet from Sultantepe.

79–81. Enlil is not conventionally the father of the gods (as restored by many), but their *māliku*. As the text is reconstructed here, it is difficult to avoid the conclusion that these three lines report Gilgameš's intentions to solicit the aid not of Enlil alone but of the great divine triad, Anu, Enlil and Ea. With the gods thus restored in ll. 78–81 compare SB I 241–2, where the prostitute warns Enkidu that the patrons of Gilgameš are Šamaš, Anu, Enlil and Ea, in that order.

83–4. The change in speaker is marked only by a ruling.

86–7. The verbs in the preterite mark this couplet out as another proverbial saying (see the note on OB III 255–6). The beginning of l. 87 looks corrupt. On the basis of Gurney's copy Parpola, *SAA Gilg.*, read *de-eš-ši* and took it as a defective orthography for *dīnšu*, though *dīna nadû* is not an expected phrase. There is not enough room for [*šá e*]*-de-eš-ši-*⟨*šú*⟩, '[what he] alone (set down)'. I am not convinced that the first preserved sign is *di*. Instead I assume the scribe meant *ultēdû*, preterite to match *iqbû*, with the middle syllable closed to mark the long vowel; for this see Chapter 9, the section on Spelling sub (b).

89. At the beginning felicitous restorations would be *ina ūmī lā šīmātīšina*, '(they go) before their time', or *ana mūt lā šīmātīšina*, 'to premature deaths', but the trace on MS **f** does not allow either. As the text stands I assume *ina* is written for *ana*.

90–171. See also the commentary on MB Ur, from which are taken many of the restorations made here.

90. This line, a slight variant of MB Ur 1: *mimma šēru ina namāri*, is a hallmark of the second half of the SB epic, occurring also at SB VIII 1, 65, 92, 213, XI 48, 97. It also appears in a literary appeal to Marduk composed by a Babylonian prince (ed. I. L. Finkel, 'The lament of Nabû-šuma-ukîn', *CDOG* 2, p. 326, 18).

91–2. The SB version's *i-na*[*m-bi*] replaces *ibakki* in MB Ur 2 and elsewhere. For other examples of this couplet see SB VI 82–3 and commentary.

93. The phrase 'precious life' recurs in a prayer to Marduk, *nap-šat nišī*(ùg)^{meš} *a-qar-t*[*u*] (W. G. Lambert, *AfO* 19 (1959–60), p. 65, 1), in comparison with which *aššu aqarti napištīya* might have been expected here; on the reversal of nouns and adjectives see Chapter 9, the section on Language and style sub (iii, iv). MS g's spelling of the last word of the phrase as zi^{tim} allows for an analysis of *aq-ra-ti* in both MSS as stative, i.e. *aššu aqrat napištī*, 'because my life is precious'. But when considered in the light of the same manuscript's *ib-ri-i* for *ibrīya* in l. 95, the spelling zi^{tim} might also stand for *napištīya*. The adjectival form *aqratu* instead of *aqartu* can be explained as elevated style: see above, Chapter 9, the section on Language and style sub (i).

93–6. These four lines offer a fuller text than their counterparts in MB Ur 4–6: *amḫurka Šamaš aššum ṣayyādi ḫābili* [*amēli*] / *ana lā'eṭi ša lā ušamṣânni mala* [*ibrīya*] / *ṣayyādu ay inṣâ mala ibrīšu*.

94. An alternative restoration at the beginning of the line is [*áš-šú*] (with MB Ur 4). It may turn out that neither proposal is right. Though the *-u* case-vowels of the LB source (MS g) do not have to be taken too seriously, the normally reliable MS **f** exhibits an accusative ending (*ḫābil*]*a* or *ḫabbil*]*a*) that suits neither *šū* nor *aššu*.

95. Though the scribe of LB MS g correctly writes *qi*]*m-mat-ti-iá* for *qimmātīya* in l. 171, his spelling *ib-ri-i* for *ibrīya* is not a mistake. Similar spellings occur in other late copies, from Babylonia (see Lambert, *Or* NS 40 (1971), p. 95) as well as Assyria (see Chapter 7, introduction to MS **e**).

99. This line is not found in MB Ur. A possible restoration is [*il bīt* (or *bītāt*)], '[the gods of the house (*or* houses)] that he enters', which would mark the hunter as one who brings bad luck wherever he goes. The lack of subjunctive after *a-š*]*ar* (MS g, coll.) is not significant in a LB copy.

102. The Kuyunjik sources can be restored to yield *š*[*i-im*]*-tu* as well as literary *š*[*i-ma*]*-tu*. The latter, which is also found in SB I 222, agrees with MB Ur 11 and is probably supported by the LB manuscript (*ši-ma-at* = *šīmat*(*a*)?). On words with unnecessary epenthetic vowels in SB Gilgameš see above, Chapter 9, the section on Language and style sub (i, ii).

102–4. The second of these three lines is additional to the text of MB Ur 11–12: *alki Šamḫat šīmata lušīmki / luzzurki izzira rabâ*.

105. The traces of MS E_1 seem to prohibit simple [*ḫa-a*]*n-ṭiš*, although that is what is expected from MB Ur 13: *ḫanṭiš ḫarpiš izzirū'a liṭḫû ana kâši*. If one prefers not to interpolate the conjunction *ù* an alternative solution would be to restore [^{ḫa}*ḫa*]*ṭ-ṭiš*. The trace of *ḫ*]*u* before *-ki ka-a-ši* on MS Z, reported by Haupt on collation of his no. 6, obv. 9 (*BA* I, p. 106), was not visible to my eyes. MS g's *-ka* for *-ki* is routine in a LB copy.

107. This line represents an addition to the text of MB Ur. Von Soden associates the hapax legomenon *ta-ḫu-ti-ki* with *taḫû* II (*AHw*, p. 1303), a rare word that refers to the young of animals and is equated with *māru*, 'son', in Explicit *Malku* I 192. The context here, as in MB Ur 14–15, is the prostitute's exclusion from the respectable wifely duty of making a household and raising a family within it, and *taḫûtu* thus describes human young. Landsberger restored the beginning of the line as [*e tu*]*-ram-mi-i* to match the form of the other prohibitions in these curses. Though the verb *rummû* means 'loosen', it would be unwise to exclude it while the middle of the line is undeciphered. It is also possible to read the verb as [*la t*]*a-ram-me*, yielding 'you are not to love (your family, etc.)', but to me the point is not that the prostitute does not love her children (or have children to love), but that she cannot provide them with a respectable home.

111–12. This couplet is evidently longer than the counterpart, MB Ur 18–19: *e taršî bīt unâti / . . . -lūtum ša paḫāri*, but apparently to the same effect: the conventional reward of respectable women, a house full of beautiful things, is not within the prostitute's expectations. Before *ša paḫāri* Landsberger suggested *ki-re-e*]*n-nu* (*RA* 62, p. 125, fn. 99). This is not out of the question according to the preserved trace, but to my mind what is required is some such phrase as 'the luxury products of the potter'; *kirinnu*, a lump of potter's clay, does not meet this need.

113–14. The couplet is certainly the counterpart of the damaged MB Ur 20–1 (note *ay irši* there for *ē tarši*, and omission of *baltu*), but until new text is discovered the decipherment of (in particular) the first line, is uncertain. Landsberger read [*šá n*]*am-ri pu-rim*, 'von dem schimmernden Alabastron', but this is doubtful. The sign he read *rim* looks to me equally like *ki* or *di* with interior damage, and the phrase itself does not convince.

115. For *dakkannu* as somewhere suitable for the slaves' quarters, see Chapter 5, the notes on MB Ur 22.

116–17. Note that *mūšabūki*, *maṣallūki* and *manzāzūki* are consistently plural (as too in the parallel passages quoted in the introduction, Ch. 10), while MB Ur 23–5 has *mūšabūki* (pl.), *mayyālaki* (sing.) and *manzāzūki* (pl.). The phrase [*išpallurtu* (or *išpallurātu*?)] *ša ḫarrāni* is the counterpart of MB Ur's *išpallurti paḫāri*.

118. The late text preserves MB Ur's *e-še-gu bal-tu* in reverse order, here as also in SB IX 188; the order *baltu u ašāgu* is conventional in later literary texts.

128. The first word was read ⌈*né-reb*⌉ by Landsberger (*RA* 62, p. 126), but the space available is not adequate for *ni*; nor do the traces of the first sign permit ⌈*ú-lap*⌉ *su-ni*, 'sanitary towel' (so Lambert in Haas (ed.), *Außenseiter*, p. 129). In my view the first sign must be A or ZA; perhaps read

a-kal? Cf. Pettinato's rendering of this and the following line: 'colui che penetra la (tua) vulva possa prendere la sifilide, la sifilide che alberga nella tua vulva possa essere il suo dono'; but this remains highly speculative. As for the word that follows, while I read the adjective in MB Ur as *šu-uḫ-ḫu-ú* (so also A. Westenholz's copy, against Lambert's *ša-aḫ-ḫu-ú*; Gadd also saw *ša*), one cannot discount the possibility that there existed a **parras*-stem adjective *šaḫḫû*, so here and in the following line there is no need take refuge in the rare value ŠAḪ = *šúḫ*. The couplet 128–9 is a fuller version of MB Ur 38: [x x *sūn*]*i šuḫḫû lū nidin* x x.

129–30. For the parallelism in vocabulary between the lines in which Enkidu remembers his seduction and the narrative of the same event (SB I 199–201), see the commentary on Tablet I.

132–3. The couplet is restored from SB IV 194–5.

135–6. This couplet is related to SB VI 27–8 and also, more distantly, to lines from the Boğazköy fragment that describes the taming of Enkidu (MB Boğ$_1$ a 14–15).

139. The phrase *ibri talīmīka* comprises construct state (*ibri* for regular *ibir*) + genitive. Unambiguous phrases in which *talīmu* is, similarly, not in apposition but comprises the *rectum* in a possessive construction are *aḫi*(šeš) *ta-li-me-šú*, 'his brother-peer' (e.g. *SAA* II 6, 86, acc.), commonly referring to Šamaš-šuma-ukīn as Aššurbanipal's sibling; a.sag.tam.ma.na = *a-pil ta-li-mi-šú*, 'his son-peer', denoting Sîn as Enlil's senior child in the bilingual Exaltation of Ištar (B. Hruška, *ArOr* 37 (1969), p. 487, 3–4); and *a-bu ta-li-m*[*e-šá*], 'her father-peer', with reference to the moon as the equal of his daughter, celestial Ištar (W. G. Lambert, *Kraus AV*, p. 198, 71, Hymn to the Queen of Nippur; Lambert translates 'father of [her twin] brother'). Analogous phrases are *mār dādī* and *abu dādī*, lit. 'son/father of love' but also 'son/father of darling', meaning 'darling son/father' (Šar-kali-šarrī dumu *da-dí*: *BE* I 2, 2, royal inscription; Anu *a-bu da-di-ša*: Lambert, *Kraus AV*, p. 198, 54, Hymn to the Queen of Nippur).

141–7. The beginnings of the lines are restored after the parallel passage in SB VIII 84–91.

143. Von Soden would emend to [*ma-al*]-*ku*! (*ZA* 53, p. 228), but there is no doubt about the preserved trace. For other spellings in Kuyunjik manuscripts that exhibit irregular inflections see Chapter 9, the section on Spelling conventions. The 'princes of the earth', who will also be offered meat at Enkidu's funeral (SB VIII 133), are the gods of the Netherworld, especially the Anunnaki. For *malku*/*maliku* (or *māliku*) in this sense see Lambert, *BWL*, p. 318 on l. 7 of the Šamaš hymn; J. F. Healey, '*Malkū : mlkm : Anunnaki*', *UF* 7 (1975), pp. 235–8; A. Tsukimoto, *Untersuchungen zur Totenpflege (*kispum*) im alten Mesopotamien* (AOAT 216), pp. 67–8; the Neo-Assyrian funerary inscription quoted in the introduction to SB VIII; and other passages quoted in *CAD* M/I, p. 168. The word *qaqqaru* is occasionally used for the realm of the dead: see *CAD* Q, p. 124.

147. For *maš-ki* as a writing of the sg. construct state (*maški* instead of *mašak*) see Chapter 9, the section on Language and style sub (ii). In the parallel line *-ma* appears in the more usual place for coordination, on the first verb, but as the text stands one cannot know whether it appears on the lion too (SB VIII 91): *altabbiš-ma mašak l*[*abbi*(*m-ma*) *arap*]*pud ṣēra*. Whether the clause *iltabbiš mašak labbim-ma* differs subtly in meaning from **iltabbiš-ma mašak labbi* is a matter for further study.

153. The spelling *li-ir-a-mu-ki* (MS L) = *lir'amūki* contrasts with MB Ur 50 *li-ra-mu-ki* = *lirāmūki*. It represents an uncontracted form of this verb unique in SB Gilgameš, and is no doubt under the influence of Assyrian dialect (strictly *lir'umūki*). For the intrusion of Assyrian forms into manuscripts of the late text, see Chapter 9, the section on Language and style sub (viii).

157. The words *ṣurra uqnâ u ḫurāṣa* replace MB Ur's *ṣupra u kišāda* (l. 54).

158. On the type of earring meant by the qualification *tutturrû* see the commentary on MB Ur 54–5. The phrase *lu-u nid-din-ki* (note the odd orthography of *nidinki*, as first deciphered by

Landsberger) replaces MB Ur's *limellâ uznīki* (l. 55). However, it does not improve the sense and is also remarkable in that it produces a more concise text. It may be that the change represents clumsy editorial work on text preserved on a damaged original, with *úz-ni-ki* misread as *nid-ni-ki*.

159. For the restoration see MB Ur 56: *ana eṭli ša kunnū {nu} kunūnūšu išpi[kkūšu ša]pkū*.

160. The Assyrian 3rd sg. precative *lušērib* (masculine!) is another example of an Assyrianism in MS L (see above, on l. 153).

162. The resoration assumes that the form written *mar-ṣa-tu* (MS L) is indicative, with a redundant 'overhanging' vowel (for comparable spellings in the same manuscript see below, on ll. 165 and 167).

162–4. These lines replace MB Ur 59–61: *Gilgāmeš ašib maḫaršu / u[št]abbal mimmu kabtatīšu / iqabbâššu ana šâšu*.

163. To my eyes *uš-[ta-ab-ba]l* looks less likely; cf. *al* elsewhere on fragments of MS L, at ll. 30 (L_2 i 4′), 140–1 (L_1 iii 12′–13′), 145 (L_1 iii 17′). Unless ventive, which seems improbable, the spelling *it-ta-lu* for *ittâl* exhibits the late convention that a syllable C$\bar{\text{V}}$C can be written CV-CV: see Chapter 9, the section on Spelling sub (g).

165. The spelling *šu-na-ta aṭ-ṭul* in MS L stands for *šunat aṭṭulu*, and in doing so accords with well-known quirks of NA orthography (CV for VC, CVC for CVCV); cf. MS g's *šu-na-at* and the same relative clause in SB I 246: *šunat aṭ-ṭu-la/lu muštīya*. Split as they are by the vocative *ibrī*, the words *mimmû* and *šunatu* do not exhibit the same syntactic relation as the genitive construction *mimmû šēri* and must form a nominal clause.

167. The spelling *az-za-zi*, probably for *azzaz*, confirms MS L as the work of a scribe who was happy to write CV for C alone, as well as for VC). Alternatively, the verb is ventive, *azzaza* (note LB variant *az-za-zu*), expressing location ('I was standing there'), as elsewhere in the epic (see OB II 179 and note).

169. The SB text omits *nā'ir*, which in MB Ur 66 qualifies Anzû. The line is identical with a phrase used in the Vision of Kummâ (quoted in the notes on MB Ur).

172. The *keppû* is more than an ordinary skipping-rope: it is the plaything of Ištar, her instrument of war, and perhaps a metaphor for the surge of battle (for a discussion see B. Landsberger, *WZKM* 56 (1960), pp. 121–3). The verb *maḫāṣu* is also found with *keppû* in the Tukultī-Ninurta Epic, where Ištar's striking of it has the effect of driving the enemy out of their senses (E. Ebeling, *MAOG* 12/II, p. 8, 32: *im-ḫa-aṣ kep-pa-ša* ^{d}*ištar*).

174. There does not seem to be the space for Landsberger's suggested *ú-kab-b]i-is* (*RA* 62, p. 130); in any case *kabāsu* refers to the step of humans not animals. The verb *raḫāṣu* is characteristic of horses and other equids, meaning 'to kick' as well as 'trample', but note its use with an ox in SB XI 108 (see further the commentary, ad loc.).

175. The sign before *pagrīya* is perhaps *ka]l* (so already Landsberger).

176. Landsberger's reading at the end, [*ul tu-še-zi*]-*ib*-[*an-ni*], is not confirmed by the extant traces.

182. The restoration is suggested by the parallels in SB VI 61 and 76.

184. Irkalla is a name of the queen of the Netherword, but its etymology indicates that it originally designated her cosmic domain (< Sum. eri.gal, 'Great City'). See further W. Röllig, *RLA* V, p. 64, who here and in parallel passages reads *šubat ilat Irkalla*, 'seat of the goddess of Irkalla'.

193. There are two alternative ways of dealing with *ana* in this line and its repetition (l. 198). Either it is a mistake for *ina* and introduces a locative phrase or it marks the indirect object of *appalsamma*. Elsewhere in SB Gilgameš *naplusu* takes a direct object (SB I 14 *itaplas samētašu*, V 2 *ittanaplasū mīlāšu*, V 3 *ittanaplasū nērebšu*, IX 141 etc. *ana palāsa arkassu*, XI 93, *ūmu ana itaplusi*, XI

139 *appalis kibrāti*), but the construction with *ana* or dative pronouns is amply documented elsewhere (see *AHw*, p. 814, s.v. N 2). A third solution, to translate 'I who entered the House of Dust', assumes an unusual word order and produces a clause that in l. 198 has no logical connection with what precedes or follows.

194. The stative *kummusū* has been interpreted to signify 'they were gathered in' and 'they were squatting down, crouching'. Given the presence of *šūt agê* in the next line, *agû* is unlikely on its own here to mean 'crowned heads' (*CAD* K, p. 117), and squatting is thus excluded. The verb *kamāsu* often means to put things away in containers. On the symbolism of the 'stowed crowns' see the introduction to Tablet VII in Chapter 10.

197. Reversal of the conventional order noun–adjective is not uncommon in Gilgameš, but the intrusion of other matter between a noun and an adjective that modifies it is rarer: for both see Chapter 9, the section on Language and style sub (iii–vii).

198. Again one expects *ina bīt epri*. Here it is hard to avoid the conclusion that the wrong preposition has been written and that *a-na* is dittography from l. 193.

199. In MS Z_1 the conjunction *u* is written over a poorly erased Ú. The variant *la ma-ga-ri* for *lagaru* (MS g) is crass in the extreme, a clumsy and unthinking corruption.

202. The spelling of Etana's name in the LB manuscript is without parallel. For the presence in the Netherworld of this legendary king see W. G. Lambert *Jacobsen Mem. Vol.*, pp. 207–8, citing lists of chthonic deities in Sumerian literary sources of the OB period (Å. W. Sjöberg, *JAOS* 103 (1983), p. 315, 97: e.ta.na; M. E. Cohen, *ZA* 67 (1977), p. 14, 78: ^{m}e.ta.na nu.bànda kur.ra.ke$_4$, 'lieutenant of the Netherworld'). Later his function is variously 'governor-in-chief' or 'minister', as witnessed by incantations that invoke the deities of the Netherworld: ^{d}e.ta.na en$_5$.si.gal kur.ra.ke$_4$: ^{d}MIN *iš-šak*!-*ku ra-bi-i šá er-ṣe-ti* (E. Ebeling, *ArOr* 21 (1953), p. 388, 77–8a; cf. Gattung III: ^{d}è.ta.na sukkal é.kur.idim.ke$_4$ (*PBS* I/2 112, 67, coll. Lambert). Lambert comments that 'one must surely assume that both Gilgamesh and Etana received their special offices in the netherworld as consolation prizes for having failed to achieve personal immortality'.

Šakkan (as Emesal Sumugan) also appears in the role of resident of the Netherworld in the Sumerian Death of Gilgameš (Cavigneaux, *Gilgameš et la Mort*, p. 23, 20: ^{d}su.mu.gán). As the god of quadrupeds, at first sight his presence in the Netherworld seems remarkable and needs explanation. According to Ebeling's interpretation, a connection of Šakkan with the realm of the dead is also found in a medical incantation:

én ^{d}*šákkan ina ṣēri*(edin) *lìb-ba-šú ka-su-šu-m*[*a*]
eper(saḫar)^{meš} *mu-ti ma-la-a rit-ta-šu*

AMT 52 no. 1, 10–11; cf. *TuL*, p. 27

Incantation: Šakkan, his heart is binding him in the wild,
his hands are full of the dust of death.

The wild is seen as a metaphor for the land of death and Šakkan, as a pastoral god, is taken as a kind of Dumuzi. However, this analysis remains speculative while the name of Šakkan does not appear in association with other dying and rising gods, for example in the liturgical lament *Edinna-usagga* (on this text see B. Alster, *CRRA* 32, p. 20; a modern translation appears in Jacobsen, *Harps*, pp. 56–84). The only sure evidence for the death of Šakkan is provided by the murderous succession myth known as the Theogony of Dunnu, where he is killed by his son (*CT* 46 43 obv. 16; for ^{d}AMA^{kan}.dù as Šakkan see W. G. Lambert, *Acta Sum* 3 (1981), p. 35). This tradition is not mainstream. Though Šakkan is the son of Šamaš in the traditional theology of An = *Anum* and its Old

Babylonian forerunner (*TCL* XV 10, 188; *CT* 24 32, 112), this does not mean that he necessarily shares in the sun god's chthonic role as judge of the dead.

However, a certain connection of Šakkan with Ereškigal's kingdom can be observed in his relationship with Nergal, the lord of the Netherworld, for there is a tradition in which, like Šakkan, Nergal too has dominion over wild animals (*PBS* I/2 119, 11: [*b*]*u-ul* ^{d}*šákkan nam-maš-šá-a qa-tuk-ka ip-qid*, '(O Nergal, Enlil) gave into your care the beasts of Šakkan, the wild animals': *šuilla*-prayer). Neo-Assyrian kings relate their success in hunting to the commission of Ninurta and Nergal (Grayson, *RIMA* 2, p. 178, 134: ^{d}*ninurta*(MAŠ) *u* ^{d}*nergal*(IGI.DU) . . . *būl*(máš.anše) *ṣēri*(edin) *ú-šat-li-mu-ni-ma e-peš ba-'u-ri iq-bu-ni*, 'Ninurta and Nergal entrusted to me the beasts of the wild and commanded me to go hunting': Tukultī-Ninurta II; cf. ibid., p. 135, 68–9: Aššur-dān II; pp. 226, 40; 291, 84–5: Aššurnaṣirpal II; *RIMA* 3, p. 41, 40–1: Šalmaneser III; etc.). These passages demonstrate that Nergal's dominion over the 'beasts of Šakkan' derives from his prowess as a hunter.

A closer relationship between Šakkan and Nergal can be inferred from lists. In the lexical text *A* I/6 Nergal is even equated, in his various manifestations, with one of the 'beasts of the wild', namely the gazelle:

$^{ma\text{-}áš\text{-}da}$maš.dà	=	*ṣa-bi-tum*
		^{d}mes.lam.ta.è.a
		^{d}nè.eri$_{11}$.gal (*var.* ^{d}lugal.[ir$_{9}$].r[a])

MSL XIV, p. 228, 126–8

Elsewhere the god of gazelles is Šakkan, of course (see above, the commentary on SB I 110). This association is given further expression in the esoteric text i.NAM.giš.ḫur.an. ki.a, according to which ^{d}*u-qur* (i.e. Nergal) and ^{d}GÌR share a mystical number (*CT* 25 50, 15, ed. Livingstone, *Mystical Works*, p. 33, rev. 4). In this list there are two other entries where divine names are paired: Bēl and Marduk (rev. 1) and Girra, or Gibil, and Nuska (rev. 5). In the first of these entries the two deities are identical: Bēl is the common name of Marduk. In the second, the first named, Girra, is the agent of the second named, Nuska, the god of fire. Since Girra is himself fire personified, the two deities are in many respects almost identical. On this evidence we would expect a close bond, if not an identity, to exist between ^{d}*u-qur* and ^{d}GÌR. With regard to this particular text I am inclined to suspect that ancient scholars would not have ignored the hidden possibilities offered by the orthography ^{d}GÌR = Šakkan. Speculative etymology of the kind practised in some scribal circles would find no difficulty in linking Šakkan with ^{d}nè(GÌR).eri$_{11}$.gal, ^{d}lugal.ir$_{9}$(GÌR).ra and ^{d}*ir*$_{9}$*-ra*, and thus extrapolating an equation of Šakkan and the lord of the Netherworld. Such an analysis would be given good cause by the observed existence of a close association of the two gods, as documented in the texts just cited.

204. As Ereškigal's scribe, Bēlet-ṣēri is the Akkadian name of the goddess also known as (Nin)-Geštinanna and Azimua, the wife of the chthonic deity Ningišzida (see W. G. Lambert, *Studies Moran*, pp. 298–9). The epithet given this goddess here is a variation on the title bestowed on her in Sumerian literature, dub.sar maḫ a.ra.li/arali, 'chief scribe of Hades', as in the Death of Ur-Nammu 126 (Kramer, *JCS* 21, p. 115; ^{d}nin.a.zi.[mú.a]), a Gattung II incantation (Ebeling, *ArOr* 21, p. 388, 66–9, = *ṭup-šar-ra-ti ṣir-ti šá* MIN*-e*, // *STT* 210, 12′; ^{d}nin.geštin.an.na), and OB and SB recensions of *Udugḫul* (Forerunners 48 and 284: Geller, *UHF*, pp. 22, 36; SB III: *CT* 16 3, 95–8, = *ṭup-šar-ra-tum ṣir-tum šá a-ra-al-le-e*, // von Weiher, *Uruk* III 64 i 27–8; cf. SB IV: *CT* 16 9 ii 4–5; ^{d}nin.geštin.na = ^{d}*be-let-ṣe-ri*). Elsewhere she is the divine scribe par excellence, in an incantation (*CT* 23 16, 15: ^{d}nin.geštin.an.na ^{f}dub.s[a]r *šá ilī*^{meš}, cf. G. Castellino, *Or* NS 24 (1955), p. 246), the Enmeduranki text (*BBR* 24, 36: ^{d}*bēlet-ṣēri šá-suk-kàt šamê*^{e} *u erṣeti*^{tim}, ed. W. G. Lambert, *Fs Borger*, p. 149), divina-

tion prayers (*BBR* 87 ii 7 // Bezold, *Cat.*, Sm 802, 7: ^{d}*bēlet-ṣēri šá-as-suk-kàt ilī*^{meš} *rabûti*[^{meš}], also OB *YOS* XI 23, 14: ^{d}geštin!(GÚ).an.na *ša-as-sú-ka-at i-li na-gi-ra-at* ^{d}*a-nim*, giving her also the specifically celestial office of 'herald of Anu'), and elsewhere (*BAM* 323, 47: ^{d}nin.geštin.na!(LA) *šam-suk-ka-tum* [. . .]; K 3424, 7′–8′: ^{d}nin.geštin.an.na *ṭup-šar-r*[*a-tu* . . .] / *šá-as-suk-kàt šamê*^{e} *u erṣeti*^{ti}[^{im} . . .]). Note that the seal inscription read by H. Limet, *Sceaux cassites*, p. 113, 11.1, 6 as ^{d}nin.geštin *ṭup-šar-ra-ti* in fact reads ^{d}nin.IN *šar-ra-ti* (coll. W. G. Lambert).

206. The superfluous DIŠ on MS Z is rather small, probably an error which the scribe neglected to erase.

209–10. The restorations are the suggestion of Landsberger, *RA* 62, p. 131, fn. 129. The pairing of *šutersû* and *kimāḫu* in this couplet recalls a line of *Ludlul* II, in which the sufferer contemplates his death: *pe-ti kimāḫu er-su-ú šu-ka-nu-u-a*, '(my) tomb was open, my funerary furnishings were ready' (Lambert, *BWL*, p. 46, 114). Note also, utilizing the same root, the phrase *tar-si-it kimāḫi*, 'funerary preparations', in a NA inscription describing the burial of an Assyrian king (*TuL*, p. 57, 12; cf. J. MacGinnis, *SAAB* 1/I (1987), p. 2, i 14′). Our passage may have Enkidu contemplating his own funerary goods—or rather lack of them, since he has been transported to the Netherworld in a dream. But more likely Ereškigal is still speaking, and follows up her preliminary enquiries as to who brought Enkidu to her realm with a further question: how did he happen to come without the vital gifts of tribute for the gods of the Netherworld?

251. The line is restored after a standard line of Gilgameš's wanderings, *ibrī ša arammūšu danniš / ittīya ittallaku kalu marṣātim* (OB VA + BM ii 0′–1′ // 2′–3′; SB X [55–6] // 132–3 // 232–3).

253. At the end Landsberger's *p*[*a-šá-ri*], 'ein Traum . . . , für den es keine Deutung gibt', is not quite compatible with the trace. Perhaps *u*[*m-taš-šá-lu*], 'a dream that will never be matched'.

256–7. According to A. Schott, *ZA* 42 (1934), p. 130, Jensen privately suggested restoring *ašib mūtu*, at least in l. 256, after the parallel in SB XI 244.

259. The broken sign on MS GG might be restored *i*[*k-ta-bit*, after MB Megiddo rev. 10: *murṣu iktabit elīšu*, but there is not sufficient agreement between the two versions of Enkidu's death to be confident of such restoration.

261. Compare MB Megiddo rev. 11′: *Enkīdu ina mayyāli na-*[*di.*

262. Enough remains of the broken sign apparently to rule out an exact equivalence of this line to MB Megiddo rev. 12′: *ilsīma Gilgāmeš ú-še-*x[. . .

TABLET VIII

3. The spelling of the predicate *ṣa-bi-ti* is presumably for a trisyllable, since the stative *ṣabīt* would not provide the required stress pattern at the line's end. The two alternative normalizations are the noun in the nominative in apposition (the parsing adopted here) or in the stative with subjunctive ending (as in MB); both are rendered *ṣabītu*.

4. The trace of *i*[*b* in the Sultantepe manuscript (MS **e**) suggested the verb *banû* to O. R. Gurney (*JCS* 8 (1954), p. 92) and all since. However, there must remain a certain reluctance to restore *banû* here, since the wild animals did not themselves bring Enkidu into the world but only reared him. It may be significant that in the Kuyunjik manuscript the preserved trace will not allow *ib-nu*]-⌈*ú*⌉-*ka*; *ib-nu-ni*]*k-ka* is possible, if less likely. Some other verb is suspected.

5–6. Von Soden was the first to restore *sirrimu* but read 4 instead of *šá* (*ZA* 53, p. 229). *CAD* has opted for *šá* but takes it as introducing an inverted genitive construction, *šá sí*[*r-ri-mi*] *še-zib-bi-šun*

(S, p. 318), with Enkidu's adopted mother and father as subject. I have treated this couplet as a tight unit, with bonds of syntax and meaning between the lines that constitute it which are greater than those that tie the couplet to the preceding text. Accordingly, *sirrimū* will be the subject of the verb and *ša* introduces a pair of relative clauses. This analysis presupposes an erroneous lack of subjunctive on the proposed verb *ušēdi* in l. 6, a partial restoration which was the idea of von Soden, loc. cit. However, in the Sultantepe manuscript which is the only witness to this word, such a lack is routine (cf. ll. 10?, 18, 24?, 30, 32, 34, 53).

7. Elsewhere in the Sultantepe manuscript the plural determinative is appended to nouns which are almost certainly singular (see ll. 17 and 22): consequently the Kuyunjik manuscript can just as well be restored *ḫar*-[*ra-nu* . . .].

8. I cannot easily make good sense of MS **e**'s text between what may be restored as [*lib-ka* (or *ki*)]-⌈*ka*⌉ and gi_6: while *la* could be taken as a reinforcement of the negative wish, i.e. 'not by night (nor) by day', it must be noted that the signs *i tur la* are clearly written on the tablet as if they were taken to be one word. In any case, in the present context *ay itūr*, 'may it not go back', is semantically difficult. Gurney suggested *a-a i-qu*!-*la*, 'may they not fall silent', and this is generally accepted by recent translators; alternatively one might propose *a-a i*-bànda-*la* < *ay ibbaṭlā*, 'may they not cease'. The problem with both proposals is that, while the sign *la* gives the 3rd fem. pl. ending required if we take kaskal^{meš} at face value, the trace on the more reliable Kuyunjik manuscript still will not agree: it is of a sign like *u*]*r*, *k*]*a* or *ša*]*r*. The first of these suggests *a-a i-tu-u*]*r* again, the second perhaps *a-a ip-par-k*]*a* or *la na-par-k*]*a* (cf. the defective writing in *CT* 16 20, 67), synonymous with *ay ibbaṭlā*.

9–10. Uruk is also preceded by the epithet *ālu rapšu* in ll. 25 and 43 (restored) of this tablet. In describing *ālu*, 'city', and other such nouns *passim* (e.g. *erṣetu* as a term for the Netherworld later in this tablet, *nišū*, 'people', and *mātu*, 'land, nation'), the adjective *rapšu*, lit. 'wide', has connotations less of spaciousness than of large population. A key witness is the poem of Atra-ḫasīs where the associated verb means 'to become well populated', as is plain from the often-repeated line *ma-tum ir-ta-pi-iš ni-šu im-ti-da*, 'the land grew populous, the people numerous' (OB I 353 // II 2; cf. Assyrian recension S iv 1, SBV 44, ed. George and Al-Rawi, *Iraq* 58 (1996), p. 176). Thus *nišū rapšātu* are the 'teeming people' on earth and *erṣetu rapaštu* is the 'densely populated Netherworld' below.

The present couplet harks back to the events that preceded Gilgameš and Enkidu's departure for the Cedar Forest. The old men will be those that repeatedly counselled caution, who are known in SB II as *mālikū rabûtu*, 'the senior advisers', but as *šībūtum* in the Yale tablet (OB III 189, 247). The crowd will be the younger men who saw the heroes off with valedictory messages (*šakkanakkū* and *eṭlūtu* according to SB III 212–14; note, in comparison with the end of SB VIII 10, that those lines end *ikarrabūšu* and *arkīšu* respectively). The preference of this and other Sultantepe manuscripts for the vowel /a/, which is seen in two words in this couplet, *lib-ku-na-ka* < *libkūnikku* and *arki-na* < *arkīni*, is one of the distinctive features collected in Chapter 7, in the introduction to MS **e**.

11. Von Soden was adamant that men should be restored before *ša šadî ḫursānī* ('wohl *eṭ*!]-*lu-ti*, "die Männer"'). Given that the following lines seem all to refer to the natural world, probably again with reference to the journey to the Cedar Forest (see especially l. 15), I would expect some more topographical allusion and follow Labat's 'les hau[ts sommets (?)]'.

12. There seems to be no room for this line on MS **e**.

14. If the Kuyunjik manuscript held *lib-ki-ka* (in agreement with the Sultantepe tablet), there would seem to be room for the name of a third tree, providing it was written with two signs only (^{giš}x). The wood *taškarinnu* is suggested because it fulfils this condition and because, like *šurmēnu* and *erēnu*, it was a timber cut in the mountains of the west, as we know from the foundation bricks of Yaḫdun-Līm that report his lumber expedition (D. R. Frayne, *RIME* 4, p. 606, 54–5: ^{giš}taškarin

^{giš}eren ^{giš}šu.ur.mìn *ù* ^{giš}*e-lam-ma-ka-am*). If, on the other hand, the expected plural form *lib-ku-nik-ku* was written, it is doubtful that more than just 'cypress and cedar' could have been mentioned.

15. The verb *ḫalāpu* in the I/3 stem is also used to describe difficult passage through forests in inscriptions of Aššurbanipal (Streck, *Asb.*, pp. 70, 83; 204, 5; 326, 20). Quite possibly his scribes had Gilgameš and Enkidu in mind.

16–17. A similar litany of wild animals occurs in SB X 259–60.

18. D. O. Edzard speculates that the use in close proximity of the adjective *qadištu* and the adverb *šamḫiš* is an intentional allusion to the prostitute Šamḫat and her kind: 'mit *šamḫiš* sollte, wie man vielleicht vermuten darf, Šamḫat, die "Prächtige", evoziert werden. Ihr Name gehört freilich einem ganz anderen Bedeutungsbereich an als *qašdu*, *qadištu*. Hier scheint ein Gegensatz unter der "Oberfläche" des Textes zu spielen' (*Or* NS 54 (1985), pp. 53–4). But I am not sure that such an allusion can be read into the text.

20. The spareness of the language means that the line is ambiguous. The passage is usually understood to refer to libations of water made to the Euphrates as a *numen loci* or on its bank. The Hittite paraphrase reports that Gilgameš and Enkidu made offerings to the sun god on the banks of the Euphrates but says nothing of where the water came from (H. Otten, *Istanbuler Mitteilungen* 8 (1958), pp. 108–9). The present line must be connected with the repeated digging of wells during the journey to the Cedar Forest (SB IV 5 // 38 // 83 // 125 // 166). According to the Yale tablet, some of the water so acquired had to be poured out in libation to Šamaš and Lugalbanda (OB III 268–71). It seems to me that the present line makes the point that the libations comprised water from the Euphrates itself. Travellers from Babylonia to Lebanon had to follow the Euphrates upstream for much of the way, and wells dug in the its vicinity could easily be imagined to contain water from the river.

21–2. This couplet continues the retrospective glance at Gilgameš and Enkidu's joint career of heroic expoits. Others have read [. . .] *tāḫāzi niṭṭulū*, i.e. 'whom we saw [in] battle', but the point is that the men of Uruk watched helplessly while Gilgameš and Enkidu took on the Bull of Heaven alone. The confusion arises from giving too much credence to the Sultantepe manuscript, which exhibits what can probably be best understood as crasis, *tāḫāzna* + (*i*)*ṭṭulū*, (*-na* for *-ni* is a variant found earlier in this manuscript, l. 10). The partial rebus orthography *a-la-āla*(uru) later stands for *alāla* (l. 24); its use here for simple *alâ* is a mistake.

23–6. The usual meaning of *šum* PN *šūlû*, 'to swear on someone's name', is not well suited to this context and I assume the expression has a special meaning here. Another solution is to take the sign *mu* in MS **e** as marking a glottal stop or glide, *ušella'ūka*. Either way, if *šūlû* is here synonymous with *ullû*, these two couplets imply that the work songs of the ploughman and some unidentified figure extol Enkidu. It is possible that there were songs sung by ploughmen that did celebrate the hero Enkidu. However, the big Sumerian text known as the Song of the Ploughing Oxen twice mentions not Enkidu but, unsurprisingly, Enkimdu, a god of ploughing and irrigation (M. Civil, *Kramer AV*, p. 89, 93.141; a Kuyunjik fragment published by A. Livingstone, *ZA* 70 (1980), pp. 55–7, attests to the survival into the late period of a bilingual version). The similarity of the two names may have resulted in a misunderstanding among ploughmen as to whom exactly they were extolling. Use of the sign URU in l. 24 as a rebus for the bisyllable /āla/ compares with the common writing *su*-URU for *su'ālu*, 'phlegm' (see further von Soden and Röllig, *Syllabar*, p. 5).

27–8. This is the first of two couplets dealing with people who provided Enkidu with, among other things, dairy products. There are difficulties in the Kuyunjik text. It is not clear why a herdsman should have brought *ḫīqu*, if this is a diluted beer. However, my suspicion is that *ḫīqu* might be any diluted liquid (cf. *ḫâqu*, 'to mix with water'), and thus sometimes a dairy product like the Turkish *ayran*. The Sultantepe manuscript understood things slightly differently, with mention of milk (cf. the spelling in l. 5) and ghee (*ḫe-e-mat* is *ḫimātu*, Assyrian dialect). There must be caution about preferring the reading of this very inferior manuscript to that of the Kuyunjik tablet, despite its apparent satisfactoriness on this occasion, and the presence of *ḫimētu* here is made suspect by its appearance in the next couplet. In trying to resolve the differences between the two sources one can only observe that Sultantepe's *ḫe-e* could otherwise be emended to *ḫe-e-⟨qa⟩*, and that the two signs that follow will match Kuyunjik if exchanged. However, *ú-šat*-GI.NA *ina pīka* does not yield good sense and thus the verb of the Kuyunjik manuscript remains uncertain.

29–30. In the Kuyunjik text the extant traces would allow this person also to be *nāqidu*, but he has already appeared in l. 27; stylistic criteria would suggest that another word is required. I cannot reconcile the traces of the two sources, so I have allowed each to have its own different synonym for herdsman. Part of the work of a shepherd boy (*kaparru*, sipa.tur) seems indeed to have been churning milk, as we learn from a line of Išbi-Erra's hymn to Nissaba: sipa.tur.ra ga ni.ib.dun$_4$ ^{dug}šakira nu.da.da, 'the shepherd boy does not churn the milk, he does not pour it in the churn' (D. Reisman, *Kramer AV*, p. 359, 30; cf. A. Berlin, *Enmerkar and Ensuḫkešdanna*, p. 86; M. Stol, 'Milch(produkte) A', *RLA* VIII, p. 195). The buttery substance *ḫimētu*, 'ghee', could be made from the milk of both cows and goats (see Stol, *RLA* VIII, pp. 194–6; id., *BSA* 7 (1993), pp. 101–2).

30. In the Sultantepe manuscript ki.ta looks unavoidable (cf. the shape of the sign TA in l. 61) but cannot be correct. I assume that *šaplīka* is an error for *šaptīka*, which is itself suggested by the traces observed on the Kuyunjik manuscript.

31–2. This couplet deals with the production of alcoholic drink, so it is very likely that MS **e**'s *šībū(tu)* is a mistake for *sābû*, 'brewer'.

33–4. If this couplet follows the pattern set in the preceding lines, the prostitute should be the subject of the relative clause as well as of *libkīka*, and the relative clause should describe an activity typical of her trade. Recent translators follow Gurney in taking *tap-pa-šiš* as 2nd masc. sg. reflexive; however, although according to the Pennsylvania tablet Enkidu did indeed anoint himself with oil when he left the wild (OB II 108: *šamnam iptašašma awīliš īwe*), the structural parallel would then be lost. My translation assumes that *tap-pa-šiš* is the Sultantepe scribe's orthography for the active *tupaššišu*, with 3rd fem. sg. prefix under Assyrian influence. The anointing of the head with oil can occur for legal reasons to mark a change of status (R. Harris, *JCS* 9 (1955), p. 92, no. 59, 10: *ša-am-na qá-qá-sú-nu pa-ši-iš*, 'their (*sc.* the buyer's and seller's) head was anointed with oil'; OB land sale), especially as a preliminary to marriage (see the Middle Assyrian Laws §§43, also the ritual *KAR* 66, 10: ì.gu.la-*a a-na qaqqadi*(sag.du)-*šú tatabbak*(dub)^{bak}, 'you pour oil pomade on (the figurine's) head' in preparation for its symbolic wedding to a piglet). However, this practice also occurs as a part of general festivities, according to the Middle Assyrian Laws §42 (*i-na u$_4$-me ra-a-qe*, 'on a holiday') and inscriptions of Sennacherib and Esarhaddon that report festivals marking the completion of building works. There the phrase is *muḫḫa šušqû*, 'to soak the crown of the head' with perfumed unguents, respectively *rūštu*, '(oil of) the first pressing, virgin oil' (Frahm, *Sanherib*, pp. 79–80, 268–73; Luckenbill, *OIP* 2, p. 125, 51), and *šaman rūšti igulâ*, 'virgin oil and oil pomade' (Borger, *Esarh.*, p. 63, vi 53). To promote an auspicious ambience Nabonidus turned the construction of the E-babbarra at Sippar into one long festival by plying his workforce with food, wine, unguents for the body and *narqīt šamni ṭābi*, 'perfume made from sweet-scented oil' for their heads, using the same phrase as his Assyrian predecessors (*OECT* I 27 iii 29–30: *nar-qí-ti* ì.giš dùg.ga *mu-uḫ-ḫa-šu-nu ú-šá-áš-qí*). It can easily be imagined that Babylonian prostitutes, who were especially visible during festivals and public holidays, would be prepared to pamper their clients with pomades. One may observe a point of literary style: the natural word order is deliberately altered to depict Enkidu's head (*muḫḫaka*) enveloped in the perfumed oil (*šamna . . . ṭāba*).

35–6. The loss of much of this couplet, with its tantalizing reference to a wedding, is particularly frustrating. If we accept the pattern established in the preceding couplets, the subject of *bakû*, and of the following relative clause, seems this time to be something to do with *emûtu*, a word that almost always occurs in the compound *bīt emûti*. The *bīt emûti* is the term that describes the house of the bride's father-in-law at the time of the wedding ceremony, and has already been met in the episode of Enkidu's wrestling match with Gilgameš (SB II 113). That episode is not necessarily the reference here, however, since allusions to the past career of the dead hero seem to stop at l. 22. The second line of the couplet is partly corrupt, one suspects, but the mention of a wife confirms that the context is nuptial. According to the pattern established in earlier lines the wife should be the object of the relative clause. The general import of the couplet thus seems to be that the bride's family and other people present at a wedding ceremony, at which Enkidu was in some way associated with a wife, will weep for him. The signs *iš ki ka* suggest *iš-qí-ka*, 'gave you to drink', but the text may well be corrupt (cf. von Soden, *Reclam*[4], p. 72: '*Im Sippenhaus des Gatten* einen Ring *gab man* dir', reading *iš-ku*!-⟨*nu*⟩-*ka* in *AHw*, p. 1422). An imaginative attempt to solve the difficulties without emendation was made by I. M. Diakonoff, *BiOr* 18 (1961), p. 62: *lib-k*[*u-ka e-ri-bu-ut*(?) *bīt*] *e-mu-tú* / *ša aššatu un-qu mil-ki-ka* [*ir-šu-ú*], 'Let those weep [over you who have entered the *bīt*] *emūti*, Who have [obtained] a wife (through) your wise(?) counsel,' with the footnote: '*ša aššatu'nqu milki-ka* [*iršû*] = *ša aššatu enqu* (= *ina enqi*) *milkika* [*iršû*] (Sandhi)'. However, it is not known that Enkidu counselled aspiring husbands. Bottéro restores boldly 'Pleurez-le, invités, qui, pour la noce, lui aviez glissé au doigt un anneau!' but comments, 'l'allusion à la coutume de "*passer un anneau au doigt*" des invités à un mariage est intéressante. Je n'en connais pas d'autre attestation' (*L'épopée*, p. 150, fn. 5). For the moment it is probably wise to suspend judgement as to the exact meaning of the line.

41. Recent translators have followed Gurney in taking *ina namêšūma* at face value ('on his steppe', etc.). The subsequent publication of MS m_2, however, shows that this phrase begins the poetic line and so qualifies the verb *abakkâkka*, a form which addresses Enkidu in the second person. For this reason I see *ina na-me-šu-ma* as an inferior variant, probably deriving from the phrase *ina ūmēšūma* through a mistake of reading (*u*$_4$ for *na*) or of hearing (crasis?). The phrase *ina ūmēšūma* has an emphatic function, signifying that what follows is heart of the matter, and here it marks the climax of the precative section of Gilgameš's peroration.

50. The word *ṭa-rid* was once also taken at face value, as an active participle in the construct state (*ṭārid*, e.g. Heidel, Speiser: 'who chased(st) the wild ass'), but the discovery of MS **e**, with its variant *ṭar-du*, encouraged Gurney and most subsequent translators to analyse it as the passive participle, lit. 'sent away, banished'. The latter parsing is confirmed correct by the phrase *ak-kan-ni ṭar-du* (var. *ṭa-ar-du*) in a potency incantation, where the image is of the recalcitrant penis as a wild donkey, unbiddable and uncooperative (Biggs, *Šaziga*, p. 17, no. 2, 7, translating 'hunted wild ass'). The nuances of the word *ṭardu* are several here. Enkidu was a famously swift runner until he was effectively banished from his homeland by the wiles of a woman. Now he is chased by death, a more lethal pursuer. He is a mule because mules, being infertile, die as he does, without offspring.

50–4. This section of five lines, a couplet and a triplet, is repeated in a slightly expanded form (three couplets) in SB X 126–31, 226–31 (also, omitting the first couplet, in IX 31–4). It is odd that the material presented in this précis of Gilgameš and Enkidu's joint career is not ordered according to the sequence of the narrative: the killing of the Bull of Heaven intrudes on the climbing of the mountains and the defeat of Ḫumbaba, which are both exploits from the story of the heroes in the Cedar Forest. The older text represented by the Megiddo fragment may have preserved a different, more chronologically correct order (MB Megiddo obv. 5′–8′).

56. For *na'duru*, 'to become darkened, eclipsed', in the sense of losing consciousness, see A. L. Oppenheim, *Or* NS 17 (1948), p. 45. The dative suffix poignantly stresses Gilgameš's personal anguish: 'you do not sense even my presence'.

58. Enclitic *-ma* attached to a noun would normally stress it. Here, however, the heart is the obvious object and needs no emphasizing. Although the particle is remote from the verb, nevertheless it coordinates the two clauses (for comparable examples see SB I 143 and commentary).

58–64. The use in the Sultantepe manuscript of the first person in many of the verbs of these lines is not consistent, since the forms *ik-tu-ma*, *i-na-as-*ḪAR and *i-na-da-a* remain in the third person. Probably it is better not to propose the existence of a variant tradition which used direct speech at this point, but instead to put these forms down to the Sultantepe manuscript's predilection for the vowel /a/ (see above, on l. 10).

61. A very similar image appears in a bilingual liturgical lament, describing Inanna: *ki-ma laḫ-ri kit-tum šá pu-ḫad-sa šu-ud-da-at*, 'like a faithful ewe forced to leave her lamb' (*PBS* I/2 125, 14; Sum. not preserved). The variant *ina šuttāte*, offered by the Sultantepe manuscript, is again an inferior variant which has the look of a corruption.

63. The restoration of *qunnuntu* is the proposal of von Soden, *ZA* 53, p. 229.

70. The second GAR is difficult. To read it as a numeral is perhaps a little clumsy; the reading *ib-ri-iá*! I owe to A. Westenholz. In the Sultantepe manuscript the possessive suffix *-ya* is written variously with *-ia* (l. 47), with *-i* (ll. 44, 47) and with *-a* (ll. 46, 48 twice) but a fourth spelling cannot be ruled out.

71. Lapis lazuli was much used in ancient statuary for dark-coloured body parts, inlays for irises and eyebrows and for beards and other hair. Good examples survive in the Royal Cemetery at Ur (see further Moorey, *Ancient Mesopotamian Materials and Industries*, pp. 26, 89). The use of lapis lazuli ($^{\text{na}_4}$za.gìn) in representations of parts of the eye is recorded in *Hh* XVI:

na$_4$.igi.za.gìn	=	*i-n*[*u*]	eye
na$_4$.igi.za$_x$(ŠID).gá.za.gìn	=	[*e*]*-gi-za-gu-ú* (RS only)	
na$_4$.igi.bar.ra.za.gìn	=	*e-gi-ba-rum* (RS only)	
na$_4$.sig$_7$.igi.za.gìn	=	*šur i-ni*	eyebrow
na$_4$.má.da.lá.za.gìn	=	*pa-ap-pat* MIN, var. *sa-sap-t*[*um*]	eye-lashes(?)

MSL X, p. 7, 89–91, incorporating p. 40, RS 66–7

For eyebrows of statues inlaid with lapis lazuli and other precious materials in other second and first-millennium texts see further *CAD* Š/III, p. 367.

The 'chest' of this line may refer to a pectoral or breastplate fastened to the statue. This seems to be the case in the Letter of Gilgameš, in which Gilgameš demands of a foreign ruler massive quantities of tribute, including gold and semi-precious stones for the decoration of Enkidu's funerary statue:

> 1 $^{\text{na}_4}$*ši-bir-ti ḫurāṣi*(kù.si[g$_{17}$]) ZI-*šú* 30 *ma-na lu šuqultašu*(ki.[l]á.bi) *ana* ⸢*i-rat*⸣ ^{d}*en-ki-dù ib-ri-ia lu-*⸢*kin*⸣ [*x*] *lim* $^{\text{na}_4}$⸢GAZ⸣ $^{\text{na}_4}$*aš-pu-u* $^{\text{na}_4}$*uqnû*(za.gìn) *abnī*(na$_4$)^{meš} *šadî*(kur) *ma-la bašû*(gál) *tak-ṣi-ri ina muḫ-ḫi lu-ban-ni*
>
> *STT* 40 // 41 // 42, 23
>
> One lump of gold—its . . . should weigh thirty minas, so I can fix it to Enkidu's breast; [*n*] thousand (beads) of GAZ-stone, jasper, lapis lazuli and mountain gems, as many kinds as there are, so I can fashion necklaces therewith.

The provision of gold for the chest or breastplate of Enkidu's funerary statue finds a parallel in an apotropaic ritual against the evil portended by a stillborn foetus (*LKA* 114 and duplicates, ed. Maul, *Zukunftsbewältigung*, pp. 336–43, to whom I am obliged for the reference). In the ritual a golden ornament of some kind is put on the foetus's head, a golden 'chest', *irat*(gaba) *ḫurāṣi*(kù.sig_{17}) (l. 12, var. adds silver), is tied to its breast and it is placed on a bed of hay while incantations are addressed to Šamaš and the divine river. Finally it is consigned to the river *itti*(ki) *ṣu-du-šú u qí-šá-ti-šú*, 'with its travel provisions and gifts' (l. 46). By these means it is clearly hoped to despatch the foetus and the bad portent attached to it safely to the Land of No Return, and one therefore suspects that the ritual simulates funerary rites for the human dead.

84–91. These lines are restored from the parallel passage (SB VII 140–7).

91. This line differs from its predecessor in the presence of coordinative *-ma* on the first verb, while SB VII 147 has this enclitic particle on the word that concludes the clause, *labbim-ma*. It is uncertain whether here one should restore *labbi* or *labbim-ma*.

94. In the light of the context, *riksu* has nothing to do with sacrificial arrangements or clothing (as previous translators have supposed), but refers to the means by which the chambers of Gilgameš's treasury were sealed. The common method of closure for the doorways of store-rooms and other chambers has been described independently by R. Zettler (*JCS* 39 (1987), pp. 210–14) and A. Malamat (in *CRRA* 30, pp. 165): a cord or hook attached to the interior of a door was tied round a peg on the exterior door-jamb; the whole could be sealed with a clay bulla for added security. Such a fastening would be well described by the word *riksu*, 'knot', and this word is indeed used by Sargon II to describe a lock captured amid the booty of Urartu: *sikkūr*(sag.kul) *ḫurāṣi*(kù.sig_{17}) . . . *ri-kis mu-ter-te*, 'a golden bolt . . . a fastening for a double door' (*TCL* III 373).

96. The reading of von Soden, *e-tep-pu-šu* (*ZA* 53, p. 229), is preferred to Thompson's]*-e lu-bu-šu*. In the absence of the preceding words it is impossible to decide whether this is active, stative or an adjective.

125. In common with the occasional practice of other LB manuscripts, the 3rd fem. sg. possessive suffix *-ša* is here written with the accusative form (cf. SB X 74–5, MS b).

128. Read perhaps *sa-an-di-*{*i*} *ḫaṭ-ṭum parzilli*, '[. . .] of carnelian, a staff of iron'.

129. If read correctly, *ṣibittu rīmu* suggests that this item was shaped in the form of a wild bull, perhaps as a memento of the triumph over the Bull of Heaven (cf. below, on l. 169). At the beginning read perhaps [. . .] *lû*, '[its . . .] was a lion (*or* steer)' (I. L.Finkel).

131. The phrase *alpū kabrūtu u immerū marûtu* is a stock expression, also used by Shalmaneser III (Grayson, *RIMA* 3, p. 31, vi 3 with var.) and Sargon II (*TCL* III 341). Among the several variants of this phrase is *alpī*(gu_4)^{meš} niga^{meš} *immerī*(udu)^{meš} niga^{meš}/*ma-ru-ú-te* (Lambert, *BWL*, p. 120, 4, translating gu_4 niga ud[u niga]; Craig, *ABRT* II 19, 9–10), in which, if one desires elegant variation, the first adjective might be read as in our line, i.e. *kabrūti* instead of *marûti*. See *A* VII/4:

ni-ig ŠE	=	*ma-ru-ú*
	=	*ka-ab-rum*

MSL XIV, p. 466–7, 31–2

132. Candidates for restoration are *tazzimtu*(i.^{d}utu), 'lamentation', and udu.ki.^{d}utu, a special sheep-offering.

133. For the 'princes of the earth' see SB VII 143 and commentary. The line signifies the participation in the funeral feast of the chthonic powers. The word written *ub-lu* and translated as plural may also be parsed as singular ventive, *ubla*, 'he brought'.

135. The restoration of *tamḫīṣu* is based upon it being some kind of wooden weapon, as determined by its association with the throwstick *addu* in *Hh* VIIA:

^{giš}LAGAB.ŠUB	=	*ad-du*
^{giš}LAGAB.ŠUB	=	*tam-ḫi-ṣu*

MSL VI, p. 89, 79–80

The throwstick was a hunting weapon naturally associated with the warlike Ištar, and thus a *tamḫīṣu* may well have been a suitable gift for her. If *kal-li-re-e* is the name of a wood it appears to be a hapax legomenon. Perhaps it should be seen as a variant of *kullaru*, a variety of *mēsu* (*MSL* V, pp. 110, *Hh* III 211: ^{giš}mes.tu = *k.*; 129, 418: ^{giš}mes.ásal = *k.*).

136. It is possible, on the face of it, to parse *uktallim* in this and the subsequent parallel lines as passive (II/2), with the grave-goods as subject. However, in l. 218 the same form of the verb is evidently active, being coordinated with *uza"inamma*, and I assume that we have II/3 throughout. The force of the modified stem is not iterative but serial, denoting the action of setting things down in a row or side by side (see *GAG*^{3} §91f).

145–6. The expansion of *erṣeti* to *erṣeti rapašti* as restored in this passage (and ll. 154–5, 159–60) relies on the parallels later in this section (ll. 177–8, 181–2). The extra word is used perhaps for metrical reasons, to fill out the line.

148. A flute is a fitting gift for a shepherd god. Dumuzi and flutes are associated in Ištar's Descent, where flutes of lapis lazuli accompany him on his passage to and from the Netherworld: gi.gíd ^{na_4}*uqnî*(za.gìn) (*CT* 15 47, 28 and 35 // 48, 24′ and 31′); and in a ritual that mimics his funeral, where a flute is one of the gifts presented to him (Farber, *Ištar und Dumuzi*, pp. 140 ff., 21, 61).

154. For Namtar as *sukkal erṣeti*, 'the vizier of the Netherworld', see the Vision of Kummâ (A. Livingstone, *Court Poetry*, p. 71, 2), and an incantation against witchcraft (W. G. Lambert, *AfO* 18 (1957–8), p. 293, 65). In *An* V his title is the vizier of Ereškigal (*CT* 25 5, 31; cf. also the myth of Nergal and Ereškigal).

159. As Namtar's wife (see W. G. Lambert, *RLA* IV, p. 522), Ḫušbišag follows him in the parallel passage of the Death of Ur-Nammu (see Chapter 10, the introduction to SB Tablet VIII), and is placed here for that reason. Her epithet is restored after a Gattung III incantation (E. Ebeling, *ArOr* 21 (1953), p. 396, 65: agrig kur.ra.ke$_4$, coll. Lambert). In the Vision of Kummâ Namtar's wife is his female aspect, ^{d}*nam-tar-tu* (Livingstone, *Court Poetry*, p. 71, 3).

164. The gender of Ereškigal's sweeper is masculine, if we accept the evidence of his title and the verb he governs (*lū ḫadi*). The name Qāssa-ṭābat, 'Her hand is light', thus refers not to his own character but to the easy relationship he enjoyed with his divine mistress, and functions like a personal name. It is uncertain whether this god is connected with the deity who bears the Sumerian version of his name, one of the cowherds of Sîn (*KAV* 172 ii 10: ^{d}šu.ni.du$_{10}$ // 179 ii 11: ^{d}šu.ni.du.ug), on whom see further T. Jacobsen, *JAOS* 103 (1983), p. 199. A name exactly opposite in meaning is attached to one of the counsellors of Lugal-Maradda, ^{d}šu.ni.dugud, 'His hand is heavy' (*CT* 25 1, 1). The pairing of Qāssa-ṭābat with the cleaner (*mušēširtu*) Ninšuluḫḫatumma confirms the menial nature of his responsibilities as *šābiṭu*, for their titles are nearly synonymous: in hemerologies the phrases *bīt-su la i-šá-biṭ*, 'he must not sweep his house' (*KAR* 176 rev. i 24 // 178 ii 71; etc.), and *bīt-su la ú-še-šèr*, 'he must not tidy his house' (C. Virolleaud, *ZA* 19 (1905–6), p. 378, 10), are interchangeable before the injunction *šēpī*^{min}*-šú là imessi*^{si}, 'he must not wash his feet'.

167. The beginning of this line is very lightly written, suggesting that, as becomes clear in ll. 168–73a, where the beginnings of some lines are left blank, the scribe was dealing with a broken original. The verb *iḫ*-NÍNDA-*ma* should thus be treated with some scepticism; perhaps it is intended for *iḫ-ḫáš-ma*, yielding *ay iḫāš libbašu ay immaraṣ*, 'he should not be anxious nor sick at heart'. The line recurs as SB VIII 174 in MS m. As noted by Cavigneaux, *Gilgameš et la Mort*, p. 43, it is remi-

niscent of a standard Sumerian poetic line, ur_5 nam.ba.e.ug_7 šà nam.ba.e.sàg.ge, which occurs in the Death of Bilgames and other texts as a stock line describing the despair of an individual faced with imminent death.

169. At this point the only significance of the Cedar Forest can be that the decorated interior of the object was a representation of it. That Enkidu's grave-goods should be embellished with mementoes of his career would seem natural. See also the dagger perhaps decorated with a representation of the Euphrates (l. 176), and cf. l. 200.

171–3 The scribe of MS m has attempted to restore these more formulaic lines, but the hesitation revealed by the tentative nature of his script indicates that he did not feel secure about what he was writing. The deity Ninšuluḫḫatumma, 'Lady Suited to the Cleansing Rites', is otherwise unknown; she has an appropriate name for one whose job is to do the housework: cf. the lexical entry *MSL* V, p. 128, *Hh* III 407: ^{giš}níg.šu.luḫ.ḫa gišimmar = *mu-še-šìr-*[*tu*]. This item is a kind of broom made of spadices of the date palm for, as seen in the hemerologies quoted above (l. 164), *šūšuru* is treated as a near-synonym of *šabāṭu*, 'to sweep'. The menial nature of the task *bīta šūšuru* is further seen in a legal document from Nuzi, in which a girl given into the service of the temple of Ištar of Nineveh for the purpose of *kisalluḫūtu*, 'cleaning the courtyard', must attend twice a month to 'tidy up and fetch water' (*HSS* 14 106, 16–17: *ú-*⌈*še-eš-še*⌉*-er mê*^{meš} *i-za-bíl*).

174. The version of this line in MS m has already occurred at l. 167, where its relationship to a stock line of Sumerian poetry has been noted. The Kuyunjik version of this line appears instead to make the deity the subject, but while the break intrudes this is not completely certain. To my eyes the traces do not allow a reading *ù' -a* (or *ú-a*) *li-iq-bi*, 'let him say, "Woe!".'

175. For *pat-ri* as a writing of the singular noun in construct state see Chapter 9, the section on Language and style sub (ii). The proposal that *katappû* here is not the word for 'bit' (the mouthpiece of a bridle) but means 'double-edged' is the perceptive idea of A. Westenholz, who draws attention to ka = *pû* in the meaning 'edge'. See further Å. W. Sjöberg, *TCS* III, p. 75, quoting the Sumerian expression ka gír.kin, 'edge of a pointed blade', used in the Enlil hymn, Falkenstein, *Götterlieder* I, p. 11, 16, and explained in *MSL* XIII, p. 244, *Kagal* D 3 : 7′: ka gír.kin = *pi-i pa-at-ri-im za-*[*aq-tim*]. The reading *ši-kìr-šu*, against *ši-rim-šu* (Parpola), is proved by the lexical entry *MSL* XIV, p. 491, *A* VIII/1 92: $^{ga\text{-}am}$gàm = *ši-ik-rum šá patri*(gìr) (so already *CAD* Š/III, p. 440).

176. The first word is of uncertain decipherment and derivation. For Parpola *mi-šil-ti* represents *mešēltu*, 'blade'. One might also propose a word *mišiltu*, 'replica' (√*mšl*), with reference to the shape of the dagger's blade or handle. In both cases the word would be a noun in construct state in an exceptional construction, with an adjective modifying the *rectum* falling between *regens* and *rectum*. To avoid this one can transfer the adjective and read in apposition *mi-ṭír-ti el-le-ti pu-rat-ti*, 'the holy water-course, the Euphrates', but note that the inverted phrase *elletu Purattu* also occurs at SB VIII 19 and was perhaps a compound. With all three readings of the first word there is no obvious syntactic connection of this line to the immediate context. Consequently it may be corrupt, and for the moment it is safer not to offer a complete translation.

177. Bibbu is otherwise known from the Vision of Kummâ, where he bears the same title (Livingstone, *Court Poetry*, p. 73, 19; I see no justification for Livingstone's translation of gír.lá = *ṭābiḫu* as 'hangman'). He appears appropriately as a death-bringing demon in an incantation, alongside the 'Snatcher', Ekkēmu (K 8104, 17′, cited in *CAD* B, p. 219). When not a general term but a specific planet, ^{d}*bibbu*(udu.til) is sometimes interpreted as Mercury (e.g. *MSL* XVII, p. 229, *Antagal* G 308: ^{d}*bi-ib-bu* = ^{d}*šiḫṭu*(udu.til.gu_4.ud)) or, with the same implication, Ninurta (see *CAD* B, p. 218), but once, in the Great Star List, it is equated with the 'red star', i.e. Mars (*CT* 26 40 iv 9: ul.sa_5 = ^{d}*bib-bu*(udu.til); cf. U. Koch-Westenholz, *Mesopotamian Astrology*, pp. 194–5, 170). This raises the possibility that a tradition existed which maintained that Mars was red because when in the

Netherworld he was, by reason of his duties there, bathed in blood. A close relationship between Bibbu and Mars (Ṣalbatānu), which is the astral manifestation of the plague god Nergal, is also found in an astronomical commentary, where they appear together in association with fatal epidemics:

^{mul}udu.til	=	*muš-mit bu-lim*	'which cuts down livestock'
^{mul}*ṣal-bat-a-nu*	=	*muš-ta-bar-ru-ú mu-ta-nu*	'which causes continual plague'

V *R* 46 no. 1, 41–2

Note that in the Gattung III incantation the name of the butcher of the Netherworld is different (*PBS* I/2 112, 66, ed. Ebeling, *ArOr* 21 (1953), p. 396): ^{d}šár.šár.bi.id gír.lá kur.ra.ke$_4$. However, in Gattung II this deity has instead the title 'dragon of the Netherworld' (Ebeling, *ArOr* 21 (1953), p. 388, 76): ^{d}šar.šar.bi.id ušumgal kur.ra.ke$_4$ // *STT* 210 rev. 18′: ^{d}šar.du.bi.da u[šumgal] kur.ra.ke$_4$.

181. In god lists there are many divine epithets [. . .]-abzu, but only a few are true divine names rather than titles or epithets. The best known of these is Dumuzi-abzu. The question is: did this deity have the chthonic connections that would support the restoration of the name in this line? At Girsu in the third millennium Dumuzi-abzu was a goddess with the title 'Lady of Kinunir' (H. Steible, *FAOS* 9/I, pp. 138, Ur-Baba 1 vi 9–10; 178, Gudea Stat. B ix 3); at Kinunir itself her name could be abbreviated simply to Dumuzi (see *House Most High*, p. 163, 1297). Kinunir is otherwise known, in the Ur III period, as a cult centre of the chthonic gods Nergal and Ningišzida (D. O. Edzard and G. Farber, *Rép. géogr.* II, p. 102). Possibly they occupied shrines in the sanctuary of the city goddess. In the big OB forerunner to An = *Anum*, Dumuzi-abzu is a name of Zarpanītum (*TCL* XV 10, 108), while in a later tradition the name is given to a male deity, a son of Enki (An II: *CT* 24 16, 30 // 28, 82). Edzard maintains that Dumuzi-abzu is not a Dumuzi figure (*RLA* V, p. 603). That may be true for the goddess of the third millennium, but the change of sex suggests that in the second and first millennia the obvious syncretism with the famous dying and rising god was accomplished. One observes that a certain cosmological confusion is sometimes apparent between abzu or Apsû, Ea's domain, and the realm of Ereškigal, both being below ground (cf. W. G. Lambert in C. Blacker and M. Loewe (eds.), *Ancient Cosmologies*, p. 48; Horowitz, *Cosmic Geography*, pp. 342–4; for *apsû* as a rare synonym of the Netherworld see *CAD* A/2, p. 196). Gods of Ea's court do occasionally appear in the Netherworld. A good example is ^{d}ḫé.dìm.(me).kug, who is sometimes the daughter of Ea, sometimes of Namtar and Ḫušbišag (see W. G. Lambert, *RLA* IV, p. 244; presumably this is the later version of the goddess ^{d}dìm.pi.(me).kug, who is one of the divine residents of the Netherworld in the Death of Bilgames and the Death of Ur-Nammu, 'standing at the side' of Ningišzida). Note also Nergal's title, ^{d}lugal.gal.abzu, 'great king of Apsû' (*CT* 25 36 rev. 3 // 37, 1), an epithet which one would have thought was the preserve of Ea. Thus the cosmological overlap of Apsû and the Netherworld also affected theology. In the light of this confusion the name Dumuzi-abzu, whatever its original application, was open to the secondary interpretation as Dumuzi in his aspect as a god resident in the Netherworld.

The word *mašḫaltappû* is a hapax legomenon but very reminiscent of the Sumerian loanword *mašḫulduppû*, 'scapegoat', and quite plausibly no more than a simple phonetic variant (see now the study of A. Cavigneaux, 'Máš-ḫul-dúb-ba', *Fs Boehmer*, pp. 53–67). Such an epithet would be highly appropriate to Dumuzi in the Netherworld, for he is held captive there in substitution for Ištar.

200. Cedar may be the material of which was made whatever object was described in this line, but one might also restore *qišti*] *erēni* (cf. above, on l. 169).

210. The phrase *dayyān Anunnakkī* is an epithet born by Gilgameš himself in the incipit of the prayer that describes his chthonic functions (Haupt, *Nimrodepos* no. 53, 1 // *KAR* 227 ii 7: di.ku$_5$ ^{d}*a-nun*-[*na-ki*], quoted in full above, in Chapter 3, the section on Gilgameš in exorcistic rituals). The

meaning of the phrase is not so much 'judge of the Anunnaki' as 'judge among the Anunnaki', i.e. the one among the number of chthonic gods whose role is judge of the shades of men. The epithet is also held by Šamaš in incantations (di.ku$_5$ ^{d}*a-nun-na-ki*: W. G. Lambert, *AfO* 18 (1957–8), p. 293, 53; *KAR* 224 rev. 11). The sun god is more likely meant here, but while the text is so damaged it is not possible to be sure.

211–12. This couplet follows the same pattern as SB I 99–100, where the mother goddess fashions Anu's *zikru* ('word, idea') 'in her heart' (*ina libbīša*), with the result that Enkidu is created. While *na-a-ri* in l. 212 could be 'singer' rather than 'river', it does not seem likely that a minstrel has been singing, and all recent translators opt for 'river'. The river is presumed to be the Ḫubur, the Babylonian Styx. What the 'word/idea' of this river might be is unknown. Instead I follow the suggestion of A. Cavigneaux that this line is related to the passage of the Death of Bilgames in which the Euphrates is diverted by damming while the hero's tomb is built in its bed (Cavigneaux, *Gilgameš et la Mort*, p. 11). The spelling ZIK-*ru* is thus for *sikru* or *sekēru*, so written because it was misunderstood under the influence of SB I 100.

216–17. Since the actions the two verbs describe are parallel, the meaning of *umtalli* cannot be much different from *umalli*. This is probably another case of an iterative stem (here II/3) denoting a serial process, resulting in rows (*GAG*^{3} §91f). With the use here of *mallatu*, a variant of *maltu*, in funeral rites compare a Sumerian lament in which water is poured from an útul.ma.al.tum.ma in a libation for the shade of the deceased (Kramer, *Finkelstein Mem. Vol.*, p. 141, 43; D. Katz, *RA* 93 (1999), p. 110).

TABLET IX

11. The trace after *a-na* is not certainly di[ngir], either here or in the apparent parallel l. 25, but the indirect object of *illikū suppû'a* is very likely a deity. The plural imperative *šullimā'inni* in l. 12 presupposes that more than one deity was invoked, and thus rules out a repetion of ^{d}*sîn* from l. 10. As the most prominent of the astral deities, Venus is perhaps the foremost candidate for restoration here, but this is uncertain while the trace before *šullimā'inni* in l. 12 is undeciphered. In the break before *ilī*^{meš} in the present line the trace that precedes *ti* could be of *ṭu* as well as *mir*, but Parpola's *ṣe-e-ti* appears inadmissible. If it is right to restore a divine name following *ana*, there is not room enough in the break also to accommodate the standard epithet *šākin(at) namirti* (used of both Sîn and Šamaš, and also the fire god: see *CAD* N/1, p. 229). As a provisional solution I propose simply DN *namirti*.

12. The first sign of this line is restored in the light of the parallel that appears to exist between ll. 10–12 and 24–6.

14. The phrase *muttiš Sîn*, if correctly restored, simply means 'at night'.

15–16. For these stock lines see the commentary on OB Ishchali 20′–1′: *ilqe ḫaṣṣinnam ina qātīšu / išlup namṣaram ina šibbīšu*, where *ina qātīšu* suggests that *idu* in the SB text is 'arm' not 'side' (*totum pro parte*!). In l. 16 the break does not seem to be wide enough to accommodate *namṣara ina*, which is the phrasing expected from the only versions of this line that survives unbroken (OB Ishchali, Nergal and Ereškigal), and the big area of blank clay before *šibbīšu* suggests that there was no preposition on this occasion. Consequently *namṣaru* is restored in construct state. The phrase *namṣar šibbi* occurs, with *ḫaṣṣin aḫi*, in a passage of Gilgameš's lament for Enkidu that is closely related to the two-line version of the present passage (SB VIII 46–7).

17. This line also appears in the company of the preceding couplet at SB X 96. Note also

something very similar in Sargon II (*TCL* III 133): *ki-i* ^{giš}*šil-ta-ḫi ez-zi i-na lib-bi-šu am-qut-ma*, 'I fell amongst them like a terrible arrow'.

19. For the last word see the commentary on SB VI 43.

37. The spelling *še-mu* for *šumu* was understood by von Soden as standing for *š*^{e}*mu* (*AHw*, pp. 1274–5). However, according to I. J. Gelb *šumu* derives from older **šimum* (*BiOr* 12 (1955), p. 105; cf. Hebrew *šēm*), so this orthography might instead derive from an archaic or dialectal variant of the word. The word displays another peculiarity, in that *še-mu-šú* exhibits triptotic declension, retaining the nominative case vowel before the possessive suffix, a formation that is exceptional with this word (one expects *šumšu*). Perhaps, in the end, the text will turn out to be corrupt (read {ŠE} *šùm-šú*). However that may be, the singular possessive suffix here and in l. 42 (*bābšu*, unless the referent there is the sun) is at first glance difficult to reconcile with the plural possessive suffixes in ll. 40–1 (*elūšunu*, *irassunu*). The solution proposed is that the Twin Mountains were indeed two mountains, one in the west and one in the east (such is the clear implication of l. 45). The singular pronouns refer to the mountain Gilgameš has reached, the plural to the mountains as a pair. On the cosmic geography see further the introduction to Tablet IX in Chapter 10.

38–9. The mountain of the sunrise bears this name nowhere else, to my knowledge. Its counterpart in the west, described as the place where the sun goes in to meet his wife at his evening homecoming, is identified as Mt Budugḫudug in SB *Hh* XXII and the *lipšur*-litany based on it, but as kur *ḫa-*[. . . = *né-r*]*e-eb* ^{d}Utu *ù* ^{d}*A-a* in the Emar version of *Hh* as given by Arnaud, *Emar* VI/4 559, 5. However, his reconstruction is open to question, for it ignores the true extent of damage on the tablet, as given in his copy. Probably the two versions of the list are much more alike, as follows:

	kur	*šá-du-ú*	mountain
	[kur *s*]*a-a-bu*	*šá-ad* ^{d}*en-líl*	mountain of Enlil
	kur ḫur.sag	*šu-bat* ^{d}*be-let-ilī*(dingir)^{meš}	seat of Bēlet-ilī
	kur *lil-mun*	*šá-ad* ^{d}*adad*(iškur)	mountain of Adad
5	kur *bu-dug-ḫu-dug*	*né-reb* ^{d}*šamši*(utu) ⟨*ana*⟩ ^{d}*a-a*	Šamaš's entrance to Aya
	kur *ḫa-ma-nu*	*šá-ad e-re-ni*	cedar mountain
	kur *ḫa-*$^{bu\text{-}ur}$*bur*	MIN MIN	ditto
	kur *ḫa-*$^{šu\text{-}ur}$*šur*	MIN MIN	ditto
	kur *si-ra-ra* (var. *si-ra-a*)	MIN MIN	ditto
10	kur *la-ab-na-nu*	MIN *šur-i-ni*	cypress mountain
	kur *a-da-lú-ur*	MIN MIN	ditto

Hh XXII 1–11 (*MSL* XI, p. 23 // von Weiher, *Uruk* III 114), with l. 5 emended after the *lipšur*-litany ed. Reiner, *JNES* 15 (1956), p. 132, 4

	kur	: *ša-du-u*	mountain
	kur x[. . .]	: *šad*(ḫur.sag) ^{d}*en-lil*	mountain of Enlil
	kur ḫu[r.sag]	: *šu-bat* ^{d}*bēlet-ilī*(nin.maḫ)	seat of Bēlet-ilī
	kur *l*[*il-mun*]	[: *ša-a*]*d* ^{d}*adad*(iškur)	mountain of Adad
5	[kur *bu-dug-ḫu-dug*]	[: *né-r*]*e-eb* ^{d}*šamaš*(utu) *ù* ^{d}*a-a*	entrance of Šamaš and Aya
	kur *ḫa-*[*ma-nu*]	[: *ša-ad e-re*]*-ni*	cedar mountain
	kur *ḫa-*{ras.}-[*šur*]	[: MIN MIN]	ditto
	kur *ḫa-bur*	: MIN [MIN]	ditto
	kur *la-ab-ba-na-na*	: MIN [*šurmēnī*?]	[*cypress*] mountain
10	kur *si-ra-ra*!	: [MIN MIN?]	[*ditto*]

Arnaud, *Emar* VI/1, Msk 74115 obv. ii 24′–33′

Read so, the Emar version duplicates the SB text except for the transpositions of ll. 7–8 and 9–10. Since the list presents the name of the mountain of sunset it is likely also to have included a name for the mountain of sunrise, and we might expect this in the next line. The cedar mountain Mt Ḫamanu, however, is the Amanus in Turkish Syria, which, from an early Mesopotamian perspective, might be another name for the mountain of sunset but cannot be associated with the sunrise. It is well known that other, mythical cedar mountains were situated in the far east (see Sjöberg, *TCS* III, p. 90; Tigay, *Evolution*, p. 77, fn. 11; Klein, *CRRA* 44/III, pp. 63–4). One of them is Mt Ḫašur, present in *Hh* XXII and also attested as a name for one of the cedar mountains in *Diri* VI ii A 10′ (cited in *CAD* Ḫ, p. 147). This mountain, whose name is taken from the timber-bearing evergreen trees that grew on it in legend (*ḫašurru* is perhaps a type of cypress or cedar), is mythical in that it is never found outside literary contexts, where it is strongly associated with the rising sun. In Enki and the World Order and a Sumerian hymn to Ninurta the sun is described as 'rising from Ḫašur (*or* from *ḫašur*-trees)' (EWO 373: ḫa.šu.úr.ta è.a; *TCL* XV 7, 13: ^{d}utu ḫa.šu.úr.[t]a è.[a]). The mountain's location in the east is confirmed by a prayer to the sun god that reports his rising at dawn:

^{d}utu an.šà kù.ga.ta e.ti.a.zu.dè
  ^{d}*šamaš*(utu) *ul-tu šamê*(an)^{e} *ellūti*(kù)^{meš} *ina a-ṣe-ka*
kur ḫa.šur.ra.ta b[a]la.dè.zu.dè
  šá-du-u ḫa-š[*u*]*r ina na-bal-kut-ti-ka*

Meek, *BA* X/1, pp. 66 and 68, K 3052+5982, 11–14, ed. ibid., p. 1

O Šamaš, as you come out from heaven's pure interior (Akk.: the pure heavens),
  as you pass over Mt Ḫašur . . .

An easterly location is also implicit in an incantation from *Udugḫul* I that describes the course of the Tigris and Euphrates from start to finish:

mû(a)^{meš} ^{id}*idiqlat*(ḫal.ḫal) *mû*(a)^{meš} ^{id}*pu-rat-ti ellūtu*(kù)^{meš}
šá iš-tu kup-pi a-na ^{kur}*ḫa-šur a-ṣu-ni*

KAR 34, 14–15

Pure waters of Tigris and waters of Euphrates,
which come forth from (their) springs to Mt Ḫašur.

The identification of Mt Ḫašur with the 'whole of the eastern Taurus and part of the northern Zagros' by M. B. Rowton (*JNES* 26 (1967) p. 268) is based on a misunderstanding of this and other literary sources. The Tigris and Euphrates were considered in antiquity to sink underground in the southern marshes and emerge again in the far east, at the place called *pî nārāti*: see Chapter 10, the introduction to SB Tablet XI.

For texts which cite mountains of sunrise and sunset together see Chapter 10, fn. 169. Other attestations of these mountains singly are a hymn to Nungal in which the expression 'mountain of the sunrise' is used figuratively, as an epithet of the E-kur (Sjöberg, *AfO* 24 (1973), p. 28, 9: kur ^{d}utu.è.a); another hymn which claims it as a mountain belonging to Nergal (*TCL* XV 26, ed. van Dijk, *Götterlieder* II, p. 37, 46: kur utu.è); and an incantation that refers to the mountain of the sunset (*Udugḫul* IV 61: ḫur.sag ^{d}utu.šú.a.šè : *ana šadî*(kur)^{i} *e-reb* ^{d}*šamši*(utu)^{ši}; courtesy M. J. Geller). The gloss [kur] *ni-pi-iḫ* ^{d}*šamši*(utu) in *Hg* B V (*MSL* XI, p. 38, b4) probably explains a lost entry in *Hh* XXI and so refers to the 'land of the sunrise', not a mountain.

39. At the end of the line there is certainly not room enough before the margin to restore *ereb*

šamši as well as *aṣê šamši*. Gilgameš is standing at the foot of only one of the Twin Mountains, identified hereby as the eastern twin.

40. I follow von Soden in analysing *e-lu-šu-nu* as a noun (*AHw*, s.v. *elu* I 'das Obere') and viewing the line as an expression of the common literary image in which mountain peaks are said to reach as high as heaven (for many instances see *CAD* E, p. 139, *emēdu* 1.a.c); the proposed restoration *in-du* is for the stative *endū* < *emdū* (*k*[*aš-du* has also been considered but is rejected on grounds of spacing and because the same word appears in l. 41). An alternative view is that *e-lu-šu-nu* is the preposition *eli* in the locative (*elušsunu*), as in *CAD* Š/3, p. 324, where this line is rendered, 'over which [extends only] the horizon'. I do not understand what such a translation would mean. The phrase *šupuk šamê* is, in any case, not clearly a synonym for *išid šamê*, 'horizon'. The word *šupku* evokes the picture of the bronze-worker casting something in a mould (*šapāku*), and is better understood as meaning the solid material of which something is made (cf. *AHw*, s.v.: 'Aufgeschüttetes'); thus *šupuk šadî*, 'the stuff of mountains', is a byword for hardness and solidity. It follows that *šupuk šamê* denotes the solid matter of heaven, beyond the stars (the term and its variants are discussed by Horowitz, *Cosmic Geography*, pp. 240–1, and p. 97, where in considering the present passage he translates *šupuk šamê* as 'firmament').

41. Elsewhere the phrase *irat šadî*, 'breast, chest of a mountain', occurs in cultic lamentations, for example as the haunt of bandits (F. Thureau-Dangin, *RA* 33 (1936), p. 104, 26–7: mu.lu.lul.la gaba kur.ra.ke$_4$: *sa-ar-ri šá i-rat šadî*^{i}, 'a criminal from the "breast" of the mountains': *Uruammairrabi*, cf. Cohen, *Lamentations*, p. 563, 144), and of porters collecting brushwood (ú.íl.íl: ibid., pp. 543, 90 // 553, 90). In the lament *Edinnausagga* the Sumerian gaba kur.ra refers to the uplands where Damu's mother seeks his body, though in the late period the phrase is given a chthonic interpretation and translated *i-rat er-ṣe-tim*, 'the breast of the Netherworld' (ibid., p. 673, 68 // 688, 98 = IV *R*^{2} 30 no. 2, 22–3; cf. Jacobsen, *Harps*, p. 71, 179′). In these passages *irat šadî* means something like 'hilltops' and is comparable with e.g. the Paps of Jura. In our line the exact opposite is the issue, for the image of mountains being grounded in the lowest levels of the cosmos is conventional. Another use of *irtu* for the base of something is in the lexical passage *Ḫḫ* V 19–21: ^{giš}gaba.gál.gigir = *ir-tum*, ŠU-*lum* (*gabagallu*), which seems to be the bottom part of a wagon (see George, *RA* 85 (1991), p. 162). Otherwise one might suspect that *irassunu* is corrupt for *išissunu*, 'their bases'.

46. Translators are divided on how to read the second verb. The least damage to orthography and grammar is done if *puluḫta u rašubbata* can be second objects of *īterim*, alongside the plural *pānīšu*. It must be admitted that in the nearest parallel (Bauer, *Asb* II, p. 90, rev. 12: *ek-le-tú pa-ni-šu li-rim-ma*, 'let him (*sc.* the moon god) cover his face with gloom'), the second object is a better instrument for producing darkness than *puluḫta u rašubbata* is here; but one must allow for metaphor in poetic language. The alternative reading of the verb, *ītekil*, assumes that the spelling *pa-ni-šu* is for *pānūšu*, nom. sg., an analysis that is quite possible, even in a Kuyunjik source. A third solution, in which *puluḫta u rašubbata* are viewed as objects of the preceding verb (Oppenheim and others), is less probable in my view, because *īmuršunūtīma* is already limited by the accusative pronoun (referring to the scorpion monsters) and should not be pressed into unaccustomed overtime.

47. On *ṭēma ṣabātu*, 'to take hold of one's senses', with the nuance of plucking up the courage to do something, see Oppenheim's translation of this passage, *Or* NS 17 (1948), p. 46. For the line's second verb von Soden prefers *ik-ru-ub*, 'grüßte', 'sich neigte' (*ZA* 53, p. 230; *Reclam*^{4}; also *CAD* K, p. 197), but it seems too early in the narrative for such a display of manners. Not until the scorpion-man has discussed with his mate the nature of the stranger does he hail him.

49. The phrase *šīr ilī* signifies that Gilgameš is immediately recognized as a king, of divine birth: see ll. 53 // 130 and the commentary on the latter.

51. This line repeats what was said of Gilgameš in the prologue (SB I 46).

53. The restoration is from the parallel in l. 130. See the commentary ad loc.

54. For the phrase *urḫa rūqta alāku* in SB Gilgameš see the commentary on SB I 9.

56. The meaning of *pašqu* is more than simply 'difficult'. The crossing of the ocean that separates Šiduri from Ūta-napišti was certainly difficult but, especially, it was fraught with danger (SB X 83 *pašqat* combined with the elative *šupšuqat*), for it was impeded by the Waters of Death. There are other passages where *pašqu* seems to convey the concept of 'dangerous': sin and oath can be so described in texts of Tukultī-Ninurta I (T-N epic vi a 24′: *gil-la-ta pa-šuq-ta šèr-ta*; *KAR* 128 rev. 4: *ma-mi-it-ka pa-šu-uq-ta*), and so too a demon in a SB medical incantation (*BAM* 471 iii 25′: *dan-na-tú pa-áš-qa-tú lem-né-tú* // *AMT* 97 no. 1, 9: *dan-na-ta pa-aš-qa-ta lem-né-ta a-a-ba-ta*). In MB Megiddo, however, *pašqu* seems to mean hard to understand (obv. 12′).

57. The trace, such as it is, agrees with Schott's proposed restoration *a-la*]*k-ta-ka* (*ZA* 42, p. 131), 'your journey', also espoused by von Soden (*ZA* 53, p. 230), but other words are possible. The goddess Šiduri asks similarly in SB X 28.

58. The restoration of *pānū* is the suggestion of A. Westenholz. The scorpion-man wants to know how Gilgameš reached him (ll. 56–7) and what his future plan is (58–9).

75. The restoration at the beginning of the line is conjectural but cf. SB X 73 // 150.

76. The restoration is taken from SB XI 7.

80. The restoration is based on the ale-wife's reaction in the OB epic to Gilgameš's proposed crossing of the ocean: *ul ibši Gilgāmeš ša kīma kâta m*[*atīma*?] (OB VA+BM iii 26).

81. The conventional restoration is *du-u*[*r-gi-šu la īmur*] (*CAD* D, p. 191: 'nobody has ever seen the inner part of the mountain'; *AHw*, p. 177), but *durgu* is otherwise only found in Assyrian royal inscriptions (from Tukultī-Ninurta II onwards) and is by no means the only possibility.

83. The end of the line is restored from the parallels later in Tablet IX.

84–7. In the light of the plural verb in l. 87, I am inclined to view this passage as a description by the scorpion-man of the gods' purpose in making the tunnels under the twin mountains of Māšu, and thus I take *ana* as 'for'. The moon evidently uses the same route as the sun, and so the mention of 'setting' in l. 86 may refer to moonset.

126. Restored from the many parallels in SB X.

130. Restored from l. 53. Use of the sign *šìr* for the construct state of *šīru* would be unusual, and although space is tight in the parallel line, I take this sign as witness to an additional word, *šarri*, intervening between Gilgameš and *šīr ilī*. The signs *šìr* and *šar* are interchangeable in Kuyunjik orthography. The resulting phrase seems to be a standard expression, for it also appears in *Ludlul* I 55: *šarru*(lugal) *šīr*(uzu) *ilī*(dingir)^{meš} ^{d}*šamšu*(utu) *šá nišī*(ùg)^{meš}-*šú*, 'the king, flesh of the gods, sun of his people'. Part of this line is quoted in the letter *ABL* 1221 rev. 13: *šīr*(uzu)^{meš} *ilī*(dingir)^{meš} ^{d}*šamaš*(utu) [*nišīšu*], where it justifies the writer's assertion that the king's word is as perfect as a god's. The idea of the king as 'flesh of the gods' is more fully articulated in the Tukultī-Ninurta epic, where it is written of the eponymous king:

ina ši-mat ^{d}*nu-dim-mud-ma ma-ni it-ti šīr*(uzu) *ilī*(dingir)^{meš} *mi-na-a-šú*
ina purussê(eš.bar) *bēl*(en)-*mātāti*(kur.kur) *ina ra-a-aṭ šassūr*(šà.tùr) *ilī*(dingir)^{meš} *ši-pi-ik-šú i-te-eš-ra*
šu-ú-ma ṣa-lam ^{d}*enlil*(idim) *da-ru-u še-e-mu pi-i nišī*(ùg)^{meš} *mi-lik māti*(kur)

W. G. Lambert, *AfO* 18 (1957–8), p. 50, 16–18 // 8–10; cf. Kuk Won Chang, *Dichtungen der Zeit Tukulti-Ninurtas I. von Assyrien* (Seoul, 1981), p. 89

By decree of Ea himself his form is reckoned as sharing the flesh of gods,
by decision of the Lord-of-the-Lands his fabric was successfully shaped in the ingot-mould of the womb of the gods.
He himself is the eternal image of Enlil, who hears the people's voice, the nation's opinion.

These passages document a belief that kings were not made of the same stuff and in the same way as men, but were fashioned by the gods. On this as a central ideology in the Assyrian imperial court and elsewhere see S. Parpola, 'The king as god's son and chosen one', *SAA* IX, pp. xxxvi–xliv. The separate creation of man (*lullû-amēlu*) and king (*māliku-amēlu*) is the subject of a mythological fragment published by W. R. Mayer, 'Ein Mythos von der Erschaffung des Menschen und des Königs', *Or* NS 56 (1987), pp. 55–68.

140–1. The restoration of this couplet here and throughout this episode relies on the better-preserved parallels in ll. 158–66. Though *palāsu* in the I/1 stem is not common, the tablet has a clear *la* (not *na*) where the word is preserved (ll. 159, 162, 166). For the significance of Gilgameš's repeated backward glances see the introduction to this episode in Ch. 10.

160. There are three verbs *ṣarāḫu* with present tense in /a/. *CAD* and others analyse *iṣarraḫ* from *ṣarāḫu* D, 'to hurry' (*CAD* Ṣ, p. 101). Another school chooses *ṣarāḫu* B, a verb of lamentation. The third verb, *ṣarāḫu* A, means 'to heat up', typically of water, in the I/1 stem and is to be discounted. The choice depends on the damaged phrase that occupies the middle of the line, which I understand as a simile introduced by *kīma*. However, other readings are possible (e.g. *šēpī*^{min}-[*šu*]?); KIMIN is ruled out, as I see the traces.

163–4. The north wind perhaps symbolizes the draught which heralds Gilgameš's approach to the far end of the tunnel. Oppenheim suggested restoring some part of the verb *napāḫu*, 'to blow', before *pānīšu* (*Or* NS 17, p. 47).

170. The phrase *lām šamši* is temporal not spatial, making it clear that Gilgameš comes out before the sun does, not into the sunshine.

171. Division of the lines into couplets makes it clear that the *namirtu* pertains not to the sun but to the magic trees of jewels (against Oppenheim, loc. cit.). Their brilliance, even before dawn, is the dazzling sight that greets Gilgameš as he escapes from the tunnel.

172. Oppenheim read *ḫi-iṣ-ṣi*, which he understood to be an enclosed garden (*Or* NS 17, p. 47, fn. 1). However, this word has not been adopted by the dictionaries. The scribal notation in the margin, a small KÚR, was not copied by Haupt, but he noted its presence in *BA* I, p. 117, and drew attention to it on other Kuyunjik tablets. Since then other examples have been discovered on tablets from Kuyunjik and Babylon and discussed by W. G. Lambert, *Kraus AV*, p. 216, who demonstrated that this was a notation marking an error, Sumerian reading kúr, Akkadian equivalence uncertain (part of *nakāru*?); cf. also Farber, *Baby-Beschwörungen*, p. 22, fn. 21. Note also the use of a single wedge as a scribal notation in SB XI 95, MS W_1. If the mark means here that something in l. 172 is actually an error, then either it will be the name of the tree, which is already so damaged that decipherment has eluded us, or perhaps the infinitive phrase *ina amāri*, which may stand instead for *ana amāri*, 'he went straight to look (at it)' (so Oppenheim, *Or* NS 17, p. 47, fn. 2).

174. With *ḫi-pat*, cf. *ḫīpāku*, 'I am attractive', as understood by W. G. Lambert, *Or* NS 36 (1967), p. 132. Another view is that of von Soden, *ZA* 53, p. 230, and *AHw*, s.v. *ḫâb/pu* I ('geputzt').

188. The stone $^{\text{na}_4}$an.za.gul.me is entered in the lexical lists as an equivalent of *zaškītu* (or *zašqītu*):

[. . .]	=	*za-áš-ki-tum*
[. . .]		
[. . .]		
[^{na_4}an.za].gul.me		

Arnaud, *Emar* VI/1, p. 123: 553, 173′–6′

Note also the reconstructed equation *Hh* XVI 344: [^{na_4}an.za.gul.me] = [ŠU] (*MSL* X, p. 13) and the entry ^{na_4}*za-áš-*[x x] in a NB list (*MSL* X, p. 67, iv 30). On the reading see Landsberger, *MSL* X, p. 27. In *Lugale* 534 this stone, written ^{na_4}an.zú.gul.me, is one of a group blessed by Ninurta and given the function of serving syrup and wine (l. 542). It also appears in a royal funerary ritual in which wine is poured on to the ground from it (or by means of it) and it is then crushed against the side of the bed (*TuL*, p. 63, 11–12). In his edition of the same text von Soden remarked of the stone that it must be 'ziemlich weich und vermutlich körnig' (*ZA* 45 (1939), p. 47). In that text the stone must be a small vessel or ladle of some kind, as also envisaged by *Lugale* (cf. *CAD* M/1, p. 267: '. . . -stone vessel'; J. A. Scurlock, *RA* 86 (1992), pp. 53–4: '*anzagullu*-vessel'; also ead. in M. Meyer and P. Mirecki (eds.), *Ancient Magic and Ritual Power* (Leiden, 1995), p. 100). Such a vessel or utensil was thus the typical use to which the stone was put. In the present line these stones take the place of sharp, pointed growths. Either the object that bore the stone's name was long and pointed like an alabastron or, if what the poet had in mind was the raw material alone, the stone itself was pointed.

191. The first word of the simile calls to mind *ḫarû*, 'palm frond', but this is a LB term (cf. older *aru*) and unlikely in SB Gilgameš. The second word is perhaps *lalikkû* = *liligû*, a type of cucumber, but it is safer not to restore.

192. For this stone see the Emar tablet of *Hh* XVI (Arnaud, *Emar* VI/1, p. 124: 553), 185′: ^{na_4}ugu.áš.g[ig] = *a-gu-zi-ig-gu* and the tablet K 4212, 4′: ^{na_4}*kunukki*(kišib) *a-gu-si-gu*, 'seal made of *a.*', between *abašmu* and *ašgikû* (áš.gi$_4$.gi$_4$). The identification of ^{na_4}áš.gì.gì, ^{na_4}áš.gi$_4$.gi$_4$ (Akk. *ašgikû* etc.) and ^{na_4}ugu.áš.gì.gì, ^{na_4}ugu.áš.gi$_4$.gi$_4$ (Akk. *agusīgu* etc.) as types of turquoise was established by F. Vallat, 'Un fragment de tablette achéménide et la turquoise', *Akkadica* 33 (1983), pp. 63–8.

195. The last word is usually read *atallukīšu*, but the traces of the first sign will not allow this. Though the first sign is badly damaged, the reading *itallukīšu* looks more promising. This form of the I/3 infinitive of *alāku* occurs quite often in SB, e.g. in a lexical text (*CT* 11 31 iv 41: *Idu* II), incantations (*CT* 16 39 i 5; *AMT* 102, 11 // *KAR* 255 i 14; IV *R*^{2} 18* no. 6 rev. 12), a medical text (*AMT* 73, 15–16), and a curse formula (Postgate, *Royal Grants* nos. 9–12, 62; SB/NA mix).

196. At the end of the line one might have expected *šâšu*.

TABLET X

3. The reading *kannu* (not *i-nu*) was first noted by von Soden, *ZA* 53, p. 230. It is conventional to restore the end of this line after the Hittite version, which states that Šiduri had [NA]M.Z[I].TUM ŠA KÙ.SI[G$_{17}$], 'a vat of gold' (*KUB* XVII 3 iii 9, ed. Friedrich, *ZA* 39, p. 22; cf. Parpola, *SAA Gilg.*). The sign *nam* is compatible with the traces, and *kannu* and *namzītu* are the two principal fittings of a brewery, well attested in numerous texts (see *CAD* K, p. 155). However, such a restoration raises a problem of agreement with the verb. Some interpret this as *ep-šu-ši*, i.e. plural stative of *epēšu*; I have followed a suggestion of A. Westenholz in taking the word from the more neutral *bašû*. However that may be, *epšū* and *ibšû* are both masculine and *namzītu* is feminine, so that for the moment it does not seem safe to restore either *n*[*am-zi-tu* or *n*[*am-za-tu* (pl.).

4. A possible restoration is *k*[*u-lu-li kul-lu-lat*], 'veiled with a veil'. This is suggested by a passage in a prayer to the constellation Ursa Major, in which *kuttumu* and *kullulu* are alternative readings (*STT* 73, 77: *kal-lat* é.kur *kul-*⌈*lul*⌉*-tu* // *YOS* XI 75, 2: *kal-lat* é.kur *kul-lul-tum* // *UET* VII 118, 22: *kal-lat* é.kur *kut-tùm-tú*).

6. At the end one might restore *naši, mali* or even *īšu*. The recovery of the penultimate word allows one to see that the phrase anticipates the action to come. The lion's skin makes Gilgameš frightening to behold, and in due course Šiduri is terrified at the sight of him.

7. The restoration is made in the light of SB IX 49: *ša illikannâši šīr ilī zumuršu*.

9. The sign *qa* is written over *qu*: the scribe originally wrote *ru-qu-ti*, as in SB 121. For this image in Gilgameš see the commentary on SB I 9; for the fem. sg. *rūqatu* see the commentary on SB III 25.

10–12. The triplet recurs, adjusted for a masculine subject, as SB X 184–6, where *uš-tam-ma* is written *uš-tam-ma-a*. The pronominal suffix on *inaṭṭalšumma*, ostensibly dative, derives from the LB manuscript and would be taken to intend the more usual accusative (CVC-CV for CV̄CV) were it not for *anaṭṭalakkumma* in SB XI 2. It appears that this verb can be construed with either case.

22. This line is restored from the Nineveh manuscript of Ištar's Descent (quoted in Chapter 10, the introduction to SB VI.

23. The Babylonian manuscript, MS b, evidently differed from MS K but not enough is preserved to allow confident restoration (*erēba*? see the apparatus).

27. The traces disallow a restoration [*bābī ē*]*di*[*lma ēteli an*]*a ūri* (after ll. 16 and 21).

28. The partial restoration relies on SB IX 57, where the Scorpion Man asks the same question.

31-71. The restoration of these lines relies on Gilgameš's recounting of his heroic adventures in his lament for Enkidu (SB VIII 52–5), and the later episodes in which Gilgameš meets, respectively, Ur-šanabi and Ūta-napišti (SB X 113–48 // 213–48).

32. There are two versions of this line. In SB VIII 53 the text reads *niṣb*[*at*]*ūma alâ* [*ninâru*] but in SB X 229 *alâ ni*[*ṣbatūma a*]*lâ ninâru*. The text at SB X 129 is entirely missing, as it is here, and cannot help decide the matter one way or the other. However, in the reprise of this line at SB X 39 MS b seems to have enough space missing for the fuller version and too much for the simpler. For this reason I suspect Tablet X uses the fuller version throughout.

34. Considered as a joint achievement, the mention of lion-slaying is new: no such feat appears in Gilgameš's lament for Enkidu. Thus it very likely refers to the episode related in SB IX 15–18, in which Gilgameš attacks a pair of lions at a mountain pass, and this is the justification for Thompson's restoration in ll. 34 // 131 // 231 of *nērebēti* before *ša šadî* (which is itself assured by l. 38). This was not an adventure in which the dead Enkidu could take part, of course, and it may be that one should restore *adūku* in the same lines (note *duk* for *duku* in l. 34, and for *duku* or *duka* in l. 38; but this is nothing unusual in LB orthography). However, the intrusion of the first person in this griefstricken reminiscence would be jarring, and I have followed other recent translators in opting for the plural.

36. The trace before *šá* is collated. Ḫumbaba's epithet 'Guardian' (of the Cedar Forest), is found in OB Ishchali 26′: *maṣṣaram* (cf. ibid. 30′, 34′: *maṣṣaru qištim*/*erēnim*; SB IV 203: *maṣṣar qišāti*). Elsewhere the word *nāṣiru* is used in the same connection but seemingly as the epithet of the god Wēr rather than of Ḫumbaba (OB III 131; cf. SB II 277).

55–60 // 132–7 // 232–7. These six lines, really four couplets, were passed down almost verbatim from the OB epic (OB VA+BM ii 0′–6′): [*ibrī ša arammūšu danniš*] / *ittīya ittallaku kalu marṣ*[*ātim*] / *Enkīdu ša arammūšu danniš* / *ittīya ittallaku kalu marṣātim* / *illikma ana šīmatu awīlūtim* / *urrī u mūšī elīšu abki* / *ul addiššu ana qebērim*.

57 // 134 // 234. The restoration relies on the OB text's similar *illikma ana šīmatu awīlūtim* (OB VA+BM ii 4′), but an alternative is offered by the funerary inscription of Yabâ, the wife of Tiglath-pileser III, which, like the SB text, uses the verb *kašādu* (Abdulilah Fadhil, *Bagh. Mitt.* 21 (1990), p. 461, 3–4): *ina mu-te šīmat*(nam) *napišti*(zi)^{ti} *ik-šu-da-še-ma ur-ḫu abbē*(ad)^{meš}*-šú ta-lik*, 'at death the doom of life overtook her and she walked the path of her fathers'.

58 // 135 // 235. On periods of six days and seven nights see the commentary on SB I 194. The word *mu-šá-a-ti* is preserved in none of these lines, but is preferred to *mu-ši* by comparison with SB XI 128.

63 // 140 // 240. The restoration of *kabtat* is compatible with the traces in l. 240, but other verbs may be possible.

74. It is also possible to read MS b [*mi-na*]-⸢*a*⸣. Note, in this and the following line, the use in this manuscript of *-ši* for possessive *-ša*, an occasional LB practice (e.g. SB VIII 125, MS m). In the parallel the Kuyunjik tablet has, correctly, *it-ta-šá* (l. 151).

76–7. This couplet expands on the OB text, as represented by OB VA+BM iii 24: *šumma naṭu ti'āmtam* [*lūbir*].

78. Note the apocopated prefixed preposition in the Babylonian manuscript, *ana šâšūma* > *aššâšūma*.

80. The sign KUR on MSK is emended out of the text by comparison with the Babylonian manuscript, though it is theoretically possible to achieve sense by reading it *ikšudu* or *kašdu*, i.e. 'anyone who, since olden days, reached here' (cf. A. R. Millard, *Iraq* 26 (1964), p. 101). The LB source has a corruption of its own, *ul* instead of *u*, producing an unsatisfactory double negative.

81. The enclitic *-ma* is here written *-mu*, as also in SB I 203 (see *AHw*, p. 664).

82. The sign AK in the Kuyunjik manuscript may most simply be explained as a corruption of the Trennungzeichen and *ba*. However, the OB text has a line *āli*[*k* . . .] *mannum* [. . .] (OB VA+BM iii 27), from which tradition AK-*la Šamaš ibbir mannu* might alternatively descend.

84. The word *birâ* cannot mean 'everywhere' here (so *CAD* B, s.v.), since the Waters of Death are located in a particular part of the ocean, way out to sea. The point is that the Waters of Death lie between (*biri*) Gilgameš and his goal, and *birâ* must take its sense accordingly, as von Soden pointed out (*OLZ* 50 (1955), 515: 'dazwischen'). The meaning of *pānātu*, 'the way forward', compares with *arkatu*, 'the way behind', in Gilgameš's race with the sun in SB IX. The feminine suffix on *pānātu* refers to *nēbertu* or *urḫu* in the previous line.

85. The first word is usually read as *a-lum-ma*, translated variously (Labat, 'par ou donc?'; von Soden, 'irgendwo einmal'; Dalley, 'wherever, then?'; *CAD* A/1, Kovacs, 'even if') or not at all (Parpola: 'meaning uncertain'). An interrogative is made unlikely by the tense of *tētebir*. Thematically this couplet takes its shape from the preceding one: first there is the problem of the dangerous ocean voyage, then there is the additional hazard of the Waters of Death. I feel that a meaning is wanted for *a-lum-ma* that emphasizes the separateness of these difficulties. The possibility of reading *aḫumma* was suggested to me by M. J. Geller. This would be a late variant of the word *aḫamma*, 'moreover', 'separately', known best from OA (with variant *aḫum*) but also present in OB.

88. Note in MS b the exceptional use of *ú* for the conjunction.

89. MS K's *li-mu-ru* may be parsed as plural or singular (CV for VC or ventive in *-u*?). The latter is preferred in order to provide an antecedent for the singular pronoun on *ittīšu* in the next line.

93–4. On these stock lines see OB Ishchali 20′–1′ and commentary. For *namṣar* (*ina*) *šibbi* see the commentary on SB IX 15–16.

96. This line repeats SB IX 17.

97. The restoration of *rigma* follows von Soden, Reclam[4], *CAD* Š/1, p. 489, et al. Though

exhibiting an accusative ending, the word is better taken as the subject of *išeppu* than as an adverbial qualification, for elsewhere in the epic this is unambiguously the case: OB Harmal$_2$ 5: *kīma lilissim liššapu rig[imka]* // SB IV 241: *[kīm]a lilissu lū šapu r[igimka]*. The spelling thus joins those peculiarities listed in Chapter 9, the section on Spelling conventions sub (j).

99. The sign after *iš* is strictly *maš*. Most emend to *iš-me*, but *ḫaṣṣinnu* is a poor object of *šemû*. Others read *iš-šú*, as in l. 93, and this is surely better. The second verb is provisionally understood as *râṣu*, a word that exactly expresses the joining of battle (see OB Atram-ḫasīs I 81 // 83, 110: *qá-ab-lum i-ru-ṣa*; SB Anzû II 56: *iš-ta-uṣ . . . qab-lu*; further George, *NABU* 1991/19). The remaining signs, *ir*-x[. . .] (where x can be *še*, *bu*, *te*, *tu*, *li*, etc.) can also be restored to give forms of *râbu*, 'tremble', *râdu*, 'quiver', *rapādu*, 'roam', *redû*, 'chase', and *ratātu*, 'shake', to give only the most obvious candidates.

101. Most translators take *ir-te-šu* as 'his chest' but *CAD* A/1, p. 61, offers the ingenious restoration [*ina sikkāt*]*i irtēšu*, 'he nailed him down [with pegs]'; a reading [*ki-ma sik-ka-t*]*i*, 'he secured him to . . . like a peg,' is also possible. In the context of tying someone down the verb *retû* calls to mind the tale of the Poor Man of Nippur:

> *ir-ṭe-ma ina dun-ni qaq-qa-ri* 5 ^{giš}*sikkāti*$^{⸢\text{meš}⸣}$
> *qātī*(šu) *šēpī*(gìr)^{min} *qaqqadu*(sag.du) *ú-pak-kir-šú*
>
> *STT* 38, 132
>
> He drove five pegs into the solid floor,
> he bound him fast by the hands, feet and head.

However, while the two signs that follow *kappašūma* in MS b defy reading and more text is not forthcoming, the conclusion of the line must remain ambiguous.

102–5. The suspense of the Stone One's fate is drawn out over these two couplets, which evidently stressed their importance for safe passage over the ocean and through the Waters of Death. Accordingly, they are likely to be an expansion of two lines which in the OB text are put into the boatman's mouth (OB VA+BM iv 22, 24): *aššum lā alappatu mê mūtim* and *šūt abnim aššum šūburim šunu ittīya*.

106. The line compares with OB VA+BM iv 1: *šunūti uḫtappi'am ina uzzīšu*.

117. The sign A, which intrudes before *šarbi*, may be partly erased, but in the parallel passages the Nimrud manuscript has it too (SB X 217 and 224) and it must be taken seriously. One solution would be to take it as the abbreviated logogram a (for a^{meš}) = *mû*, common in rituals and prescriptions, yielding *mê šarbi*, 'icy water' or winter rain. However, the phrase *ina šarbi u ṣēti* is also found in SB IX 126 (partly restored), which suggests that the writing A *šar-ba* stands for *šarbu* alone. Since the logogram for *šarbu* is šèg (A.AN), I suspect that the spelling A *šar-ba* descends from a glossed orthography A.AN$^{\textit{šar-bi}}$.

118. Thanks to Assyrian MS **z** this line is now complete. The idiom *pān* X *šakin* means to have the appearance of X (see *CAD* Š/1, p. 133). As we know from SB VII 147 // VIII 91, Gilgameš is clad in a lion's skin.

153. Note the use of the sign TU for *ṭú*, an example of MB orthography which is edited out in the next line.

157. The reading *tattabak* is assured by the parallel in l. 106.

158. The reading of the end of this line is made in the light of l. 88, where *urna qatāpu* seems to be a necessary prelude to the safe passage of Ur-šanabi's boat. One could also read ⸢*šu*⸣-*nu ul* [. . .], but the traces seem to disallow von Soden's reading *baq-nu ul-*[*lu-šu-nu*] (*AHw*, p. 1410).

160. This and the parallel line (166) are restored after OB VA+BM iv 26: *parīsī ša ṣuppā* 5 *šūšī iksam*. I agree with M. A. Powell, who writes: 'the usual restoration [2.UŠ] for these lines is based, I believe on a misunderstanding of Gilgameš X iv 8 [= 180]' (*ZA* 72 (1982), p. 94, fn. 30). He argues that 2.UŠ in the latter line is not the number of poles used, but the distance travelled (see below, ad loc.). An additional argument in favour of this would point out that, as a general rule, numbers in the older text are either reproduced accurately or exaggerated, but not reduced. According to this observation the 300 poles of OB VA+BM are not likely to diminish to as little as 120 in the later tradition. On *parīsu* see the commentary on the OB text. On the imperative *erid* instead of regular *rid* see von Soden, *GAG*[3] §103n.

161. The word translated 'boss', *tulû*, is lit. 'teat' or 'nipple'. In the OB text the parallel phrase is *šukun ṣe-re-tim* (OB VA+BM iv 27). In the later periods *tulû* was the more common word, for it explains *ṣertu* in commentaries (see *MSL* IX, p. 35, *Hg* B IV 33: uzu.$^{\text{a-ka-ni}}$UBUR = *ṣer-tum* = *tu-lu-u*; cf. the commentaries on *Šumma izbu*, ed. Leichty, *Izbu*, p. 221, 325?–7 // von Weiher, *Uruk* II 37, 41; p. 231, 376g). On the nature of the 'teat' of a punting-pole see further Chapter 5, the note on the OB text.

162. The writing of the ventive imperative with a closed syllable suggests a secondary lengthening of that syllable, *billa* or *bīla*; cf. the orthography *bi-i-la* in SB IV 42.

164–5. On these stock lines see OB Ishchali 20′–1′ and commentary.

169–70. This couplet is restored from its repetition in SB XI 271–2. The verb *rakābu*, which occurs twice in the couplet, before the launch and afterwards, utilizes both its meanings, (a) to ride aboard a boat and (b) to embark (as in Adapa, *BRM* IV 3, 19). The significance of the verb on its repetition, with subject independently marked, is that in the absence of the crew Ur-šanabi and Gilgameš are more than passengers. They must do the job of propelling the boat and steering it. The *magillu* is an ocean-going boat typically used in long-distance trading ventures, as we know from Enki and the World Order:

^{giš}má.[g]i$_4$.lum me.luḫ.ḫa^{ki}.a.ke$_4$	Let the *magillu*-boat of Meluḫḫa
kù.sig$_{17}$ kù.babbar bala.šè ḫé.ak.e	transport gold and silver.

EWO 126–7, ed. I. Bernhardt and S. N. Kramer, *WZJ* 9 (1959–60), p. 234

Note also Bilgames and Huwawa A 111–13:

ba.su.a.ba ba.su.a.ba	After it sank, after it sank,
u$_4$ ^{giš}má má.gan.na ba.su.a.ba	after the boat of Magan sank,
^{giš}má.gur$_8$ ^{giš}má.gi$_4$.lum ba.su.a.ba	after the ship, the *magillu*-boat sank.

D. O. Edzard, *ZA* 81 (1991), pp. 203–4

The verb *nadû* with the nuance 'to launch (a boat)' is documented in *CAD* N/1, p. 80.

171. The phrase *mālak arḫi u šapatti ina šalši ūmi* is standard for long journeys in SB Gilgameš: see SB IV 4 // 37 // 82 // 123.

174. The tablet has more than simply Thompson's *dup-pir*: Haupt copied UM MEŠ TE, and noted in the margin '*um* nicht *dup*!' (*Nimrodepos*, pl. 70). I agree with him, though the interior wedge of TE is damaged. This is a meaningless combination of signs, of course, and the text is certainly corrupt.

175. For *iltapit* instead of *iltapat* see the commentary on SB IV 239.

180. As noted already, I follow Powell's understanding of 2.UŠ as a metrological notation (see above, on l. 160; one UŠ = 60 *nindan*). The reading of the unit UŠ as giš is adopted in the light of

the Sumerian homophone gíš, 'sixty' (as already observed in George, *Topog. Texts*, p. 135, fn. 24; according to J. Krecher, *Matouš Festschrift* II, pp. 42 and 47, both are /g̃iš/). In this I disagree with Powell, who refers to Akkadian *šūš(i)* and speculates that 'UŠ is perhaps originally a phonetic complement indicating a reading šuš, "sixty"' (loc. cit.). In the present line Powell takes 2.UŠ as 120 *nindan*, i.e. about 7200 metres, and goes on to calculate the rate of progress per punt, which at 2.4 metres seems ridiculously unheroic, especially for such an enormous man wielding such immense poles. Powell puts this slow progress down to the depth of the sea being not much less than the length of the poles, but it is certainly futile to speculate on the depth of the ocean and its effect on the length of each punt: this is epic! However, the solution adopted here is to take 2.UŠ as a notation for 2 × 60 units, i.e. 7200 *nindan*, which is a little over forty-three kilometres, yielding, if it is relevant, a rate of progression of 144 metres per punt. The use in the translation of the word 'furlong' is not meant to give an exact equation with the ancient measure; it is a term coined for lack of a suitable unit in English (two furlongs is a quarter of mile, just over 400 metres; one UŠ is about 360 metres).

181. On *qabla paṭāru*, 'to undress', the opposite of *q. rakāsu*, see A. L. Oppenheim, *Or* NS 14 (1945), p. 239; cf. R. Borger, *Or* NS 27 (1958), p. 148 (on Erra IIIc 49). The restoration of Ur-šanabi at the end of the line is the suggestion of A. Westenholz, the change of subject being signposted by *u šū* at the beginning of the line. Confirmation comes from the verb *ḫamāṣu*, which is used of taking off someone else's clothing—not one's own—and by force: see *CAD* Ḫ, p. 60, where the sense of this line is already suggested in the translation 'Gilgamesh stripped off his (Ur-šanabi's?) clothing'.

184–5. The ends of these lines are restored from the parallel, ll. 10–11.

187. The significance of the small horizontal wedge in the margin of MS K between column iv and v is unknown. This is not a manuscript which keeps count of its lines with wedges in the margin at every tenth line ('decimal markers'). It may be an incomplete notation KÚR, marking an error (on which see the commentary on SB IX 172).

195. The trace is not of *a-na-a*]*ṭ-ṭ*[*a-lam-ma*.

226–7. The beginning of the second line of the couplet, preserved only on Assyrian MS **z** (*kūdanu ṭar*[*idu*), is expected to read *Enkīdu ibrī kūdanu ṭardu* or *Enkīdu kūdanu ṭardu*, after SB VIII 51. Since the repetition of a line with an added proper noun is a standard device in Babylonian poetry (and Sumerian before that), either the extant text is defective at this point or the line division was so placed by the Nimrud scribe that the missing material was appended to the indented overrun of the preceding line.

250. That *umma* can introduce thought as well as speech has recently been pointed out by M. Stol, *BiOr* 49 (1992), 146. At the beginning von Soden read *tu-ku-um-ma*, 'wohlan!' (*AHw*, p. 1369), but the space available does not permit this. The abbreviated pronominal suffix on *idabbubū-š* is (if not vernacular) a mark of elevated style of a kind rare in SB Gilgameš.

254. The signs at the beginning of the line in MS f are marked aside by means of the Trennungzeichen. They cannot be overrun from column vi, for that was written after this line, of course. If the first sign were clearly DIŠ the phrase could be read *anāku umma*, as restored in l. 250, and taken as dittography, but this does not look feasible either. In fact, it looks more like [*n*]*u*, as Lambert's copy indicates. I am unable to explain the significance of this interpolation.

257. The omission of this essential line by the Kuyunjik manuscript can be put down to the carelessness that engendered other errors of substance in this source (see ll. 80, 82, 117, 318).

258. With the beginning of the line cf. SB IX 6.

259–60. Cf. the rather similar litany of wild animals in Gilgameš's lament for Enkidu (SB VIII 16–17).

261. The parallel line in the OB epic reads simply *[iltab]aš maškīšunu ikkal šīram* (OB VA+BM i 2′). Here the verb that follows *maškīšunu* cannot be any part of *labāšu* but is likely to refer to some technique of turning raw animal pelt into a skin fit to wear. The expression *mašku ṭubbuḫu* (once *ṭubbuḫtu*, inexplicably) can be read in three MB documents, as documented by the writer, with the help of K. Deller, in *NABU* 1991/19 (*UET* VII 40, 7: ⌜3! *mašak*(kuš) *alpi*(gu$_4$) *ṭú*⌝-*bu*-[*ḫu*]; K. Kessler, *Bagh. Mitt.* 13 (1982), p. 63, 15: *mašak*(kuš) *alpi*(gu$_4$) *ṭú*-[*ub*?]-*bu*-[*ḫu*]; *CT* 43 59, 21: *ma-áš-ka ṭú-bu-uḫ-ta il-te-en*). There the phrase in this line was translated literally, 'I carved up their hides'. I suppose that *ṭubbuḫu* is here a synonym for *kâṣu*, 'to flay'. The Seleucid source MS f seems to have room for extra material after the verb, perhaps 'for clothing' or something like it. Something similar also happens in l. 310 and one wonders whether, in fact, it is the (uncharacteristically unreliable) Kuyunjik manuscript that is in error.

264. The games that Gilgameš looks forward to are not only the activities described in SB Tablet I and the Sumerian tale of Bilgames and the Netherworld. As is well known, the religious festivals of Babylonia were events accompanied by general merrymaking and considerable *mēlulu*. It may be recalled that, before leaving for the Cedar Forest, Gilgameš promises to celebrate the principal religious festival of Uruk twice on his return (SB II 268–9 // III 31–2), which implies that it had to be suspended in his absence. This situation no doubt also obtained during the absence of the king on his quest for Ūta-napišti. Accordingly the restoration of *ušabṭalū*, *uqattû* or some such word in l. 264 looks probable.

265. In response to MS b's variant (see the apparatus) I have been encouraged to reject the hapax legomenon **pa-ad-di-'* (Thompson; von Soden, *AHw*, p. 808), and opt for a known word. The context recommends *ḫaddû* < *ḫaddi'u* (*parris) over *ḫaṭṭi'u*, 'sinner' (I owe this preference to the insight of A. Westenholz). The word intentionally echoes the prostitute's description of Gilgameš as *ḫaddi'u amēlu* (SB I 234), and evokes the happy frame of mind and life of carefree pleasure that was his in the good old days.

272. The spelling *šur-šum-me* looks construct state and since this word often appears qualified by *šikaru* I have restored accordingly. At the end of the line one should probably restore an adjective describing good-quality ghee (e.g. 'fresh, pure').

273. The words *tuḫḫī* (var. *tuḫḫu*) and *kukkuša* are ostensibly accusative, so the subject of the missing verb will be the fool.

274. The root of *mašḫandu*, √*šḫn*, shows it to be a garment worn for warmth; evidently in this context it is a rude item of no sophistication.

277. Negation with *lā* indicates that the verb is subordinated, presumably by *aššu* in l. 276.

278. While the idiom *rēša našû*, 'to lift (someone's) head', can mean 'to hold in honour' (e.g. SB XII 149), here it more likely conveys the sense of showing concern for another, as in a letter of Burnaburiaš to Amenhophis IV (*EA* 7, 17): *am-me-ni re-e-ši la iš-*[*ši*], 'why has he shown no concern for me?' Other examples of the phrase where the parties concerned are a superior and an inferior, as here, are omen apodoses such as *i-lu-um re-eš a-wi-lim i-na-aš-ši* (*CT* 5 6, 69; OB). This need not refer to a god's promotion or 'exaltation' of an individual, merely to his solicitude for him: 'a god will show concern for a man'. PNs of the type DN-*rēša*/*rēšī-iššī* can be rendered likewise, 'the god So-and-so showed concern (for me)'.

279. The first word of this line might be restored as [*man*]-*nu* (so already Parpola), yielding a question reminiscent of a proverbial saying preserved in an OB or MB tablet from Nippur: *ša la i-šu-ú šar-ra-am ù šar-ra-tam be-el-šu ma-an-nu-um*, 'the man who has no king or queen—who is his master?' (Lambert, *BWL*, p. 277, 13–14). The implication for the present context would be that Ūta-napišti reminds Gilgameš of the duties of his position.

287. A possessive suffix on *tappûtu* usually denotes the object of the aid, so I suspect the word refers to the aid that gods traditionally gave kings in ancient Mesopotamian ideology.

297. Jacobsen's translation 'why do you howl?' implies a reading *ta-šag-gum*, but the middle sign is to my eyes better read as *al*, with Lambert (*CRRA* 26, p. 54, 6). The final vowel is wrong for *leqû*, but indifference to the quality of vowels of final open syllables is a well-known and all-pervading feature of LB orthography, though it extends less commonly to the vowels of III weak verbs (the first example in SB Gilgameš is *ip-tu* for *ipte* in I 5, MS d).

300. For other examples of an adjective separated from its noun by the verb that they qualify see Chapter 9, the section on Language and style sub (vi).

301. The syntax of this line is open to two interpretations, depending on whether the last two words are analysed as the predicate (Lambert) or as part of the relative clause. The spelling of the verb, whether *ḫa-ṣi-pi*! or *ḫa-ṣi-ip*! (Lambert: *ḫa-ṣi*-PI+IP), does not decide the issue, since in a LB source any such writing can be indicative or subjunctive. For literary reasons I prefer a long relative clause, *ša kīma qanê api ḫaṣpu šumšu*, and no main verb. Note that this line begins a section whose opening and closing lines report the same fact, from the points of view of first the object of the action and then the subject (l. 307). It is fitting that they should be similarly constructed, both being nominal sentences in which the predicate is a descriptive phrase: 301 subject : pronoun + relative clause, 307 subject : participial phrase.

308. Recent translators are divided as to whether to understand the adverb *immatīma* in this and the following lines as introducing a statement or a rhetorical question. The translation of *CAD* M/1, p. 410, 'do we build a house forever?', is a mistranslation based on the ambiguity of English, for *immatīma*, 'at some time (past, present or future)', is not a synonym for e.g. *ana dūr dār*, 'for ever and ever'. The translation 'did/do we ever . . . ?' (Heidel et al.) succeeds, in my view, only when 'ever' is understood as 'forever'; translated into unambiguous language, the questions 'do we at any time build a household, start a family, etc.?', seem, as rhetorical questions, to be encouraging a negative answer and consequently ill suited to the context. Lambert evidently saw this difficulty, for he translates 'for how long . . . ?' (*CRRA* 26, p. 55, 17–21). This view assumes that *immatīma* means the same as *adi mati*, for which I can find no substantiation; elsewhere the interrogative *ina matīma* means 'when?' Thus I join those who take the lines as plain statements of fact, observations on the daily life of men and their generations.

309. Collation confirms the reading of *CAD* Q, p. 81.

310. Note the extra word in the Babylonian manuscript, and cf. the commentary on l. 261.

311. In MS K the restoration at the end of the line, after *ina*, can only be of a single, rather small sign, to judge from the spacing. The only trace of this word, on MS f, is compatible with ⌈kur⌉, and I have followed the solution suggested by W. G. Lambert's reading *ma-ti*, though in fact those signs are not actually preserved together anywhere. MS b's variant is not absolutely certain. The traces might be read *ma-t*[*im*!?], but *ma-r*[*u-tú*] is also possible and might be a more satisfying end to the couplet. Because a paternal estate was divided unequally between those with the status of 'sonship' (*mārūtu*)—the chosen heir (*aplu*) receiving more than the less favoured sons—there would always be possibility for jealousy and resentment among brothers. I translate *zērūtu* as 'feud' since, whether *māti* or *mārūti*, the reference seems to be mutual hostility breaking out among an extended family.

313. The failure of MS K to write the first syllable of *iqqeleppâ* explicitly may be put down to crasis: *kulīl(u)-iqqeleppâ*. The *kulīlu* is known in Sumerian as the 'river locust' (buru$_5$.íd.da) and, according to omen texts, Mesopotamian rivers in flood habitually carry with them large numbers of these insects (*CT* 39 19, 110–19: *Šumma ālu* LXI A; *ACh Šamaš* 14, 14; *Ištar* 2, 51: both *Enūma Anu Enlil*; Hunger, *SAA* VIII 461, 3). This phenomenon could be observed until recently on the Tigris,

which at the time of the spring flood carried large quantities of mayflies, *Sialis lutaria*, Arabic *klil*, according to M. Drower (as reported in E. D. van Buren, *Fauna of Ancient Mesopotamia*, p. 108; cf. E. Ebeling, 'Fliege', *RLA* III, p. 87; W. Heimpel, *RLA* V, p. 106; A. D. Kilmer, *Studies Reiner*, pp. 176–7). The ephemeral nature of the mayfly is proverbial, and for this reason (as well as the Arabic cognate) I prefer to take *kulīlu* as 'mayfly' rather than the customary 'dragonfly'. As Dalley notes (*Myths*, p. 133, n. 121), the image evokes a passage of Atra-ḫasīs in which the mother goddess likens those drowned in the Deluge to mayflies borne along by a river: *ki-ma ku-li-li im-la-a-nim na-ra-am*, 'they fill the river like mayflies' (OB Atram-ḫasīs III iv 6).

316. Though some translators cling to Heidel and Oppenheim's old idea of emending *šal-lu* to *ṣallu*, 'sleeper', I ally myself with those who do not see the need. The point of *šallu*, however, is not just any 'prisoner' (Lambert), so much as one who has been forcibly abducted (von Soden: 'der Verschleppte', Jacobsen: 'the one snatched away'). The usual reference of the term is to someone carried off in an enemy raid, taken prisoner in battle or press-ganged into permanent slavery or other service. Such a person, unable to send word of his fate to his family, would be lost to them more completely than, say, a man locked up in the local jail. Given up for dead, he would be for all practical purposes no more alive than the dead man with whom he is coupled here.

318. Recent translations opt for one of two interpretations in the first half of this line, in MS K reading either *e-ṭil* (vocative or stative of *eṭlu*) or *e-dil*. All take the second half of the line as looking forward to what follows in the next lines. These consist essentially of a reminder that the gods, among them the mother goddess, who, as man's creator, is given special mention, at some time in the past had made a distinction between life and death. Von Soden proposed in 1959 (*ZA* 53, p. 231) that the phrase *ultu ikrubu* in the Kuyunjik source alludes to the events described in Tablet XI, when Enlil blesses Ūta-napišti and his wife and confers on them the life of the gods (ll. 200–2). This interpretation looks sound at first sight and all have followed. When, after the publication of MSS bf, it became apparent that the LB manuscripts differ substantially from the Kuyunjik tablet, Lambert maintained the existing understanding of the line by dismissing their readings as corrupt. This follows accepted practice in dealing with sources for SB literary texts; tablets from Aššurbanipal's libraries are given precedence over late manuscripts and this is usually a demonstrably reliable procedure. However, in the case of MS K I am not so confident of Kuyunjik reliability: as we have seen, this manuscript has, for an Aššurbanipal tablet, rather a high proportion of corruptions (cf. above, on l. 257), and twice these have involved the intrusion of a sign not present in the late manuscripts (ll. 80, 117). Accordingly, in Tablet X one feels inclined to give more weight to the LB sources than one might in other texts.

The question then arises: does the Kuyunjik manuscript ring true? And then: do the LB sources yield sense? To deal with the first question first, it must be asked whether Enlil's blessing and deification of Ūta-napišti on his survival of the Deluge is really the occasion referred to in the following lines. The LB manuscripts make it unlikely that Enlil's name is to be restored in MS K at the end of this line, as von Soden originally proposed (and there was precious little room for ^{d}*en-lil* in any case). And would not such a reference anticipate the knowledge revealed to Gilgameš in the telling of the Flood story—the whole point of which is to prepare the ground for Gilgameš's disillusionment—and thus reduce its effectiveness? Before narrating that story Ūta-napišti tells Gilgameš that he is about to reveal to him a 'secret of the gods' (SB XI 9–10). Such a promise hardly rings true if Gilgameš has been told in advance of Ūta-napišti's blessing by the gods. Apart from this the description here of the proceedings of the divine assembly does not fit the episode in which Enlil deifies Ūta-napišti: l. 321 states that the gods 'established death and life', but no one is condemned to die in

SB XI 201–3; quite the reverse. There is in that assembly no trace of the business conducted in OB Atram-ḫasīs III vi 47–8, in which the mother goddess imposes death on postdiluvian man to keep down his numbers (see on this point Chapter 10, the introduction to Tablet X).

If we take the two final couplets of Tablet X together, they stand independently very well. And in isolation the reference becomes clear: the assembly described is that convened when the gods for the first time had to make a distinction between the respective destinies of those beings that were to be immortal and those that were to be mortal. As discussed in the introduction, in the tradition passed on by the poets of Babylonian Gilgameš epic this event took place at man's creation, not after the Flood.

If SB X 319–22 refer to events which took place at man's first creation, MS K's phrase *ultu ikrubū* [. . .] loses the context conventionally assigned to it and becomes still less satisfactory. Is it then corrupt, with *ul-tu* developed from *ul*? And if it is, is the immediately preceding text, which also disagrees with the LB manuscripts, also corrupt? The sense of the phrase *lullû-amēlu edil* is appropriate enough, as demonstrated in Lambert's exegesis (*CRRA* 26, p. 56), so on the criterion of meaning the text passes. But if we place confidence in the Kuyunjik manuscript, and take its Trennungzeichen to mark the boundary between two lines of poetry, it has to be remarked that we are left with two exceedingly short lines. Writing with regard to this phrase, Lambert supposed that 'the reading of the Babylonian copies, LÚ.BAD, is no doubt a corruption of LÚ DIL and the Glossenkeil' (p. 56). The truth might just as easily lie the other way around, with MS K's LÚ DIL and the Glossenkeil a corruption of the Babylonian LÚ.BAD.

This brings us to the second question posed above, as to whether good sense can be had from the late sources. These themselves differ, but only with regard to the tail end of the line: MS f, like MS K, has only space for two signs after the verb *ikruba/u*, and must have lacked *ka-ra-bi*. The line therefore reminds us of other lines in Tablet X where an extra word has been present after the verb in some sources but not in others (ll. 261, 310). From the point of view of syntax, the Babylonian line looks satisfactory in both its versions: two nouns, which might be analysed as object and subject (or, disregarding the case vowel of *lullâ*, subject and object), then the verb, negated, then a second object or paronomastic infinitive, cognate with the verb, and finally a prepositional phrase (to my eyes the wedge that follows *ka-ra-bi* in MS f is too elongated to be part of a MU, and has to be AŠ). The line itself, then, as preserved in the LB sources, presents on its own no difficulty to the literal translator. The difficulty lies in interpreting the import of what is written. I take it to mean that the dead, once their shades are successfully delivered to the Netherworld, have no further contact with the living. The preterite verb can be explained as 'gnomic', indicative of a proverbial saying (see on this Chapter 5, the note on OB III 255–6).

Thus the line is a second reminder of the finality of death. The imagery is not simple—and this explains the editorial changes made to produce the text preserved in MS K—but much of the imagery in Ūta-napišti's homily, and in wisdom literature generally, is not immediately accessible. In my view the text of the Kuyunjik manuscript is inferior on literary grounds, since it pre-empts the revelation of Ūta-napišti's story and in doing so has to place an unsatisfactory interpretation on the following two couplets; and on stylistic grounds, since the division of l. 318 into two lines results in a pair of overly short lines. Thus I see the Babylonian manuscripts' text as the more original version of the line and MS K's text as an inferior, though not meaningless, corruption.

320. Here again the Kuyunjik manuscript offers, in comparison with the Babylonian tablets, an expansion. This time I suspect the LB sources of telescoping *bānât šīmti ittīšunu* into *bānât šīmtīšu(nu)*, for the suffixless *bānât šīmti* is an attested epithet of the mother goddess (OB

Atram-ḫasīs III vi 47, quoted in the introduction to this Tablet; NA Atra-ḫasīs MS S iii 11). The enclitic *-me* in MS b has been explained as *-ma* coloured by vowel harmony (see *AHw*, p. 639: 'n/spB, nA selten nach *e* od[er] *im*').

322. As Lambert noted, both LB manuscripts preserve a variant *ultēdû*, introduced by the conventional notation, *šanîš*, 'alternatively'. Though he is surely right to remark that 'the TE is no doubt a graphic corruption of UD' (*ul-te-du-ú* from *ul ud-du-ú*), if *ultēdû* replaces *ul uddû* in its entirety, exactly the opposite sense is placed on the line through the loss of the negative. Such a wrong-headed variant is not likely to have been thought so worth preserving that it entered the copying tradition as a permanent part of the text, and I suggest that, no matter the origins of the variant through corruption of UD to TE, *ultēdû* was understood as a variant for *uddû* only.

TABLET XI

5. The phrase *gummurka libbī* is literally 'in respect to you my heart was fully concentrated (on doing battle)'. Some older translations attribute bellicosity to Ūta-napišti, not Gilgameš, relying on an original idea of T. Jacobsen (Heidel, *Gilgamesh*, p. 80, fn. 164). The translation put forward here follows Jacobsen's revised interpretation (*Treasures*, p. 206). It is Gilgameš's instinct to obtain his desires by the sword, not Ūta-napišti's.

6. At the beginning [*ana-k*]*u*? is possible but not secure. As so often in Gilgameš the prepositional phrase *elu ṣēri* is not literal but means 'in the presence of' (see above, on SB I 145 // 166). Thus I follow von Soden, *ZA* 53, p. 232, in preferring *nadât* to the apparent variant *nadâta*. MS W's *na-da-at-ta* does not have to be a second-person form: the trisyllabic spelling of a finally weak verb in stative 3rd fem. sg. can be paralleled elsewhere in seventh-century Assyrian orthography (see *GAG*³ §75c, n. 11) and the expression of a long vowel in non-final position by writing the syllable as closed is also attested in late orthography; see Chapter 9, the section on Spelling conventions sub (b). The phrase *aḫa nadû*, often rendered as 'to be negligent', also means 'to procrastinate, let up' (cf. *nīd aḫi*). Gilgameš, wearied by his exertions and perhaps intimidated in the presence of the venerable sage, no longer has the energy or the will to wrestle Ūta-napišti's secret out of him, and holds back from violence.

7. Cf. SB IX 76. On the last word (*teš'û*) see W. G. Lambert, *JSS* 24 (1979), pp. 271–2, against W. von Soden, *ZA* 53, p. 232. Here *balāṭa še'û*, which describes the success of Ūta-napišti in attaining what Gilgameš imagines was his goal, is used in contrast to *bālāṭa bu'û* (l. 206) and *balāṭam saḫārum* (OB VA+BM iii 2), which describe the vain quest of Gilgameš himself: *še'û* thus has the nuance of to seek successfully (cf. its meaning 'to visit, seek out', e.g. deities in their sanctuaries, as used constantly by the pious kings of the Chaldaean Dynasty).

9–10. The couplet is repeated later in the Tablet (ll. 281–2).

11. The variant *Šurippak* for Šuruppak also occurs in l. 23, where [*šu-r*]*i-ip-pa-ku-ú* and *šu-ru-up-pa-ku-ú* are both attested, and in *Hg* E, commenting on a lost line of *Hh* XXI: LAM × KUR.RU^{ki} = *šu-ri-*[*ip*]*-pak*; note also the OB personal name ^{m}*awīl*(lú)*-šu-ri-pak* (Ni 373 i′ 21′, cited in Nashef, *Rép. géogr.* V, p. 253). The conventional reading is based on (a) *Diri* IV: šu-ru-pag SU.KUR.RU^{ki} ku-uš ku-ru šu-ub ki-ki *šu-ru-up-pak* (*CT* 11 49, 33). Note also (b) a bilingual incantation that equates LAM × KUR.RU^{ki} and *šu-ru-ub-ba-ak* (*CT* 16 36, 5; *Udugḫul*), and (c) the spelling ^{m}*šu-ru-u*[*p-pak*?] in the Akkadian version of the Instructions of Šuruppak (*KAR* 27 obv. 1, ed. Lambert, *BWL*, p. 95). Contra Zadok, *Rép. géogr.* VIII, p. 209, the relevant entry in Proto-*Diri* = *OECT* IV 153 occurs at iii 40 not ii 40 and reads LAM.KUR.RU[^{ki} = *šu-ri/ru*]*-pa-ak* not LAM × KUR.RU^{ki} = *šu-rup-*[*pa-ak*].

12. The trace on MS W might also be read ⸢*i*⸣-[*na*; that on MS j, *a-ḫ*]*i*.

13. In common with most recent translators I take the second clause as nominal, with the locative *qerbuššu* (var. *qerbuš*) as a prepositional phrase (cf. Borger, *BAL*^{2}, p. 145). Note, however, von Soden's 'die Götter waren ihr nah', i.e. *qerbūšu* (Reclam^4).

15–18. The painful history of the decipherment of the first word of l. 15 is reported by J. C. C. Kamminga, *Akkadica* 36 (1984), pp. 19–20. The rest of these two couplets is taken over from Atra-ḫasīs, where they are the stock phrases that enumerate the hierarchy of divine taskmasters who lorded it over the assembly of the gods (OB Atram-ḫasīs I 7–10; cf. 124–7 // 136–9). There the text before Ennugi reads not *gugallašunu* but *ù ga-al-lu-šu-nu* // *ù gal-lu-ku-nu* (so also the late version, SB Atra-ḫasīs I 7–10, II 11–14 // 23–6, ed. George and Al-Rawi, *Iraq* 58 (1996), pp. 153, 163). Ennugi's title is conventionally *guzalû* (see Lambert and Millard, *Atra-ḫasīs*, pp. 147–8), but Ninurta seems to have the prerogative of that function here. As noted by Lambert, *gallû*, 'constable', is very suitable while *gugallu* is a title 'quite inappropriate for an officer in a divine assembly'. He saw the change of title as a corruption, put down to a knowledge of Ennugi's riverine activities in *Šurpu* IV 103 (also the hemerology *KAR* 178 iv 58: ^{d}*en-nu-gi* ⸢ugu?⸣.gal *šá* ^{d}*a-nim*).

19. For Ea's title *niššīku* see still W. G. Lambert, *Atra-ḫasīs*, pp. 148–9. The binding of Enki by oath is described more fully in Atra-ḫasīs, where the verb is *tummûm* (OB II vii 38, 42). On this account the old reading of the last word, *ta-šib*, is rejected in favour of the stative *tami*. The force of the stative is not that it is active (so *AHw*, p. 1317) but that Ea did not swear of his own accord, being placed under oath against his will; compare the common adjuration *lū tamâta*, lit. 'be you sworn', addressed to evil spirits and ghosts in exorcism. For the function of enclitic *-ma* here see *GAG*^{3} §12a: 'gleichfalls'.

21–2. The older text is differently worded (OB Atram-ḫasīs III i 20–1; cf. the Assyrian recension, MS U obv. 15–16). The alliteration of sibilants, and in particular *ḫissas*, perhaps evokes the sound of whispered words. Though an *igāru* need not always be made of mud brick (cf. *i.* of the ark in l. 58), in a domestic context it normally is, so in *kikkišu* and *igāru* the present couplet presents a contrasting pair. Between them they constitute the permanent and temporary divisions of a house, its courtyard and enclosure wall. Thus the fabric of Ūta-napišti's house (or, in the Assyrian recension of Atra-ḫasīs, Ea's temple) is the intermediary that passes on Ea's message in what is only much later identified specifically as a dream (l. 197; see the commentary below).

23. This line appears to quote verbatim a line of the Akkadian translation of the Instructions of Šuruppak. On this, and the name Ubār-Tutu, see Chapter 4, the section on Ūta-napišti.

24–7. These two couplets, which developed from OB Atram-ḫasīs III i 22–4, have been discussed by H. A. Hoffner, *Kramer AV*, pp. 241–5. He has an understanding of OB *ú-bu-ut bi-ta* and *ma-ak-ku-ra zé-e-er-ma* very different ('flee your home', 'build a huge boat') from the translations usually put forward, and proposed that the replacing of these phrases in SB Gilgameš by *uqur bīta* and *makkūru zērma* significantly altered the sense and structure of the passage and may have been the result of editorial misunderstandings. This idea has been developed by Scott B. Noegel, who transferred Hoffner's lexical proposals to the SB text on the grounds that, when so read, the text presents an example of 'Janus' parallelism (*Acta Sum* 13 (1991), pp. 419–21). The philological evidence that Hoffner adduces in support of his translation is very tenuous, however (see already the remarks of M. Malul, *Acta Sum* 17 (1995), pp. 339–40, fn. 6). As far as the lines of SB Gilgameš are concerned, there is little doubt in my mind that the conventional modern understanding is that which would also have been current in the first millennium BC.

28–31. Cf. OB Atram-ḫasīs III i 25–31. In our l. 29 note the II/1 stative *mundudā* in the LB manuscript. The verb of l. 31 has sometimes been translated as from *ṣalālu*, 'to rest', with reference to mooring the boat *on* the Apsû (reading [*e*]-*ma apsî*, 'wherever the A.'); see most recently P. Naster, '*ṣullulu* dans Gilgamesh XI, 31', *Symbolae Böhl*, pp. 295–8. However, a II stem of that *ṣalālu* remains unparalleled and the preposition *ēma* is not felicitous; the traces of the sign before *ma* on MSW may have suggested *e* to Thompson but to my eyes (as well as Haupt's) the sign ends in a single vertical wedge. In the OB poem the preposition is in any case clearly ⌈*ki*⌉-*ma* (*CT* 46 3 i 29). The obvious derivation of *ṣullulu* as a denominative verb from *ṣulūlu*, 'roof', remains a much better idea. Note that in OB Atram-ḫasīs III i 31: *lu-ú ṣú-ul-lu-la-at e-li-iš ù ša-ap-li-iš*, 'let it be roofed over "above and below"', the adverbial phrase signifies 'fore and aft' (see A. Shaffer, *RA* 75 (1981), pp. 188–9).

33. As can best be seen from the following line, where only the sign *at* is missing, there is not space enough at the beginning of the line for von Soden's [*zik-r*]*a* (*ZA* 53, p. 232), and the horizontal wedges are, in any case, rather too long for *ra*. As well as [*am-g*]*ur* ('performative' preterite, *GAG*³ §79b*), [*mit-g*]*ur* might be read: 'What you told me thus, master, is agreed.'

35. The word *kī* with enclitic -*mi* is otherwise found only in the Dialogue of Pessimism, and there as an exclamation of consent (ll. 36, 40, 63, 71). The city comprises the council of elders and the rest, a bipartite division that recalls the similar arrangements described for Uruk in the narrative of the preparations for the journey to the Cedar Forest (OB III, SB II–III; cf. also SB VIII 9–10).

38. Von Soden proposed [*eṭ*]-*lu* at the beginning of the line (*ZA* 53, p. 232), but it is doubtful whether there is quite enough space for this. As I read it, the conjunction introduces the additional information: 'as well as telling the people you are building a boat, this too you will tell them'.

39. On *minde* see Ch. 5, the note on OB II 17. This line begins a sequence in which all but one of seven lines terminate with the enclitic particle. In all of them it is a mark of emphatic exclamation, emphasizing the whole clause. Other examples occur in Ūta-napišti's monologue, certainly XI 114: *ilū iptalḫū abūbam-ma* and 124: *kī mārī nūnī umallâ tâmtam-ma*.

40–2. Cf. OB Atram-ḫasīs III i 47–9, where the reason given for the hero's flight is that Enlil and Enki were quarrelling.

44. The first word is restored from Atra-ḫasīs, which for this line reads *ḫi-iṣ-bi iṣ-ṣú-ri bu-du-ri nu-ni* (OB Atram-ḫasīs III i 35; see further Lambert's note, op. cit., p. 159). The word *bu-du-ri* was evidently unknown to one or other editor of Gilgameš, who replaced it with *puzru*, 'secret, hidden thing', perhaps because this was the nearest word he knew with an appropriate meaning (i.e. 'secret stock', 'hidden supply'? cf. von Soden's 'Bergung', 'Verborgenes').

45. The traces after the break in MS T do not appear to allow the reading -*kunūši*. Evidently the first half of the line contains more than just the missing verb.

46. At the start of this line and its parallels (ll. 88, 91) the old reading *mu-ir* is finally discounted by the unambiguous disposal of the signs in the new manuscript, $\mathbf{c}_1$. In all three lines the noun *šēr* appears to be in the absolute state. The frequency with which the expression *ina šēri* occurs in other texts makes it unlikely that *ina šēr* numbers with the 'bestimmte lokale und temporale Ausdrücke' noted as employing the absolute state in *GAG*³ §62h; but another explanation escapes me.

49. The use of the epithet Atra-ḫasīs, 'Exceeding-Wise', in this line is a indication, if one were needed, of the source of the Flood narrative in Gilgameš. From a literary point of view Ūta-napišti's self-reference in the third person does not sit well with the use of the first person in rest of the narration; it is perhaps an indication that the adaptation of the story was not carried out as expertly as it might have been.

50–6. Thanks to the new manuscript, $\mathbf{c}_1$, this passage is easier to reconstruct and can now be seen to number seven lines not six. From here on the traditional modern numeration of lines has therefore been abandoned. The passage corresponds to three couplets of Atra-ḫasīs, which fall in a slightly different order:

e[*ṭ-lu-tum* . . . . . .]	Young [men . . . . . . ,]
ši-bu-[*tum* . . . . . .]	old [men . . . . . .]
na-ga-[*ru* . . . . . .]	The carpenter [. . . . . . ,]
at-ku-up-[*pu* . . . . . .]	the reed-worker [. . . . . .]
ku-up-ra [. . . . . .]	Pitch [brought the rich man(?),]
la-ap-nu [. . . . . .]	the poor man [. . . . . .]

OB Atram-ḫasīs III ii 9–14

The comparison reveals that SB XI 52 represents an interpolation padding out the preceding couplet and that MS **c** has ll. 53–4 in reverse order. Alternative restorations of the final words of ll. 50–1 have been offered by von Soden, namely *pa-a*[*s-ri*], 'poles' (*AHw*, p. 839; cf. Reclam^4: 'Holzpfosten'), and whatever lies behind the translation '*Klammern*'; Labat's sacrificial lambs and rams go back to an older idea of von Soden, *ZA* 53, p. 232, now discarded. I follow the idea put forward by W. G. Lambert in his note on the couplet of Atra-ḫasīs, that what the craftsmen are bringing here are their tools of trade, the axe for trimming timber and the stone for flattening reed (Lambert and Millard, *Atra-ḫasīs*, p. 160). For the carpenter and reed-worker in the context of shipbuilding see for example, in an OB letter, the injunction ^{lú}*naggārū*(nagar)^{meš} ^{lú}*malāḫū*(má.laḫ$_5$)^{meš} *ù atkuppū*(ad.⌜KID⌝)^{meš} . . . *našpakam*(má.ì.dub) *li-pu-šu*, 'let the carpenters, shipwrights and reed-workers . . . build a cargo-boat' (*LIH* 8 rev. 7′–10′, ed. *AbB* II 8).

52. The third craftsman of the passage just quoted, *malāḫu*, is an obvious candidate for restoration as the one who carries the *agasilikku*. The writing of this word is unique but clearly more closely based on the Sumerian aga.šilig than other phonetic orthographies, which vary as to the vowels of the second element but all exhibit the unvoiced final consonant expected in a borrowing from Sumerian (OB *a-ga-sa-la-ki-im*, Mari AGA-*si-li-ki*, *a-ga-sa-li-ik-ki-im*, Shemshara *a-ga-sa-li-ki*, *a-ga-sa-li-kam*, SB lex. ŠU-*kum*, etc.: see *CAD* A/1, pp. 148–9; the restoration of this word in K 1356 by A. Livingstone, *NABU* 1990/87, is uncertain). Since the line is an interpolation the spelling may be symptomatic of a learned editor at work. The tool in question, a heavyweight axe, has recently been discussed by Danielle Cadelli in publishing a letter from Mari that is concerned with tools for felling timber (*Florilegium marianum* 2, p. 167). Elsewhere it is carried as a weapon by Ninurta (*Angim* 133) and wielded as an implement of demolition by Narām-Sîn (Curse of Akkade 114). In Sumerian Gilgameš the hero has his smiths cast such an axe for his expedition to the Cedar Forest (Bilgames and Huwawa A 55), but there it can have dual purpose, for battle and for cedar-felling. Its use in the present context, however, as a tool brought to a shipbuilding, must be much the same as the carpenter's *pāšu* (l. 50), for cutting the ship's timbers to size.

53. The second word looks like a verb. The copyist of the new manuscript noted of the broken sign 'das Zeichen nach *i* am ehesten SU zu lesen' (S. M. Maul, private communication). Neither *isūrū* (or *isurrū*) nor *ikuššū* rings true in this context, but *i-gu*[*š-šu*], 'they were rushing' (< *gâšu*) is not impossible; however, what is really wanted is a verb of carrying and the decipherment is left open for the moment.

54. Now that the passage is better preserved, Dalley's *pitilta* looks the best candidate for the damaged word that terminates this line. As a kind of rope, twisted by hand from fibres of the date-palm, this is an appropriate object to bring to a shipbuilding, and the only known lexeme *pi . . . tu* that can be considered such (on *pitiltu* see B. Landsberger, *Date Palm*, p. 21). The traces do not allow a reading *pi-ti-il-ta* but may represent *til* over an erasure.

55. The new manuscript at last decides the first word of this line, which was something of a crux. The solution had already been anticipated by M. Stol, *AfO* 35 (1988), p. 78, who argued that MS

C's *šar-ru* (as he read it then) was an orthography for *šarû*, 'rich', and drew attention to other examples of what he considered unexpected gemination of consonants in this Tablet (ll. 58 *šaq-qa-a*, 69 *ni-iq-qu*, 88 *ú-šá-az-na-an-nu*, all of which have good morphological or orthographic explanations, however). One can now see that MS C begins *šar-ru-ú* and postulate the existence of a **parras*-type adjective *šarrû*.

57. I do not accept the suggestion of D. G. M. de Rooij, as published by Stol, op. cit., that '*būna nadû* [57] introduces the construction of the Ark on the horizontal level(s), and . . . *lāna nadû* [60] is followed by the erection of the stories, vertically'. The idea is neater than the reality, for the height of the boat is detailed in l. 58 not l. 60. I see the contrast as between the external dimensions of the hull, bottom, sides and top (*būnu*), and the interior subdivision of the boat's body into compartments (*lānu*).

58. The form *šaqqâ* (hardly an Assyrian II/1 stative) is an example of the use of the **parras* stem for the plural of adjectives of dimension (on this see N. J. C. Kouwenberg, *Gemination in the Akkadian Verb* (Assen, 1997), pp. 52–7; D. O. Edzard, *ZA* 90 (2000), p. 293).

60. Note, in MS W, the use of the accusative suffix -*ši* for genitive -*ša* (l. 60); this is exceptional at Kuyunjik but well attested in LB copies (e.g. above, SB VIII 125). W. L. Moran's alternative exegesis of *la-an-ši* as *lā amši*, 'I did not forget' (reported by H. A. Hoffner, *Kramer AV*, p. 244), avoids the need to question MS W's reliability at this point. MS W, however, is a source that sometimes exhibits final vowels that are wrong by the standards of earlier grammar (at least seven examples are collected in Chapter 9, the section on Spelling conventions). Moreover, the conventional interpretation of the line yields a pleasing symmetry, verb + object || object + verb.

62–3. Note in both lines, on *aptaras* and *qerbītu*, masculine suffixes with reference to a feminine boat (cf. also l. 80). This is rare at Kuyunjik (another inescapable example is *kašādīšu* in l. 164), but use of the masc. sg. possessive suffix for the feminine is common in LB copies, and on nouns can be seen as another incidence of a shift from final /a/ to /u/ (which is first observed in the change in the acc. sg. case ending, but also, as is less generally known, in ventives in -*u*; see Chapter 9).

64. The *sikkāt mê* were probably bilge plugs: see F. Schmidtke, 'Wasserpflöcke (Gilg. XI 63)', *Festschrift Friedrich*, pp. 427–34. MS T's *amḫassi*, if not an error, suggests a variant of the line in with the verb is qualified with two accusatives, the pegs and the boat.

68. Like many others, I translate as if the text reads *šalšat šār šamnu ša izabbilū nāš sussullī*. The odd word order is explicable as a literary device to avoid monotony (so D. O. Edzard, 'Gilgameš XI 65–69', in A. S. Kaye (ed.), *Semitic Studies in Honor of Wolf Leslau*, p. 395).

69. The great obscurity here is the word *ni-iq-qu*; the various renderings of recent translators are collected by Edzard, loc. cit. These either translate ad hoc, with the word seen as a technical term in shipbuilding, or they associate it with a known word (e.g. *niqqu*, 'fig pollen'; *nīqu*, 'sacrifice'), or they surrender to an ellipsis. For waterproofing the fabric of an ancient Mesopotamian boat, shipbuilders needed oil or fat of some kind (*šamnu* in such usage is found with the verbs *peḫû*, 'to seal, caulk', and *kapāru*, 'to smear': see *CAD* Š/1, p. 324). The problem posed by *ni-iq-qu* may be resolved by a Sumerian document from Girsu which records the disbursement of oil or fat for preparing various cultic barges for a procession of the gods on water (R. Kutscher, *Acta Sum* 5 (1983), pp. 60–1; Šulgi). Some of the oil is to be used for caulking the boats (ì má.du$_8$.a), some for smearing on the hulls (ì sa.bíl.la), some for reducing friction at the dockside (ì má kar.re tag.ga), some for the teams of hauliers (ì érin [lú]má.gíd) and some for 'sacrifice' (ì sískur.ra). The last would translate into Akkadian as *šaman nīqi*/*niqî* and appears to vindicate those translators of Gilgameš who interpret *ni-iq-qu* as a late orthography of *nīqu*; for the convention of expressing a long vowel in an open syllable by closing the syllable see Chapter 9, the section on Spelling conventions sub

(b). Evidently shipbuilding was attended by some ritual in which oil was ceremoniously poured out, presumably over the hull, as an offering to secure the vessel's safety. Nowadays shipbuilders use champagne.

70. The remaining oil, to be stowed away by the boatman, is obviously for future use, whether this be for re-waterproofing or lubrication of the gunwales, for consumption by those on board or, as Edzard proposes, for the boatman's illicit profit (op. cit., p. 396).

74. The restoration follows Heidel and others. An alternative restoration, *um-ma-r*[*i iš-tu-u*], 'they drank soups', is offered by von Soden (*ZA* 53, p. 232; *AHw*, p. 1414; Reclam[4]), but offers one object too many (see the objection of M. Streck, *Or* NS 64 (1995), p. 67, fn. 141).

76. I have followed the usual convention in placing ^{d}utu (MS j ii 20′) at the beginning of this line. However, this manuscript does double lines up on occasion, and therefore it is possible that this last extant line of the column is l. 77, not 76, which would yield a variant *šamšu* [*ina rabê*] for *lām šamši rabê* in that line. As currently read this line throws up a problem of sense, since it is not clear how salving with oil could be the finishing touch with which the boat was completed. Perhaps what is referred to is the lubrication of the hull to facilitate launching or the ritual libation proposed in the commentary on l. 69. Others have had different solutions: Labat associated *piššatu* with the preceding festivities and took *qātī addi* to mean a cessation of labour. Von Soden rejects *piš-šá-ti* as to do with oil and translates *ad sensum*: '*bei Sonnenaufgang* legte ich Hand an, das *Letzte* zu tun' (Reclam[4]). In Babylonian of the first millennium the expression *qāta nadû* means to touch sacrilegiously (*CAD*, N/1, p. 94) but it did not always carry that nuance, for the OA king Erišum I uses it in the sense to start a job of work (Grayson, *RIMA* 1, p. 22, 15–17).

77. At the beginning of this line Borger reads [*it-t*]*i* (*BAL*^{2}, p. 107; cf. p. 145). However, to my eyes the big oblique wedge that is all that remains of the word is a little low for the end of *ti*. The use of *lām*(*a*) with the infinitive is common (cf. Lambert and Millard, *Atra-ḫasīs*, p. 126, 4: *la-am a-bu-bi wa-ṣe-e*), and the present phrase is thus the opposite of the standard *lām šamši napāḫi*.

79. The history of reading of the first five signs has been given by O. R. Gurney (*RA* 73 (1979), pp. 89–90; 75 (1981), p. 189). Gurney discarded the dictionaries' *germadê* (as originally proposed by Salonen, *Wasserfahrzeuge*, p. 93), in favour of Thompson's emendation, *gir*(*ri*) *tarkullī* (or *tarkullāti*). As understood by A. L. Oppenheim (*Or* NS 17 (1948), p. 53) and Gurney, this was a slipway comprising rollers that had to be moved from back to front as the ark was slowly launched from the bank. On the nuance of *eliš u šapliš*, 'front and/to back' on the horizontal plane, see A. Shaffer, *RA* 75 (1981), pp. 188–9. With regard to the sign that follows *gi-ir* má.dù^{meš}, I do not agree with Gurney's contention that 'the sign can just as well be *it* [as *uš*]'; to my eyes the oblique wedge is too low—and too deep—to allow the reading *it*, and the faint interior trace suggests the head of an upright: on this evidence the verb must be UŠ-*tab-ba-lu*. All difficulties of parsing from *šutābulu* disappear if we read instead *nittabbalu* (I/3 ventive).

80. Most translators follow the understanding of Oppenheim (op. cit.: '(when eventually afloat) two thirds of it (i.e. the craft) [stood out of the water]') or Schott and von Soden (Reclam[2]: '*bis das Schiff zu* zwei Dritteln *im Wasser* schwamm'). In the light of ll. 62–3, one may disregard Speiser's warning that the masculine suffix on *šinipāt* means 'the antecedent cannot be the feminine *eleppu*' (*ANET*^{3}, p. 94, fn. 201).

81–4. These two couplets pad out OB Atram-ḫasīs III ii 30–1.

82. The spelling *i-ṣe-en-ši* in MS T, ostensibly third person, might be thought a legacy of an imperfect transfer of Ūta-napišti's narrative to the first person. More probably it represents an unusual spelling of first-person *eṣēnši*; comparable spellings of other verbs in the first person can be found in first-millennium manuscripts (see above, the commentary on SB III 127).

88. MS J's orthography *ú-šá-az-na-an-nu* for *ušaznan* + V (sg.: cf. ll. 43–7) contains two peculiarities, a ventive in *-u* and the repetition of the final consonant at the morpheme boundary. The former feature is unremarkable in late SB and the latter is an occasional orthographic habit of Neo-Assyrian scribes (for both see above, Chapter 9). Despite Šamaš's intrusion the subject of this verb is Enlil, if the text is consistent (cf. l. 43).

91. I take this as direct speech, i.e. Ūta-napišti's announcement to the city folk as he loads his cargo, an encouraging reminder of the coming fulfilment of the divine promise. Others have taken it as narrative but this is awkard, for the storm has not yet begun.

95. The tiny horizontal wedge at the beginning of the line in MS W is evidently a scribal notation of some sort. The line is without obvious fault, so the wedge is unlikely to be an abbreviated example of the marginal notation KÚR discussed above in the commentary on SB IX 172.

99. The variant of MS W, [*iš*(*t*)*ag*]*gum* (or [*ir*(*t*)*ag*]*gum*), recalls OB Atram-ḫasīs III ii 53: ^{d}*adad i-ša-ag-gu-um i-na er-pé-ti*, and is probably more original than MS J's *irtammamma* (the latter is preferred in the composite text only because it is fully preserved). The description of the storm's onset is otherwise very different in Atra-ḫasīs.

100. The deities Šullat and Ḫaniš are twin agents of destruction identified as aspects of Šamaš and Adad respectively (*An* III 243–6: see further D. O. Edzard and W. G. Lambert, *RLA* IV, pp. 107–8.). Ḫaniš's destructive force is also found in Erra IV 145, where the devastated vegetation of Mt Šaršar is likened to woodland over which ' Ḫaniš had passed'. The image is probably one of trees flattened by a gale. Here, as in the parallel line OB Atram-ḫasīs II vii 49–50, Šullat and Ḫaniš are the vanguards of the storm, and thus the harbingers of Adad. The word *guzalû* in the following line can also refer to them, in which case they are specifically his 'throne-bearers', attendant on his progress.

101. The words *šadû u mātum* are unlikely to display locative case endings, for these are not expected in SB Gilgameš. They are instead accusatives of place (so Borger, *BAL*^{2}, p. 146). The expression finds a close parallel in a letter of Yasmaḫ-Addu from Mari: *i-na a-ta-lu-ki-ia bi-ri-it ma-a-tim ù šadî*(kur)^{i}, 'by my constant travelling between interior and uplands' (*ARM* V 66, 7–9).

102–3. This couplet appears, slightly modified and with lines transposed, in the Assyrian recension of Atra-ḫasīs, MS U rev. 14–15: [*il*]*-lak* ^{d}*nin-urta mi-iḫ-ra* [*ú-šar-di*] / ^{d}*èr-ra-kal ú-na-sa-ḫa t*[*ar-kul-li*]. That the Gilgameš epic preserves the original order of the lines can be seen from OB Atram-ḫasīs II vii 51–3: *ta-ar-ku-ul-li* ^{d}*er-*[*ra-kal li-na-si-iḫ*] / *li-il-li-i*[*k* ^{d}*nin-urta*] *li-ir-*[*de mi-iḫ-ra*]. In both versions of Atra-ḫasīs *nasāḫu* is used in the intensive stem, as in our MS C. Streck interprets *illak* as 'iterierend-pluralische Sachverhalte der Vergangenheit, wobei . . . der Sachverhalt verläuft in verschiedene Richtungen' (*Or* NS 64 (1995), pp. 49–50). To my mind this is an over-interpretation. The present tense describes circumstance attending an action in the past: just by moving on the water, Ninurta drove it into great waves. The god was present in the gale itself.

Neither Erra nor Ninurta is mentioned at random. According to Erra IV 118–20 the god of plague and war considered pulling out mooring poles one of his duties. There the chaos of boats floating loose on the river is a metaphor for the anarchy of civil war. Here the fuller form of his name allows the poet to anticipate the consonants of *tarkullī*. Ninurta had a particular association with weirs, as recorded in the god list *An = Anu ša amēli*, where ^{d}nu.nir = ^{d}*nin-urta šá me-eḫ-ri* (*CT* 24 41, 63).

106. Adad's *šuḫarratu* is the 'calm before the storm'. Since this noun is singular, the verb it governs, *ibā'u*, must be viewed as exhibiting a ventive in *-u*.

107. Since Thompson's edition the broken word in the middle of the line has customarily been read *e-ṭu-ti*, 'darkness', though very little of it remains. In fact the first sign seems much too long for *e* (see also Haupt's copy). It is not a complete *da*, either, but the general shape is better and I am

encouraged to restore *da'ummati* in the light of the stock idiom *ūmu namru ana da'ummati târu* (III *R* 41 = *BBSt* 7 ii 20: Marduk-nādin-aḫḫē; SB Anzû II 16; cf. OB Anzû II 68: *u_4-mu nam-rum da-um-ma-tam li-we-šum*). No such usage is found with *eṭûtu*. The endingless spelling *da-'-um-mat* in MS C (there is not room on that tablet for *da-'-um-ma-ti* etc.) is of the kind collected in Chapter 9, sub (c). The question then is whether the first word is *mim-ma*, as usually read, or *u_4-ma* for *ūmu*. A horizontal trace before *ma*, suggesting [*mi*]*m*, was seen by George Smith (*TSBA* 3 (1874), p. 551, 50; IV *R*[1] 50 ii 50), though not by Pinches (IV *R*[2] 43) or Haupt (p. 97). However, Thompson's copy also shows it (pl. 47). A reading [*u_4*]-*ma* is probably to be discounted on other evidence, for no trace of any head of an upright wedge is visible to the left of *ma*. At the end is yet another ventive in *-u*. The repeated /m/ sounds of this line, as restored, may be deliberate, to match the gloomy picture described.

108. In Atra-ḫasīs the subject of this line is Anzû (OB III iii 9–10; Assyrian recension, MS U rev. 17). Despite *ki-ma karpati*(dug) in the Assyrian recension, the sign after gim in the present line, though somewhat abraded at the end, appears to be more nearly gu_4 than dug. The verb *raḫāṣu* is typical of equids but appears with a bovine subject in SB VII 174 (*kīma rīmi dan*[*ni irḫ*]*iṣ elīy*[*a*]) and in the context of storms generally, where the bellowing storm god trampling the land and harvest is a metaphor that evokes a bull on the rampage (*Adad iraḫḫiṣ, passim* in omen apodoses and elsewhere). The end of the line can also be read *iḫ-p*[*i māta*(kur)] or even *iḫ-p*[*u-u*], but probably not *iḫ-ḫ*[*e-pi*]. What precedes it is witnessed by the solitary trace of an upright wedge from the end of the word (which comprised three signs at most). This trace rules out *kar-pa-niš* and *kīma karpati*(dug), but if the simile of the Assyrian recension is still desired *kar-pa-ti*]*š* might be considered, though to my knowledge this exact form is not yet attested.

110–13. George Smith's copies of these lines (*TSBA* 3 (1874), p. 551; IV *R*[1] 50) preserve wedges, and sometimes entire signs, that were already missing by the time Delitzsch (1885) and Pinches and Haupt (both 1891) published their copies. Smith's copies relied on MS J_1 only at this point, since the single other source for these lines currently extant, the fragment 82-5-22, 316 (now part of MS T_2), was not excavated until 1878 at the earliest (it came to the British Museum as part of the collection registered in May 1882, which included, among much Babylonian material, Rassam's penultimate consignment of tablets from Kuyunjik). While Delitzsch and Haupt acknowledged the missing signs of MS J_1 in footnotes, Thompson was evidently unaware of the tablet's earlier deterioration and the lost text is missing from his edition (except in l. 113, where, curiously enough, his copy even completes the end of the line as if it were intact). This omission has meant that later translators of the text have also failed to take account of all Smith's original readings.

110. At the end of the line Smith's text could be read *ši-mat a-m*[*e-lu-ti*], but though the coming destruction certainly sent most of mankind to its destiny, the phrase does not ring true at this point in the narrative. Instead, the restoration of *abūbu* as the last word of the line relies on the parallel couplet in Atra-ḫasīs, in the first line of which (OB Atram-ḫasīs III iii 11) only this word, *a-bu-bu*, remains (though the Assyrian recension has: . . .] ⌈*i*⌉-*ta-ṣa-a a-bu-bu*, MS U rev. 18). The preceding word in Gilgameš, *šadâ*, could refer to the upland north, the source of river-borne floods, but note that a wind is blowing earlier in the line and that the east wind, *šadû*, is especially considered the bringer of rain, as found in a proverb (Alster, *Proverbs*, p. 114, 4.9, 2): im.sa_{12}.ti.um im im.šèg.ga, 'the east wind is the rain wind', and in a passage of *Udugḫul* (*BIN* II 22, 51–2 // K 4625 obv. 16′–17′, ed. O. R. Gurney, *AAA* 22 (1935), p. 78): ^{im}sa_{12}.tùm im.ma an.ta ⌈šèg⌉ = *šad-du-ú šá* [*iš-tu*] *šamê*[e] *e-liš ú-šá-az-na-nu*, 'east wind that brings rain from the heavens'.

111. From Smith's copy it can be seen that this line is almost identical with the second line of the Atra-ḫasīs couplet, as preserved in the OB text and the Assyrian recension (OB III iii 12: [*ki-ma*

qá-ab-l]*i*⸢*e*⸣*-li ni-ši i-ba-a'ka-šu-šu* // MS U rev. 19). I have restored the end of the line accordingly. The form *ibā'* in Atra-ḫasīs is much preferable to our *ú-ba-'-ú*, ostensibly from *bu''û*, 'to seek', and it seems that MS J is unreliable here, as it clearly is elsewhere.

112–13. OB Atram-ḫasīs has the verb of the first line in the preterite, ⸢*i*⸣*-mu-ur* (III iii 13). Careful copying also reveals what was not seen previously, that MS C appears to agree with OB Atram-ḫasīs III iii 14 in concluding the line with the words *ina karāši* (though *ina* ⸢*ka-šu*⸣-[*ši*] is also possible). Since this manuscript's readings are usually superior to MS J's, I have relegated to the apparatus the latter's variant, conventionally read *ina šamê*. Note that only the sign AN is preserved on this manuscript: the last sign of the line is lost entirely, a situation that already obtained in George Smith's day. In presenting *šamê*(an)^{e} as if it were completely preserved, Thompson's copy is guilty of a misleading fiction. For the interpretation of this variant as 'in the rain' rather than 'from heaven' see George, 'Notes on two extremes of weather', *RA* 79 (1985), p. 69. It should be added that as well as *šamê*[^{e}] in this meaning one might also read *šamū*-[*ti*]. The survival of *karāšu* from the OB text in MS C vindicates the attempt to find a semantic correspondence between the two versions of the line.

114. The word *abūbam-ma* hardly needs the enclitic for its own sake. This is a case where the particle serves to emphasize the extraordinariness of the information conveyed by the clause as a whole (see above, on SB XI 39).

117. It is customary to take ^{d}*iš-tar* as a proper noun. However, the following line, which develops the idea further, shows that the mother goddess is the subject here. Though Ištar and Bēlet-ilī can be identified in the more syncretistic theological traditions (*CT* 25 30, 12), they are normally quite separate deities. Ištar is quite out of place as the lamenting goddess on this occasion. The parallel passage of OB Atram-ḫasīs has a similar couplet with *il-tum* in the first line and ^{d}*ma-mi* in the second (III iii 32–3); thus I take ^{d}*iš-tar* as a common noun, anticipating *bēlet-ilī* (cf. Bottéro, p. 191, fn. 2; for another example in SB Gilgameš see SB I 274, where ^{d}*ištari ummīšu*, 'the goddess, his mother', is Ninsun). The word *ištaru*, feminine and singular, provides a stark contrast with *ilū*, masculine and plural, in the previous line. The compassionate reaction of the individual most affected by the disaster is set against the selfish reaction of the crowd. The mother goddess initiates the lamentation for, as she will herself emphasize, it is her offspring who have been destroyed. The phrase *kīma ālitti* provides an advance clue to the goddess's identity, for Bēlet-ilī is the archetypal female in childbirth. MS J's *ma-li-ti* is ostensibly a different word, but since this is a root *primae*-w it cannot be excluded that it is an orthographic variant only, akin to *mar-šu-ti* for *aršūti* in SB VI 3.

118. Note the contrast between the two halves of the line. The sweet tones with which a mother soothes her baby are replaced by the dissonant shrieks of grief.

119. This line ultimately derives from OB Atram-ḫasīs III iii 34–5: *u*$_4$*-mu-um li-id-da-*⸢*i*⸣-[*im*] / *li-tu-ur li-ki-*[*il*], 'let the day turn to gloom, let it become again dark' (cf. C. Saporetti, *Egitto e Vicino Oriente* 5 (1982), p. 60), but it has been radically adapted to serve a different purpose. Here the words *lū itūr* convey emphasis more probably than retrospective wish; the usage of the particle *lū* to stress a verb in the preterite is more common outside royal inscriptions than the grammars suggest (*GAG*^{3} §81f: 'sehr selten'); in OB it can carry considerable emotion, as in the juridical document in which a distraught father swears to his parentage of a disputed baby: ^{m}*a-ḫa-su-nu lu-ú ma-ar-ti a-na ku-ul-lu-pa-at a-na šu-nu-qí lu ad-di-iš-ši*, 'Aḫassunu really is my daughter. I really did hand her over to Kullupat [the contesting party's servant] for suckling' (G. Boyer, *Contribution à l'histoire juridique de la première dynastie babylonienne*, 143, 25–7). Emotion is appropriate in the present line, too. The particle *lū* can also be present without modifying the meaning of the verb in any obvious way: compare an example in this episode, *sikkāt mê ina qablīša lū amḫaṣ* (SB XI 64).

Translations such as Landsberger's 'jener tag, möge er doch zur Erde werden' (in E. Lehmann, *Textbuch zur Religionsgeschichte* (Leipzig, 1912), p. 92), and many since, are predicated on the alternative assumption, that *lū itūr* expresses wish (strictly retrospective wish, however; Landsberger's rendering matches *litūr*, not *lū itūr*). In such an analysis *ūmu ullû* would refer to the day that the gods made their fateful decision to send the Deluge, which, to paraphrase the metaphor, 'should never have existed'. Jacobsen's novel translation of this line as 'O that you day had turned to clay', with the suggestion that the goddess is 'cursing the day', stalls on the third person *lū itūr* (T. Jacobsen and K. Nielsen, *Scandinavian Journal of the Old Testament* 6 (1992), p. 192).

The expression *ana ṭiṭṭi târu* does not sit easily with a given day, but if *ūmu* refers to the age gone by, and all that lived in it, the image becomes meaningful. An objection is that references to periods of time in general, either past or future, are commonly expressed with the plural (e.g. *ūmū ullûtu*); but there are exceptions that suggest we need not let the number of *ūmu* force us down a difficult path unnecessarily (e.g. *ūm ṣâti*). The old world is gone forever, and Bēlet-ilī's grief is compounded by the realization that her human family has been wiped out because of a divine conspiracy at which she herself connived.

120–1. Cf. OB Atram-ḫasīs III iii 36–7. The comparison reveals that MS C's *pu-ḫur* is taken over from the older text; MS J's *ma-ḫar* is secondary and inferior.

123. With this line compare Enki's words in Atra-ḫasīs, *a-na-ku-ma ú-ul-la-da* [*a-bu-ba*?] (OB Atram-ḫasīs II vii 46). In our line the orthography of the first word is unexpected: mimation is not wanted on *anāku*. Labat and Borger chose to circumvent this problem by reading *anāku umma* ('moi, (ai-je pu dire)'), but the resulting speech within a speech is not convincing. Borger's translation of the remainder of the line as 'meine Leute zeugen/gebären zwar' (*BAL*^{2}, p. 146) also fails to satisfy. The most straightforward solution is to reckon the spelling *a-na-ku-um-ma* with others that mark a long vowel (here long by virtue of stress, *anākú-ma*) in an open syllable by closing the syllable: see Chapter 9, the section on Spelling sub (b). Most translators distort the grammar of *nišū'a* to make it serve as the object of *ullada*. The word occupies a whole half-line and is best taken as a nominal clause.

124. For the final enclitic see above, the commentary on SB XI 39.

125. Cf. OB Atram-ḫasīs III iv 15. At the end of the line MS J writes *šá* over a partially erased *ia*.

126. Lambert's comments on the relationship of this line to Atra-ḫasīs (OB Atram-ḫasīs III iv 18–19a) have been elaborated by C. Saporetti, who puts forward the suggestion that MS J's line should be interpreted more closely with the older text, with *aš-ru áš-bi* taken as *ašar ašbū*: 'gli dei, dove (lei) stava, in pianto ⟨stavano⟩' (*Egitto e Vicino Oriente* 5 (1982), pp. 59–61). However, I find it difficult to believe that, if the scribe of MS J meant *ašar*, he could have failed to use the standard orthography, and I maintain Lambert's interpretation of *ašrū* < *ašāru* as a clumsy corruption. Lambert saw MS T's *ina nurub nissati* as probably the result of 'editorial work on a corruption of *aš-ru áš-bu ina nissati*', but this manuscript is usually more reliable than MS J, and I suspect that matters were the other way around. It is possible to imagine that *ina nurub nissati* (marginally the *lectio difficilior*, on account of the rare word *nurbu*) was original to Gilgameš but was later corrupted (MS J) by contamination with a similar line of Atra-ḫasīs: **ilū ašrū ašbū* (*i-na* > *i-lu*, *nu* > *aš*, *ru* > *ru aš*, *ub* > *bi*). The last derivation, in particular, would explain the presence of the irregular orthography *áš-bi* for *ašbū*. The phrase *nurub nissati* is a vivid image evoking the streaming eyes and nose of a person in tears (cf. *ḫé-ḫé-en*, 'nasal mucus' = *nu-ru-ub ap-pi*, 'wetness of the nose', in a commentary on *Šumma izbu*, ed. Leichty, *Izbu*, p. 231, 376 l).

127. Cf. OB Atram-ḫasīs III iv 21. This line is discussed at length by Lambert in his note on III

iii 29 of that text. Again, the *lectio difficilior* is preserved in MS T, while MS J has replaced the problem with an easier word (for *šaptī katāmu*, 'to close the lips', see *Enūma eliš* IV 98; von Weiher, *Uruk* II 24, 11).

128–30. Once again one must refer to Smith's copies to establish the true reading of MS J, on which a blistering effect has resulted in deterioration of the surface in the middle of the lines.

128. Already by the time of Delitzsch MS J's *ù mušâti* (clear to George Smith and still entirely visible on the old photograph reproduced as Fig. 12) had begun to look like traces of *u* 7 *mušâti*, although Haupt rejected this possibility (*Nimrodepos*, p. 108, fn. 12). On the duration of the Deluge in days and nights, see further Chapter 10, the introduction to SB XI.

129. On MS J *a-bu-bu* is no longer as obvious as it was, but the signs were clear to George Smith. At the end of the line, the sign kur is written over what is probably an erased *šá* (Smith read the whole thing *-nu*). Here again MS T is closer than MS J to the older text, *il-li-ik ra-⌈du⌉ me-ḫu-⌈ú⌉ [a-bu-bu]* (OB Atram-ḫasīs III iv 25), though the line has been expanded almost to the weight of a couplet by the addition of extra material now lost on MS T. It is presumed that MS J's *isappan māta* can be restored to fill this gap, though this is not completely certain, given the variation between the two sources in other lines.

130–1. This line of tablet is two lines of poetry, not one, and from here on the line numbering becomes still more removed from Thompson's. The problematical phrase *it-ta-ra*K *meḫû* may be clarified by reference to the Old Akkadian verb listed in *MAD* III, pp. 299 f., TRK, for which A. Westenholz proposes a meaning 'to take pity, intercede on someone's behalf', noting *li-*D*a-ar-*G*a-am-ma* in *RTC* 78 (private communication). The OAkk PNs *i-*D*a-ra-a*K/K*i-*(*i*)*-li* and *i*D*-ra-a*K*-ì-li* thus mean very plausibly 'My god (has) relented' (against *AHw*, p. 1325, 'grüngelb, blau werden'). This verb survives into the late period in the name of the demon Lā-tarāK, 'Unrelenting' (cf. Lā-gamāl, 'Unsparing'). The explanation of this name in one late commentary, namely *la ta-ri-qu* (cited by W. G. Lambert, *RLA* VII, s.v. Lulal), gives the radicals unambiguously, at least as they were then understood (another commentary records the less plausible exegesis *lā tarāk*, 'unthrashable', citing as justification *ta-ra-ku*=*na-ṭù-u*: BM 62741, 26, quoted by *CAD* N/2, p. 132). The evidence thus points to a verb *tarāqu* (*a*/*a*), used in the I/1 and I/2 stems.

The middle of the line was already damaged on MS J in Smith's day. In his second copy he read the signs between *ka-šá-a-di* and *šu-ú* as [*zunnu*(A) *šá*]*-mu-ut* (*TSBA* 3 (1874), p. 555, 21), but in his first he saw more, ŠE-[x]*-mu-ut* (IV *R*[1] 50 iii 21). The visible wedges Pinches noted as looking 'like *mu-ut* or *rik*(?)' (IV *R*[2] 43, fn. 86); Delitzsch and Haupt also opted for *rik*. Since MSS CT have what appears to be the I/2 stem *ittaraq* it seems possible that MS J had a stative form of the same verb, with passive meaning. The traces of the beginning of the word observed by Smith in his first copy suggest that the whole word was *te-riq*. However, *ta-riq* would be expected, and *šu-ú* itself looks strange (cf. Borger, *BAL*[2], p. 109: 'korrupt'); so, too, perhaps, does the end of the line (Borger: 'lies [*qab-la*] etwa *ik-la*?'; *CAD* Q, p. 15: 'emend possibly to *ik-la*'). The decipherment of MS J must therefore remain open to question.

132–3. The presence of 'Janus' parallelism in ll. 131–3, advocated by M. Malul, *Acta Sum* 17 (1995), pp. 338–42, relies on an unattested meaning of Akkadian *ḫayyāltu* (Heidel and Speiser: 'army'). Once it is seen that the metrical balance of ll. 132–3 would be better served if the line division came after *tâmtu* (note the perfect chiasmus that results in the rest of l. 133), it becomes clear that all three manuscripts preserve a false division of lines. Accordingly, the relative clause of l. 132 and its simile *kīma ḫayyālti* describe the sea in l. 133 (so already *CAD* M/1, p. 82, Hecker), not the Deluge of l. 131. The grounds for interpreting *ḫayyāltu* as anything other than 'woman in childbirth'—and for the 'Janus' parallelism—then disappear.

134. The variant of MS J apparently resulted from an old misreading of *u₄-ma* as *tam-ma-⟨ta⟩*, or even of *-am-ma u₄-ma* as *ta!-ma-tam-ma*, and can be marked as inferior.

137,139. On the phrase *dūr appi* and the standard epic line that uses it, see Chapter 5, the note on OB III 229.

140. There is no agreement as to whether the word written *pa-tu* in MSS CJ is *pāṭu*, *pattu* or *pātu*; I have translated *ad sensum*. Von Soden thinks it may be an error (*AHw*, p. 849), and one is left wondering what followed *ana* in MS T.

141. In the matter of the number I have given precedence once again to the reading of the more reliable MS T over that of MS J. Most translators prefer 'twelve' and assume that this figure is a measure of length and that a metrological unit must be understood. However, this does not account for the distributive determinative, and I am more sympathetic to Oppenheim's idea that the reference is to direction rather than distance (*Or* NS 17 (1948), p. 54: 'in each (of the) 14 directions'). The use of *nagû* evokes the famous world 'map' ('diagram' would be the more accurate term), in which areas of land depicted as beyond the Bitter Sea, at the edge of the world, are so termed (*CT* 22 48). Ūta-napišti sees a similar view, an expanse of water relieved at intervals by distant islands (the evidence for *nagû* with reference to islands is collected by W. Horowitz in his discussion of the map, *Cosmic Geography*, pp. 30–2). Oppenheim took the figure fourteen as significant: 'instead of the seven *nagû*-mountains depicted on the well-known Babylonian *mappa mundi*, we have here double the amount (the variant "12" of one copy is to be emendated)', and he referred for confirmation to H. and J. Lewy's 'seven-direction-system' (*HUCA* 17 (1943), pp. 8–13). However, it is by no means certain that the map, when complete, showed seven such islands: some commentators presume eight to be more likely (W. G. Lambert in C. Blacker and M. Loewe (eds.), *Ancient Cosmologies*, p. 60; Horowitz, loc. cit.).

148 // 151 // 154. Unlike other translators I prefer here to take *šūṣû* in the meaning 'to fetch out', as in SB VIII 215, rather than 'send out': this action thus precedes the actual release. As matters now stand, more manuscripts have *ú-maš-šar* than have *ú-maš-šir*, which appears only in MS J. However, confusion between the signs ŠAR and ḪIR was rife at Nineveh, and it is almost certain that the two spellings do not mark variations in the tense of the verb.

149 // 152. All recent translators prefer the easy variant of MS J to MSS CW's *i-pi-ra-am-ma*. Since the suspicion is that MS J or one of its predecessors replaced the difficult verb exactly because of its obscurity (apparently by ignoring a wedge, and reading *i-tú-ra-am-ma*), MSS CW's reading must be taken as the more original. The return of the birds is, in any case, reported in the following lines (*issaḫra*). Since the birds' first instinct on release would be to find food (cf. l. 156), perhaps one might derive the word in question from *epēru*, 'to provide food', and assume a nuance of 'to forage' (seeking and finding being activities often conveyed by the same verb: cf. *amāru* and *še'û*). There is also the verb *i-pi-ra-ni* in broken context in SB III 42 to consider. As it stands, it is better to withhold judgement.

150 // 153. While MS C reads *īpâššimma* MSS JWc all have *īpâššumma*. This need not be an error, for the two nouns to which the pronominal suffixes refer are both written logographically and can be read as masculine (*summu*, *sinūnu*) as well as feminine (*summatu*, *sinūntu*).

156. Part of this line finds a parallel in an *ikrib* prayer to Šamaš and Adad (Craig, *ABRT* I 60, 19: *e-kal i-šá-ḫa u i-ta-ra*; coll. W. Mayer, *AHw*, p. 1589). The context there is the behaviour of a gazelle kid. Both verbs after *ikkal* are problematical and are translated from context alone. I connect *i-šá-aḫ-ḫi* with a passage of the omen text *Šumma ālu*, describing behaviour typical of a raven: DIŠ {mušen} *arabû*(ára.bu)^{mušen} *kīma*(gim) *aribi*(buru₅)^{mušen} *išpil/uštappil*?(ki.ta)*-ma i-šá-'-i*, 'if a waterfowl . . . low like a raven' (*CT* 40 49, 32). *CAD* places the verb of the omen under *šâ'u*, 'to

swoop', even though the trisyllabic form is not good (Š/2, pp. 244: 'anomalous'). Two such 'anomalies' begin to make a case for a variant form of the verb. Von Soden originally thought similarly (*OLZ* 38 (1935), 146: '*i.* steht für *išā'(ī)* . . . "er flattert umher"'), but later rejected this decipherment (*AHw*, p. 1133, Reclam[4]: '*scharrte*'; otherwise Dalley: 'preened(?)'; Bottéro: 'croassa(?)'). Consideration of the contexts leads us to reject a derivation from *šâ'u* and consider another verb entirely. What does a gazelle kid do when eating that a raven also does? Certainly not fly. The third verb of the line used to be translated *ad sensum*, e.g. 'caw', but has been more recently associated by von Soden with *zibbata tarû*, 'to hold the tail raised', behaviour attributed to pigs and dogs in a number of omen texts (see *AHw*, p. 1336). The two verbs together may describe a jerky movement of an animal or bird when feeding, perhaps the motion head down, tail up and vice versa. Note that the traces in MS W are incompatible with *i-tar-ri* (and *i-ta-ri*, etc.); it may have held a different text.

157–9. These lines are remarkable in that they all display final stress (*niqâ*, *šadî*, *uktīn*). Such stresses occur sporadically in Gilgameš, as in other poetry, but to find a group of three makes one wonder whether they are deliberate. Further investigation of such stresses may shed light on the question, but for the moment it will suffice to draw attention to the sequence as noteworthy.

157. Of the parallel in Atra-ḫasīs only *a-na ša-a-r[i* remains (OB Atram-ḫasīs III v 30). Most recent translators have assumed that the implicit object of *ušēṣīma* is the occupants, animal and human, of Ūta-napišti's boat, with reference perhaps to Genesis 8: 19. S. J. Lieberman takes it intransitively, 'I came out' (in M. deJ. Ellis (ed.), *Nippur at the Centennial*, p. 131). Both renderings seem to me unjustified: *šūṣû* means to fetch something out of something (as with the birds in ll. 148–54, and the table in SB VIII 215), and here describes the preparations for the sacrifice. The winds, which symbolize the four corners of the earth, are thus not the directions in which the boat's cargo disperses but those in which the sacrifices are made (so also Lieberman and *CAD* N/1, p. 339, though otherwise Š/2, p. 136).

158. The phrase *ziqqurrat šadî* is an unusual coinage, but reminds us that religious ritual in ancient Mesopotamia was essentially urban and temple-bound. The juxtaposition between the manmade and the natural also evokes a theme essential to the epic, the contrast between the city and the wilderness. Perhaps the alliteration *surqinnu* . . . *ziqqurrat* also affected the choice of words. Incense is burnt to attract the gods to the sacrifice, of course, as is explicit in, for example, an OB divination prayer recited in preparation for extispicy: ^{d}⌜*šamaš a-ša-ka*⌝*-an a-na pi-i qú-ut-ri-nim ša m*[*a-aḫ-r*]*i-i-ka* ^{giš}*erēnam*(eren) *el-la-am li-ši-ib qú-ut-ri-nu li-iq-ri-am i-li ra-bu-tim*, 'O Šamaš, I am putting pure cedar into the mouth of the censer that is before you: let the censer rest, let it invite the great gods here' (*YOS* XI 22, 14–16; ed. A. Goetze, *JCS* 22 (1968–9), p. 28).

159–60. These two lines explain in detail how Ūta-napišti made the first ritual offering of food to the gods and therefore elaborate on the phrase *surqinna šakānu* in l. 158. The word *uktīn* can be parsed as II/1 perfect but perhaps also as II/3 preterite, not iterative but serial, with the nuance of setting in rows or one by one (see *GAG*[3] §91f). The objects set up in this manner, called *adagurru* (or *atakurru*), are small vessels that contain liquid for rituals of libation. Around their bases Ūta-napišti puts perfumed leaves and resin. It has been suggested that these were thrown on to fire beneath the vessels (*CAD* A/1, p. 93), but this does not tally with what we know of the function of the *adagurru*. This container is nowhere directly associated with fire and we do not expect libations to be warm. It remains true that the aromatics' function in such rituals was to attract the gods' attention to their meal, and that to that end they were usually burnt on a censer. This understanding informs the ritual quoted in the preceding paragraph and is expressed directly in an incantation prayer to Girra, the fire god (*LKA* 139, 49): [*ilū*^{m}]^{eš} *e-ri-ša-am ul iṣ-ṣi-nu* ⌜*ba*⌝-

lu-uk-ka, 'without you [the gods] cannot smell the aroma'. Perhaps aromatic leaves and gum were on some occasions thought pungent enough nevertheless to reach the gods' nostrils without being burnt as incense. Further study is required of the various ways in which the gods of Babylonia could be fed.

161–7. This passage is parallel to OB Atram-ḫasīs III v 34–vi 4 but very much condensed.

166–7. The couplet's syntax has caused difficulties (the most recent exegesis is by J. N. Postgate, *NABU* 1998/30). It is best understood in the light of the parallel OB Atram-ḫasīs III vi 2–4, where a nominal clause modified with precative *lū* is followed by a clause with the voluntative *luḫsus*: *zu-ub-bu-ú a*[*n-nu-tum*] *lu-ú uq-ni ki-ša-di-i*[*a-a-ma*] / *lu-uḫ-sú-ús-ma* u_4*-mi* [*an-nu-tim*] *zi*-[. . .], 'these flies [shall be] the lapis lazuli (beads) around my neck, so that I remember [these] days [. . .]' (cf. W. von Soden, *TUAT* III/4, p. 643). The phrase *ay amši* in our l. 166 is preserved only on MS J (W does not hold it) and is suspicious for this very reason; in the light of the OB text it can be ignored as dittography from l. 167. The uncertainty of the sources regarding the verb of the second line has led previous commentators to read *aḫsusamma*, with or without *lū*, but neither form makes sense (*lū* with the preterite denotes retrospective wish, 'I should have . . .', or reports past fact, 'I did . . .'). Reference to the OB text encourages me instead to read MS C as *lu-ú-uḫ-su-sa-am-ma*, an orthography comparable with the same tablet's *lu-ú-up-te* in SB XI 281 (note also ⌈*lu-u*⌉*-uš-pu-uk* in SB VI 30, Kuyunjik MS). The other manuscripts' *aḫsusamma* is corrupt.

168–9. The heavy repetition of the consonant /l/ in the phrases *ilū lillikūnim* and *Ellil ay illika* may be intentional, to suggest that the mother goddess uttered her words in a kind of ululation.

170–1. Cf. OB Atram-ḫasīs III iii 53–4 // v 42–3: *ša lā imtalkūma iškunu abūba* / *nišī ikmisu ana karāši* (where the subject is not Enlil but Anu).

173–4. Cf. ibid., vi 5–6: *makurra ītamar q*[*urādu Ellil*] / *libbāti mali ša Ig*[*īgī*].

175. As Lambert remarked in his note on the parallel couplet of Atra-ḫasīs (OB III vi 9–10), the older text's *a-ia-a-nu* indicates that MS **c** (which is better restored [*a-a-n*]*u-* than Borger's [*man*]-*nu-*, *BAL*[2], p. 110) has the better tradition of reading in this line, since it avoids the conflict of gender between *ayyumma* and *napištu*. The same manuscript also confirms that ll. 175–6 are a couplet, not a single line.

176. The vetitive *ay ibluṭ* normally (if not always) denotes wish in the present-future, 'may he not survive', though in this line it is nevertheless conventionally translated as if referring to the past (e.g. von Soden, Reclam[5]: 'überleben sollt' niemand'). Further research is needed to discover whether the negation of past *lū iblut*, 'would that he had survived', can really be *ay iblut* and not, as expected, *lū lā iblut* (cf. in form positive and negative wish with the stative, *lū damqat* : *lū lā damqat*).

177–82. Cf. OB Atram-ḫasīs III vi 11–17, where, however, there are two differences: first, it is Anu who suggests to Enlil the culprit's identity. The reason for his substitution by Ninurta is not clear. Second, Enki addresses his reply to 'the great gods', i.e. all the gods in assembly.

183. The choice of epithets is surely loaded with irony.

185–6. i.e. punish the guilty but not the innocent. A slightly different version of this couplet survives on the newly discovered NB copy of SB Atra-ḫasīs (courtesy W. G. Lambert):

be-el š[*e-er-ti*] ⌈*e*⌉*-mid še-ret-s*[*u*]
be-el [*gíl-la-t*]*i e-mid gíl-lat-s*[*u*]

MMA 86.11.378A rev. v 11–12, ed. Lambert, *CTMMA* 2 forthcoming

187. Cf. OB Atram-ḫasīs III vi 24: [. . .] *ù ru-um-mi*. In trying to make this line fit the specific context of the punishment of sinful mankind, most translators have followed the spirit of A. L.

Oppenheim's rendering: 'but be careful lest (an innocent) might be punished, act gently that an(other) might not [come to harm]!' (*Or* NS 17 (1948), p. 55, with fn. 2: 'the verbs *ramû* II and *šadâdu* have here the nuance "to go slow, to let loose"'). I can find no support for this. While *šadādu* can be 'to heed', even without *ina/ana libbi* (as in SB XII 32) and *rummû* can be 'to relax' (trans.), so far from being synonyms they are more commonly antonyms, 'to pull taut' and 'to slacken, loosen'; and *ay ibbatiq* has nothing to do with punishment. Heidel translates more accurately ('let loose, that he shall not be cut off; pull tight, that he might not ge[t (too) loose]', but still identifies the anonymous third person singular with 'man'. I do not find this convincing. In my view the line is proverbial, using the imagery of hauling a boat upstream (*šadādu* is the usual verb for this work). The point is that the appropriate amount of force must be applied: too much, and the rope will snap under the boat's inertia; too little, and momentum will be lost as the line goes slack. Enlil's retribution has been out of all proportion to what was required, and Ea goes on to list the less dire means that are suitable for the reduction of human numbers.

188–9. These lines, and the six that follow, are conventionally translated as if the precatives *litbâmma* and *liššakinma* were *lū itbâmma* and *lū iššakinma*, in other words, as retrospective wishes. The Deluge is certainly past (*taškunu*) but this does not allow us to ignore the grammar and force the alternative means of reducing the population into the past also. Ea uses the precative because the alternatives remain at Enlil's disposal and should be used in future.

193 and 195. The end of the l. 193 could also be read *mātu li*[*m-ṭi*], 'so that the land became diminished'. Other translators have had various ideas. For reasons of literary structure I prefer an active verb, parallel with *liṣaḫḫir* (ll. 189 and 191). Similarly, if *māta lišgiš* is the correct reading in l. 195, so too it must be in l. 193 (thus also Borger, *BAL*^{2}, p. 111). MS J's variant *nišī* in l. 195 is rejected as upsetting the carefully balanced repetition of these lines. The phrase *Erra* (nom.) *šagāšu* is a standard literary expression for the ravages of plague (cf. Erra V 57; *STT* 71, 16, ed. W. G. Lambert, *RA* 53 (1959), p. 135: prayer to Nabû); the use of the same verb with *ḫušaḫḫu*, as if this last were a demonic personification of famine, appears to be an original figure.

197. Curiously, both extant manuscripts (CJ) write the verb's prononimal suffix as dative (-*šum*-) when an accusative is wanted. This may be an orthographic feature rather than an error of grammar (see already the commentary on SB I 220).

198. Since Ea is addressing only Enlil, I take the first word of the phrase *milikšu milku* as the verb, not the second, which makes a less satisfactory singular imperative.

200. Notice the alliteration on the liquid /l/ and the bilabials /m/, /b/ and /p/. The meaning of *šūlû* here is now discovered not to be 'to put (aboard)' as it was in ll. 27 and 85 and as it has conventionally been understood, but 'to remove', effectively the opposite. This has become clear from a new manuscript of SB Atra-ḫasīs that gives a variant account of this episode (courtesy W. G. Lambert):

> *i-lam-ma* [^{d}*en-l*]*íl a-na lìb-bi* ^{gi}[^{š}*eleppi*(má)]
> *iṣ-bat qa-ta* [*u*]*l-te-la-an-ni ul-te lìb-bi* [^{giš}*eleppi*]
>
> MMA 86.11.378A rev. v 15–16, ed. Lambert, *CTMMA* 2 forthcoming
>
> Enlil came up into the [boat,]
> he took hold of my hand, he took me out of [the boat.]

It does, indeed, make better sense if Enlil removes Ūta-napišti and his wife from the ark before spiriting them away. That way they are blessed and immortalized in full view of the gods whose number they join.

202. The spelling *bi-ri-in-ni* can be taken as an example of late spelling (see Chapter 9, the

section on Spelling sub b) or as a morphological development, *birīni* > *birinni* (*GAG*³ §20d; for other examples see Borger, *BAL*², p. 142 on 125). The repetition of the syllable /put/ is perhaps intended to suggest the pat of Enlil's hand on the foreheads of Ūta-napišti and his wife. Enlil's action is also reported in the new fragment of Atra-ḫasīs, MMA 86.11.378A rev. v 21: [*i*]*l-pu-ut pu-ta u pu-us-s*[*a*], 'he touched my forehead and her forehead'. Lambert comments that 'this ceremony was no doubt based on a custom in human society, perhaps the OB rite of freeing a slave', comparing an OB expression used in those circumstances, *pūtam ullulum*, lit. 'to render the forehead pure'.

208. The spelling *tu-ut-ta-a* is ambiguous (as too is *ut-ta* in l. 317): it is uncertain whether a I stem or a II stem of *atû* is at issue. An example of this verb exhibiting an unambiguous II/1 stem occurs on a Kassite-period cylinder seal: see W. G. Lambert, *AfO* 23 (1970), p. 47: *balāṭa*(ti.la) *lu-ut-ti*, 'may I find life' (I am obliged to Lambert for this reference).

212. For the rare word *marḫītu* see the note on OB VA+BM iii 13.

213. Thompson's *amēla danna* was accepted by Heidel and others but von Soden rejected it in favour of *amēla eṭla* (*ZA* 53, p. 233). Others have presumed that lú is a determinative and I agree with them. In Gilgameš the orthography ˡᵘ́guruš = *eṭlu* is not usual, but is also found in l. 53 of this Tablet, in SB I 77 and MB Boğ$_2$ obv. 15 (note also guruš.lú in MB Ur 56 and 65).

217–18. This couplet distantly echoes the words of the prayers and valedictions made at the beginning of Gilgameš's heroic career (OB III 214–15, SB III 29–30). This may be an intentional signal that at last his journey is over. A more prosaic formulation of *ḫarrān illika litūr ina šulmi* is to be found in the *namburbi* of the broken chariot (*CT* 34 8, 8): *ina ḫarrān*(kaskal) *illiku*(gin)^*ku* *šal-mu-us-su ana māti*(kur)*-šú i-tur-ra*, 'so he will come back safely to his land by the way he went' (for this text and its duplicates see now Maul, *Zukunftsbewältigung*, pp. 387–99).

220. The first sign of the line had already lost clarity when Haupt saw it (*Nimrodepos*, p. 111, fn. 2: 'sehr undeutlich'), but it is unquestionably a complete *rag* on the old photograph (Fig. 13). The spelling *a-me-lut-tu* could be taken as an Assyrianism (*GAG*³ §56s), for there are several certain Assyrian dialect forms in Kuyunjik manuscripts of Gilgameš (see Chapter 5, the section on Language and style sub viii, ix), but the suffix *-ūtu* is so spelled in many Babylonian tablets, too.

221. The verb *šitakkanī* (with *ištakkan* in l. 223) is an unambiguous example of the serial nuance of the iterative infix /tan/ found especially with verbs of placing: the subject puts things in position in turn, or one by one, to form a row of them (see *GAG*³ §91f). A comparable use if the I/3 stem of the same verb occurs in an inscription of Nebuchadnezzar II in which he sets in position a row of cedar logs to form the deck of a bridge (*aš-tàk-ka-an*: George, *RA* 82 (1988), p. 149, 26).

226 and 238. It is conventional to derive *muš-šu-kàt* from *mussuku*, which means 'to be ugly, foul, vile'. According to the attestations of this verb and associated words in the dictionaries, this root never uses /š/ as its middle radical. Semantically it is not obviously appropriate. Its most common use is of tarnished reputation and it is not found with foodstuffs. Bread in any case does not putrefy in the open: it goes mouldy and hard. Thus I feel emboldened to posit as a denominative verb *muššuku*, 'to turn (something) into leather', for bread, particularly Mesopotamian bread, goes leathery as it dries out. (It is only proper to note that long after reaching this conclusion I found that the translation of *muššukat* as 'leathery' already occurs in J. Gardner and J. Maier, *Gilgamesh, Translated from the Sîn-leqi-unninni Version* (New York, 1985), pp. 241 and 245.)

230 and 241. Most translators read *ina pittimma* and take it as a unique adverb of time (see *AHw*, p. 871), qualifying *ilpussūma* or the bread. A derivation from *pēmtu* is preferable, as already seen by Oppenheim (*Or* NS 17 (1948), p. 57: 'in the oven').

244. The 'Thief' is a metaphor for death and almost a demonic personification, as in *Bīt mēsiri* II (G. Meier, *AfO* 14 (1941–4), p. 144, 80): *lu-ú mu-tum lu-ú ek-ke-mu lu-ú šag-gi-šu lu-u ḫab-bi-lu*,

'be it Death or the Thief, be it the Butcher or the Robber' (other, better-known demons follow). The verb is singular ventive, as the variant in MS J proves (for the ventive in *-u* see Chapter 9, the section on Spelling sub v). As object of the verb *CAD* E, p. 69, restores specifically [*šīrī*]-*ia*, 'my [flesh]', but von Soden prefers [*qerbē*]-*ia* (*ZA* 53, p. 233); other words are also possible.

246. Haupt's denial that the broken sign on MS J was *uš* (*Nimrodepos*, p. 112, fn. 7) seems to my eyes unfounded. All recent translators restore the missing word as *šēpīya*, 'my feet' (cf. l. 41), often without square brackets, but it seems to me that the less specific *pānī šakānu* is the better idiom; it often occurs after the conjunction *ašar* (usually in the stative, e.g. *ašar pānūšu šaknū*, 'where he intends to go').

248. The new MS **b** proves correct the restoration of the first verb in *CAD* Z, p. 99, against von Soden's reading (*ZA* 53, p. 233), [*li-šam*]-*ṭi-ka*, '[may it] humiliate you'.

254 // 263. Note the heavy alliteration on /l/ and /m/. *CAD* E, p. 106, takes *ellu* here as a synonym of *ramku*, with reference to a class of priest bathed to ensure cultic purity. Most other translators render *kīma elli* as 'like snow', a translation that, as far as I can see, is based entirely on the synonym list *Malku* VI 217–18 (*CT* 18 23, K 2036 // 4190+, 9–10), where *ḫal-pu-u*, 'frost', and *ku-uṣ*, 'winter' are matched with *el-lum*, 'pure'. These two entries are not necessarily to be taken as exact synonyms, however. In another synonym list *ellu* is itself explained as the metals copper (*erû*) and bronze (*siparru*) because they are bright and shiny (*CAD* N/1, p. 240, citing 'An VII 34 and 48'). The equation of *ellu* with ice and snow in *Malku* need only be to their shining purity. Jacobsen translated the phrase *kīma elli* 'as if with clear oil' (*Studies Moran*, p. 242; in this analysis *ellu* is elliptical for *šamnu ellu*, a type of sesame oil). None of these proposed similes seems satisfactory to me. Instead I compare the idiom with *Maqlû* III 70: *e-te-lil ki-ma nam-ru*. There is no class of priest known as *namru* and the phrase seems to mean 'I have become as pure as pure can be'. The commentary on this line offers the explanation *nam-ru* = ^{d}*šá-maš*, 'pure = sun' (*KAR* 94, 44), but this explanation is not convincing and probably represents a late scholar's ad hoc rendering of an old idiom that had perhaps fallen out of use. Previous commentators have failed to notice that Sumerian possesses a similar construction, as seen in the stock phrase ḫúl.la.gim im.ma.na.ni.ib.gar in Gudea's hymn on cylinders (Cyl. A xiv 5–6, xvii 28, xx 4, 12), translated as 'it made him extremely happy', in my view correctly, by D. O. Edzard, *RIME* 3/I, pp. 77–81. In a building inscription of Samsuiluna the same Sumerian phrase relates the pleasure felt by Šamaš at the destiny Enlil has decreed for Sippar. An Akkadian translation is extant: *ki-ma ḫi-du-tim it-ta-aš-ka-an-šum* (Frayne, *RIME* 4, p. 376, 23–4 // 31–2). This looks very much like a mechanical rendering of a construction that was not properly understood. I conclude that both languages, Akkadian and Sumerian, can express the superlative by construing an adjective with *kīma* // gim.

256 // 265. The inversion of the noun and its adjective, a device that serves to emphasize the latter, is compounded by the intrusion between them of the verb; for both devices see Chapter 9, the section on Language and style sub (iii–vii).

268–70. The omission of these three lines in MS J can no doubt be put down to a simple slip of the eye, from *tēdiqu* in l. 267 to the same word in l. 270.

271–2. The couplet is repeated from SB X 169–70.

273. The form *tattannaššu* is perfect not, as most translators have it, present-future. The assimilation is typical of MB and later dialects (see *CAD* N/1, p. 44). Ūta-napišti's repetition of his wife's words in the same tense (l. 280) is by way of exclamation, a rhetorical question begging the answer 'nothing'.

281–2. The couplet is repeated from earlier in this Tablet (ll. 9–10).

283–4. The copies of Haupt and Thompson were made after the last three lines of MS J lost some legibility, with the result that recent attempts at deciphering the end of l. 283 have been made without using the full evidence (e.g. *CAD* E, p. 23: *š*]*ur-šu-šu*). George Smith read the two signs *šá ri* (*TSBA* 3 (1874), p. 579, 48; IV R^1 51 v 48; cf. Haupt, *Nimrodepos*, p. 113, fn. 10; Pinches, IV R^2 44 vi 4), but the old photograph clearly shows the middle of the last sign to be missing (Fig. 13), leaving the possibility of reading the more suitable *š*]*á-k*[*i*]*n*. There is a lack of agreement in the dictionaries as to the exact identification of the plant *amurdinnu*: *CAD* proposes 'bramble', *AHw* suggests 'Rose?'. I. Diakonoff compared the description of the plant given here with the mention of its fragrance in the episode of the snake (now l. 305), and wrote: 'no wonder that all commentators, from George Smith to the *AHw*, have always thought the magic plant was or looked like a rose, with its prickles and its magic odour' (*Rocznik Orientalistyczny* 41/II (1980), p. 20). He goes on to show that the plant *amurdinnu* was known as an aromatic and argues that it is more likely the wild rose, *Rosa canina*, than a bramble. This I accept, but one should stress that it is not the scent of the *amurdinnu* that is the issue in the imagery of this couplet. Only its thorniness is important. The fact that the magic plant described by Ūta-napišti, and in due course recovered by Gilgameš, also had a strong scent—appealing to snakes in particular—would appear to be coincidence, even if it led earlier commentators to the right conclusion. Nothing need be held in common by the *amurdinnu* and the magic plant except their thorns.

285–6. Note the preponderance of /š/. The spacing of the signs on the line shows that there is too much text yet to come for this line of tablet to be a single line of poetry, and so I presume a Trennungszeichen to follow *qātāka*. The second part of what is thus a couplet is usually restored along the lines of 'you will find life' or 'you will become young again'. This line is effectively the precursor of SB XI 296, in which Gilgameš reports the plant's rejuvenating effect to Ur-šanabi. Perhaps read accordingly [*atta ina libbīšu takaššad napšatka*], 'by means of it you can recapture your vitality'.

288. The word *rāṭu* is restored from Gilgameš's later recollection of what he did in this episode, l. 316.

289. There is no option but to read the traces *kab-tu-t*[*a*, here and in l. 292, with Thompson (against von Soden, *ZA* 53, p. 233). The orthography, for *kabtūti*, is another example of late scribal indifference to the final vowel, even at Kuyunjik.

291. Since Thompson's edition it has been conventional to restore *is-ḫ*[*u-ul qātīšu*] here, but to me the damaged sign looked more as Haupt suggested (*Nimrodepos*, p. 104, fn. 9: 'kann aber *ba* sein'), and *nasāḫu* is then the obvious verb.

293. The ostensibly masculine suffix on *kib-ri-šú* (MS j) refers to the feminine *tâmtu*; this is not problematical in a LB manuscript. There is therefore no reason to suppose that the bank belongs to the Apsû (so W. G. Lambert, 'The Apsû', *CRRA* 44/III, p. 77).

295. The meaning of the phrase *šam-mu ni-kit-ti* has been something of a crux. Many have analysed the second word as *niqittu*, a medical term for the most critical or life-threatening phase of a disease or condition (e.g. von Soden, *ZA* 53, p. 233: 'die Pflanze gegen Unruhe'; Kovacs: 'a plant against decay(?)'; Dalley: 'a plant to cure a crisis'). A plant so named could therefore be viewed as a herb reserved for use on someone in grave danger of dying, the 'plant of death's door'. Others have opted for slightly different interpretations of the same word (Labat: 'un remède contre l'angoisse'; Bottéro: 'la plante spécifique de la peur(-de-la-mort)'; Pettinato: 'la pianta dell'irrequietezza', i.e. of youthful vigour). In discussing this problem K. Watanabe has since compared the name of the plant with a passage in a NA letter which reads *a-ke-e la-ab-laṭ a-li ni-kit-ti da-me-e-a ina lìb-bi-ia e-tab-lu*, 'How can I survive? Where is my *n.*? The blood has dried from my heart' (*ABL* 455, 12–14),

and concludes, undoubtedly correctly, 'demnach wäre *niqittu/nikittu* "Herzschlag, pulsierendes Leben"' (*Bagh. Mitt.* 25 (1994), p. 583, fn. 6). I read *nikittu* and not *niqittu* because, in Gilgameš, the associated verb, meaning 'to beat' (of the heart), is *nakādu* (SB VIII 58). The plant is thus one which ensures that fundamental sign of life, the healthy heartbeat of youth and the strong pulse that accompanies it.

296. For the expression *napišta kašādu*, 'to regain one's vigour', see the OB letter *TCL* XVIII 91, 5–6: *iš-tu an-ni-iš al-li-kam am-ra-aṣ-ma na-pí-iš-tam ak-šu-ud*, 'after I came here I fell ill but then I recovered (my) health'. This makes less probable von Soden's suggested reading of the last word as *nab-laṭ!-su*, 'seine Genesung' (*ZA* 53, p. 233, following T. Bauer).

299. The old reading of the first word, *šumša*, is suspect. The antecedent of feminine *-ša* would have to be the masculine *šammu*. This is not impossible on a Gilgameš tablet from Kuyunjik, for careless writings of final vowels abound (see Chapter 9), but there are other grounds for doubt. The first word of l. 299 is only certainly preserved on MS C, where it was already so indistinct in George Smith's day that he read the two signs together as *il* (*TSBA* 3 (1874), p. 581, 9; IV R^1 51 vi 9). While admitting that the second sign was badly damaged, Haupt read *šum-ša*, claiming to detect at the end of the damaged sign two vertical heads and a trace of an oblique wedge high in front of them (*Nimrodepos*, p. 104, fn. 11). However, Delitzsch, who copied the tablet at much the same time as Haupt, saw *šum-šu* (AL^3, p. 109, 267). Haupt, having nailed his colours to the mast, promptly condemned this as 'entschieden falsch' (*BA* 1 (1889), p. 143). Thompson followed Haupt. Given that the signs were already indistinct in Smith's lifetime, I suspect that Haupt's reading *šum-ša* was influenced by knowledge of MS W's *šá*, about which he wrote, 'die Variante *ša* = *gar* von C ist richtig' (loc. cit.). Though MS W's *šá* has been taken to represent [*šum*]-*šá* ever since, it may just as easily be seen as a vestige of the preceding line, [*lu*]-*šá*-[*kil*], with ll. 298–9 then occupying the same line of tablet. Accordingly it has no bearing on how to read MS C's *šum*-x. I cannot see on MS C as much as Haupt. All that is visible now is one final upright wedge and, less distinct, a long horizontal wedge low down. This suggests *šum-šu*, with Delitzsch, or even *šum-ma*. The former reading provides a pronoun that agrees with the gender of *šammu* and *šību*. The latter allows a very different interpretation. The implications have already been discussed in the introduction to SB Tablet XI.

301–2. This couplet, much used on the outbound leg of Gilgameš's first great journey (SB IV *passim*), is found again in ll. 319–20. Its use on the return leg of his last great journey is a literary device intentionally suggesting a kind of symmetry in the hero's adventures.

306. The restoration of the first word follows von Soden, *ZA* 53, p. 233. Others have restored [*ina mê*(a)^{m}]^{eš} (Heidel, Speiser).

309. Cf. above, SB XI 139.

310. To judge from MS j there is not enough space for a standard line on the model of l. 322, i.e. *Gilgāmeš ana šâšūma izakkara ana Ur-šanābi malāḫi*. An abbreviated version must have been used. However, the traces of the first word, extant only on MS W, are not certainly of *Gilgāmeš*, of *ana šâšūma* or of *izakkara*; perhaps an adverb opened the line.

314. The identity of the 'Lion of the Earth' has recently been discussed by A. W. Sjöberg, 'Eve and the chameleon', in W. Boyd Barrick and J. R. Spencer (eds.), *In the Shelter of Elyon: Essays . . . in Honor of G. W. Ahlström* (Sheffield, 1984), pp. 221–2. He traces the phrase back to Ebla (*na-iš gàr-ga-rí-im*), and, more revealingly, notes the semantic equation between *nēš*(*u ša*) *qaqqari* and Greek χαμαιλεον, both meaning 'earth-lion', and also the long-known equation entered in the pharmaceutical series *Uruanna* III, *nēš*(ur.maḫ) *qaq-qa-ri* = *ḫu-la-m*[*e-šú*], which is itself commonly rendered chameleon (*MSL* VIII/2, p. 58). Sjöberg thus proposes that the animal that makes off with

Gilgameš's plant could have been a chameleon and that 'either "earth-lion" (*nēšu ša qaqqari*) was interpreted as an epithet of the snake or *ṣēru* might have been the more general "reptile"'. Since underhand behaviour of the kind Gilgameš encounters here is universally the mark of snakes rather than lizards, I am inclined to keep *nēšu ša qaqqari* in our line separate from *nēš qaqqari* the chameleon. The 'Lion of the Earth' is an epithet well suited to the snake, which when alarmed is a threat every bit as dangerous to human beings as the more obviously threatening four-legged version. In ancient Mesopotamia lions and snakes were more of a kind than one might think, for they held an equal terror for the Babylonian traveller. According to the common omen apodoses *šiḫiṭ nēši* and *šiḫiṭ ṣēri*, 'attack by lion' and 'attack by snake', the two most feared encounters in the open were with exactly these two animals, and these alone: according to the dictionaries no other animal appears in this phrase in such texts (*AHw*, p. 1209; *CAD* Š/2, p. 416). For MS C's spelling of first-person *ētepuš* with initial *i-* see SB XI 82 and commentary.

315. For *ana* 20 *bēr* as signifying 'a long way' see also SB VII 41 and commentary. With the rest of the line compare Sennacherib's description of the incoming tide (III *R* 12 no. 2, 28, ed. Luckenbill, *OIP* 2, p. 74, 74: *e-du-ú ta-ma-ti gap-šiš* [*iš*]*-šá-am-ma*, 'the tide of the sea rose against me in a great swell'). The verb *našû* is here intransitive. Diakonoff has a very different understanding of this and the following lines:

> . . . at twenty leagues distance the tide rocks the flower [*ināš šamma*],
> When I opened the well I lost my tools,
> Something I've found that to me is a sign: it's my fate to renounce it [*luḫḫis*],
> And even the boat I've left on the shore.
>
> M. Diakonoff, *Rocznik Orientalistyczny* 41/II (1980), p. 19

Quite apart from the fact that *nâšu* is intransitive, his reading *edû ināš šamma* is now precluded by the new variant *inaššâ edû* (Assyrian MS **z**).

316. The verb *tabāku* of tools means to drop them where one stands (cf. the omen passages cited by von Soden, *ZA* 53, p. 233; also *CT* 31 45, 5: *nakr*[*u*](kúr) [gi]]š*kakkī*(tukul)[meš]*-šú tu-šat-bak-šú*, 'you will force the enemy to abandon his weapons'). A reading *it-ta-bak*, as put forward by *CAD* (E, p. 36), seems to be discounted by the traces.

317. On *ut-ta* see above, the commentary on l. 208.

317–18. Most take the final clause of l. 317 as an avowal of future intentions—the abandonment of the quest—with the mention of leaving the boat tacked on as a curious afterthought (e.g. Diakonoff, quoted above). Metrical as well as semantic considerations suggest that there is something wrong with the text: if the afterthought is an unsatisfactory anticlimax, the lines are unevenly balanced. Bottéro solved these problems by placing *anāku lū aḫḫis* after l. 318, which then yields '"J'ai laissé la barque au rivage / Et j'(en) suis (trop) loin"' (*L'épopée*, p. 204). For me the couplet reads just as well, and acquires metrical balance, with the words left in the order that has come down to us but with a different line division, so that *anāku lū aḫḫis* introduces l. 318 rather than concluding l. 317. It is then a lament that Gilgameš did not leave the boat on the shore and turn back (cf. *CAD* N/1, p. 128; Reclam[2]). This must be a reference to the initial crossing of the ocean, to which, significantly, the alternative was 'coming away', using the same word as here (SB X 91: *iḫis*). The point is that if Gilgameš had never reached Ūta-napišti he would not have suffered the successive failures that so demoralize him. How much better had he given up his quest when he first reached the ocean, just as the wise Šiduri had advised him.

323–8. See already SB I 18–23 and commentary.

324. The spelling *ḫi-i-ṭi-ma* (MS C) for the masculine imperative *ḫīṭma* displays a CV sign in use for VC or C alone; for other examples among the Kuyunjik manuscripts see Chapter 9, the section on Spelling sub (a) and (w).

TABLET XII AND BILGAMES AND THE NETHERWORLD 172–END

1. The identification of the *pukku* and *mikkû* has exercised the minds of many scholars. The lesser problem is the *mikkû* (Sum. GIŠ.E.KID/KÌD.ma, probably to be read ^{giš}e.ke$_4$/kè.ma). This, fashioned in Bilgames and the Netherworld from a branch of Inanna's *ḫuluppu*-tree, must clearly have been some kind of long stick. The *pukku* (Sum. ^{giš}ellag) was made from the base of the tree; that fact, together with the sign which is used to write the Sumerian word (LAGAB), suggests that it was round. Scholars have interpreted the pair variously as drum and drumstick, hoop and stick, musical scraper and stick, and ball and stick (for a synopsis of the discussion see D. O. Edzard, *RLA* VIII, p. 34; not mentioned there is the singular contribution by M. Schneider, 'Pukku und mikku: ein Beitrag zum Aufbau und zum System der Zahlenmystik des Gilgamesch-Epos', *Antaios* 9 (1967), pp. 262–83). Two well-known passages about Inanna-Ištar mention *pukku* in connection with the war goddess's bloody sport (on this see most recently A. D. Kilmer, *AoF* 18 (1991), p. 15). To Ištar the mortal fray of battle is just a game. This is nowhere more clear than in the bilingual Exaltation of Inanna:

^{d}inanna ti.sùḫ giš.lá éšemen(KI.E.NE.DI.^{d}INNIN).gin$_7$ ù.mi.ni.íb.sar.sar
^{d}iš-tar a-na-an-ti u tu-qu-un-ta ki-ma kep-pe-e šu-tak-pi-ma
$^{e\text{-}lag}$ellag giš.dù.a.gin$_7$ nin.mè.a ur.a.ra sè.sè.ga.ba.ni.íb
ki-ma pu-uk-ku ù me-ek-ke-e be-let ta-ḫa-zi šu-tam-ḫi-ṣu tam-ḫa-ru

B. Hruška, *ArOr* 37 (1969), p. 488, 3–6

O Inanna (Akk. Ištar), make fight and combat ebb and flow (lit. bend back) like a skipping rope,
O lady of battle, make the fray clash together like *pukku* and *mekkû*!

Here the imagery derives in my view from the different outdoor games of girls and boys: girls skip, boys play *pukku*. A related passage occurs in the cultic lament *Uruammairrabi*, in which Inanna describes how she revels in the business of hand-to-hand combat:

sag.du ^{giš}ellag.gur$_4$.ra.àm mi.ni.íb.gur$_4$.gur$_4$.re.e.en
qaq-qa-da-a-ti kīma(gim) *pu-uk-ki ku-ub-bu-ti uš-ta-nag-ra-ar*
^{giš}mes gu.ni gùn.nu.a mi.ni.íb.sar.sar.re.e[n]
kep-pé-a šá qû(gu)*-šá bit-ra-mu em-me-li-l*[*u*$_4$]

SBH 56 rev. 45–8 // Rm 218 iii 4′–5′, ed. Volk, *Balağ-Komposition*, p. 200

I send heads rolling like heavy *pukku*s,
I play with my skipping rope whose cord is specked (with blood?).

Decapitated heads do not roll like drums, hoops or scrapers. As Landsberger saw when this passage was fully recovered for the first time (*WZKM* 57 (1961), p. 23), the terms ^{giš}ellag and *pukku* mean a solid, wooden ball (note, however, that the phonetic similarity between *pukku* and 'puck', which is related to 'pocket', is entirely coincidental). A child's ball, too, makes a good missile, as one reads in the Sumerian proverb:

> ur.gi$_7$ ^{giš}ellag (*var.* illar) ra.a.gin$_7$ dum.dam an.da.ab.za (*var.* ì.íb.za)
>
> Alster, *Proverbs*, 3.95 // 5.93
>
> He (*or* she) howls like a dog struck by a ball (*var.* throw-stick).

Though the identification of *pukku* as 'ball' was repudiated as 'hardly acceptable' by M. Duchesne-Guillemin ('Pukku and mekkû', *Iraq* 45 (1983), p. 153), her objection was based on an erroneous interpretation of *tebû* in SB I 66 and can be disregarded (as, indeed, it has been by Jacobsen, Cooper, Kilmer and others). It is in the light of ball-games that one must understand *pukku* and *mekkû* in the Sumerian poem of Bilgames and the Netherworld. Gilgameš makes the playthings for himself and involves the young men of his city in a game that lasts all day. As play is about to resume one morning the womenfolk complain to the gods and the playthings disappear into the bowels of the earth:

e.ne úr.bi ^{giš}ellag.a.ni.šè ba.da.ab.dím.me
pa.bi ^{giš}e.ke$_4$.ma.ni.šè ba.ab.dím.me
^{giš}ellag al.du$_{11}$.du$_{11}$.ge (*var.* in.du$_6$?.du$_6$?.e) sila ùr.ra ^{giš}ellag na.mu.un.è (*var.* e, è.dè)
IM.DI (*var.* KA.DI, ME.DI) du$_{11}$.du$_{11}$.ge (*var.* in.du$_6$?.du$_6$?.e) sila ùr.ra IM.DI (*var.* KA.DI, ^{giš}ellag) na.mu.un.è (*var.* e, è.dè)
guruš uru.na.ka ^{giš}ellag al.du$_{11}$.du$_{11}$.ga.ne
e.ne érin dumu nu.mu.un.su.a.ke$_4$.ne íb.ba u$_5$.a
a gú.mu a íb.ba.mu a.nir.ni im.gá.gá.ne
ama.tuku dumu.ni.ir ninda mu.na.ab.túm
nin$_9$.tuku šeš.a.ni.ir a mu.na.dé.e
ú.sa$_{11}$.an.e um.ma.kar.ta
ki ^{giš}ellag gar.ra.ka.ni giš.ḫur in.ḫur.re
^{giš}ellag.a.ni igi.ni.a mu.ni.in.íl é.a.ni.šè mu.un.túm
á.gú.zi.ga.ta ki giš.ḫur in.ḫur.ra íb.ba u$_5$.a
šu.dù.dù.a nu.mu.un.su.a.ta
i.^{d}utu ki.sikil tur.ra.ta
^{giš}ellag.a.ni ù ^{giš}e.ke$_4$/kè.ma.ni dúr kur.ra.šè ba.da.an.šub

Bilgames and the Netherworld 149–64, ed. Shaffer, 'Sumerian Sources', pp. 66–7

As for himself he fashions its base into his ball,
he fashions its branch into his mallet.
Playing with the ball he took the ball out in the city square,
playing with the . . . he took the . . . out in the city square.
The young men of his city were *playing* with the ball,
with him riding piggyback (*lit.* on the hips) (among) a band of widows' sons.
'O my neck! O my hips!' they kept groaning.
The son who has a mother, she brought him bread,
the brother who has a sister, she pours him water.
After evening drew nigh,

making a mark (at) the place where his ball was situated (*lit.* his place where the ball was situated),
he lifted his ball up before him and carried it off to his house.
At dawn, on (his) mounting piggyback at the place where he had made the mark,
at the complaint of the widows
the outcry of the young girls,
his ball and his mallet fell down to the bottom of the Netherworld.

Different renderings are possible for ll. 151–3, which are plagued by substantive variants and were evidently open to different interpretations in antiquity. The sequence of signs al.du$_{11}$.du$_{11}$-(g) can also be interpreted as al—dug$_4$, 'to want' (though its phonetically spelled variant undermines that position); IM.DI and KA.DI ought, by reason of the parallel, to refer to the mallet (otherwise ^{giš}E.KID/KÌD.ma) but have also been very plausibly interpreted as ní.silim and ka.silim, 'self-glorification', construed with the verb e, 'to vaunt oneself'. The variant ME.DI (*UET* VI 57 rev. 3, coll.) is obscure. See further P. Attinger, *Eléments de linguistique sumérienne*, p. 676; J. Klein, 'A new look at the "oppression of Uruk" episode in the Gilgameš epic', *Jacobsen Mem. Vol.*, p. 194, fn. 26. These details, however, do not affect the point under discussion.

It was Landsberger who first supposed that the *pukku* and *mekkû* were the equipment used to play 'eine Art Polo oder Croquet' (loc. cit.). But this was not polo or croquet as we know it. The reason for the young men's discomfort and their womenfolk's outcry is that the youths of Uruk have to carry the giant Gilgameš as he wields his huge mallet and great wooden ball. The ball evidently came to rest on the ground, for its position could be marked in the dust while the game was suspended for the night. The logical conclusion is that Gilgameš struck the ball from one place to the next with the mallet. It would seem that the game was a kind of piggyback golf or solo polo. Klein reached a similar conclusion independently (Klein, op. cit., pp. 192–4).

4–5. The Akkadian text is witness to a tradition in which the Sumerian of BN 175–6 evidently read simply ^{giš}ellag.mu kur.šè mu.da.šub / ^{giš}E.KID.ma.mu ganzir.šè mu.da.šub. As regards the restoration of the final word, *imqutannīma* is suggested by XII 57–8 but *imqutanni* by XII 65–6.

6. Here the Akkadian follows the tradition of Sumerian MS H (BN 177), rather than those of MSS rVW.

8. In retaining *ūma* this line follows MSS rVW not MS H, which omits u$_4$.da (l. 179).

16. The Akkadian *ana irīšīšu* renders the Nippur tradition of MSS HYZ (ir.si.im.bi.šè), not the Ur tradition of MS r (ir.sim.zu.šè).

17. The preposition *ana*, when *ina* is expected, is the result of a misparsing of Sum. kur.ra as kur and dative instead of kur and locative.

19. As its etymology suggests (cf. *šabāṭu*, 'to strike'), the *šabbiṭu*, a rod of cornel wood (Sum. ^{giš}ma.nu), is not a badge of office but a deliverer of violence. As such it is carried by soldiers (cf. *CAD* Š/I s.v. *šabbiṭu* B) and, according to the poet of the Vision of Kummâ, brandished at new arrivals in the Netherworld by Nergal, the terrible king of the Babylonian Hades, as a death-dealing instrument (Livingstone, *Court Poetry* no. 32 rev. 15–16): *šab-bi-ṭu si-mat ilu-ti-šú . . . i-šá-a-ṭa a-na da-ke-*[*ia*], 'he was wielding the staff appropriate to his divine office (as if) to kill [me]'. This allusion, in particular, explains why the shades of the dead will tremble in terror.

22. The Sumerian sources for BN 194 disagree as to what word precedes the verb. MS r, from Ur, has KA, which is best read as gù (so Gadd, *RA* 30 (1933), p. 133, and Shaffer, 'Sumerian Sources', p. 75) and provides the translator's *rigmu*. Shaffer saw that the trace in MS Y, from Nippur, was of a different sign but he offered no decipherment. Help is provided by the narrative

parallel, where Nippur MSS HZ and MS V appear to have du_6.(du_6)-n and BUL.BUL = tu_{13}.tu_{13} respectively (BN 216). Since the latter means 'to quake', the former may be taken as an orthographic variant for synonymous BÚR.BÚR = du_9.du_9 or dun_5.dun_5 (for both verbs in lexical equations with *nâšu* see *CAD* Ṇ/2, p. 113). The trace of MS Y in BN 194 seems to be this verb in its conventional spelling. The Nippur tradition is thus that the wearing of shoes in the Netherworld upsets the shades of the dead by making the ground shake. The shift from the idea of shaking to the idea of noise, in which the Ur manuscript is followed by the Akkadian text, perhaps came about through a misunderstanding of du_9 or du_6 as du_{11} = KA = gù.

28. The epithet 'mother of Ninazu' is also used of Ereškigal in the doxology of the Death of Bilgames in the version from Mê-Turan (Cavigneaux, *Gilgameš et la Mort*, p. 36, 305). For Ninazu as Ereškigal's son see further the Collection of Sumerian Temple Hymns 182 etc. (Å. W. Sjöberg, *TCS* III, p. 27; cf. W. G. Lambert, *CRRA* 26, p. 61; F. A. M. Wiggermann, *RLA* IX, p. 330).

29–30. As Shaffer had already implied, the Akkadian of these lines renders the Sumerian of Inanna's Descent 232–3 // 259–60 more nearly than that of BN 202–3. The adjective kù = *ellu*, used of shoulders, has connotations of colour: like other residents of the Netherworld Ereškigal is deprived of sun, and her gleaming white flesh stands out in the dark. The bur.šagan is translated here as *pūr šappāti* but in l. 50 as *pūr šikkati*, reflecting the dual entries in lexical texts:

[ša-gan	dug.šagan]	=	[*šik*]-*ka-t*[*u*]
			[*šap*]-*pa-t*[*u*]

Diri V 256–7 (*CAD* Š/1, p. 477); cf. *Hh* X 103–4

These equations suggest that the bur.šagan was a vessel shaped like wine jar (*šappatu*) or an oil flask (*šikkatu*), i.e. narrow of neck and bulbous of body. It was typically made of stone (for three instances of ^{na4}bur.šagan in administrative documents see *PSD* B, p. 183). According to *Lugale* 599, where ^{na4}bur.šagan is also translated *pu-ú-ru šik-ka-tum*, this stone was ^{na4}mar.ḫu.ša = *marḫušû*, commonly rendered 'marcasite', and the vessel was used for filtration of water, oil or wine (see F. N. H. Al-Rawi, *Iraq* 57 (1995), p. 220, and my note on p. 222 of that volume).

The verb at the end of l. 30 has caused difficulty in the past. The correspondence with gíd in Inanna's Descent 233 // 260 makes *šadādu*, 'to pull, draw', the obvious derivation, though von Soden read *naddāta* (*ZA* 53 (1959), p. 234: 'ist nicht behängt'; followed by W. R. Sladek, 'Inanna's Descent', p. 209). I assume that the verb matches gada búr in BN 203 and so conveys not the shape of the breast or the bowl ('drawn out') but the drawing over the breast of a garment (so already Heidel; for the phrase *šidda*/*ṣubāta šadādu* see *CAD* Š/1, p. 22). Most recent translations have lost sight of the reference of the simile, which applies to the breast and not the draping. Speiser already saw the point, translating 'her cruse-shaped breasts are not wrapped in cloth'. Ereškigal's breasts, the clothing rent from them in mourning, are seen hanging pale and pendulous like twin flasks of marcasite.

31–2. These lines represent an expansion of the original Sumerian, at least as it is given in MSS HAA (BN 206).

37a. This line, present in the tablets from Nineveh but absent from the Babylonian manuscript and the Sumerian text, probably derives from dittography of l. 40.

48–54. These lines are absent from the Nippur recension of the Sumerian poem, though the last three survive at two appropriate points later in the narrative (BN 227–9, 235–7). The Mê-Turan recension offers a parallel but is not an exact match (BN 221a–g, MS pp). Evidently the Akkadian version is based on some other, similarly divergent edition of the Sumerian text.

51. As this line stands this line has no obvious verb, unless one emends the first word to *i-nu-q*[*a*!], 'he wailed' (Penguin). However, in this tablet verbs fall at the ends of clauses. It is better to assume that the end of the line is defective. The newly recovered Mê-Turan version of Bilgames and the Netherworld supports for this idea, reading at this point (BN 221b, MS pp): šubur.ra.a.ni ^{d}en.ki.du$_{10}$.{ra} kur.ta nu.mu.un.è.de.

53 // 61 // 69 // 77. With the joining of N 2696 to MSY of the Sumerian poem and the collation of MS AA, the phrase *lā pādû* can now be seen to be the counterpart of two Sumerian epithets, sag šu.nu.ba (BN 228, MSS YAA) and sag šu.nu.du$_7$ (BN 237, MSS HTT). The former epithet became a divine name in its own right, for in *An*V 108 ^{d}sag.šu.nu.ba appears as one of the four counsellors of Baba of Girsu (ed. Litke, *God-Lists*, p. 178, where other references are also cited).

55. The Mê-Turan tablet also offers a partial Sumerian counterpart to this line (BN 221c, MS pp): lugal.e i.lu mu.un.na.bé é[r gi]g še$_x$(A.IGI).še$_x$(A.IGI). This new evidence allows the sign before *mār Ninsun* to be read correctly for the first time. At the beginning of the line it is also possible to read *i-nu-u*[*q-ma*, 'he wailed'.

59 // 67 // 75. The word provisionally restored as *ūrdu* renders the problematical Sumerian ì.gi$_4$-(n) (BN 226 // 234). The latter can hardly be the modal particle ì.ge$_4$.en discussed by C. Wilcke, *JNES* 27 (1968), pp. 239–40. Perhaps it stands for ì.g̃en, 'he went', though strictly speaking the opening consonants of gi$_4$ and g̃en are different.

61–2 // 77–8. In the order of these lines the Akkadian translation follows Sumerian MSS Y, TT and pp; the majority of Nippur sources (MSS H, W, AA, BB, GG, JJ and UU) have them transposed.

81. Restored after l. 85.

83. For *utukku* as a near synonym of *eṭemmu*, 'ghost', see, in an astrological report (Hunger, *SAA* VIII 477, 7), the omen apodosis *utukki*(udug) *ḫab-lim māta*(kur) *iṣabbat*(dab)^{bat}-*ma mūtānu*(nam.úš)^{meš} *ina māti*(kur) *ibaššû*(gál)^{meš}, 'the shade of someone wronged will seize the land and there will be pestilence in the land'. The two words are also semantically related in Sumerian, for the sign udug is a variant of gidim, 'ghost', and occurs in its stead often enough to earn the value gidim$_4$.

85. The beginning of the Sumerian counterpart of this line has now come to light on the tablet in the Schøyen Collection, SC 3361 (BN 241a, MS rr$_2$).

86. Comparison with the Sumerian shows that *lūman* is an error generated by l. 82 (cf. already *CAD* L, p. 245).

87–9. The sole witness to this episode, MS G$_1$, is badly scuffed at this point. My readings of the last words of each of the three lines differ from those of previous commentators, but produce in each case a text that is more predictable from the Sumerian. Since the Dtt stem is not found in Babylonian I assume that *ut-ta-taš-šá-qu* (l. 88) represents *uttaššaqū* rather than *uttataššaqū*. The erroneous equivalence kúš.ù, 'to become exhausted' (BN 245) = *malāku* (l. 89) is based on the equation šà.kúš.ù = *ma-li-ku* (*MSL* XVI, p. 84, *Nabnītu* IV 196; XII, p. 118, *Lu* II ii 8–10).

92. The translation *ul aqabbâkkum* disregards the /š/ of the preformative nu.uš- and ignores the first-person dative infix in the verbal prefix chain: the Sumerian nu.uš.ma.ab.bé.en (BN 247) can only mean 'if only you would tell me'.

96–9. These lines have now to be interpreted in the light of MS rr, the new source for BN 250–3. In the Sumerian it transpires that there Enkidu describes the corruption not of his own body but of the corpse of a woman who had been Gilgameš's sexual partner. The tradition that there were such women is found in the unpublished Ur III fragment IM 70101 = 6N-T 450 (see Chapter 1, fn. 16). The decomposition of her body is symbolized graphically by the decay of her genitals. The new text also shows more clearly than before how the Akkadian translator altered the thrust of the passage in translation. While evidently keeping the two lines that frame the passage he adapted BIN 251–2 freely, imposing on the text a parallelism not present in the Sumerian, and converting the third-person subject of giš šu bí.in.tag.ga (BN 250), i.e. the owner of the gal_4.la (BN 252–3), into the second person (*talputu*), i.e. Gilgameš. In this way the Akkadian lines appear at first glance to describe the decomposition of a both a male and a female body. It has always been suspected, however, that what Enkidu reports in the translation is the decay of his own corpse and in my view this is still the case. Enkidu had a penis but surely no vulva. Sumerian gal_4.la has three common counterparts in Akkadian, *biṣṣūru* and *qallû*, both meaning 'vulva', and *ūru*, 'crotch'; the last of these is attested as part of a man's body as well as a woman's. In this way it was open to the translator to apply both sets of parallel lines to Enkidu, and that is exactly what I assume was done. In short, the newly revealed explicitness of the Sumerian passage, as reworded in the Akkadian version, is further evidence for the often doubted sexual relationship between Gilgameš and Enkidu.

97. For *kalmatu*, lit. 'louse', as a term for the grub of the clothes moth see the lexical entry *Hh* XIV 267: uḫ.túg.ba = *kal-mat ṣu-ba-ti* (*MSL* VIII/2, p. 30). For ME with the value tuba, meaning 'cloak', in the Sumerian line (BN 252, MS rr), see OB Proto-*Ea* (*MSL* XIV, pp. 34, 73: $^{\text{tu-ba}}$ME; 128, 23: $^{\text{tu-ba}}$ME = *na-al-ba-šum*).

100–1. This couplet combines the two different versions of the Sumerian exhibited by the Nippur sources on the one hand (MS H, at least) and MS rr on the other (BN 254). Compare two other bilingual passages: saḫar.ḫub.ba ba.dúr : *ina e-pe-ri it-ta-pal-saḫ* (Haupt, *ASKT*, p. 120, rev. 5–6); saḫar.ra durun.na.eš.àm : *ina e-per it-ta-pal-si-ḫu* (Meek, *BA* X/1, p. 109, no. 27 obv. 12–13).

102. The writing *ta-mu-ru* here and in succeeding lines of MSS UKK is taken as a spelling in which the final CV sign marks the preceding syllable as stressed, *tāmúr*; for comparable spellings of long closed syllables see Chapter 9, the section on Spelling conventions sub (g). MSS GN use the regular spelling, *ta-mur* (ll. 144–52).

103. As Shaffer noted, the peg in the wall is a mark of ownership: 'the implication seems to be that the house has changed hands' ('Sumerian Sources', p. 149; further Tournay and Shaffer, p. 265, fn. g; Bauer, *Studies Sjöberg*, p. 22). Where a house has been pledged as collateral security for a loan, such a peg can also mark the creditor's interest in his debtor's property. As the debtor weeps in the realization that the future of his household is precarious, so the father of a single son laments the lack of family to provide his shade with water.

107. The original Sumerian line (BN 260) is now explained by M. Civil, *Studies Reiner*, p. 47, where the meaning of dag.si = *dakšû* is also elucidated.

111. C. Wilcke has translated á.ni gál bí.in.tag_4 = *issu petât* as 'läßt er (beim Gehen) die Arme weit schwingen' (*Lugalbandaepos*, p. 180). However, the phrase seems to have some other meaning in scribal context, as we learn from Enkitalu and Enkiḫegal 112 (*PSD* A/2, p. 2): á.ni gál bí.in.tak_4 šìr.gíd.da nu.ub.bé, 'he "opened his arm", he cannot recite a "long song"'. Heidel took the phrase to mean 'his arm is bared' (also Speiser), while von Soden translated 'arbeitsbereit' (Reclam[4]). I see an 'open' arm as a more positive attribute, one that can obtain a scribe a coveted position in the palace administration. Presumably then it means a swift and nimble hand (cf. Tournay and Shaffer, 'son bras se remue').

118. The place of this line soon after the section dealing with numbers of sons leads one to compare it with BN a–e, which have in common that their subjects are childless. The presence of *tubqu* makes a correlation with ub.dug_4.ga (BN b) highly attractive. Though *šurinnu damqu* is not an exact match for pa a.la.la ḫu.ru/ḫur.ra, 'a useless *alala*-stick', a standard and a stick are at

least comparable items (see further A. R. George, 'Sumerian tiru = "eunuch"', *NABU* 1997/97). Since it may be assumed that palace eunuchs, like soldiers, wore some kind of uniform or standardized dress, the simile of the 'fine standard' perhaps draws attention to the fellow's splendid livery. The next line represents an expansion of the original and, were it legible, it might provide a rendering nearer the Sumerian of BN b. The line asking after the palace eunuch begins the second section of Gilgameš and Enkidu's dialogue in four of six manuscripts of the Sumerian poem (MSS FHDDFF *v.* MSS VDDD), so I assume that it comes first in the Akkadian version too. Since the preceding section is restorable line by line up to l. 116, Gilgamesh's first query of the new section will fall at l. 117. The place of this line, MS G v 1, as Enkidu's corresponding answer, is thus fixed by restoration at 118, confirming Thompson's calculation from the physical shape of MS G.

144. For *tarkullu*, not 'mast' but 'mooring-pole', see SB XI 102 and A. Salonen, *Wasserfahrzeuge*, p. 127.

145. Though the two lines do not exhibit a verbatim correspondence, the Akkadian phrase *ina nasīḫ sikkāt*[*im*] evidently corresponds to the Sumerian ^{giš}má.GAG bu.ra.ni/ba.a (BN 297). The Akkadian verb is an example of the construct state of the I/1 infinitive in *parīs* (or *parēs*; for this see *GAG*^{3} §87k; W. R. Mayer, *Or* NS 59 (1990), p. 452). The oldest datable attestation of such an infinitive is in an inscription of Sargon II from Dūr-Šarrukēn (now Fuchs, *Sargon*, p. 78, 30: *za-qip*), but the presence of another such construct state in the SB epic, *qabī* (var. *qabê*) in SB VI 154, alongside the various other SB attestations adduced by Mayer, is evidence that points to an older origin for the usage. The word *sikkatu*, 'peg', is elicited from gag, and though there is plenty of evidence for such a thing in nautical life (e.g. SB XI 64), there may be a confusion with the peg of ownership encountered above in l. 103. In any case, it seems the unfortunate shade will find no rest, being spurred into constant motion every time a peg is pulled out. In the Sumerian poem the variant ti bu.ra.ni 'his rib being pulled out' (BN k, Ur MS mm), suggests that the antecedent of this line is one of several dealing with people who have been maimed—in this case the subject was impaled in a boating accident.

146. The text of the line's Sumerian counterpart (BN s 1) can now be properly read for the first time, thanks to MS rr, and this allows at last the correct reading of the Akkadian. The phrase *mūt ilīšu*, lit. 'death (decided) by one's god', occurs in omen apodoses. See especially *YOS* X 18, 55–6: *awīlum*(lú) *ina ḫarrān*(kaskal) *illaku*(du) *i-ma-ra-aṣ-ma i-ma-a-*⌈*at*⌉, ⌈*u*$_4$⌉*-ma-am r*[*e-q*]*á-a-am mu-ut ili*(dingir)*-šu awīlum*(lú) *i-ma-a-at*, 'a man will fall ill and die on a journey he undertakes; (or else) at some future time the man will die "the death of his god"'. Other instances of the phrase are *YOS* X 56 i 16 (ed. Leichty, *Izbu*, p. 202), *Šumma izbu* VIII 67′ (ed. Leichty, *Izbu*, p. 108), *Šumma manzāzu* VI 72 (ed. Koch-Westenholz, *Liver Omens*, p. 112), *Pān tākalti* IX 180 and commentary (ed. Koch-Westenholz, *Liver Omens*, pp. 374, 432). According to the dictionaries the expression signifies a death of natural causes (as opposed to death by violence or disease) and is therefore a synonym of the more common *mūt šīmti* (or *šīmāti*). The significance of the present passage would then be that those who enjoy the goodwill of a divine guardian in life will also be blessed after death.

147. The second clause is absent from the Nippur sources of the Sumerian poem but now appears on the tablet currently in Norway (BN s 2, MS rr$_2$). The water is 'clear' as opposed to the foul and polluted water (a ki.lul.la a lù.a) which many shades have to drink (see especially the continuation of the Sumerian poem in the Ur tradition).

149. The Akkadian follows a tradition in which the first verb is not negated. Both the legible Sumerian manuscripts have a clear negative (BN o 2, MSS mm and rr); the Nippur sources are broken at the crucial point (MSS DD and SS).

150–1. These lines have no counterpart in the Nippur manuscripts of the Sumerian poem but derive from a tradition represented by the Norwegian tablet (BN p, MS rr_2): [lú] ad_6.da.ni edin.na an.ná (unfortunately not complete).

153. For *šukkultu* see K. Deller and K. Watanabe, '*šukkulu(m), šakkulu*, "abwischen, auswischen"', *ZA* 70 (1980), pp. 211–12. The Akkadian translation ignores the word following ninda. pad.pad.rá.(ni) in BN q 2: MS V has PA.a, MS DD probably the same (on collation the damaged traces suggested KAL) and MSS ll and rr have PA.

BIBLIOGRAPHY

The following bibliography lists principally those works cited in the preceding chapters and does not pretend to provide a comprehensive bibliography of the Babylonian Gilgameš epic. There have been three successive bibliographies dedicated to Gilgameš:

1960 De Meyer, L.: Introduction bibliographique, in Garelli, *Gilg.*, pp. 1–30
1964 Matouš, L.: Zur neueren Literatur über das Gilgameš-Epos, *BiOr* 21, pp. 3–10
1997 Maier, J.: A Gilgamesh bibliography to 1994, in Maier (ed.), *Gilgamesh. A Reader*, pp. 357–491[1]

Many of the abundant inaccuracies that mar the last of these can be corrected from its predecessors and also from:

1982 Tigay, J. H.: Works cited, in Tigay, *Evolution*, pp. 309–33

Abel, L., and H. Winckler: *Keilschrifttexte zum Gebrauch bei Vorlesungen*. Berlin, 1890

Abusch, T.: Gilgamesh's Request and Siduri's Denial, Part I: The meaning of the dialogue and its implications for the history of the epic, *Studies Hallo*, pp. 1–14

——Gilgamesh's Request and Siduri's Denial, Part II: An analysis and interpretation of an Old Babylonian fragment about mourning and celebration, *ANES* 22 (1993), pp. 3–17

——Ishtar's proposal and Gilgamesh's refusal: an interpretation of the Gilgamesh Epic, Tablet 6, lines 1–79, *History of Religions* 26, 2 (1986), pp. 143–87

——Mesopotamian anti-witchcraft literature: texts and studies, Part 1: The nature of *Maqlû*: its character, divisions and calendrical setting, *JNES* 33 (1974), pp. 251–63

——Mourning the death of a friend: some Assyriological notes, in Walfish (ed.), *Talmage Memorial Volume* 1, pp. 53–62

——(ed.): *Riches Hidden in Secret Places: Studies in Memory of Thorkild Jacobsen*. Winona Lake, Ind., 2002

——The Epic of Gilgamesh and the Homeric epics, in Whiting (ed.), *Mythology and Mythologies*, pp. 1–6

——P.-A. Beaulieu, J. Huehnergard, P. Machinist and P. Steinkeller (eds.): *Historiography in the Cuneiform World*. CRRA 45, 1. Bethesda, Md., 2001

——J. Huehnergard and P. Steinkeller (eds.): *Lingering over Words: Studies in Ancient Near Eastern Literature in Honor of William L. Moran*. HSS 37. Atlanta, 1990

——and K. van der Toorn (eds.): *Mesopotamian Magic: Textual, Historical and Interpretative Perspectives*. Groningen, 1999

Aelian: *De natura animalium*. Cited from the Loeb edn, trans. A. F. Scholfield, 2 vols. London, 1959

Alberti, A., and F. Pomponio: *Pre-Sargonic and Sargonic Texts from Ur Edited in UET 2, Supplement*. Studia Pohl SM 13. Rome, 1986

Albright, W. F.: Notes on Assyrian lexicography and etymology, *RA* 16 (1919), pp. 173–94

[1] One item entered in Maier's list is Buchanan, W.: *Gilgamesh, a Bibliography*. Philadelphia: University of Pennsylvania, 1979. I have not been able to obtain access to this work, either in Philadelphia or elsewhere.

Albright, W. F.: The mouth of the rivers, *AJSL* 35 (1919), pp. 161–95
Ali, Fadhil Abdulwahid: Sumerian Letters: Two Collections from the Old Babylonian Schools. PhD dissertation, University of Pennsylvania, 1964. Ann Arbor, Mich., 1970
Allotte de la Fuÿe, F.-M.: *Documents présargoniques*. 5 vols. Paris, 1908–20
Al-Rawi, F. N. H.: Nabopolassar's restoration work on *Imgur-Enlil* at Babylon, *Iraq* 47 (1985), pp. 1–13
——with an appendix by A. R. George: Tablets from the Sippar Library IV. *Lugale*, *Iraq* 57 (1995), pp. 199–223
——and A. R. George: *Enūma Anu Enlil* XIV and other early astronomical tables, *AfO* 38–9 (1991–2), pp. 52–73
————Tablets from the Sippar library III: two royal counterfeits, *Iraq* 56 (1994), pp. 135–48
————Tablets from the Sippar library V: an incantation from *mīs pî*, *Iraq* 57 (1995), pp. 225–8
————Tablets from the Sippar library VI: Atra-ḫasīs, *Iraq* 58 (1996), pp. 147–90
Alster, B.: A note on the Uriah letter in the Sumerian Sargon legend, *ZA* 77 (1987), pp. 169–73
——(ed.): *Death in Mesopotamia*. CRRA 26. Mesopotamia 8. Copenhagen, 1980
——Dilmun, Bahrain, and the alleged paradise in Sumerian myth and literature, in Potts (ed.), *Dilmun*, pp. 39–74
——*Dumuzi's Dream: Aspects of Oral Poetry in a Sumerian Myth*. Mesopotamia 1. Copenhagen, 1972
——Edin-na ú-sag-gá: Reconstruction, history, and interpretation of a Sumerian cultic lament, *CRRA* 32, pp. 19–31
——Incantation to Utu, *Acta Sum* 13 (1991), pp. 27–96
——Interaction of oral and written poetry in early Mesopotamian literature, *Mesopotamian Epic Literature*, pp. 23–69
——Lugalbanda and the early epic tradition in Mesopotamia, *Studies Moran*, pp. 59–72
——Marriage and love in the Sumerian love songs, *Studies Hallo*, pp. 15–27
——*Proverbs of Ancient Sumer*. 2 vols. Bethesda, Md., 1997
——*The Instructions of Suruppak*. Mesopotamia 2. Copenhagen, 1974
——The mythology of mourning, *Acta Sum* 5 (1983), pp. 1–16
——The paradigmatic character of Mesopotamian heroes, *RA* 68 (1974), pp. 49–60
——The Sumerian Poem of Early Rulers and related poems, *OLP* 21 (1990), pp. 5–25
——Two Sumerian short tales reconsidered, *ZA* 82 (1992), pp. 186–201
——and M. J. Geller: *Sumerian Literary Texts*. CT 58. London, 1990
——and H. Vanstiphout: Lahar and Ashnan: Presentation and analysis of a Sumerian disputation, *Acta Sum* 9 (1987), pp. 1–43
Amiet, P.: Le problème de la représentation de Gilgameš dans l'art, in Garelli, *Gilg.*, pp. 169–73
Ankum, J. A., R. Feenstra and W. F. Leemans (eds.): *Symbolae iuridicae et historicae Martino David dedicatae* 2. *Iura Orientis antiqui*. Leiden, 1968
Annus, A.: Babylonian flood story in the Nag Hammadi writings, *NABU* 2000, no. 68
Anonymous: *A Guide to the Collections in the Iraq Museum*. Baghdad, 1937
Arnaud, D.: La bibliothèque d'un devin à Meskéné-Emar (Syrie), *CRAI* 1980, pp. 375–88
——*Recherches au pays d'Aštata*. *Emar* 6. 4 vols. Paris, 1985–7
——Traditions urbaines et influences semi-nomades à Emar, in J.-Cl. Margueron (ed.), *Le moyen Euphrate. Zone de contacts et d'échanges*. Leiden, 1980, pp. 245–64
Aro, J.: *Die akkadischen Infinitivkonstruktionen*. StOr 26. Helsinki, 1961
——*Studien zur mittelbabylonischen Grammatik*. StOr 20. Helsinki, 1955

Aro, Sanna, and R. M. Whiting (eds.): *The Heirs of Assyria*. Melammu Symposia 1. Helsinki, 2000
Attinger, P.: *Eléments de linguistique sumérienne*. Fribourg and Göttingen, 1993
——Enki et Ninḫursağa, *ZA* 74 (1984), pp. 1–52
——Inanna et Ebiḫ, *ZA* 88 (1998), pp. 164–95
Baqir, Taha: Tell Harmal, a preliminary report, *Sumer* 2 (1946), pp. 22–30 and pls.
Barnett, R. D.: *Illustrations of Old Testament History*. London, 1966
Barrelet, Marie-Thérèse: Remarques sur une découverte faite à Tell al Rimah: 'Face de Humbaba' et conventions iconographiques, *Iraq* 30 (1968), pp. 206–14
Barrick, W. B., and J. R. Spencer (eds.): *In the Shelter of Elyon. Essays . . . in Honor of G. W. Ahlström*. Sheffield, 1984
Battini, Laura: La localisation des archives du palais sud-ouest de Ninive, *RA* 90 (1996), pp. 33–40
Bauer, J.: *Altsumerische Wirtschaftstexte aus Lagasch*. Studia Pohl 9. Rome, 1972
——Der 'schlimme Tod' in Mesopotamien, *Studies Sjöberg*, pp. 21–7
——R. K. Englund and M. Krebernik: *Mesopotamien. Späturuk-Zeit und Frühdynastische Zeit*. OBO 160, 1. Freiburg and Göttingen, 1998
Bauer, T.: *Akkadische Lesestücke*. 3 vols. Rome, 1953
——*Das Inschriftenwerk Assurbanipals vervollständigt und neu bearbeitet*. 2 vols. AB NF 1–2. Leipzig, 1933
——Ein viertes altbabylonisches Fragment des Gilgamesch-Epos, *JNES* 16 (1957), pp. 254–62
Bayliss, Miranda: The cult of dead kin in Assyria and Babylonia, *Iraq* 35 (1973), pp. 115–25
Beaulieu, P.-A.: A land grant on a cylinder seal and Assurbanipal's Babylonian policy, in Graziani (ed.), *Studi sul Vicino Oriente antico*, pp. 25–45
——*Ayakkum* in the Basetki inscription of Narām-Sîn, *NABU* 2002 no. 36
——*Legal and Administrative Texts from the Reign of Nabonidus*. YOS 19. New Haven, Conn., 2000
——New light on secret knowledge in Late Babylonian culture, *ZA* 82 (1992), pp. 98–111
——The cult of AN.ŠÁR/Aššur in Babylonia after the fall of the Assyrian empire, *SAAB* 11 (1997), pp. 55–73
——The descendants of Sîn-lēqi-unninni, *Fs Oelsner*, pp. 1–16
Beckman, G.: Emar and its archives, in Chavalas (ed.), *Emar*, pp. 1–12
——Mesopotamians and Mesopotamian learning at Ḫattuša, *JCS* 35 (1983), pp. 97–114
——Month XII, *NABU* 2000, no. 46
Beek, M. A., A. A. Kampman, C. Nijland and J. Ryckmans (eds.): *Symbolae biblicae et mesopotamicae Francisco Mario Theodoro de Liagre Böhl dedicatae*. Leiden, 1973
Behrens, H.: *Die Ninegalla-Hymne: Die Wohnungnahme Inannas in Nippur in altbabylonischer Zeit*. FAOS 21. Stuttgart, 1998
——Darlene Loding and Martha T. Roth (eds.): *DUMU-E_2-DUB-BA-A: Studies in Honor of Åke W. Sjöberg*. OPBF 11. Philadelphia, 1989
Bergmann, E.: *Codex Hammurabi, textus primigenius*. Rome, 1953
Berlin, Adele: *Enmerkar and Ensuḫkešdanna: A Sumerian Narrative Poem*. OPBF 2. Philadelphia, 1979
Bernhardt, Inez, and S. N. Kramer: Enki und die Weltordnung, ein sumerischer Keilschrifttext über die 'Lehre der Welt' in der Hilprecht-Sammlung und im University Museum of Pennsylvania, *WZJ* 9 (1959–60), pp. 231–56
————*Sumerische literarische Texte aus Nippur* 1. *Mythen, Epen, Weisheitsliteratur und andere Literaturgattungen*. 2. *Hymnen, Klagelieder, Weisheitstexte und andere Literaturgattungen*. TuM NF 3–4. Berlin, 1961 and 1967

Beyer, K.: *Die aramäischen Texte vom Toten Meer.* Göttingen, 1984
——*Die aramäischen Texte vom Toten Meer, Ergänzungsband.* Göttingen, 1994
Bezold, C.: *Catalogue of the Cuneiform Tablets in the Kouyunjik Collection.* 5 vols. London, 1889–99
Biggs, R. D.: An archaic version of the Kesh Temple Hymn from Tell Abū Ṣalābīkh, *ZA* 61 (1971), pp. 193–207
——An esoteric Babylonian commentary, *RA* 62 (1968), pp. 51–8
——*Inscriptions from Tell Abū Ṣalābīkh.* OIP 99. Chicago, 1974
——review of *UET* VIII, *JNES* 27 (1968), pp. 145–6
——*Šà.zi.ga. Ancient Mesopotamian Potency Incantations.* TCS 2. Locust Valley, NY, 1967
[Biggs, R. D., and J. A. Brinkman (eds.):] *Studies Presented to A. Leo Oppenheim, June 7, 1964.* Chicago, 1964
Bing, J. D.: Gilgamesh and Lugalbanda in the Fara period, *ANES* 9 (1977), pp. 1–4
——On the Sumerian Epic of Gilgamesh, *ANES* 7 (1975), pp. 1–11
Birot, M.: *Lettres de Yaqqim-Addu, gouverneur de Sagarâtum.* ARM IV. TCM 1. Paris, 1976
——*Tablettes économiques et administratives d'époque babylonienne ancienne conservées au Musée d'Art et d'Histoire de Genève.* Paris, no date
Bittel, K.: Das Archiv in Gebäude K, *MDOG* 91 (1958), pp. 57–61
——2. Vorläufiger Bericht über die Ausgrabungen in Boğazköy 1934, *MDOG* 73 (1935), pp. 13–39
——Ph. H. J. Houwink ten Cate and Erica Reiner (eds.): *Anatolian Studies Presented to H. G. Güterbock.* Istanbul, 1974
Bjorkman, Judith, K.: *Meteors and Meteorites in the Ancient Near East.* Tempe, Ariz., 1973. Also published in *Meteoritics* 8 (1973), pp. 91–132
Black, J. A.: Babylonian ballads: a new genre, *JAOS* 103 (1983), pp. 25–34
——*Reading Sumerian Poetry.* London, 1998
——Some structural features of Sumerian narrative poetry, *Mesopotamian Epic Literature*, pp. 71–101
——The alleged 'extra' phonemes of Sumerian, *RA* 84 (1990), pp. 107–18
——and F. N. H. Al-Rawi: A contribution to the study of Akkadian bird names, *ZA* 77 (1987), pp. 117–26
——and A. Green: *Gods, Demons and Symbols of Ancient Mesopotamia: An Illustrated Dictionary.* London, 1992
——and Susan M. Sherwin-White: A clay tablet with Greek letters in the Ashmolean Museum, and the 'Graeco-Babyloniaca' texts, *Iraq* 46 (1984), pp. 131–40
——et al.: Electronic Text Corpus of Sumerian Literature: www-etcsl.orient.ox.ac.uk
Blacker, Carmen, and M. Loewe (eds.): *Ancient Cosmologies.* London, 1975
Böck, Barbara: *Die babylonisch-assyrische Morphoskopie. AfO* Beiheft 27. Vienna, 2000
——Eva Cancik-Kirschbaum and T. Richter (eds.): *Munuscula Mesopotamica. Festschrift für Johannes Renger.* AOAT 267. Münster, 1999
Boese, J.: Mesanepada und der Schatz von Mari, *ZA* 68 (1978), pp. 6–33
Böhl, F. M. Th. de Liagre: Das Problem ewigen Lebens im Zyklus und Epos des Gilgameschs, in id., *Opera minora. Studies en bijdragen op Assyriologisch en Oudtestamentisch terrein.* Groningen, 1953, pp. 234–62
——Die Fahrt nach dem Lebenskraut, *ArOr* 18, 1 (1950), pp. 107–22
——Gilgameš B. Nach akkadischen Texten, *RLA* 3 (1957–71), pp. 364–72
——*Het Gilgamesj-epos.* Amsterdam, 1952

Böhl, F. M. Th. de Liagre: *Mededeelingen uit de Leidsche verzameling van spijkerschrift-inscripties*. 3 vols. Amsterdam, 1933

Boissier, A.: *Choix des textes relatifs à la divination assyro-babylonienne*. Geneva, 1905–6

——*Documents assyriens relatifs aus présages*. 3 vols. Paris, 1894–9

Böllenrücher, J.: *Gebete und Hymnen an Nergal*. LSS 1, 6. Leipzig, 1904

Borger, R.: *Assyrisch-babylonische Zeichenliste*. AOAT 33. Kevelaer and Neukirchen-Vluyn, 1978

——*Babylonische-assyrische Lesestücke*. 1st edn: 3 vols. Rome, 1963. 2nd edn: 2 vols. AnOr 54. Rome, 1994

——*Beiträge zum Inschriftenwerk Assurbanipals*. Wiesbaden, 1996

——*Die Inschriften Asarhaddons, Königs von Assyrien*. *AfO* Beiheft 9. Graz, 1956

——Die Kuyunjik-Sammlung 1982–1983, *AfO* 31 (1984), pp. 331–6

——Einige Texte religiösen Inhalts IV. Ein neues Gilgameš-Fragment, *Or* NS 54 (1985), pp. 25–6

——W. Hinz and W. H. Ph. Römer: *Historisch-chronologische Texte* 1. TUAT 1, 4. Gütersloh, 1984

——and W. G. Lambert: Ein neuer Era-Text aus Ninive (K 9956+79-7-8, 18), *Or* NS 27 (1958), pp. 136–49

Boscawen, W. St Chad: Notes on the religion and mythology of the Assyrians, *TSBA* 4 (1876), pp. 267–301

Bottéro, J.: *L'épopée de Gilgameš*. Paris, 1994

——La mythologie de la mort en Mésopotamia ancienne, *CRRA* 26, pp. 25–52

——Le substitut royal et son sort en Mésopotamie ancienne, *Akkadica* 9 (1978), pp. 2–24

——Les inventaires de Qatna, *RA* 43 (1949), pp. 1–40, 137–215

——Les morts et l'au-delà dans les rituels en accadien contre l'action des 'revenants', *ZA* 73 (1983), pp. 153–204

——*Mesopotamia: Writing, Reasoning, and the Gods*. Chicago and London, 1992

——and S. N. Kramer: *Lorsque les dieux faisaient l'homme. Mythologie mésopotamienne*. Paris, 1989

Boyer, G.: *Contribution à l'histoire juridique de la première dynastie babylonienne*. Paris, 1928

Braun-Holzinger, Eva Andrea: *Mesopotamische Weihgaben der frühdynastischen bis altbabylonischen Zeit*. HSAO 3. Heidelberg, 1991

Brinkman, J. A.: Merodach-baladan II, *Studies Oppenheim*, pp. 6–53

British Museum: *The Babylonian Story of the Deluge and the Epic of Gilgamesh*. Ed. C. J. Gadd. London, 1929

Buccellati, G.: On poetry—theirs and ours, *Studies Moran*, pp. 105–35

——Wisdom and not: the case of Mesopotamia, *JAOS* 101 (1981), pp. 35–47

Buren, Elisabeth D. van: *The Fauna of Ancient Mesopotamia as Represented in Art*. AnOr 18. Rome, 1939

Burkert, W.: *The Orientalizing Revolution: Near Eastern Influence on Greek Culture in the Early Archaic Age*. Cambridge, Mass., 1992

Burrows, E.: *Archaic Texts*. UET 2. London, 1935

——Tilmun, Baḥrain, Paradise, *Or* 30 (1928), pp. 1–34

Burstein, S. M.: *The Babyloniaca of Berossus*. SANE 1, 5. Malibu, Calif., 1978

Butler, Sally A. L.: *Mesopotamian Conceptions of Dreams and Dream Rituals*. AOAT 258. Münster, 1998

Cadelli, Danielle: Lieux boisés et bois coupés, *Florilegium marianum* 2, pp. 159–73

Çağırgan, G.: Three more duplicates to Astrolabe B, *Belleten* 48 (1984), pp. 399–417

Cagni, L.: *Briefe aus dem Iraq Museum (TIM II)*. AbB 8. Leiden, 1980

——(ed.): *Il bilinguismo a Ebla*. Naples, 1984

Calmeyer, P., K. Hecker, Liane Jakob-Rost and C. B. F. Walker (eds.): *Beiträge zur altorientalischen Archäologie und Altertumskunde. Festschrift für Barthel Hrouda zum 65. Geburtstag*. Wiesbaden, 1994

Caplice, R.: Further namburbi notes, *Or* NS 42 (1973), pp. 508–17

——Namburbi texts in the British Museum, I, *Or* NS 34 (1965), pp. 105–31

——Namburbi texts in the British Museum, V, *Or* NS 40 (1971), pp. 133–83

Carroué, F.: *Études de géographie et de topographie sumériennes* III. *L'Iturungal et le Sud sumérien*, *Acta Sum* 15 (1993), pp. 11–69

Cassin, Elena: Cycles du temps et cadres de l'espace en Mésopotamie ancienne, *Revue de synthèse* 90 (1969), pp. 241–57

Castellino, G. R.: *Two Šulgi Hymns*. Studi semitici 42. Rome, 1972

Cavigneaux, A.: Au sources du Midrash: l'herméneutique babylonienne, *Aula Or* 5 (1987), pp. 243–55

——Die sumerisch-akkadischen Zeichenlisten. Überlieferungsprobleme. PhD dissertation, University of Munich, 1976

——Máš-ḫul-dúb-ba, *Fs Boehmer*, pp. 53–67

——*Textes scolaires du temple de Nabû ša ḫarê* 1. Baghdad, 1981

——*Uruk. Altbabylonische Texte aus dem Planquadrat Pe XVI-4/5*. AUWE 23. Mainz, 1996

——and F. N. H. Al-Rawi: *Gilgameš et la Mort. Textes de Tell Haddad VI*. Cuneiform Monographs 19. Groningen, 2000

————Gilgameš et Taureau de Ciel (Šul.mè.kam). Textes de Tell Haddad IV, *RA* 87 (1993), pp. 97–129

————La fin de Gilgameš, Enkidu et les Enfers d'après les manuscrits d'Ur et de Meturan, *Iraq* 62 (2000), pp. 1–19

————New Sumerian literary texts from Tell Haddad (ancient Meturan): a first survey, *Iraq* 55 (1993), pp. 93–5

——H. G. Güterbock, Martha T. Roth and Gertrud Farber: *The Series Erimḫuš = anantu and An-ta-gál = šaqû*. MSL 17. Rome, 1985

——and J. Renger: Ein altbabylonischer Gilgameš-Text aus Nippur, *Studies Lambert*, pp. 91–103

Charpin, D.: A propos du site de Tell Harmal, *NABU* 1987, no. 117

——Inanna/Eštar, divinité poliade d'Uruk à l'époque paléo-babylonienne, *NABU* 1994, no. 39

——La chronologie des souverains d'Ešnunna, *Mélanges Birot*, pp. 51–66

——Les champions, la meule et le fleuve, *Florilegium marianum* 1, pp. 29–38

——Les malheurs d'un scribe ou de l'inutilité du sumérien loin de Nippur, in Ellis (ed.), *Nippur at the Centennial*, pp. 7–27

——Postures de table, *NABU* 1992, no. 123

——review of Greengus, *Ishchali*, *RA* 82 (1988), pp. 185–6

——Toponymie amorrite et biblique: la ville de Ṣîbat/Ṣobah, *RA* 92 (1998), pp. 79–92

——Usages épistolaires des chancelleries d'Ešnunna, d'Ekallâtum et de Mari, *NABU* 1993, no. 110

——and J.-M. Durand (eds.): *Florilegium marianum 2. Receuil d'études à la mémoire de Maurice Birot*. Paris, 1994

——and F. Joannès (eds.): *Marchands, diplomates et empereurs. Études . . . offertes à Paul Garelli*. Paris, 1991

Chavalas, M. W. (ed.): *Emar: The History, Religion, and Culture of a Syrian Town in the Late Bronze Age*. Bethesda, Md., 1996

Chiera, E.: *Sumerian Epics and Myths*. OIP 15. Chicago, 1934

Chiera, E.: *Sumerian Lexical Texts from the Temple School at Nippur*. OIP 11. Chicago, 1929
——*Sumerian Religious Texts*. Upland, Pa., 1924
——*Sumerian Texts of Varied Contents*. OIP 16. Chicago, 1934
Chiodi, Silvia M.: Il prigioniero e il morto. Epopea di Gilgameš Tav. X r. 318–320, *Orientis antiqui miscellanea* 2. Rome, 1995, pp. 159–71
——*Offerte 'funebri' nella Lagaš presargonica*. 2 vols. Rome, 1997
Çığ, Muazzez, Hatice Kızılyay and S. N. Kramer: *Sumer Edebî Tablet ve Parçaları (Sumerian Literary Tablets and Fragments)*. 2 vols. Istanbul, 1969 and 1976
Ciraola, L., and J. Seidel (eds.): *Magic and Divination in the Ancient World*. Groningen, forthcoming
Civil M.: Ancient Mesopotamian lexicography, in Sasson (ed.), *Civilizations of the Near East*, pp. 2305–14
——Feeding Dumuzi's sheep: the lexicon as a source of literary inspiration, *Studies Reiner*, pp. 37–55
——From Enki's headaches to phonology, *JNES* 32 (1973), pp. 57–61
——Medical commentaries from Nippur, *JNES* 33 (1974), pp. 329–39
——Notes on Sumerian lexicography, I, *JCS* 20 (1966), pp. 119–24
——Reading Gilgameš, *Aula Or* 17–18 (1999–2000), pp. 179–89
——review of *CT* 44, *JNES* 28 (1969), pp. 70–2
——Sin-iddinam in Emar and SU.A = Šimaški, *NABU* 1996, no. 41
——Sur un texte sumérien d'Ugarit, *RA* 63 (1969), p. 179
——The 10th tablet of úru àm-ma-ir-ra-bi, *Aula Or* 1 (1983), pp. 45–54
——*The Farmer's Instructions: A Sumerian Agricultural Manual*. Aula Or Suppl. 5. Madrid, 1994
——The song of the plowing oxen, *Kramer AV*, pp. 82–95
——The texts from Meskene-Emar, *Aula Or* 7 (1989), pp. 5–25
——R. D. Biggs, H. G. Güterbock, H. J. Nissen and Erica Reiner: *The Series Lú = ša and Related Texts*. MSL 12. Rome, 1969
——Margaret W. Green and W. G. Lambert: *Ea A = nâqu, Aa A = nâqu, with their Forerunners and Related Texts*. MSL 14. Rome, 1979
——O. R. Gurney and D. A. Kennedy: *The Sag-Tablet, Lexical Texts in the Ashmolean Museum, Middle Babylonian Grammatical Texts, Miscellaneous Texts*. MSL SS 1. Rome, 1986
——H. G. Güterbock, W. W. Hallo, H. A. Hoffner and Erica Reiner: *Izi = išātu, Ká-gal = abullu and Níg-ga = makkūru*. MSL 13. Rome, 1971
Clay, A. T.: *A Hebrew Deluge Story in Cuneiform and Other Epic Fragments in the Pierpont Morgan Library*. YOR 5, 3. New Haven, 1922
——*Documents from the Temple Archives of Nippur Dated in the Reigns of Cassite Rulers* [1] *Complete Dates*. BE 14. Philadelphia, 1906
——*Documents from the Temple Archives of Nippur Dated in the Reigns of Cassite Rulers* [3]. PBS 2, 2. Philadelphia, 1912
——*Epics, Hymns, Omens, and Other Texts*. BRM 4. New Haven, Conn., 1923
——*Letters and Transactions from Cappadocia*. BIN 4. New Haven, Conn., 1927
——*Miscellaneous Inscriptions in the Yale Babylonian Collection*. YOS 1. New Haven, Conn., 1915
Cocquerillat, Denise: *Palmeraies et cultures de l'Eanna d'Uruk (559–520)*. ADFU 8. Berlin, 1968
Cohen, M. E.: Another Utu hymn, *ZA* 67 (1977), pp. 1–19
——*Sumerian Hymnology: The Eršemma*. HUCA Supplement 2. Cincinnati, 1981
——*The Canonical Lamentations of Mesopotamia*. 2 vols. Bethesda, Md., 1988
——*The Cultic Calendars of the Ancient Near East*. Bethesda, Md., 1993

Cohen, M. E., D. C. Snell and D. B. Weisberg (eds.): *The Tablet and the Scroll: Near Eastern Studies in Honor of William W. Hallo*. Bethesda, Md., 1993

Cohn-Sherbok, D. (ed.): *A Traditional Quest: Essays in Honour of Louis Jacobs*. Sheffield, 1991

Cole, S. W.: The crimes and sacrileges of Nabû-šuma-iškun, *ZA* 84 (1994), pp. 220–52

—— and H. Gasche: Levees, floods, and the river network of northern Babylonia, *CDOG* 2, pp. 87–110

—— and P. Machinist: *Letters from Priests to the Kings Esarhaddon and Assurbanipal*. SAA 13. Helsinki, 1998

Collon, Dominique: *Ancient Near Eastern Art*. London, 1995

Cooper, J. S.: Apodotic death and the historicity of 'historical' omens, *CRRA* 26, pp. 99–105

—— Babbling on: recovering Mesopotamian orality, *Mesopotamian Epic Literature*, pp. 103–22

—— Bilinguals from Boghazköi I, *ZA* 61 (1971), pp. 1–22

—— Bilinguals from Boghazköi II, *ZA* 62 (1972), pp. 62–81

—— Gilgamesh dreams of Enkidu: the evolution and dilution of narrative, *Finkelstein Mem.Vol.*, pp. 39–44

—— gìr-KIN 'to stamp out, trample', *RA* 66 (1972), pp. 81–3

—— Studies in Sumerian lapidary inscriptions, II, *RA* 74 (1980), pp. 101–10

—— *Sumerian and Akkadian Royal Inscriptions* 1. *Presargonic Inscriptions*. New Haven, Conn., 1986

—— Symmetry and repetition in Akkadian narrative, *JAOS* 97 (1977), pp. 508–12

—— *The Curse of Agade*. Baltimore, 1983

—— The fate of mankind: death and afterlife in ancient Mesopotamia, in Obayashi (ed.), *Death and the Afterlife*, pp. 19–33

—— and W. Heimpel: The Sumerian Sargon legend, *JAOS* 103 (1983), pp. 67–82

—— and G. M. Schwartz (eds.): *The Study of the Ancient Near East in the Twenty-First Century*. Winona Lake, Ind., 1996

Cornil, P.: Textes de Boghazköy. Liste des lieux de trouvaille, *Hethitica* 7 (1987), pp. 5–72

Craig, J. A.: *Assyrian and Babylonian Religious Texts*. AB 13. 2 vols. Leipzig, 1895–7

Curtis, J. E., and J. E. Reade (eds.): *Art and Empire. Treasures from Assyria in the British Museum*. London, 1995

Dalley, Stephanie: *A Catalogue of the Cuneiform Tablets in the Collections of the Royal Scottish Museum, Edinburgh*. Edinburgh, 1979

—— Assyrian court narratives in Aramaic and Egyptian: historical fiction, in Abusch et al. (eds.), *Historiography in the Cuneiform World*, pp. 149–61

—— Authorship, variation and canonicity in Gilgamesh and other ancient texts, *Interaction: Journal of the Tureck Bach Foundation* 2 (1999), pp. 31–47

—— Gilgamesh and Manichaean themes, *Aram* 3 (1991), pp. 23–33

—— Gilgamesh in the Arabian Nights, *JRAS* NS 1 (1991), pp. 1–17

—— *Myths from Mesopotamia*. Oxford, 1989

—— Old Babylonian tablets from Nineveh; and possible pieces of early Gilgamesh epic, *Iraq* 63 (2001), pp. 155–63

—— The tale of Bulūqiyā and the *Alexander Romance* in Jewish and Sufi mystical circles, in Reeves (ed.), *Tracing the Threads*, pp. 239–69

—— A. T. Reyes, D. Pingree, A. Salvesen and H. McCall: *The Legacy of Mesopotamia*. Oxford, 1998

Damerji, Muayad Sa'id Basim: *Gräber assyrischer Königinnen aus Nimrud*. Mainz, 1999. Reprinted from *Jahrbuch des Römisch-Germanischen Zentralmuseums* 45 (1998)

Dandamaev, M. A.: *Slavery in Babylonia from Nabopolassar to Alexander the Great (626–331 BC)*. Transl. V. A. Powell. DeKalb, Ill., 1984

—— (ed.): *Societies and Languages of the Ancient Near East: Studies in Honour of I. M. Diakonoff*. Warminster, UK, 1982

David, M.: *Die Adoption im altbabylonischen Recht*. Leipzig, 1927

David, Madeleine V.: L'épisode des oiseaux dans les récits du déluge, *Vetus Testamentum* 7 (1957), pp. 189–90

Davila, J. R.: The Flood hero as King and priest, *JNES* 54 (1995), pp. 199–214

Day, J., R. P. Gordon and H. G. M. Williamson (eds.): *Wisdom in Ancient Israel: Essays in Honour of J. A. Emerton*. Cambridge, 1995

De Graeve, Marie-Christine: *The Ships of the Ancient Near East (c. 2000–500 B.C.)*. OLA 7. Leuven, 1981

Deimel, A.: *Die Inschriften von Fara*. 3 vols. WVDOG 40, 43, 45. Leipzig, 1922–4

—— *Šumerisches Lexikon* 2. *Vollständige Ideogramm-Sammlung*. 4 vols. Rome, 1928–33

—— *Šumerisches Lexikon* 4. *Pantheon babylonicum*. Rome, 1950

Delitzsch, F.: *Assyrische Lesestücke*. 3rd edn. Leipzig, 1885

Deller, K.: Studien zur neuassyrischen Orthographie, *Or* NS 31 (1962), pp. 186–96

—— The sacred burial chamber, *SAAB* 1, 2 (1987), pp. 69–71

—— Zweisilbige Lautwerte des Typs KVKV im Neuassyrischen, *Or* NS 31 (1962), pp. 7–26

—— W. R. Mayer and W. Sommerfeld: Akkadische Lexikographie: *CAD* N, *Or* NS 56 (1987), pp. 176–218

—— and Kazuko Watanabe: *šukkulu(m)*, *šakkulu*, 'abwischen, auswischen', *ZA* 70 (1980), pp. 198–226

Delougaz, P.: *Pottery from the Diyala Region*. OIP 63. Chicago, 1952

—— and T. Jacobsen: *The Temple Oval at Khafājah*. OIP 53. Chicago, 1940

Dever, W. G., and M. Tadmor: A copper hoard of the Middle Bronze Age I, *IEJ* 26 (1976), pp. 163–9

Dhorme, E.: Rituel funéraire assyrien, *RA* 38 (1941), pp. 57–66

Diakonoff, I. M.: review of Böhl, *Het Gilgamesj-epos*, and Matouš, *Epos o Gilgamešovi*, *BiOr* 18 (1961), pp. 61–7

—— Thorns and roses, *Rocznik Orientalistyczny* 41, 2 (1980), pp. 19–24

—— and N. B. Jankowska: An Elamite Gilgameš text from Argištihenele, Urartu (Armavir-blur, 8th century BC), *ZA* 80 (1990), pp. 102–23

Dietrich, M.: 'Ein Leben ohne Freude . . .'. Studie über eine Weisheitskomposition aus den Gelehrtenbibliotheken von Emar und Ugarit, *UF* 24 (1992), pp. 9–29

—— and O. Loretz (eds.): *Dubsar anta-men. Studien zur Altorientalistik. Festschrift für W. H. Ph. Römer zur Vollendung seines 70. Lebensjahres*. AOAT 253. Münster, 1998

—— —— (eds.): *Vom Alten Orient zum Alten Testament. Festschrift für Wolfram Freiherrn von Soden zum 85. Geburtstag*. AOAT 240. Kevelaer and Neukirchen-Vluyn, Germany, 1995

Dijk, J. J. A. van: *Cuneiform Texts: Old Babylonian Contracts and Juridical Texts*. TIM 4. Wiesbaden, 1967

—— *Cuneiform Texts: Old Babylonian Contracts and Related Material*. TIM 5. Wiesbaden, 1968

—— *Cuneiform Texts: Old Babylonian Letters and Related Material*. TIM 2. Wiesbaden, 1965

—— *Cuneiform Texts: Texts of Varying Content*. TIM 9. Leiden, 1976

—— Die Inschriftenfunde, *UVB* 18, pp. 39–62

—— Ein spätaltbabylonischer Katalog einer Sammlung sumerischer Briefe, *Or* NS 58 (1989), pp. 441–52

Dijk, J. J. A. van: IM. 52615: un songe d'Enkidu, *Sumer* 14 (1958), pp. 114–21
——Inanna, le bon augure de Samsu'iluna, *Studies Lambert*, pp. 119–29
——Inanna raubt den 'großen Himmel'. Ein Mythos, *Fs Borger*, pp. 9–31
——*Literarische Texte aus Babylon.* VAS 24. Berlin, 1987
——*Nicht-kanonische Beschwörungen und sonstige literarische Texte.* VAS NF 1 (17). Berlin, 1971
——*Sumerische Götterlieder* 2. Heidelberg, 1960
——Textes divers du musée de Baghdad II, *Sumer* 13 (1957), pp. 65–7
——Textes divers du musée de Baghdad III, *Sumer* 15 (1959), pp. 5–14
——VAT 8382: ein zweisprachiges Königsritual, *HSAO* I, pp. 233–68
——A. Goetze and Mary I. Hussey: *Early Mesopotamian Incantations and Rituals.* YOS 11. New Haven, Conn., 1985
——and W. Mayer: *Texte aus dem Rēš-Heiligtum in Uruk-Warka. Bagh. Mitt.* Beiheft 2. Berlin, 1980
Dirven, Lucinda: The exaltation of Nabû: a revision of the relief depicting the battle against Tiamat from the temple of Bel in Palmyra, *WO* 28 (1997), pp. 96–116
Dossin, G.: Enkidou dans l' 'Épopée de Gilgameš', *Bulletin de l'Académie royale de Belgique, Classe des lettres*, Series 5, 42 (1956), pp. 580–93
——Inscriptions de fondation provenant de Mari, *Syria* 21 (1940), pp. 152–69
——*La correspondance féminine.* ARM 10. TCL 31. Paris, 1967
——*La pâleur d'Enkidu.* Louvain, 1931
——*Lettres.* ARM 5. TCL 26. Paris, 1951
——*Lettres de la première dynastie babylonienne.* 2 vols. TCL 17–18. Paris, 1933–4
Driel, G. van: *The Cult of Aššur.* Assen, 1969
——T. J. H. Krispijn, M. Stol and K. R. Veenhof (eds.): *Zikir Šumim: Assyriological Studies Presented to F. R. Kraus.* Leiden, 1982
Duchesne-Guillemin, Marcelle: Pukku and mekkû, *Iraq* 45 (1983), pp. 151–6
Durand, J. M.: *Archives épistolaires de Mari* 1, 1. ARM 26, 1. Paris, 1988
——*Documents cunéiformes de la IVe Section de l'École Pratique des Hautes Études.* Geneva, 1982
——(ed.): *Florilegium marianum. Recueil d'études en l'honneur de Michel Fleury.* Mémories de NABU 1. Paris, 1992
—— 'Hittite' *tišanuš* = mariote *tišânum*, *NABU* 1998, no. 15
—— *Textes administratifs des salles 134 et 160 du palais de Mari.* ARMT 21. Paris, 1983
——*tutturum*, *NABU* 1992, no. 34
——Un commentaire à TDP I, AO 17661, *RA* 73 (1979), pp. 153–71
——and J.-R. Kupper (eds.): *Miscellanea babylonica. Mélanges offerts à Maurice Birot.* Paris, 1985
Durham, J. W.: Studies in Boğazköy Akkadian. PhD dissertation, Harvard University, 1976
During Caspers, Elisabeth C. L.: In the footsteps of Gilgamesh: in search of the 'prickly rose', *Persica* 12 (1987), pp. 57–95
——Of corals and ailments in the ancient Near East, *Proceedings of the Seminar for Arabian Studies* 16 (1986), pp. 25–31
——Pearl fishery in the Arabian Gulf and the 'prickly rose' of Gilgamesh, *BiOr* 40 (1983), 31–49
Ebeling, E.: *Bruchstücke eines politischen Propagandagedichtes aus einer assyrischen Kanzlei.* MAOG 12, 2. Berlin, 1938
——*Die akkadische Gebetsserie 'Handerhebung' von neuem gesammelt und herausgegeben.* Berlin, 1953
——Fliege, *RLA* 3 (1957–71), p. 87
——*Keilschrifttexte aus Assur juristischen Inhalts.* WVDOG 50. Leipzig, 1927
——*Keilschrifttexte aus Assur religiösen Inhalts.* 2 vols. WVDOG 28 and 34. Leipzig, 1919 and 1923

Ebeling, E.: *Literarische Keilschrifttexte aus Assur.* Berlin, 1953

——Mittelassyrische Rezepte zur Bereitung (Herstellung) von wohlriechenden Salben, *Or* NS 17 (1948), pp. 129–45, 299–313

——review of Thompson, *Gilgamish*, *AfO* 8 (1932–3), pp. 226–32

——Sammlungen von Beschwörungsformeln, *ArOr* 21 (1953), pp. 357–423

—— *Tod und Leben nach den Vorstellungen der Babylonier.* Berlin and Leipzig, 1931

——B. Meissner, E. Weidner, W. von Soden and D. O. Edzard (eds.): *Reallexikon der Assyriologie.* Berlin, 1928–

Edzard, D. O.: Enmebaragesi von Kiš, *ZA* 53 (1959), pp. 9–26

——Gilgameš XI 65–69, in Kaye (ed), *Semitic Studies in Honor of Wolf Leslau* 1 pp. 392–6

——Gilgamesch und Huwawa, *TUAT* III/3, pp. 540–9

——Gilgameš und Huwawa A. I. Teil, *ZA* 80 (1990), pp. 165–203

——Gilgameš und Huwawa A. II. Teil, *ZA* 81 (1991), pp. 165–233

——'*Gilgameš und Huwawa'. Zwei Versionen der sumerischen Zedernwaldepisode nebst einer Edition von Version 'B'.* BAW Sitzungsberichte 1993, 4. Munich, 1993

—— *Gudea and his Dynasty.* RIME 3, 1. Toronto, 1997

[Edzard, D. O. (ed.):] *Heidelberger Studien zum alten Orient, Adam Falkenstein zum 17. September 1966.* Heidelberg, 1967

——*Hymnen, Beschwörungen und Verwandtes aus dem Archiv L. 2769.* ARET 5. Rome, 1984

——Kinunir, Kiniršа, *RLA* 5 (1976–80), pp. 603–4

——Kleine Beiträge zum Gilgameš-Epos, *Or* NS 54 (1985), pp. 46–55

——Königslisten und Chroniken. A. Sumerisch, *RLA* 6 (1980–3), pp. 77–86

——mekkû, pukku und, *RLA* 8 (1993–7), p. 34

——namir 'er ist glänzend', *Acta Sum* 16 (1994), pp. 1–14

——review of *CAD* R, *ZA* 90 (2000), pp. 292–5

——*Sumerische Rechtsurkunden des III. Jahrtausends.* Munich, 1968

——U 7804 // *UET* VI/1 26: 'Gedicht von der Hacke', *Studies Lambert*, pp. 131–5

——Zahlen, Zählen und Messen im Gilgameš-Epos, in Gross et al. (eds.), *Texte, Methode und Grammatik*, pp. 57–66

——Zu den akkadischen Nominalformen parsat-, pirsat- und pursat, *ZA* 72 (1982), pp. 68–88

——and Gertrud Farber: *Répertoire géographique des textes cunéiformes 2. Die Orts- und Gewässernamen der Zeit der 3. Dynastie von Ur.* Beihefte zum Tübinger Atlas des vorderen Orients B 7 [1]. Wiesbaden, 1974

——and W. G. Lambert: Ḫaniš, Šullat und, *RLA* 4 (1972–5), pp. 107–8

Ehelolf, H.: *Mythen und Rituale.* KUB 17. Berlin, 1926

—— *Texte verschiedenen Inhalts (vorwiegend aus den Grabungen seit 1931)* [2]. KUB 30. Berlin, 1939

—— *Texte verschiedenen Inhalts (vorwiegend aus den Grabungen 1931 und 1932).* KUB 34. Berlin, 1944

Eichler, B. L. (ed.): *Kramer Anniversary Volume.* AOAT 25. Kevelaer, Neukirchen-Vluyn, 1976

Eisser, G., and J. Lewy: *Die altassyrischen Rechtsurkunden vom Kültepe* 1. MVAG 33. Leipzig, 1930

Ellis, Maria deJ.: An Old Babylonian adoption contract from Tell Harmal, *JCS* 27 (1975), pp. 130–51

——(ed.): *Essays on the Ancient Near East in Memory of Jacob Joel Finkelstein.* Hamden, Conn., 1977

——(ed.): *Nippur at the Centennial.* CRRA 35. OPBF 14. Philadelphia, 1992

——Old Babylonian texts from Tell Harmal—and elsewhere?, *Studies Sachs*, pp. 119–41

Erkanal, H., V. Donbaz and Ayşegül Uğuruğlu (eds.): *XXXIV. Uluslararası Assiriyoloji Kongresi*. CRRA 34. Ankara, 1998

Fadhil, Abdulilah: Die Grabinschrift der Mullissu-mukannišat-Ninua aus Nimrud/Kalḫu und andere in ihrem Grab gefundene Schriftträger, *Bagh. Mitt.* 21 (1990), pp. 471–82

—— Die in Nimrud/Kalḫu aufgefundene Grabinschrift der Jabâ, *Bagh. Mitt.* 21 (1990), pp. 461–70

Fales, F. M., and B. J. Hickey (eds.): *Austen Henry Layard tra l'oriente e Venezia*. Rome, 1987

—— and J. N. Postgate: *Imperial Administrative Records* 1. *Palace and Temple Administration*. SAA 7. Helsinki, 1992

Falkenstein, A.: *akiti*-Fest und *akiti*-Haus, *Festschrift Friedrich*, pp. 147–82

—— *Die Inschriften Gudeas von Lagaš* 1. *Einleitung*. AnOr 30. Rome, 1966

—— Gilgameš. A. Nach sumerischen Texten, *RLA* 3 (1957–71), pp. 357–64

—— *Grammatik der Sprache Gudeas von Lagaš*. AnOr 28. Rome, 1949

—— *Literarische Keilschrifttexte aus Uruk*. Berlin, 1931

—— *Sumerische Götterlieder* 1. Heidelberg, 1959

—— Sumerische religiöse Texte 1. Drei 'Hymnen' auf Urninurta von Isin, *ZA* 49 (1950), pp. 80–150

—— Sumerische religiöse Texte 2. Ein Šulgi-Lied, *ZA* 50 (1952), pp. 61–91

—— *Topographie von Uruk* 1. *Uruk zur Seleukidenzeit*. ADFU 3. Leipzig, 1941

—— Zwei Rituale aus seleukidischer Zeit, *UVB* 15, pp. 36–44

Falkowitz, R.: Round Old Babylonian school tablets, *AfO* 29–30 (1983–4), pp. 18–45

Farber, W.: Altbabylonische Adverbialbildungen auf *-āni*, *Kraus AV*, pp. 37–47

—— *Beschwörungsrituale an Ištar und Dumuzi*. Wiesbaden, 1977

—— *Mannam lušpur ana Enkidu*: some new thoughts about an old motif, *JNES* 49 (1990), pp. 299–321

—— Neues aus Uruk. Zur 'Bibliothek des Iqīša', *WO* 18 (1987), pp. 26–42

—— *Schlaf, Kindchen, Schlaf! Mesopotamische Baby-Beschwörungen und -Rituale*. Mesopotamian Civilizations 2. Winona Lake, Ind., 1989

—— The city wall of Babylon: a belt-cord?, *NABU* 1991, no. 72

Farkas, Ann E., Prudence O. Harper and Evelyn B. Harrison (eds.): *Monsters and Demons in the Ancient and Medieval Worlds: Papers Presented in Honor of Edith Porada*. Mainz, 1987

Feigin, S. I.: Ḫum-Ḫum, *Miscellanea Orientalia dedicata Antonio Deimel*. AnOr 12. Rome, 1935, pp. 82–100

—— and A. L. Oppenheim: *Legal and Administrative Texts of the Reign of Samsu-iluna*. YOS 12. New Haven, Conn., 1979

Ferrara, A. J.: *Nanna-Suen's Journey to Nippur*. Studia Pohl SM 2. Rome, 1973

Figulla, H. H.: *Cuneiform Texts from Babylonian Tablets in the British Museum* 42. London, 1959

—— *Letters and Documents of the Old Babylonian Period*. UET 5. London, 1953

—— *Old Babylonian Letters*. CT 43. London, 1963

Finet, A. (ed.): *Actes de la XVIIe Rencontre Assyriologique Internationale*. CRRA 17. Brussels, 1970

—— La lutte entre Gilgameš et Enkidu, *Mélanges Limet*, pp. 45–50

Finkbeiner, U., R. Dittmann and H. Hauptmann (eds.): *Beiträge zur Kulturgeschichte Vorderasiens. Festschrift für Rainer Michael Boehmer*. Mainz, 1995

Finkel, I. L.: Adad-apla-iddina, Esagil-kīn-apli, and the series SA.GIG, *Studies Sachs*, pp. 143–59

—— Bilingual chronicle fragments, *JCS* 32 (1980), pp. 65–80

—— Necromancy in ancient Mesopotamia, *AfO* 29–30 (1983–4), pp. 1–17

—— On some dog, snake and scorpion incantations, *Mesopotamian Magic*, pp. 213–50

Finkel, I. L.: Tablets for Lord Amherst, *Iraq* 58 (1996), pp. 191–205
——The dream of Kurigalzu and the tablet of sins, *AnSt* 33 (1983), pp. 75–80
——The lament of Nabû-šuma-ukîn, *CDOG* 2, pp. 323–42
——and M. Civil: *The Series SIG₇.ALAN = Nabnītu*. MSL 16. Rome, 1982
——and M. J. Geller (eds.): *Sumerian Gods and their Representations*. Cuneiform Monographs 7. Groningen, 1997
Finkelstein, J. J.: *Ana bīt emim šasū*, *RA* 61 (1967), pp. 127–36
——Cuneiform texts from Tell Billa, *JCS* 7 (1953), pp. 111–76
——*Late Old Babylonian Documents and Letters*. YOS 13. New Haven, Conn., 1972
——On some recent studies in cuneiform law, *JAOS* 90 (1970), pp. 243–56
——The genealogy of the Hammurapi dynasty, *JCS* 20 (1966), pp. 95–118
Fishbane, M., and E. Tov (eds.): *'Shaʿarei Talmon': Studies in the Bible, Qumran, and the Ancient Near East Presented to Shemaryahu Talmon*. Winona Lake, Ind., 1992
Flückiger-Hawker, Esther: *Urnamma of Ur in Sumerian Literary Tradition*. OBO 166. Fribourg and Göttingen, 1999
Forsyth, N.: Huwawa and his trees: a narrative and cultural analysis', *Acta Sum* 3 (1981), pp. 13–29
Foster, B. R.: A postscript to the Gilgamesh letter, *AnSt* 32 (1982), pp. 43–4
——*Before the Muses: An Anthology of Akkadian Literature*. 2 vols. Bethesda, Md., 1993
——Gilgamesh: sex, love and the ascent of knowledge, *Essays Pope*, pp. 21–42
——OB Gilgamesh Pa i 22, *RA* 77 (1983), p. 92
——review of *CRRA* 26, *BiOr* 38 (1981), 619–26
——*The Epic of Gilgamesh*. New York, 2001
——The siege of Armanum, *ANES* 14 (1982), pp. 27–36
——Wisdom and the gods in ancient Mesopotamia, *Or* NS 43 (1974), pp. 344–55
Foxvog, D. A.: A manual of sacrificial procedure, *Studies Sjöberg*, pp. 167–76
——Sumerian brands and branding-irons, *ZA* 85 (1995), pp. 1–7
Frahm, E.: *Einleitung in die Sanherib-Inschriften*. *AfO* Beiheft 26. Horn, Austria, 1997
——Nabû-zuqup-kēnu, das Gilgameš-Epos und der Tod Sargons II., *JCS* 51 (1999), pp. 73–90
Frame, G.: *Rulers of Babylonia from the Second Dynasty of Isin to the End of the Assyrian Domination (1157–612 BC)*. RIMB 2. Toronto, 1995
Frank, C.: Ein Klagelied der Muttergöttin aus Uruk, *ZA* 40 (1931), pp. 81–93
Frankena, R.: *Briefe aus dem Berliner Museum*. AbB 6. Leiden, 1974
——*Briefe aus dem British Museum (LIH und CT 2–33)*. AbB 2. Leiden, 1966
——Nouveaux fragments de la sixième tablette de l'Épopée de Gilgameš, in Garelli, *Gilg.*, pp. 113–22
Frayne, D. R.: *Old Babylonian Period (2003–1595 BC)*. RIME 4. Toronto, 1990
——review of Klein, *Šulgi*, *BiOr* 40 (1983), 92–101
——*Sargonic and Gutian Periods (2334–2113 BC)*. RIME 2. Toronto, 1993
——The birth of Gilgameš in ancient Mesopotamian art, *Bulletin CSMS* 34 (1999), pp. 39–49
——*Ur III Period (2112–2004 BC)*. RIME 3, 2. Toronto, 1997
Freedman, R. D.: The dispatch of the reconnaissance birds in Gilgamesh XI, *ANES* 5 (1973), pp. 123–9
Freedman, Sally M.: *If a City is Set on a Height* 1. OPBF 17. Philadelphia, 1998
Freydank, H., and C. Saporetti: *Bābu-aḫa-iddina: die Texte*. Rome, 1989
Friedrich, J.: Die hethitischen Bruchstücke des Gilgameš-Epos, *ZA* 39 (1930), pp. 1–82

Fronzaroli, P. (ed.), *Literature and Literary Language at Ebla*. Quaderna di semitistica 18. Florence, 1992
Frost, Honor: Gilgamesh and the 'Things of Stone', *Report of the Department of Antiquities, Cyprus* 1984, pp. 96–100
Fuchs, A.: *Die Inschriften Sargons II. aus Khorsabad*. Göttingen, 1994
Gadd, C. J.: *Cuneiform Texts from Babylonian Tablets in the British Museum* 38. London, 1925
—— *Cuneiform Texts from Babylonian Tablets in the British Museum* 39. London, 1926
—— *Cuneiform Texts from Babylonian Tablets in the British Museum* 40. London, 1927
—— *Cuneiform Texts from Babylonian Tablets in the British Museum* 41. London, 1931
—— Some contributions to the Gilgamesh Epic, *Iraq* 28 (1966), pp. 105–21
—— The Epic of Gilgameš, Tablet XII, *RA* 30 (1933), pp. 127–43
—— The Harran inscriptions of Nabonidus, *AnSt* 8 (1958), pp. 35–69
—— and S. N. Kramer: *Literary and Religious Texts*. 2 vols. UET 6, 1–2. London, 1963 and 1966
—— L. Legrain and S. Smith: *Royal Inscriptions*. UET 1. London, 1928
—— and R. C. Thompson: A Middle Babylonian chemical text, *Iraq* 3 (1936), pp. 87–96
Gallery, Maureen L.: Service obligations of the *kezertu*-women', *Or* NS 49 (1980), pp. 333–8
Ganter, Annette: Zum Ausgang von *Gilgameš und Huwawa* Version B, *NABU* 1995, no. 41
Gardner, J., and J. Maier: *Gilgamesh, Translated from the Sîn-leqi-unninni Version*. New York, 1985
Garelli, P. (ed.): *Gilgameš et sa légende*. CRRA 7. Paris, 1960
—— (ed.): *Le palais et la royauté*. CRRA 19. Paris, 1974
Geers, F. W.: N (unpublished folio)
Gelb, I. J.: *A Study of Writing*. Chicago and London, 1952
—— *Glossary of Old Akkadian*. MAD 3. Chicago, 1957
—— Homo ludens in early Mesopotamia, *StOr* 46 (1975), pp. 43–77
—— *Hurrians and Subarians*. SAOC 22. Chicago, 1944
—— Notes on von Soden's grammar of Akkadian, *BiOr* 12 (1955), pp. 93–111
—— *Old Akkadian Writing and Grammar*. MAD 2. 2nd edn. Chicago, 1961
—— Terms for slaves in ancient Mesopotamia, *Studies Diakonoff*, pp. 81–97
—— P. Steinkeller and R. M. Whiting: *Earliest Land Tenure Systems in the Near East: Ancient Kudurrus*. OIP 104. Chicago, 1991
Geller, M. J.: A Middle Assyrian tablet of *Utukkū, lemnūtu*, Tablet 12, *Iraq* 42 (1980), pp. 23–51
—— Akkadian medicine in the Babylonian Talmud, in Cohn-Sherbok (ed.), *A Traditional Quest*, pp. 102–12
—— *Forerunners to Udug-hul: Sumerian Exorcistic Incantations*. FAOS 12. Stuttgart, 1985
—— Incipits and rubrics, *Studies Lambert*, pp. 225–58
—— More Graeco-Babyloniaca, *ZA* 73 (1983), pp. 114–20
—— New duplicates to *SBTU* II, *AfO* 35 (1988), pp. 1–23
—— The influence of ancient Mesopotamia on Hellenistic Judaism, in Sasson (ed.), *Civilizations of the Ancient Near East*, pp. 43–54
—— The Last Wedge, *ZA* 87 (1997), pp. 43–95
—— The survival of Babylonian Wissenschaft in later tradition, in Aro and Whiting (eds.), *The Heirs of Assyria*, pp. 1–6
—— J. C. Greenfield and M. P. Weitzman (eds.): *Studia Aramaica: New Sources and New Approaches*. JSS Supplement 4. Oxford, 1995
Genouillac, H. de: *Époque présargonique, époque d'Agadé, époque d'Ur*. ITT 5. Paris, 1925
—— Inscriptions diverses, *RA* 10 (1913), pp. 101–2

Genouillac, H. de: *Textes économiques d'Oumma de l'époque d'Our.* TCL 5. Paris, 1922

—— *Textes religieux sumériens du Louvre.* 2 vols. TCL 15–16. Paris, 1930

George, A. R.: Babylonian texts from the folios of Sidney Smith, Part One, *RA* 82 (1988), pp. 139–62

—— Babylonian texts from the folios of Sidney Smith, Part Two: prognostic and diagnostic omens, *RA* 85 (1991), pp. 137–67

—— *Babylonian Topographical Texts.* OLA 40. Leuven, 1992

—— Four temple rituals from Babylon, *Studies Lambert*, pp. 259–99

—— Gilgamesh and the cedars of Lebanon, *Archaeology and History in Lebanon*, autumn 2001 (London), pp. 8–12

—— *House Most High: The Temples of Ancient Mesopotamia.* Mesopotamian Civilizations 5. Winona Lake, Ind., 1993

—— How women weep? Reflections on a passage of Bilgames and the Bull of Heaven, in Parpola and Whiting (eds.), *Sex and Gender in the Ancient Near East.* CRRA 47. Helsinki, forthcoming

—— Ninurta-pāqidāt's Dog Bite, and notes on other comic tales, *Iraq* 55 (1993), pp. 63–75

—— Notes on two extremes of weather, *RA* 79 (1985), pp. 69–71

—— review of Arnaud, *Emar* VI, *BSOAS* 53 (1990), pp. 323–5

—— review of *OECT* XI, *ZA* 80 (1990), pp. 155–60

—— review of Pedersén, *Archives and Libraries* 1, *JRAS* 1987, pp. 99–102

—— review of von Weiher, *Uruk* III, *JNES* 52 (1993), pp. 300–3

—— review of von Weiher, *Uruk* IV, *BiOr* 52 (1995), 730–2

—— Seven words, *NABU* 1991, no. 19

—— Studies in cultic topography and ideology, *BiOr* 53 (1996), 363–95

—— Sumerian tiru = 'eunuch', *NABU* 1997, no. 97

—— The bricks of E-sagil, *Iraq* 57 (1995), pp. 173–97

—— The city wall of Babylon : a belt cord, *NABU* 1991, no. 101

—— The Day the Earth Divided: a geological aetiology in the Babylonian Gilgameš Epic, *ZA* 80 (1990), pp. 214–19, reprinted in Erkanal et al. (eds.), *XXXIV. Uluslararası Assiriyoloji Kongresi.* CRRA 34. Ankara, 1998, pp. 179–83

—— *The Epic of Gilgamesh: The Babylonian Epic Poem and Other Texts in Akkadian and Sumerian.* Harmondsworth, 1999. Reprinted as *The Epic of Gilgamesh. A New Translation.* Penguin Classics. Harmondsworth, 2000

—— and F. N. H. Al-Rawi: Tablets from the Sippar library VI. Atra-ḫasīs, *Iraq* 58 (1996), pp. 147–90

—— and F. N. H. Al-Rawi: Tablets from the Sippar Library VII. Three wisdom texts, *Iraq* 60 (1998), pp. 187–206

—— and I. L. Finkel (eds.): *Wisdom, Gods and Literature: Studies in Assyriology in Honour of W. G. Lambert.* Winona Lake, Ind., 2000

Gerardi, Pamela: *A Bibliography of the Tablet Collections of the University Museum.* OPBF 8. Philadelphia, 1984

Gesche, Petra: *Schulunterricht in Babylonien im ersten Jahrtausend v. Chr.* AOAT 275. Münster, 2001

Glassner, J.-J.: La division quinaire de la terre, *Akkadica* 40 (1984), pp. 17–35

—— L'Etemenanki, armature du cosmos, *NABU* 2002, no. 32

—— L'hospitalité en Mésopotamie ancienne: aspect de la question de l'étranger, *ZA* 80 (1990), pp. 60–75

—— Sargon 'roi du combat', *RA* 79 (1985), pp. 115–26

Gnoli, G.: Babylonian influences on Iran, *Encyclopaedia Iranica* 3, 3. London, 1988, pp. 334–6

Goedicke, H., and J. J. M. Roberts (eds.): *Unity and Diversity*. Baltimore, 1975
Goetze, A.: An Old Babylonian prayer of the divination priest, *JCS* 22 (1968–9), pp. 25–9
—— Historical allusions in the Old Babylonian omen texts, *JCS* 1 (1947), pp. 253–66
—— *Old Babylonian Omen Texts*. YOS 10. New Haven, Conn., 1947
—— The Akkadian dialects of the Old Babylonian mathematical texts, *MCT*, pp. 146–51
—— The sibilants of Old Babylonian, *RA* 52 (1958), pp. 137–49
—— The vocabulary of the Princeton Theological Seminary, *JAOS* 65 (1945), pp. 223–37
—— and S. Levy: Fragment of the Gilgamesh Epic from Megiddo, *'Atiqot* 2 (1959), pp. 121–8
Gökçe, N., and S. Lloyd: 1951 Yılında Millî Eğitim Bakanlığı ve İngiliz Arkeoloji Enstitüsü tarafından yapılan Sultantepe (Urfa) Kazısı, *Ankara Üniversitesi Dil ve Tarih-Coğrafya Fakültesi Dergisi* 11, 1 (1953), pp. 109–23
Gordon, E. I.: Mesilim and Mesannepadda: are they identical?, *BASOR* 132 (1953), pp. 27–30
—— Sumerian proverbs: 'Collection four', *JAOS* 77 (1957), pp. 67–70
Gray, C. D.: *The Šamaš Religious Texts*. Chicago, 1901. Reprinted in *AJSL* 17 (1900–1), pp. 129–45, 222–43
Grayson, A. K.: *Assyrian and Babylonian Chronicles*. TCS 5. Locust Valley, NY, 1975
—— *Assyrian Rulers of the Early First Millennium BC* 1. *(1114–859 BC)*. RIMA 2. Toronto, 1991
—— *Assyrian Rulers of the Early First Millennium BC* 2. *(858–745 BC)*. RIMA 3. Toronto, 1996
—— *Assyrian Rulers of the Third and Second Millennia BC*. RIMA 1. Toronto, 1987
—— *Babylonian Historical-Literary Texts*. Toronto, 1975
—— The Epic of Gilgamesh, additions to Tablets V–VIII and X, *ANET*, 3rd edn with Supplement, pp. 503–7
—— and D. B. Redford: *Papyrus and Tablet*. Englewood Cliffs, NJ, 1973
Graziani, Simonetta (ed.): *Studi sul Vicino Oriente antico dedicati alla memoria di Luigi Cagni*. 4 vols. Naples, 2000
Green, A.: Myths in Mesopotamian art, *Sumerian Gods*, pp. 137–9
Green, Margaret W., and H.-J. Nissen: *Zeichenliste der archaischen Texte aus Uruk*. Archaische Texte aus Uruk 2. ADFU 11. Berlin, 1987
Greenfield, J. C.: The Wisdom of Ahiqar, *Essays Emerton*, pp. 43–52
—— and M. Sokoloff: Astrological and related omen texts in Jewish Palestinian Aramaic, *Journal of Near Eastern Studies* 48 (1989), pp. 201–14
Greengus, S.: Old Babylonian marriage ceremonies and rites, *JCS* 20 (1966), pp. 55–72
—— *Old Babylonian Tablets from Ishchali and Vicinity*. Leiden and Istanbul, 1979
—— The Old Babylonian marriage contract, *JAOS* 89 (1969), pp. 505–32
Grégoire, J.-P.: *Inscriptions et archives administratives cunéiformes* 1. MVN 10. Rome, 1981
Gresseth, G. K.: The Gilgamesh epic and Homer, *Classical Journal* 70 (Apr.–May 1975), pp. 1–18
Groneberg, Brigitte R. M.: *ḫabābu-ṣabāru*, *RA* 80 (1986), pp. 188–90
—— Die sumerisch-akkadische Inanna/Ištar: Hermaphroditos?, *WO* 17 (1986), pp. 25–46
—— Philologische Bearbeitung des Agušayahymnus, *RA* 75 (1981), pp. 107–35
—— *Répertoire géographique des textes cunéiformes* 3. *Die Orts- und Gewässernamen der altbabylonischen Zeit*. Beihefte zum Tübinger Atlas des vorderen Orients B 7, 3. Wiesbaden, 1980
—— *Syntax, Morphologie und Stil der jungbabylonischen 'hymnischen' Literatur*. 2 vols. FAOS 14. Stuttgart, 1987
—— Terminativ- und Lokativadverbialis in altbabylonischen literarischen Texten, *AfO* 26 (1978–9), pp. 15–29
—— Zu den 'gebrochenen Schreibungen', *JCS* 32 (1980), pp. 151–67

Groneberg, Brigitte R. M.: Zu den mesopotamischen Unterweltsvorstellungen: das Jenseits als Fortsetzung des Diesseits, *AoF* 17 (1990), pp. 245–61

Gross, W., H. Irsigler and T. Seidl (eds.): *Texte, Methode und Grammatik. Wolfgang Richter zum 65. Geburtstag*. St Ottilien, 1991

Grottanelli, C.: The story of Combabos and the Gilgamesh tradition, in Whiting (ed.), *Mythology and Mythologies*, pp. 19–27

Gruber, M. I.: *Aspects of Nonverbal Communication in the Ancient Near East*. 2 vols. Studia Pohl 12. Rome, 1980

Guichard, M.: Trophées de Huppipi, *NABU* 1994, no. 74

Günbattı, C.: Kültepe'den akadlı Sargon'a âit bir tablet, *Archivum Anatolicum* 3. Bilgiç Memorial Volume. Ankara, 1997, pp. 131–55

Gurney, O. R.: Babylonian prophylactic figures and their rituals, *AAA* 22 (1935), pp. 31–96

——Gilgamesh XI 78, Descent of Ishtar 90, *RA* 73 (1979), pp. 89–90

——Gilgamesh XI 78, *RA* 75 (1981), p. 189

——Hittite fragments in private collections, in Hoffner and Beckman (eds.), *Kaniššuwar*, pp. 59–68

——*Literary and Miscellaneous Texts in the Ashmolean Museum*. OECT 11. Oxford, 1989

——review of *KUB* XXXVII, *JSS* 2 (1957), pp. 201–2

—— *The Middle Babylonian Legal and Economic Texts from Ur*. London, 1983

—— *The Sultantepe Tablets* 1. Corrigenda, *AnSt* 8 (1958), pp. 245–6

——The Sultantepe tablets V. The tale of the Poor Man of Nippur, *AnSt* 6 (1956), pp. 145–64

——The Sultantepe tablets VI. A letter of Gilgamesh, *AnSt* 7 (1957), pp. 127–35

——The Sultantepe tablets. A preliminary note, *AnSt* 2 (1952), pp. 25–35

——The tale of the Poor Man of Nippur and its folktale parallels, *AnSt* 22 (1972), pp. 149–58

——Two fragments of the Epic of Gilgamesh from Sultantepe, *JCS* 8 (1954), pp. 87–95

——J. J. Finkelstein and P. Hulin: *The Sultantepe Tablets*. 2 vols. London, 1957 and 1964

Güterbock, H. G.: Die Texte aus der Grabung 1934 in Boğazköy, *MDOG* 73 (1935), pp. 29–39

——*Kumarbi. Mythen vom churritischen Kronos aus den hethitischen Fragmenten zusammengestellt, übersetzt und erklärt*. Istanbuler Schriften 16. Zurich, 1936

——and H. A. Hoffner: *The Hittite Dictionary*. Vol. 3, L–N; Chicago, 1989. Vol. 4, 1, P–parā; 1984

[Güterbock, H. G., and T. Jacobsen (eds.):] *Studies in Honor of Benno Landsberger on his Seventy-Fifth Birthday*. AS 16. Chicago, 1965

——and H. Otten: *Texte aus Gebäude K*, 1. KBo 10. WVDOG 72. Berlin, 1960

Haas, V. (ed.): *Außenseiter und Randgruppen*. Xenia 32. Konstanz, 1992

—— (ed.): *Hurriter und Hurritisch*. Xenia 21. Konstanz, 1988

Hackman, G. G.: *Sumerian and Akkadian Administrative Texts from Predynastic Times to the End of the Akkad Dynasty*. BIN 8. New Haven, Conn., 1958

Haller, A. von: Die Stadtmauer, *UVB* 7, pp. 41–5

Hallo, W. W.: *Early Mesopotamian Royal Titles*. AOS 43. New Haven, 1957

——Lugalbanda excavated, *JAOS* 103 (1983), pp. 165–80

——On the antiquity of Sumerian literature, *JAOS* 83 (1963), pp. 167–76

——Royal ancestor worship in the biblical world, *Studies Talmon*, pp. 381–401

——Šullanu, *RA* 74 (1970), p. 94

——The birth of kings, *Essays Pope*, pp. 45–52

—— (ed.): *The Context of Scripture* 1. *Canonical Compositions from the Biblical World*. Leiden, 1997

——The coronation of Ur-Nammu, *JCS* 20 (1966), pp. 133–41

——The road to Emar, *JCS* 18 (1964), pp. 57–88

Hämeen-Anttila, J.: Descent and ascent in Islamic myth, in Whiting (ed.), *Mythology and Mythologies*, pp. 47–67
Handcock, P. S. P.: *Cuneiform Texts from Babylonian Tablets in the British Museum* 28. London, 1910
—— *Cuneiform Texts from Babylonian Tablets in the British Museum* 30. London, 1911
—— *Cuneiform Texts from Babylonian Tablets in the British Museum* 31. London, 1911
Hansman, J.: Gilgamesh, Humbaba and the land of the ERIN-trees, *Iraq* 38 (1976), pp. 23–35
Harper, R. F.: *Assyrian and Babylonian Letters*. 14 vols. London and Chicago, 1892–1914
Heimerdinger, Jane W.: *Sumerian Literary Fragments from Nippur*. OPBF 4. Philadelphia, 1979
Harris, Rivkah: *Gender and Aging in Mesopotamia: the Gilgamesh Epic and Other Ancient Literature*. Norman, Okla., 2000
—— Images of women in the Gilgamesh epic, *Studies Moran*, pp. 219–30
—— The archive of the Sin temple at Khafajah (Tutub) (conclusion), *JCS* 9 (1955), pp. 91–120
Haupt, P.: *Akkadische und sumerische Keilschrifttexte nach den Originalen im Britischen Museum copirt*. AB 1. Leipzig, 1882
—— *Das babylonische Nimrodepos*. 2 vols. AB 3. Leipzig, 1884 and 1891
—— *Die akkadische Sprache*. Berlin, 1883
—— *Die keilinschriftliche Sintfluthbericht*. Leipzig, 1881
—— Die zwölfte Tafel des babylonischen Nimrod-Epos, *BA* 1. Leipzig, 1890, pp. 48–79
—— Ergebnisse einer erneuten Collation der Izdubar-Legenden, *BA* 1. Leipzig, 1890, pp. 94–152
—— On a modern reproduction of the eleventh tablet of the Babylonian Nimrod Epic and a new fragment of the Chaldean account of the Deluge, *PAOS* April 1893, pp. ix–xiii
—— pls. 1–4 in Jeremias, *Izdubar-Nimrod*
Healey, J. F.: *Malkū : mlkm : Anunnaki*, *UF* 7 (1975), pp. 235–8
Hecker K.: Das akkadische Gilgamesch-Epos, *TUAT* III/4, pp. 646–744
—— *Untersuchungen zur akkadischen Epik*. AOAT Sonderreihe 8. Kevelaer and Neukirchen-Vluyn, 1974
—— W. G. Lambert, G. G. W. Müller, W. von Soden and A. Ünal: *Mythen und Epen* 2. TUAT 3, 4. Gütersloh, 1994
—— and W. Sommerfeld (eds.): *Keilschriftliche Literaturen*. CRRA 32. BBVO 6. Berlin, 1986
Heidel, A.: A Neo-Babylonian Gilgamesh fragment, *JNES* 11 (1952), pp. 140–3
—— *The Gilgamesh Epic and Old Testament Parallels*. 2nd edn. Chicago, 1949
Heimpel, W.: A catalogue of Near Eastern Venus deities, *Syro-Mesopotamian Studies* 4, 3 (1982), pp. 9–22
—— Insekten, *RLA* 5 (1976–80), pp. 105–9
—— The sun at night and the doors of heaven in Babylonian texts, *JCS* 38 (1986), pp. 127–51
Held, G. F.: Parallels between the Gilgamesh Epic and Plato's *Symposium*, *JNES* 42 (1983), pp. 133–41
Heltzer, M.: *The Suteans*. Naples, 1981
Henning, W. B.: The Book of Giants, *BSOAS* 11 (1943–6), pp. 52–74
Hill, H. D., T. Jacobsen and P. Delougaz: *Old Babylonian Public Buildings in the Diyala Region*. OIP 98. Chicago, 1990
Hilprecht, H. V.: *Old Babylonian Inscriptions Chiefly from Nippur*. BE 1. TAPS 18, 1 and 3. 2 vols. Philadelphia, 1893 and 1896
Hilprecht Anniversary Volume: Studies in Assyriology and Archaeology Dedicated to Hermann V. Hilprecht. Leipzig, 1909
Hinz, W.: Elams Vertrag mit Narām-Sîn von Akkade, *ZA* 58 (1967), pp. 66–96

Hirsch, H.: Die Heimkehr des Gilgamesch, *Archivum Anatolicum* 3. Bilgiç Memorial Volume. Ankara, 1997, pp. 173–90

——The Prince and the Pauper, *AfO* 35 (1988), pp. 109–10

——and H. Hunger (eds.): *Vorträge gehalten auf der 28. Rencontre Assyriologique Internationale in Wien.* CRRA 28. *AfO* Beiheft 19. Horn, 1982

Hoffner, H. A.: Enki's command to Atraḫasis, *Kramer AV*, pp. 241–5

——and G. M. Beckman (eds.): *Kaniššuwar: A Tribute to Hans G. Güterbock on his Seventy-Fifth Birthday.* AS 23. Chicago, 1986

Horowitz, W.: *Mesopotamian Cosmic Geography.* Mesopotamian Civilizations 8. Winona Lake, Ind., 1998

——The Babylonian map of the world, *Iraq* 50 (1988), pp. 147–65

Hrouda, B., S. A. S. Ayoub, Eva A. Braun-Holzinger, J. Boessneck, A. von den Driesch, Martha Haussperger, K. Karstens, M. Kokabi, W. Rauert, W. Schirmer, Agnès Spycket, Eva Strommenger, C. B. F. Walker, C. Wilcke and G. Ziegelmayer: *Isin-Išān Baḥrīyāt* 2. *Die Ergebnisse der Ausgrabungen 1975–1978.* BAW Abhandlungen 87. Munich, 1981

——M. R. Behm-Blancke, J. Boessneck, A. von den Driesch, Martha Haussperger, P. Spanos, Agnès Spycket, C. Wilcke, G. Ziegelmayer and R. Ziegler: *Isin-Išān Baḥrīyāt* 3. *Die Ergebnisse der Ausgrabungen 1983–1984.* BAW Abhandlungen 94. Munich, 1987

Hrozný, F.: *Keilschrifttexte aus Boghazköi* 5–6. WVDOG 36. Leipzig, 1921

Hruška, B.: Das spätbabylonische Lehrgedicht 'Inannas Erhöhung', *ArOr* 37 (1969), pp. 473–522

——and G. Komoróczy (eds.): *Festschrift Lubor Matouš.* 2 vols. Assyriologica 4–5. Budapest, 1978

Huehnergard, J.: *A Grammar of Akkadian.* HSS 45. Atlanta, 1997

——*The Akkadian of Ugarit.* HSS 34. Atlanta, 1989

——Meskene (Imar/Emar), *RLA* 8 (1993–7), p. 83

Hunger, H.: *Astrological Reports to Assyrian Kings.* SAA 8. Helsinki, 1992

——*Babylonische und assyrische Kolophone.* AOAT 2. Kevelaer and Neukirchen-Vluyn, 1968

——Die Tafeln des Iqīšâ, *WO* 6 (1971), pp. 163–5

——*Spätbabylonische Texte aus Uruk* 1. ADFU 9. Berlin, 1976

Hurowitz, V. A.: An Old Babylonian bawdy ballad, *Studies Greenfield*, pp. 543–58

Hussein, Laith M., and P. Miglus: Tell Ḥarmal: die Frühjahrskampagne 1997, *Bagh. Mitt.* 29 (1998), pp. 35–46

Huxley, Margaret: The gates and guardians in Sennacherib's addition to the temple of Assur, *Iraq* 62 (2000), pp. 109–37

——The shape of the cosmos according to cuneiform sources, *JRAS* NS 7 (1997), pp. 189–98

Hyatt, J. P.: *The Treatment of Final Vowels in Early Neo-Babylonian.* YOR 23. New Haven, Conn., 1941

Jacobsen, T.: Death in Mesopotamia, *CRRA* 26, pp. 19–24

——Early political development in Mesopotamia, *ZA* 52 (1957), pp. 91–140

——How did Gilgameš oppress Uruk?, *Acta Or* 8 (1930), pp. 62–74

——Lad in the desert, *JAOS* 103 (1983), pp. 193–200

——Lugalbanda and Ninsuna, *JCS* 41 (1989), pp. 69–86

——Pictures and pictorial language (the Burney relief), in Mindlin et al. (eds.), *Figurative Language in the Ancient Near East*, pp. 1–11

——Religious drama in ancient Mesopotamia, in Goedicke and Roberts (eds.), *Unity and Diversity*, pp. 65–95

——The Akkadian ablative accusative, *JNES* 22 (1963), pp. 18–29

Jacobsen, T.: The Gilgamesh epic: romantic and tragic vision, *Studies Moran*, pp. 231–49
—— *The Harps that Once . . . : Sumerian Poetry in Translation*. New Haven, Conn., 1987
—— The sister's message, *ANES* 5 (1973), pp. 199–212
—— *The Sumerian King List*. AS 11. Chicago, 1939
—— The Sumerian verbal core, *ZA* 78 (1988), pp. 161–220
—— *The Treasures of Darkness*. New Haven, Conn., 1976
—— and Kirsten Nielsen: Cursing the day, *Scandinavian Journal of the Old Testament* 6 (1992), pp. 186–205
Jacoby, F.: *Die Fragmente der griechischen Historiker* III C 1. Leiden, 1958
Jason, Heda: The Poor Man of Nippur: an ethnopoetic analysis, *JCS* 31 (1979), pp. 189–215
Jastrow, M.: Adam and Eve in Babylonian literature, *AJSL* 15 (1899), pp. 193–214
—— and A. T. Clay: *An Old Babylonian Version of the Gilgamesh Epic*. YOR 4, 3. New Haven, Conn., 1920
Jean, C.-F.: *Lettres*. ARM 2. TCL 23. Paris, 1941
—— *Tell Sifr, textes cunéiformes conservés au British Museum, réédités*. Paris, 1931
—— Vocabulaire du Louvre AO 6447, *RA* 32 (1935), pp. 161–74
Jensen, P.: *Assyrisch-babylonische Mythen und Epen*. KB 6, 1. Berlin, 1900
—— *Das Gilgamesch-Epos in der Weltliteratur*. 2 vols. Strasbourg, 1906; Marburg, 1929
—— Das Gilgameš-Epos und Homer. Vorläufige Mitteilung, *ZA* 16 (1902), pp. 125–34; Nachträge zu meinen Thesen über die griechischen Gilgamiš-Sagen, pp. 413–14
Jeremias, A.: *Izdubar-Nimrod, eine altbabylonische Heldensage*. Leipzig, 1891
Jestin, R.: *Nouvelles tablettes sumériennes de Šuruppak au Musée d'Istanbul*. Paris, 1957
—— *Tablettes sumériennes de Šuruppak conservées au Musée de Stamboul*. Paris, 1937
Jeyes, Ulla: A compendium of gall-bladder omens extant in Middle Babylonian, Nineveh and Seleucid versions, *Studies Lambert*, pp. 345–73
—— *Old Babylonian Extispicy. Omen Texts in the British Museum*. Uitgaven van het Nederlands Historisch-Archaeologisch Instituut te Istanbul 64. Leiden and Istanbul, 1989
Joannès, F.: Metalle und Metallurgie A. I. In Mesopotamien, *RLA* 8 (1993–7), pp. 96–112
—— Palmyre et les routes du désert au début du deuxième millénaire av. J.-C., *MARI* 8 (1997), pp. 393–415
Johns, C. H. W.: *Assyrian Deeds and Documents*. 4 vols. Cambridge, 1898–1923
Jordan, J.: *Ausgrabungen in Uruk-Warka 1928/29*. UVB 1. Berlin, 1930
Kämmerer, T. R.: *šimâ milka. Induktion und Reception der mittelbabylonischen Dichtung von Ugarit, Emār und Tell el-ʿAmarna*. AOAT 251. Münster, 1998, pp. 146–55
Kamminga, J. C. C.: Einige Bemerkungen zu Gilgameš P, Y und Nin. XI 15, *Akkadica* 36, 1 (1984), pp. 18–21
Kataja, Laura, and R. Whiting: *Grants, Decrees and Gifts of the Neo-Assyrian Period*. SAA XII. Helsinki, 1995
Katz, Dina: Enmebaragesi king of Kiš a sister of Gilgameš?, *NABU* 1995, no. 29
—— *Gilgamesh and Akka*. Groningen, 1993
—— The messenger, Lulil and the cult of the dead, *RA* 93 (1999), pp. 107–18
Kaye, A. S. (ed.): *Semitic Studies in Honor of Wolf Leslau*. 2 vols. Wiesbaden, 1991
Keiser, C. E., and Shin Theke Kang: *Neo-Sumerian Account Texts from Drehem*. BIN 3. New Haven, Conn., 1971
Kessler, K.: Kassitische Tontafeln vom Tell Imlihiye, *Bagh. Mitt.* 13 (1982), pp. 51–116

Kienle, R. von, A. Moortgat, H. Otten, E. von Schüler and W. Zaumseil (eds.): *Festschrift Johannes Friedrich zum 65. Geburtstag gewidmet.* Heidelberg, 1959

Kilmer, Anne D.: A note on an overlooked word-play in the Akkadian Gilgamesh, *Kraus AV*, pp. 128–32

——An oration on Babylon, *AoF* 18 (1991), pp. 8–22

——Crossing the Waters of Death: the 'Stone Things' in the Gilgamesh Epic, *WZKM* 86 (1986), pp. 213–17

——Notes on Akkadian *uppu*, *Finkelstein Mem.Vol.*, pp. 129–38

——The first tablet of *malku* = *šarru* together with its explicit version, *JAOS* 83 (1963), pp. 421–46

——The symbolism of the flies in the Mesopotamian flood myth and some further implications, *Studies Reiner*, pp. 175–80

King, L.W.: A new fragment of the Gilgamesh Epic, *PSBA* 36 (1914), pp. 64–8

——*Babylonian Boundary Stones and Memorial Tablets in the British Museum.* 2 vols. London, 1912

——*Babylonian Magic and Sorcery.* London, 1896

——*Catalogue of the Cuneiform Tablets in the Kouyunjik Collection, Supplement.* London, 1914

——*Cuneiform Texts from Babylonian Tablets in the British Museum* 5. London, 1898

——*Cuneiform Texts from Babylonian Tablets in the British Museum* 13. London, 1901

——*Cuneiform Texts from Babylonian Tablets in the British Museum* 15. London, 1902

——*Cuneiform Texts from Babylonian Tablets in the British Museum* 24. London, 1908

——*Cuneiform Texts from Babylonian Tablets in the British Museum* 25. London, 1909

——*Cuneiform Texts from Babylonian Tablets in the British Museum* 26. London, 1909

——*Cuneiform Texts from Babylonian Tablets in the British Museum* 29. London, 1910

——*Cuneiform Texts from Babylonian Tablets in the British Museum* 32. London, 1912

——*Cuneiform Texts from Babylonian Tablets in the British Museum* 33. London, 1912

——*Cuneiform Texts from Babylonian Tablets in the British Museum* 34. London, 1914

——*The Letters and Inscriptions of Hammurabi, King of Babylon.* London, 1898

——*The Seven Tablets of Creation.* 2 vols. London, 1902

Kingsley, P.: Ezekiel by the Grand Canal: between Jewish and Babylonian tradition, *JRAS* NS 2 (1992), pp. 339–46

Kinnier Wilson, J. V.: On the fourth and fifth tablets of the Epic of Gilgameš, in Garelli, *Gilg.*, pp. 103–11

——Texts and fragments: miscellaneous literary Kuyunjik texts, *JCS* 42 (1990), pp. 88–97

Klein, J.: A new look at the 'oppression of Uruk' episode in the Gilgameš epic, *Jacobsen Mem.Vol.*, pp. 187–201

——A new Nippur duplicate of the Sumerian Kinglist in the Brockmon Collection, University of Haifa, *Aula Or* 9 (1991), pp. 123–9

——A self-laudatory Šulgi hymn fragment from Nippur, *Studies Hallo*, pp. 124–31

——Additional notes to 'The Marriage of Martu', *Kutscher Mem.Vol.*, pp. 93–106

——Building and dedication hymns in Sumerian literature, *Acta Sum* 11 (1989), pp. 27–67

——Šulgi and Gilgameš: two brother-peers (Šulgi O), *Kramer AV*, pp. 270–93

——The god Martu in Sumerian literature, *Sumerian Gods*, pp. 99–116

——*The Royal Hymns of Shulgi King of Ur: Man's Quest for Immortal Fame.* TAPS 71, 7. Philadelphia, 1981

——*Three Šulgi Hymns.* Ramat Gan, Israel, 1981

——and K. Abraham: Problems of geography in the Gilgameš epics: the journey to the 'Cedar Forest', *CRRA* 44, 3, pp. 63–73

Klein, J. and A. Skaist (eds.): *Bar-Ilan Studies in Assyriology.* Ramat Gan, Israel, 1990
Klengel, H.: *Texte verschiedenen Inhalts.* KUB 60. Berlin, 1990
Knudtzon, J. A., O. Weber and E. Ebeling: *Die El-Amarna-Tafeln.* VAB 2. Leipzig, 1915
Kobayashi, T.: The ki-a-nag of Enentarzi, *Orient* 21 (1985), pp. 10–30
Koch, Heidemarie: Elamisches Gilgameš-Epos oder doch Verwaltungstafel?, *ZA* 83 (1993), pp. 219–36
Koch, J.: review of W. Papke, *Die Sterne von Babylon. Die geheime Botschaft der Gilgamesch, WO* 24 (1993), pp. 213–22
Koch-Westenholz, Ulla: *Babylonian Liver Omens: The Chapters manzāzu, padānu and pān tākalti of the Babylonian Extispicy Series Mainly from Aššurbanipal's Library.* Carsten Niebuhr Institute Publications 25. Copenhagen, 2000
—— *Mesopotamian Astrology: An Introduction to Babylonian and Assyrian Celestial Divination.* Copenhagen, 1995
Köcher, F.: Der babylonische Göttertypentext, *MIO* 1 (1953), pp. 57–107
—— *Die babylonische-assyrische Medizin in Texten und Untersuchungen.* 6 vols. Berlin, 1963–80
—— *Literarische Texte in akkadischer Sprache.* KUB 37. Berlin, 1953
—— and A. L. Oppenheim: The Old-Babylonian omen text VAT 7525, *AfO* 18 (1957–8), pp. 62–77
Koefed, A.: Gilgames, Enkidu and the Nether World, *Acta Sum* 5 (1983), pp. 16–23
Komoróczy, G.: Akkadian epic poetry and its Sumerian sources, *Acta Acad. Scient. Hung.* 23 (1975), pp. 40–63
—— Berosos and the Mesopotamian literature, *Acta Acad. Scient. Hung.* 21 (1973), pp. 125–52
—— Zur Ätiologie der Schrifterfindung im Enmerkar-Epos, *AoF* 3 (1975), pp. 19–24
Kouwenberg, N. J. C.: *Gemination in the Akkadian Verb.* Assen, 1997
Kovacs, Maureen Gallery: *The Epic of Gilgamesh.* Stanford, Calif., 1989
Kramer, S. N.: A new literary catalogue from Ur, *RA* 55 (1961), pp. 169–76
—— *From the Tablets of Sumer.* Indian Hills, Colo., 1956
—— *Gilgamesh and the Ḫuluppu-Tree: A Reconstructed Sumerian Text.* AS 10. Chicago, 1938
—— Gilgamesh and the land of the living, *JCS* 1 (1947), pp. 3–46
—— *History Begins at Sumer.* 2nd edn. London, 1961
—— *Sumerian Literary Texts from Nippur in the Museum of the Ancient Orient at Istanbul.* AASOR 23. New Haven, Conn., 1944
—— Sumerian literature and the British Museum, *PAPS* 124 (1980), pp. 294–313
—— *Sumerian Mythology.* Revised edn, New York, 1961
—— The death of Gilgamesh, *BASOR* 94, pp. 2–12
—— The death of Ur-nammu and his descent to the netherworld, *JCS* 21, pp. 104–22
—— The Epic of Gilgameš and its Sumerian sources: a study in literary evolution, *JAOS* 64 (1944), pp. 7–23
—— The GIR$_5$ and the ki-sikil: a new Sumerian elegy, *Finkelstein. Mem. Vol.*, pp. 139–42
—— The oldest literary catalogue, *BASOR* 88 (1942), pp. 10–19
Kraus, F. R.: Akkadische Wörter und Ausdrücke, I–III, *RA* 64 (1970), pp. 53–61
—— *Briefe aus dem British Museum (CT 43 und 44).* AbB I. Leiden, 1964
—— Der Brief des Gilgameš, *AnSt* 30 (1980), pp. 109–21
—— Ein Sittenkanon in Omenform, *ZA* 43 (1936), pp. 77–113
—— review of *YOS* X, *JCS* 4 (1950), pp. 141–54
Krebernik, M.: Die Götterlisten aus Fāra, *ZA* 76 (1986), pp. 161–204
—— Die Texte aus Fāra und Tell Abū, Ṣalābīḫ, in Bauer et al., *Mesopotamien*, pp. 237–427

Krebernik, M.: Ein Keulenkopf mit Weihung an Gilgameš im Vorderasiatischen Museum, Berlin, *AoF* 21 (1994), pp. 5–12

——Meru, *RLA* 8 (1993–7), p. 73

——Mesopotamian myths at Ebla: *ARET* 5, 6 and *ARET* 5, 7, in Fronzaroli (ed.), *Literature and Literary Language at Ebla*, pp. 63–159

——Zu Syllabar und Orthographie der lexikalischen Texte aus Ebla. Teil 1, *ZA* 72 (1982), pp. 178–236

——Zur Einleitung der z à - m e -Hymnen aus Tell Abū Ṣalābīḫ, in Calmeyer et al. (eds.), *Beiträge zur altorientalischen Archäologie und Altertumskunde*, pp. 151–7

Krecher, J.: Das sumerische Phonem /g̃/, *Matouš Festschrift* 2, pp. 7–73

Kuk Won Chang: *Dichtungen der Zeit Tukulti-Ninurtas I. von Assyrien*. Seoul, 1981

Kupper, J.-R. (ed.): *La civilisation de Mari*. CRRA 15. Paris, 1967

——Les différentes versions de l'épopée de Gilgameš, in Garelli, *Gilg.*, pp. 97–102

Kutscher, R.: A torchlight festival in Lagaš, *Acta Sum* 5 (1983), pp. 59–67

——The cult of Dumuzi/Tammuz, in Klein and Skaist (eds.), *Bar-Ilan Studies in Assyriology*, pp. 29–44

Kwasman, T.: A new join to the Epic of Gilgameš Tablet I, *NABU* 1998, no. 99

——and S. Parpola: *Legal Transactions of the Royal Court of Nineveh*, 1. *Tiglath-Pileser III through Esarhaddon*. SAA 6. Helsinki, 1991

Labat, R.: *Commentaires assyro-babyloniens sur les présages*. Bordeaux, 1933

——L'Épopée de Gilgamesh, in Labat et al., *Les religions du Proche-Orient asiatique*, pp. 145–226

—— *Traité akkadien de diagnostics et pronostics médicaux*. 2 vols. Leiden, 1951

——A. Caquot, M. Sznycer and M. Vieyra: *Les religions du Proche-Orient asiatique. Textes babyloniens, ougaritiques, hittites*. Paris, 1970

Lacheman, E.-R.: *Excavations at Nuzi* 5: *Miscellaneous Texts from Nuzi* 2. HSS 14. Cambridge, Mass., 1950

Lackenbacher, Sylvie: Note sur l'ardat-lilî, *RA* 65 (1971), pp. 119–54

Laessøe, J.: *Studies on the Assyrian Ritual and Series bît rimki*. Copenhagen, 1955

——and T. Jacobsen: Šikšabbum again, *JCS* 42 (1990), pp. 127–78

Lafont, B., and Fatma Yıldız: *Tablettes cunéiformes de Tello au Musée d'Istanbul datant de l'époque de la IIIe dynastie d'Ur*. 2 vols. Leiden and Istanbul, 1989 and 1996

Lambert, W. G.: A catalogue of texts and authors, *JCS* 16 (1962), pp. 59–77

——A further attempt at the Babylonian 'Man and his God', *Studies Reiner*, pp. 187–202

——A Late Assyrian catalogue of literary and scholarly texts, *Kramer AV*, pp. 313–18

——A new Babylonian Descent to the Netherworld, *Studies Moran*, pp. 289–300

——A new fragment from a list of antediluvian kings and Marduk's chariot, *Symbolae Böhl*, pp. 271–80

——A part of the ritual for the substitute king, *AfO* 18 (1957–8), pp. 109–12

——A rare exorcistic fragment, *Jacobsen Mem. Vol.*, pp. 203–10

——An address of Marduk to the demons, *AfO* 17 (1954–6), pp. 310–21

——An incantation of the *maqlû* type, *AfO* 18 (1957–8), pp. 288–99

——Ancestors, authors and canonicity, *JCS* 11 (1957), pp. 1–14, 112

——Atra-ḫasīs: 86.11.378A, *CTMMA* 2, forthcoming

——*Babylonian Wisdom Literature*. Oxford, 1960

——*Catalogue of the Cuneiform Tablets in the Kouyunjik Collection of the British Museum. Third Supplement*. London, 1992

——Critical notes on recent publications, *Or* NS 40 (1971), pp. 90–8

Lambert, W. G.: Devotion: the languages of religion and love, in Mindlin et al. (eds.), *Figurative Language in the Ancient Near East*, pp. 25–39
—— Dingir.šà.dib.ba incantations, *JNES* 33 (1974), pp. 267–322
—— Divine love lyrics from the reigh of Abī-ešuḫ, *MIO* 12 (1966), pp. 41–56
—— Gilg. I i 41, *RA* 73 (1979), p. 89
—— Gilgameš in religious, historical and omen texts, and the historicity of Gilgameš, in Garelli, *Gilg.*, pp. 39–56
—— Gilgamesh in literature and art: the second and first millennia, *Papers Porada*, pp. 37–52 with pls. 7–11, reprinted in abridged form in Maier (ed.), *Gilgamesh*, pp. 50–62
—— Ḫedimmeku, *RLA* 4 (1972–5), p. 244
—— Ḫušbiša, *RLA* 4 (1972–5), p. 522
—— Interchange of ideas between southern Mesopotamia and Syria-Palestine as seen in literature, in Nissen and Renger (eds.), *Mesopotamien und seine Nachbarn*, pp. 311–16
—— Ištarān, *RLA* 5 (1976–80), p. 211
—— Literary style in first-millennium Mesopotamia, *JAOS* 88 (1968), pp. 123–32
—— Lulal/Lātarāk, *RLA* 7 (1987–90), pp. 163–4
—— Manz'at/Mazzi'at/Mazzât/Mazzêt, *RLA* 7 (1987–90), pp. 344–6
—— Nebuchadnezzar, King of Justice, *Iraq* 27 (1965), pp. 1–11
—— New evidence for the first line of Atra-ḫasīs, *Or* NS 38 (1969), pp. 533–8
—— New fragments of Babylonian epics, *AfO* 27 (1980), pp. 71–82
—— New light on the Babylonian flood, *JSS* 5 (1960), pp. 113–23
—— Niṣir or Nimuš?, *RA* 80 (1986), pp. 185–6
—— Notes on a work of the most ancient Semitic literature, *JCS* 41 (1989), pp. 1–32
—— Objects inscribed and uninscribed, *AfO* 23 (1970), pp. 46–51
—— Prostitution, in Haas (ed.), *Außenseiter und Randgruppen*, pp. 127–57
—— review of *AHw* Lief. 12, *JSS* 24 (1979), pp. 268–73
—— review of *CTN* IV, *AfO* 46–7 (1999–2000), pp. 149–55
—— review of Dalley, *Myths*, *Classical Review* 41, 1 (1991), pp. 113–15
—— review of Limet, *Sceaux cassites*, *BiOr* 32 (1975), pp. 219–23
—— review of *OIP* 99, *BSOAS* 39 (1976), pp. 428–32
—— review of Tigay, *Evolution*, *Journal of Biblical Literature* 104, 1 (1985), pp. 115–18
—— Some new Babylonian wisdom literature, *Essays Emerton*, pp. 30–42
—— Studies in Nergal, *BiOr* 30 (1973), pp. 355–63
—— The Apsû, *CRRA* 44, 3, pp. 75–7
—— The cosmology of Sumer and Babylon, in Blacker and Loewe (eds.), *Ancient Cosmologies*, pp. 42–65
—— The Gula hymn of Bulluṭsa-rabi, *Or* NS 36 (1967), pp. 105–32
—— The Hymn to the Queen of Nippur, *Kraus AV*, pp. 173–218
—— The language of *ARET* V 6 and 7, in Fronzaroli (ed.), *Literature and Literary Language at Ebla*, pp. 41–62
—— The language of Mari, in Kupper (ed.), *La civilisation de Mari*, pp. 29–38
—— The month names of Old Babylonian Sippar, *NABU* 1989, no. 90
—— The names of Umma, *JNES* 49 (1990), pp. 75–80
—— The pantheon of Mari, *MARI* 4 (1985), pp. 525–39
—— The problem of the Love Lyrics, in Goedicke and Roberts (eds.), *Unity and Diversity*, pp. 98–135
—— The qualifications of Babylonian diviners, *Fs Borger*, pp. 141–58

Lambert, W. G.: The reading of AMA.GAN.ŠA, *Acta Sum* 3 (1981), pp. 31–6
——The reading of the divine name Šakkan, *Or* NS 55 (1986), pp. 152–8
——The section *An*, in Cagni (ed.), *Il bilinguismo a Ebla*, pp. 393–401
——The Sultantepe Tablets IX: the birdcall text, *AnSt* 20 (1970), pp. 111–17
——The Sultantepe tablets: a review article, *RA* 53 (1959), pp. 119–38
——The theology of death, *CRRA* 26, pp. 53–66
——Three literary prayers of the Babylonians, *AfO* 19 (1959–60), pp. 47–66
——Three new pieces of Atra-ḫasīs, *Mélanges Garelli*, pp. 411–14
——Three unpublished fragments of the Tukulti-Ninurta epic, *AfO* 18 (1957–8), pp. 38–51
——Ur- or Sur-?, *RA* 75 (1981), pp. 61–2
——Ur- or Sur- again, *RA* 76 (1982), pp. 93–4
——Zum Forschungsstand der sumerisch-babylonischen Literatur-Geschichte, *ZDMG* Suppl. 3 (1975), pp. 64–73
——and A. R. Millard: *Atra-ḫasīs: The Babylonian Story of the Flood*. Oxford, 1969
————*Babylonian Literary Texts*. CT 46. London, 1965
————*Catalogue of the Cuneiform Tablets in the Kouyunjik Collection of the British Museum. Second Supplement*. London, 1968
Landsberger, B.: Assyriologische Notizen, *WO* 1 (1947–52), pp. 362–76
——Babylonisch-assyrische Texte, in Lehmann (ed.), *Textbuch zur Religionsgeschichte*, pp. 73–134
——Die babylonische Theodizee, *ZA* 43 (1936), pp. 32–76
——Einige unerkannt gebliebene oder verkannte Nomina des Akkadischen, *WZKM* 56 (1960), pp. 109–29
——Einige unerkannt gebliebene oder verkannte Nomina des Akkadischen [Fortsetzung], *WZKM* 57 (1961), pp. 1–23
——Einleitung in das Gilgameš-Epos, in Garelli, *Gilg.*, pp. 31–6
——Jahreszeiten im Sumerisch-akkadischen, *JNES* 8 (1949), pp. 249–97
——Jungfräulichkeit: ein Beitrag zum Thema 'Beilager und Eheschliessung', *David AV* 2, pp. 41–105
——*The Date Palm and its By-Products According to the Cuneiform Sources*. *AfO* Beiheft 17. Graz, 1967
——*The Fauna of Ancient Mesopotamia* 1. [*ḪAR-ra = ḫubullu*] *Tablet XIII*. MSL 8, 1. Rome, 1960
——*The Fauna of Ancient Mesopotamia* 2. *ḪAR-ra = ḫubullu Tablets XIV–XVIII*. MSL 8, 2. Rome, 1962
——*The Series ḪAR-ra = ḫubullu Tablets I–IV*. MSL 5. Rome, 1957
——*The Series ḪAR-ra = ḫubullu Tablets V–VII*. MSL 6. Rome, 1957
——*The Series ḪAR-ra = ḫubullu Tablets VIII–XII*. MSL 7. Rome, 1959
——Zur vierten und siebenten Tafel des Gilgamesch-Epos, *RA* 62 (1968), pp. 97–135
——and M. Civil: *The Series ḪAR-ra = ḫubullu Tablet XV and Related Texts*. MSL 9. Rome, 1967
——A. Falkenstein, T. Jacobsen and R. Hallock: *Emesal Vocabulary, Old Babylonian Grammatical Texts, Neo-Babylonian Grammatical Texts*. MSL 4. Rome, 1956
——Erica Reiner and M. Civil: *The Series ḪAR-ra = ḫubullu Tablets XVI, XVII, XIX and Related Texts*. MSL 10. Rome, 1970
Langdon, S.: A fragment of a series of ritualistic prayers to astral deities in the ceremonies of divination, *RA* 12 (1915), pp. 189–92
——*Babylonian Liturgies, Sumerian Texts from the Early Period and from the Library of Ashurbanipal*. Paris, 1913

Langdon, S.: *Babylonian Penitential Psalms, to which are Added Fragments of the Epic of Creation.* OECT 6. Paris, 1927
——*Historical and Religious Texts from the Temple Library of Nippur.* BE 31. Munich, 1914
——Notes on the Philadelphia and Yale tablets of the Gilgamesh epic, *JRAS* 1929, pp. 343–6
—— *The Epic of Gilgamish.* PBS 10, 3. Philadelphia, 1917
—— *The H. Weld-Blundell Collection in the Ashmolean Museum: Sumerian and Semitic Religious and Historical Texts.* OECT 1. Oxford, 1923
—— *The Herbert Weld Collection in the Ashmolean Museum: Pictographic Inscriptions from Jemdet Nasr Excavated by the Oxford and Field Museum Expedition.* OECT 7. Oxford, 1928
Laroche, E.: *Catalogue des textes hittites.* Paris, 1971
——Emar, étape entre Babylone et le Hatti, in Margueron (ed.), *Le moyen Euphrate,* pp. 235–44
—— *Glossaire de la langue hourrite.* Paris, 1980
——La bibliothèque de Ḫattuša, *ArOr* 17, 2 (1949), pp. 7–23
——Textes mythologiques hittites en transcription, deuxième partie. Mythologie d'origine étrangère, XII. Gilgameš, *RHA* 26 (1968), pp. 121–38 (82, pp. 7–24)
Layard, A. H.: *Nineveh and Babylon.* 2 vols. London, 1853
Lebeau, M., and P. Talon (eds.): *Reflet des deux fleuves. Volume de mélanges offerts à André Finet.* Peeters, 1989
Legrain, L.: *Business Documents of the Third Dynasty of Ur.* 2 vols. UET 3. London, 1937 and 1947
——*Royal Inscriptions and Fragments from Nippur and Babylon.* PBS 15. Philadelphia, 1926
Lehmann, E. (ed.): *Textbuch zur Religionsgeschichte.* Leipzig, 1912
Leichty, E.: *The Omen Series Šumma Izbu.* TCS 4. Locust Valley, NY, 1970
——Maria deJ. Ellis and Pamela Gerardi (eds.): *A Scientific Humanist: Studies in Memory of Abraham Sachs.* OPBF 9. Philadelphia, 1988
——A. K. Grayson, J. J. Finkelstein and C. B. F. Walker: *Catalogue of the Babylonian Tablets in the British Museum* 6–8. *Tablets from Sippar* 1–3. London, 1986–8
Lenzen, H., A. von Haller, J. van Dijk and Eva Strommenger: *XVIII. Vorläufiger Bericht über die von dem Deutschen Archäologischen Institut und der Deutschen Orient-Gesellschaft aus Mitteln der Deutschen Forschungsgemeinschaft unternommenen Ausgrabungen in Uruk-Warka. Winter 1959/60.* UVB 18. Berlin, 1962
——A. von Müller, G. Peschken and A. Falkenstein: *XV. Vorläufiger Bericht über die von dem Deutschen Archäologischen Institut und der Deutschen Orient-Gesellschaft aus Mitteln der Deutschen Forschungsgemeinschaft unternommenen Ausgrabungen in Uruk-Warka. Winter 1956/57.* UVB 15. Berlin, 1959
Lerberghe, K. van: New data from the archives found in the house of Ur-Utu at Tell ed-Dēr (résumé), *CRRA* 28, pp. 280–3
Lewy, Hildegard, and J. Lewy: The origin of the week and the oldest West Asiatic calendar, *HUCA* 17 (1943), pp. 1–152
Lewy, J.: *Textes cappadociennes, troisième série.* 3 vols. TCL 19–21. Paris, 1935–7
Lie, A. G.: *The Inscriptions of Sargon II, King of Assyria* 1. *The Annals.* Paris, 1929
Lieberman, S. J.: A Mesopotamian background for the so-called *Aggadic* 'measures' of biblical hermeneutics, *HUCA* 58 (1987), pp. 157–225
——Nippur: city of decisions, in Ellis (ed.), *Nippur at the Centennial,* pp. 127–36
Limet, H.: *L'anthroponymie sumérienne dans les documents de la 3ᵉ dynastie d'Ur.* Paris, 1968
——*Le travail du métal au pays de Sumer au temps de la IIIᵉ dynastie d'Ur.* Paris, 1960
——*Les légendes des sceaux cassites.* Brussels, 1971

Lion, Brigitte, and Cécile Michel: Criquets et autres insectes à Mari, *MARI* 8 (1997), pp. 707–24

Lipiński, E.: El's abode: mythological traditions related to Mount Hermon and to the mountains of Armenia, *OLP* 2 (1970), pp. 13–69

Litke, R. L.: *A Reconstruction of the Assyro-Babylonian God-Lists, AN:^{d}A-nu-um and AN:Anu ša amēli*. Texts from the Babylonian Collection 3. New Haven, Conn., 1998

Littmann, E.: Alf layla wa-layla, *Encyclopedia of Islam, New Edition* 1. Leiden, 1960, pp. 358–64

Liverani, M.: *Studies in the Annals of Ashurnasirpal II, 2. Topographical Analysis*. Quaderni di Geografica Storica 4. Rome, 1992

Livingstone, A.: A fragment of a work song, *ZA* 70 (1980), pp. 55–7

—— *Court Poetry and Literary Miscellanea*. SAA 3. Helsinki, 1989

—— *Mystical and Mythological Explanatory Works of Assyrian and Babylonian Scholars*. Oxford, 1986

—— *Šērtu*, 'ring', *šeršerratu*, 'chain', *NABU* 1990, no. 87

Lloyd, Seton, and Nuri Gökçe: Sultantepe: Anglo-Turkish joint excavations, 1952, *AnSt* 3 (1953), pp. 27–47

Longman, T., III: *Fictional Akkadian Autobiography*. Winona Lake, Ind., 1991

Lord, A. B.: Gilgamesh and other epics, *Studies Moran*, pp. 371–80

Loretz, O.: *Texte aus Chagar Bazar und Tell Brak*. AOAT 3. Kevelaer and Neukirchen-Vluyn, 1969

Loud, G.: *Megiddo* II. OIP 62. Chicago, 1948

Luckenbill, D. D.: Shut-abni, 'Those of Stone', *AJSL* 38 (1922), pp. 97–102

—— *The Annals of Sennacherib*. OIP 2. Chicago, 1924

Lutz, H. F.: *Early Babylonian Letters from Larsa*. YOS 2. New Haven, Conn., 1917

—— *Selected Sumerian and Babylonian Texts*. PBS 1, 2. Philadelphia, 1919

—— *The Verdict of a Trial Judge in a Case of Assault and Battery*. UCP 9, 6. Berkeley, Calif., 1930

MacGinnis, J.: A Neo-Assyrian text describing a royal funeral, *SAAB* 1, 1 (1987), pp. 1–12

MacMillan, K. D.: *Some Cuneiform Tablets Bearing on the Religion of Babylonia and Assyria*. BA 5, 5, pp. 531–712. Leipzig, 1906

Maddin, R., and T. Stech Wheeler: Metallurgical study of seven bar ingots, *IEJ* 26 (1976), pp. 170–3

Maeda, T.: Collation of G. A. Barton, *Haverford Library Collection of Cuneiform Tablets or Documents*, *Acta Sum* 2 (1980), pp. 197–224

Magnusson, M.: *BC: The Archaeology of the Bible Lands*. London, 1977

Maier, J. (ed.): *Gilgamesh: A Reader*. Wauconda, Ill., 1997

Malamat, A.: 'Doorbells' at Mari: a textual-archaeological correlation, *CRRA* 30, pp. 160–7

—— *Mari and the Early Israelite Experience*. Oxford, 1989

Malbran-Labat, Florence: La découverte épigraphique de 1994 à Ougarit (les textes akkadiens), *Studi micenei ed egeo-anatolici* 36 (1995), pp. 103–11

—— Les archives de la maison d'Ourtenou, *CRAI* 1995, pp. 443–9

Malul, M.: A possible case of Janus parallelism in the Epic of Gilgamesh XI, 130, *Acta Sum* 17 (1995), pp. 338–42

Mander, P. A.: Gilgamesh e Dante: due itinerari alla ricerca dell'immortalità, *Miscellanea di studi in onore di Raffaele Sirri*. Naples, 1995, pp. 281–97

—— *Il pantheon di Abu-Ṣālabīkh*. Naples, 1986

Marchesi, G.: Ì-a lullum$_x$ ú-luh-ha sù-sù. On the incipit of the Sumerian poem Gilgamesh and Huwawa B, in Graziani (ed.), *Studi sul Vicino Oriente antico* 2, pp. 673–84

Margueron, J.-Cl.: Emar: un example d'implantation hittite en terre syrienne, in Margueron (ed.), *Le moyen Euphrate*, pp. 285–312

Margueron, J.-Cl. (ed.): *Le moyen Euphrate. Zone de contacts et d'échanges.* Actes du Colloque de Strasbourg 10–12 mars 1977. Leiden, 1980
——Meskene. B. Archäologisch, *RLA* 8 (1993–7), pp. 84–93
——Quatre campagnes de fouilles à Emar (1972–1974): un bilan provisoire, *Syria* 52 (1975), pp. 53–85
——Rapport préliminaire sur les 3e, 4e, 5e et 6e campagnes de fouilles à Meskéné-Emar, *AAAS* 32 (1982), pp. 233–46
——Une tombe monumentale à Mari, *MARI* 3 (1984), pp. 197–215
Marks, J. H., and R. M. Good (eds.): *Love and Death in the Ancient Near East: Essays in Honor of Marvin H. Pope.* Guilford, Conn., 1987
Marzahn, J., and H. Neumann (eds.): *Assyriologica et Semitica, Festschrift für Joachim Oelsner.* AOAT 252. Münster, 2000
Matouš, L.: *Die lexikalischen Tafelserien der Babylonier und Assyrer in den Berliner Museen* 1. *Gegendstandlisten (Serie ḪAR-ra = ḫubullu).* Berlin, 1933
——Les rapports entre la version sumérienne et la version akkadienne de l'épopée de Gilgameš, in Garelli, *Gilg.*, pp. 83–94
——Zur neueren Literatur über das Gilgameš-Epos, *BiOr* 21 (1964), pp. 3–10
Mattila, Raija: *Legal Transactions of the Royal Court of Nineveh 2. Assurbanipal through Sin-šarru-iškun.* SAA XIV. Helsinki, 2002
Maul, S. M.: *Die Inschriften von Tall Bderi.* BBVO Texte 2. Berlin, 1992
—— (ed.): *Festschrift für Rykle Borger zu seinem 65. Geburtstag am 24. Mai 1994. tikip santakki mala bašmu* . . . Cuneiform Monographs 10. Groningen, 1998
—— *'Herzberuhigungsklagen'. Die sumerisch-akkadischen Eršaḫunga-Gebete.* Wiesbaden, 1988
——*Kurgarrû* und *assinnu* und ihr Stand in der babylonischen Gesellschaft, in Haas (ed.), *Außenseiter und Randgruppen*, pp. 159–71
——Neue Textvertreter der elften Tafel des Gilgamesch-Epos, *MDOG* 133 (2001), pp. 33–50
——Reste einer frühneuassyrischen Fassung des Gilgamesch-Epos aus Assur, *MDOG* 133 (2001), pp. 11–32
——Wer baute die babylonische Arche? Ein neues Fragment der mesopotamischen Sintfluterzählung aus Assur, *MDOG* 131 (1999), pp. 155–62
——*Zukunftsbewältigung.* BaF 18. Mainz, 1994
Maxwell-Hyslop, Kathleen R.: *Western Asiatic Jewellery.* London, 1971
Mayer, W.: Sargons Feldzug gegen Urartu—714 v. Chr. Text und Übersetzung, *MDOG* 115 (1983), pp. 65–132
Mayer, W. R.: Das 'gnomische Präteritum' im literarischen Akkadisch, *Or* NS 61 (1992), pp. 373–99
——Ein Hymnus auf Ninurta als Helfer in der Not, *Or* NS 61 (1992), pp. 17–57
——Ein Mythos von der Erschaffung des Menschen und des Königs, *Or* NS 56 (1987), pp. 55–68
——Ein neues Königsritual gegen feindliche Bedrohung, *Or* NS 57 (1988), pp. 145–64
——Ein Ritual gegen Feindschaft im Museo Nazionale d'Arte Orientale zu Rom, *Or* NS 59 (1990), pp. 14–33
——Sechs Šu-ila Gebete, *Or* NS 59 (1990), pp. 449–90
——*Untersuchungen zur Formensprache der babylonischen 'Gebetsbeschwörungen'.* Studia Pohl SM 5. Rome, 1976
McCall, Henrietta: *Mesopotamian Myths.* London, 1990
McCown, D. E., and R. C. Haines: *Nippur* 1. *Temple of Enlil, Scribal Quarter, and Soundings.* OIP 78. Chicago, 1967

McEwan, G. J. P.: *Priest and Temple in Hellenistic Babylonia.* FAOS 4. Wiesbaden, 1981
Meek, T. J.: *Cuneiform Bilingual Hymns, Prayers and Penitential Psalms.* BA 10, 1. Leipzig, 1913
Meer, P. E. van der: *Syllabaries A, B¹ and B with Miscellaneous Lexicographical Texts.* OECT 4. Oxford, 1938
—— *Textes scolaires de Suse.* MDP 27. Paris, 1935
Meier, G.: Die zweite Tafel der Serie *bīt mēseri*, *AfO* 14 (1941–4), pp. 139–52
—— Kommentare aus dem Archiv der Tempelschule in Assur, *AfO* 12 (1937–9), pp. 237–46
Meier, S. A.: Women and communication in the ancient Near East, *JAOS* 111 (1991), pp. 540–7
Meissner, B.: *Assyriologische Studien* 4. MVAG 12, 3. Berlin, 1908
—— *Beiträge zum assyrischen Wörterbuch.* 2 vols. AS 1 and 4. Chicago, 1931–2
—— *Ein altbabylonisches Fragment des Gilgamos Epos.* MVAG 7, 1. Berlin, 1902
Menzel, Brigitte: *Die assyrische Tempel.* 2 vols. Studia Pohl SM 10. Rome, 1981
Merkel, J. F., and W. G. Dever: Metalworking technology at the end of the Early Bronze Age in the southern Levant, *Institute for Archaeo-Metallurgical Studies* 14 (1989), pp. 1–4
Messerschmidt, L.: *Die Inschrift der Stele Nabuna'ids, des Königs von Babel.* MVAG 1, 1. Berlin, 1896
Meyer, M., and P. Mirecki (eds.): *Ancient Magic and Ritual Power.* Leiden, 1995
Michalowski, P.: History as charter, *JAOS* 103 (1983), pp. 237–48
—— Orality and literacy and early Mesopotamian literature, *Mesopotamian Epic Literature*, pp. 227–45
—— review of *OECT* V, *JNES* 37 (1978), pp. 343–5
—— Sailing to Babylon, reading the dark side of the moon, in Cooper and Schwartz (eds.), *The Study of the Ancient Near East in the Twenty-First Century*, pp. 177–93
—— *The Lamentation over the Destruction of Sumer and Ur.* Mesopotamian Civilizations 1. Winona Lake, Ind., 1989
—— Tudanapšum, Naram-Sin and Nippur, *RA* 75 (1981), pp. 173–6
Michel, Cécile: Les 'diamants' du roi de Mari, *Florilegium marianum* 1, pp. 127–36
Michel, E.: Die Assur-Texte Salmanassars III. (858–824), *WO* 1 (1947–52), pp. 5–20
Milano, L., S. de Martino, F. M. Fales and G. B. Lanfranchi (eds.): *Landscapes: Territories, Frontiers and Horizons in the Ancient Near East.* 3 vols. CRRA 44. Padua, 1999–2000
Milik, J. T.: *The Books of Enoch: Aramaic Fragments of Qumran Cave 4.* Oxford, 1976
Millard, A. R.: Gilgamesh X: A new fragment, *Iraq* 26 (1964), pp. 99–105
—— The sign of the Flood, *Iraq* 49 (1987), pp. 63–9
Mindlin, M., M. J. Geller and J. E. Wansbrough (eds.): *Figurative Language in the Ancient Near East.* London, 1987
Moorey, P. R. S.: *Ancient Mesopotamian Materials and Industries.* Oxford, 1994
Moran, W. L.: *duppuru* (*dubburu*)—*ṭuppuru*, too?, *JCS* 33 (1981), pp. 44–7
—— Ovid's *blanda voluptas* and the humanization of Enkidu, *JNES* 50 (1991), pp. 121–7
—— The Epic of Gilgamesh: a document of ancient humanism, *Bulletin CSMS* 22 (1991), pp. 15–22
—— and W. W. Hallo: The first tablet of the SB recension of the Anzu-myth, *JCS* 31 (1979), pp. 65–115
Morony, M. G.: *Iraq after the Muslim Conquest.* Princeton, NJ, 1984
Muhly, J. D.: Kupfer B. Archäologisch, *RLA* 6 (1980–3), pp. 348–64
—— Metalle B. Archäologisch, *RLA* 8 (1993–7), pp. 119–36
Müller, E. W. (ed.): *Geschlechtsreife und Legitimation zur Zeugung.* Munich, 1985

Müller, H.-P.: Gilgameschs Trauergesang um Enkidu und die Gattung der Totenklage, *ZA* 68 (1978), pp. 233–50

Müller-Kessler, Christa: Interrelations between lead rolls and incantation bowls, *Mesopotamian Magic*, pp. 197–209

——and K. Kessler: Spätbabylonische Gottheiten in spätantiken mandäischen Texten, *ZA* 89 (1999), pp. 65–87

Myrhman, D.: *Babylonian Hymns and Prayers*. PBS 1, 1. Philadelphia, 1911

Nakamura, M.: Zum hurritischen Gilgameš-Epos: ein neuer Zusammenschluß, *SCCNH* 10, pp. 375–8

Nashef, K.: The deities of Dilmun, *Akkadica* 38 (1984), pp. 1–38

——*Répertoire géographique des textes cunéiformes* 5. *Die Orts- und Gewässernamen der mittelbabylonischen und mittelassyrischen Zeit*. Beihefte zum Tübinger Atlas des vorderen Orients B 7, 5. Wiesbaden, 1982

Nasrabadi, B. M.: *Untersuchungen zu den Bestattungssitten in Mesopotamien in der ersten Hälfte des ersten Jahrtausends v. Chr.* BaF 23. Mainz, 1999

Naster, P.: *ṣullulu* dans Gilgamesh XI, 31, *Symbolae Böhl*, pp. 295–8

Neugebauer, O., and A. Sachs: *Mathematical Cuneiform Texts*. AOS 29. New Haven, Conn., 1945

Neve, P.: *Büyükkale. Die Bauwerke*. Berlin, 1982

——Die Ausgrabungen in Boğazköy-Ḫattuša 1983, *Archäologischer Anzeiger* 1984, 3, pp. 329–81

Nies, J. B., and C. E. Keiser: *Historical, Religious and Economic Texts and Antiquities*. BIN 2. New Haven, Conn., 1920

Nissen, H.-J.: The city wall of Uruk, in Ucko et al. (eds.), *Man, Settlement and Urbanism*, pp. 793–8

——and J. Renger (eds.): *Mesopotamien und seine Nachbarn*. CRRA 25. BBVO 1. Berlin, 1982

Noegel, S. B.: A Janus parallelism in the Gilgamesh Flood story, *Acta Sum* 13 (1991), pp. 419–21

——An asymmetrical Janus parallelism in the Gilgamesh Flood story, *Acta Sum* 16 (1994), pp. 306–8

Nöldeke, A., H. Lenzen, A. von Haller and W. Göpner: *Siebenter Vorläufiger Bericht über die von der Deutschen Forschungsgemeinschaft unternommenen Ausgrabungen in Uruk-Warka*. UVB 7. PAW Abhandlungen 1935, 4. Berlin, 1935

Nötscher, F.: *Die Omen-Serie šumma âlu ina melê šakin (CT 38–40)*. 2 vols. Or 39–42 and 51–4. Rome, 1929–30

Nougayrol, J.: *Le palais royal d'Ugarit* 4. *Textes accadiens des archives sud (archives internationales)*. MRS 9. Paris, 1956

——Textes hépatoscopiques d'époque ancienne conservés au Musée du Louvre, *RA* 38 (1941), pp. 67–88

——Textes hépatoscopiques d'époque ancienne conservés au Musée du Louvre (III), *RA* 44 (1950), pp. 1–44

——Textes religieux, *RA* 66 (1972), pp. 141–5

——Un chef-d'œuvre inédit de la littérature babylonienne, *RA* 45 (1951), pp. 169–83

——Une version ancienne du 'Juste Souffrant', *RB* 59 (1952), pp. 239–50

——E. Laroche, C. Virolleaud and C. F. A. Schaeffer: *Ugaritica* V. *Nouveaux textes accadiens, hourrites et ugaritiques des archives et bibliothèques privées d'Ugarit*. MRS 16. Paris, 1968

Obayashi, H. (ed.): *Death and the Afterlife: Perspectives of World Religion*. Westport, Conn., 1991

Oelsner, J.: Aus dem Leben babylonischer 'Priester' in der 2. Hälfte des 1. Jahrtausends v. Chr. (am Beispiel der Funde aus Uruk), in Julia Zabłocka and S. Zawadzki (eds.), *Šulmu* IV. *Everyday Life in Ancient Near East*. Poznań, 1993, pp. 253–42

Oelsner, J.: Ein Beitrag zu keilschriftlichen Königstitulaturen in hellenistischer Zeit, *ZA* 56 (1964), pp. 262–74

Offner, Gratianne: Jeux corporels en Sumer. Documents relatifs à la compétition athlétique, *RA* 56 (1962), pp. 31–8

——L'épopée de Gilgameš, a-t-elle été fixée dans l'art?, in Garelli, *Gilg.*, pp. 175–81

Oinas, F. J. (ed.): *Heroic Epic and Saga: An Introduction to the World's Great Folk Epics.* Bloomington, Ind., 1978

Opificius, Ruth: *Das altbabylonische Terrakottarelief.* Berlin, 1961

——Gilgamesch und Enkidu in der bildenden Kunst, in H. Pohle and G. Mahr (eds.), *Festschrift zum hundertjährigen Bestehen der Berliner Gesellschaft für Anthropologie, Ethnologie und Urgeschichte, 1869–1969.* Berlin, 1970, pp. 286–92

Oppenheim, A. L.: *Ancient Mesopotamia: Portrait of a Dead Civilization.* Chicago, 1964

——Idiomatic Akkadian (lexicographical researches), *JAOS* 61 (1941), pp. 251–71

——Mesopotamian mythology II, *Or* NS 17 (1948), pp. 17–58

——Studies in Akkadian lexicography II, *Or* NS 14 (1945), pp. 235–41

—— *The Interpretation of Dreams in the Ancient Near East, with a Translation of an Assyrian Dream-Book.* TAPS 46, 3. Philadelphia, 1956

——et al.: *The Assyrian Dictionary of the Oriental Institute of the University of Chicago.* Chicago, 1956–

Osten-Sacken, Elisabeth von der: Hürden und Netze, *MDOG* 123 (1991), pp. 133–48

Otten, H.: Archive und Bibliotheken in Ḫattuša, *CRRA* 30, pp. 184–90

——*Aus dem Bezirk des Grossen Tempels* [1]. KBo 19. WVDOG 84. Berlin, 1970

——Die erste Tafel des hethitischen Gilgamesch-Epos, *Istanbuler Mitteilungen* 8 (1958), pp. 93–125

——Die Tontafelfunde aus Haus 16, *Archäologischer Anzeiger* 1984, pp. 372–5

——*Mythische und magische Texte in hethitischer Sprache.* KUB 33. Berlin, 1943

—— *Texte aus Stadtplanquadrat L/18*, 2. KBo 13. WVDOG 78. Berlin, 1967

—— *Texte der Grabungen 1953 und 1954.* KBo 8. WVDOG 69. Berlin, 1955

—— *Vorwiegend Mythen, Epen, Gebete und Texte in althethitischer Sprache.* KUB 36. Berlin, 1955

—— *Vorwiegend Texte der Grabungen 1955 und 1956.* KBo 9. WVDOG 70. Berlin, 1957

——Zur Überlieferung des Gilgameš-Epos nach den Boğazköy-Texten, in Garelli, *Gilg.*, pp. 139–43

——and Christel Rüster: *Aus dem Bezirk des Grossen Tempels* [2]. KBo 22. WVDOG 90. Berlin, 1974

———— *Die hurritisch-hethitische Bilingue und weitere Texte aus der Oberstadt.* KBo 32. Berlin, 1990

Owen, D. I.: *Neo-Sumerian Archival Texts Primarily from Nippur in the University Museum, the Oriental Institute and the Iraq Museum.* Winona Lake, Ind., 1982

——The world's great epics III. Gilgamesh, *Horizon* 15, 1 (1974), pp. 112–16

——and G. Wilhelm (eds.): *Nuzi at Seventy-Five.* SCCNH 10. Bethesda, Md., 1999

Panaino, A.: Between Mesopotamia and India: some remarks about the Unicorn cycle in Iran, in Whiting (ed.), *Mythology and Mythologies*, pp. 149–79

Parker, R. A., and W. H. Dubberstein: *Babylonian Chronology 626 B.C.–A.D. 75.* Providence, RI, 1956

Parpola, S.: A letter from Šamaš-šuma-ukīn to Esarhaddon, *Iraq* 34 (1972), pp. 21–34

——Assyrian library records, *JNES* 42 (1983), pp. 1–29

——*Assyrian Prophecies.* SAA 9. Helsinki, 1997

——Assyrians after Assyria, *Journal of the Assyrian Academic Society* 12, 2 (2000), pp. 1–16

Parpola, S.: *Letters from Assyrian and Babylonian Scholars*. SAA 10. Helsinki, 1993
——*Letters of Assyrian Scholars to the Kings Esarhaddon and Ashurbanipals*. 2 vols. AOAT 5. Kevelaer and Neukirchen-Vluyn, Germany, 1970 and 1983
——The Assyrian cabinet, *Festschrift von Soden* 1995, pp. 279–401
——The Assyrian Tree of Life: tracing the origins of Jewish monotheism and Greek philosophy, *JNES* 52 (1993), pp. 161–208
——*The Correspondence of Sargon II*, 1. *Letters from Assyrian and the West*. SAA 1. Helsinki, 1987
——The esoteric meaning of the name of Gilgamesh, *CRRA* 43, pp. 315–29
——The forlorn scholar, *Studies Reiner*, pp. 257–78
——The royal archives of Nineveh, *CRRA* 30, pp. 223–36
——*The Standard Babylonian Epic of Gilgamesh*. SAACT 1. Helsinki, 1997
——Transliteration of Sumerian: problems and prospects, *StOr* 46 (1975), pp. 239–57
——and Kazuko Watanabe: *Neo-Assyrian Treaties and Loyalty Oaths*. SAA 2. Helsinki, 1988
——and R. M. Whiting (eds.): *Assyria 1995*. Helsinki, 1997
—— —— (eds.): *Sex and Gender in the Ancient Near East*. CRRA 47, 1. Helsinki, forthcoming
Parrot, A.: *Glyptique mésopotamienne, fouilles de Lagash (Tello) et de Larsa (Senkereh) (1931–1933)*. Paris, 1954
Paul, S. M.: Euphemistically 'speaking' and a covetous eye, *Hebrew Annual Review* 14 (1994), pp. 193–204
——The 'plural of ecstasy' in Mesopotamian and biblical love poetry, *Studies Greenfield*, pp. 585–97
Pearce, Laurie E., and L. T. Doty: The activities of the Anu-belšunu, *Fs Oelsner*, pp. 331–41
Pedersén, O.: *Archives and Libraries in the City of Assur*. 2 vols. Uppsala, 1985–6
Pettinato, G.: *Catalogo dei testi cuneiformi di Tell Mardikh-Ebla*. MEE 1. Naples, 1979
——*Ebla. Un impero inciso nell'argilla*. Milan, 1979
——*La saga di Gilgamesh*. Milan, 1992
Pfann, S. J.: *Qumran Cave 4 26. Cryptic Texts*. P. Alexander et al.: *Miscellanea* Part 1. Discoveries in the Judaean Desert 36. Oxford, 2000
Pietersma, A.: *The Apocryphon of Jannes and Jambres the Magicians*. Leiden, 1994
Pinches, T. G.: A Babylonian tablet dated in the reign of Aspasinē, *BOR* 4 (1889–90), pp. 131–5
——*Cuneiform Texts from Babylonian Tablets in the British Museum* 6. London, 1898
——Exit Gišṭubar!, *BOR* 4 (1889–90), p. 264
——Gilgameš and the hero of the Flood, *PSBA* 25 (1903), pp. 113–22, 195–201
——*Miscellaneous Texts*. CT 44. London, 1963
——*Texts in the Babylonian Wedge-Writing, Autographed from the Original Documents*. London, 1882
Pingree, D.: Legacies in astronomy and celestial omens, in Dalley et al., *Legacy of Mesopotamia*, pp. 125–37
Pitard, W. T.: Care of the dead at Emar, in Chavalas (ed.), *Emar*, pp. 123–40
——The archaeology of Emar, in Chavalas (ed.), *Emar*, pp. 13–23
Poebel, A.: *Historical and Grammatical Texts*. PBS 5. Philadelphia, 1914
——The root forms sì(m) and su(m), 'to give', in Sumerian, *JAOS* 57 (1937), pp. 33–72
Pohl, A.: *Neubabylonische Rechtsurkunden aus den Berliner Staatlichen Museen*. 2 vols. AnOr 8–9. Rome, 1933–4
Pomponio, F.: *La prosopografia dei testi presargonici di Fara*. Studia semitici 3. Rome, 1987

Pongratz-Leisten, Beate: *Ina Šulmi Īrub. Die kulttopographische und ideologische Programmatik der* akītu-*Prozession in Babylonien und Assyrien im 1. Jahrtausend v. Ch.* BaF 16. Mainz, 1994

Postgate, J. N.: *Neo-Assyrian Royal Grants and Decrees.* Studia Pohl SM 1. Rome, 1969

—— *The Governor's Palace Archive.* CTN 2. London, 1973

—— Two lines in Gilgamesh, *NABU* 1998, no. 30

Potts, D. T. (ed.): *Dilmun. New Studies in the Archeology and Early History of Bahrain.* BBVO 2. Berlin, 1983

Powell, M. A.: Epistemology and Sumerian agriculture: the strange case of sesame and linseed, *Aula Or* 9 (1991), pp. 155–64

—— Maße und Gewichte, *RLA* 8 (1993–7), pp. 457–516

—— The adverbial suffix *-ā* and the morphology of the multiples of ten in Akkadian, *ZA* 72 (1982), pp. 89–105

Pritchard, J. B. (ed.): *Ancient Near Eastern Texts Relating to the Old Testament.* 3rd edn with supplement. Princeton, NJ, 1969

Prosecký, J. (ed.): *Intellectual Life of the Ancient Near East.* CRRA 43. Prague, 1998

Puech, É.: *Qumrân Grotte 4 22. Textes araméens, première partie.* Discoveries in the Judaean Desert 31. Oxford, 2001

Radau, H.: Miscellaneous Sumerian texts from the temple library of Nippur, *HAV*, pp. 374–457

Radner, Karen, and Heather D. Baker (eds.): *The Prosopography of the Neo-Assyrian Empire.* Helsinki, 1998–

Rainey, A. F. (ed.): *kinattūtu ša dārâti. Raphael Kutscher Memorial Volume.* Tel Aviv, Occasional Publications 1. Tel Aviv, 1993

Ranke, H.: *Babylonian Legal and Business Documents from the Time of the First Dynasty of Babylon, Chiefly from Sippar.* BE 6, 1. Philadelphia, 1906

Ravn, O. E.: Selected passages in Enuma eliš and Gilgameš, *Acta Or* 22 (1955), pp. 28–54

—— The passage on Gilgamesh and the wives of Uruk, *BiOr* 10 (1953), pp. 12–13

Rawlinson, H. C., and E. Norris: *The Cuneiform Inscriptions of Western Asia* 1. *A Selection from the Historical Inscriptions of Chaldea, Assyria, and Babylonia.* London, 1861

—— —— *The Cuneiform Inscriptions of Western Asia* 2. *A Selection from the Miscellaneous Inscriptions of Assyria.* London, 1866

—— and T. G. Pinches: *The Cuneiform Inscriptions of Western Asia* 4. *A Selection from the Miscellaneous Inscriptions of Assyria.* 2nd edn. London, 1891

—— —— *The Cuneiform Inscriptions of Western Asia* 5. *A Selection from the Miscellaneous Inscriptions of Assyria and Babylonia.* 2 vols. London, 1880 and 1884

—— and G. Smith: *The Cuneiform Inscriptions of Western Asia* 3. *A Selection from the Miscellaneous Inscriptions of Assyria.* London, 1870

—— —— *The Cuneiform Inscriptions of Western Asia* 4. *A Selection from the Miscellaneous Inscriptions of Assyria.* 1st edn. London, 1875

Reade, J. E.: Alexander the Great and the Hanging Gardens of Babylon, *Iraq* 62 (2000), pp. 195–217

—— Archaeology and the Kuyunjik archives, *CRRA* 30, pp. 213–22

—— Ninive, *RLA* 9 (1998–2001), pp. 388–433

—— Rassam's Babylonian collection: the excavations and the archives, in E. Leichty, *Catalogue* VI, pp. xiii–xxxvi

Reeves, J. C.: *Jewish Lore in Manichaean Cosmogony.* Cincinnati, 1992

—— (ed.): *Tracing the Threads: Studies in the Vitality of Jewish Pseudepigraphia.* Atlanta, Ga., 1994

Reeves, J. C.: Utnapishtim in the Book of Giants?, *JBL* 112 (1993), pp. 110–15

Reiner, Erica: A Sumero-Akkadian hymn of Nanâ, *JNES* 33 (1974), pp. 221–36

——*Damqam īnim* revisited, *StOr* 55 (1984), pp. 177–82

——*Lipšur* litanies, *JNES* 15 (1956), pp. 129–49

——New light on some historical omens, in Bittel et al. (eds.), *Anatolian Studies Presented to H. G. Güterbock*, pp. 257–61

——*Šurpu: A Collection of Sumerian and Akkadian Incantations. AfO* Beiheft 11. Graz, 1958

——The etiological myth of the 'Seven Sages', *Or* NS 30 (1961), pp. 1–11

——The location of Anšan, *RA* 67 (1973), pp. 57–62

——and M. Civil: *The Series ḪAR-ra = ḫubullu Tablets XX–XXIV and Related Texts.* MSL 11. Rome, 1973

——and H. G. Güterbock: The Great Prayer to Ištar and its two versions from Boğazköy, *JCS* 21 (1967), pp. 255–66

Reisman, D.: A 'royal hymn' of Išbi-Erra to the goddess Nisaba, *Kramer AV*, pp. 357–66

Reisner, G. A.: *Sumerisch-babylonische Hymnen nach Thontafeln griechischer Zeit.* Berlin, 1896

Reiter, Karin: *Die Metalle im Alten Orient unter besonderer Berücksichtigung altbabylonischer Quellen.* AOAT 249. Münster, 1997

Renger, J. (ed.): *Babylon: Focus mesopotamischer Geschichte, Wiege früher Gelehrsamkeit, Mythos in der Moderne.* CDOG 2. Saarbrücken, 1999

——*Gilg.* P ii 32 (*PBS* 10/3), *RA* 66 (1972), p. 190

——Mesopotamian epic literature, in Oinas (ed.), *Heroic Epic and Saga*, pp. 27–48

——Zur fünften Tafel des Gilgameschepos, *Studies Reiner*, pp. 317–26

Reuther, O.: *Die Innenstadt von Babylon (Merkes).* WVDOG 47. Leipzig, 1926

Richter, T.: *Untersuchungen zu den lokalen Panthea Süd- und Mittelbabyloniens in altbabylonischer Zeit.* AOAT 257. Münster, 1999

Ridley, R. T.: The saga of an epic: Gilgamesh and the constitution of Uruk, *Or* NS 69 (2000), pp. 341–67

Riemschneider, K. K.: *Babylonische Geburtsomina in hethitischer Übersetzung.* StBoT 9. Wiesbaden, 1970

Riftin, A. P.: *Staro-Vavilonskie iuridicheskie i administrativnye dokumenty v sobraniiakh SSSR.* Moscow and Leningrad, 1937

Robson, Eleanor: Three Old Babylonian methods for dealing with 'Pythagorean' triangles, *JCS* 49 (1997), pp. 51–72

Rochberg, Francesca: Scribes and Scholars: the *ṭupšar Enūma Anu Enlil*, Fs Oelsner, pp. 359–75

Rochberg-Halton, Francesca (ed.): *Language, Literature, and History: Philological and Historical Studies Presented to Erica Reiner.* AOS 67. New Haven, Conn., 1987

Röllig, W.: Götterzahlen, *RLA* 3 (1957–71), pp. 499–500

——Im, *RLA* 5 (1976–80), pp. 63–5

Römer, W. H. Ph.: *Das sumerische Kurzepos 'Bilgameš und Akka'.* AOAT 209/I. Kevelaer and Neukirchen-Vluyn, Germany, 1980

——Die sumerische Königsliste, *TUAT* I/4, pp. 328–37

——Die Tontafeln Utuchegals von Unug, *TUAT* I/4, pp. 316–19

——Kleine Beiträge zur Grammatik des Sumerischen: 1. Das modale grammatische Element nu-uš, *Kramer AV*, pp. 371–8

——Miscellanea Sumerologica II. zum sog. Gudam-Text, *BiOr* 48 (1991), 363–78

Römer, W. H. Ph.: Studien zu den altbabylonischen hymnisch-epischen Texten. Ein *kummu*-Lied auf Adad (CT 15, 3–4), *HSAO* I, pp. 185–99
——*Sumerische 'Königshymnen' der Isin-Zeit.* Leiden, 1965
——Zur Siegesinschrift des Königs Utuḫeĝal von Unug (±2116–2110 v. Chr., *Or* NS 54 (1985), pp. 274–88
——and D. O. Edzard: *Mythen und Epen* 1. TUAT 3, 3. Gütersloh, 1993
Roth, Martha T.: The Slave and the Scoundrel: CBS 10467, a Sumerian morality tale?, *JAOS* 103 (1983), pp. 275–82
Roth, W. M. W.: The numerical sequence x/x + 1 in the Old Testament, *Vetus Testamentum* 12 (1962), pp. 300–11
Rowton, M. B.: The woodlands of ancient Western Asia, *JNES* 26 (1967), pp. 261–77
Rubio, G.: On the alleged 'pre-Sumerian substratum', *JCS* 51 (1999), pp. 1–16
Russell, J. M.: *The Final Sack of Nineveh.* New Haven, Conn., 1998
Rüster, Christel, and E. Neu: *Hethitisches Zeichenlexikon.* StBoT Beiheft 2. Harrassowitz, 1989
Saggs, H. W. F.: Additions to Anzu, *AfO* 33 (1986), pp. 1–29
Sallaberger, W.: *Der kultische Kalender der Ur III-Zeit.* 2 vols. Berlin, 1993
Salonen, A.: *Die Landfahrzeuge des alten Mesopotamien.* AASF 72, 3. Helsinki, 1951
——*Die Türen des alten Mesopotamien.* AASF 124. Helsinki, 1961
——*Die Wasserfahrzeuge in Babylonien.* StOr 8, 4. Helsinki, 1939
——*Vögel und Vogelfang im alten Mesopotamien.* AASF 180. Helsinki, 1973
Salvesen, Alison: Babylon and Nineveh in Aramaic sources, in Dalley et al., *The Legacy of Mesopotamia*, pp. 139–61
Salvini, M.: Die hurritischen Überlieferungen des Gilgameš-Epos und der Keššі-Erzählung, in Haas (ed.), *Hurriter und Hurritisch*, pp. 157–72
Saporetti, C.: Qualche punto problematico nella narrazione del diluvio, *Egitto e Vicino Oriente* 5 (1982), pp. 59–61
——tùn.bar = 'tagliare', in Cagni (ed.), *Il bilinguismo a Ebla*, pp. 403–4
Sasson, J. M. (ed.): *Civilizations of the Ancient Near East.* 4 vols. New York, 1995
——Some literary motifs in the composition of the Gilgamesh epic, *Studies in Philology* 69, 3 (July 1972), pp. 259–79
Savignac, J. de: La sagesse du Qôhéléth et l'épopée de Gilgamesh, *Vetus Testamentum* 28 (1978), pp. 318–23
Schaeffer, C. F.-A.: *Textes en cunéiformes alphabétiques des archives sud, sud-ouest et du petit palais.* PRU 5. MRS 11. Paris, 1965
Schaudig, H.: *Die Inschriften Nabonids von Babylon und Kyros' des Großen.* AOAT 256. Münster, 2001
Scheil, V.: *Actes juridiques susiens.* MDP 22. Paris, 1930
——Catalogue de la collection Eugène Tisserant, *RA* 18 (1921), pp. 1–33
——Le poème d'Agušaya, *RA* 15 (1918), pp. 169–82
——*Textes élamites-sémitiques, première série.* MDP 2. Paris, 1900
Schmidt, B. B.: The gods and the dead of the domestic cult at Emar: a reassessment, in Chavalas (ed.), *Emar*, pp. 141–63
Schmidt, J.: Uruk-Warka. Zusammenfassender Bericht über die 27. Kampagne 1969, *Bagh. Mitt.* 5 (1970), pp. 51–96
——D. Duda, H. Fenner, U. Finkbeiner, M. Hoh, D. Sack and E. von Weiher: *XXIX. und XXX. Vorläufiger Bericht über die von dem Deutschen Archäologischen Institut aus Mitteln der Deutschen*

Forschungsgemeinschaft unternommenen Ausgrabungen in Uruk-Warka, 1970/71 und 1971/72. UVB 29–30. Berlin, 1979

Schmidtke, F.: Wasserpflöcke (Gilg. XI 63), *Festschrift Friedrich*, pp. 427–34

Schmökel, H.: *Das Gilgamesch-Epos*. Stuttgart, 1966

Schneider, M.: Pukku und mikku. Ein Beitrag zum Aufbau und zum System der Zahlenmystik des Gilgamesch-Epos, *Antaios* 9 (1967), pp. 262–83

Schneider, N.: *Die Götternamen von Ur III*. AnOr 19. Rome, 1939

Schott, A.: *Das Gilgamesch-Epos*. Neu übersetzt und mit Anmerkungen versehen von Albert Schott. Durchgesehen und ergänzt von W. von Soden. Reclam, 2nd edn. Stuttgart, 1958

——Die inschriftliche Quellen zur Geschichte Eannas, *UVB* 1, pp. 45–67

——review of Dossin, *La pâleur d'Enkidu*, *OLZ* 36 (1933), 519–22

——Zu meiner Übersetzung des Gilgameš-Epos, *ZA* 42 (1934), pp. 92–143

Schramm, W.: Ein Adapa-Fragment aus Ninive, *Or* NS 43 (1974), pp. 162–4

——Zu Gilgameš Tf. VII, III, Z. 9 (Thompson, *EG* S. 45), *RA* 64 (1970), p. 94

Schroeder, O.: *Altbabylonische Briefe*. VAS 16. Leipzig, 1917

——*Die Tontafeln von El-Amarna*. 2 vols. VAS 11–12. Lepzig, 1915

——*Keilschrifttexte aus Assur verschiedenen Inhalts*. WVDOG 35. Leipzig, 1920

Schwartz, M.: Qumran, Turfan, and Arabic magic, in *Charmes et sortilèges. Magie et magiciens.* Res Orientales 15. Forthcoming 2002

Schwemer, D.: *Akkadische Rituale aus Ḫattuša. Die Sammeltafel KBo XXXVI 29 und verwandte Fragmente*. Texte der Hethiter 23. Heidelberg, 1998

Scurlock, Jo Ann: K 164 (*BA* 2, p. 635): new light on the mourning rites for Dumuzi?, *RA* 86 (1992), pp. 53–67

——*KAR* 267 // *BMS* 53: A ghostly light on *bīt rimki*?, *JAOS* 108 (1988), pp. 203–9

——Magical uses of Mesopotamian festivals, in Meyer and Mirecki (eds.), *Ancient Magic and Ritual Power*, pp. 93–107

——Soul emplacements in ancient Mesopotamian funerary rites, in Ciraola and Seidel (eds.), *Magic and Divination in the Ancient World*, forthcoming

——*Taklimtu*: a display of grave goods?, *NABU* 1991, no. 3

Sefati, Y.: *Love Songs in Sumerian Literature. Critical Edition of the Dumuzi-Inanna Songs.* Ramat Gan, Israel, 1998

Selz, G.: *Untersuchungen zur Götterwelt des altsumerischen Stadtstaates von Lagaš.* OPBF 13. Philadelphia, 1995

Shaffer, A.: Gilgamesh, the Cedar Forest and Mesopotamian history, *JAOS* 103 (1983), pp. 307–13

——Sumerian Sources of Tablet XII of the Epic of Gilgameš. PhD dissertation, University of Pennsylvania. Ann Arbor, Mich., 1963

——'Up' and 'down', 'front' and 'back'; Gilgamesh, XI 78 and *Atrahasis* III 29–31, *RA* 75 (1981), pp. 188–9

——הרקע המיסופוטאמי של קוהלת ד, ט-יב [The Mesopotamian background to Ecclesiastes 4: 9–12], *Eretz-Israel* 8 (1967), pp. 246–50

——ידיעות חדשות על מקור 'החוט המשלש' [New light on the three-ply cord], *Eretz-Israel* 9 (1969), pp. 159–60

Siegelová, Jana: Ein hethitisches Fragment des Atra-ḫasīs Epos, *ArOr* 38 (1970), pp. 135–9

Sigrist, M.: On the bite of a dog, *Essays Pope*, pp. 85–8

——D. I. Owen and G. D. Young: *The John Frederick Lewis Collection* 2. MVN 13. Rome, 1984

Silva Castillo, J.: *Nagbu*: totality or abyss in the first verse of Gilgamesh, *Iraq* 60 (1998), pp. 219–21

Sims-Williams, N. J.: From Babylon to China: astrological and epistolary formulae across two millennia, in *La Persia e l'Asia centrale da Alessandro al X secolo*. Atti dei convegni Lincei 127. Rome, 1996, pp. 77–84

Sjöberg, Å. W.: A blessing of King Urninurta, *Finkelstein Mem. Vol.*, pp. 189–95

——An Old Babylonian schooltext from Nippur, *ZA* 83 (1993), pp. 1–21

——Beiträge zum sumerischen Wörterbuch, *AS* 16, pp. 63–70

——*Der Mondgott Nanna-Suen in der sumerischen Überlieferung* 1. Uppsala, 1960

——Die göttliche Abstammung der sumerisch-babylonischen Herrscher, *Or Suec* 21 (1972), pp. 87–112

——Eve and the chameleon, in Barrick and Spencer (eds.), *In the Shelter of Elyon*, pp. 217–25

——in-nin šà-gur$_4$-ra: a hymn to the goddess Inanna by the en-priestess Enḫeduanna, *ZA* 65 (1975), pp. 161–253

——Miscellaneous Sumerian texts I, *Or Suec* 23–4 (1974–5), pp. 159–81

——Nungal in the Ekur, *AfO* 24 (1973), pp. 19–46

——The first Pushkin Museum elegy and new texts, *JAOS* 103 (1983), pp. 315–20

——Zu einigen Verwandtschaftsbezeichnungen im Sumerischen, *HSAO* I, pp. 201–31

——and E. Bergmann: *The Collection of Sumerian Temple Hymns*. G. B. Gragg: *The Keš Temple Hymn*. TCS 3. Locust Valley, NY, 1969

——et al.: *The Sumerian Dictionary of the University Museum of the University of Philadelphia*. Philadelphia, 1984–

Sladek, W.: Inanna's Descent to the Netherworld. PhD dissertation, Johns Hopkins University, Baltimore, 1974. Ann Arbor, Mich., 1974

Smith, G.: *Assyrian Discoveries*. London, 1875

—— *The Chaldean Account of Genesis*. London, 1876

——The Chaldean account of the Deluge, *TSBA* 2 (1973), pp. 213–34

——The eleventh tablet of the Izdubar legends: the Chaldean account of the Deluge, *TSBA* 3 (1874), pp. 534–87

Smith, S.: *Babylonian Historical Texts Relating to the Capture and Downfall of Babylon*. London, 1924

——The face of Humbaba, *AAA* 11 (1924), pp. 107–14

Soden, W. von: *Akkadisches Handwörterbuch*. 3 vols. Wiesbaden, 1965–81

——Aramäische Wörter in neuassyrischen und neu- und spätbabylonischen Texten. Ein Vorbericht, II (n–z und Nachträge), *Or* NS 37 (1968), pp. 261–71

——Assyrisch *ana ʾīni* < *ana mīni* und *suʾʾu* < *summu*, *AfO* 20 (1963), p. 82

——Aus einen Ersatzopferritual für den assyrischen Hof, *ZA* 45 (1939), pp. 42–61

——Beiträge zum Verständnis des babylonischen Gilgameš-Epos, *ZA* 53 (1959), pp. 209–35

—— (ed.): *Das Gilgamesch-Epos. Übersetzt und mit Anmerkungen versehen von Albert Schott*. Neu herausgegeben von Wolfram von Soden. Reclam, 4th edn, Stuttgart, 1982. 5th edn, Stuttgart, 1989

——Der große Hymnus an Nabû, *ZA* 61 (1971), pp. 46–71

——Der hymnisch-epische Dialekt des Akkadischen, *ZA* 40 (1931), pp. 163–227, *ZA* 41 (1933), pp. 90–183

——Die erste Tafel des altbabylonischen Atramḫasīs-Mythus. 'Haupttext' und Parallelversionen, *ZA* 68 (1978), pp. 50–95

——*Die lexikalischen Tafelserien der Babylonier und Assyrer in den Berliner Museen* 2. *Die akkadischen Synonymenlisten*. Berlin, 1933

——Ein spät-altbabylonisches *pārum*-Preislied für Ištar, *Or* NS 60 (1991), pp. 339–43

Soden, W. von: Gab es in Babylonien die Inanspruchname des *ius primae noctis*?, *ZA* 71 (1981), pp. 103–6
—— *Grundriss der akkadischen Grammatik*, 3rd edn. AnOr 33. Rome, 1995
—— Kleine Beiträge zu Text und Erklärung babylonischer Epen. 1. Ein neues altbabylonisches Bruchstück zum Gilgameš-Epos, *ZA* 58 (1967), pp. 189–92
—— review of Böhl, *Het Gilgamesj-Epos*, *OLZ* 50 (1955), 513–16
—— review of *Finkelstein Mem. Vol.*, *ZA* 69 (1979), pp. 155–7
—— review of Reclam^4, *ZA* 72 (1982), p. 162
—— review of Schott, *Das Gilgamesch-Epos* (Reclam^1), *OLZ* 38 (1935), 143–6
—— Status rectus-Formen vor dem Genitiv im Akkadischen und die sogenannte uneigentliche Annexion im Arabischen, *JNES* 19 (1960), pp. 163–71
—— Untersuchungen zur babylonischen Metrik, Teil I, *ZA* 71 (1981), pp. 161–204
—— Vokalfärbigen im Akkadischen, *JCS* 2 (1948), pp. 291–303
—— and W. Röllig: *Das akkadische Syllabar.* 4th edn. AnOr 42. Rome, 1991
Soldt, W. H. van: *Letters in the British Museum* [1]. AbB 12. Leiden, 1990
—— (ed.): *Veenhof Anniversary Volume: Studies Presented to Klaas R. Veenhof on the Occasion of his Sixty-Fifth Birthday.* Leiden, 2001
Sollberger, E.: Deux pierres de seuil d'Entena, *ZA* 50 (1952), pp. 1–28
—— *Pre-Sargonic and Sargonic Economic Texts.* CT 50. London, 1972
—— *Royal Inscriptions, Part II.* UET VIII. London, 1965
—— Selected texts from American collections, *JCS* 10 (1956), pp. 11–31
—— *The Babylonian Legend of the Flood.* London, 1971
—— The Rulers of Lagaš, *JCS* 21 (1967), pp. 279–91
—— The Tummal inscription, *JCS* 16 (1962), pp. 40–7
—— Une lecture du signe GÍN, *AfO* 16 (1953), p. 230
Sommerfeld, W.: Die mittelbabylonische Grenzsteinurkunde IM 5527, *UF* 16 (1984), pp. 299–306
—— Zu einigen seltenen akkadischen Wörtern, *Or* NS 53 (1984), pp. 444–7
Sonnek, F.: Die Einführung der direkten Rede in den epischen Texten, *ZA* 46 (1940), pp. 225–35
Sørenssen, Elizabeth G.: The Schøyen Collection. www.nb.no/baser/schoyen
Spaey, J.: Some notes on kù.babbar/*nēbiḫ kezēr(t)i(m)*, *Akkadica* 67 (Mar.–Apr. 1990), pp. 1–9
Speiser, E. A.: A note on certain Akkadian terms for door-equipment, *JCS* 2 (1948), pp. 225–7
—— Southern Kurdistan in the annals of Ashurnasirpal and today, *AASOR* 8 (1926–7), pp. 1–41
—— The Epic of Gilgamesh, *ANET*, pp. 73–99
Spek, R. J. van der: The Babylonian temple during the Macedonian and Parthian domination, *BiOr* 42 (1985), 541–62
Stamm, J. J.: *Die akkadische Namengebung.* MVAG 44. Leipzig, 1939
Starr, I.: Notes on some published and unpublished historical omens, *JCS* 29 (1977), pp. 157–66
Stefanini, R.: Enkidu's dream in the Hittite 'Gilgamesh', *JNES* 28 (1969), pp. 40–7
Steible, H.: *Die altsumerischen Bau- und Weihinschriften.* 2 vols. FAOS 5. Stuttgart, 1982
—— *Die Bau- und Weihinschriften der Lagaš-II- und Ur-III-Zeit.* 2 vols. FAOS 9. Stuttgart, 1989
Steiner, G.: Ḫuwawa und sein 'Bergland' in der sumerischen Tradition, *Acta Sum* 18 (1996), pp. 187–215
Steiner, R. C.: Ashurbanipal and Shamash-shum-ukin: a tale of two brothers from the Aramaic text in Demotic script, *RB* 92 (1985), pp. 60–81
—— Papyrus Amherst 63: A new source for the language, literature, religion, and history of the Aramaeans, in Geller et al. (eds.), *Studia Aramaica*, pp. 199–207

Steiner, R. C.: The Aramaic text in Demotic script, in Hallo (ed.), *The Context of Scripture* 1, pp. 309–27

Steinkeller, P.: Comments on the seal of Aman-Eshtar, *NABU* 1993, no. 9

——On rulers, priests and sacred marriage: tracing the evolution of early Sumerian kingship, in Watanabe (ed.), *Priests and Officials in the Ancient Near East*, pp. 102–37

——On the identity of the toponym LÚ.SU(.A), *JAOS* 108 (1988), pp. 197–202

——(z)a-áš-da = *kiššatum*, *RA* 74 (1980), pp. 178–9

Stephens, F. J.: collations of the Yale tablet (OB III), reported in *Or* NS 25 (1956), p. 273

Stol, M.: Diagnosis and therapy in Babylonian medicine, *JEOL* 32 (1991–2), pp. 42–65

——*Epilepsy in Babylonia*. Cuneiform Monographs 2. Groningen, 1993

——Gilgamesh Epic XI, 54, *AfO* 35 (1988), p. 78

——*Letters from Collections in Philadelphia, Chicago and Berkeley*. AbB 11. Leiden, 1986

——Milch(produkte). A. In Mesopotamien, *RLA* 8 (1993–7), pp. 189–201

——Milk, butter and cheese, *BSA* 7 (1993), pp. 99–113

——Old Babylonian fields, *BSA* 4 (1988), pp. 173–88

——review of *Studies Moran*, *BiOr* 49 (1992), 145–8

——*Studies in Old Babylonian History*. Leiden and Istanbul, 1976

——Suffixe bei Zeitangaben im Akkadischen, *WZKM* 86 (1996), pp. 413–24

Stone, Elizabeth C.: *Nippur Neighborhoods*. SAOC 44. Chicago, 1987

Streck, M.: *Assurbanipal und die letzten assyrischen Könige*. VAB 7. Leipzig, 1916

Streck, M. P.: *Die Bildersprache der akkadischen Epik*. AOAT 264. Münster, 1999

——*ittašab ibakki* 'weinend setze er sich'. *iparras* für die Vergangenheit in der akkadischen Epik, *Or* NS 64 (1995), pp. 33–91

——*Zahl und Zeit. Grammatik der Numeralia und des Verbalsystems im Spätbabylonischen*. Groningen, 1995

Stuckenbruck, Loren T.: *The Book of Giants from Qumran: Texts, Translation, and Commentary*. Tübingen, 1997

Sumner, W. M.: Tall-e Maljān, *RLA* 7 (1987–90), pp. 306–20

Szlechter, E.: *Tablettes juridiques et administratives de la III*[e] *Dynastie d'Ur et de la I*[re] *Dynastie de Babylone*. Paris, 1963

Talbot, H. F.: Ishtar and Izdubar, being the sixth tablet of the Izdubar series, *TSBA* 5 (1877), pp. 97–121

Talon, P.: *Enūma eliš* and the transmission of Babylonian cosmology to the West, in Whiting (ed.), *Mythology and Mythologies*, pp. 265–77

Théodore bar Koni: *Livre des scolies* I, trans. R. Hespel and R. Draguet. Louvain, 1981

Theodorus bar Kōnī: *Liber scholiorum* I. Louvain, 1954

Thompson, R. C.: *A Dictionary of Assyrian Chemistry and Geology*. Oxford, 1936

——A selection from the cuneiform historical texts from Nineveh (1927–32), *Iraq* 7 (1940), pp. 85–131

——*Assyrian Medical Texts*. London, 1923

——*Cuneiform Texts from Babylonian Tablets in the British Museum* 11. London, 1900

——*Cuneiform Texts from Babylonian Tablets in the British Museum* 12. London, 1901

——*Cuneiform Texts from Babylonian Tablets in the British Museum* 16. London, 1903

——*Cuneiform Texts from Babylonian Tablets in the British Museum* 17. London, 1903

——*Cuneiform Texts from Babylonian Tablets in the British Museum* 18. London, 1904

——*Cuneiform Texts from Babylonian Tablets in the British Museum* 22. London, 1906

—— *Cuneiform Texts from Babylonian Tablets in the British Museum* 23. London, 1906
—— *The Epic of Gilgamish*. Oxford, 1930
Thompson, R. C. and M. E. L. Mallowan: The British Museum excavations at Nineveh, 1931–32, *AAA* 20 (1933), pp. 71–186 and pls. 35–106
Thomsen, Marie-Louise: *The Sumerian Language*. Mesopotamia 10. Copenhagen, 1984
Thureau-Dangin, F.: *Lettres et contrats de l'époque de la première dynastie babylonienne*. [TCL 1.] Paris, 1910
—— *Receuil des tablettes chaldéennes*. Paris, 1903
—— Rituel et amulettes conte Labartu, *RA* 18 (1921), pp. 161–98
—— *Rituels accadiens*. Paris, 1921
—— *Tablettes d'Uruk à l'usage des prêtres d'Anu au temps des Séleucides*. Paris, 1922
—— Un hymne à Ištar de la haute époque babylonienne, *RA* 22 (1925), pp. 169–77
—— Une acte de donation de Mardouk-zâkir-šumi, *RA* 16 (1919), pp. 117–56
—— Une lamentation sur la dévastation du temple d'Ištar, *RA* 33 (1936), pp. 103–11
—— *Une relation de la huitième campagne de Sargon*. TCL 3. Paris, 1912
Tigay, J. H.: *The Evolution of the Gilgamesh Epic*. Philadelphia, 1982
Tinney, S.: *The Nippur Lament*. OPBF 16. Philadelphia, 1996
—— On the curricular setting of Sumerian literature, *Iraq* 61 (1999), pp. 159–72
Toorn, K. van der: Echoes of Gilgamesh in the Book of Qohelet? A reassessment of the intellectual sources of Qohelet, *Veenhof AV*, pp. 503–14.
—— *Family Religion in Babylonia, Ugarit and Israel. Continuity and Changes in the Forms of Religious Life*. Leiden, 1996
—— Gods and ancestors in Emar and Nuzi, *ZA* 84 (1994), pp. 38–59
Tournay, R. J., and A. Shaffer: *L'épopée de Gilgameš*. Paris, 1994
Tropper, J.: 'Beschwörung' des Enkidu? Anmerkungen zur Interpretation von GEN 240–243 // Gilg. XII, 79–84, *WO* 17 (1986), pp. 19–24
Tsukimoto, A.: *Untersuchungen zur Totenpflege (kispum) im alten Mesopotamien*. AOAT 216. Kevelaer and Neukirchen-Vluyn, Germany, 1985
Tunca, Ö., and Danielle Deheselle (eds.): *Tablettes et images aux pays de Sumer et d'Akkad. Mélanges offerts à Monsieur H. Limet*. Liège, 1996
Ucko, P. J., Ruth Tringham and G. W. Dimbleby (eds.): *Man, Settlement and Urbanism*. London, 1972
Unger, E.: *Babylon, die heilige Stadt*. Berlin and Leipzig, 1931
Ungern-Sternberg, J. von, and H. Reinau (eds.): *Vergangenheit in mündlicher Überlieferung*. Colloquium Rauricum 1. Stuttgart, 1988
Ungnad, A.: *Das Gilgamesch-Epos*. Göttingen, 1911
—— *Neubabylonische Urkunden*. 4 vols. VAS 3–6. Leipzig, 1907–8
—— Zwei neue Veröffentlichungen der Yale-Universität, *ZA* 34 (1922), pp. 15–23
Vallat, F.: Epopée de Gilgameš ou tablette économique de Persépolis? Ni l'un, ni l'autre!, *NABU* 1995, no. 46
—— Un fragment de tablette achéménide et la turquoise, *Akkadica* 33 (1983), pp. 63–8
Vanstiphout, H. L. J.: A further note on Ebiḫ, *NABU* 1991, no. 103
—— Reflections on the dream of Lugalbanda, *CRRA* 43, pp. 397–412
—— Shamshum aj-Jabbar: on the persistence of Mesopotamian literary motifs, *Veenhof AV*, pp. 515–27
—— The craftmanship of Sîn-leqi-unninnī, *OLP* 21 (1990), pp. 45–79
Veenhof, K. R. (ed.): *Cuneiform Archives and Libraries*. CRRA 30. Leiden and Istanbul, 1986

Veenhof, K. R.: Three Old Babylonian marriage contracts involving *nadītum* and *šugītum*, *Mélanges Finet*, pp. 181–9

Velde, C.: Enkidu's Rede vor den Weisen von Uruk: SpTU II 30 +(?) IV 123, *NABU* 1995, no. 78

Veldhuis, N.: Kassite exercises: literary and lexical extracts, *JCS* 52 (2000), 67–94

——review of Parpola, *SAA Gilg.*, *BiOr* 56 (1999), 388–92

Vincente, C.-A.: The Tall Leilān recension of the Sumerian King List, *ZA* 85 (1995), pp. 234–70

Virolleaud, C.: De quelques survivances de la légende babylonienne concernant la plante de vie, *Journal asiatique* 239 (1951), pp. 127–32

——*L'astrologie chaldéenne.* Fascicles 2 and 6. *Shamash.* Paris, 1907, 1905

——*L'astrologie chaldéenne.* Fascicles 3 and 7. *Ishtar.* Paris, 1908–9

——Quelques textes cunéiformes inédits, *ZA* 19 (1905–6), pp. 377–85

Vleeming, S. P., and J. W. Wesselius: *Studies in Papyrus Amherst 63*, 1. Amsterdam, 1985

Vogelzang, Marianna E., and H. L. J. Vanstiphout (eds.): *Mesopotamian Epic Literature: Oral or Aural?* Lampeter, UK, 1992

Volk, K.: *Die Balaĝ-Komposition Úru àm-ma-ir-ra-bi.* FAOS 18. Stuttgart, 1989

——*Inanna und Šukaletuda.* Wiesbaden, 1995

Vulpe, Nicola: Irony and the unity of the Gilgamesh epic, *JNES* 53 (1994), pp. 275–83

Waetzoldt, H.: Die eblaitische Entsprechung und die Bedeutung von nì-anše-aka, *NABU* 1990, no. 96

Walfish, B. (ed.): *The Frank Talmage Memorial Volume.* 2 vols. Haifa, 1993

Walker, C. B. F.: *Cuneiform Texts from Babylonian Tablets in the British Museum. Index to Parts I–L.* London, 1974

——Introduction, in Leichty, *Catalogue* VIII, pp. xi–xxv

——*Old Babylonian Letters.* CT 52. London, 1976

——The Kouyunjik collection of cuneiform texts: formation, problems, and prospects, in Fales and Hickey (eds.), *Austen Henry Layard tra l'oriente e Venezia*, pp. 183–93

——The second tablet of *ṭupšenna pitema*, an Old Babylonian Naram-Sin legend, *JCS* 33 (1981), pp. 191–5

——and M. Dick: *The Induction of the Cult Image in Ancient Mesopotamia: The Mesopotamian Mīs Pî Ritual.* SAALT 1. Helsinki, 2001

——and C. Wilcke: Preliminary report of the inscriptions, autumn 1975, spring 1977, autumn 1978, *Isin* II, pp. 91–102

Wasserman, N.: review of West, *East Face of Helicon*, *Scripta Classica Israelica* 20 (2001), pp. 261–7

——*Style and Form in Old Babylonian Literary Texts.* Leiden, forthcoming

Watanabe, Kazuko: Lebenspendende und todbringende Substanzen in Altmesopotamien, *Bagh. Mitt.* 25 (1994), pp. 579–96

——(ed.): *Priests and Officials in the Ancient Near East.* Heidelberg, 1999

Weadock, Penelope N.: The *giparu* at Ur, *Iraq* 37 (1975), pp. 101–28

Wegner, Ilse: *Gestalt und Kult der Ištar-Šawuška in Kleinasien.* AOAT 36. Kevelaer and Neukirchen-Vluyn, Germany, 1981

Weidner, E.: Altbabylonische Götterlisten, *AfK* 2 (1924–5), pp. 1–18, 71–82

——Ein neues Bruchstück der XII. Tafel des Gilgameš-Epos, *AfO* 10 (1936), pp. 363–5

——*Keilschrifturkunden aus Boghazköi* 4. Berlin, 1922

——*Keilschrifturkunden aus Boghazköi* 8. Berlin, 1924

Weiher, E. von: Die Tontafelfunde der XXIX. und XXX. Kampagne, *UVB* 29–30, pp. 95–111

——Ein Fragment der 5. Tafel des Gilgameš-Epos aus Uruk, *Bagh. Mitt.* 11 (1980), pp. 90–105

——Ein Fragment des Gilgameš-Epos aus Uruk, *ZA* 62 (1972), pp. 222–9
——Gilgameš und Enkidu: die Idee einer Freundschaft, *Bagh. Mitt.* 11 (1980), pp. 106–19
Weiher, E. von: *Spätbabylonische Texte aus Uruk* 2. ADFU 10. Berlin, 1983
——*Spätbabylonische Texte aus Uruk* 3. ADFU 12. Berlin, 1988
——*Uruk. Spätbabylonische Texte aus dem Planquadrat U 18* [*Spätbabylonische Texte aus Uruk*] 4. AUWE 12. Mainz, 1993
——*Uruk. Spätbabylonische Texte aus dem Planquadrat U 18* [*Spätbabylonische Texte aus Uruk*] 5. AUWE 13. Mainz, 1998
Weinfeld, M.: 'Partition, partition; wall, wall, listen': 'leaking' the divine secret to someone behind the curtain, *AfO* 44–5 (1997–8), pp. 222–5
Weippert, M.: Libanon, *RLA* 6 (1980–3), pp. 641–50
Weissbach, F. H.: *Die Inschriften Nebukadnezars II im Wâdī Brîsā und am Nahr el-Kelb.* WVDOG 5. Leipzig, 1906
Weissert, E.: Royal hunt and royal triumph in a prism fragment of Ashurbanipal (82-5-22, 2), in Parpola and Whiting (eds.), *Assyria 1995*, pp. 339–58
West, M. L.: Akkadian poetry: metre and performance, *Iraq* 59 (1997), pp. 175–87
—— *The East Face of Helicon.* Oxford, 1997
Westenholz, A.: *Old Sumerian and Old Akkadian Texts in Philadelphia* 2. *The 'Akkadian' Letters, the Enlilemaba Archive, and the Onion Archive.* Copenhagen, 1987
——review of R. A. di Vito, *Studies in Third Millennium Sumerian and Akkadian Personal Names*, *AfO* 42–3 (1995–6), pp. 217–22
——and Ulla Koch-Westenholz: Enkidu — the noble savage?, *Studies Lambert*, pp. 437–51
Westenholz, Joan Goodnick: A forgotten love song, *Studies Reiner*, pp. 415–25
——*Legends of the Kings of Akkade: The Texts.* Mesopotamian Civilizations 7. Winona Lake, Ind., 1997
——Oral traditions and written texts in the cycle of Akkade, *Mesopotamian Epic Literature*, pp. 123–54
Westenholz, Ulla, and A. Westenholz: *Gilgamesh, Enuma elish. Guder og mennesker i oldtidens Babylon.* Denmark, 1997
Whiting, R. M. (ed.): *Mythology and Mythologies.* Melammu Symposia 2. Helsinki, 2001
Wiggermann, F. A. M.: *Mesopotamian Protective Spirits.* Cuneiform Monographs 1. Groningen, 1992
——Nin-azu, *RLA* 9 (1998–2001), pp. 329–35.
Wilcke, C.: *Das Lugalbandaepos.* Wiesbaden, 1969
——Das modale Adverb i-gi$_4$-in-zu im Sumerischen, *JNES* 27 (1968), pp. 229–42
——Die akkadischen Glossen in TMH NF 3 Nr. 25 und eine neue Interpretation des Textes, *AfO* 23 (1970), pp. 84–7
——Die Anfänge der akkadischen Epen. 12. Gilgameš-Epos, *ZA* 67 (1977), pp. 200–11
——Die Emar-Version von 'Dattelpalme und Tamariske'. Ein Rekonstruktionsversuch, *ZA* 79 (1989), pp. 161–90
——Die Inschriftenfunde der 7. und 8. Kampagnen (1983 und 1984), *Isin* III, pp. 83–120
——Die Sumerische Königsliste und erzählte Vergangenheit, in von Ungern-Sternberg and Reinau (eds.), *Vergangenheit in mündlicher Überlieferung*, pp. 113–40
——Ein Schicksalentscheidung für den toten Urnammu, *CRRA* 17, pp. 81–92
——Ein weiteres Gilgameš-Fragment aus Emar?, *NABU* 1989, no. 5
——Familiengründung im Alten Babylonien, in Müller (ed.), *Geschlechtsreife und Legitimation zur Zeugung*, pp. 213–317

Wilcke, C.: Genealogical and geographical thought in the Sumerian King List, *Studies Sjöberg*, pp. 557–71

——'Gilgameš und Akka'. Überlegungen zur Zeit von Enstehung und Niederschrift wie auch zum Text des Epos mit einem Exkurs zur Überlieferung von 'Šulgi A' und von 'Lugalbanda II', *Fs Römer*, pp. 457–85

——Ḫuwawa/Ḫumbaba, *RLA* 4 (1972–5), pp. 530–5

——*Kollationen zu den sumerischen literarischen Texten aus Nippur in der Hilprecht-Sammlung Jena*. Berlin, 1976

——Liebesbeschwörungen aus Isin, *ZA* 75 (1985), pp. 188–208

——Lugalbanda, *RLA* 7 (1987–90), pp. 117–32

——Ninsun, *RLA* 9 (1998–2001), pp. 501–4

——Philologische Bemerkungen zum *Rat des Šuruppag* und Versuch einer neuen Übersetzung, *ZA* 68 (1978), pp. 196–232

——review of Hunger, *Uruk* I, *BiOr* 39 (1982), 141–5

——*Wer las und schrieb in Babylonien und Assyrien*. BAW Sitzungsberichte 2000, 6. Munich, 2000

——Zum Königtum in der Ur III-Zeit, *CRRA* 19, pp. 177–232

Wilhelm, G. (ed.): *Die orientalische Stadt: Kontinuität, Wandel, Bruch*. CDOG 1. Saarbrücken, 1997

——*Literarische Texte in sumerischer und akkadischer Sprache*. KBo 36. Berlin, 1991

——Neue akkadische Gilgameš-Fragmente aus Ḫattusa, *ZA* 78 (1988), pp. 99–121

——Zur babylonisch-assyrischen Schultradition in Hattuša, in *Uluslararası 1. Hititoloji Kongresi Bildirileri (First International Congress of Hittitology)*. Ankara, 1990, pp. 83–93

Winckler, H.: Vorläufige Nachrichten über die Ausgrabungen in Boghaz-köi im Sommer 1907. I. Die Tontafelfunde, *MDOG* 35 (1907), pp. 1–59

Wiseman, D. J.: A Gilgamesh epic fragment from Nimrud, *Iraq* 37 (1975), pp. 157–63

——A Late Babylonian tribute list?, *BSOAS* 30 (1967), pp. 495–504

——Additional Neo-Babylonian Gilgamesh fragments, in Garelli, *Gilg.*, pp. 123–35

——The Nabu temple texts from Nimrud, *JNES* 27 (1968), pp. 248–50

——and J. A. Black: *Literary Texts from the Temple of Nabû*. CTN 4. London, 1996

Woestenburg, Els, and B. Jagersma: The continuing story of Sippar-Amnānum = Sippar-rabûm, *NABU* 1992, no. 28

Wolff, Hope N.: Gilgamesh, Enkidu, and the heroic life, *JAOS* 89 (1969), pp. 392–8

Woodington, Nancy R.: A Grammar of the Neo-Babylonian Letters of the Kuyunjik Collection. PhD dissertation, Yale University, 1982. Ann Arbor, Mich., 1983

Woolley, C. L.: *The Royal Cemetery, a Report on the Predynastic and Sargonid Graves Excavated between 1926 and 1931*. UE 2. London and Philadelphia, 1934

Wu Yuhong: The earliest war for the water in Mesopotamia: Gilgamesh and Agga, *NABU* 1998, no. 103

Yang Zhi: *Inscriptions from Adab*. Changchun, 1989

Zadok, R.: *Répertoire géographique des textes cunéiformes* 8. *Geographical Names According to New- and Late-Babylonian Texts*. Beihefte zum Tübinger Atlas des vorderen Orients B 7, 8. Wiesbaden, 1985

—— *The Elamite Onomasticon*. Naples, 1984

Zettler, R.: Sealings as artifacts of institutional administration in ancient Mesopotamia, *JCS* 39 (1987), pp. 197–240

—— *The Ur III Temple of Inanna at Nippur: The Operation and Organization of Urban Religious Institutions in Mesopotamia in the Late Third Millennium B.C.* BBVO 11. Berlin, 1992

Zevit, Z., S. Gitin and M. Sokoloff (eds.): *Solving Riddles and Untying Knots: Biblical, Epigraphic and Semitic Studies in Honor of Jonas C. Greenfield.* Winona Lake, Ind., 1995

Zgoll, Annette: *Der Rechtsfall der En-ḫedu-Ana im Lied nin-me-šara.* AOAT 246. Münster, 1997

Ziegler, Nele: *Le harem de Zimrî-Lîm.* Florilegium marianum 4. Mémoires de NABU 5. Paris, 1999

Zimmern, H.: *Beiträge zur Kenntnis der babylonischen Religion.* AB 12. Leipzig, 1901

——Ein vorläufiges Wort über babylonische Metrik, *ZA* 8 (1893), pp. 121–4

——*Sumerische Kultlieder aus altbabylonischer Zeit.* 2 vols. VAS 2 and 10. Leipzig, 1912–13

——Ueber Rhythmus im Babylonischen, *ZA* 12 (1897), pp. 382–92

GENERAL INDEX

PHILOLOGICAL INDEX

SELECTIVE INDEX OF QUOTATIONS, PREVIOUS PUBLICATION, AND OTHER CITATIONS

INDEX OF CUNEIFORM TABLETS AND OTHER OBJECTS BY MUSEUM NUMBER

This list includes an entry for all cuneiform tablets used as sources of the Babylonian Gilgameš epic and of Bilgames and the Netherworld 172—end, for other cuneiform tablets published in the plates and for objects published in the figures. The abbreviations of period signal the chapter in which the tablets are edited, *viz.* OB (Old Babylonian) = Chapter 5, MB (Middle Babylonian) = Chapter 6, Ass (Assyrian) = Chapter 7, SB (Standard Babylonian) = Chapter 11, Sum (Sumerian) = Chapter 12. BN = Bilgames and the Netherworld.

Museum number		Period	Tablet	Siglum	Plate
Aleppo: National Museum					
M 9204n (Msk 7498n)+ 9211z (74104z)+9301d (74159d)		MB	—	MB Emar$_2$ a	29
M 9211z	see M 9204n+				
M 9212m (Msk 74105m)		MB	—	?	28
M 9238d (Msk 74128d)		MB	—	MB Emar$_1$	28
M 9301d	see M 9204n+				
Msk 7498n	= M 9204n+				
Msk 74104z	see M 9204n+				
Msk 74105m	= M 9212m				
Msk 74128d	= M 9238d				
Msk 74159d	see M 9204n+				
Ankara: Museum of Anatolian Civilizations					
Bo 284/d		MB	—	MB Boğ$_3$	25
S.U. 51/7		SB	VIII	**e**	34
S.U. 51/129A		SB	VII	**f**	98–9
S.U. 51/187	see Ch. 8, fn. 81				
S.U. 51/216	see Ch. 8, fn. 81				
Baghdad: Iraq Museum					
H 154		Sum	BN	pp	—
H 157		Sum	BN	qq	—
HL^3 286	= IM 52615				
HL^3 295	= IM 52750				
IM 21180*x*		OB	—	OB IM	14–15
IM 52615 (HL^3 286)		OB	—	OB Harmal$_1$	11
IM 52750 (HL^3 295)		OB	—	OB Harmal$_2$	12–13

Museum number		Period	Tablet	Siglum	Plate
IM 57836 (2N-T 75)		MB	—	MB $Nippur_2$	20
IM 58451 (3N-T 376)		OB	—	OB Nippur	10
IM 67564 (ND 4381)		Ass	(X–XI)	**z**	32–3
IM 67577 (ND 4405/4)		SB	I	**g**	46
IM 76873 (W 23130)		SB	III	aa	66–7
IM 76941 (W 22729/9)[1]		SB	II	bb	57
IM 76973 (W 22744/1 b)		SB	I	cc	52
IM 76985 (W 22554/7)		SB	V	dd	74–6
ND 4381	= IM 67564				
ND 4405/4	= IM 67577				
W 22554/7	= IM 76985				
W 22729/9	= IM 76941				
W 22744/1 b	= IM 76973				
W '23018' (23013?)		SB	II	ee	58
W 23130	= IM 76873				
2N-T 75	= IM 57836				
3N-T 376	= IM 58451				

Berlin: Vorderasiatisches Museum

VAT 4105		OB	—	OB VA+BM_1	17–19
VAT 9667 (Ass 21600r)		SB	VI	$\mathbf{a}_1$	89–91
VAT 10217		Ass	(IV)	**x**	28
VAT 10585b		Ass	(II)	$\mathbf{y}_1$	31
VAT 10586		SB	XI	**b**	137
VAT 10916		Ass	(II)	$\mathbf{y}_2$	31
VAT 11000		SB	XI	$\mathbf{c}_1$	138–9
VAT 11087		SB	XI	$\mathbf{c}_2$	138–9
VAT 11294		SB	XI	$\mathbf{c}_3$	138–9
VAT 11576		SB	VI	**d**	87
VAT 12890		MB	—	MB $Boğ_2$	26–7
VAT 14512		SB	IV	w_1	71
VAT 14513		SB	IV	w_2	71
VAT 17234		SB	I	x	51
VAT 19286 (BE 27125)		SB	III	y	68
Ass 21600r	= VAT 9667				
BE 27125	= VAT 19286				

Boğazkale, Turkey: Site Museum

Bo 83/614		MB	—	MB $Boğ_1$ c	24
Bo 83/615		MB	—	MB $Boğ_1$ d	25
Bo 83/625		MB	—	MB $Boğ_1$ a	24

[1] This tablet was on loan to the provincial museum of Misan at Amara when it was looted during the uprising in early 1991. The tablet's present whereabouts are unknown.

Museum number		Period	Tablet	Siglum	Plate
Bo 83/627+641+658		MB	—	MB Boğ$_1$ e	25
Bo 83/634		MB	—	MB Boğ$_1$ f	25
Bo 83/641	see Bo 83/627+				
Bo 83/658	see Bo 83/627+				
Bo 83/666		MB	—	MB Boğ$_1$ b	24
Chicago: Oriental Institute Museum					
A 3444		SB	II	z	56
A 22007 (Ishchali 35-T 117)		OB	—	OB Ishchali	16
A 29934 (2N-T 79)		MB	—	MB Nippur$_1$	20
Ishchali 35-T 117	= A 22007				
2N-T 79	= A 29934				
Istanbul: Archaeological Museum					
A 122+123		SB	VI	**a**$_2$	90–1
A 123	see A 122+				
A 124 B and C	see Ch. 8, fn. 73	SB	VI?	**a**?	91
Ni 2378		Sum	BN	BB	—
Ni 4249		Sum	BN	f	—
Ni 4585		Sum	BN	GG	—
Ni 9626		Sum	BN	JJ	—
Ni 9847		Sum	BN	HH	—
Jena: Hilprecht Sammlung					
HS 1482+2502+2612		Sum	BN	V	—
HS 2502	see HS 1482+				
HS 2612	see HS 1482+				
Jerusalem: Israel Museum					
Israel Museum 55-2		MB	—	MB Megiddo	30
Israel Museum 70.71.571	Clay plaque, see p. 477				Fig. 14
London: British Museum					
K 231		SB	VI	A$_1$	78–81
K 913+2756+2756E+2756F +6541+81-7-27, 93		SB	I	B$_1$	36–40
K 2252+2602+3321+4486+ Sm 1881		SB	XI	C	118–23
K 2360+3060		SB	IX	D	106–7
K 2589		SB	VII	E$_1$	92–3

Museum number		Period	Tablet	Siglum	Plate
K 2602	see K 2252+				
K 2756	see K 913+				
K 2756A+2756B+13874		SB	I	B_2	37–9
K 2756B	see K 2756A+				
K 2756C		SB	I	B_3	37
K 2756D+20778		SB	I	F_1	41
K 2756E	see K 913+				
K 2756F	see K 913+				
K 2774		SB	XII	G_1	142–5
K 3060	see K 2360+				
K 3252+8561		SB	V	H	72–3
K 3321	see K 2252+				
K 3375		SB	XI	J_1	124–7
K 3382+Rm 621		SB	X	K_1	108–13
K 3389		SB	VII	L_1	94–5
K 3423+Sm 2097+Rm 579		SB	III	M_1	61–2
K 3475+DT 13+81-2-4, 327		SB	XII	N	146
K 3588		SB	VII	L_2	94–5
K 3990+4579+DT 2+ Rm 578+Rm II 197		SB	VI	O_1	82–5
K 4465+9245+22153+ Sm 2133		SB	I	P	42–5
K 4474		SB	III	M_2	61
K 4486	see K 2252+				
K 4579	see K 3990+				
K 4579A+8018		SB	VI	Q_1	86–8
K 5335		SB	VI	A_2	79, 81
K 6497	see Ch. 8, fn. 68				
K 6541	see K 913+				
K 6899+8564+9716+ Rm II 262		SB	VIII	R	100–1
K 7017		SB	I	F_2	41
K 7224		SB	IV	S	65
K 7752+81-2-4, 245+ 296+460		SB	XI	T_1	128–30
K 8018	see K 4579A+				
K 8225		SB	XII	G_2	143–4
K 8226		SB	XII	U_1	143
K 8281		SB	VIII	V_1	103
K 8517+8518+8569+ 8593+8595		SB	XI	W_1	132–6
K 8518	see K 8517+				
K 8558		SB	III	M_3	61
K 8561	see K 3252+				

Museum number		Period	Tablet	Siglum	Plate
K 8564	see K 6899+				
K 8565+9997		SB	VIII	V_2	102
K 8569	see K 8517+				
K 8573		SB	III	M_4	62
K 8574		SB	II	X_1	55
K 8579		SB	X	K_2	109, 111
K 8584		SB	I	F_3	41
K 8586		SB	IV	Y_1	69
K 8587		SB	VIII	V_3	102–3
K 8589+Sm 1681		SB	X	K_3	108–9, 112–13
K 8590		SB	VII	Z_1	97
K 8591		SB	IV	AA	70
K 8593	see K 8517+				
K 8594+21502		SB	XI	W_2	136
K 8595	see K 8517+				
K 9196		SB	VII	E_2	93
K 9245	see K 4465+				
K 9716	see K 6899+				
K 9885+80-7-19, 306		SB	III	BB_1	63–5
K 9997	see K 8565+				
K 10777		SB	IV	CC	69–70
K 11659		SB	VII	E_3	92
K 12000Q		SB	I	F_4	41
K 13525		SB	IV	DD	69
K 13874	see K 2756A+				
K 13880	see p. 136	SB	?	—	35
K 14945 (Rm unnumbered)		SB	VI	Q_2	86, 88
K 15145 (Rm unnumbered)		SB	I	d_2	47
K 15193 (Rm unnumbered) +Sm 401+Sm 2194		SB	VI	Q_3	86–8
K 16024		Ass	?	YY	35
K 17343		SB	XI	W_3	136
K 18183		SB	IX	EE	102
K 19276		Ass	?	ZZ	35
K 19325		SB	VII	Z_2	97
K 19549		SB	VIII	V_4	102–3
K 20013		SB	VII	E_4	93
K 20778	see K 2756D				
K 21502	see K 8594+				
K 22153	see K 4465+				
DT 2	see K 3990+				
DT 13	see K 3475+				
DT unnumbered	see Sm 2112+				

Museum number		Period	Tablet	Siglum	Plate
Sm 401	see K 15193+				
Sm 1040		SB	IV	Y_2	69
Sm 1681	see K 8589+				
Sm 1754	see p. 739	SB	?	FF	35
Sm 1881	see K 2252+				
Sm 2097	see K 3423+				
Sm 2112+DT unnumbered		SB	VI	O_2	82–4
Sm 2131+2196+Rm II 383 +390+82-5-22, 316		SB	XI	T_2	128–9, 131
Sm 2132		SB	VII	GG	96
Sm 2133	see K 4465+				
Sm 2194	see K 15193+				
Sm 2196	see Sm 2131+				
Rm 289+unnumbered		SB	II	X_2	54–5
Rm 535	omens, see p. 113				35
Rm 578	see K 3990+				
Rm 579	see K 3423+				
Rm 616		SB	XI	J_2	124
Rm 621	see K 3382+				
Rm 751+BM 34853 (Sp II 357)+35546 (Sp III 52)		SB	X	f	116–17
Rm 785+956+1017+ BM 34248 (Sp 355)+ 34357 (Sp 472)		SB	I	d_1	47
Rm 853		SB	IV	u	71
Rm 907	see Ch. 8, fn. 52				
Rm 933		SB	XII	U_2	145
Rm 956	see Rm 785+				
Rm 964		SB	XII	HH	142
Rm 1017	see Rm 785+				
Rm unnumbered	see K 14945, 15145,15193				
Rm II 197	see K 3990+				
Rm II 262	see K 6899+				
Rm II 383	see Sm 2131+				
Rm II 390	see Sm 2131+				
Rm II 399		SB	VII	Z_3	96
Sp 265	= BM 34160				
Sp 297	= BM 34191				
Sp 299	= BM 34193, see BM 34160+				
Sp 355	= BM 34248, see Rm 785+				

Museum number		Period	Tablet	Siglum	Plate
81-2-4, 296	see K 7752+				
81-2-4, 327	see K 3475+				
81-2-4, 460	see K 7752+				
81-6-25, 454	= BM 41835, see BM 34191+				
81-6-25, 482	= BM 41862				
81-7-6, 314	= BM 45883				
81-7-6, 446	= BM 46002				
81-7-27, 93	see K 913+				
81-11-3, 840	= BM 48131				
82-5-22, 316	see Sm 2131+				
82-5-22, 466	= BM 54325				
82-5-22, 1230	= BM 54900, see BM 54325+				
82-9-18, 12726	= BM 72719				
83-1-21, 1788	= BM 93052				
83-1-21, 2238	= BM 99876				
1902-10-11, 28	= BM 96974				
Ki 1904-10-9, 19	= BM 98990				
1973-6-18, 1	= BM 135909				
BM 30559+32418 (S† 76-11-17, 286+2152)		SB	XII	a	147
BM 32418	see BM 30559+				
BM 34160+34193+35174+35348+35413+35628 (Sp 265+299+Sp II 726+922+998+Sp III 140)		SB	X	b	114–15
BM 34191+41835 (Sp 297+81-6-25, 454)		SB	III	c	59
BM 34193	see BM 34160+				
BM 34248	see Rm 785+				
BM 34314 (Sp 426)	see p. 136	SB	?	—	115
BM 34357	see Rm 785+				
BM 34449 (Sp 573)		SB	II	e	53
BM 34853	see Rm 751+				
BM 34873 (Sp II 380)		SB	VII	g_1	77
BM 34916+35419 (Sp II 431+1006)		SB	I	h	48–9
BM 35079+35103 (Sp II 614+645)		SB	III	i	68
BM 35103	see BM 35079+				
BM 35174	see BM 34160+				
BM 35245 (Sp II 812)		SB	VII	g_2	77
BM 35348	see BM 34160+				
BM 35380 (Sp II 960)		SB	XI	j	140–1

Museum number		Period	Tablet	Siglum	Plate
BM 35413	see BM 34160+				
BM 35419	see BM 34916+				
BM 35546	see Rm 751+				
BM 35567 (Sp III 74)		SB	II	k	53
BM 35628	see BM 34160+				
BM 36909+37023 (80-6-17, 660+767)+F 235		SB	VIII	m_1	104–5
BM 37023	see BM 36909+				
BM 37163 (80-6-17, 913) +F 234		SB	I	n	50
BM 37189 (80-6-17, 942)		SB	VIII	m_2	104
BM 38538 (80-11-12, 422)		SB	I	o	50
BM 38833 (80-11-12, 718)		SB	II	p	53
BM 41862 (81-6-25, 482)		SB	XII	q	147
BM 41835	see BM 34191+				
BM 45883 (81-7-6, 314)		SB	IV	r	71
BM 46002 (81-7-6, 446)		SB	VII	g_3	77
BM 54325+54900 (82-5-22, 466+1230)		Sum	BN	kk_1	—
BM 54900	see BM 54325+				
BM 72719 (82-9-18, 12726)		SB	II	s	55
BM 93052 (83-1-21, 1788)		SB	IV	t	52
BM 96974 (1902-10-11, 28)		OB	—	OB VA+BM_2	18–19
BM 98990 (Ki 1904-10-9, 19)		SB	III	BB_2	63–5
BM 99876 (83-1-21, 2238)		Sum	BN	kk_2	—
BM 135909 (1973-6-18, 1)		SB	XII	KK	144–5
F 234	see BM 37163+				
F 235	see BM 36909+				
U 9364		Sum	BN	r	—
U 16874		Sum	BN	t	—
U 16878		Sum	BN	ll	—
U 17900L		Sum	BN	nn	—
U unnumbered (UET VI 59)		Sum	BN	mm	—
U unnumbered (UET VI 394)		MB	—	MB Ur	22–3

New Haven: Yale Babylonian Collection

YBC 2178		OB	III	OB III	4–6

Oxford: Ashmolean Museum

Ash. 1924.1795	See Ch. 8, fn. 46				

Philadelphia: University Museum

CBS 7771		OB	II	OB II	1–3
CBS 10400		Sum	BN	W	—

Museum number		Period	Tablet	Siglum	Plate
CBS 13116+15360		Sum	BN	DD	—
CBS 14167		MB	—	MB Nippur$_4$	21
CBS 15150+19950+UM 29-13-438+N 3280+ 3474+3634		Sum	BN	H	—
CBS 15360	see CBS 13116+				
CBS 19950	see CBS 15150+				
N 1470		Sum	BN	CC	—
N 2696	see UM 29-16-463+				
N 3162	see UM 29-16-463+				
N 3280	see CBS 15150+				
N 3474	see CBS 15150+				
N 3634	see CBS 15150+				
N 4507		Sum	BN	TT	—
UM 29-13-438	see CBS 15150+				
UM 29-13-536		Sum	BN	FF	—
UM 29-13-570		OB	—	OB UM	7
UM 29-15-847		OB	BN	SS	—
UM 29-15-993		Sum	BN	AA	—
UM 29-16-58		Sum	BN	Z	—
UM 29-16-463+ N 2696+3162		Sum	BN	Y	—
UM 29-16-606		MB	—	MB Nippur$_3$	21
3N-T 902, 66		Sum	BN	UU	—
3N-T 908, 302		Sum	BN	CCC	—
3N-T 918, 443		Sum	BN	DDD	—
3N-T 923, 498		Sum	BN	EEE	—
3N-T 923, 500		Sum	BN	FFF	—
3N-T 927, 527		Sum	BN	EE	—

Private collections: Schøyen Collection, Norway

SC 1989	Cylinder seal, see p. 101				Fig. 1
SC 2652/5		OB	—	OB Schøyen$_1$	7
SC 2887		Sum	BN	rr$_1$	Fig. 15
SC 3025		OB	—	OB Schøyen$_2$	8–9
SC 3361		Sum	BN	rr$_2$	Fig. 15
SC 4577	Macehead, see p. 123				Fig. 2

Private collections: anonymous owners

—		MB	—	MB Emar$_2$ b	29
—		MB	—	MB Emar$_2$ c	29
—		SB	IV	v	52

CBS 7771

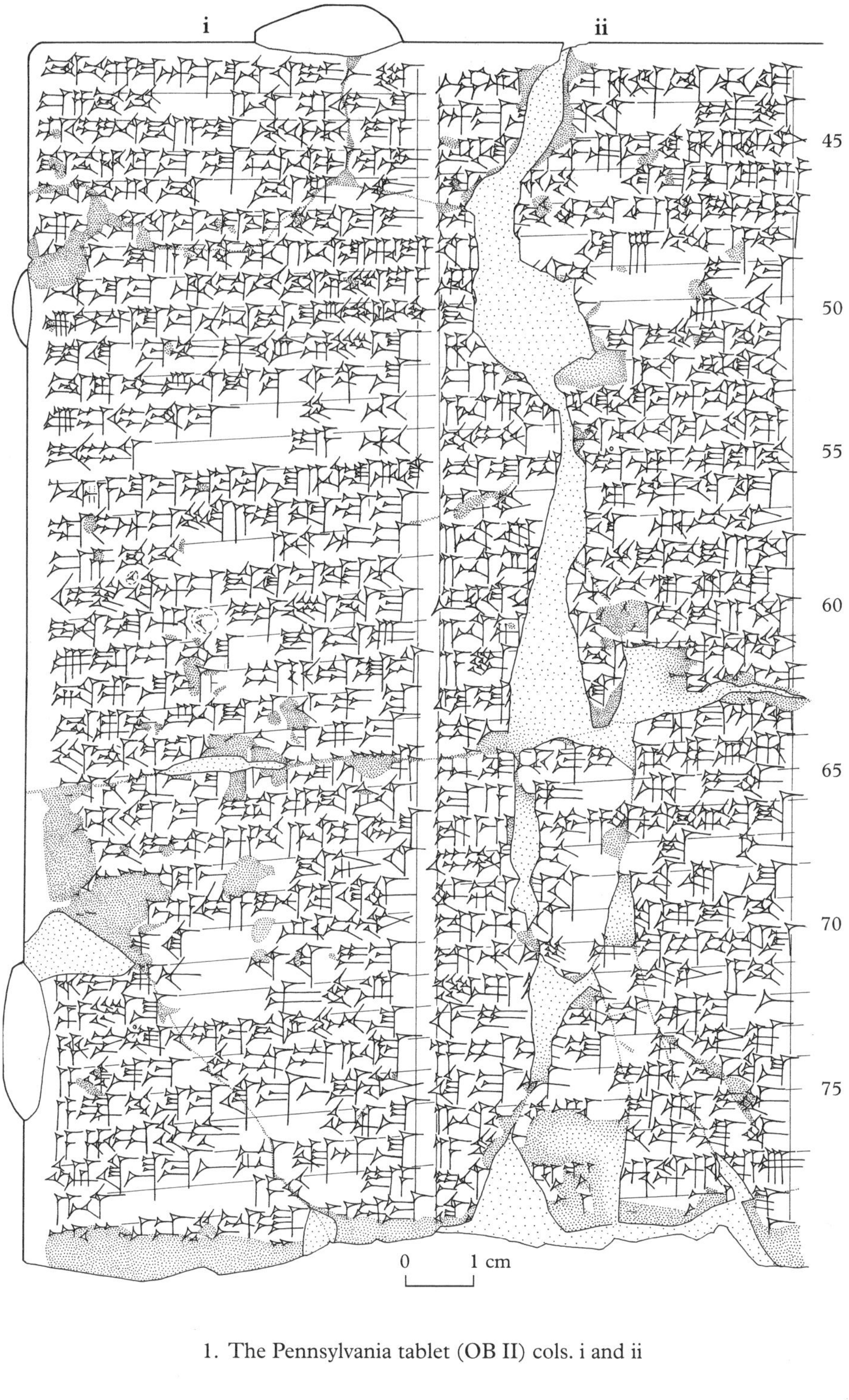

1. The Pennsylvania tablet (OB II) cols. i and ii

CBS 7771

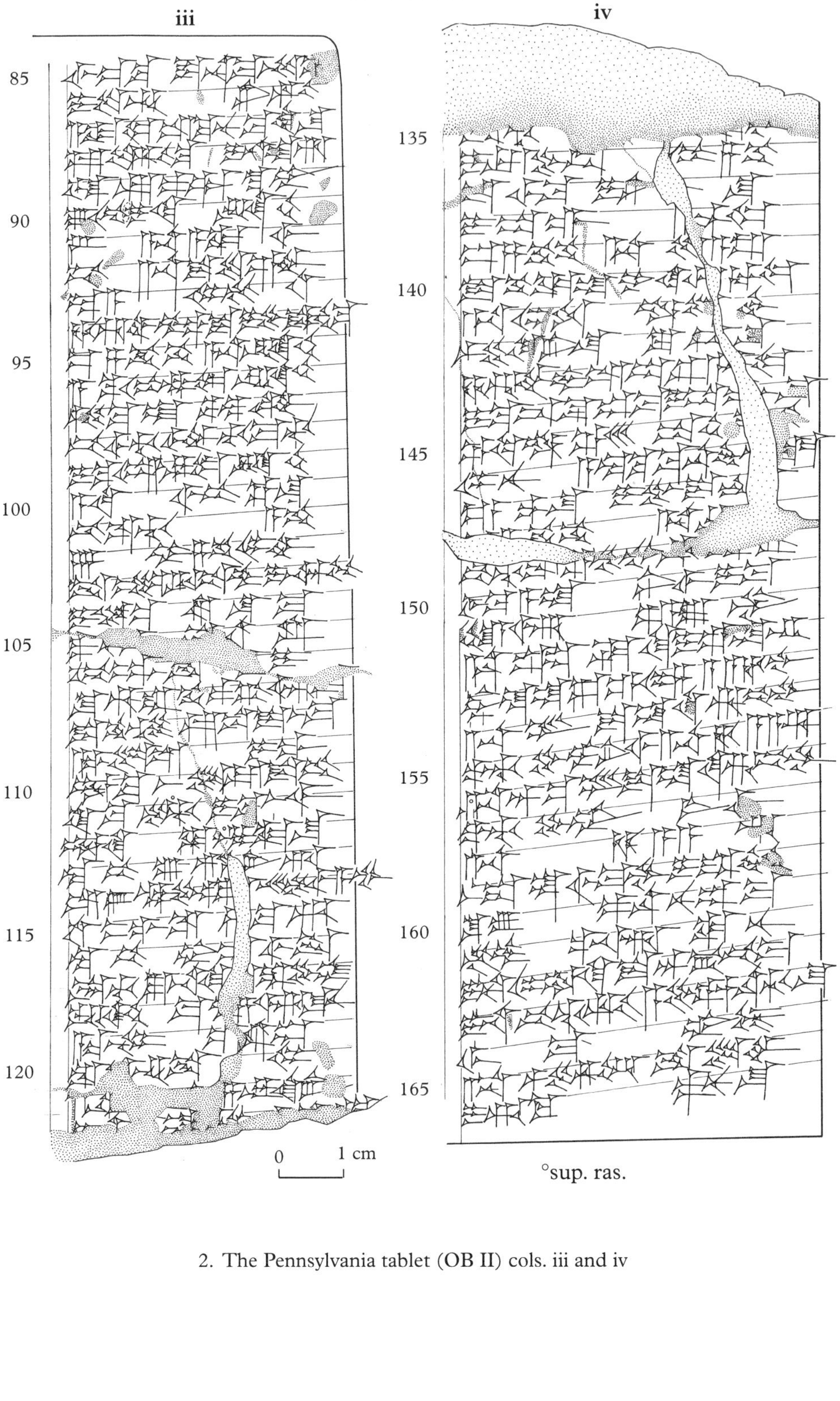

2. The Pennsylvania tablet (OB II) cols. iii and iv

CBS 7771

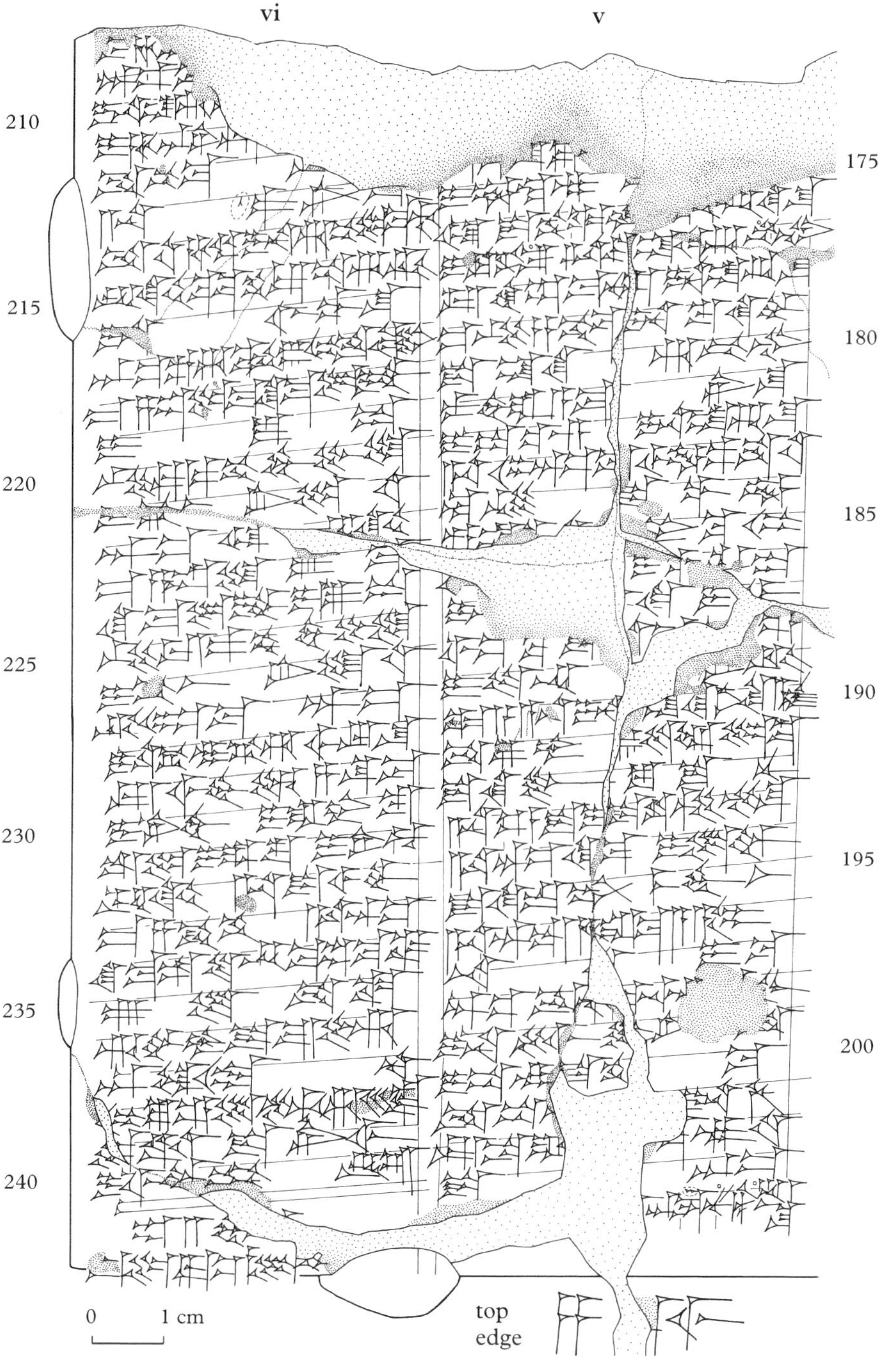

3. The Pennsylvania tablet (OB II) cols. v and vi

YBC 2178

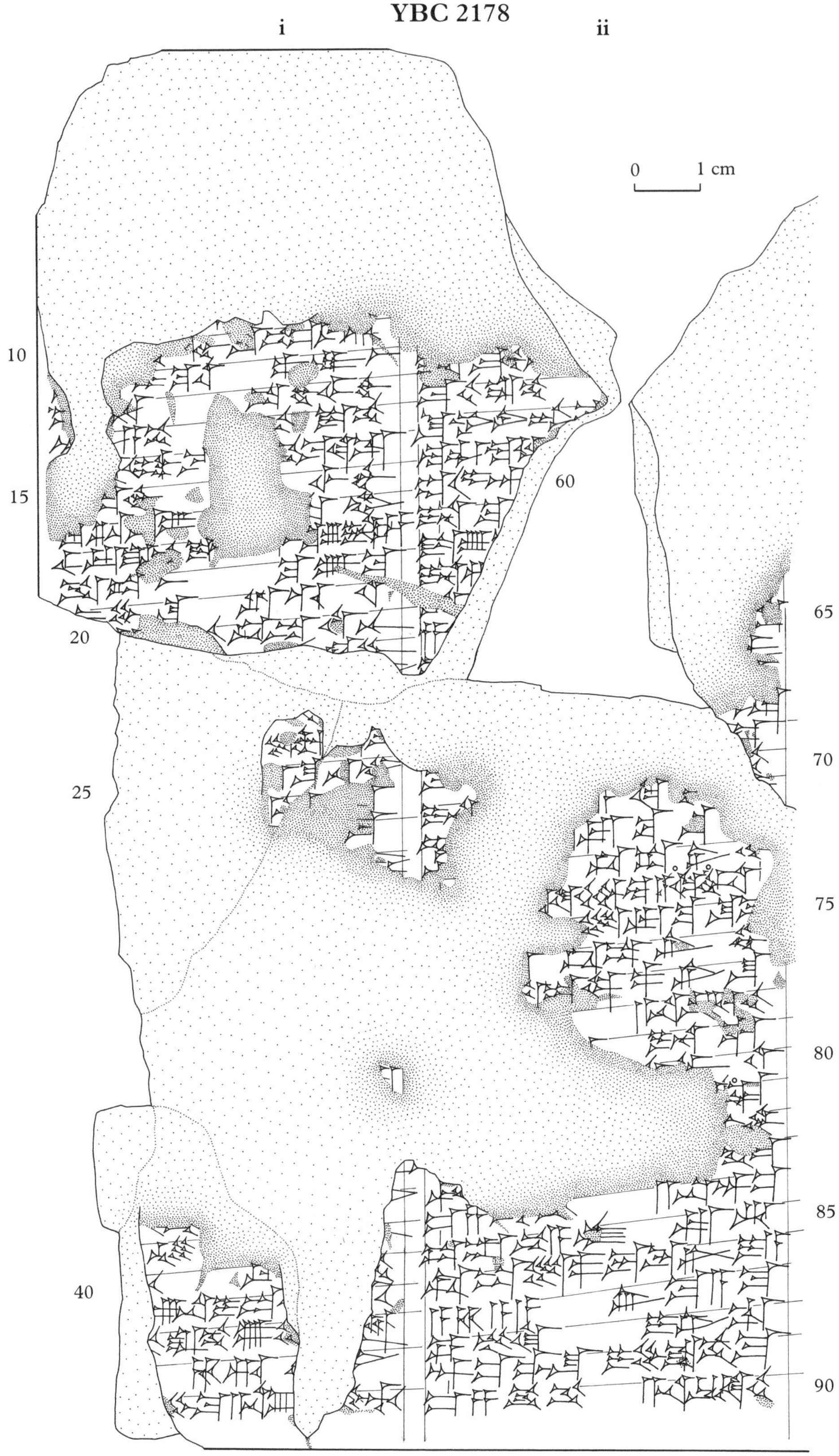

4. The Yale tablet (OB III) cols. i and ii

YBC 2178

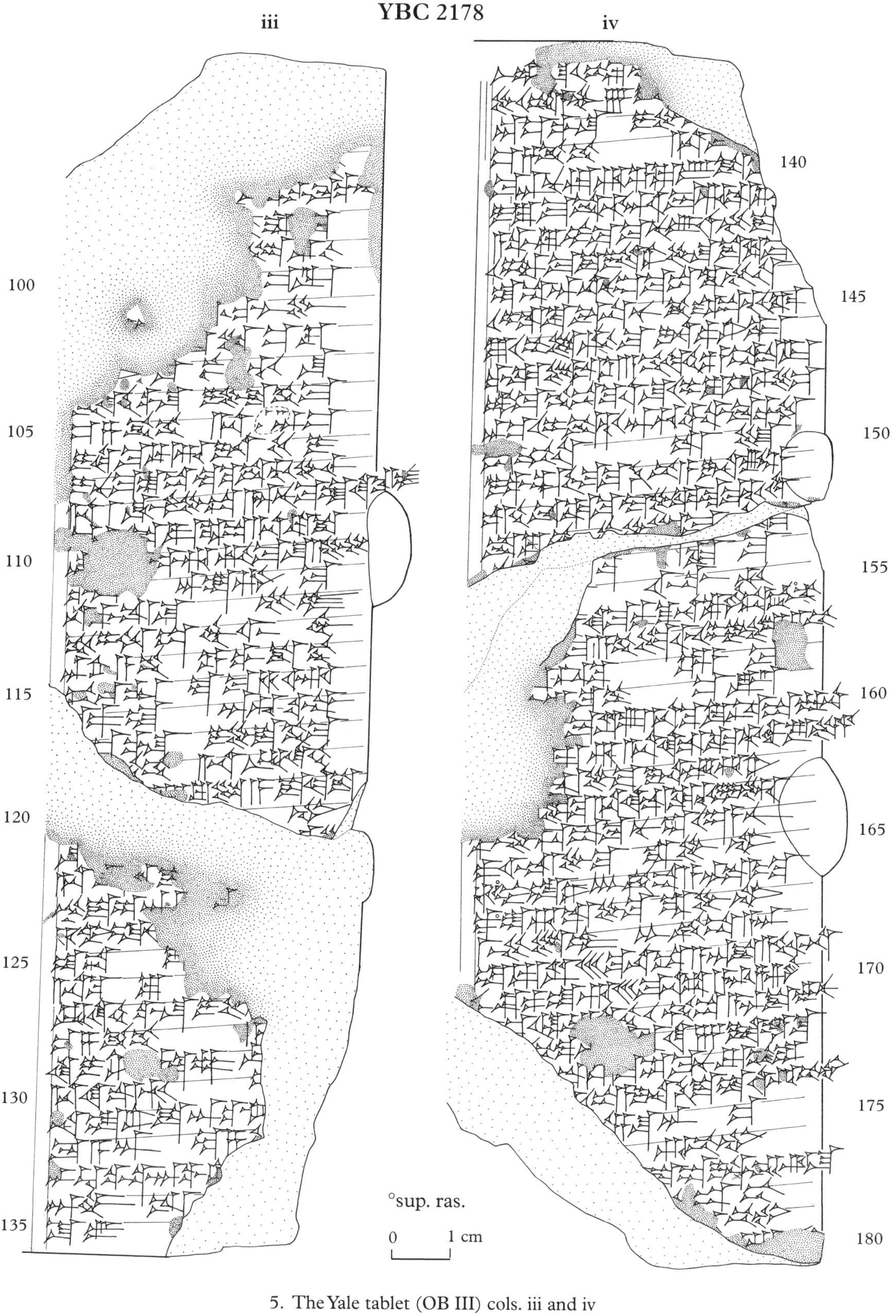

5. The Yale tablet (OB III) cols. iii and iv

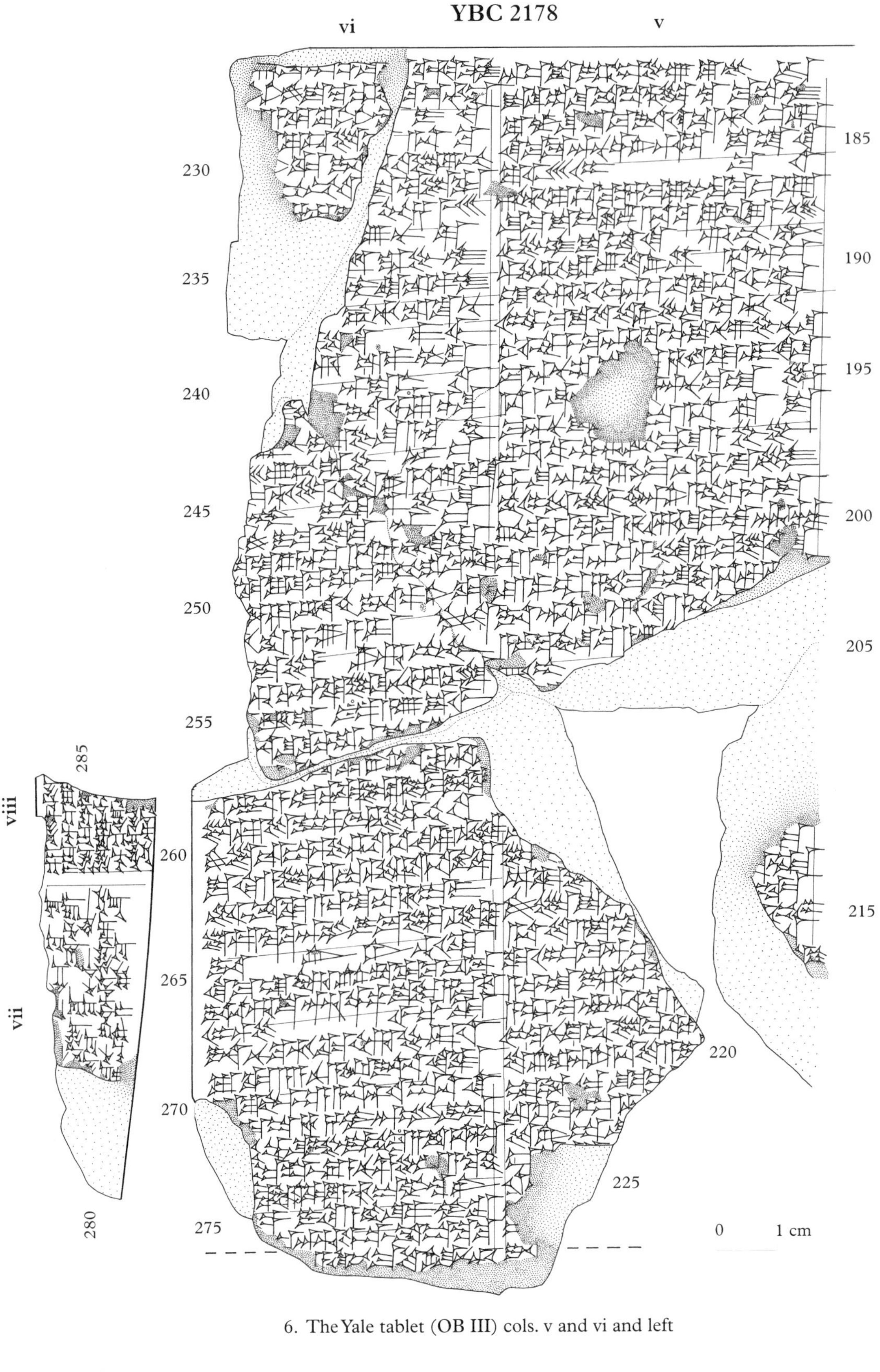

6. The Yale tablet (OB III) cols. v and vi and left

UM 29-13-570

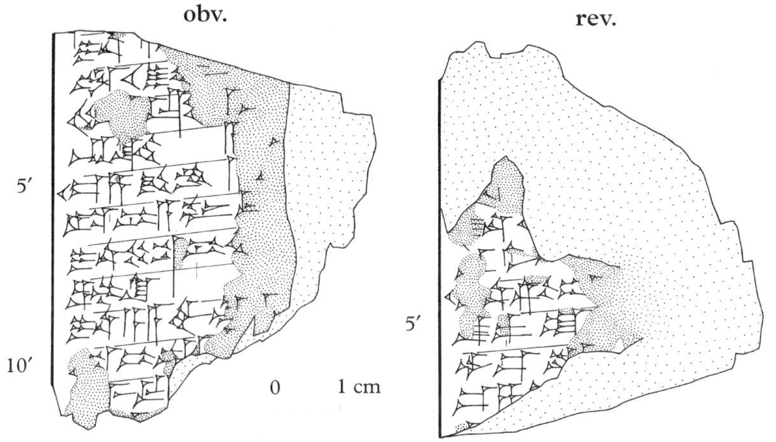

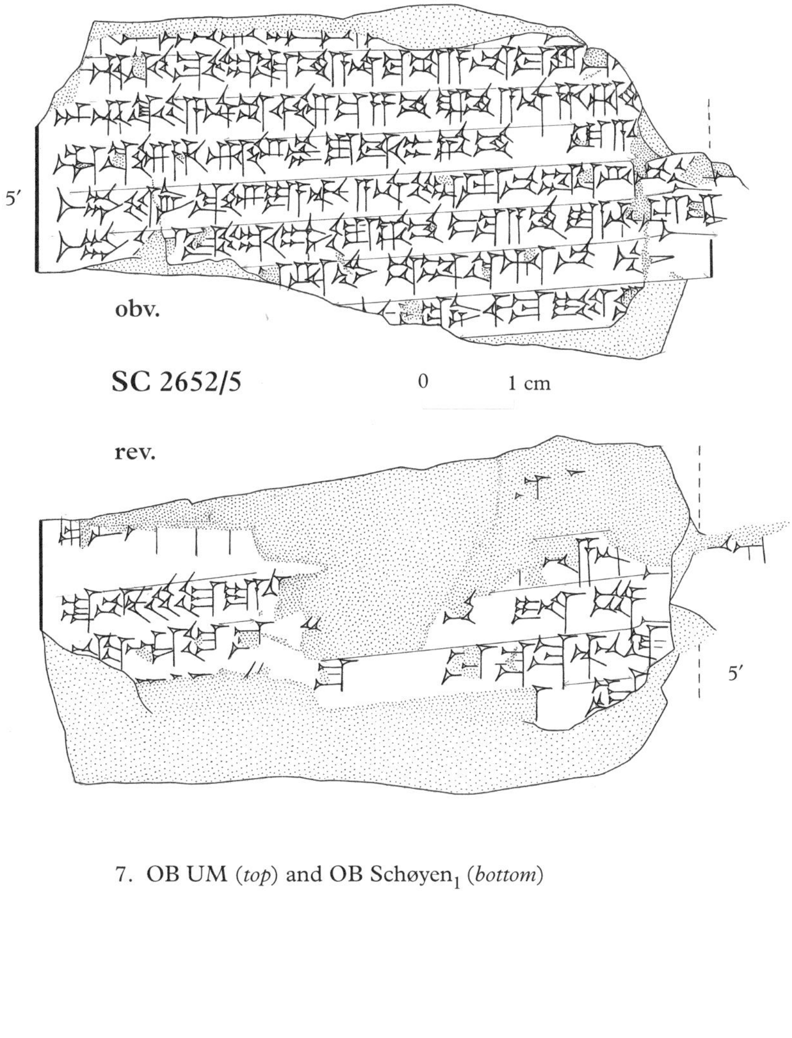

7. OB UM (*top*) and OB Schøyen$_1$ (*bottom*)

SC 3025

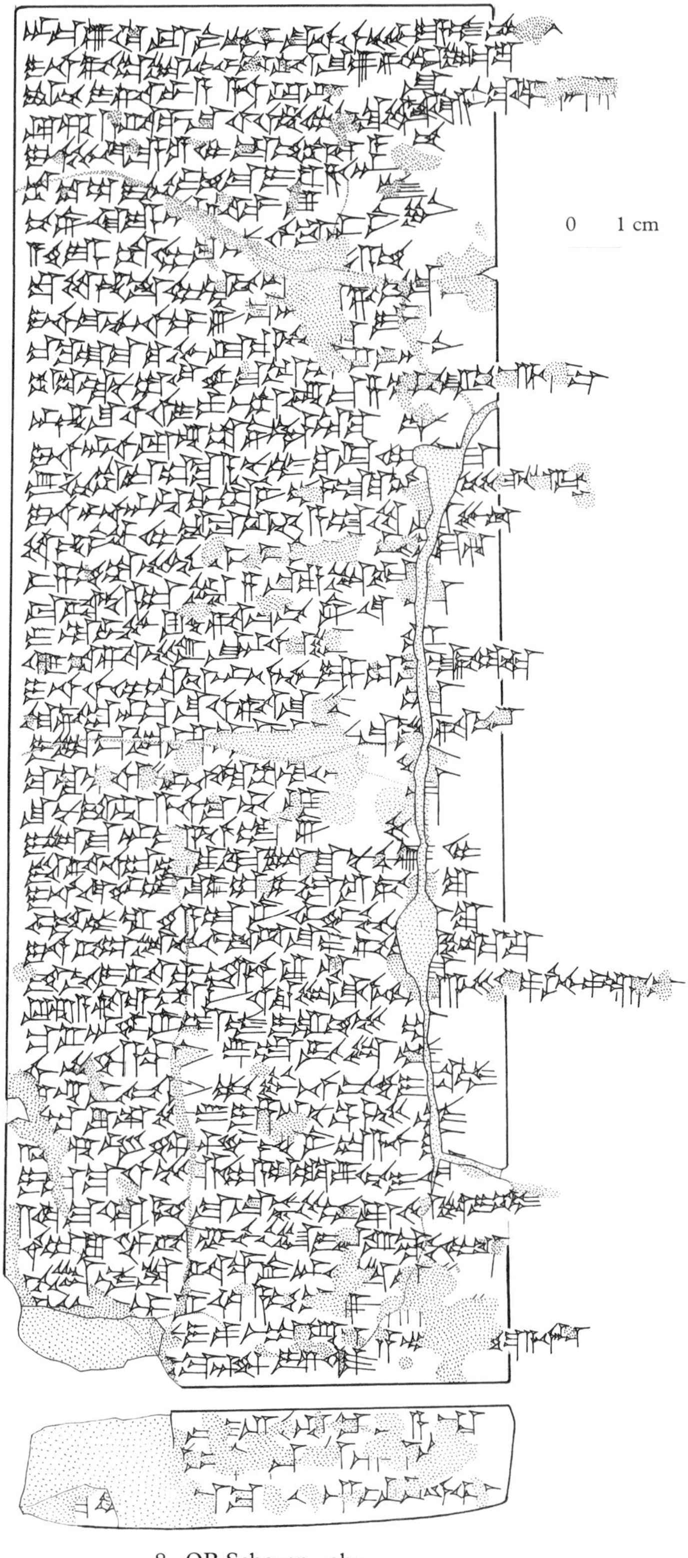

8. OB Schøyen$_2$ obv.

SC 3025

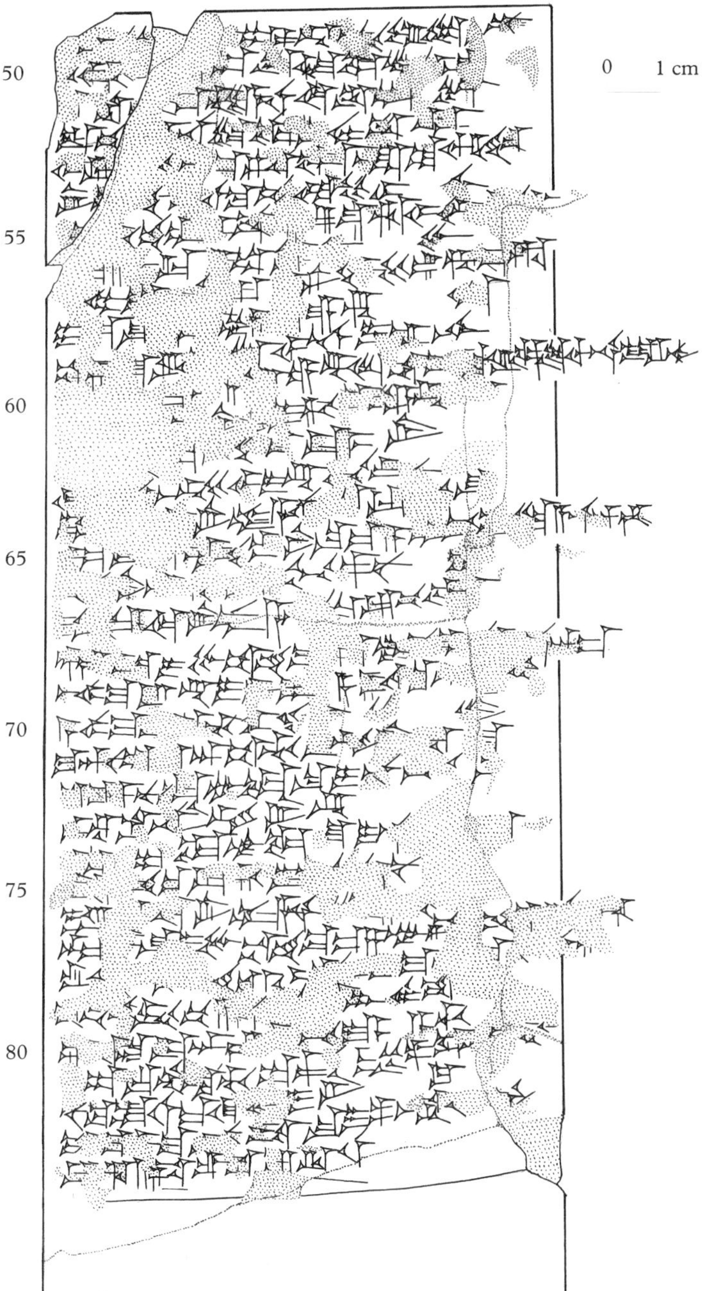

9. OB Schøyen$_2$ rev.

IM 58451

obv. rev.

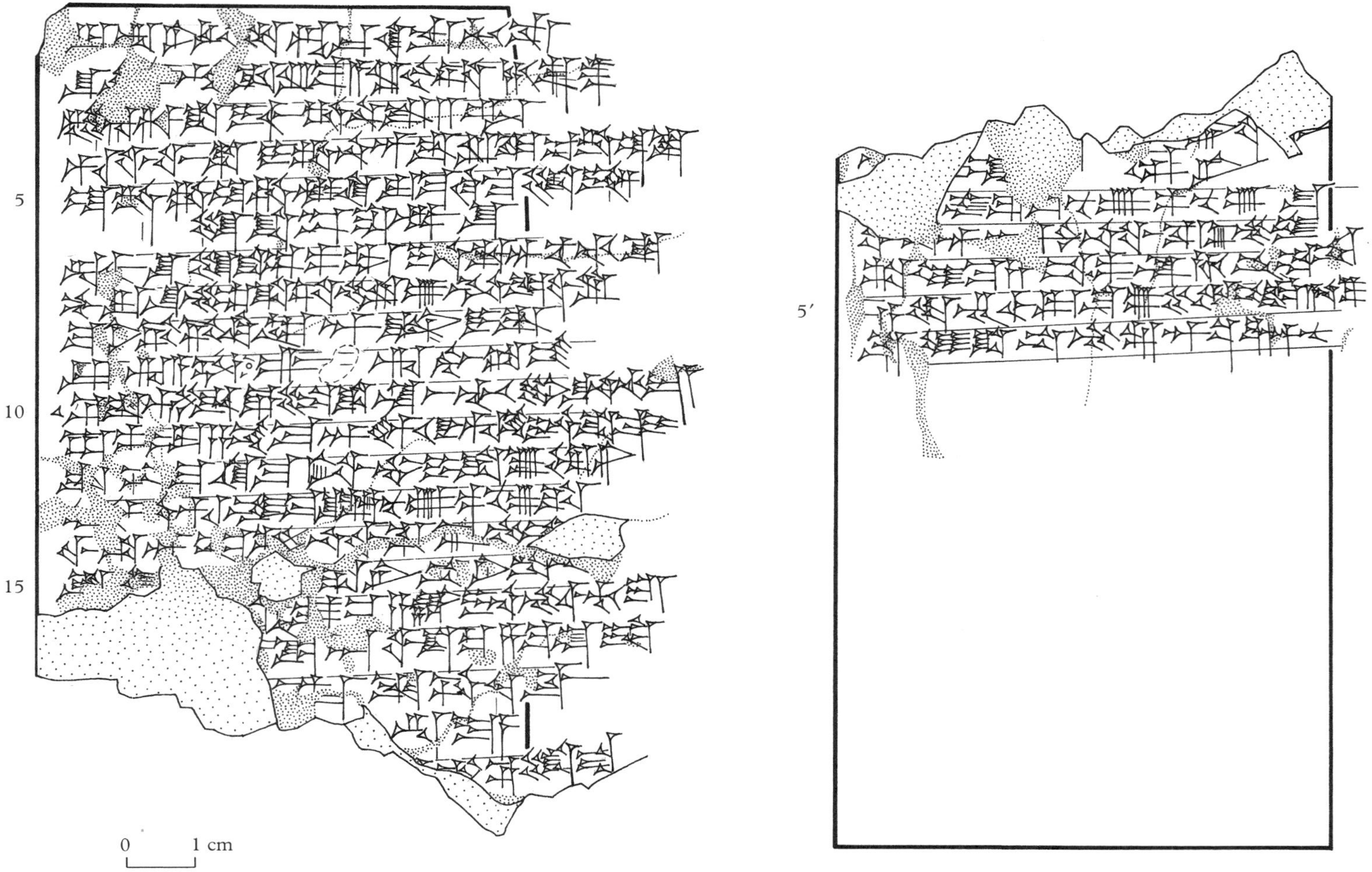

10. OB Nippur

IM 52615

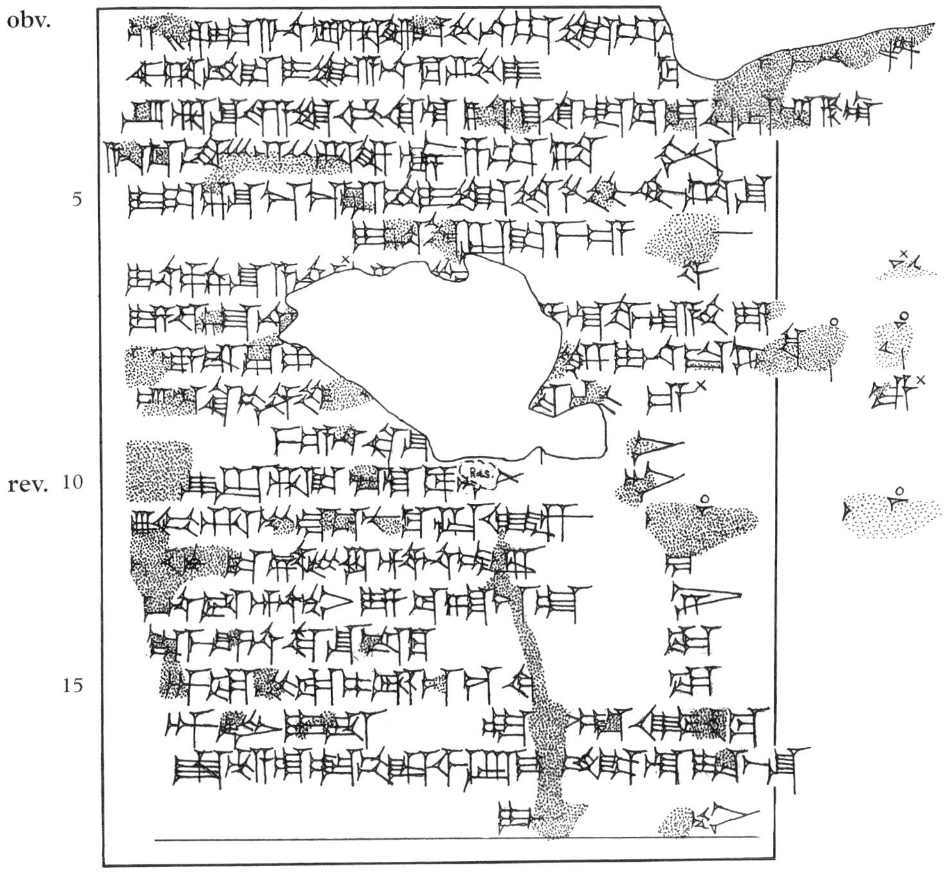

11. OB Harmal$_1$. Copy by W. G. Lambert, collations by the author

IM 52750 obv.

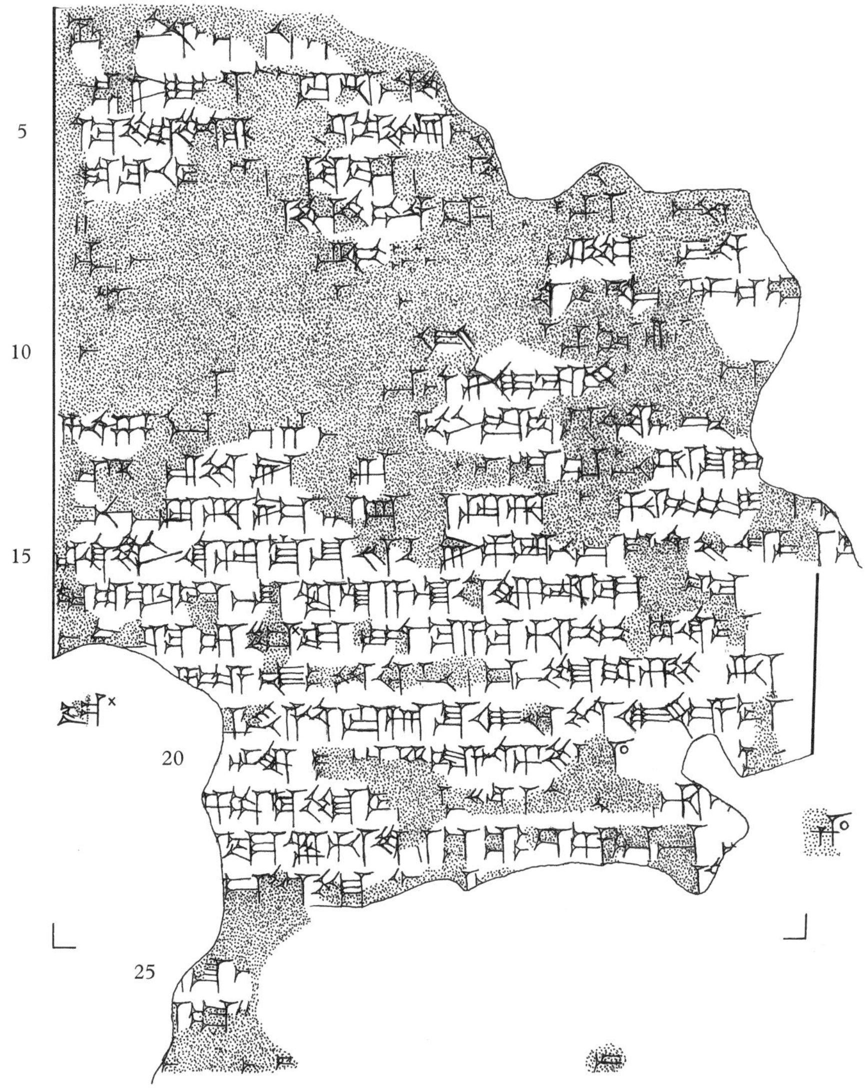

12. OB Harmal$_2$ obv. Copy by W. G. Lambert, collations by the author

IM 52750 rev.

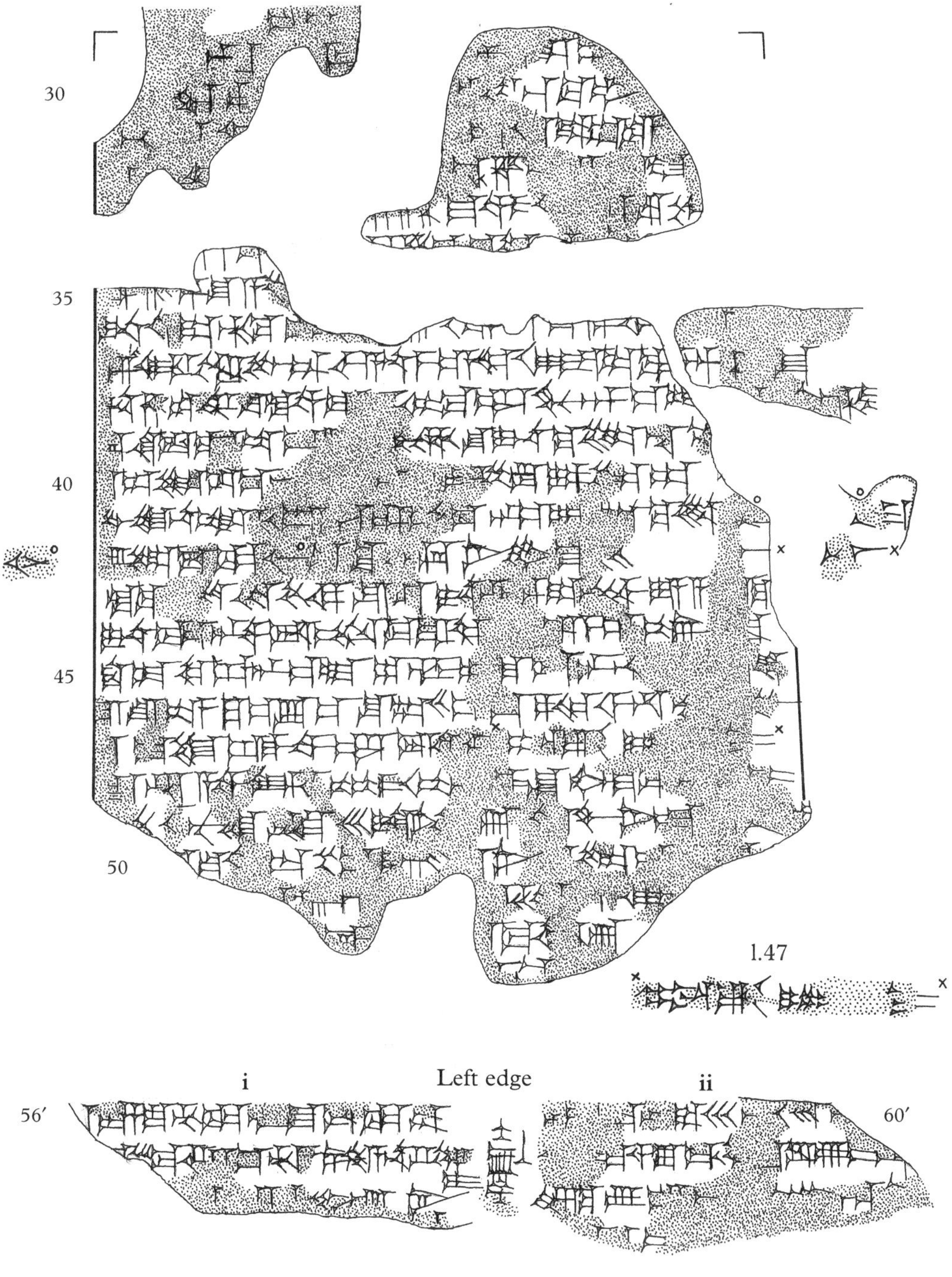

13. OB Harmal$_2$ rev. Copy by W. G. Lambert, collations by the author

IM 21180*x*

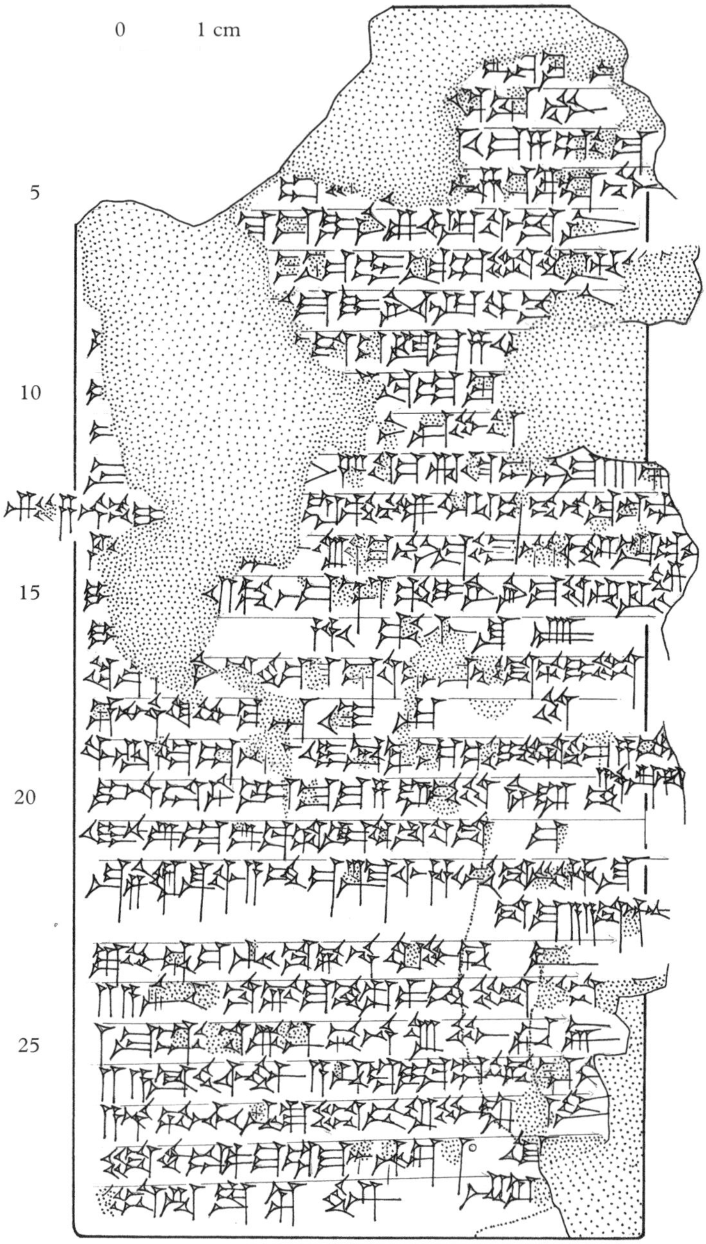

°ras. ?

14. OB IM obv.

IM 21180*x*

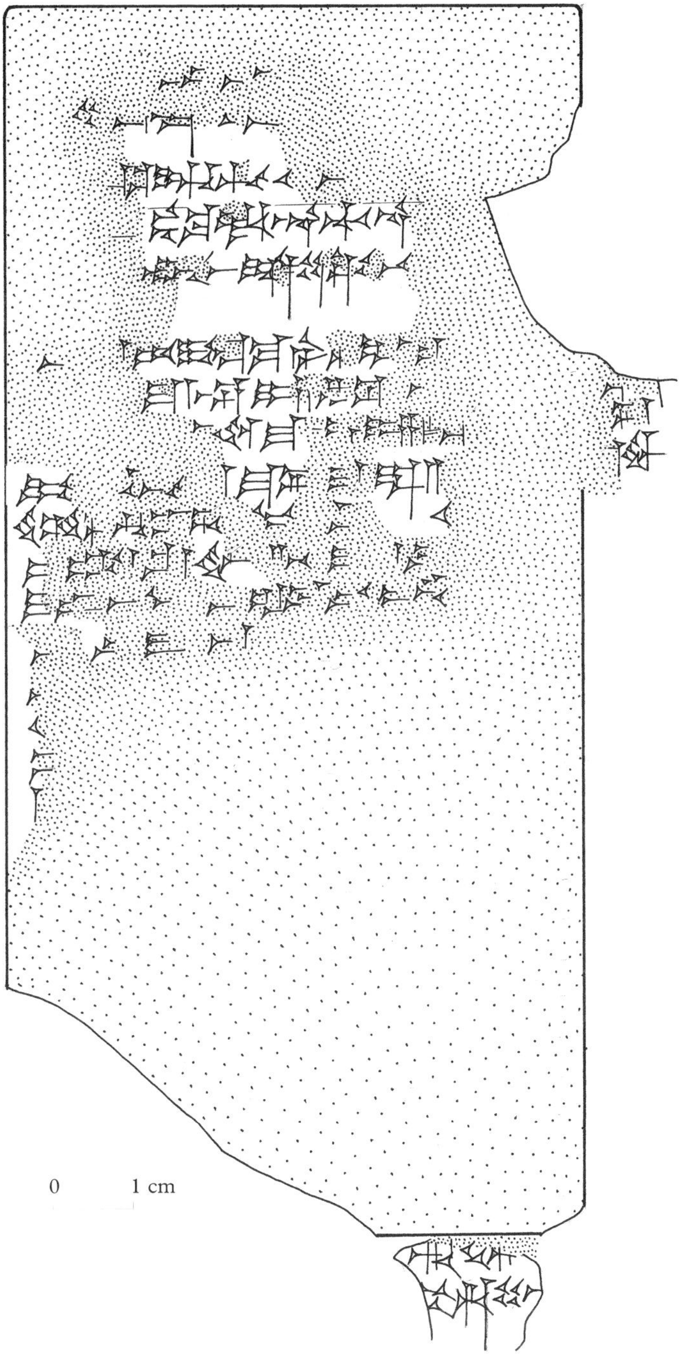

15. OB IM rev. and top edge

A 22007

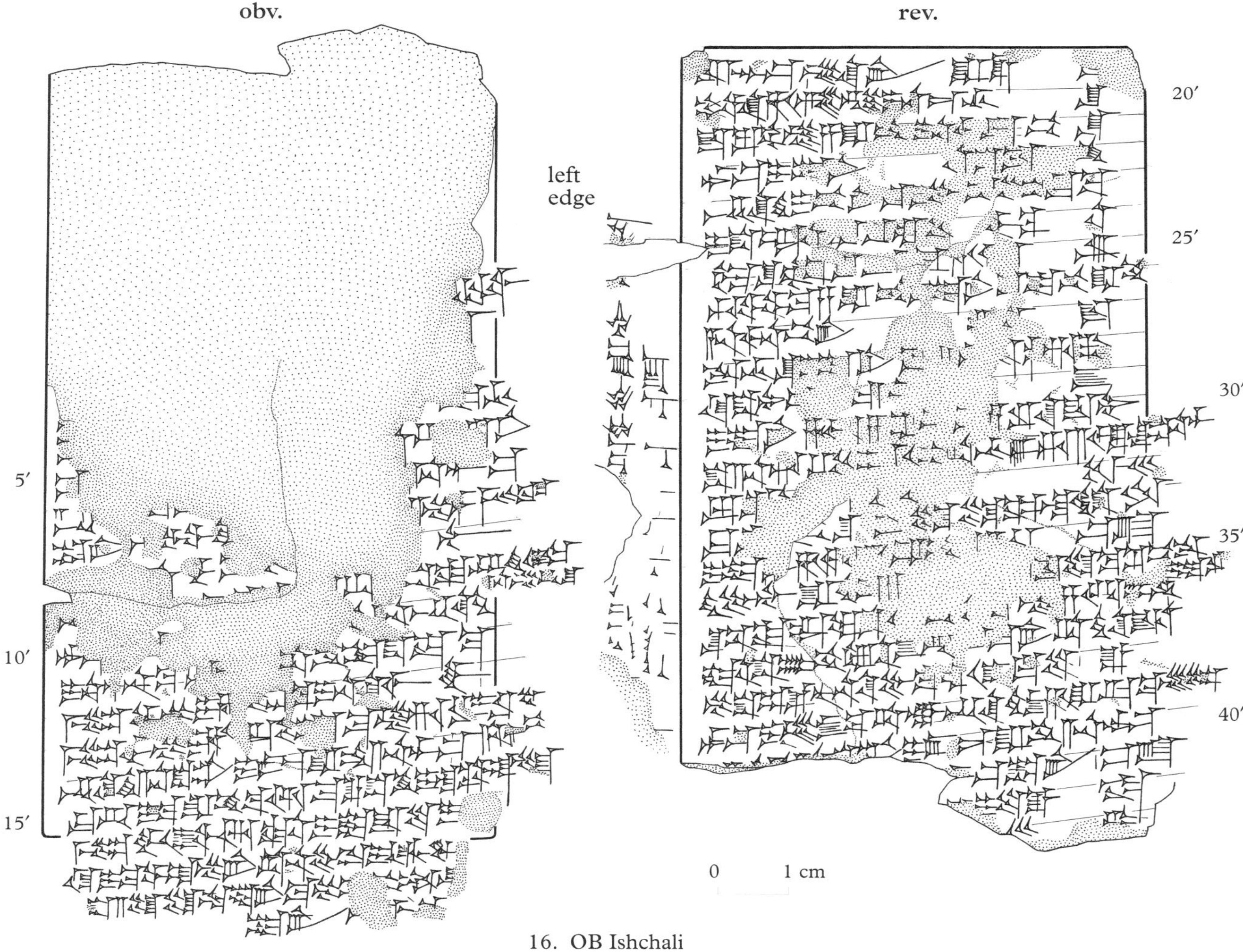

16. OB Ishchali

VAT 4105+ obv.

i

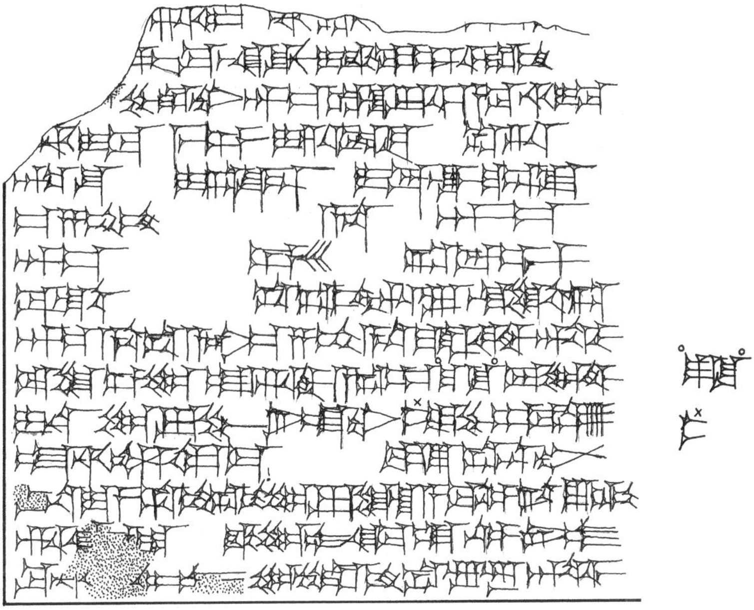

ii

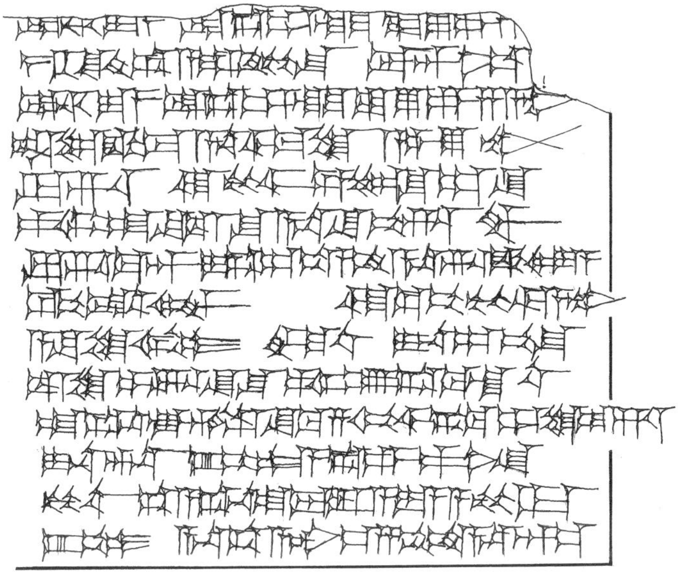

17. OB VA+BM obv. Copy by W. G. Lambert, collations by the author

VAT 4105+ iv

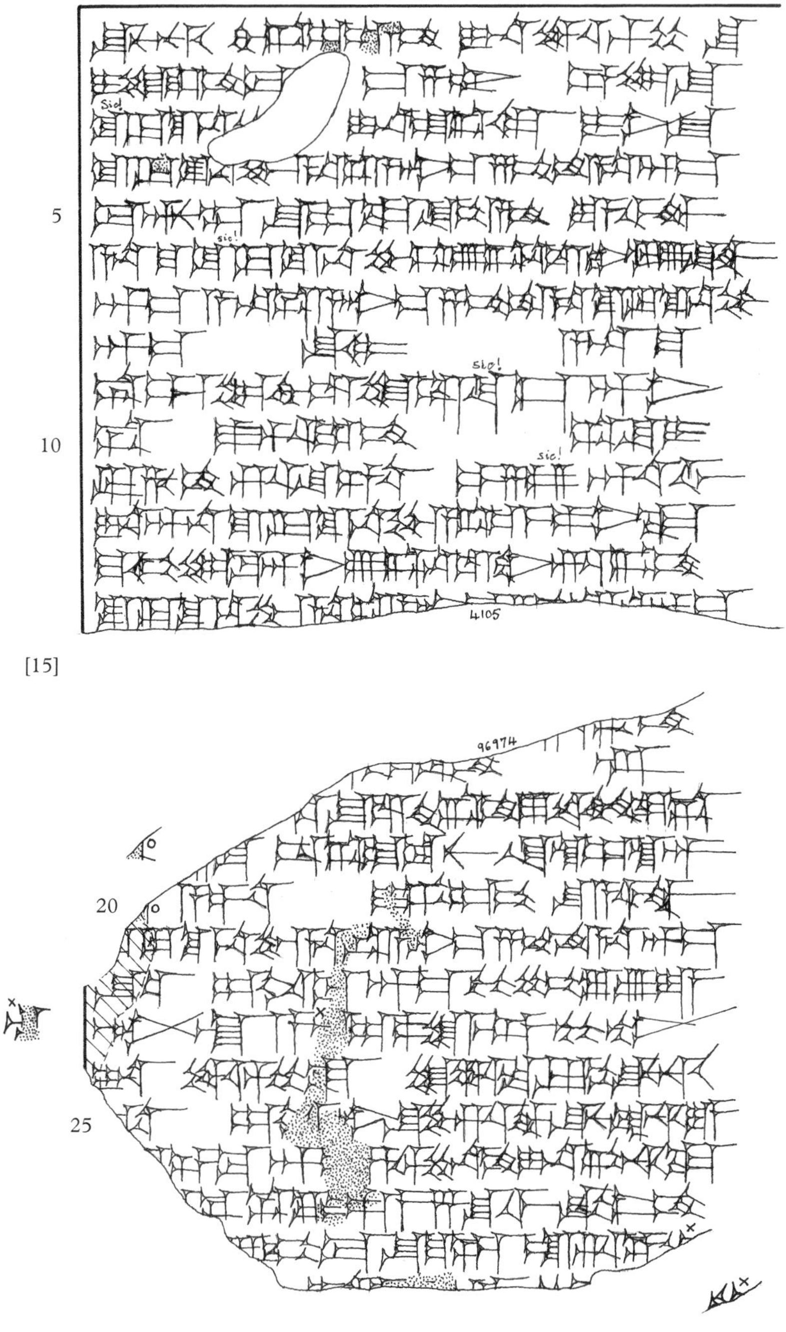

18. OB VA+BM col. iv. Copy by W. G. Lambert, collations by the author. The hatched area is restored from Millard's copy (*CT* 46 no.16)

VAT 4105+ iii

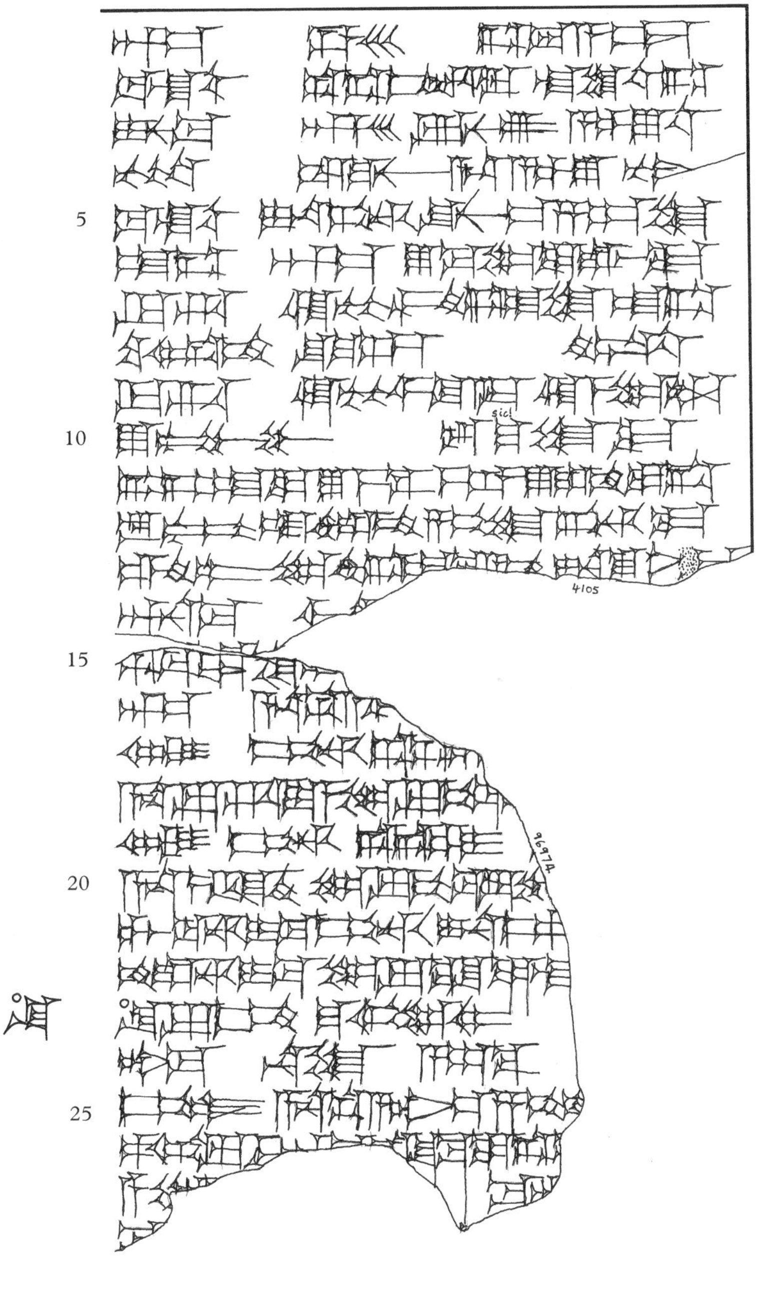

19. OB VA+BM col. iii. Copy by W. G. Lambert, collation by the author

A 29934

obv.

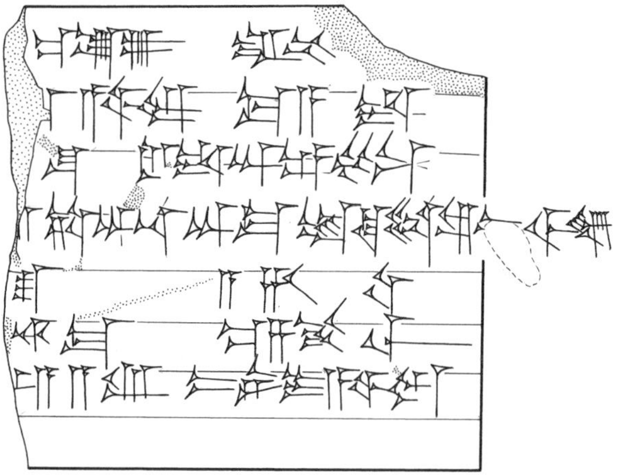

rev.

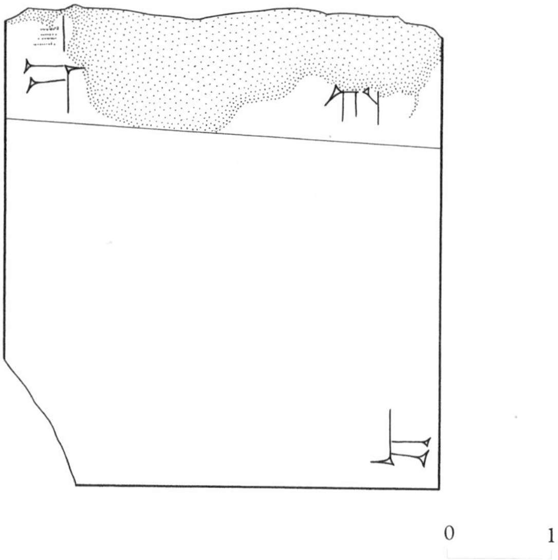

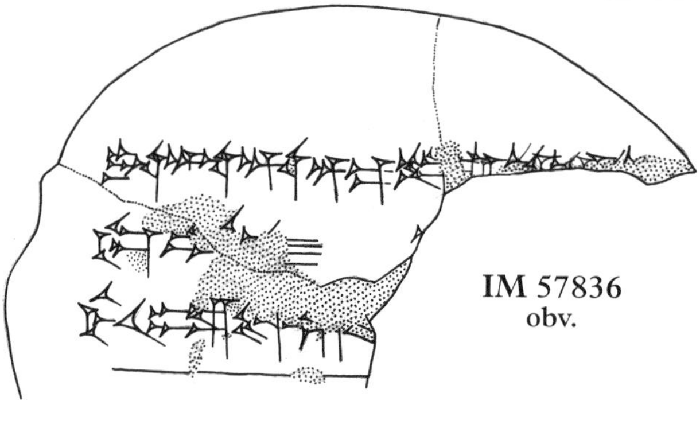

IM 57836
obv.

20. MB Nippur$_1$ (*top and middle*) and MB Nippur$_2$ obv. (*bottom*)

obv.

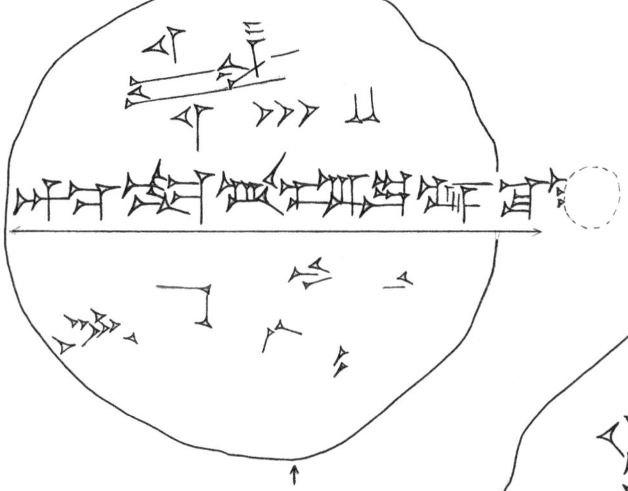

CBS 14167

rev.

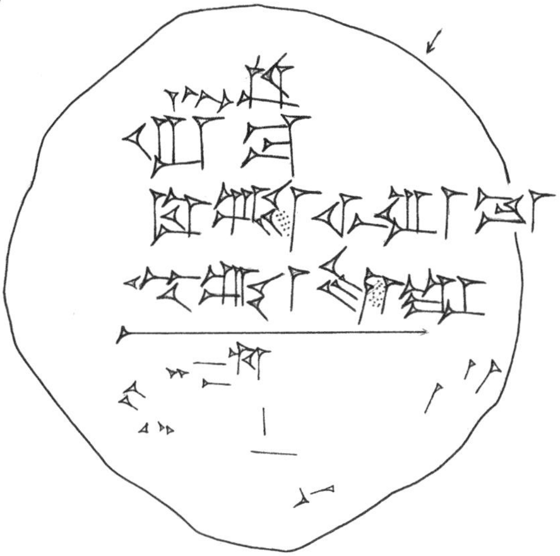

0 1 cm

obv.

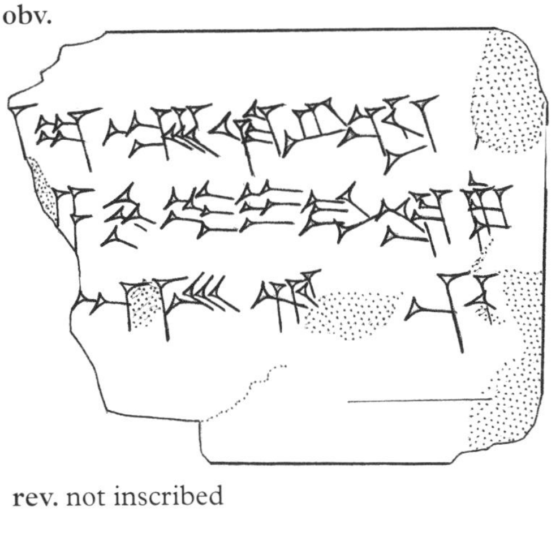

UM 29-16-606

rev. not inscribed

21. MB Nippur$_3$ (*top and middle*) and MB Nippur$_4$ (*bottom*)

UET 6/394

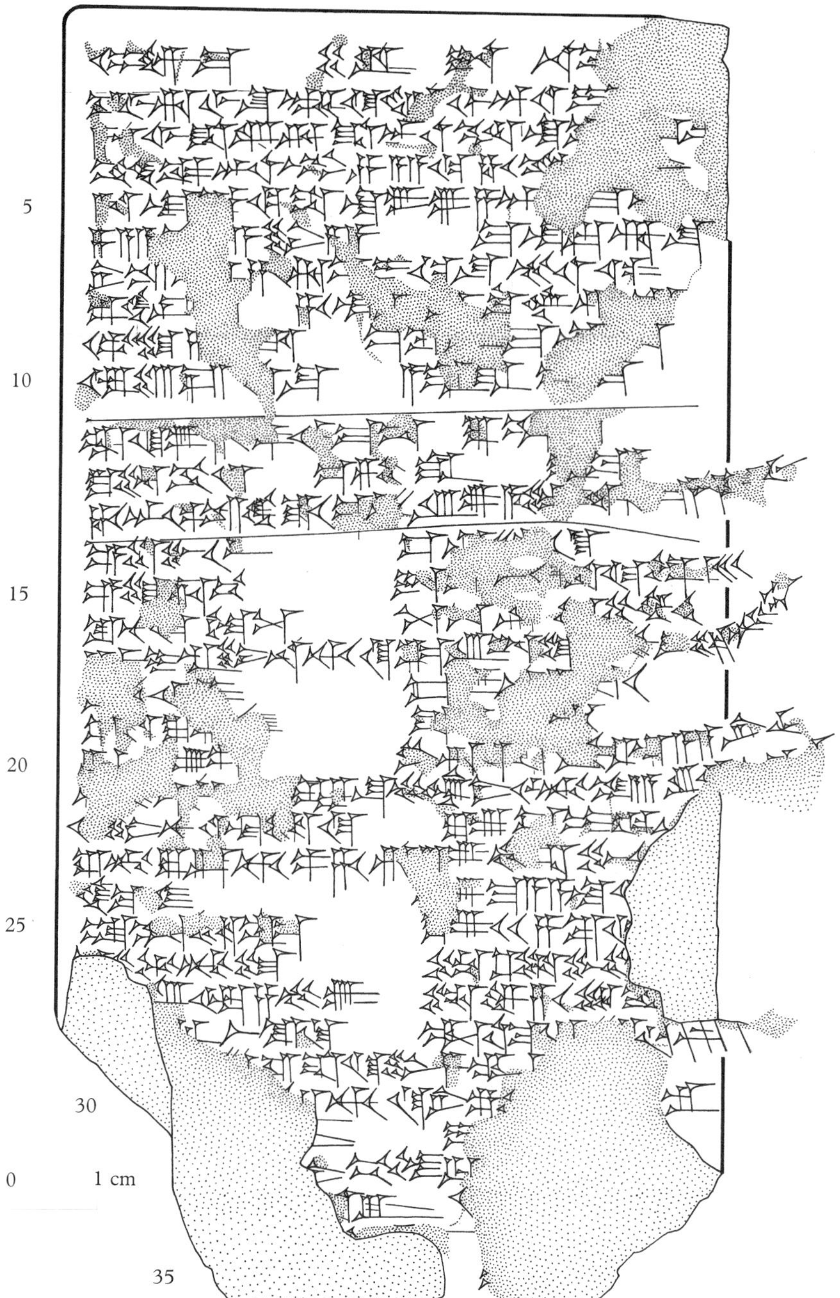

22. MB Ur obv.

UET 6/394

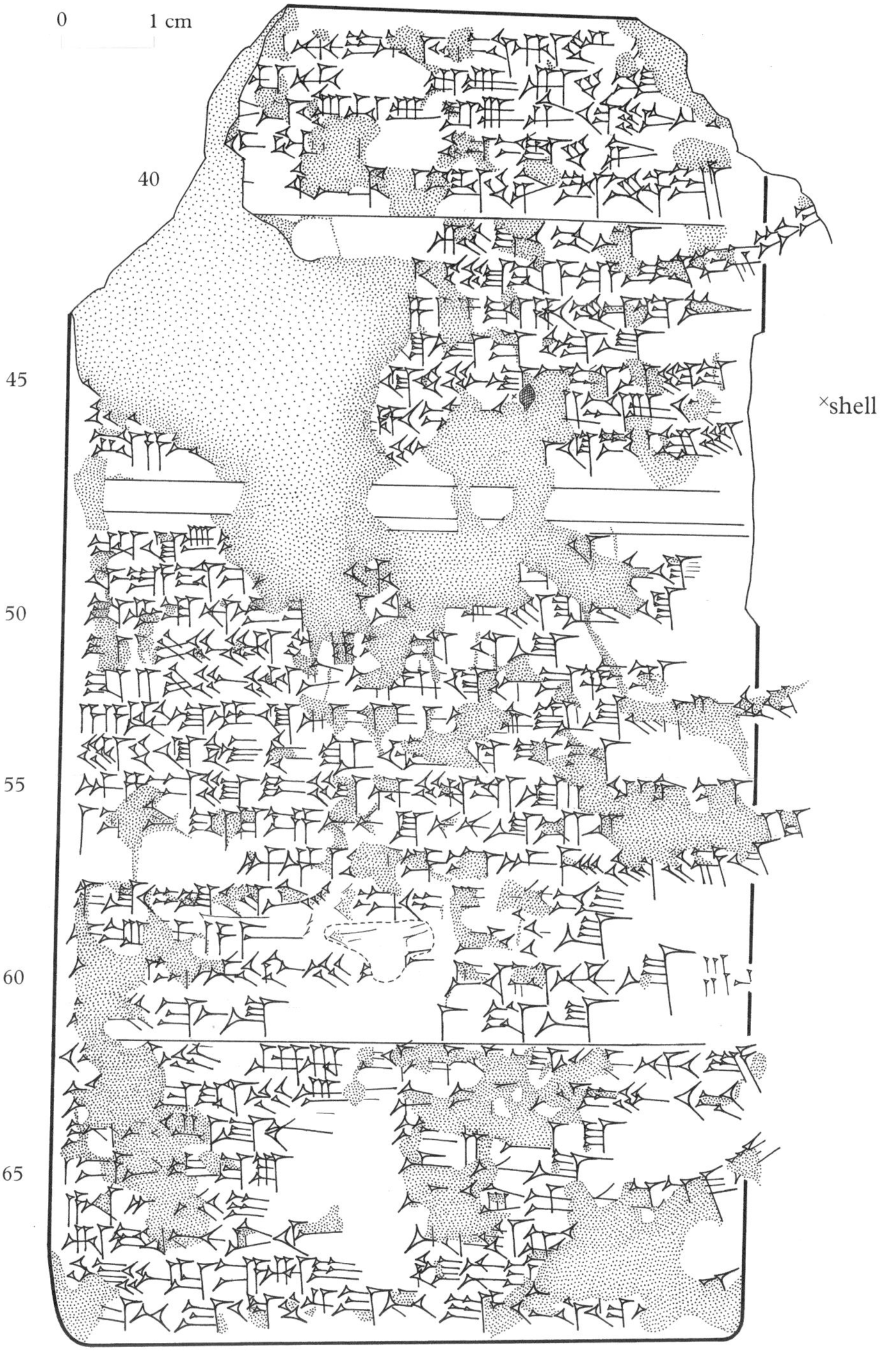

23. MB Ur rev.

(a) **Bo 83/625**

obv.

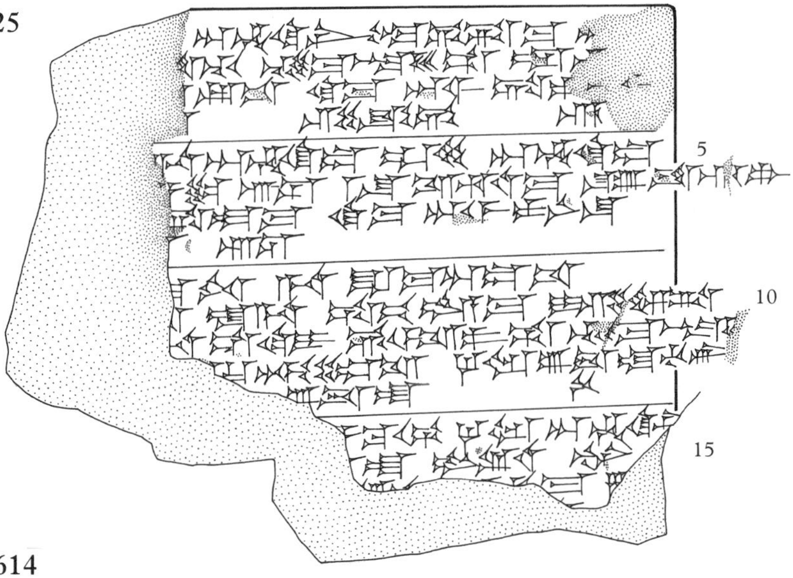

(c) **Bo 83/614**

0 1 cm

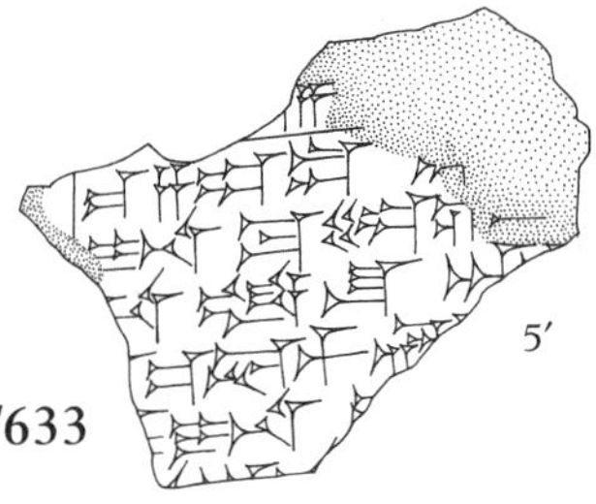

(b) **Bo 83/633**

(a) **Bo 83/625**

rev.

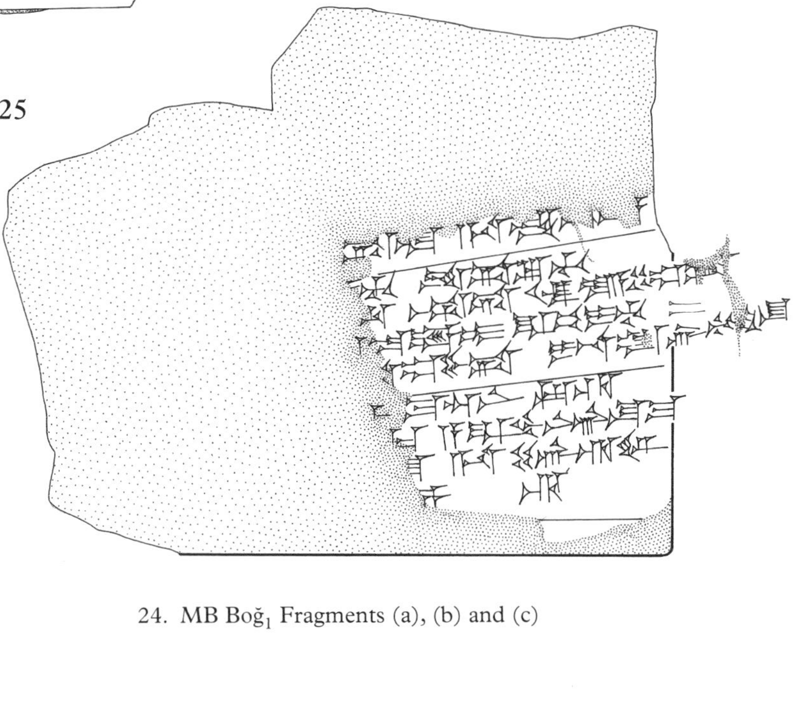

24. MB Boğ$_1$ Fragments (a), (b) and (c)

(d) **Bo 83/615**

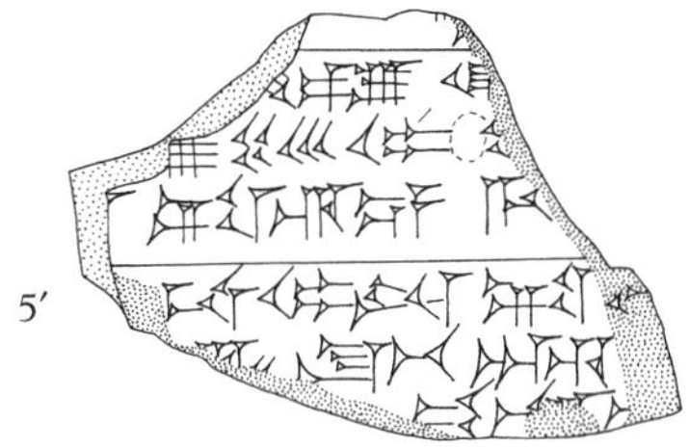

(e) **Bo 83/634**

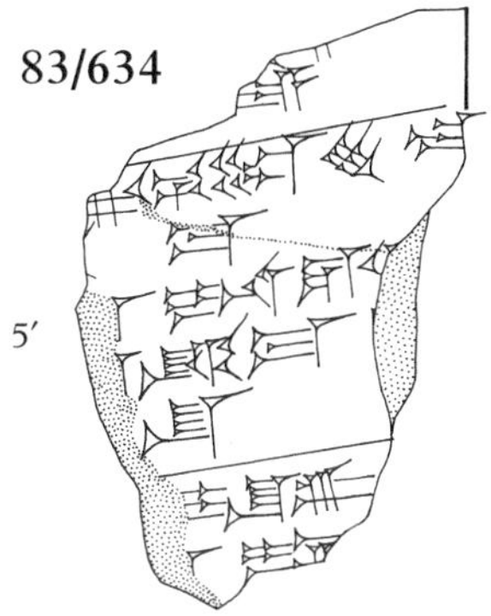

(f) **Bo 83/627+641+658**

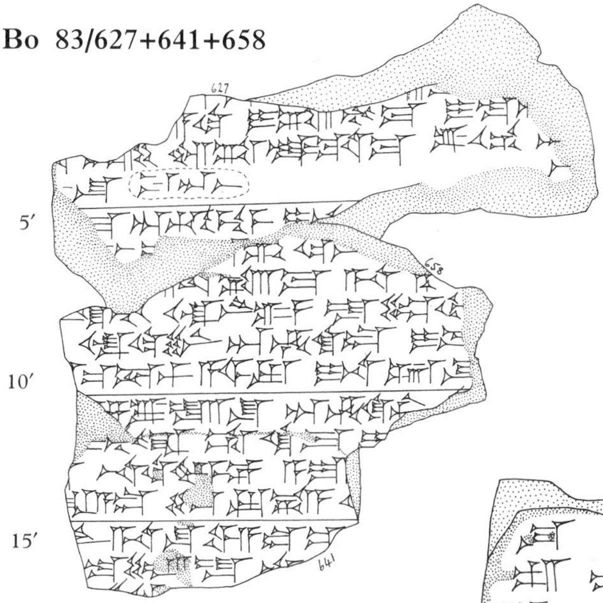

MB Boğ$_3$
Bo 284/d

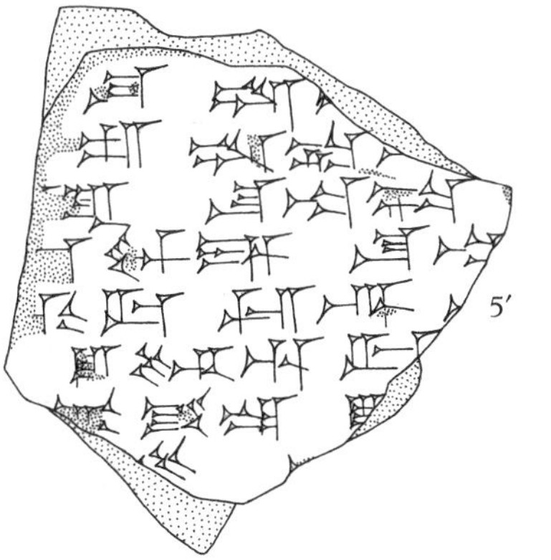

25. MB Boğ$_1$ Fragments (d), (e) and (f) (*top and middle*), MB Boğ$_3$ (*bottom right*)

VAT 12890

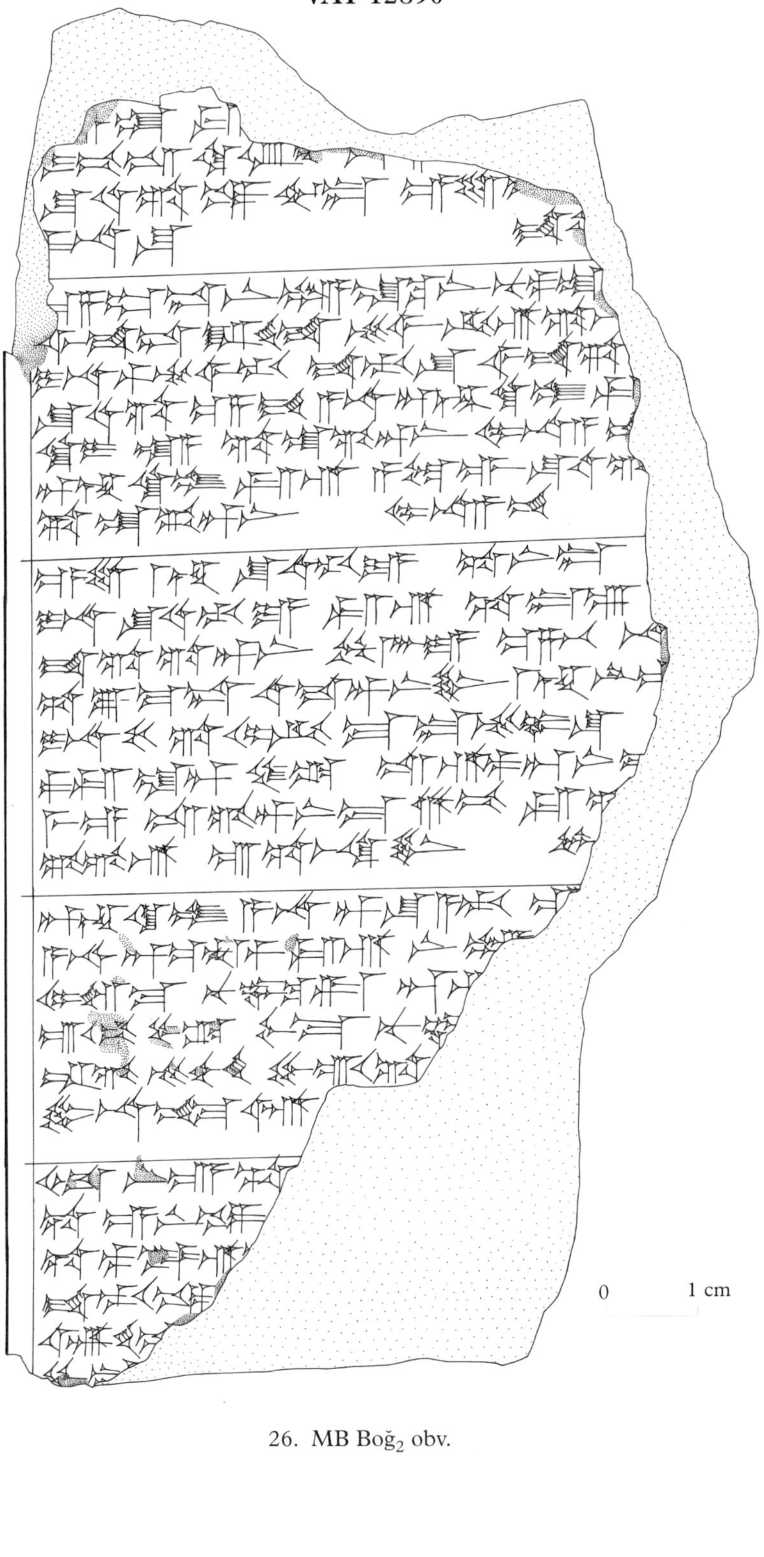

26. MB Boğ$_2$ obv.

VAT 12890

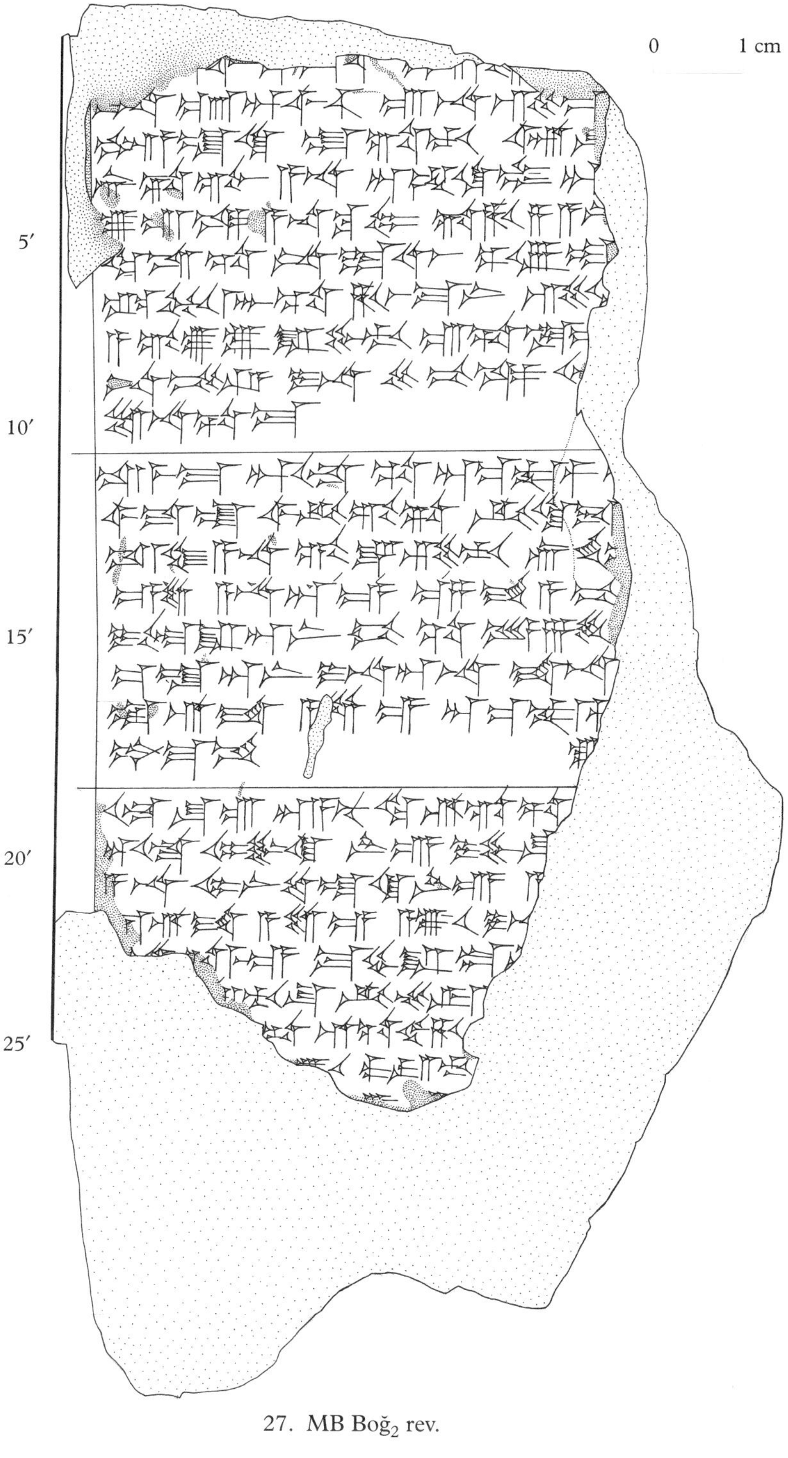

27. MB Boğ$_2$ rev.

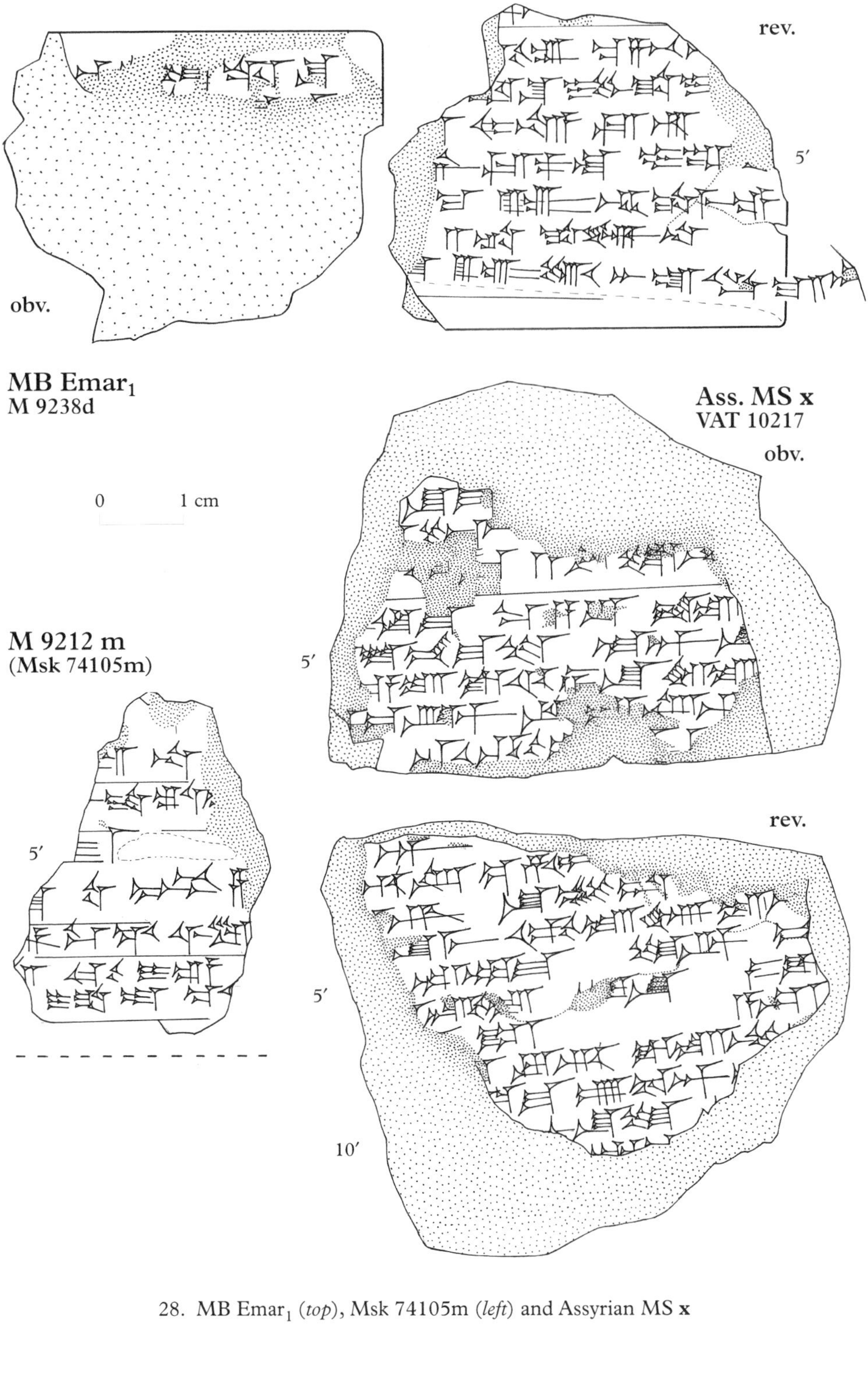

28. MB Emar$_1$ (*top*), Msk 74105m (*left*) and Assyrian MS **x**

M 9204n+9211z+9301d (+) unnumbered

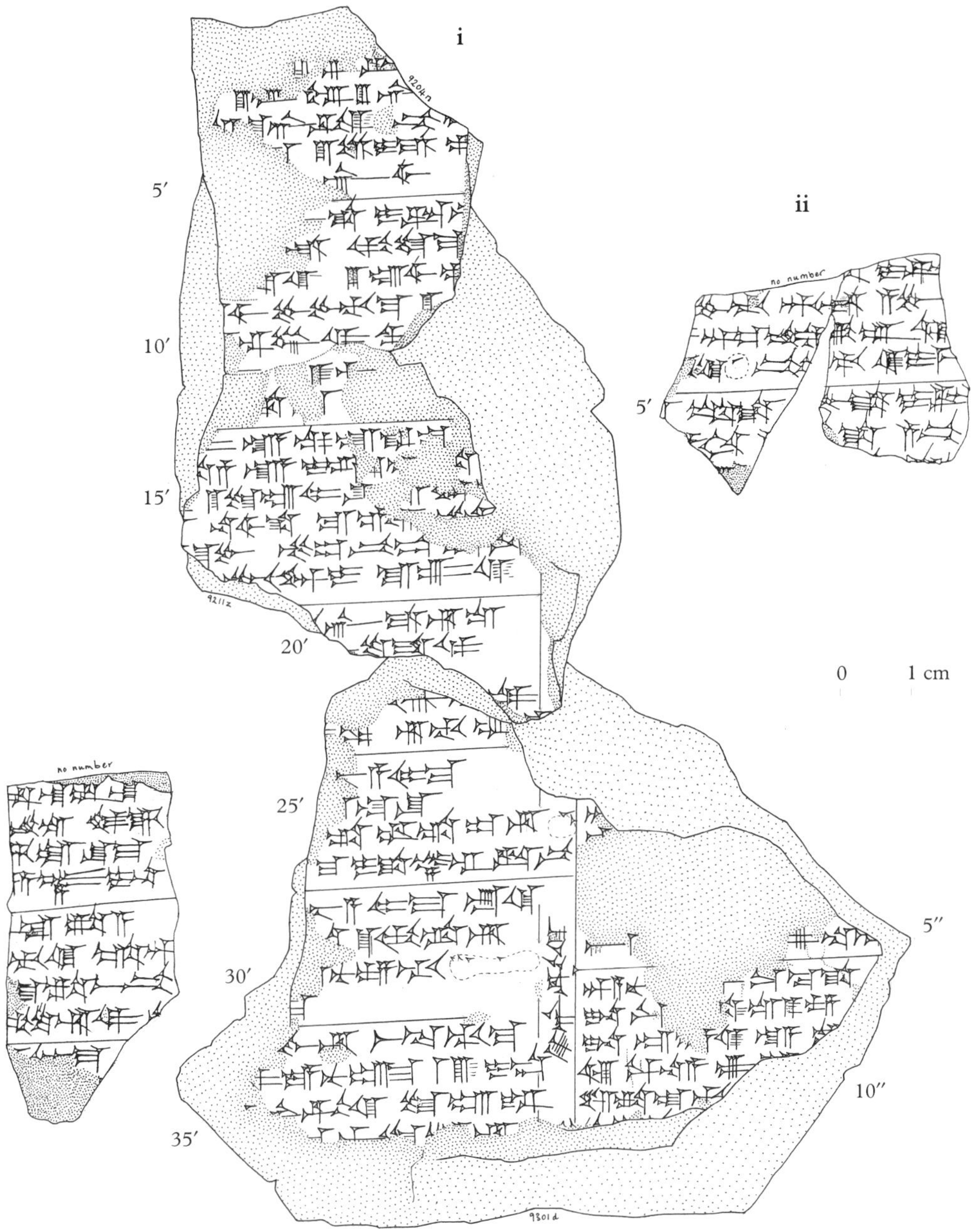

29. MB Emar$_2$. Unnumbered fragments copied by I. L. Finkel

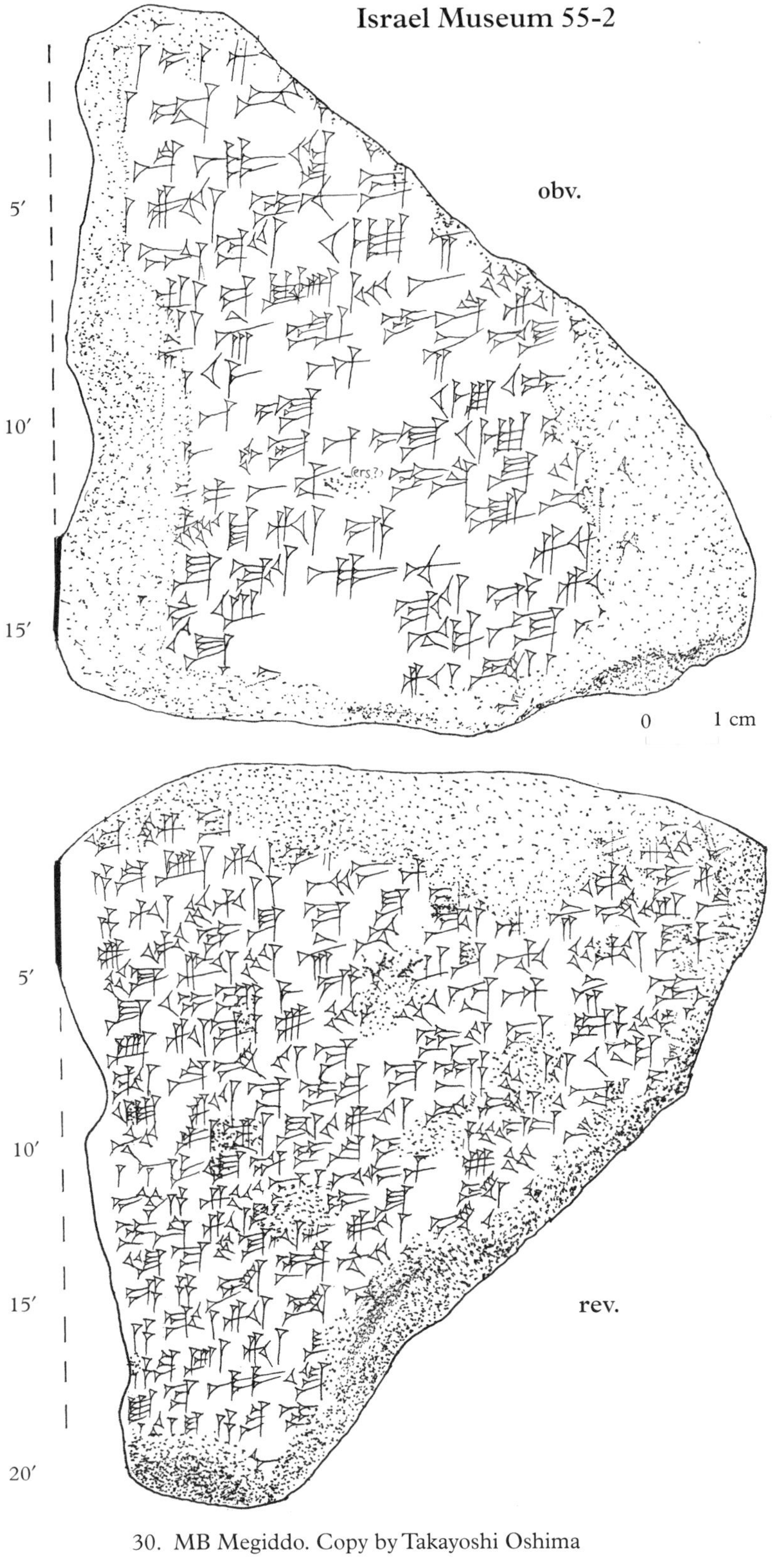

30. MB Megiddo. Copy by Takayoshi Oshima

y_1 VAT 10585b

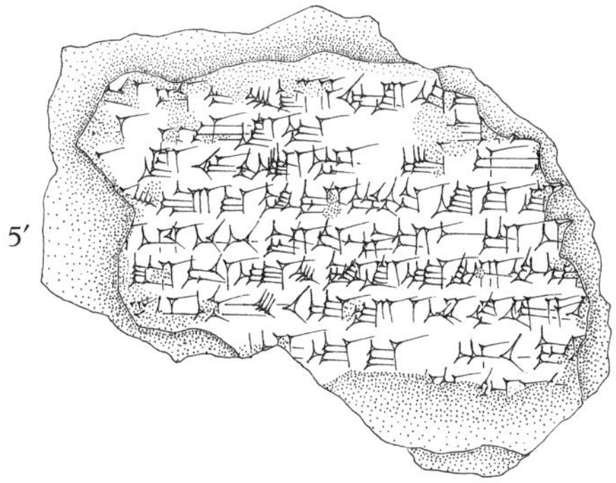

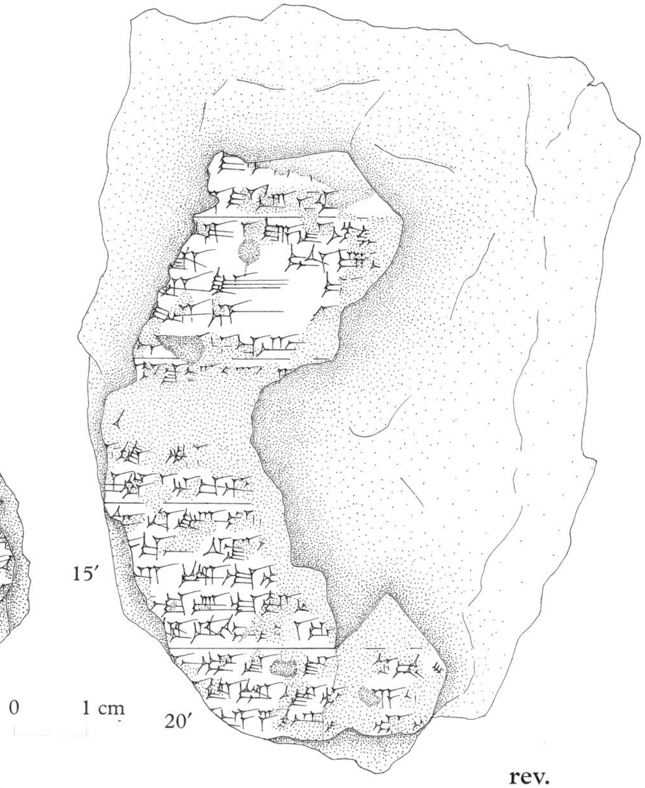

rev.

y_2 VAT 10916

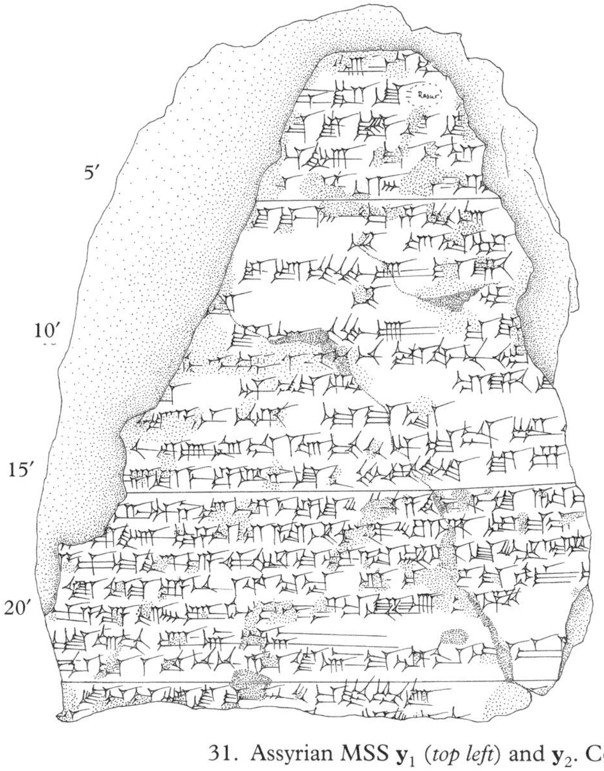

obv.

31. Assyrian MSS $\mathbf{y}_1$ (*top left*) and $\mathbf{y}_2$. Copies by Stefan M. Maul

IM 67564

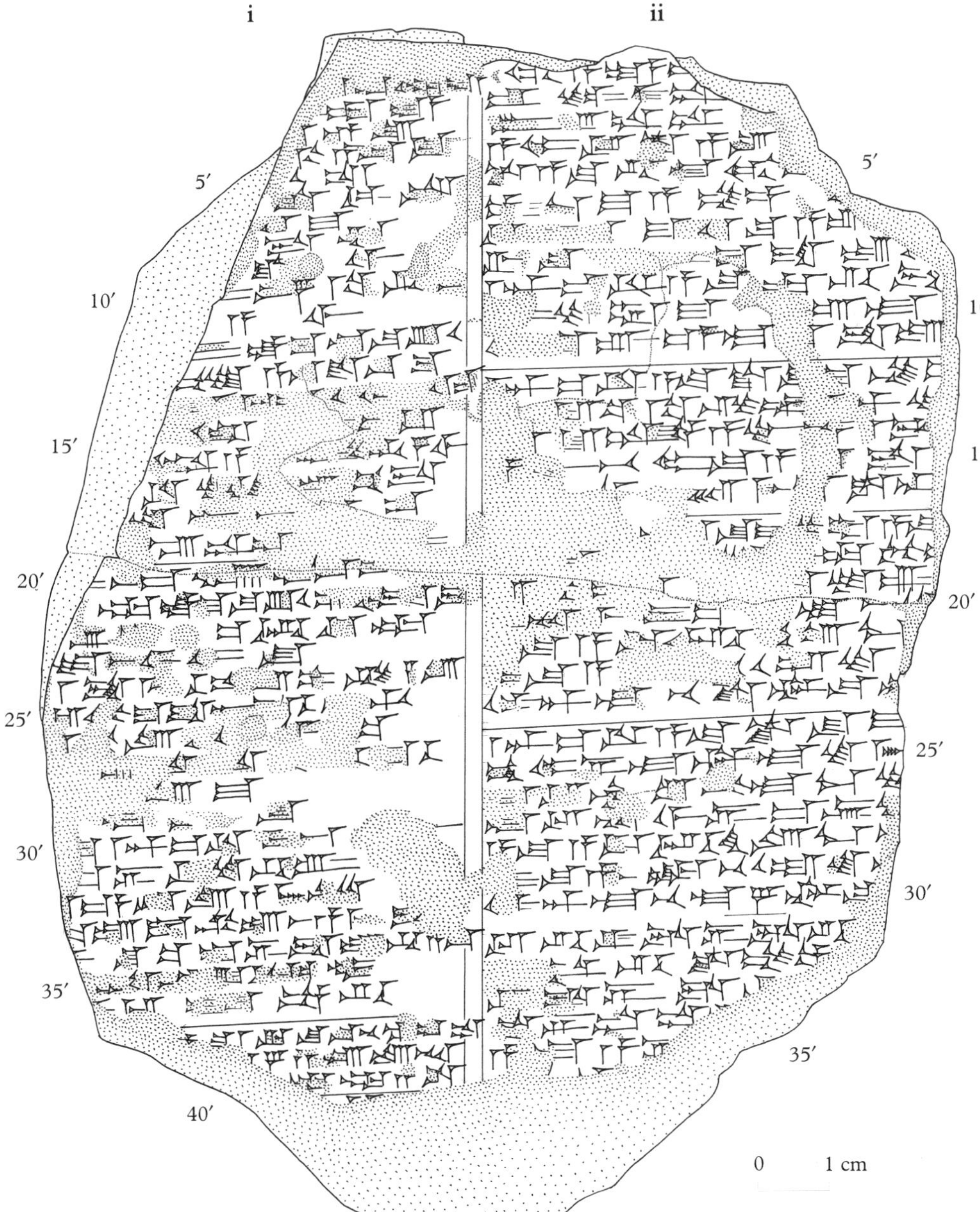

32. Assyrian MS **z** obv.

IM 67564

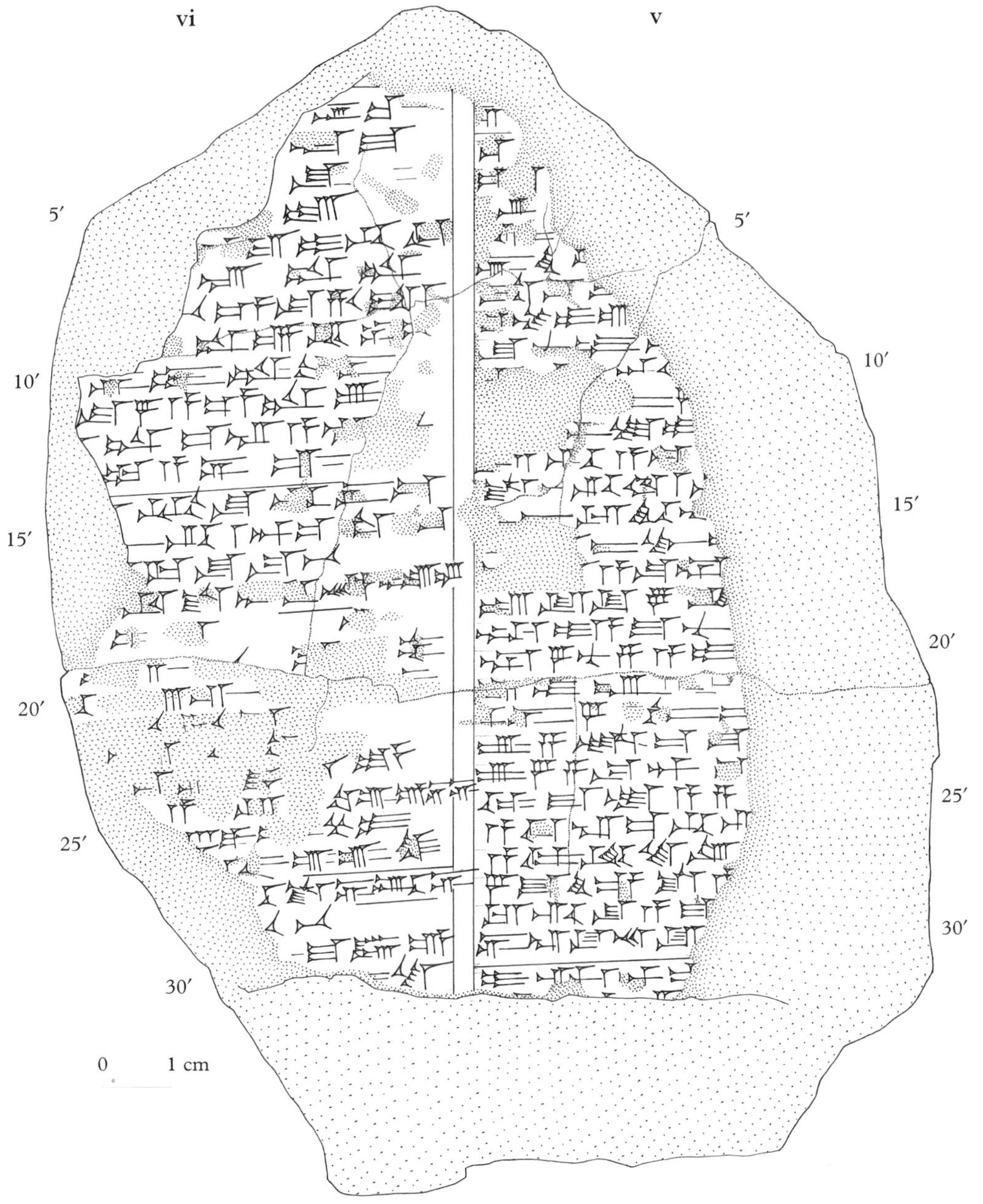

33. Assyrian MS **z** rev.

S.U. 51/7

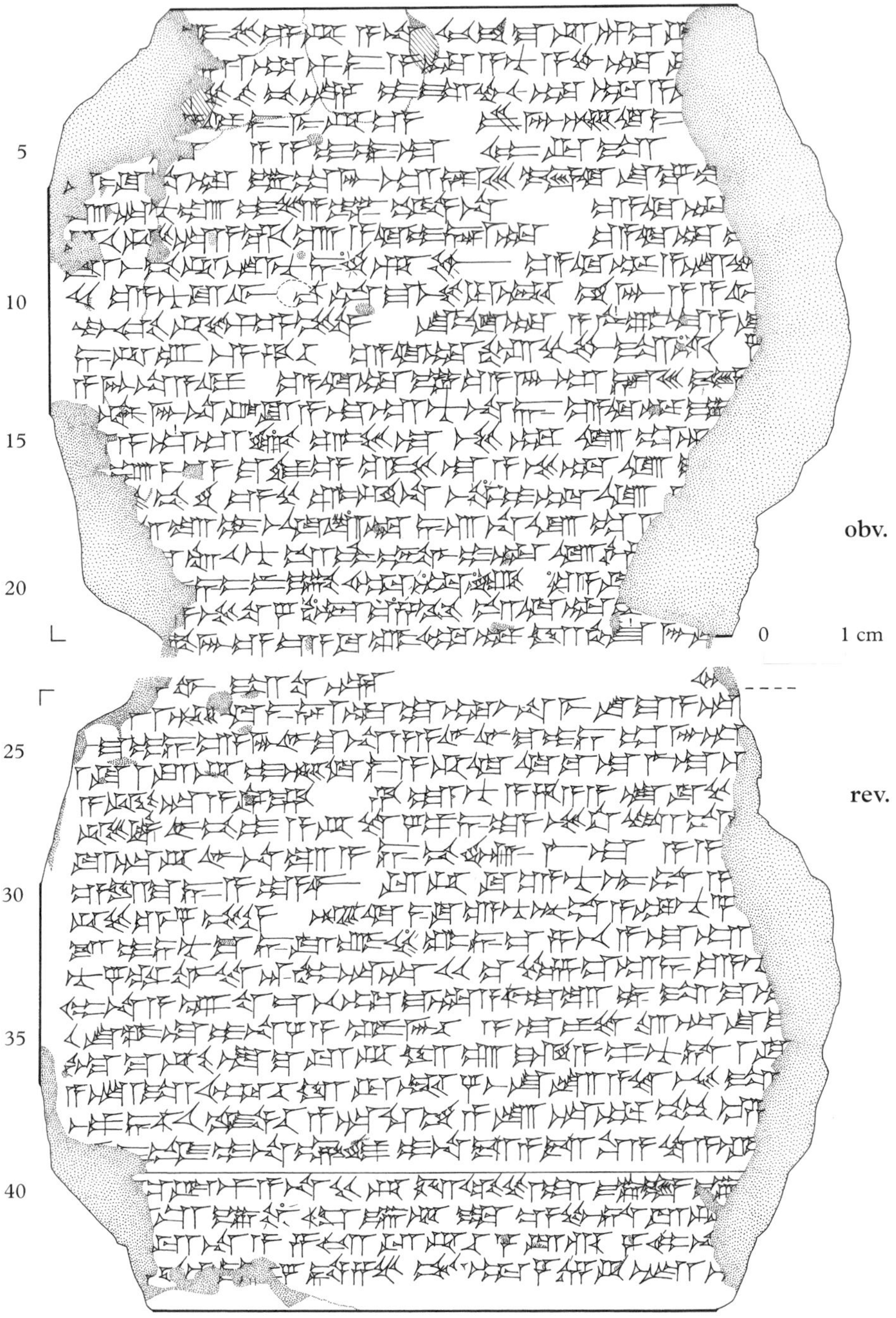

34. Assyrian MS **e**. The hatched areas are restored from the photograph

ZZ K 19276

obv.

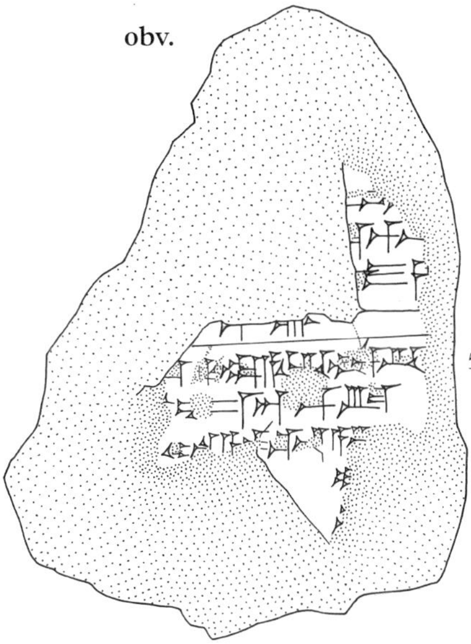

rev.

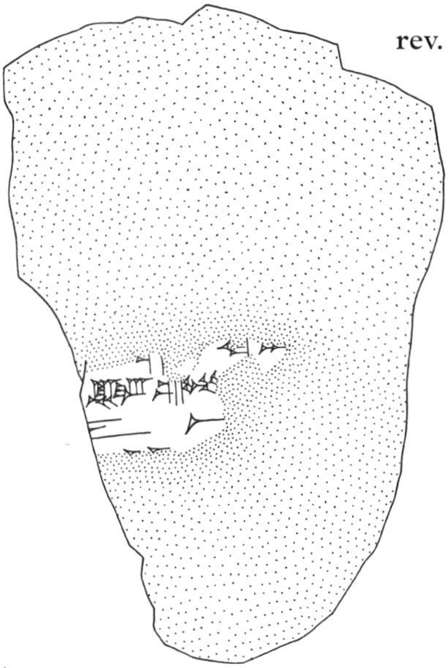

0 1 cm

YY K 16024

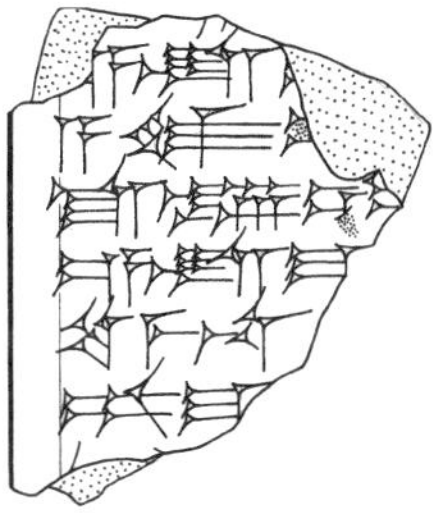

Rm 535 obv.?

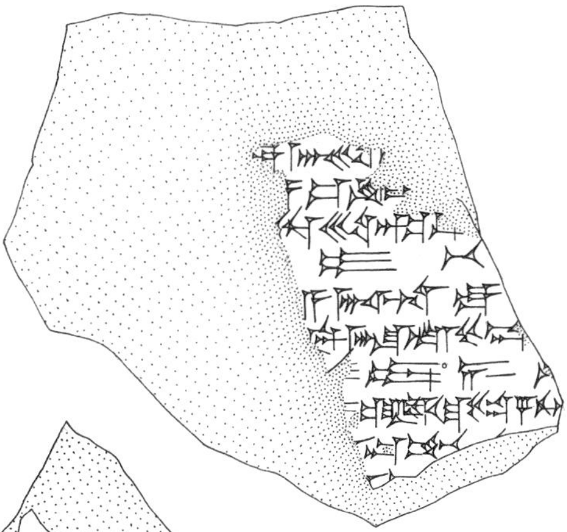

K 13880

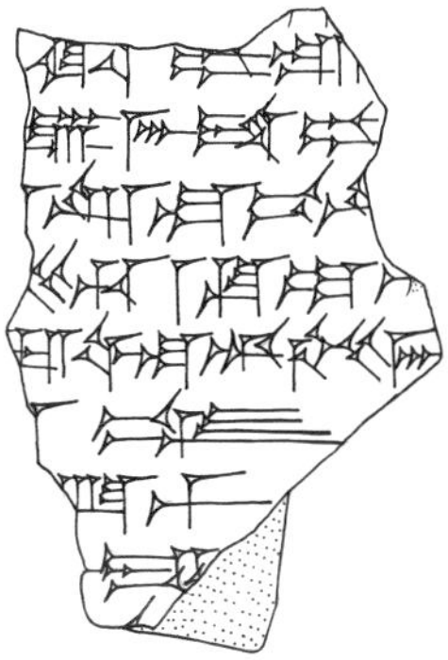

FF Sm 1754

35. Kuyunjik MSS ZZ and YY, unplaced fragment K 13880, colophon fragment SB MS FF, omen fragment Rm 535

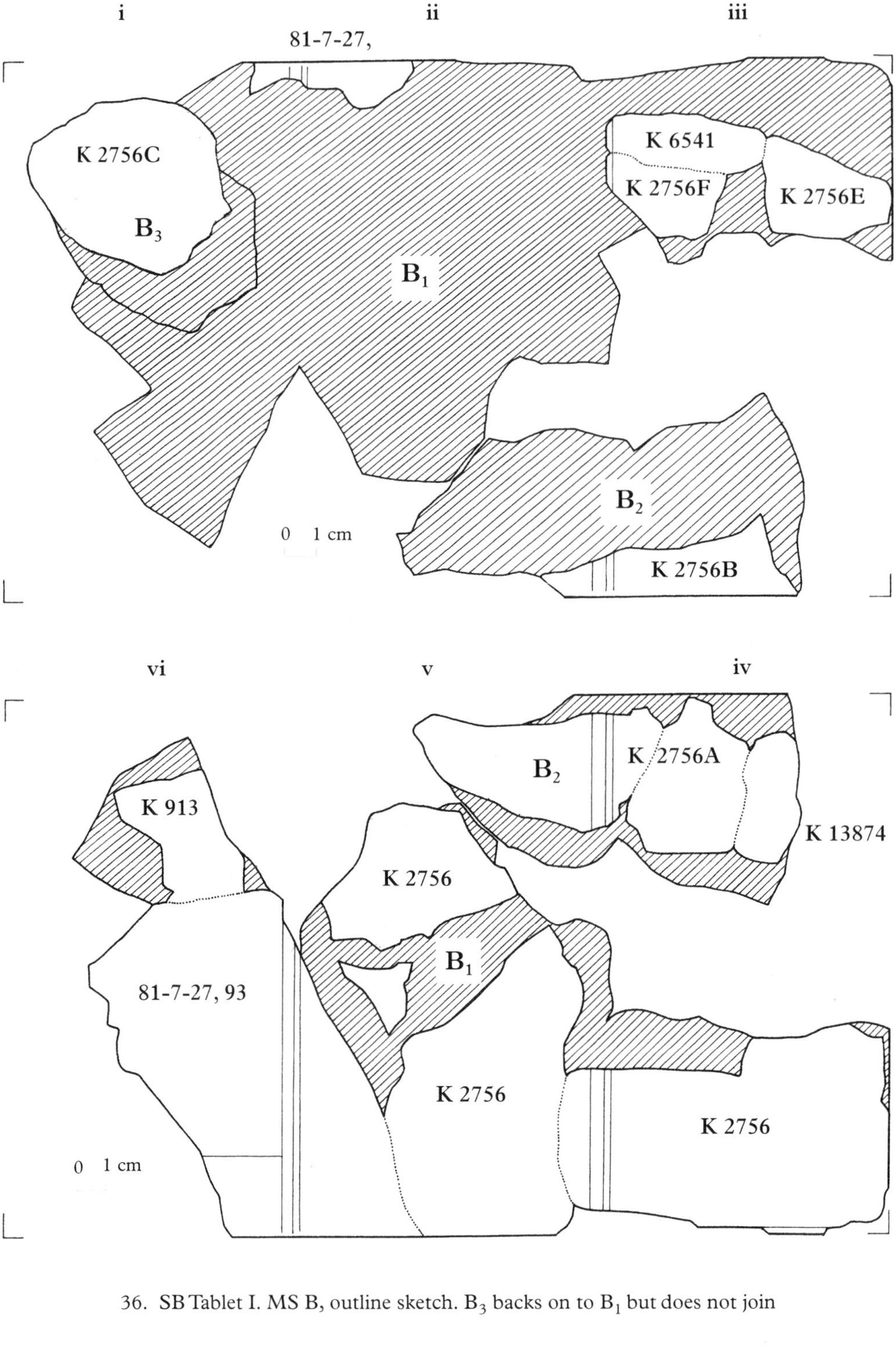

36. SB Tablet I. MS B, outline sketch. B_3 backs on to B_1 but does not join

B_1 K 913+

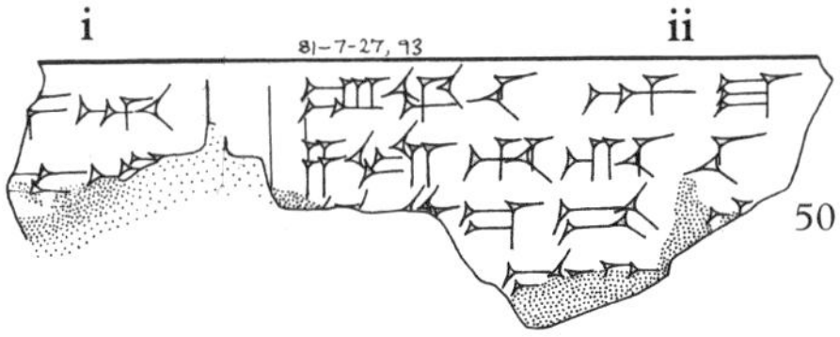

B_3 K 2756C

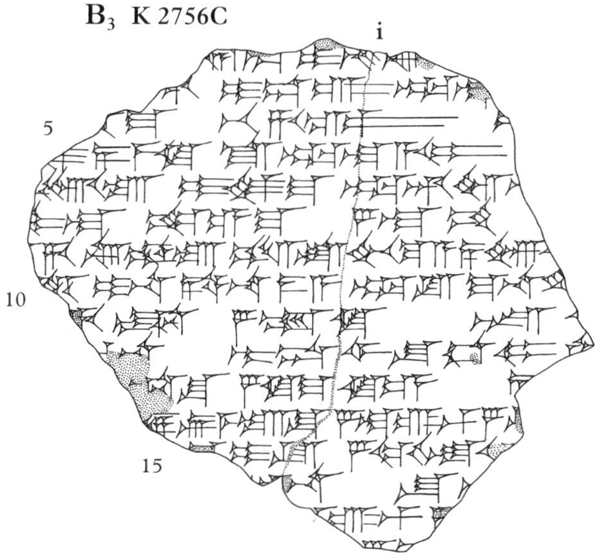

B_1 K 913+ iii

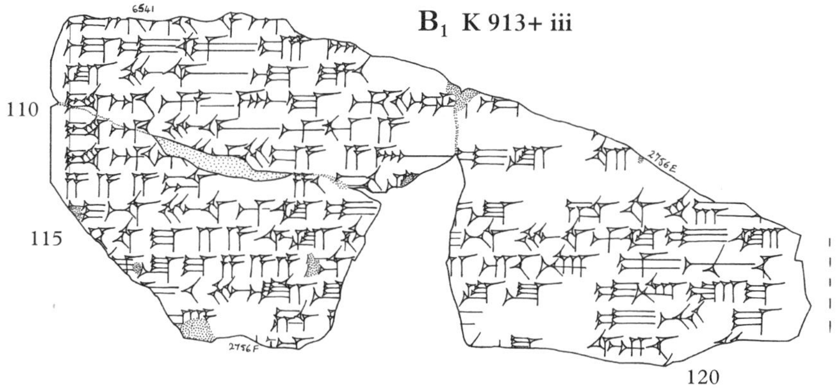

B_2 K 2756A+

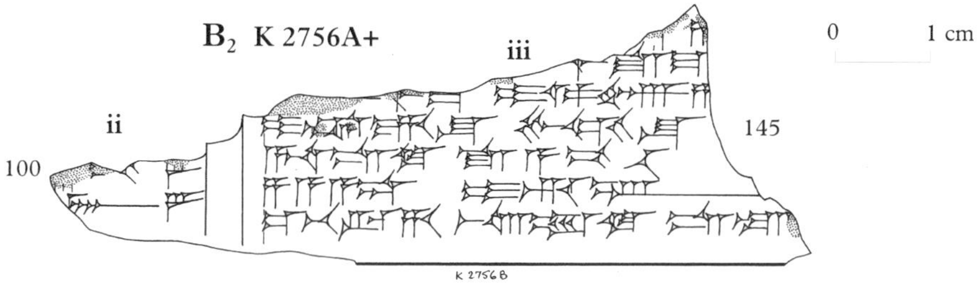

37. SB Tablet I. MS B obv.

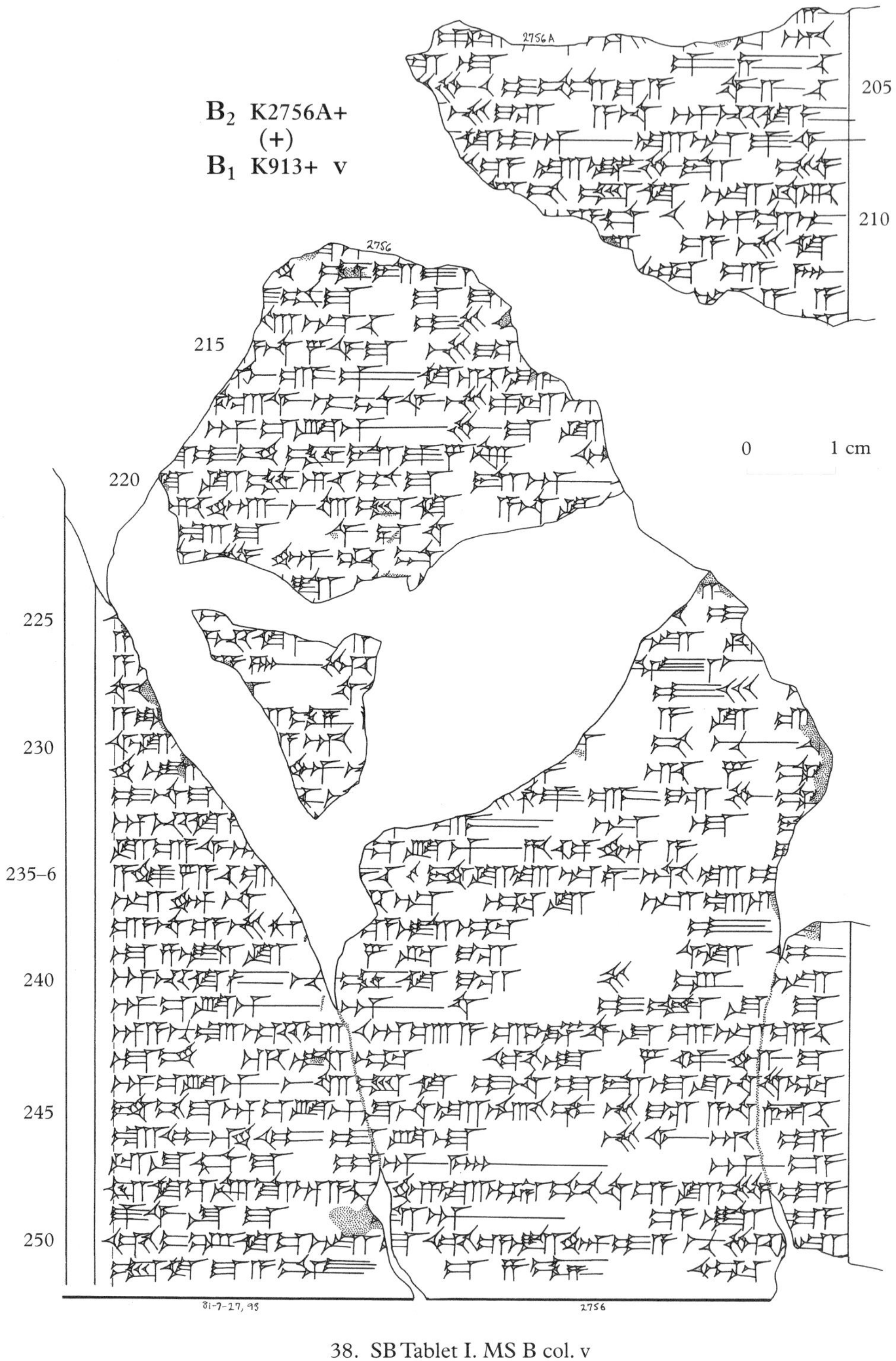

38. SB Tablet I. MS B col. v

B_2 K 2756A+ iv

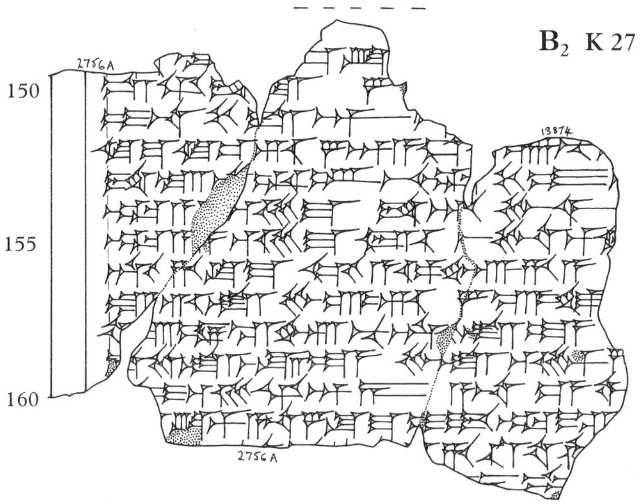

0 1 cm

B_1 K913+ iv

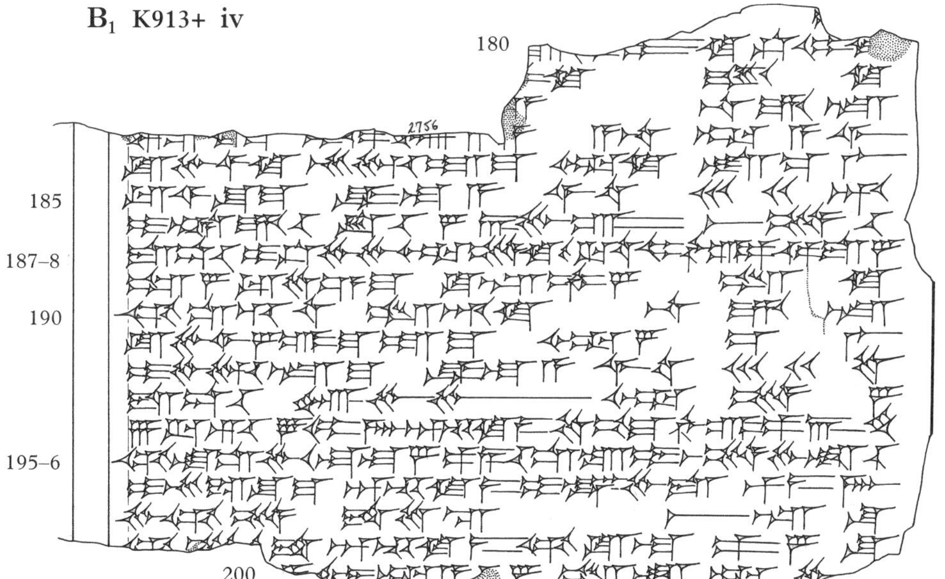

39. SB Tablet I. MS B col. iv

B_1 **K 913+ vi**

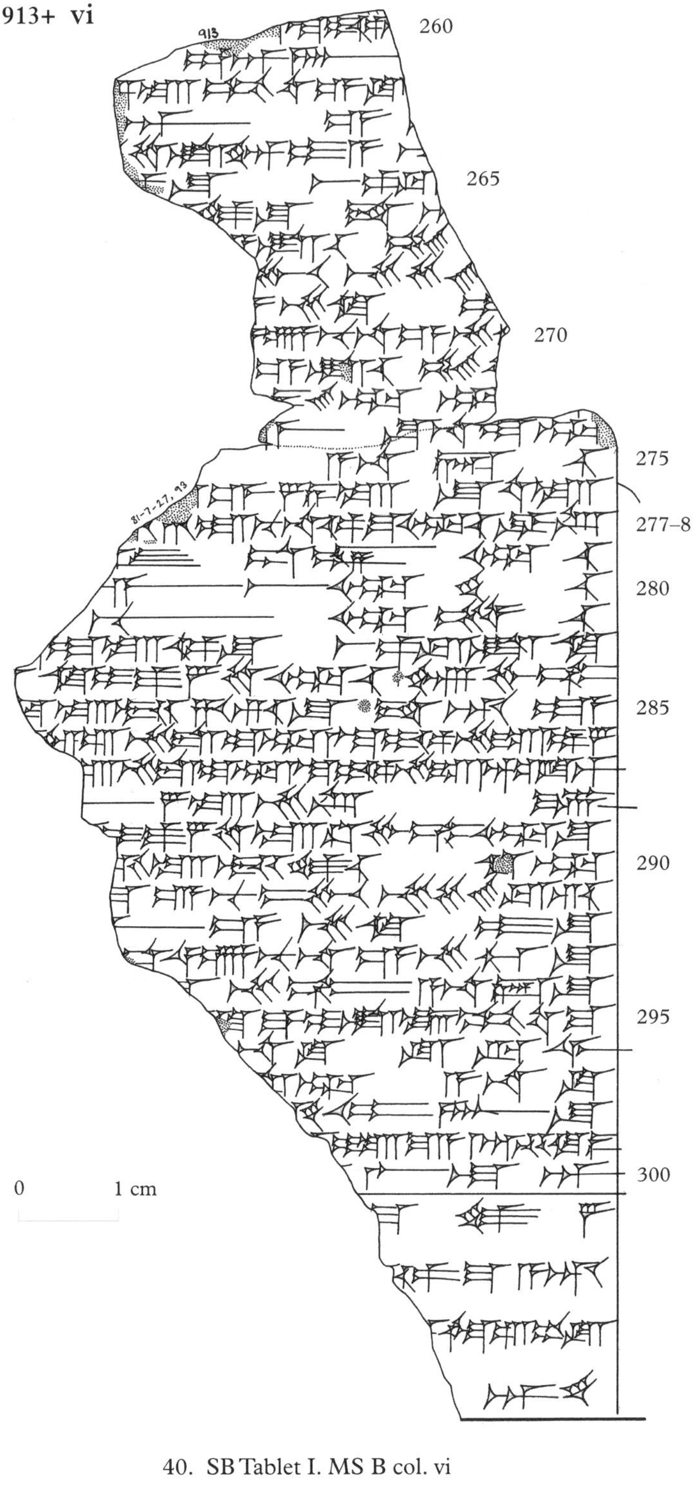

40. SB Tablet I. MS B col. vi

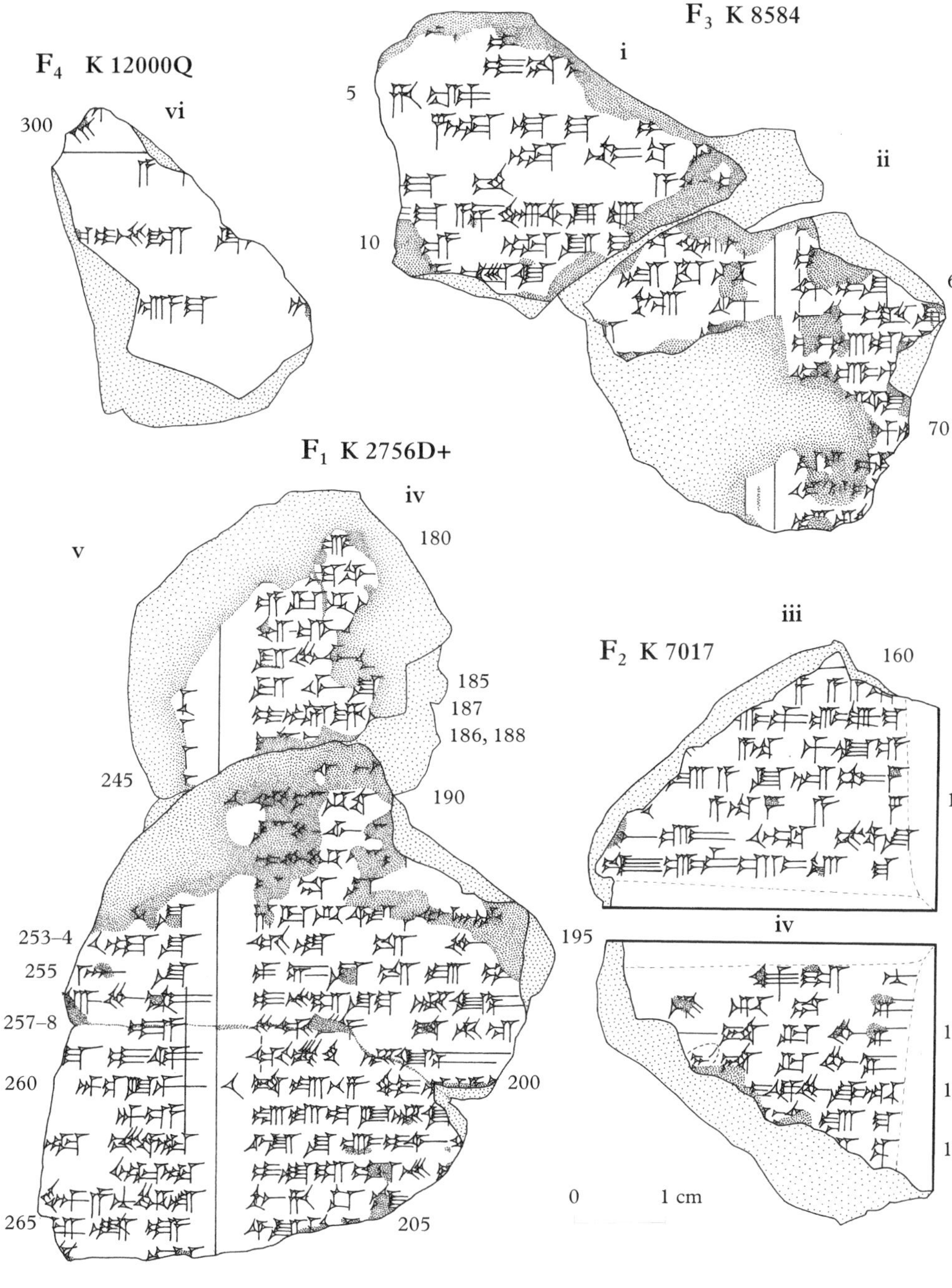

41. SB Tablet I. MS F

P **K4465+ ii**

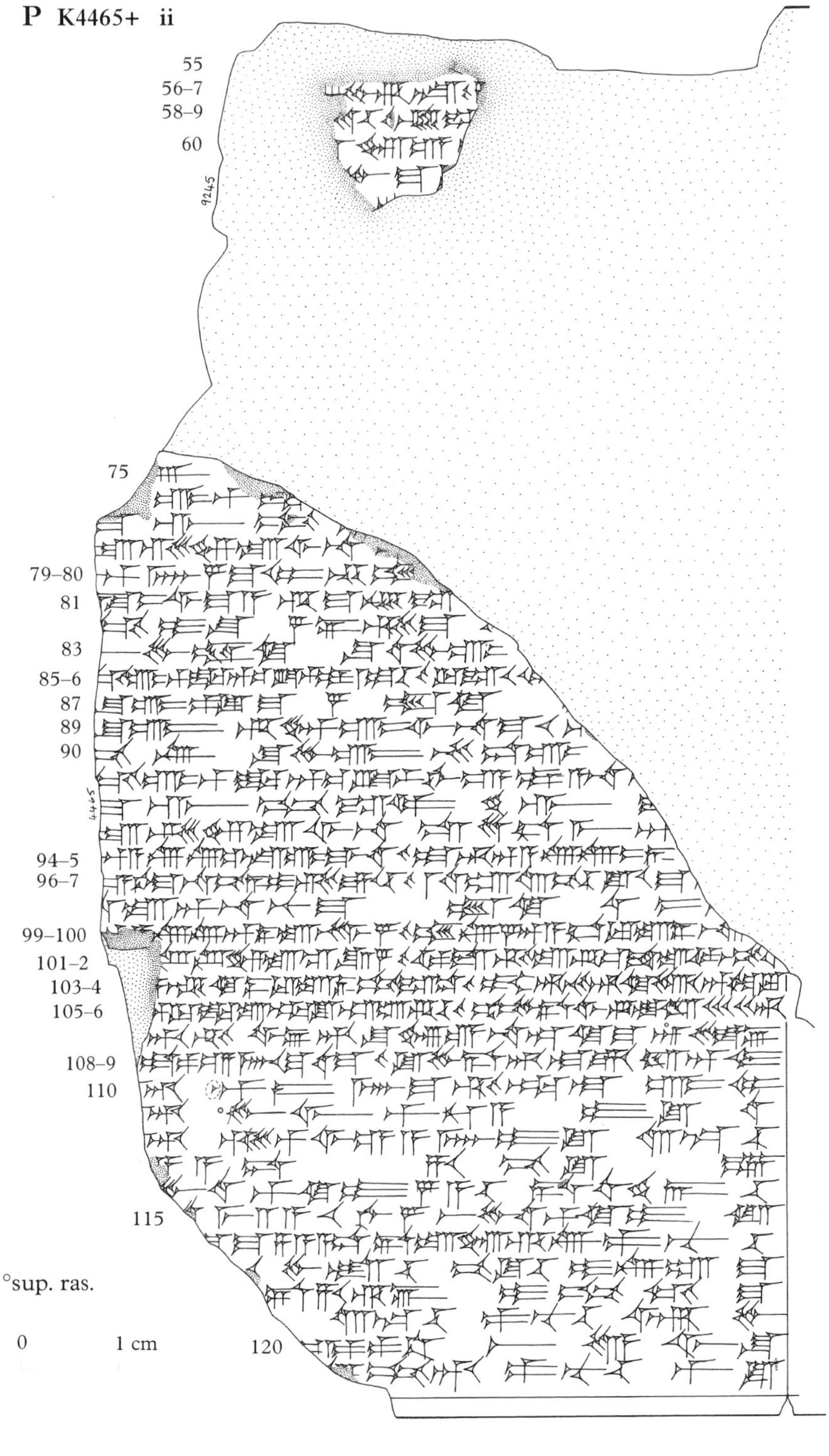

42. SB Tablet I. MS P col. ii

P K 4465+ iii

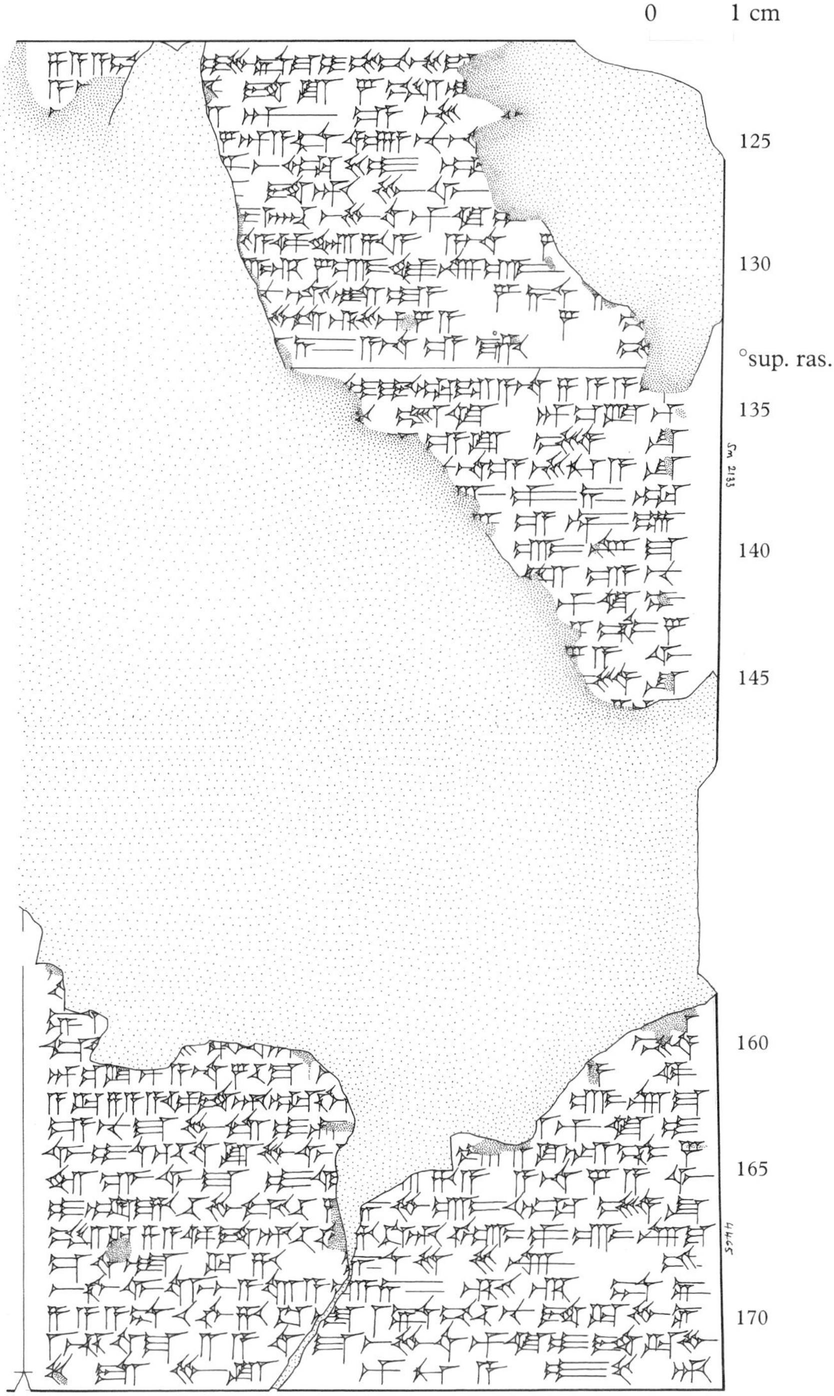

43. SB Tablet I. MS P col. iii

P K 4465+

v

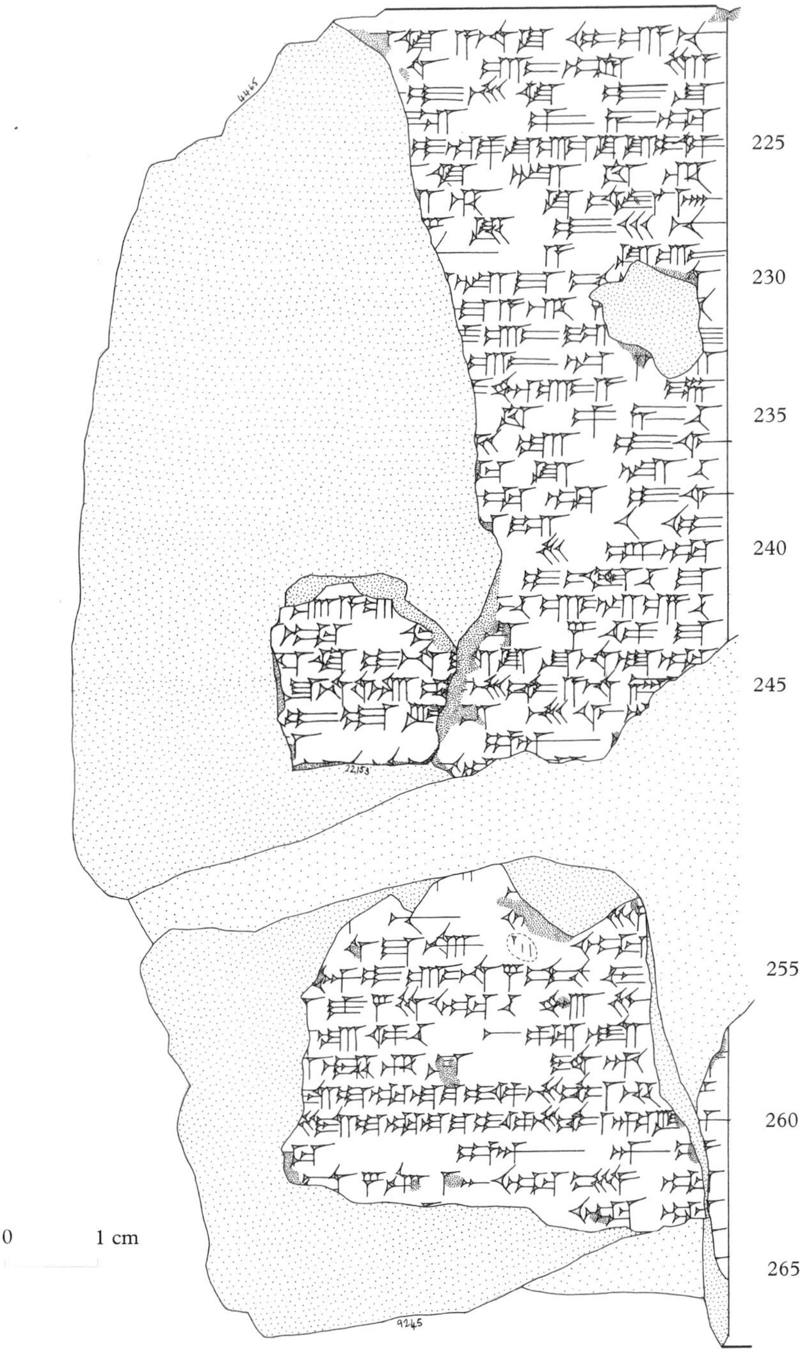

44. SB Tablet I. MS P col. v

P K 4465+

iv

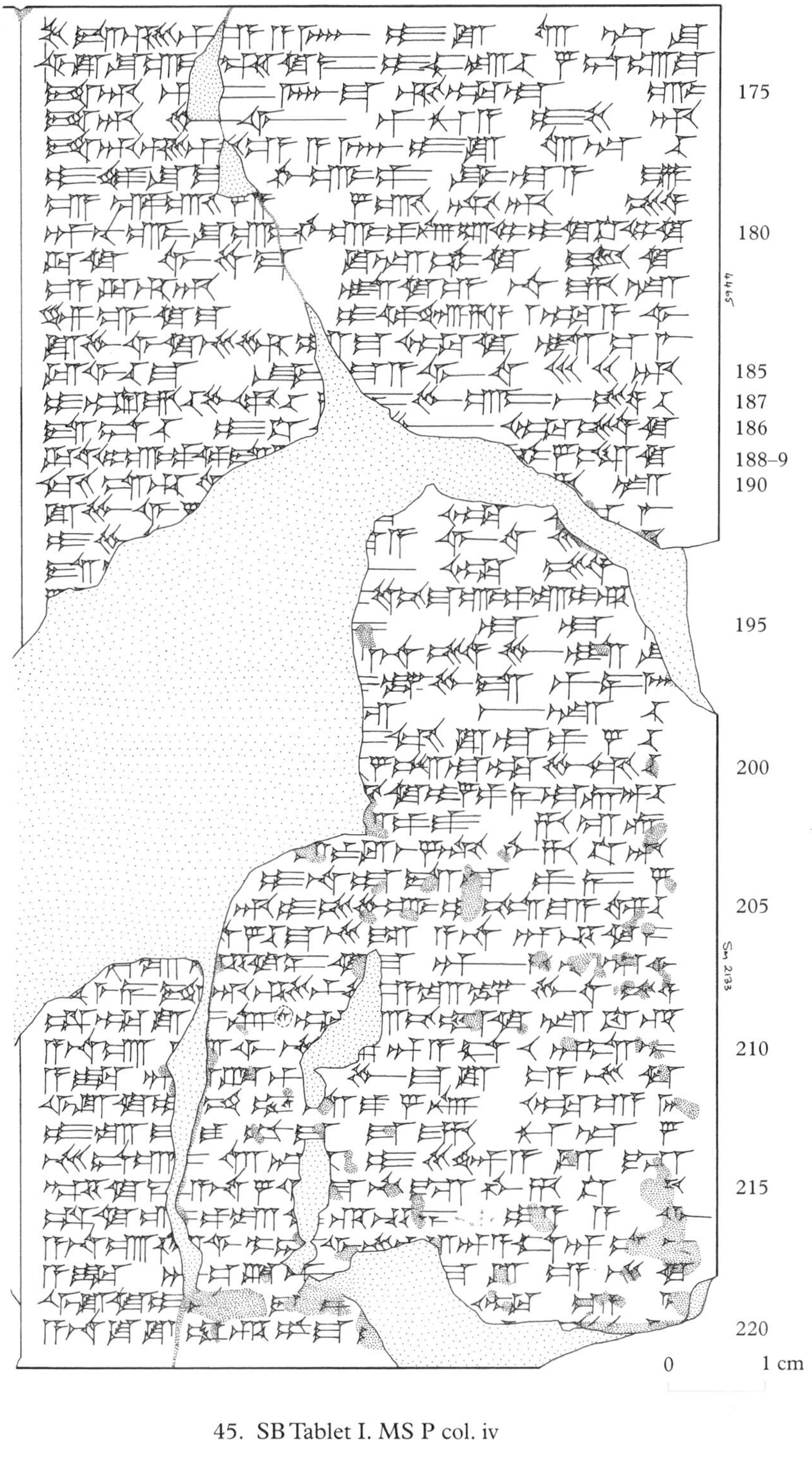

45. SB Tablet I. MS P col. iv

g IM 67577

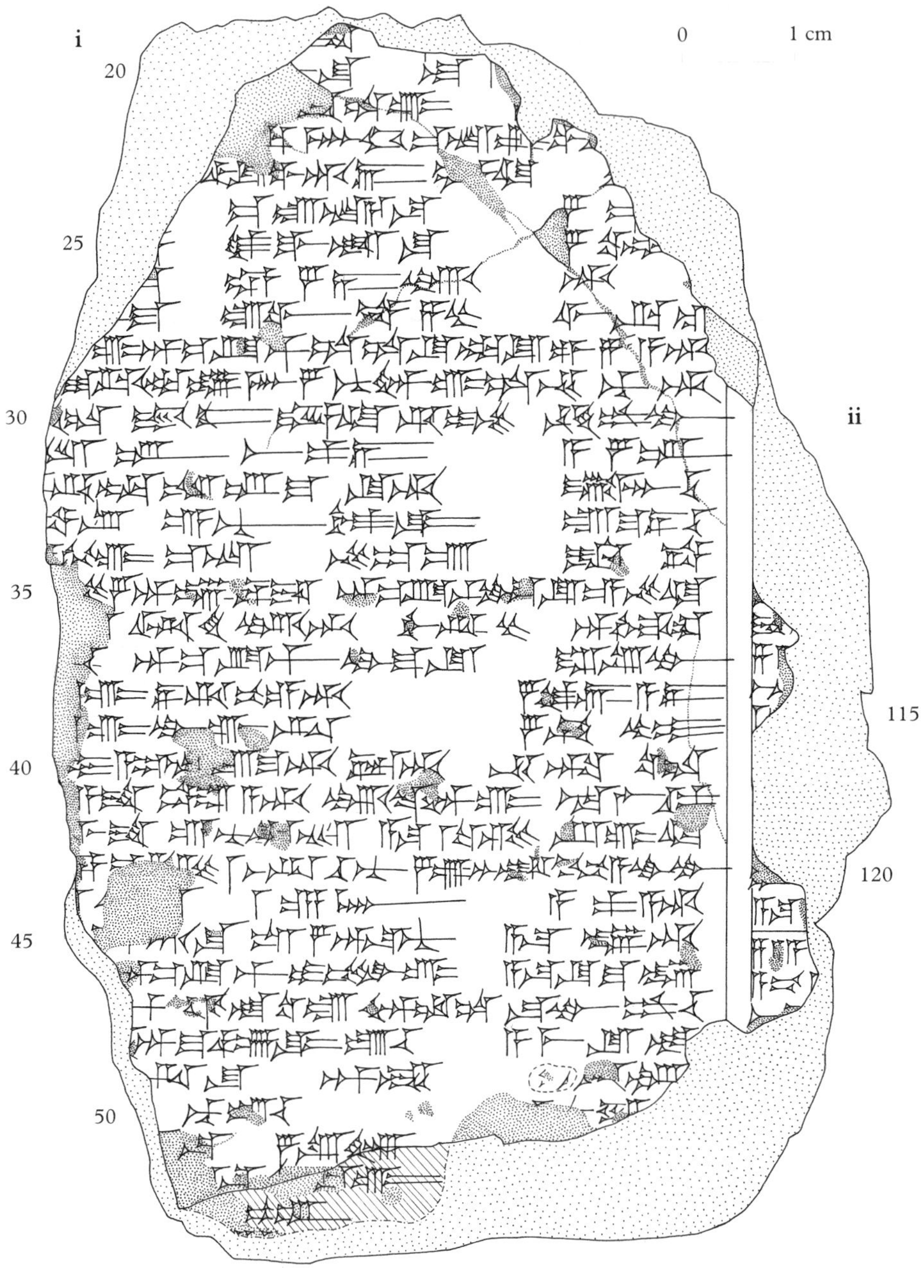

46. SB Tablet I. MS **g.** The hatched area is restored from the photograph

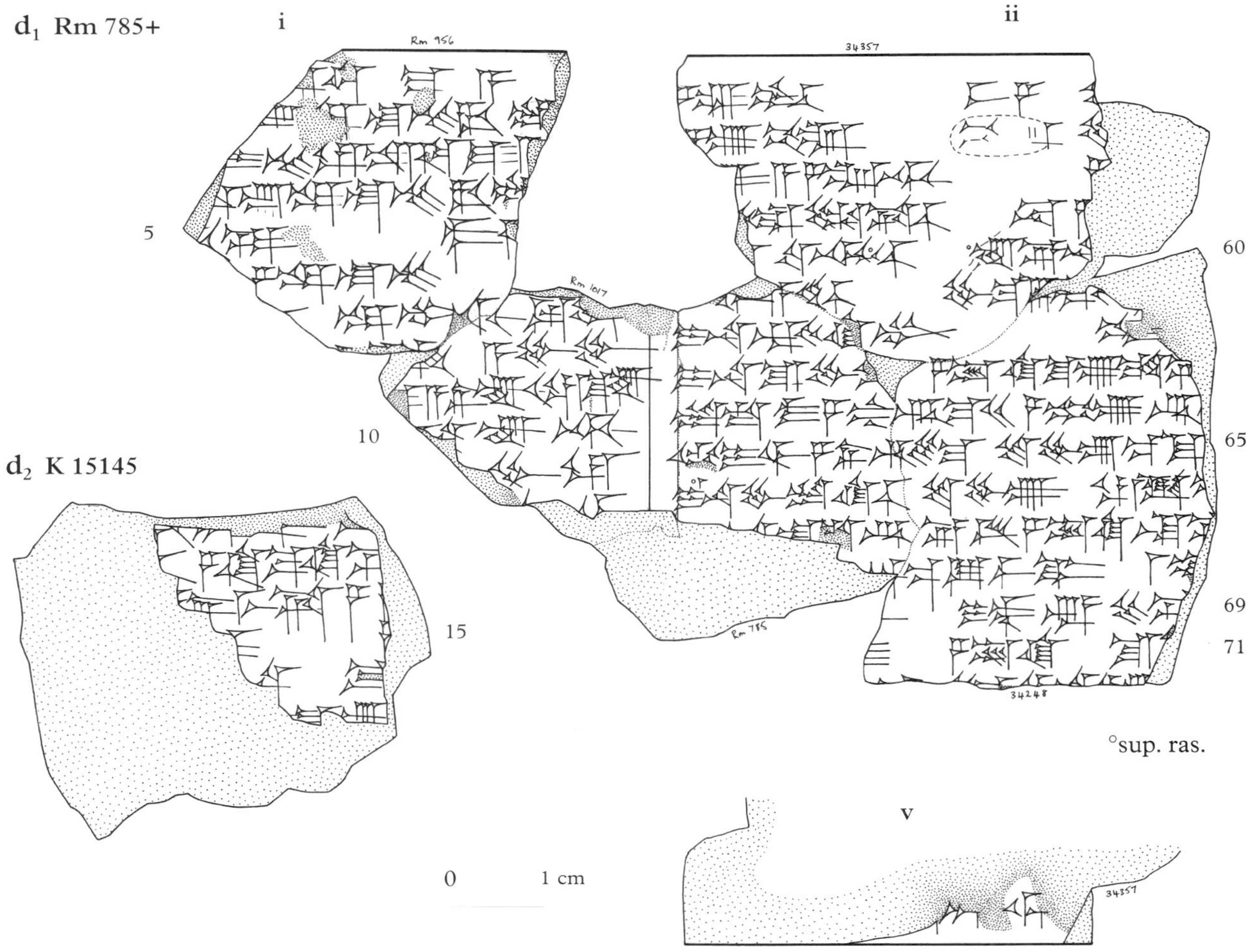

47. SB Tablet I. MS d

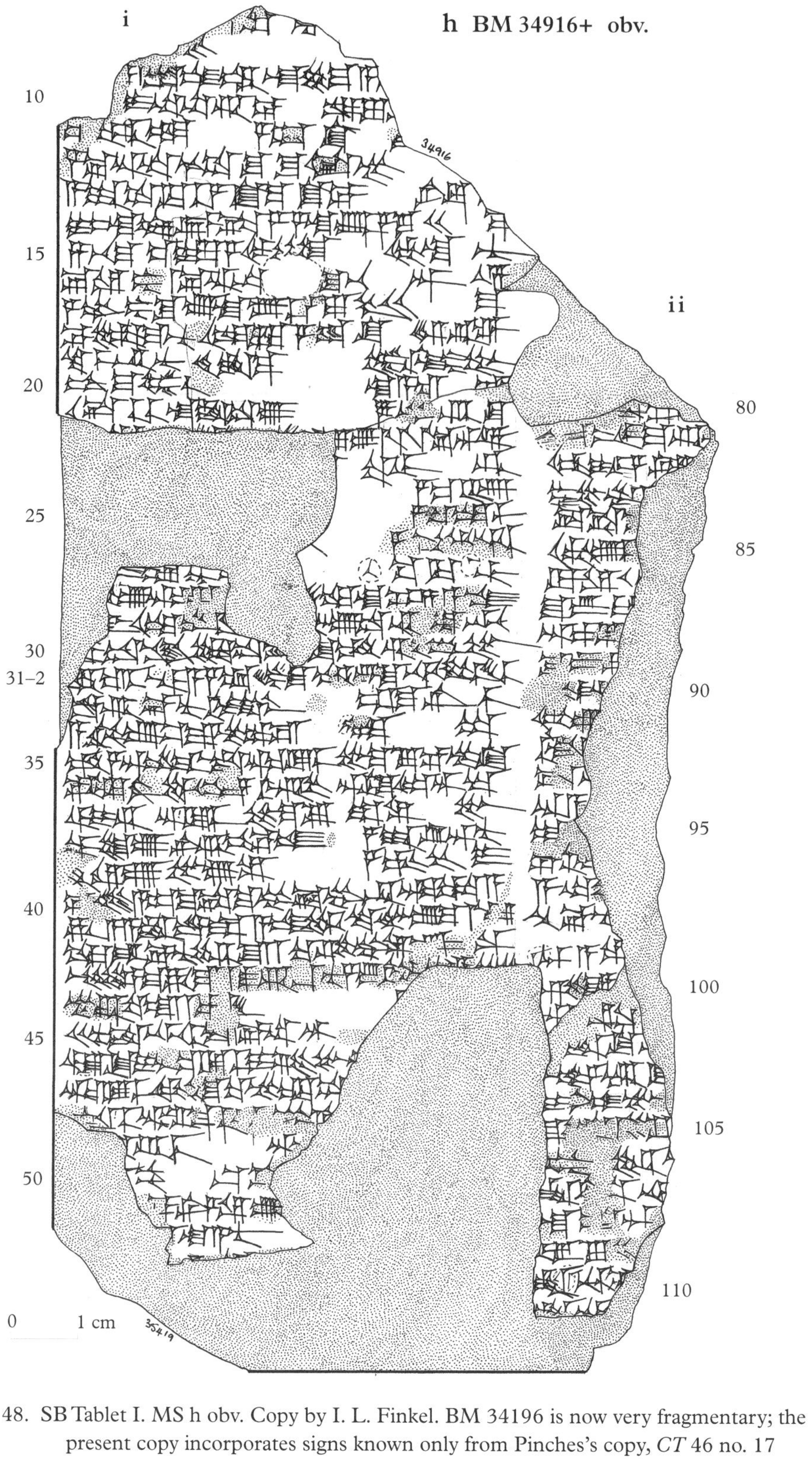

48. SB Tablet I. MS h obv. Copy by I. L. Finkel. BM 34196 is now very fragmentary; the present copy incorporates signs known only from Pinches's copy, *CT* 46 no. 17

h BM 34916+ rev.

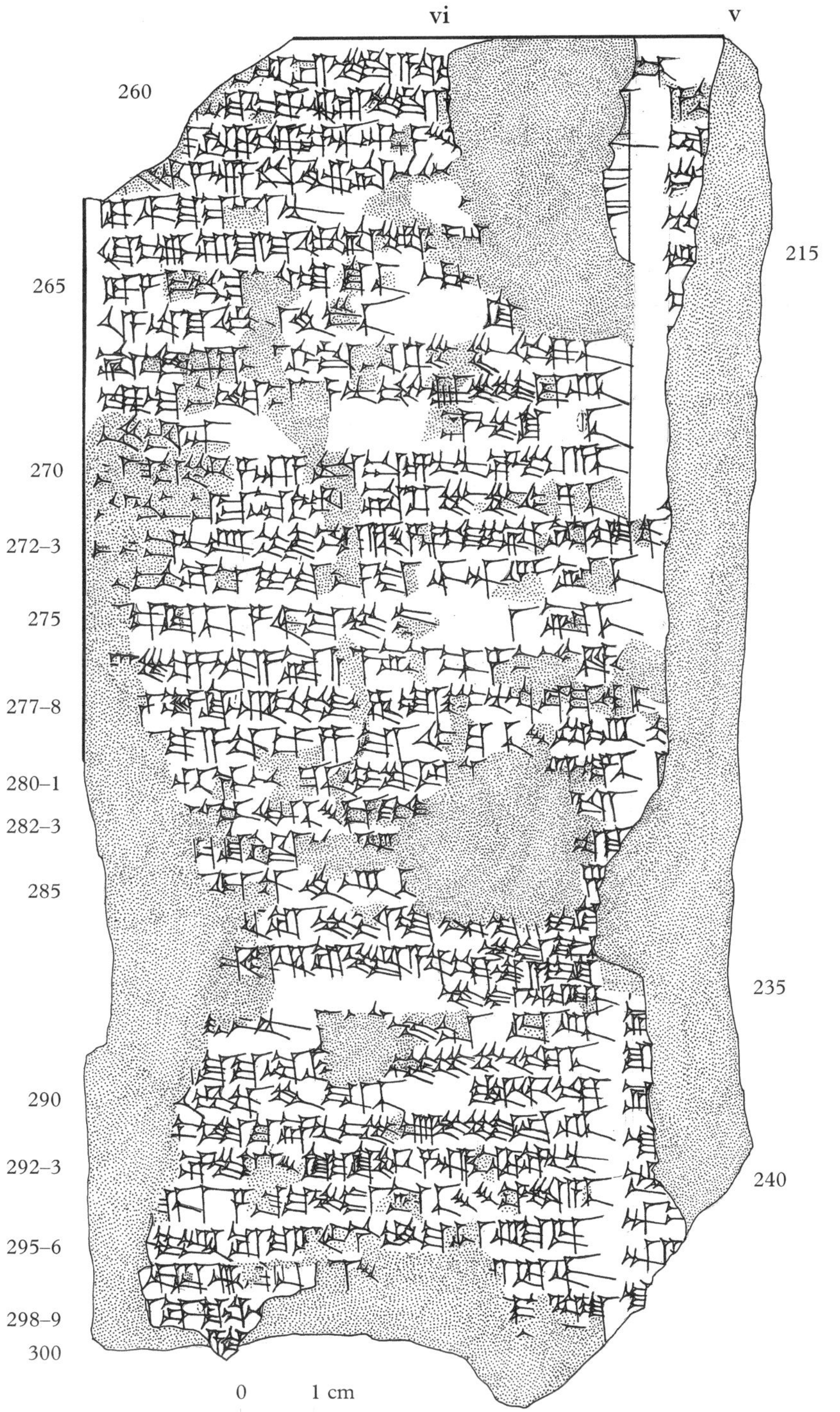

49. SB Tablet I. MS h rev. Copy by I. L. Finkel

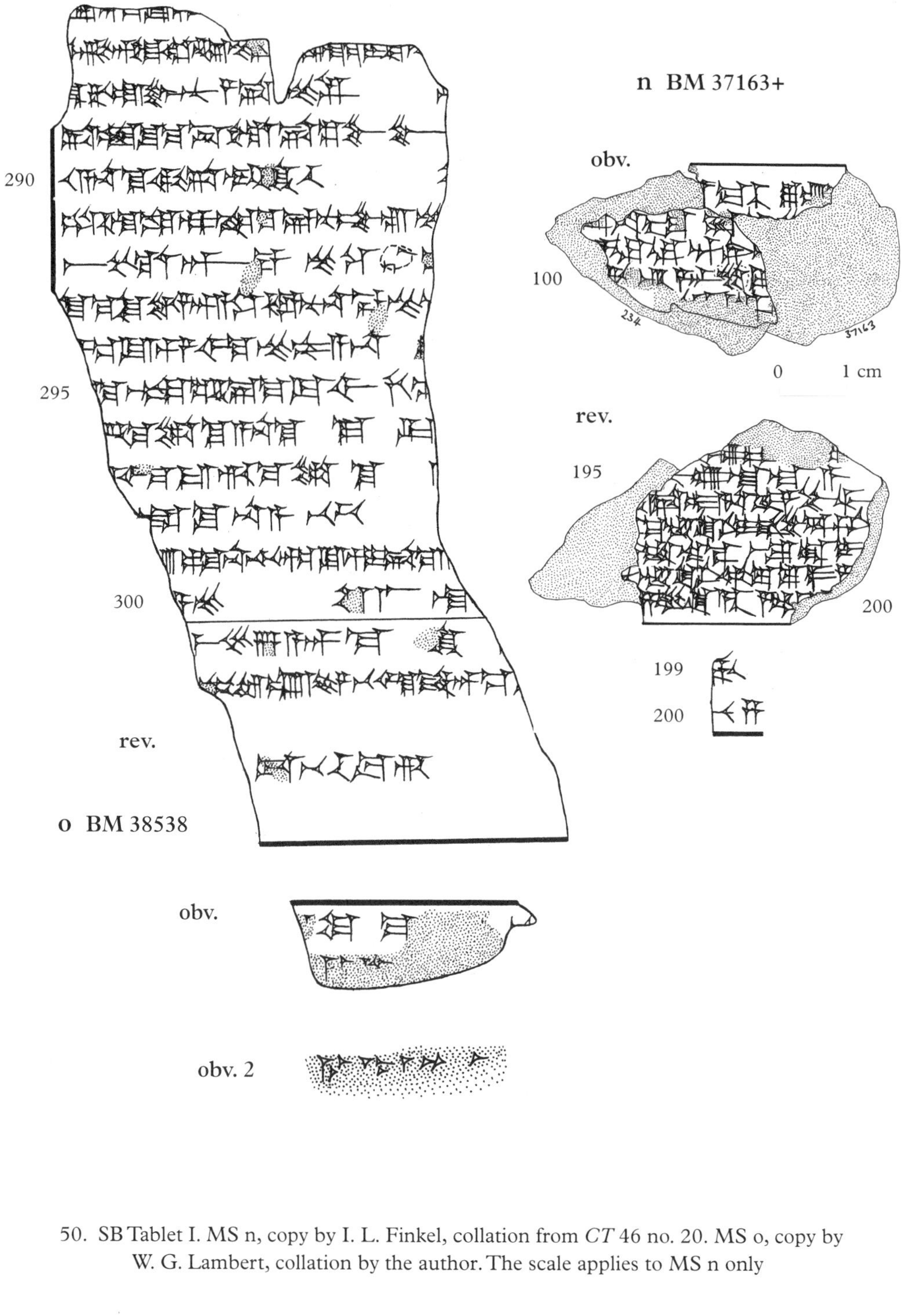

50. SB Tablet I. MS n, copy by I. L. Finkel, collation from *CT* 46 no. 20. MS o, copy by W. G. Lambert, collation by the author. The scale applies to MS n only

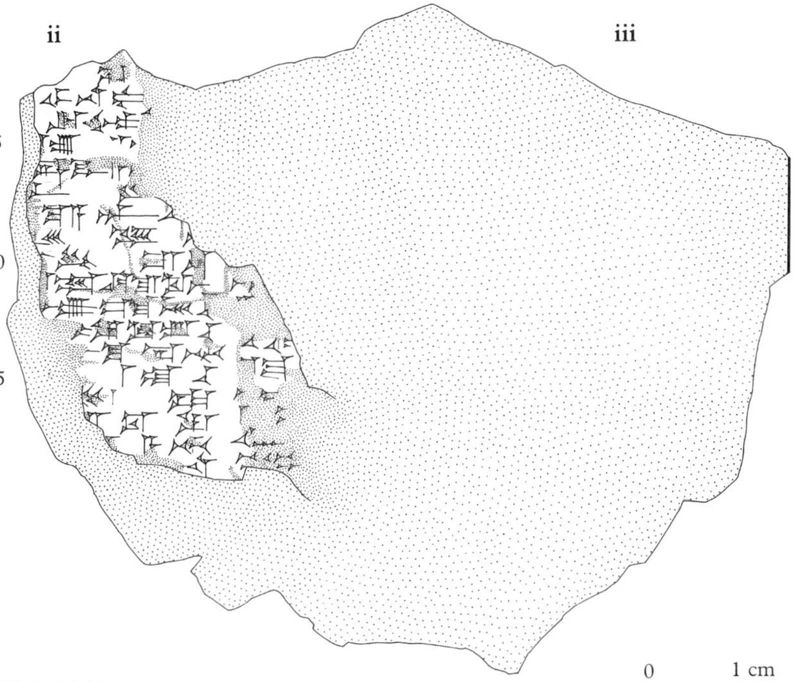

x VAT 17234

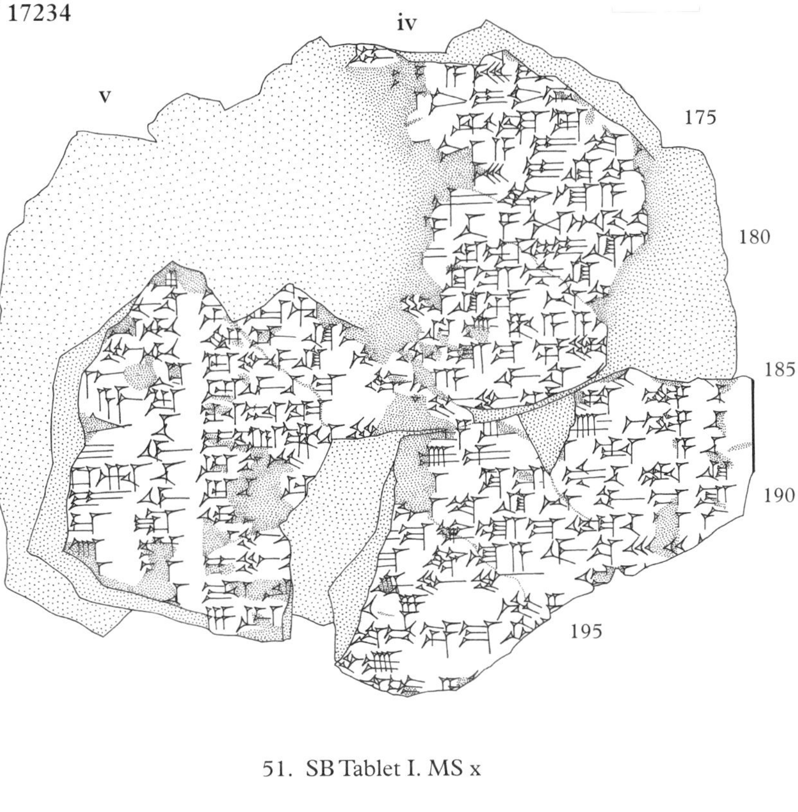

51. SB Tablet I. MS x

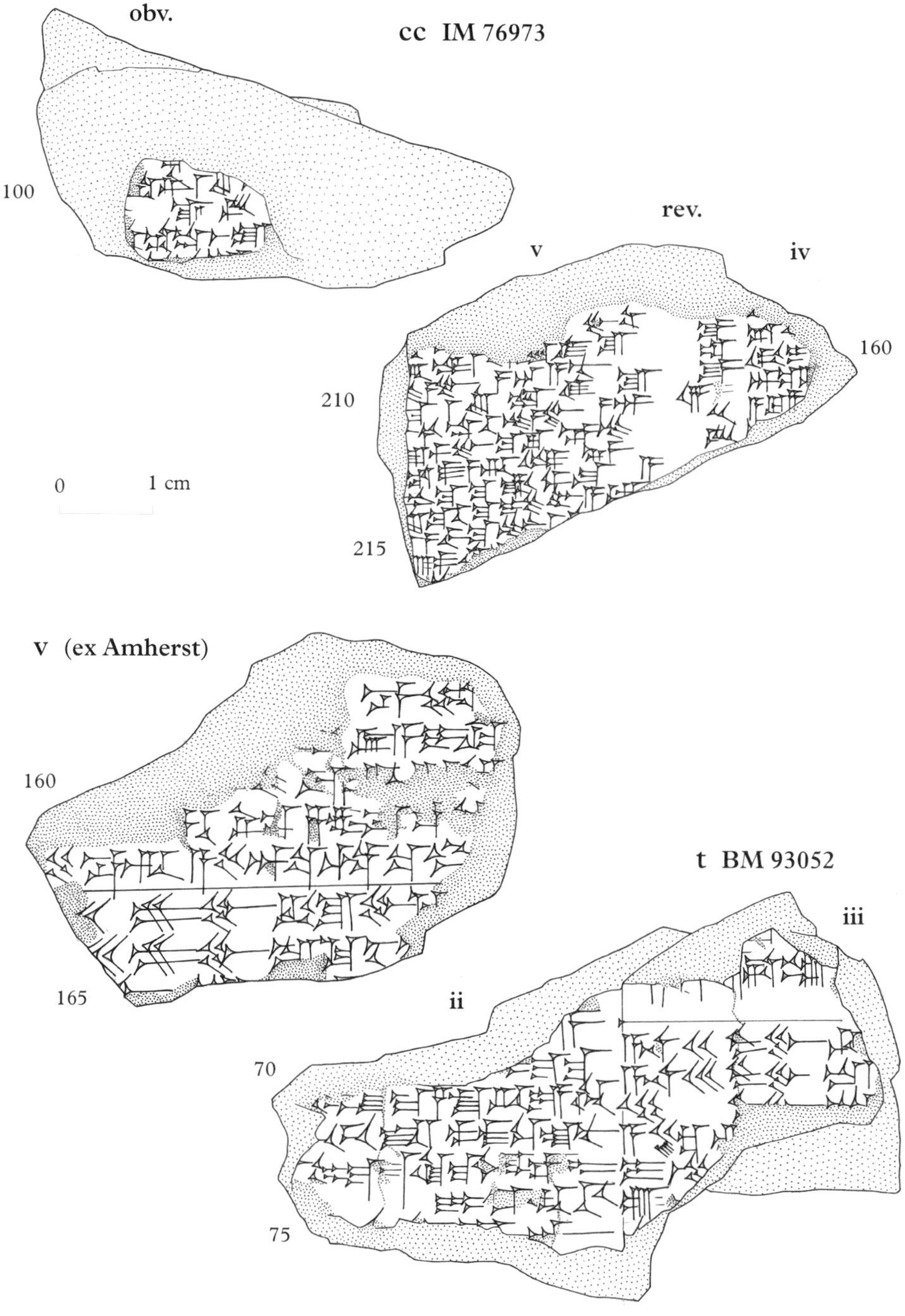

52. SB Tablet I, MS cc. Tablet IV, MSS t and v

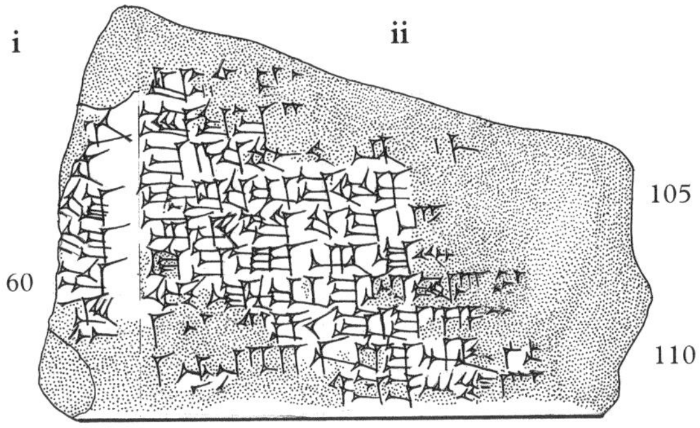

k BM 35567

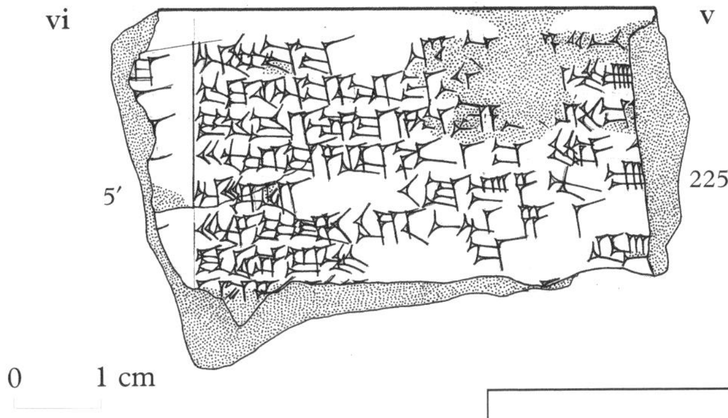

e BM 34449

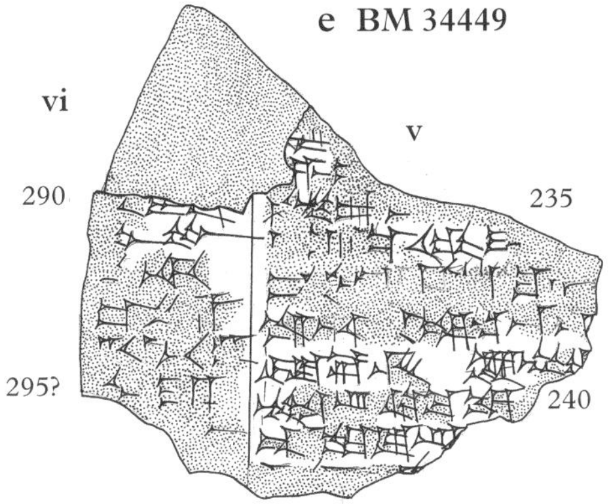

p BM 38833

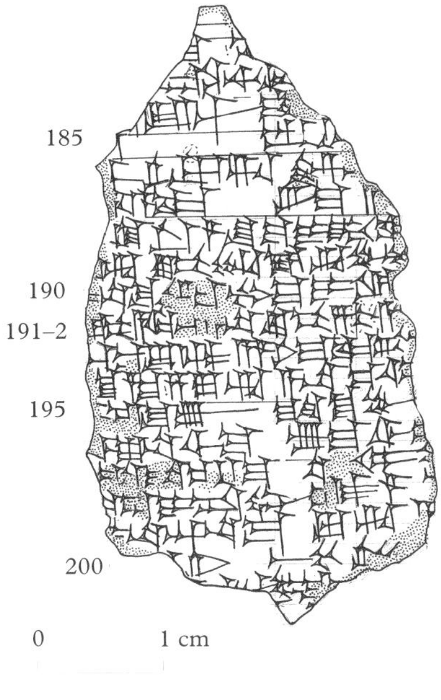

53. SB Tablet II. MSS e, k and p. Copies by I. L. Finkel

X_2 Rm 289+

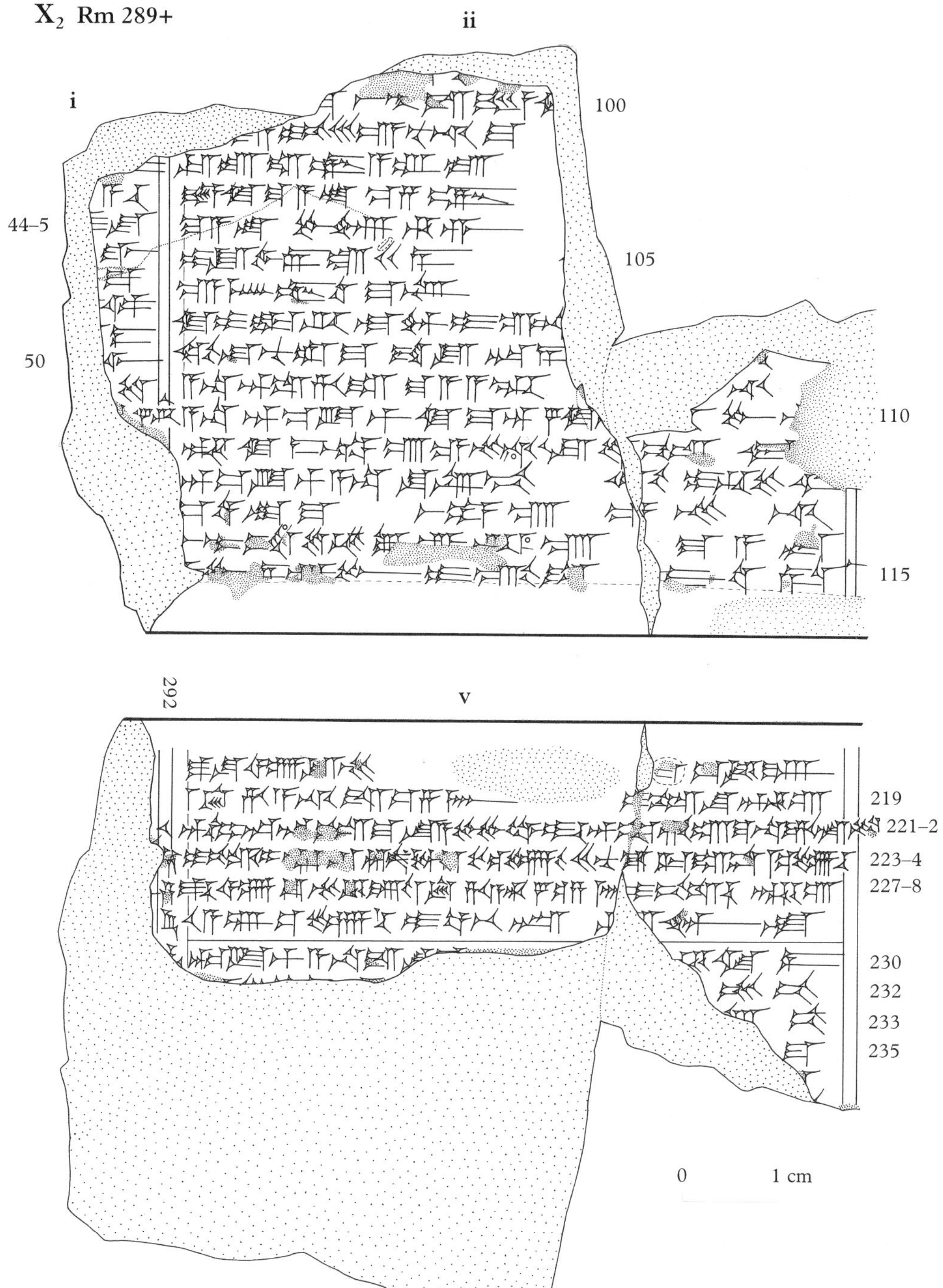

54. SB Tablet II. MS X_2 cols. i, ii and v

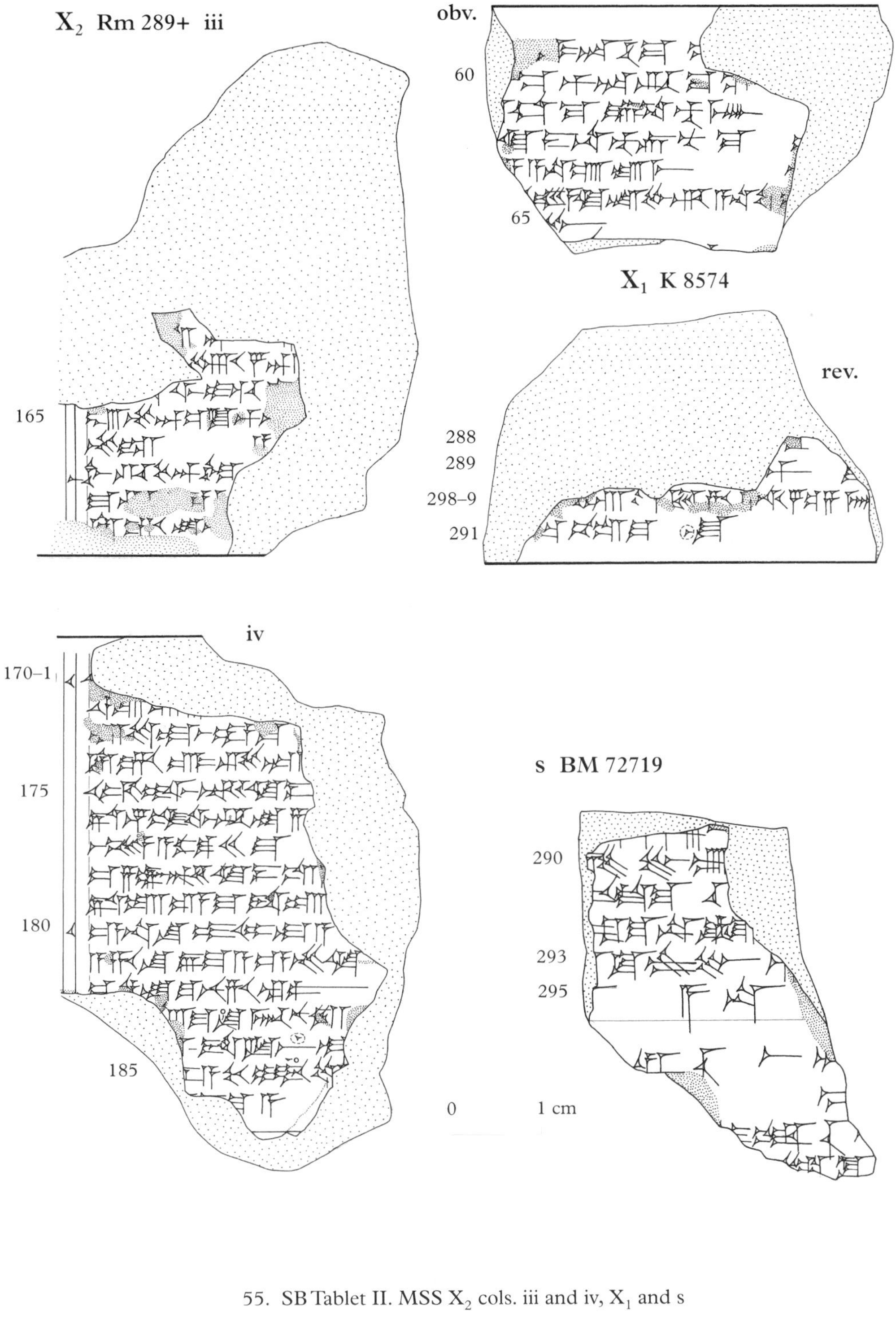

55. SB Tablet II. MSS X$_2$ cols. iii and iv, X$_1$ and s

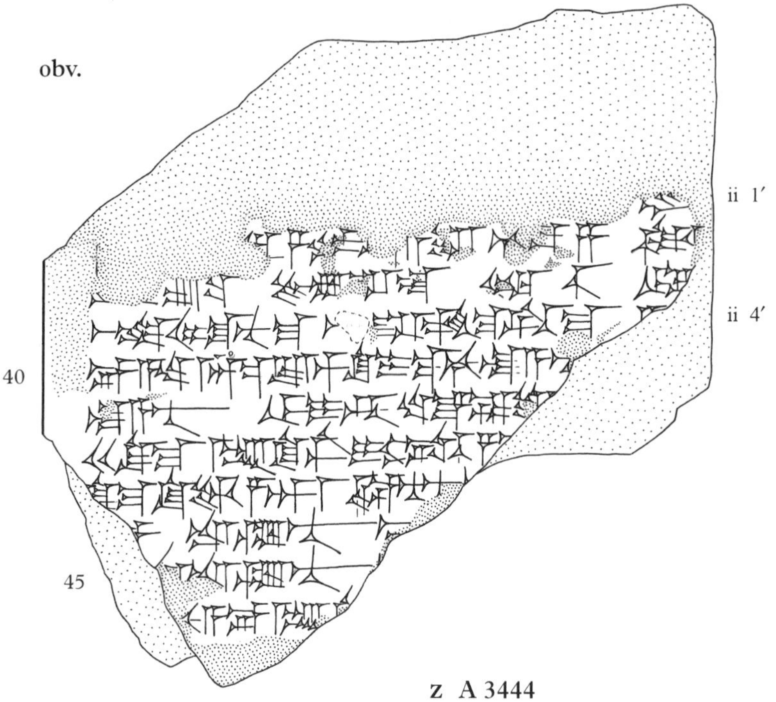

z A 3444

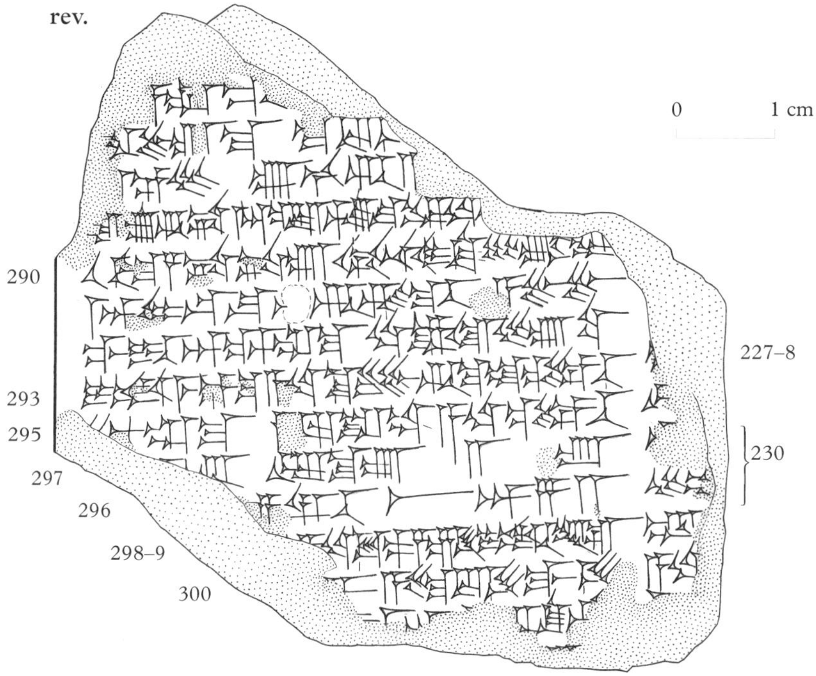

56. SB Tablet II. MS z

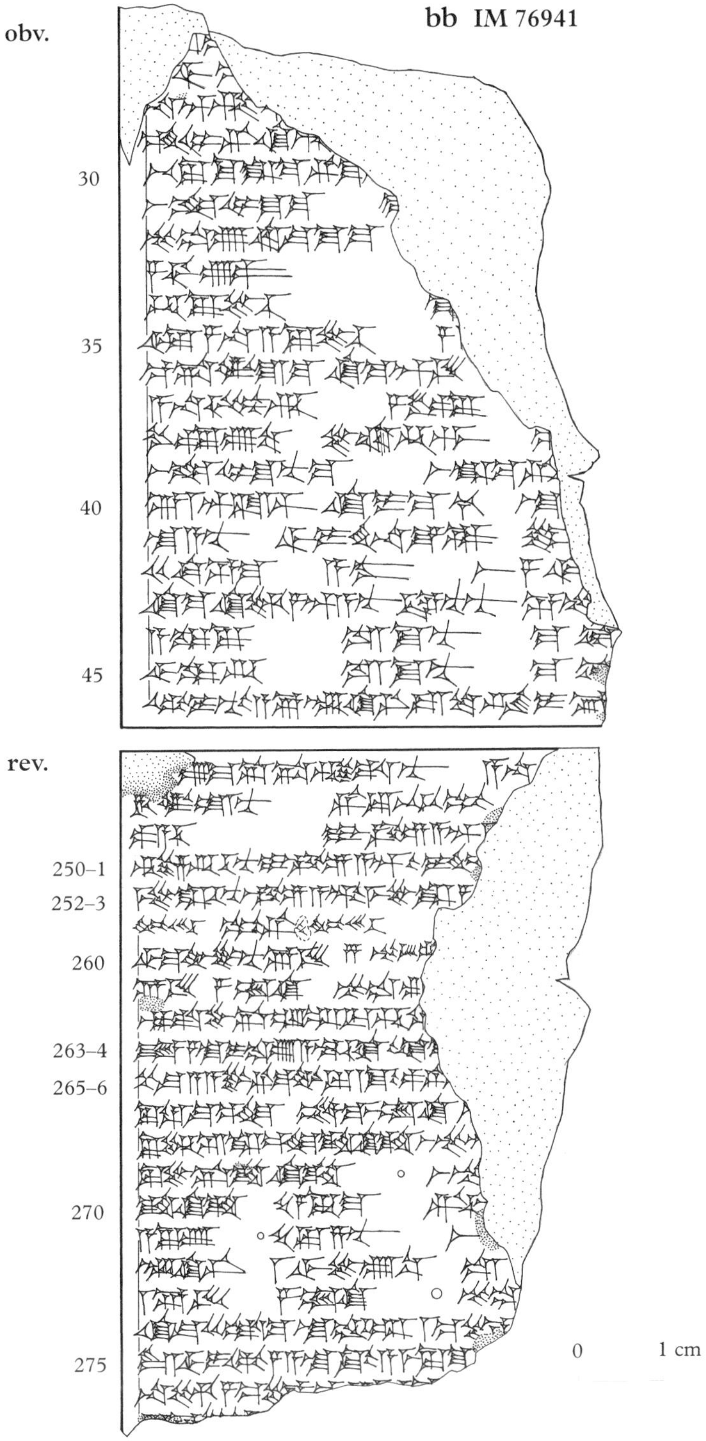

57. SB Tablet II. MS bb

ee W ‘23018’ (23013?)

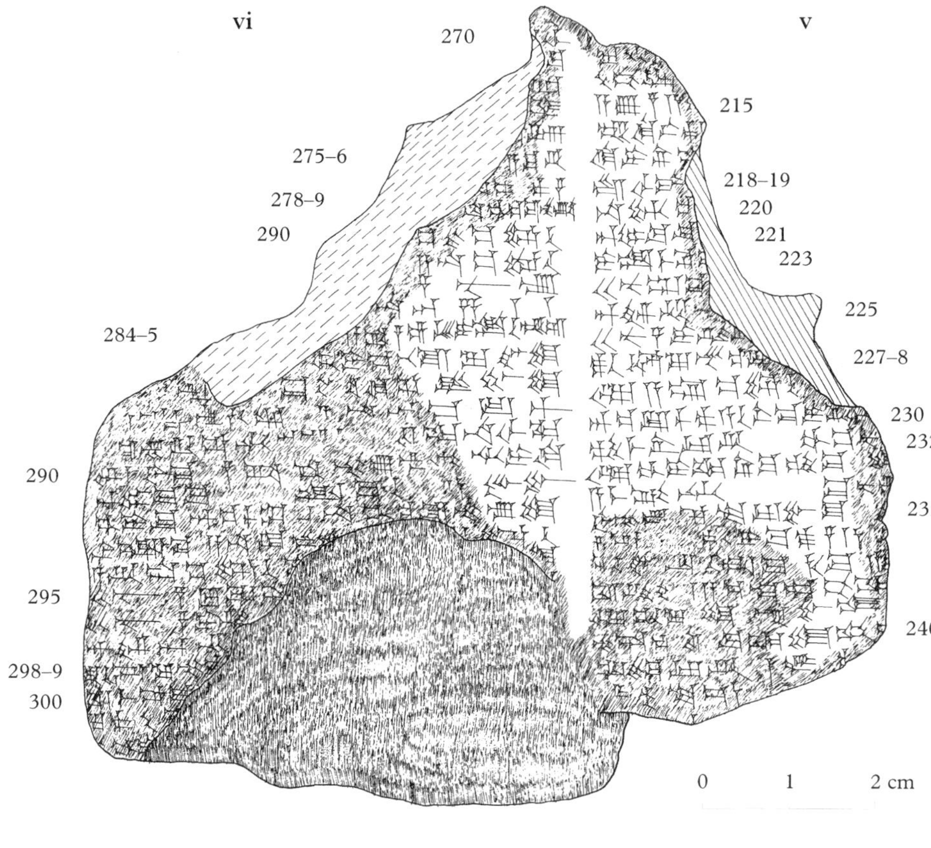

58. SB Tablet II. MS ee. Copy by E. von Weiher

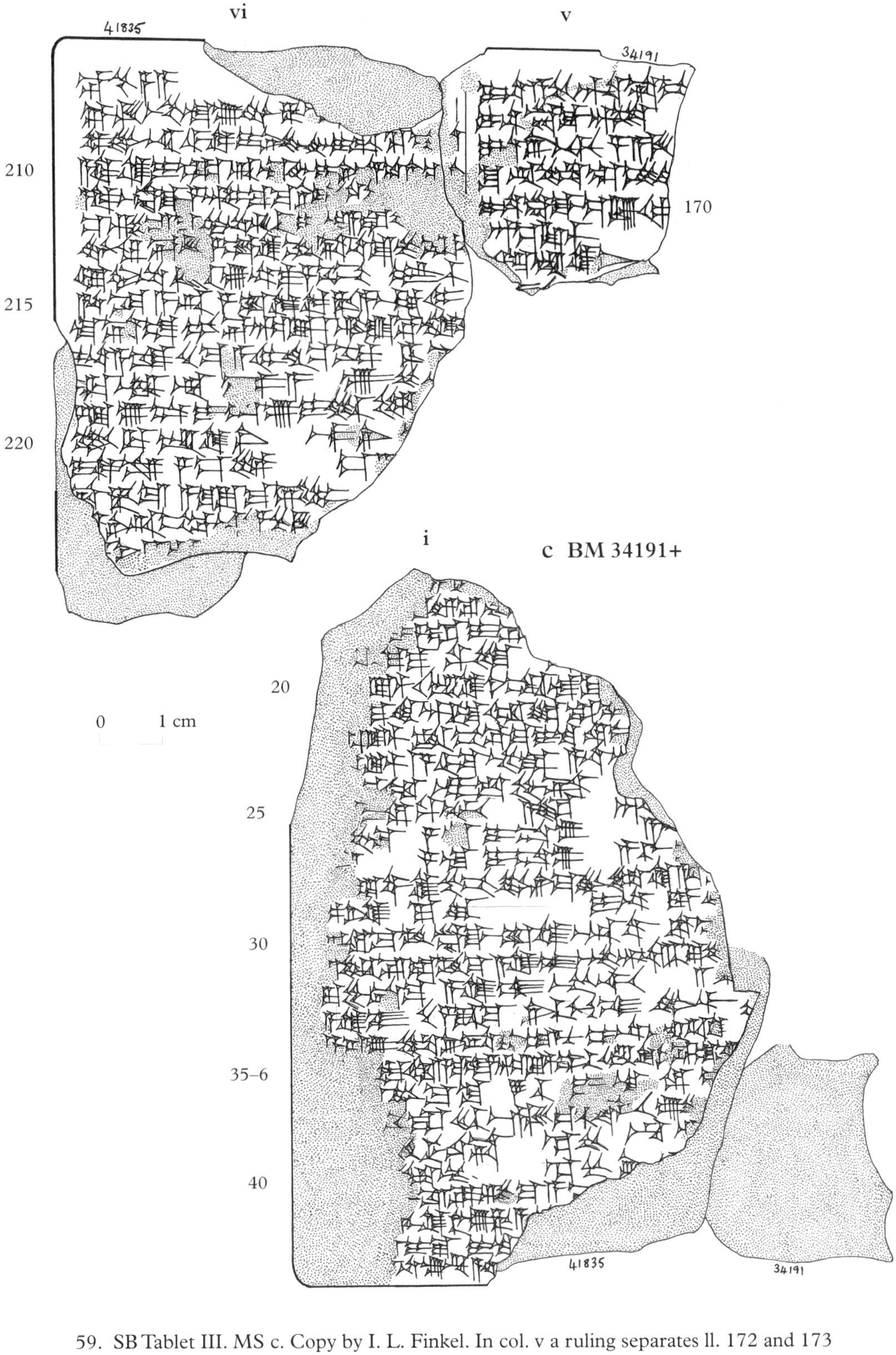

59. SB Tablet III. MS c. Copy by I. L. Finkel. In col. v a ruling separates ll. 172 and 173

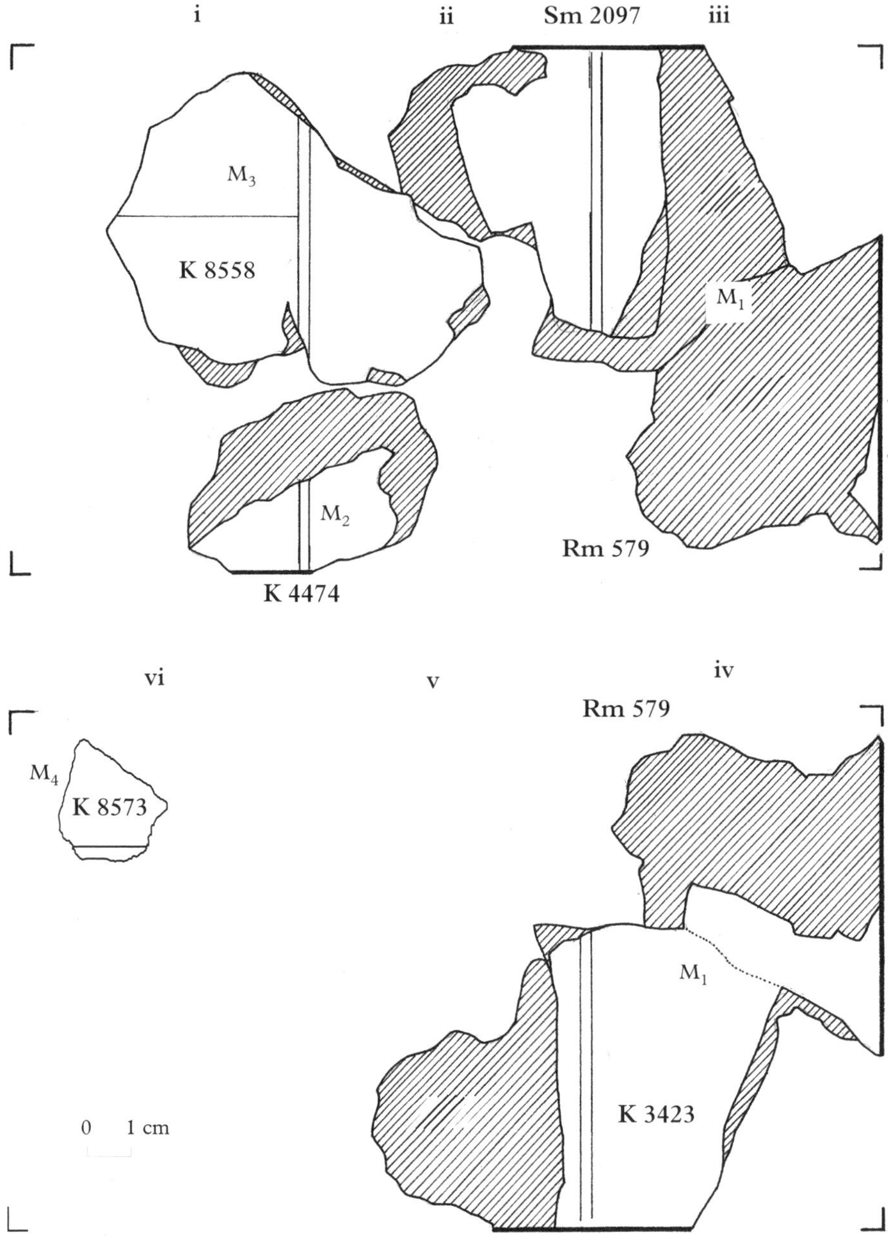

60. SB Tablet III. MS M, outline sketch. The position of M_4 is uncertain

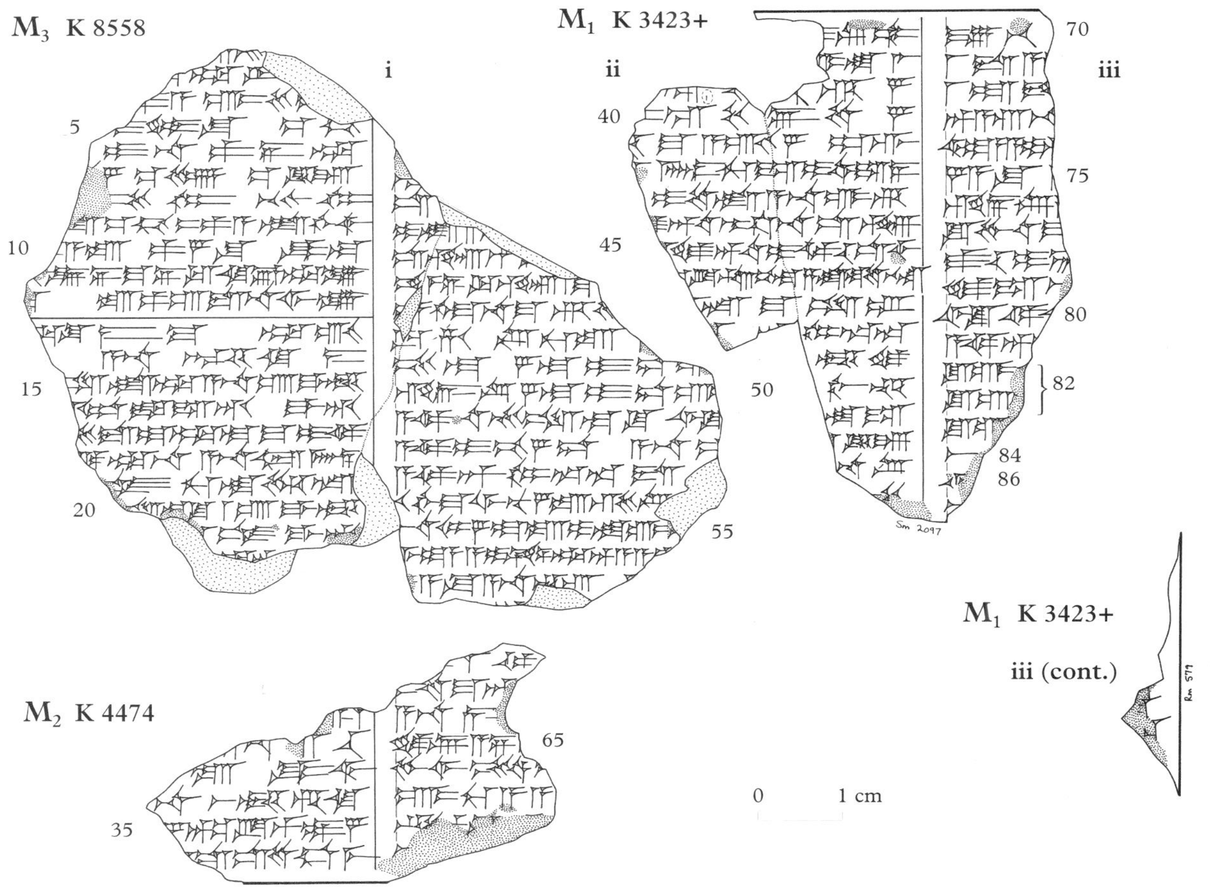

61. SB Tablet III. MS M obv.

M_4 K 8573

M_1 K 3423+

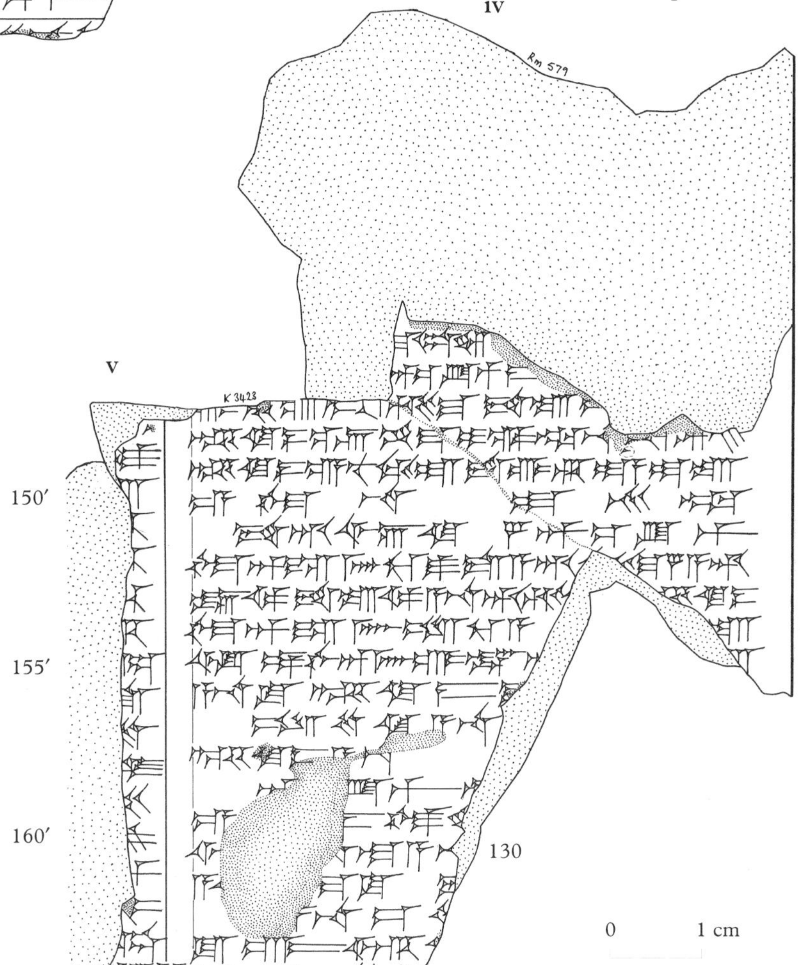

62. SB Tablet III. MS M rev.

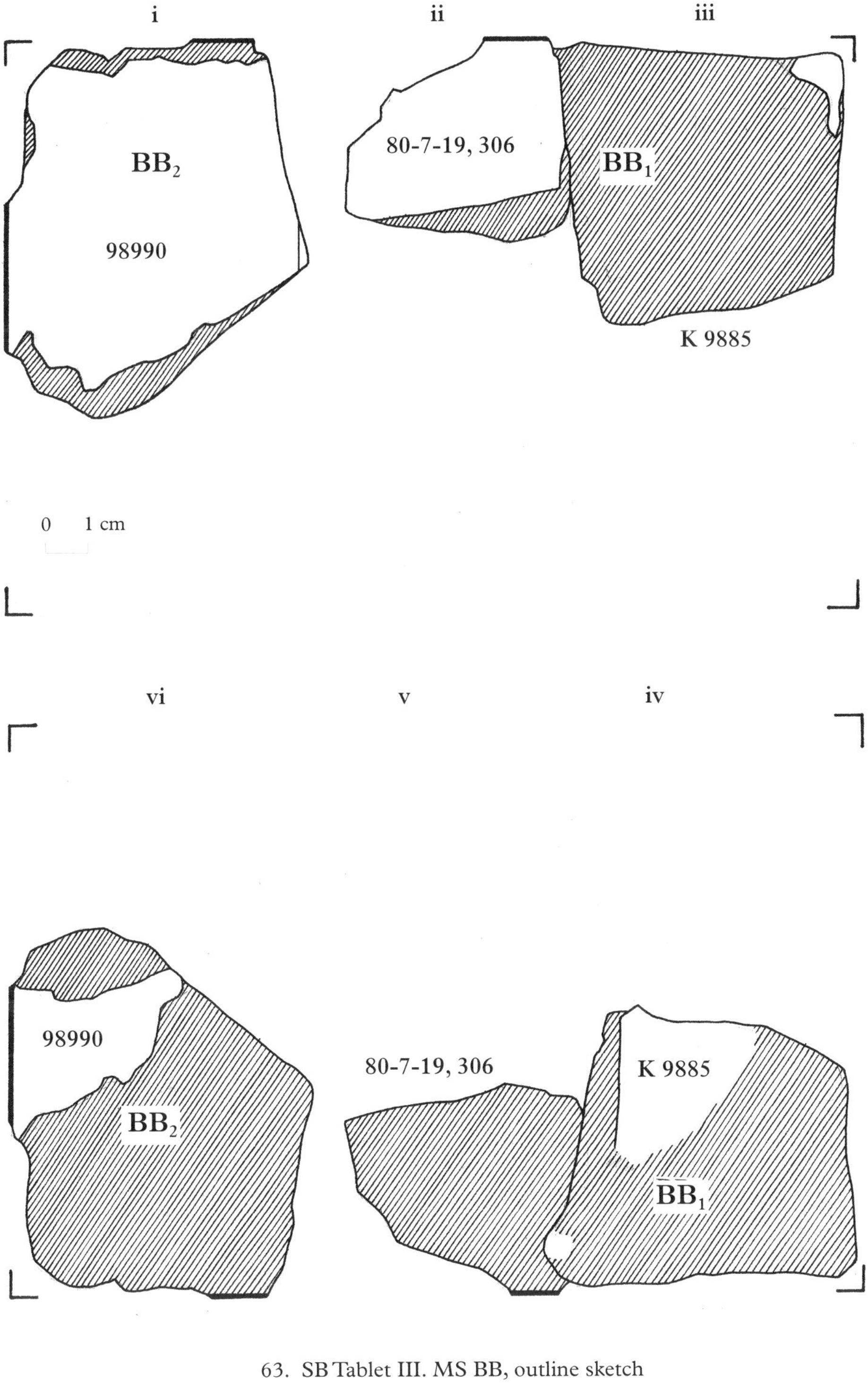

63. SB Tablet III. MS BB, outline sketch

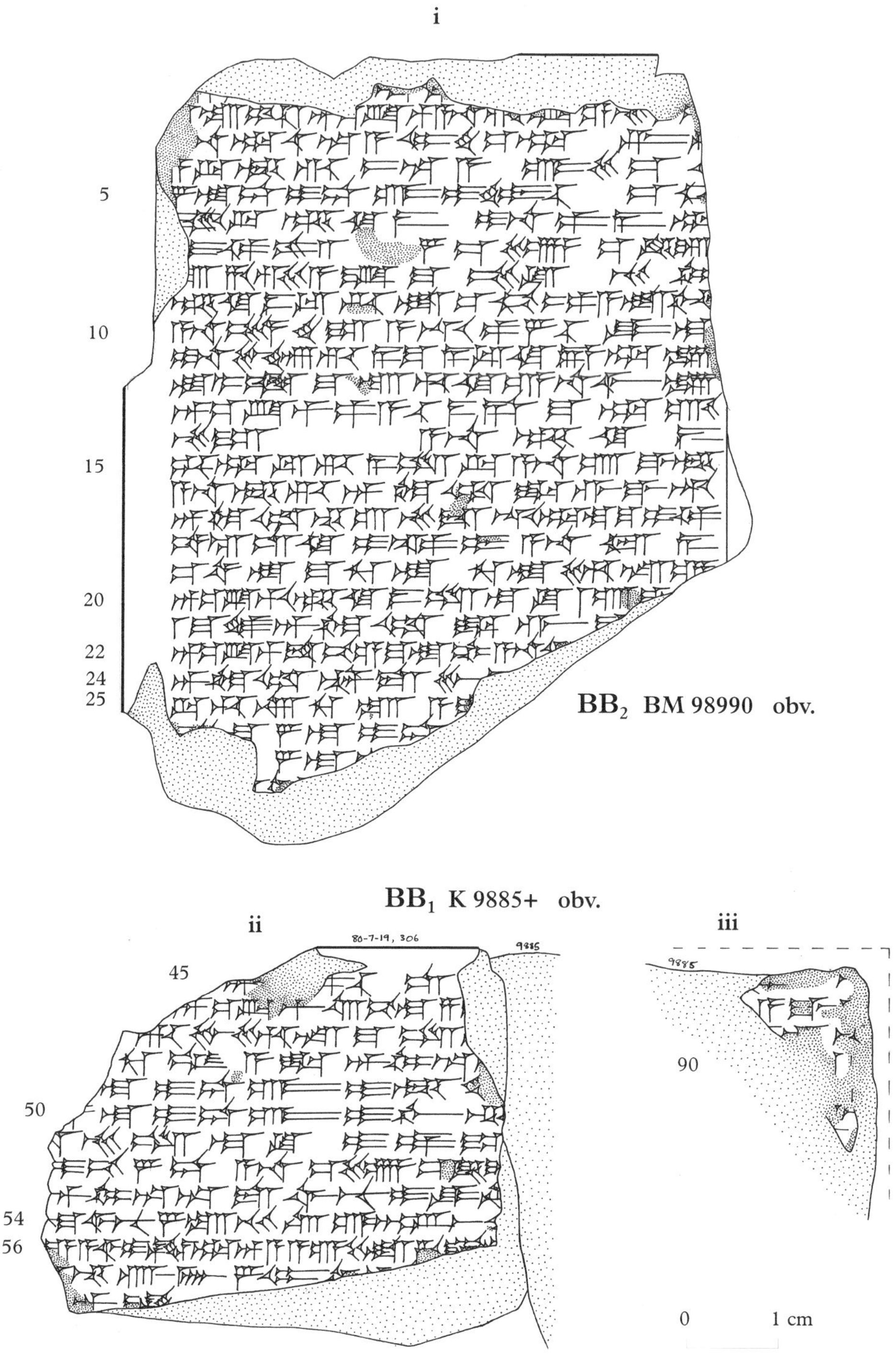

64. SB Tablet III. MS BB obv.

BB$_1$ K 9885+ rev.

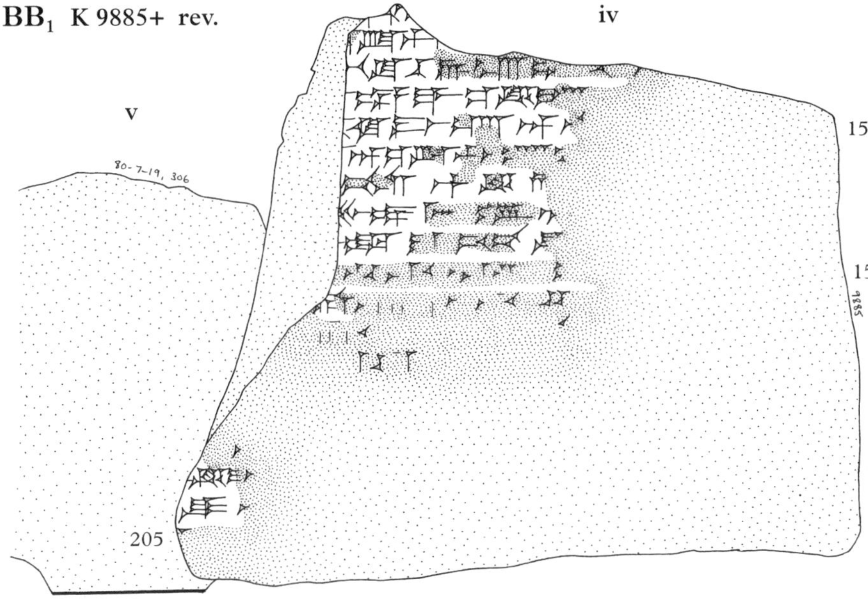

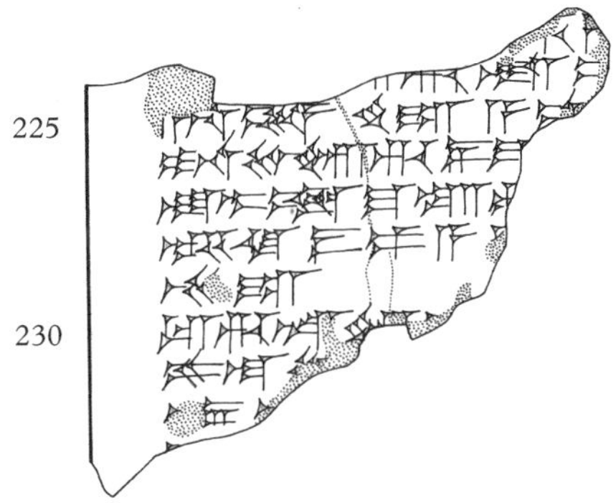

BB$_2$ BM 98990 rev.

S K 7224

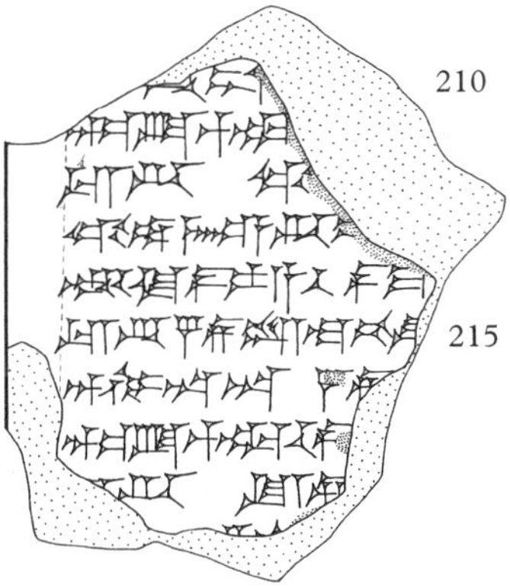

0 1 cm

65. SB Tablet III. MS BB rev.
Tablet IV(?). MS S

aa IM 76873

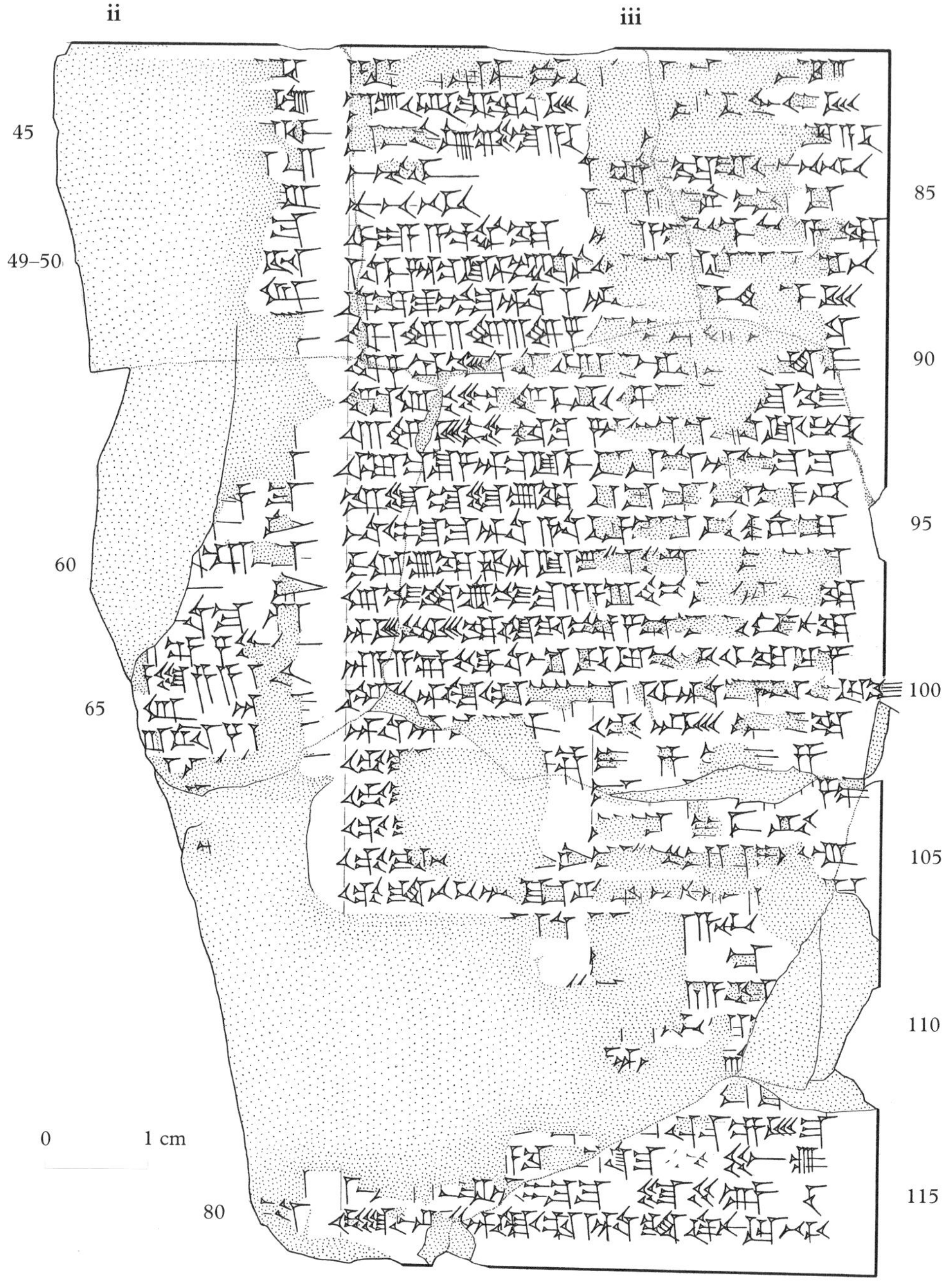

66. SB Tablet III. MS aa obv.

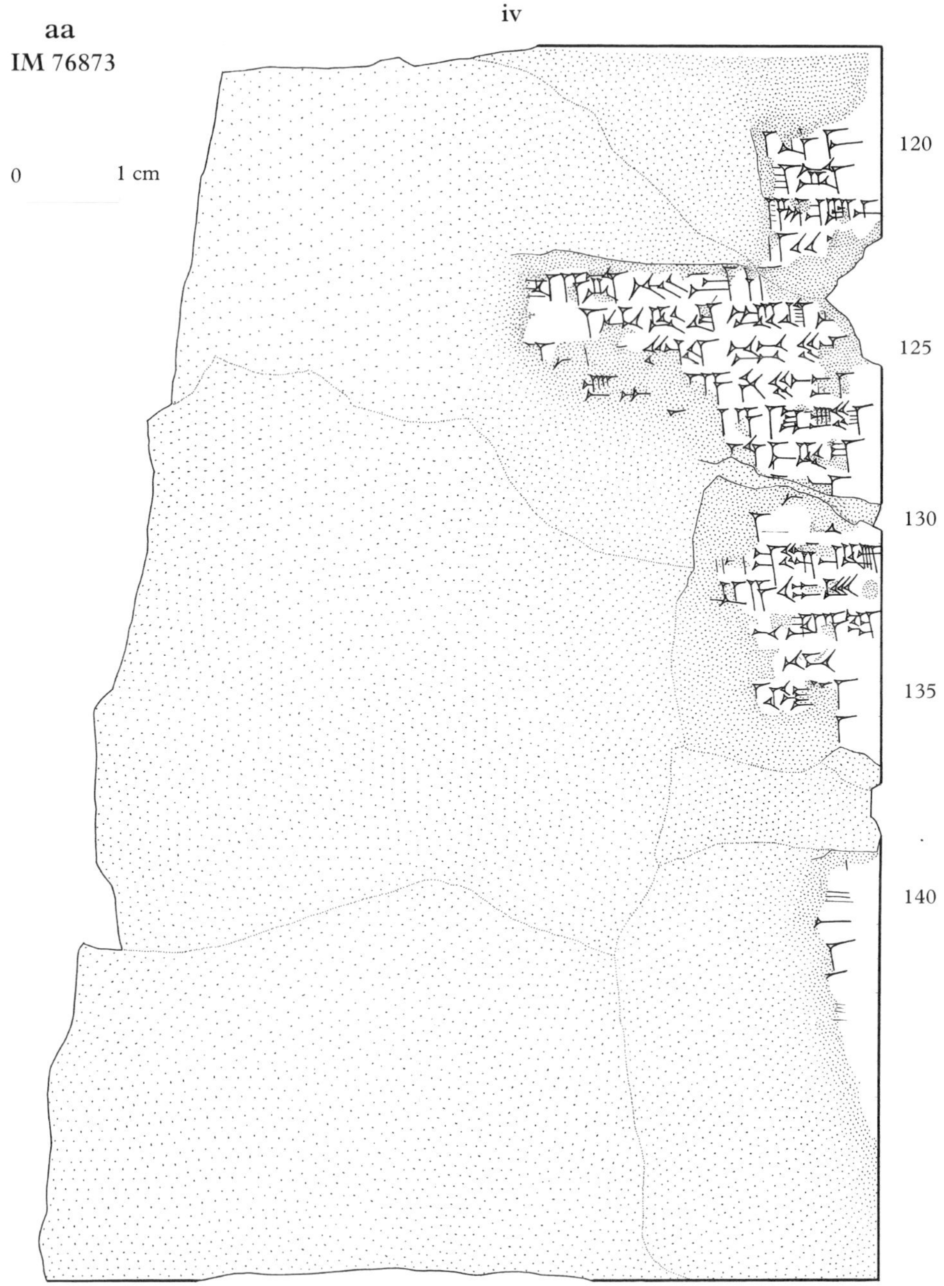

67. SB Tablet III. MS aa rev.

i BM 35079+

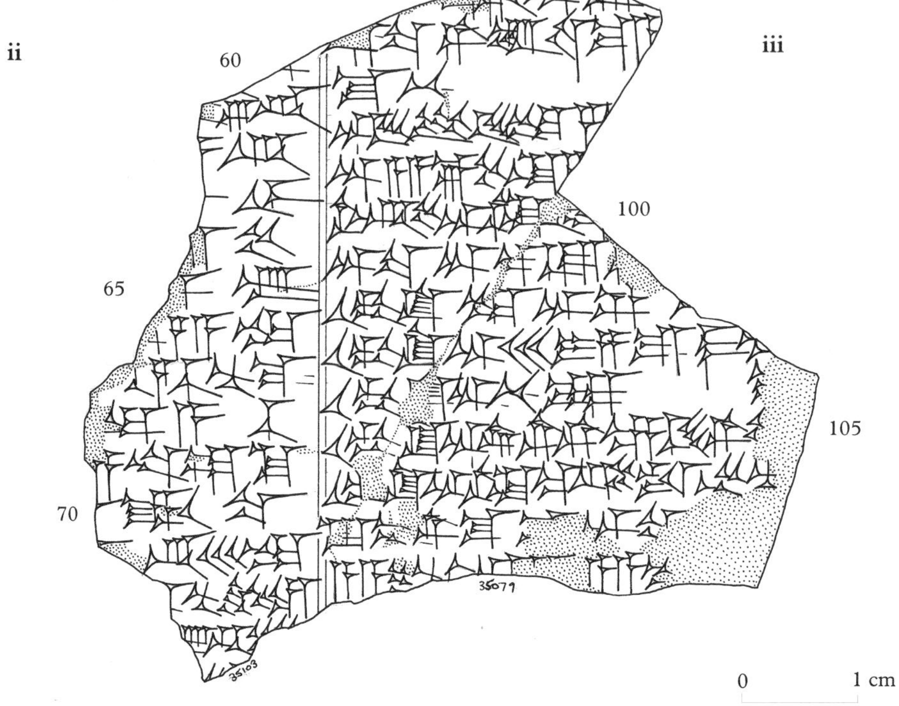

y VAT 19286 rev.

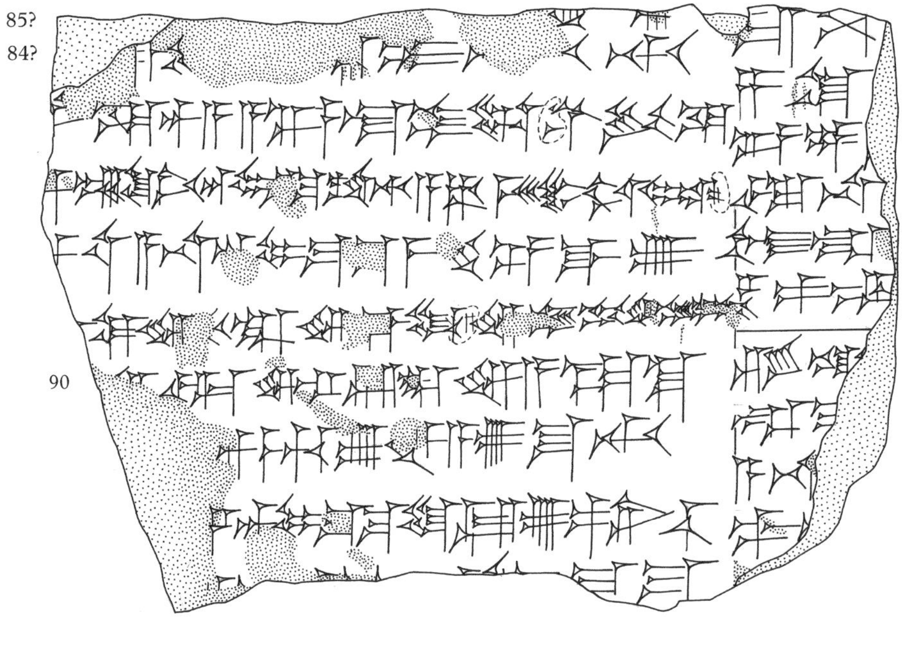

68. SB Tablet III. MSS i and y

iii Y$_2$ Sm 1040

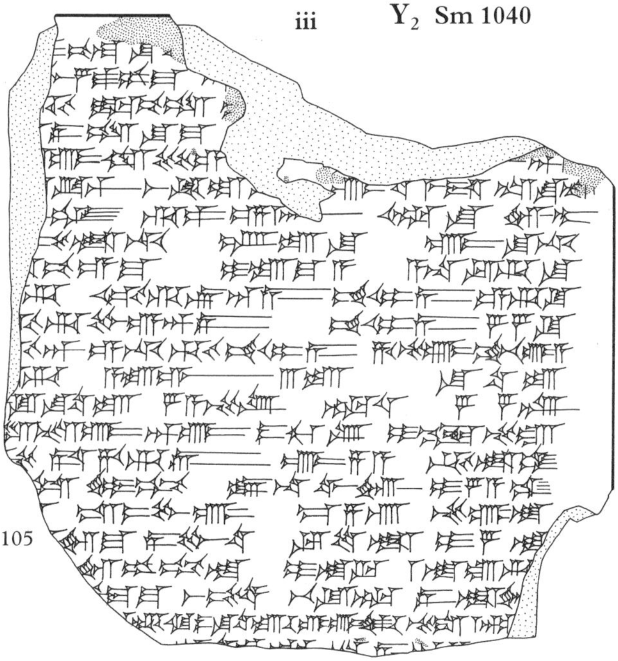

DD K 13525

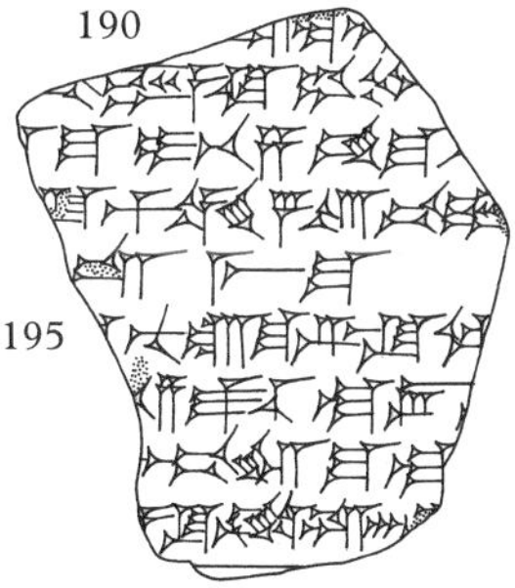

Y$_1$ K 8586

i

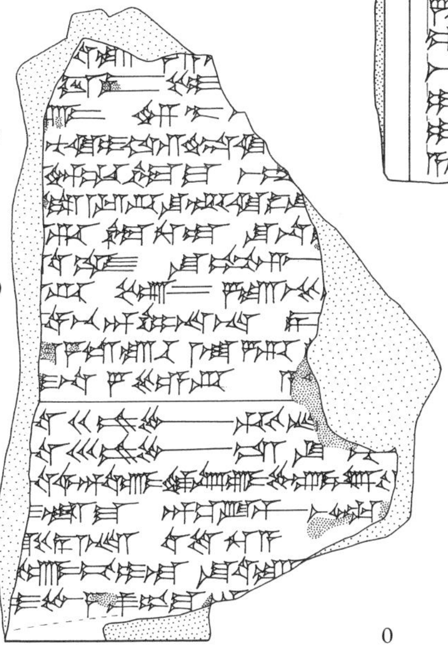

Y$_3$ 79-7-8, 342

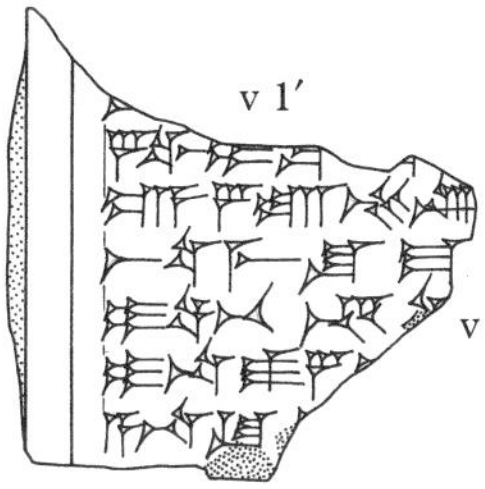

CC K 10777 obv.

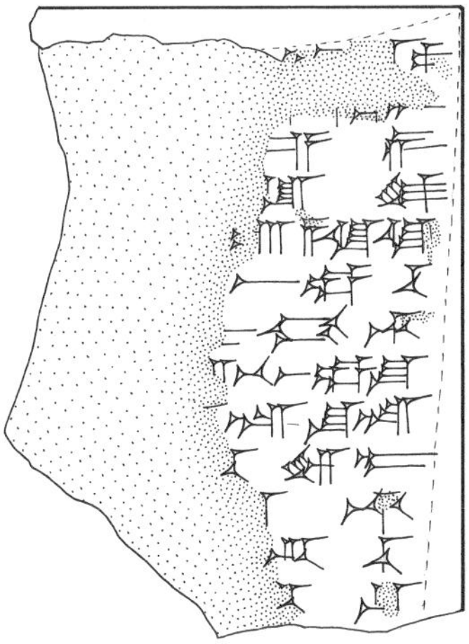

0 1 cm

69. SB Tablet IV. MSS Y, DD and CC obv.

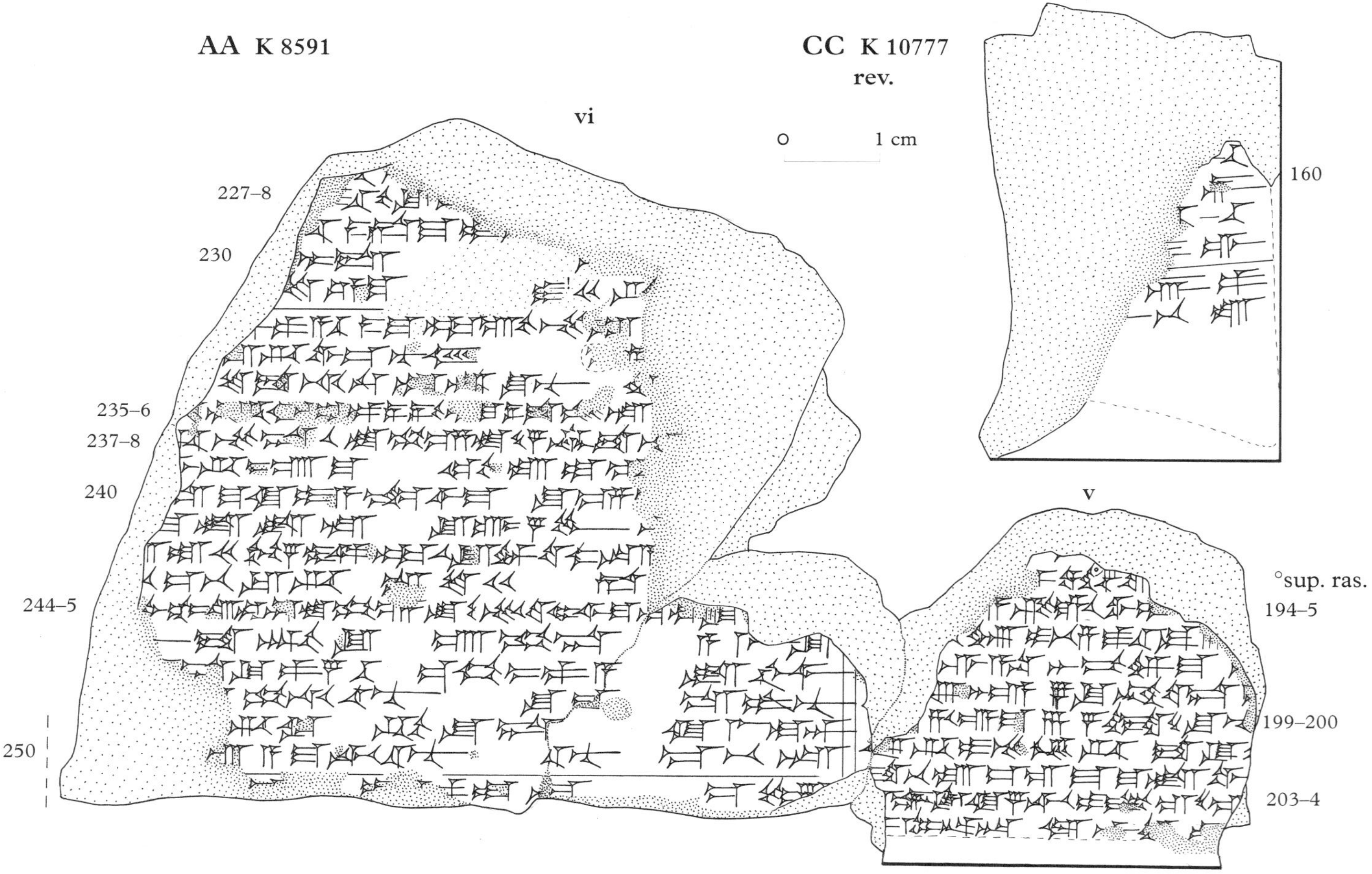

70. SB Tablet IV. MSS AA and CC rev.

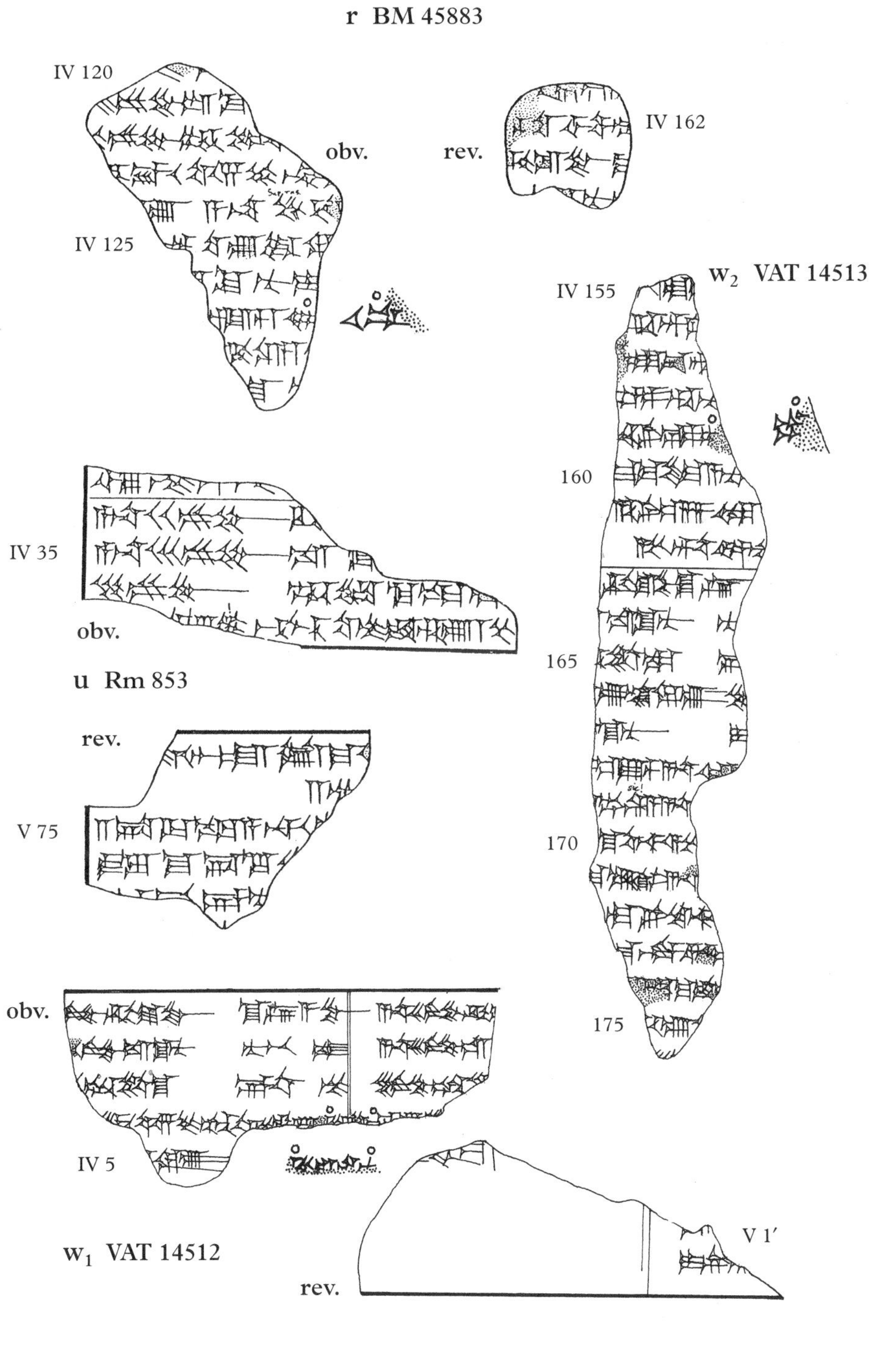

71. SB Tablets IV–V. MSS r, u and w. Copies by W. G. Lambert, collations by the author

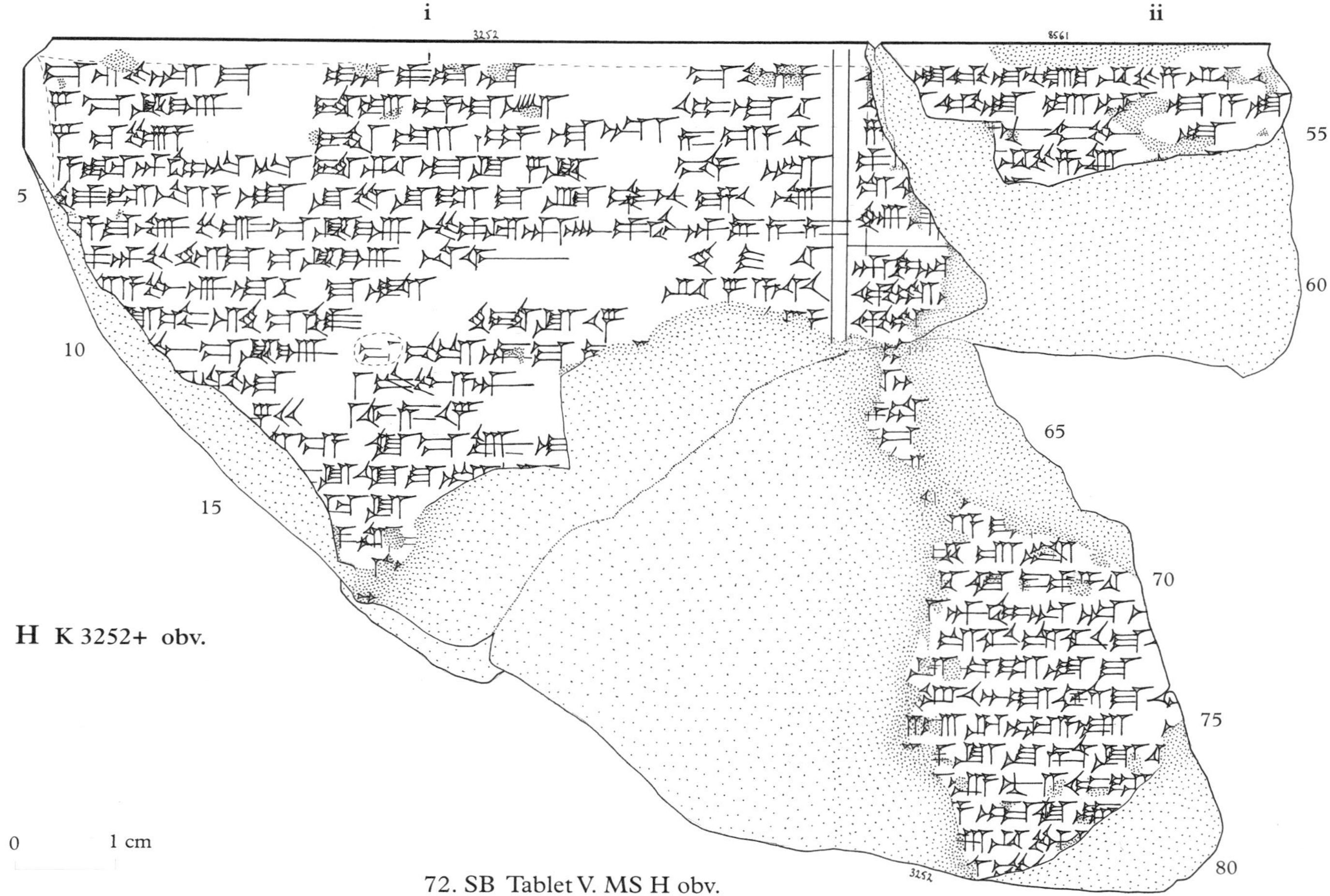

72. SB Tablet V. MS H obv.

H K 3252+ rev.

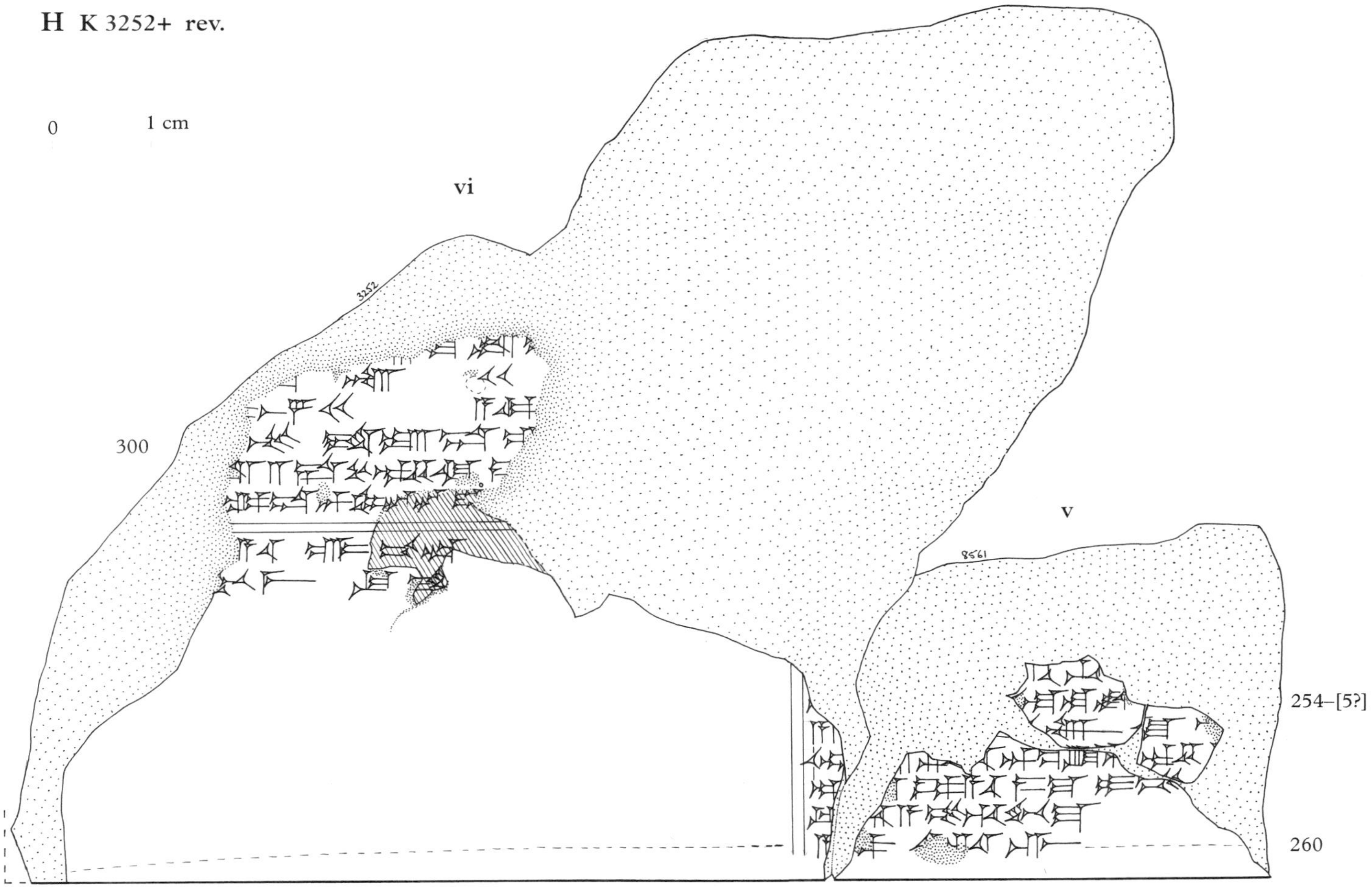

° so Delitzsch; Haupt: *ab*

73. SB Tablet V. MS H rev. The hatched area is restored from Haupt's copy

dd IM 76985

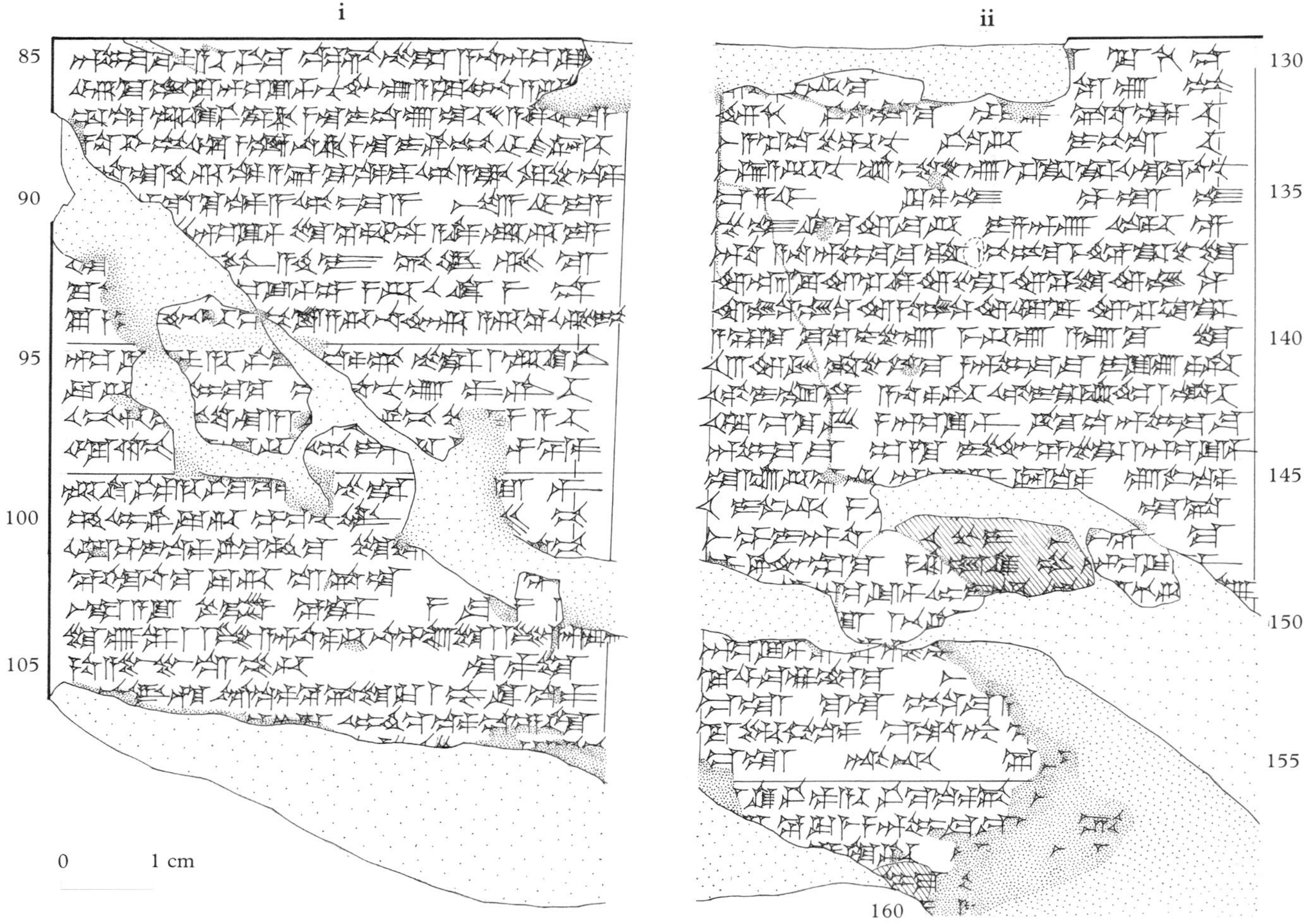

74. SB Tablet V. MS dd cols. i and ii. The hatched areas are restored from the photograph

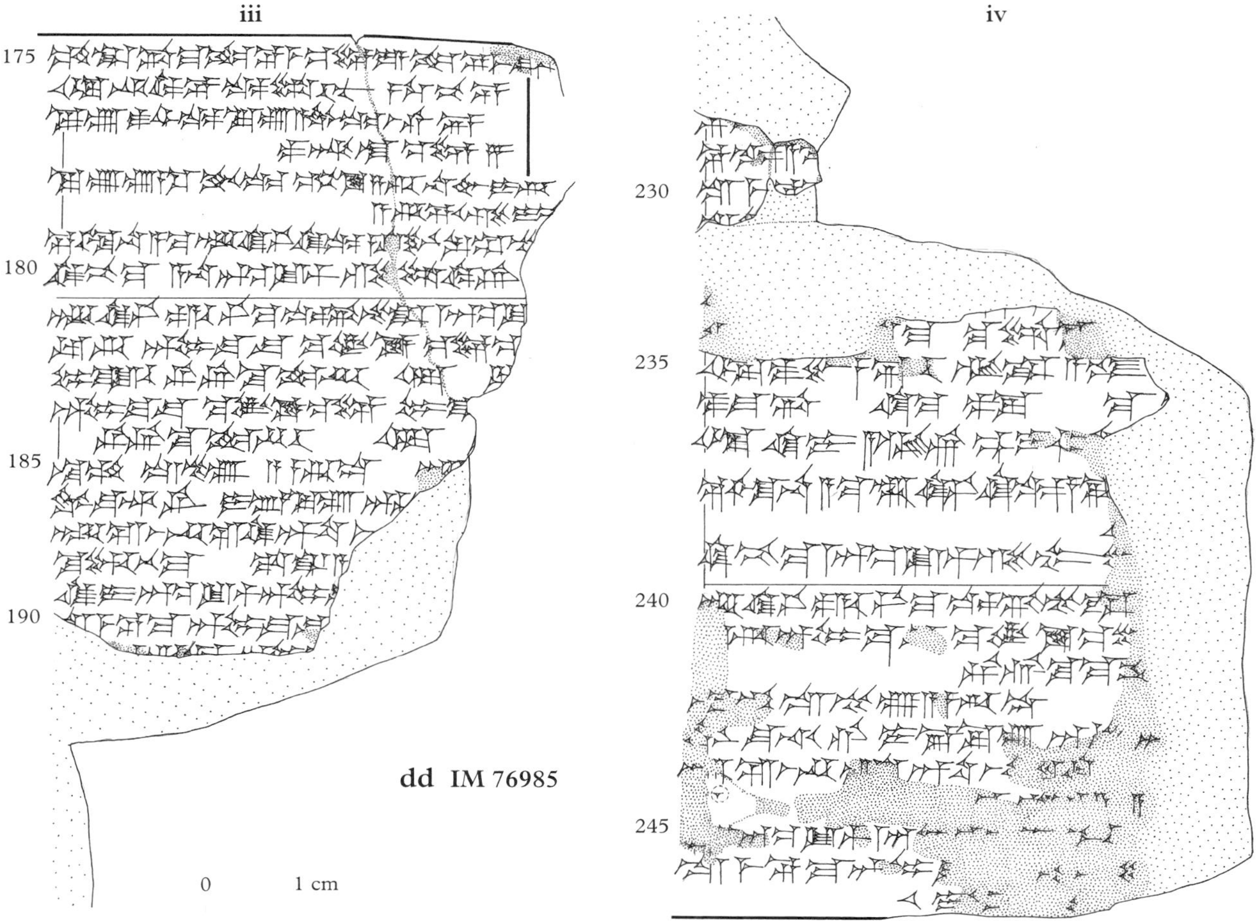

75. SB Tablet V. MS dd cols. iii and iv

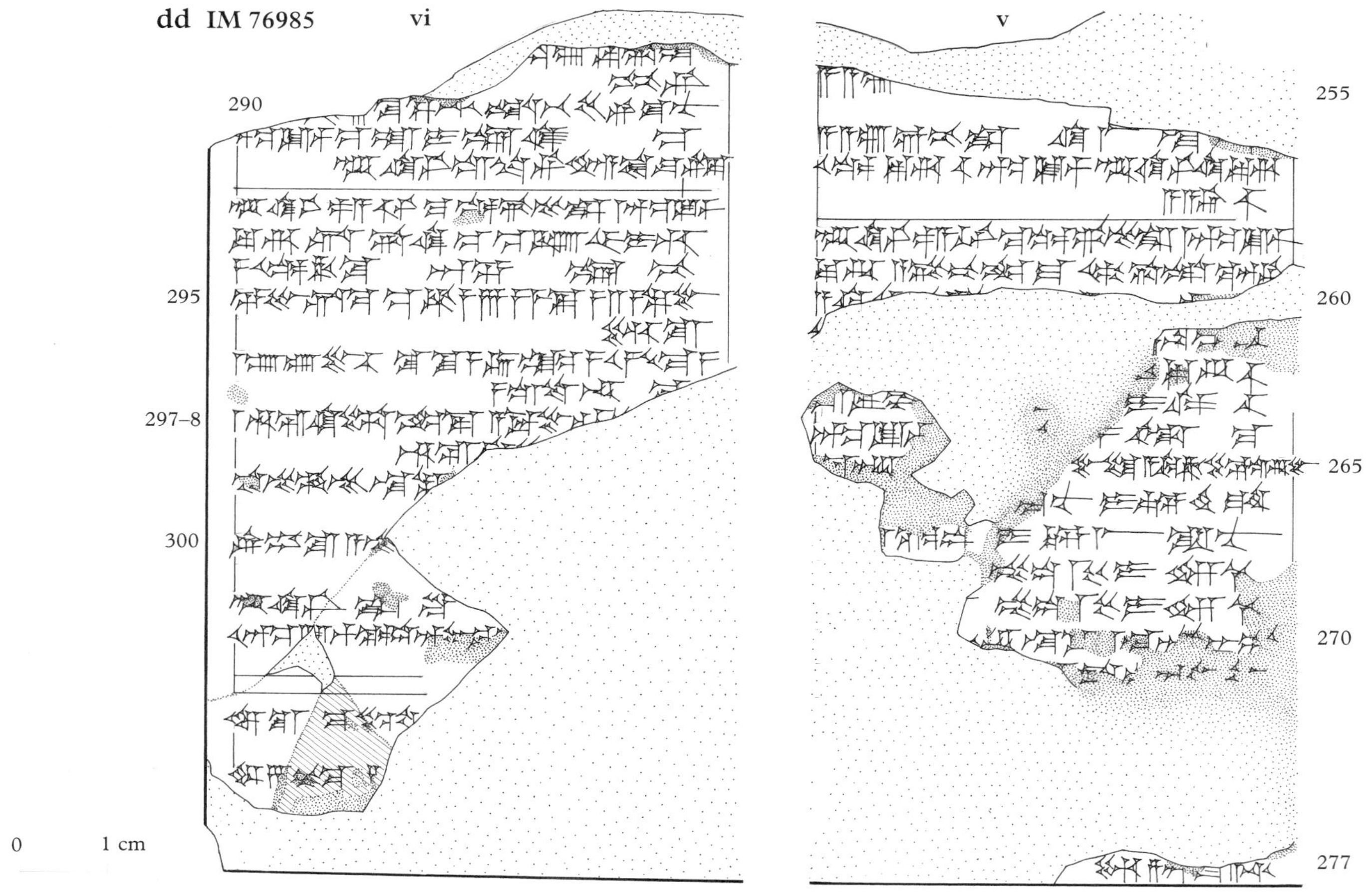

76. SB Tablet V. MS dd cols. v and vi. The hatched area is restored from the photograph

g_3 **BM 46002**

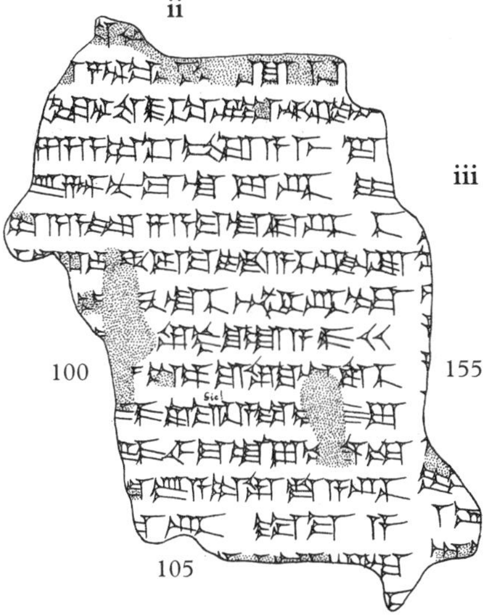

g_1 **BM 34873 obv.**

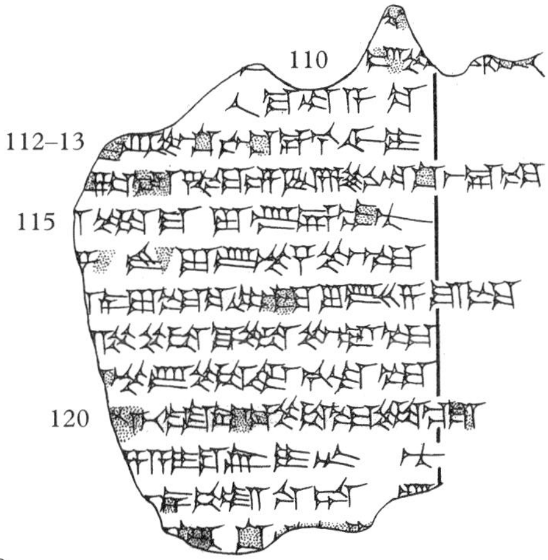

g_3

91 *a-n*]*a* ⌜igi⌝ [

92 *šá* ᵈutu-

96 *-du*

97 ⌜*lu-ú*⌝ *-liq-ma*

98 [ḫ]a.la-*šú*

99 *-ru-ub*

101 *lib-*

105]-⌜*ú?-a liṭ-ḫu-ka*⌝ *ka-*/[*a-š*]*i*

g_2 **BM 35245**

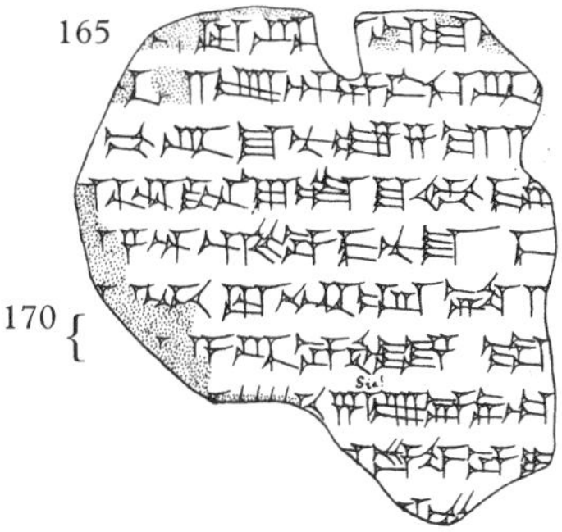

g_1

109 *li-šaḫ*]-

110 *-ú l*[*i-ba*]*l-*⌜*lil*⌝

113 *ri bu*

118 *li-qal-li-pu*

120 *be-let*

i]*l-ta-na-as-su ina*

g_1 **BM 34873 rev.**

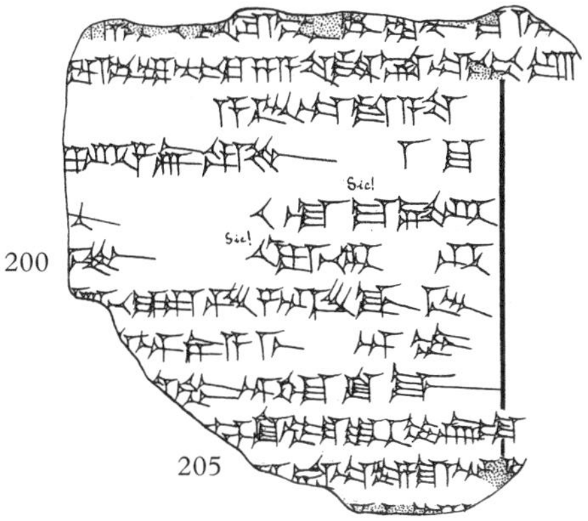

g_2

167 *bi-ri-šu-nu*

168 1+*en*

170 *-ti*

-mu

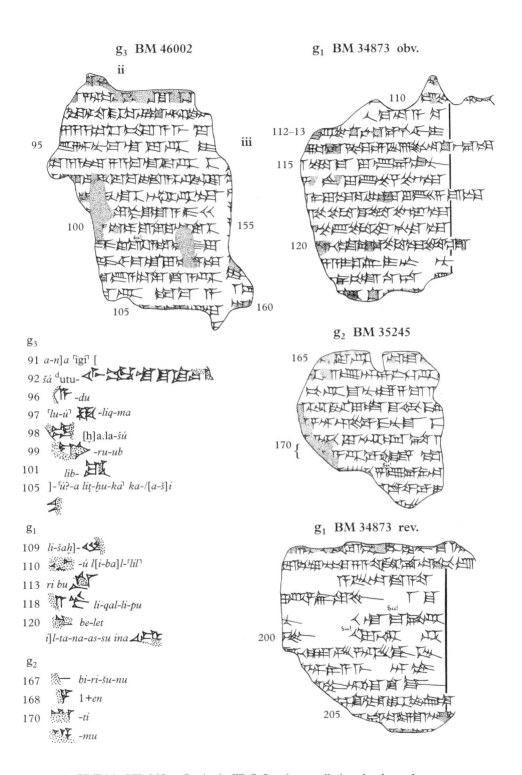

77. SB Tablet VII. MS g. Copies by W. G. Lambert, collations by the author

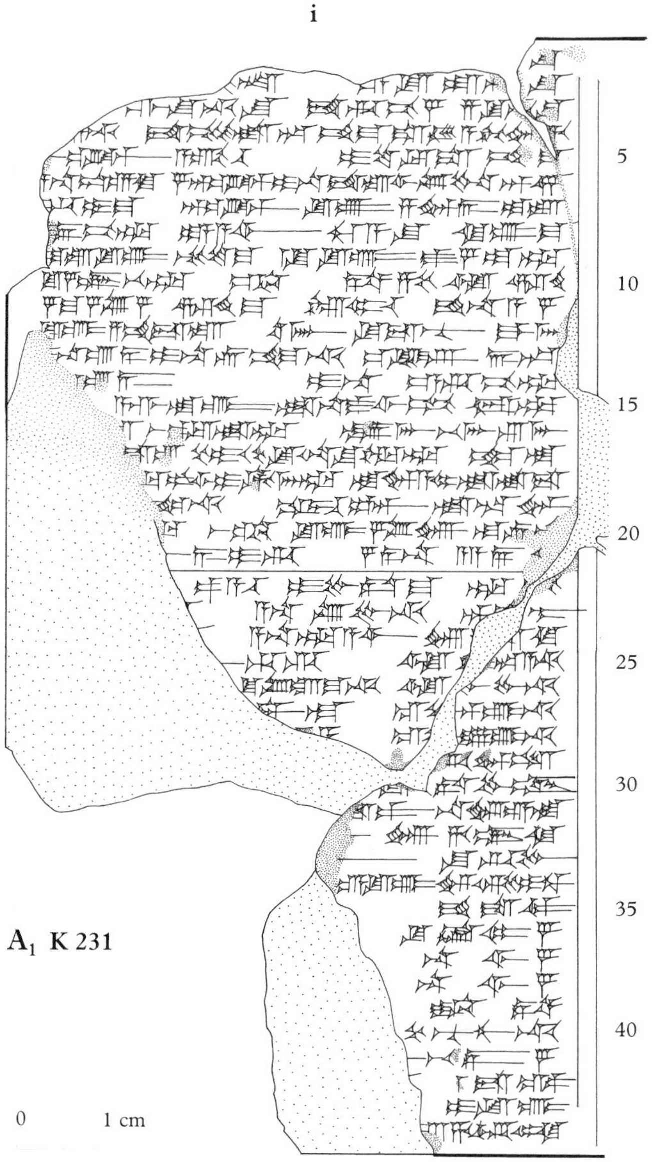

78. SB Tablet VI. MS A col. i

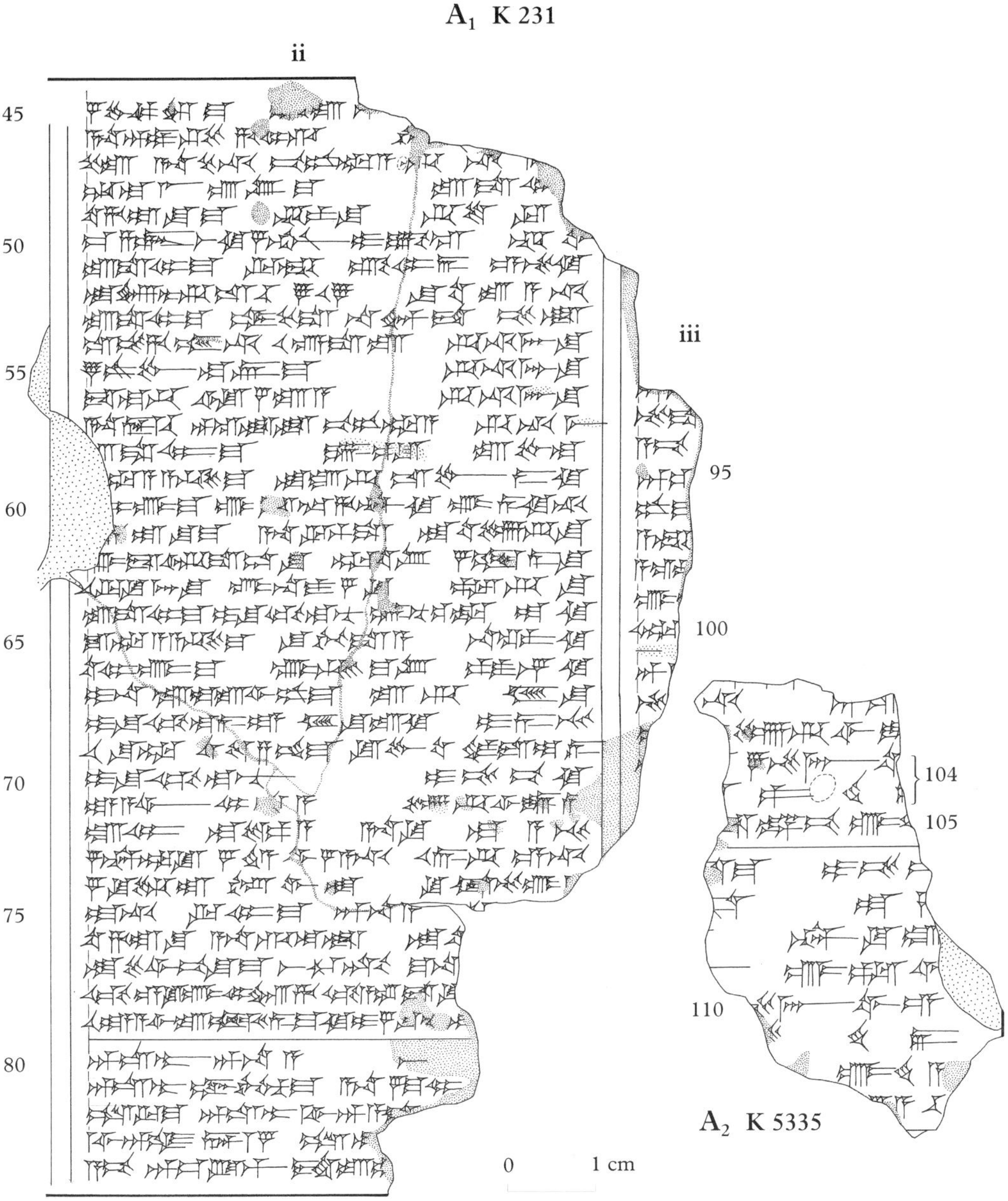

79. SB Tablet VI. MS A cols. ii and iii

A$_1$ **K 231** **vi**

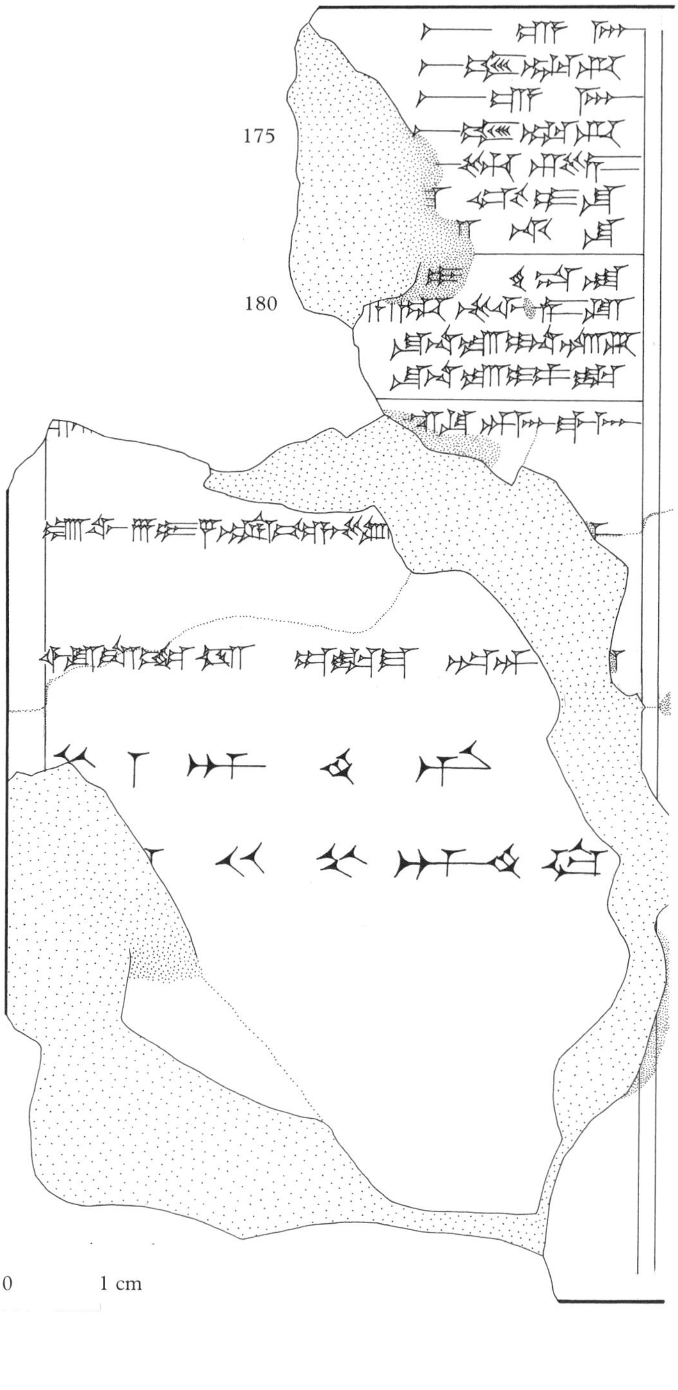

80. SB Tablet VI. MS A col. vi

A_1 **K 231**

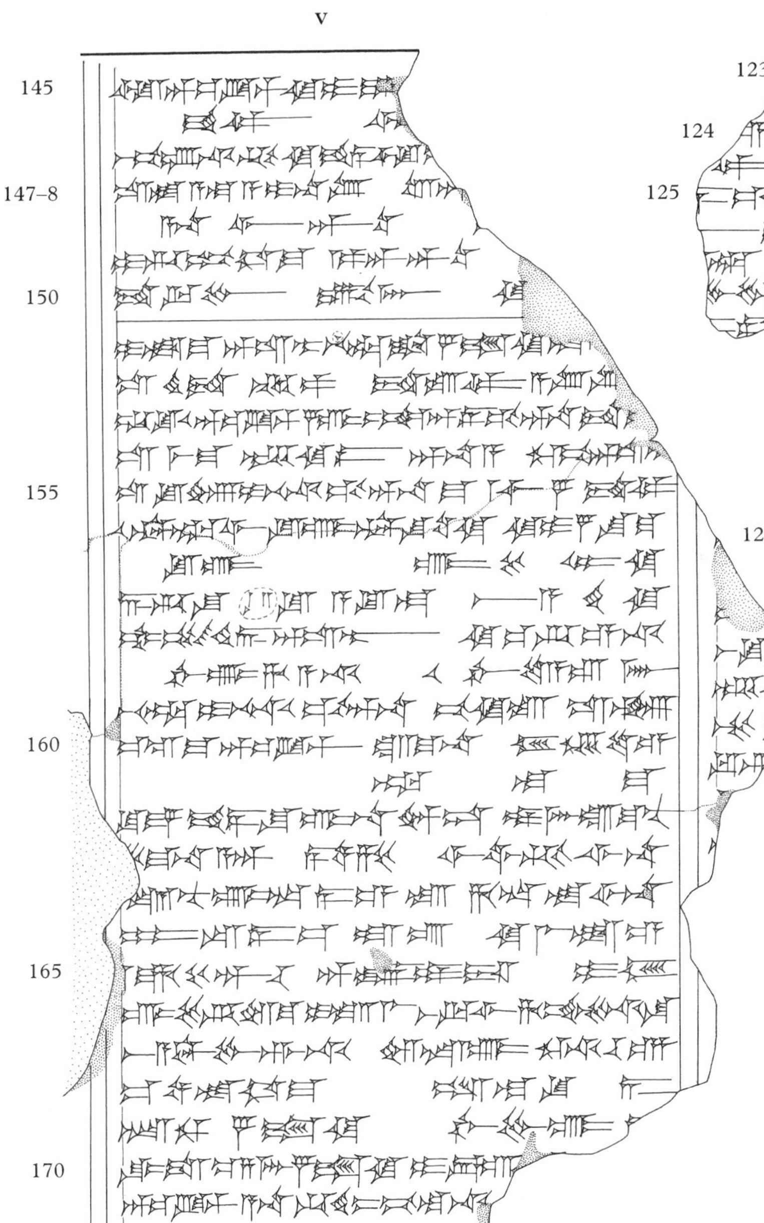

A_2 **K 5335**

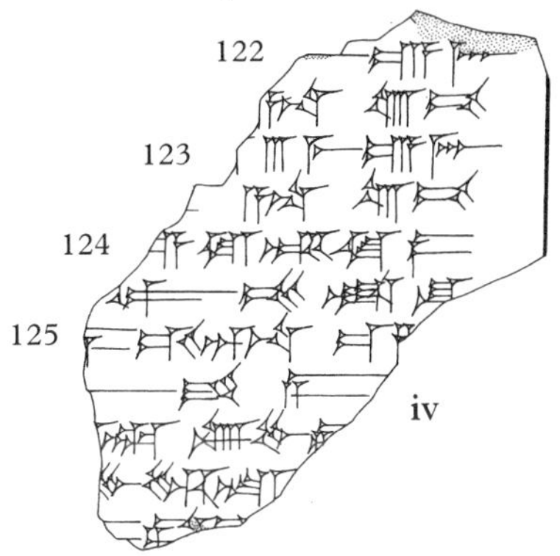

81. SB Tablet VI. MS A cols. iv and v

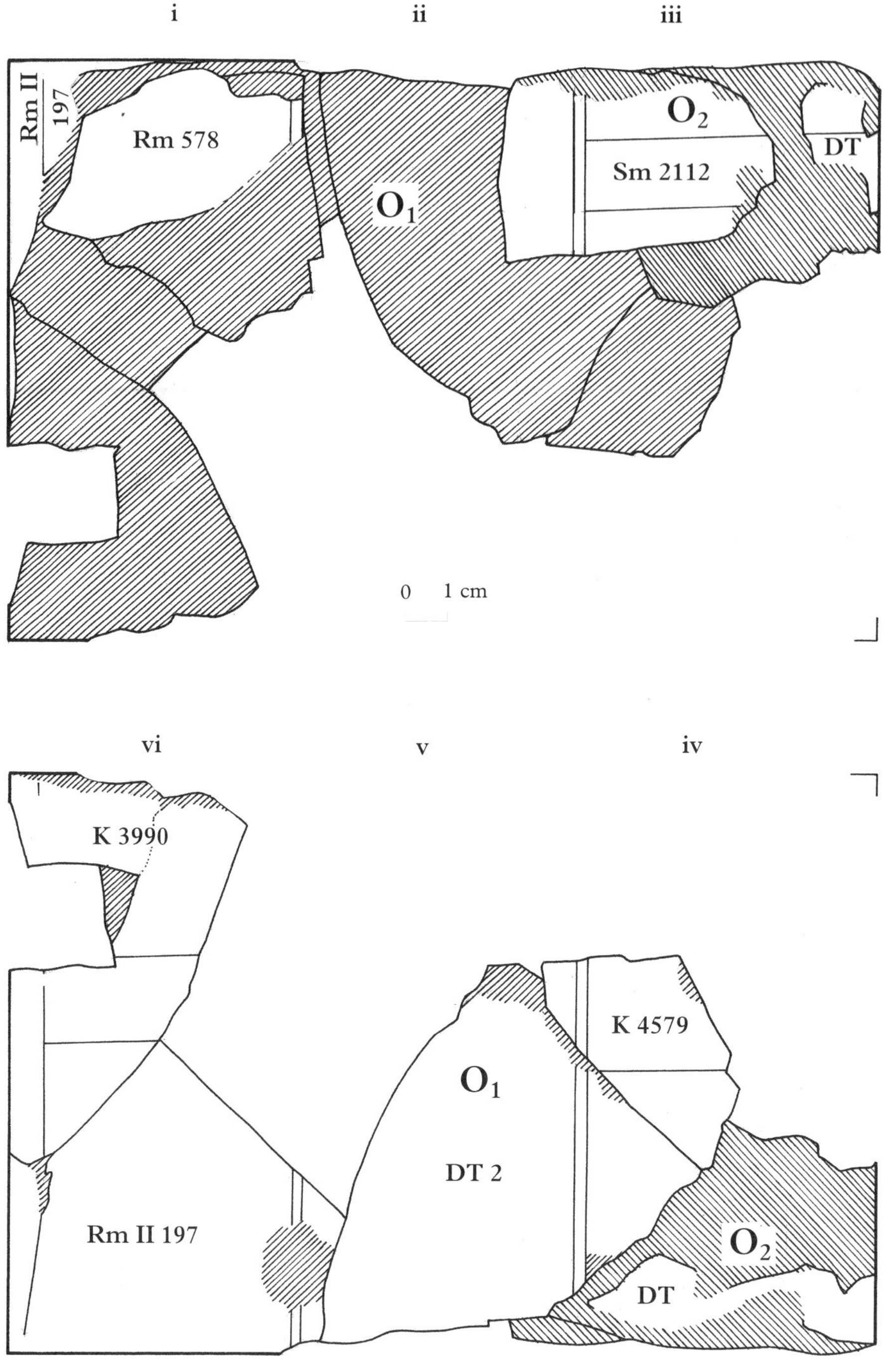

82. SB Tablet VI. MS O, outline sketch. O_1 and O_2 touch but do not join

O_1 K 3990+

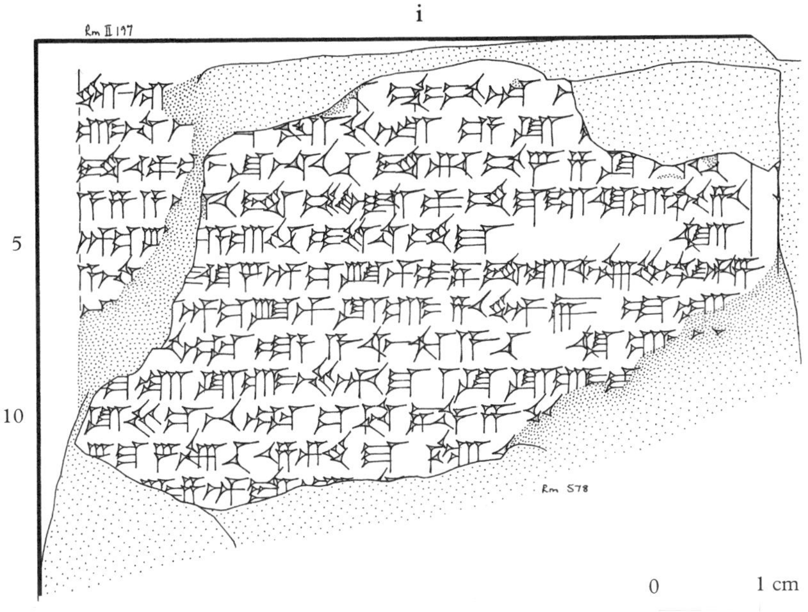

O_2 Sm 2112+

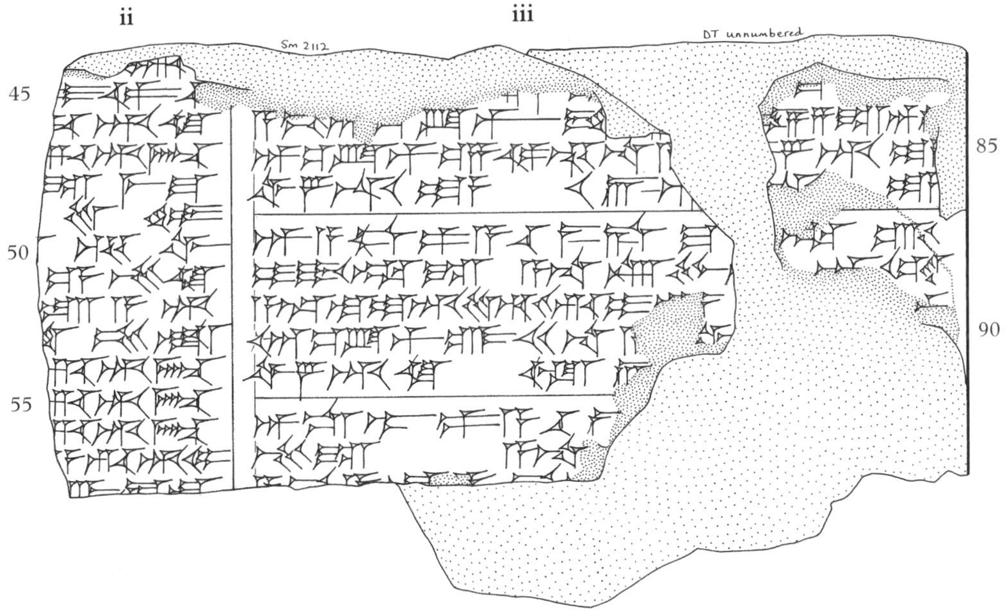

83. SB Tablet VI. MS O obv.

O_1 K 3990+ (+) O_2 Sm 2112

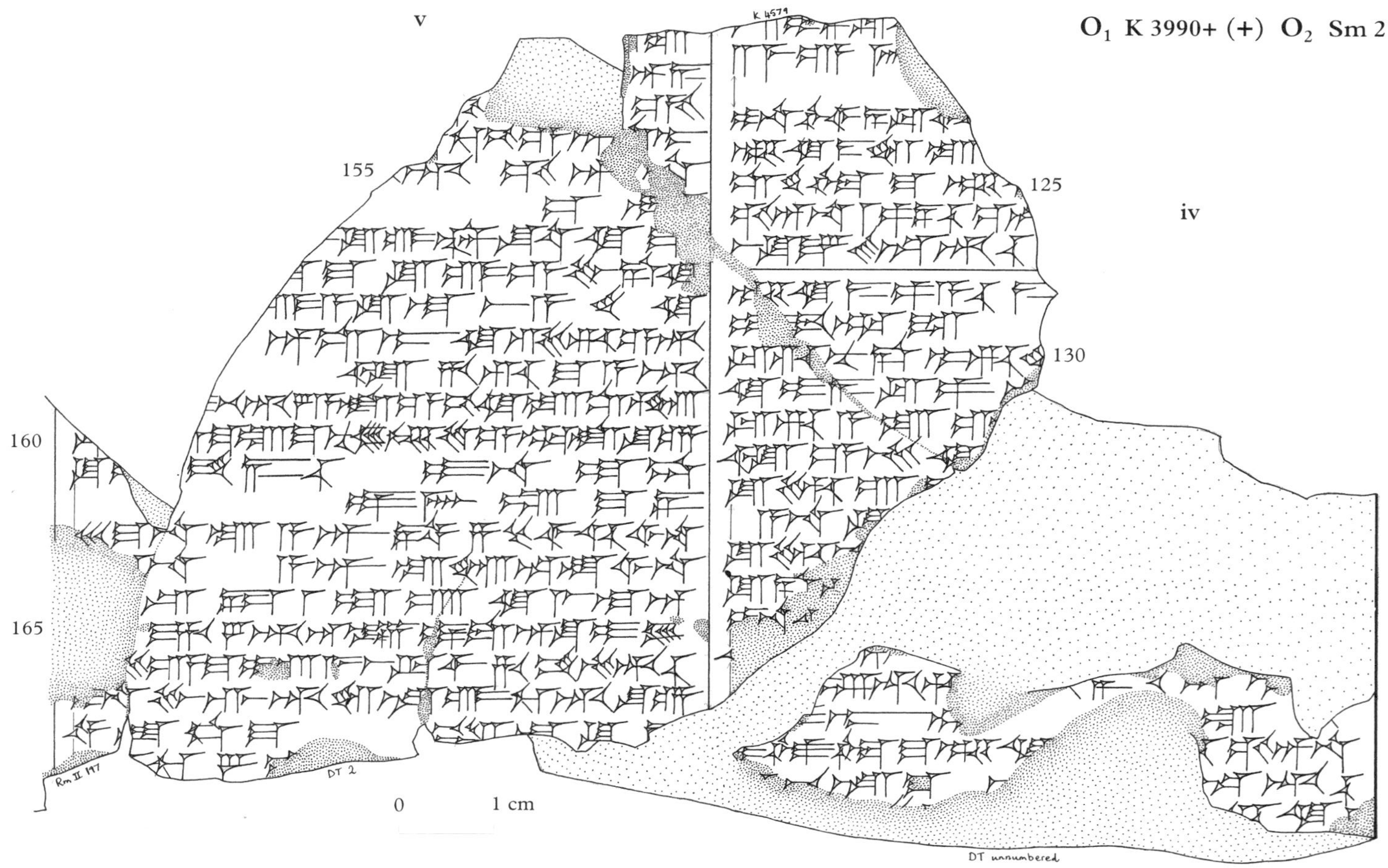

84. SB Tablet VI. MS O, cols. iv and v

O_1 K 3990+ vi

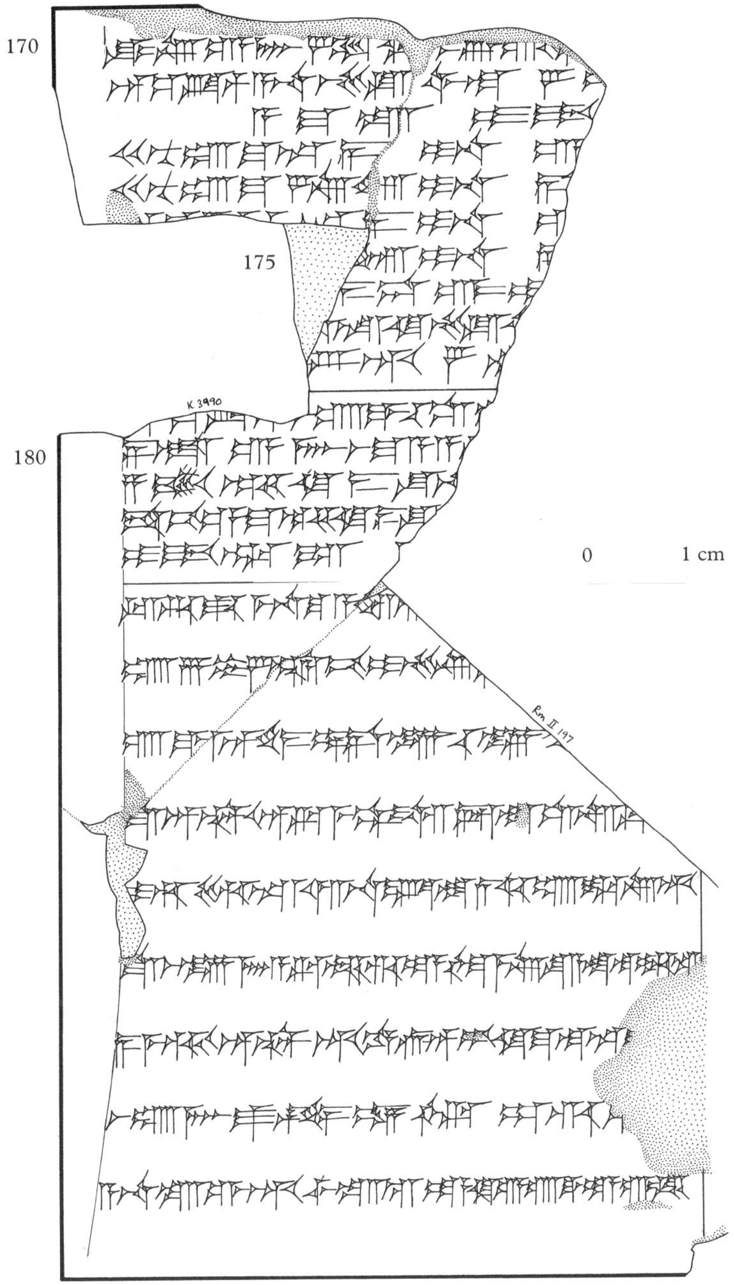

85. SB Tablet VI. MS O, col. vi

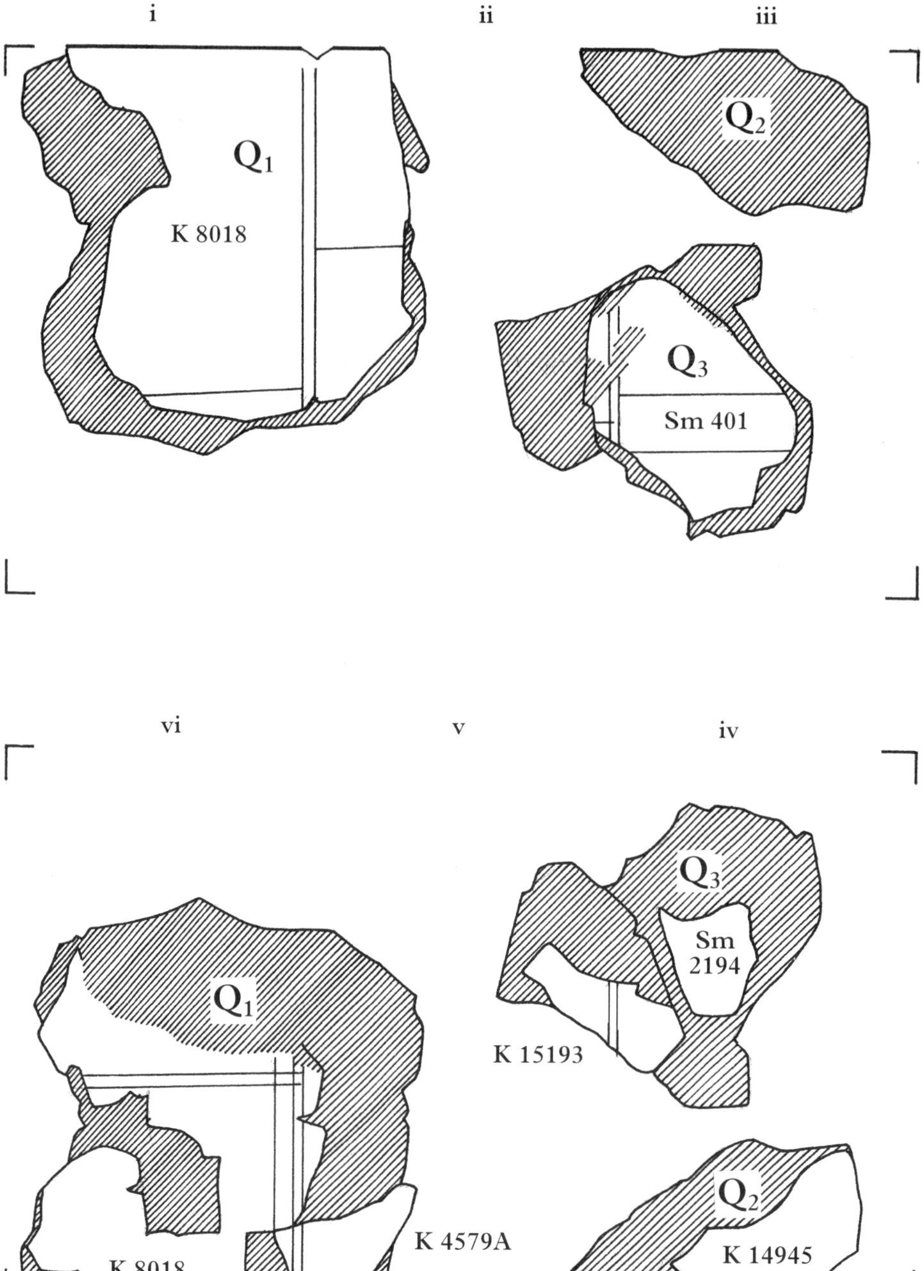

86. SB Tablet VI. MS Q, outline sketch. The positions of Q_2 and Q_3 are approximate

Q_1 K 4579A+

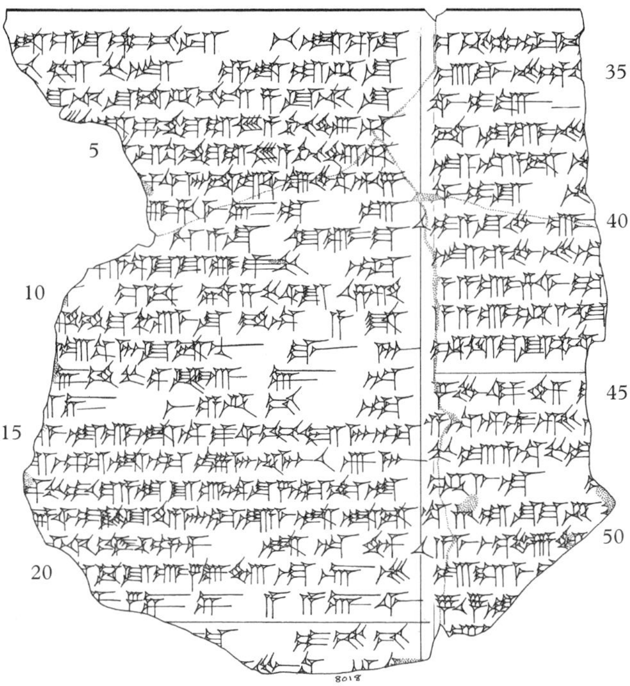

Q_3 K 15193+

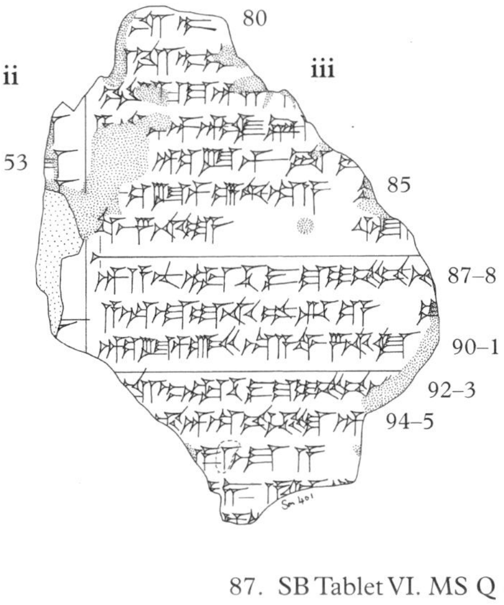

d VAT 11576

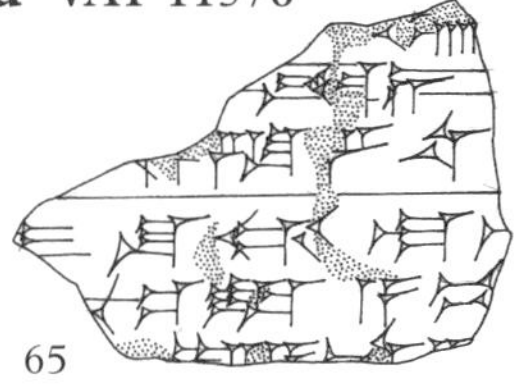

0 1 cm

87. SB Tablet VI. MS Q obv., MS **d**

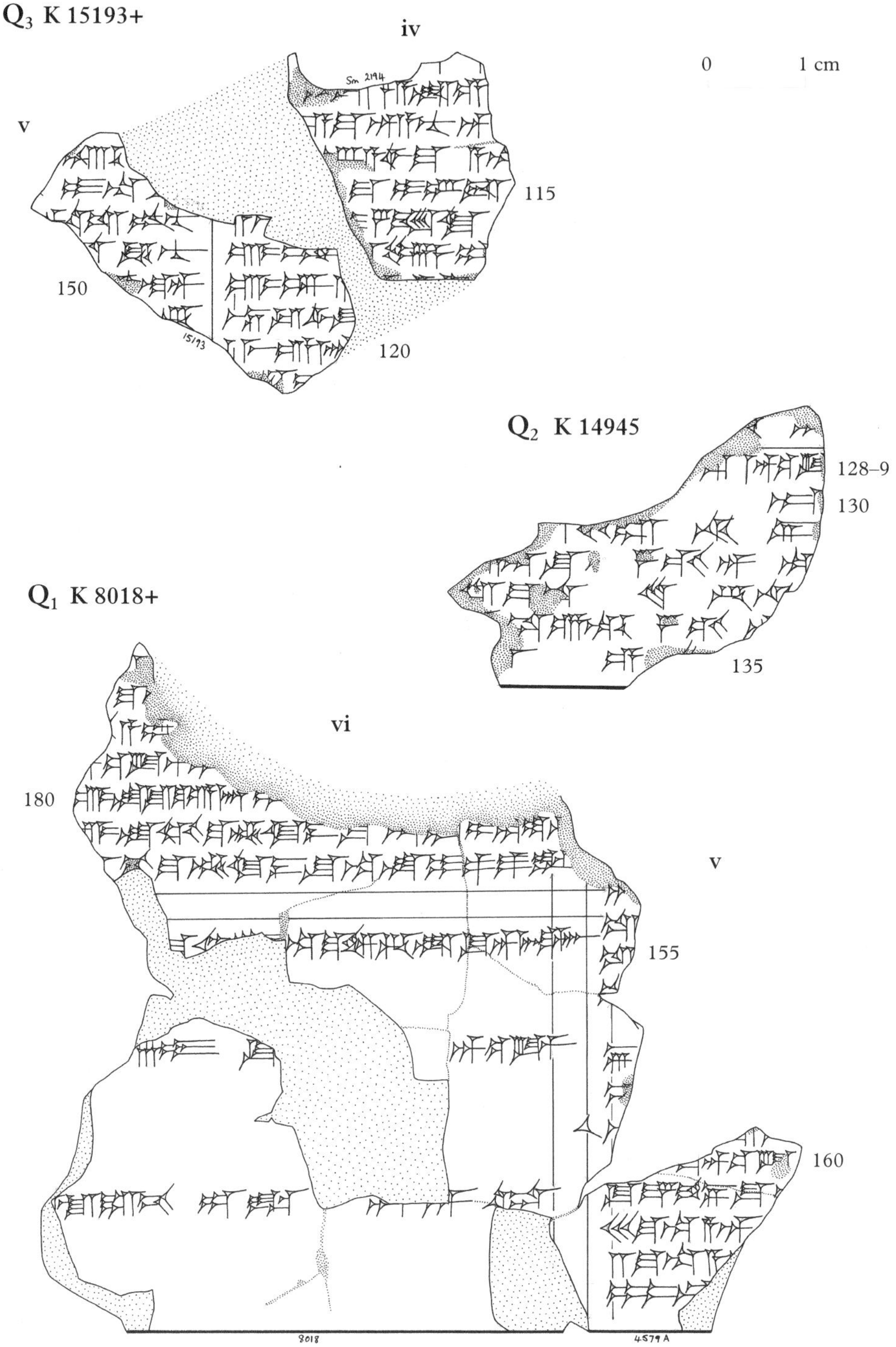

88. SB Tablet VI. MS Q rev.

a_1 VAT 9667

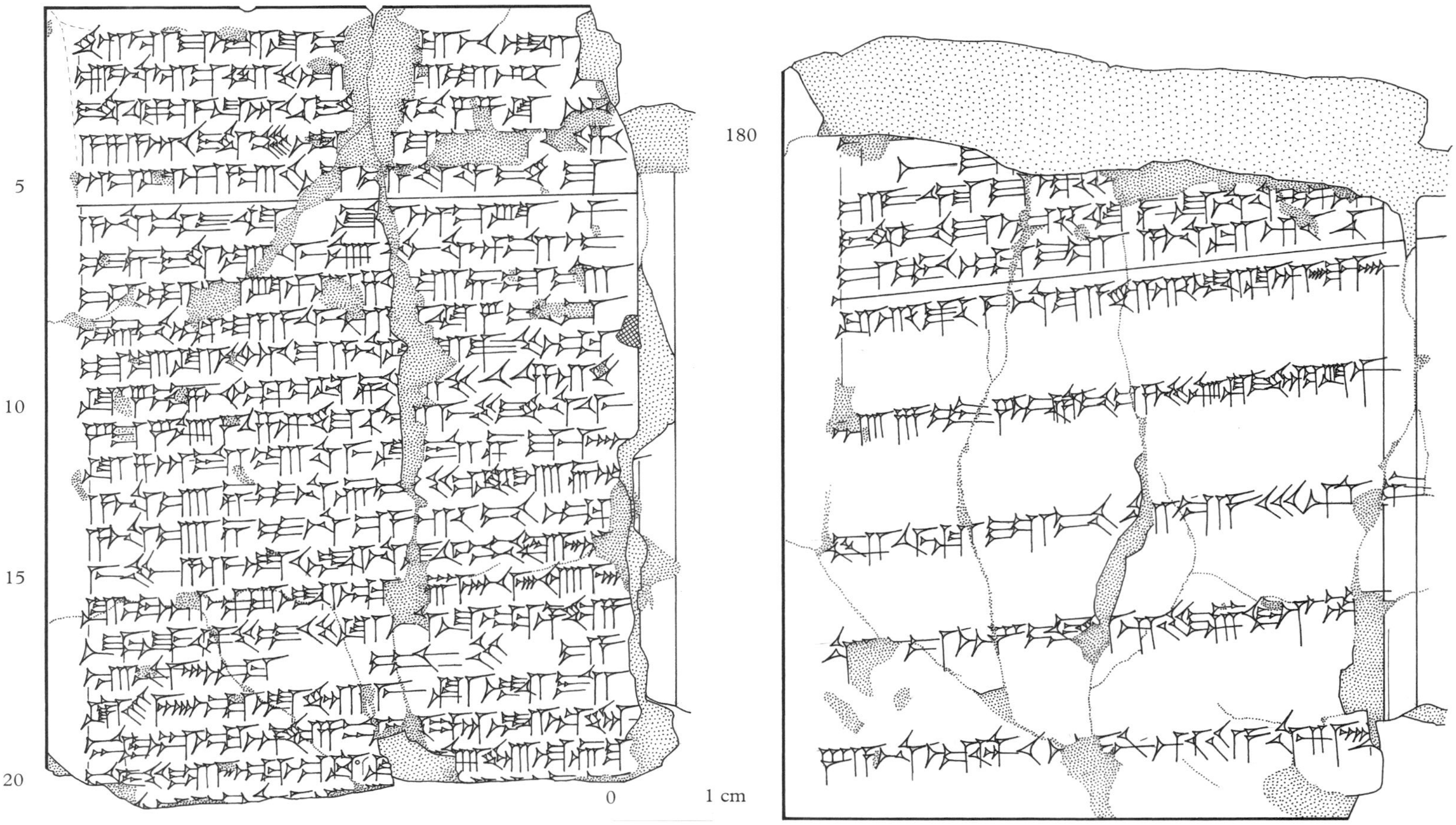

89. SB Tablet VI. MS **a** cols. i and vi

a_1 VAT 9667 (+) a_2 A 122+

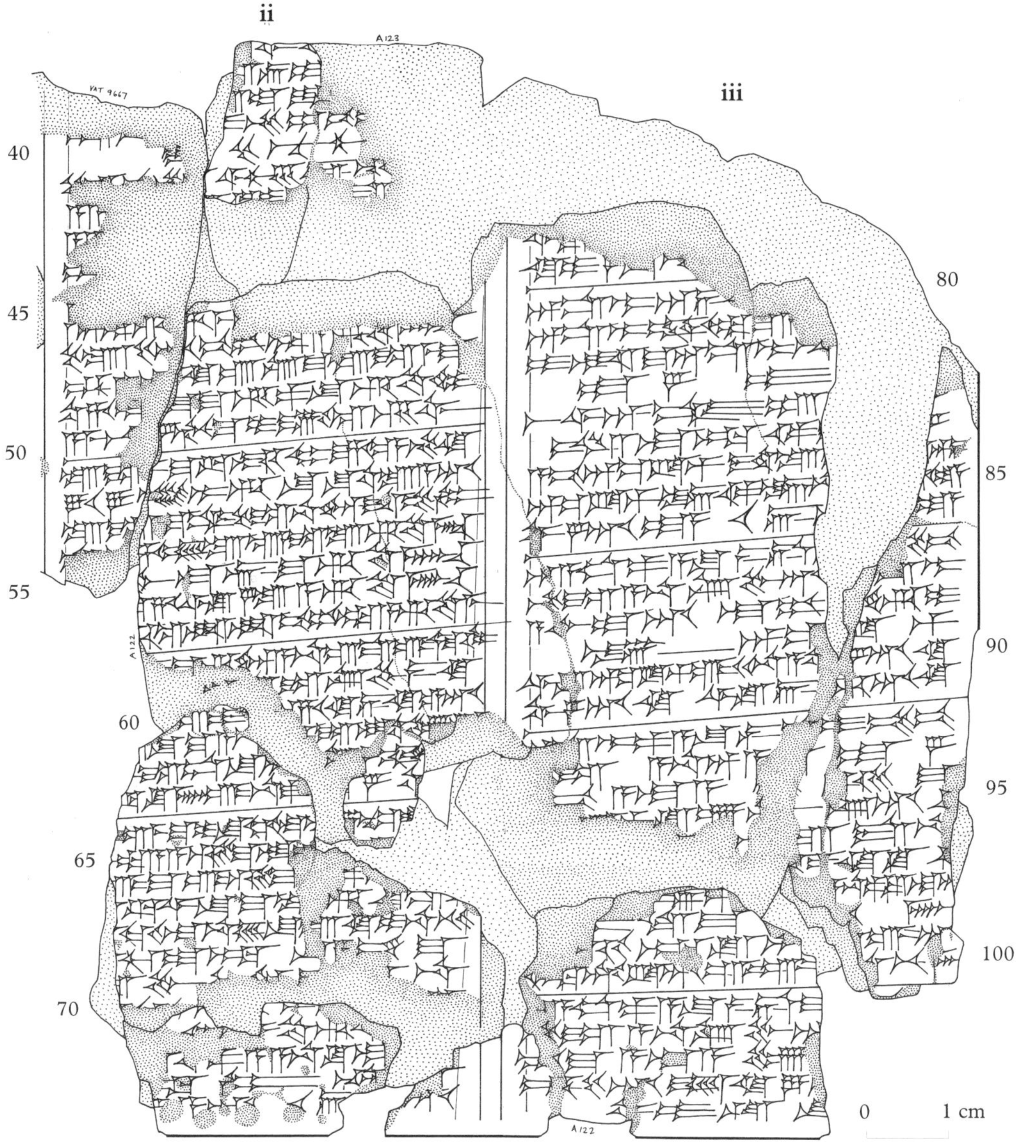

90. SB Tablet VI. MS **a** cols. ii and iii

a_1 VAT 9667 (+) a_2 A 122+

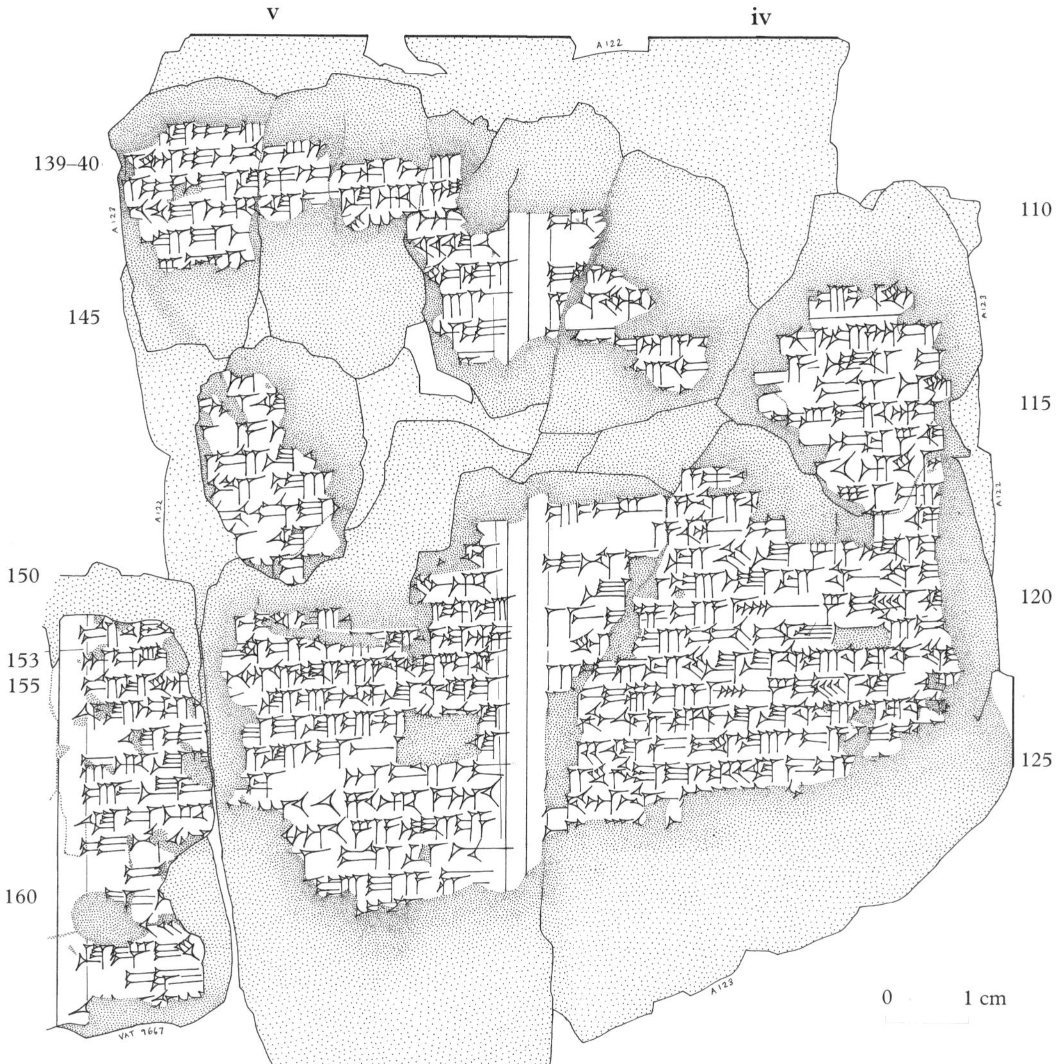

A 124 C

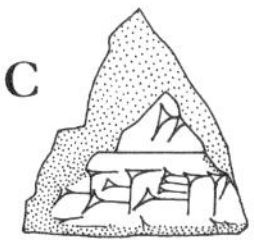

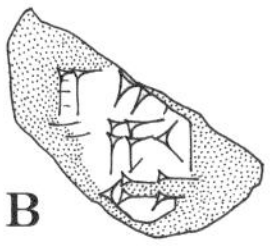

A 124 B

91. SB Tablet VI. MS **a** cols. iv and v, and two unplaced fragments, possibly of **a**

iii

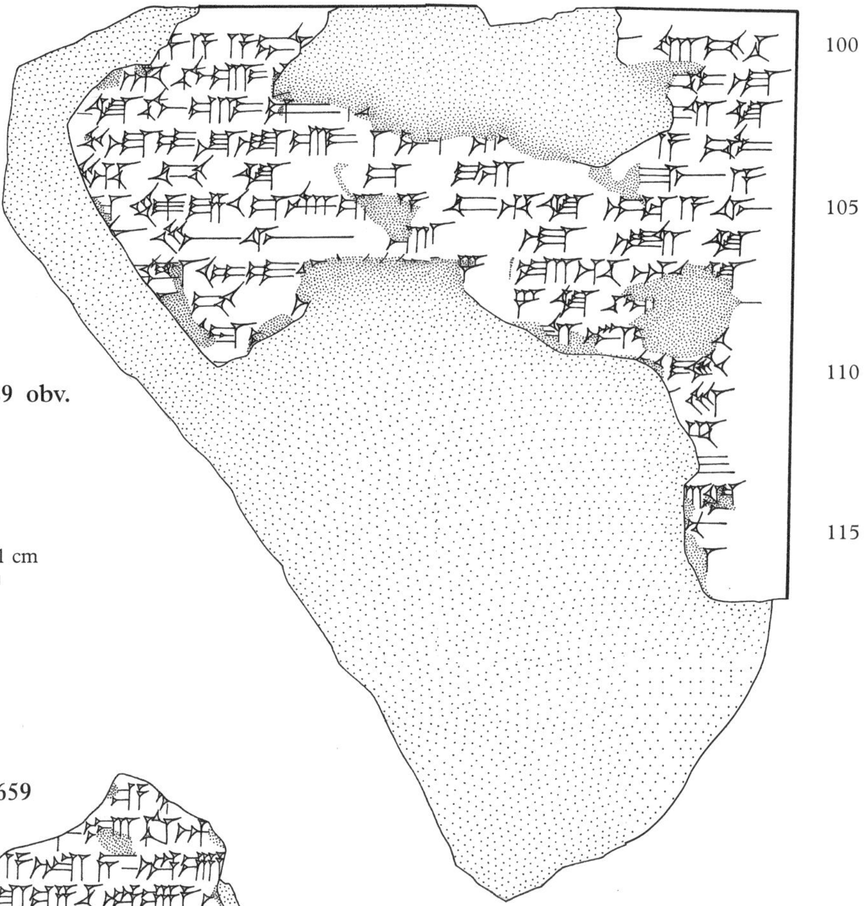

E_1 K 2589 obv.

0 1 cm

E_3 K 11659

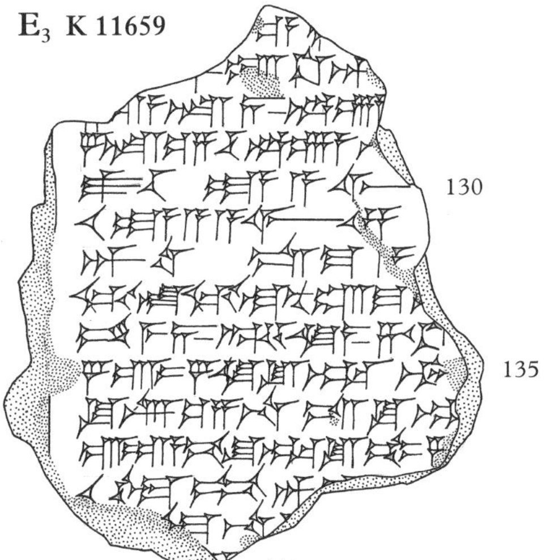

92. SB Tablet VII. MS E obv.

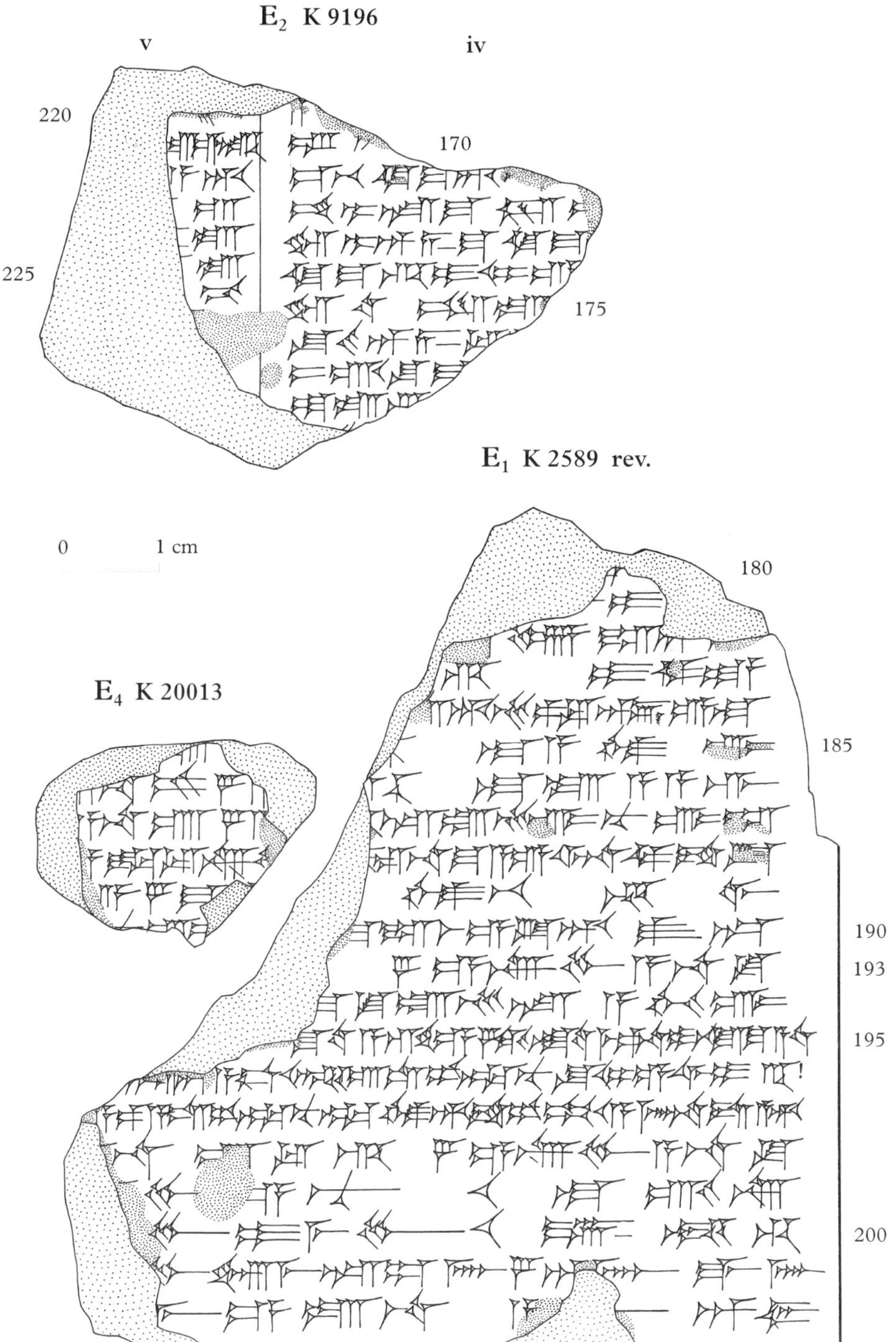

93. SB Tablet VII. MS E rev.

L$_2$ K 3588 obv.

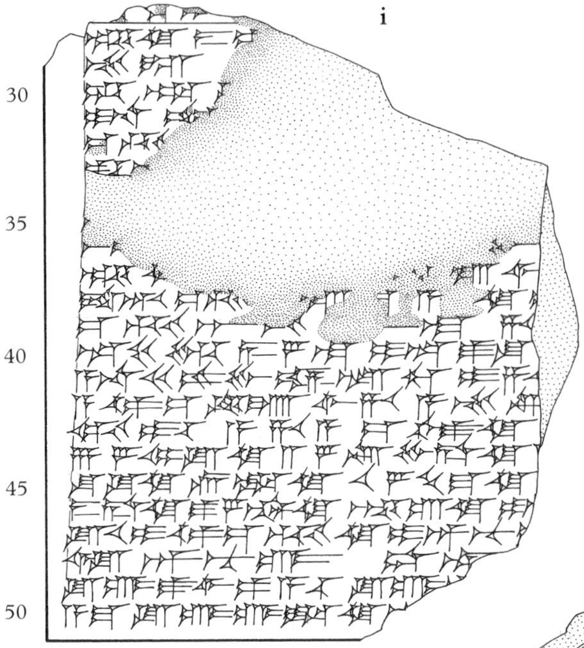

L$_1$ K 3389 obv.

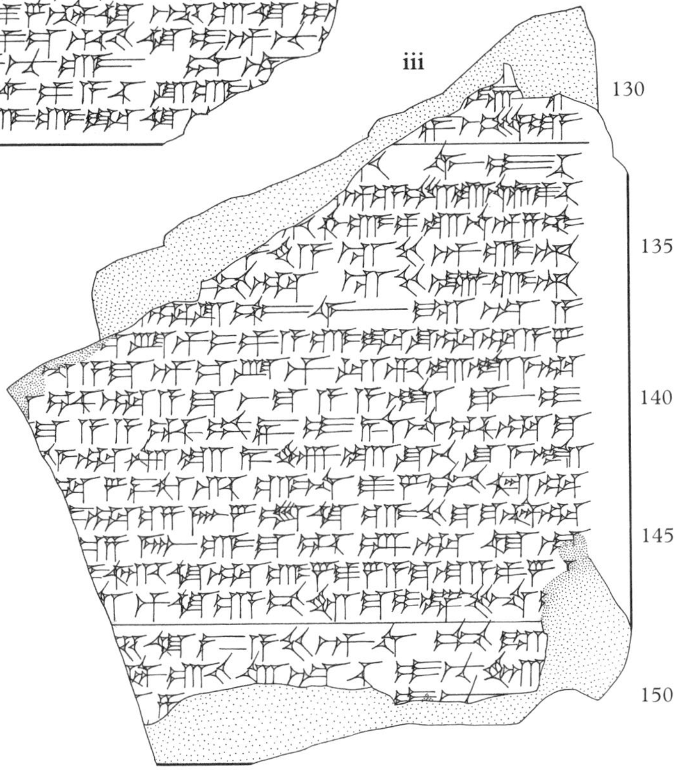

94. SB Tablet VII. MS L obv.

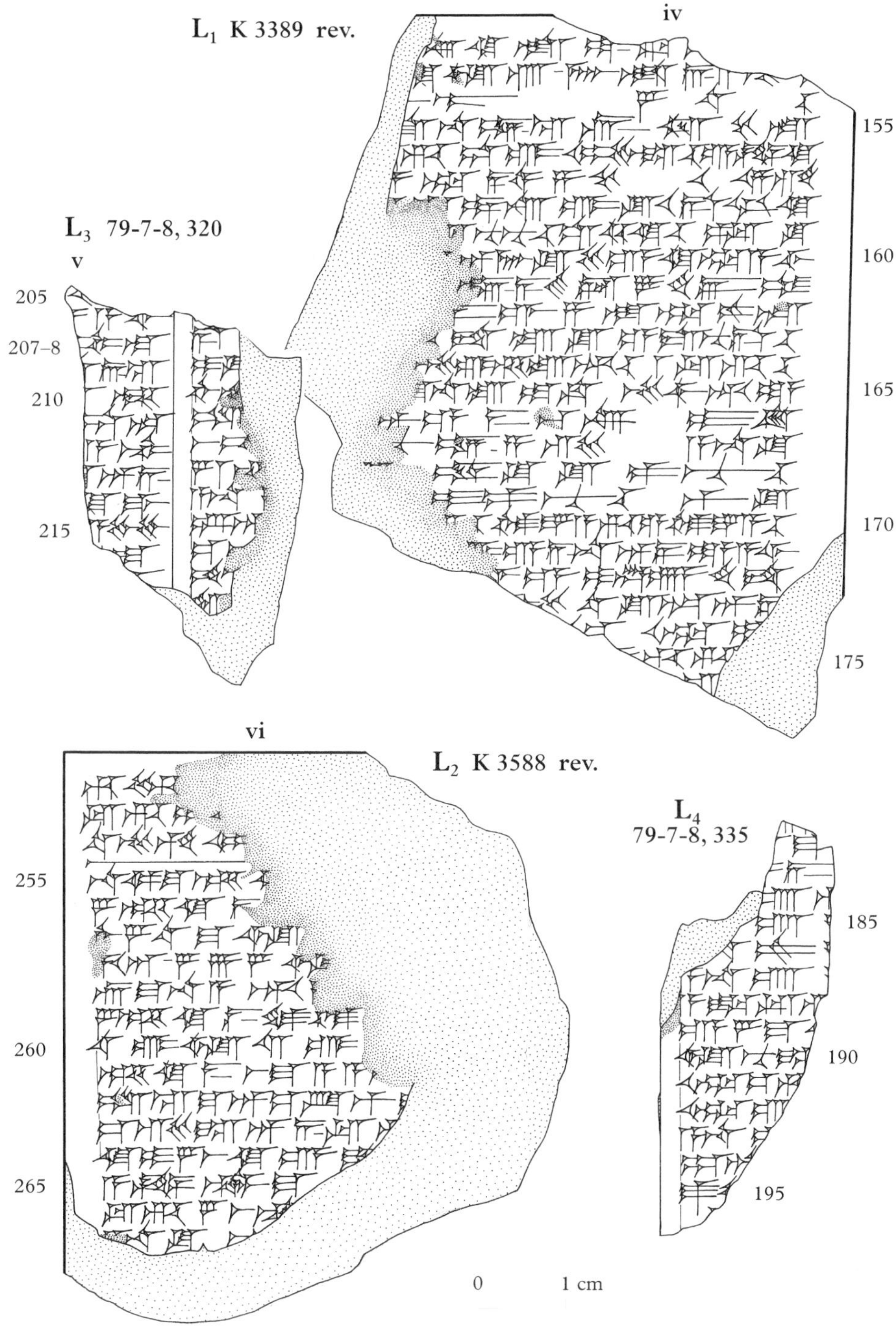

95. SB Tablet VII. MS L rev. L$_1$ and L$_3$ overlap but do not join

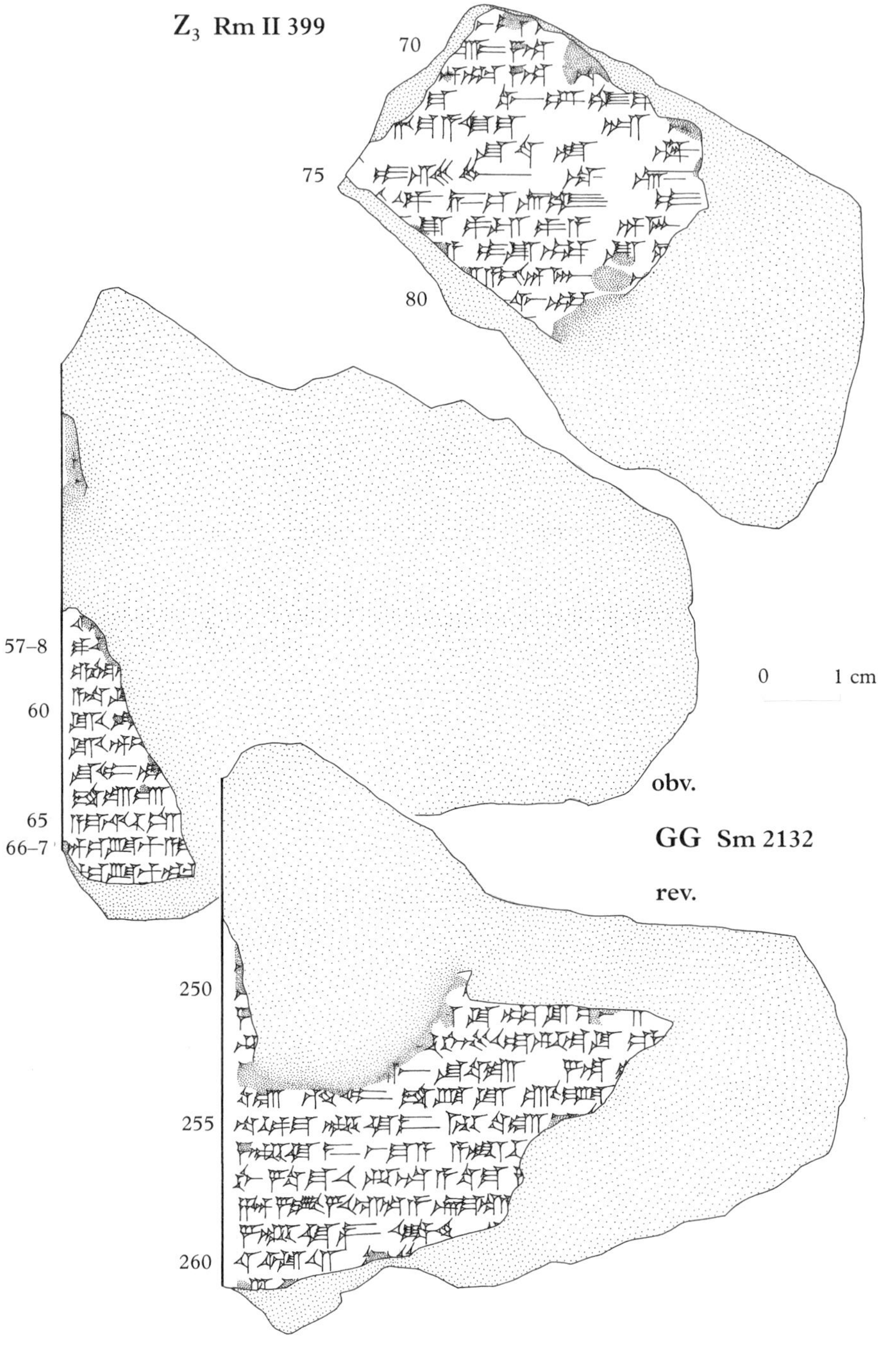

96. SB Tablet VII. MS Z col. ii, MS GG

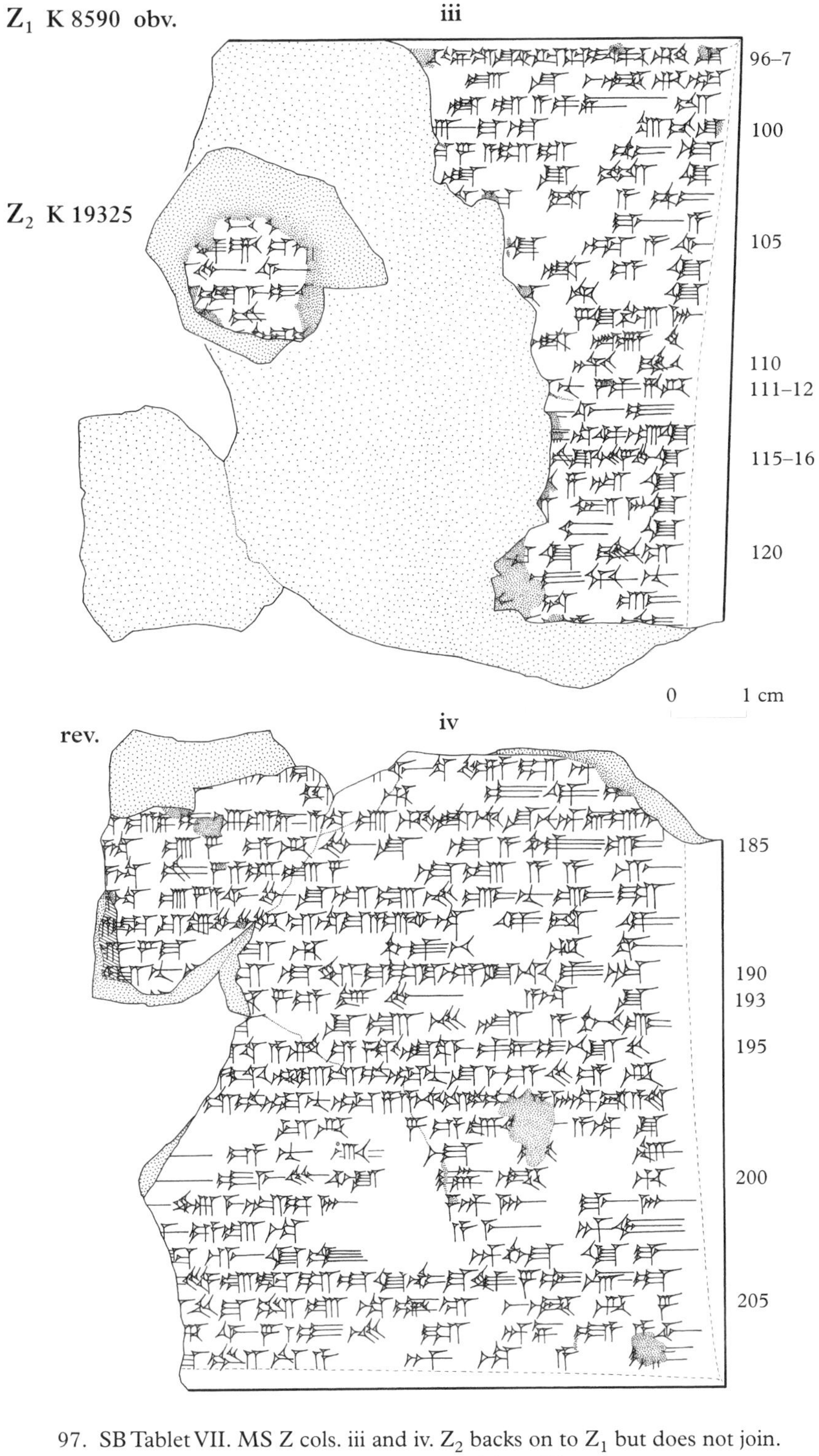

97. SB Tablet VII. MS Z cols. iii and iv. Z_2 backs on to Z_1 but does not join.
The hatched area is restored from Haupt's copy

f S.U. 51/129 A

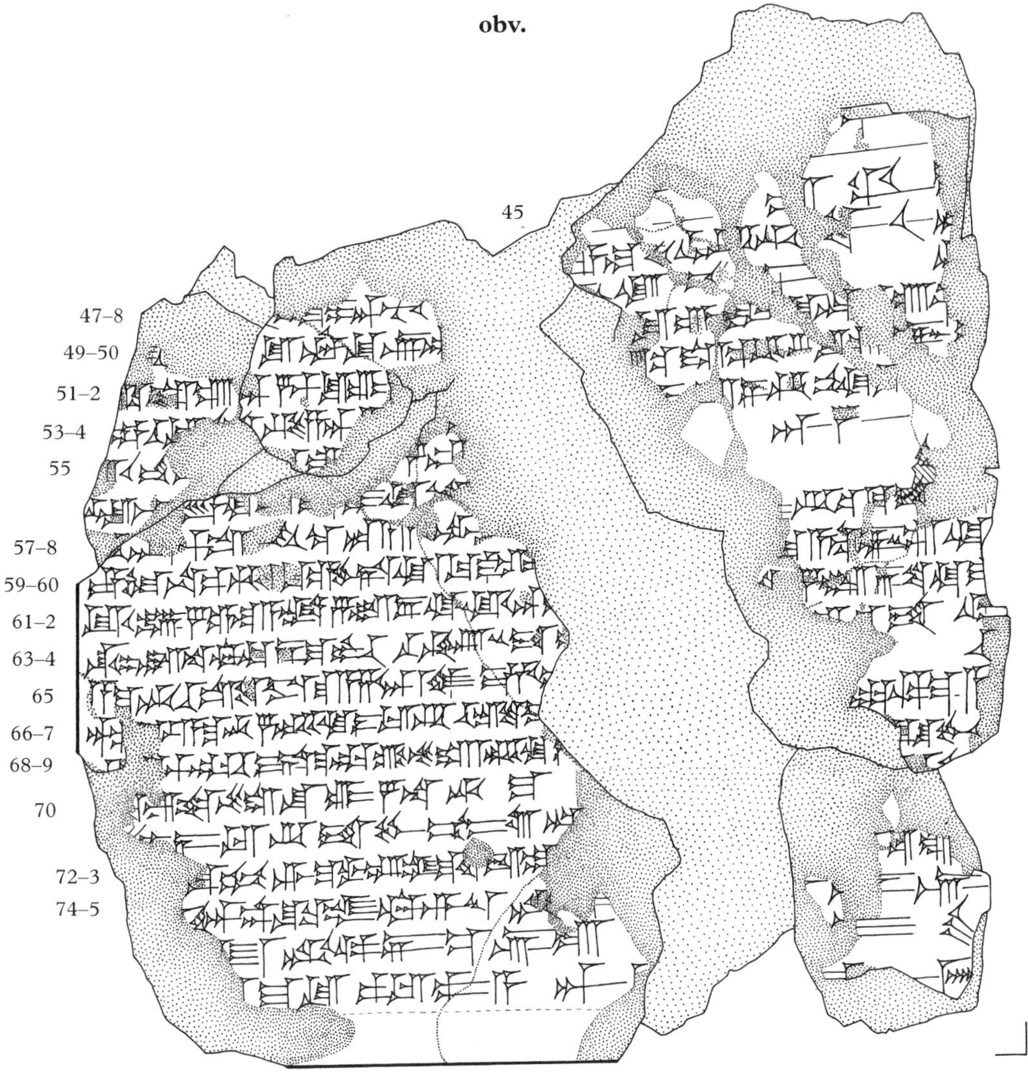

98. SB Tablet VII. MS **f** obv. The hatched area is restored from an old photograph

f S.U. 51/129A rev.

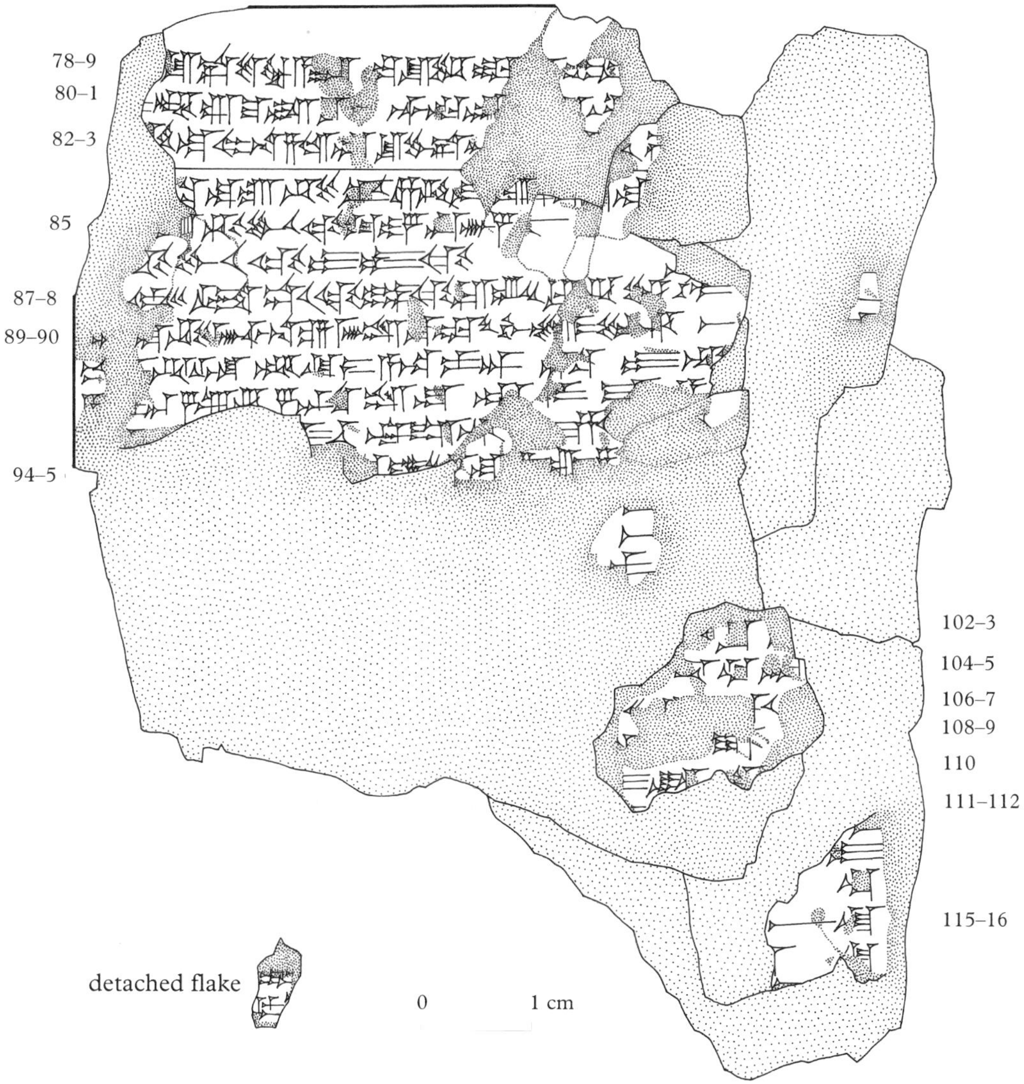

99. SB Tablet VII. MS **f** rev.

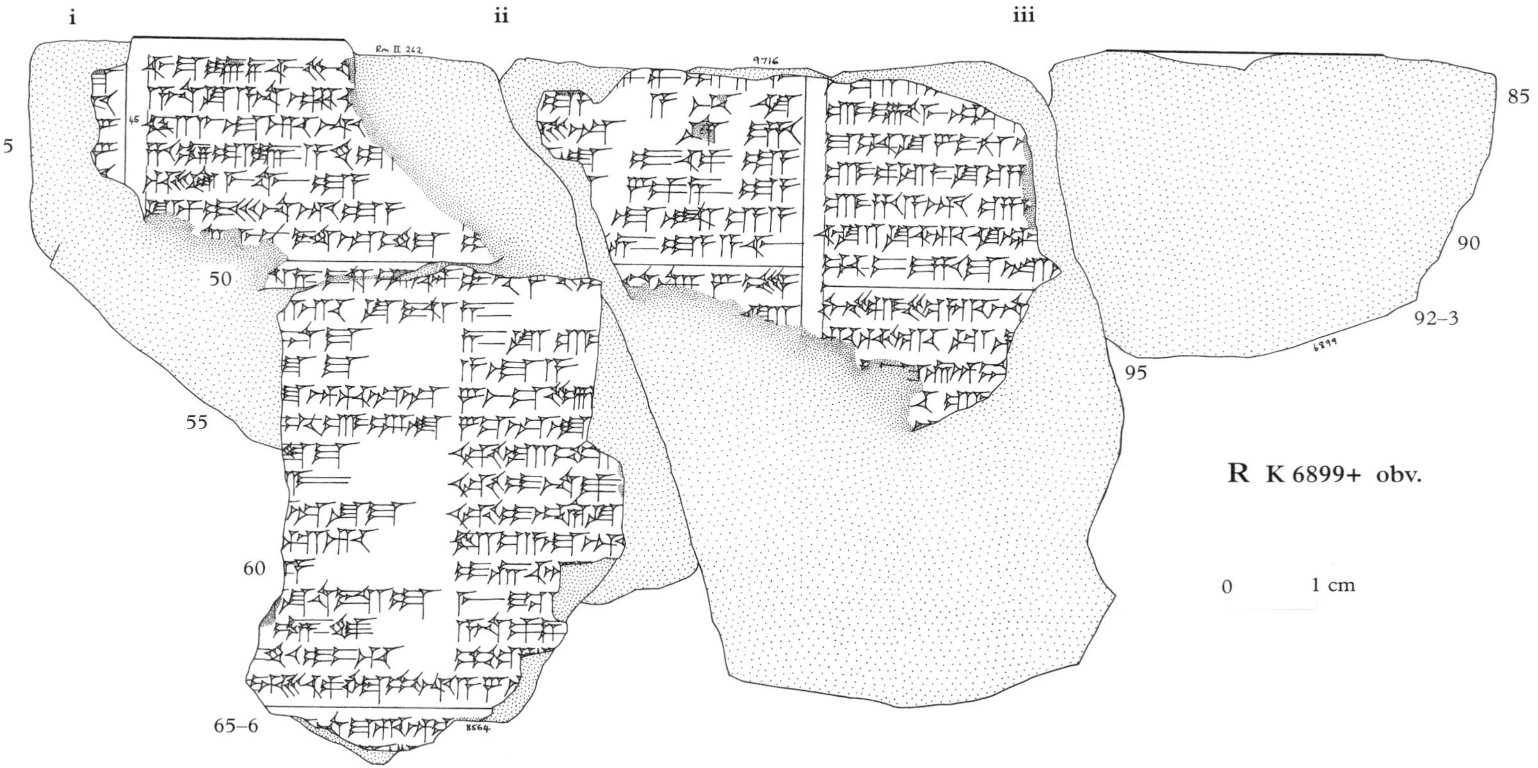

100. SB Tablet VIII. MS R obv.

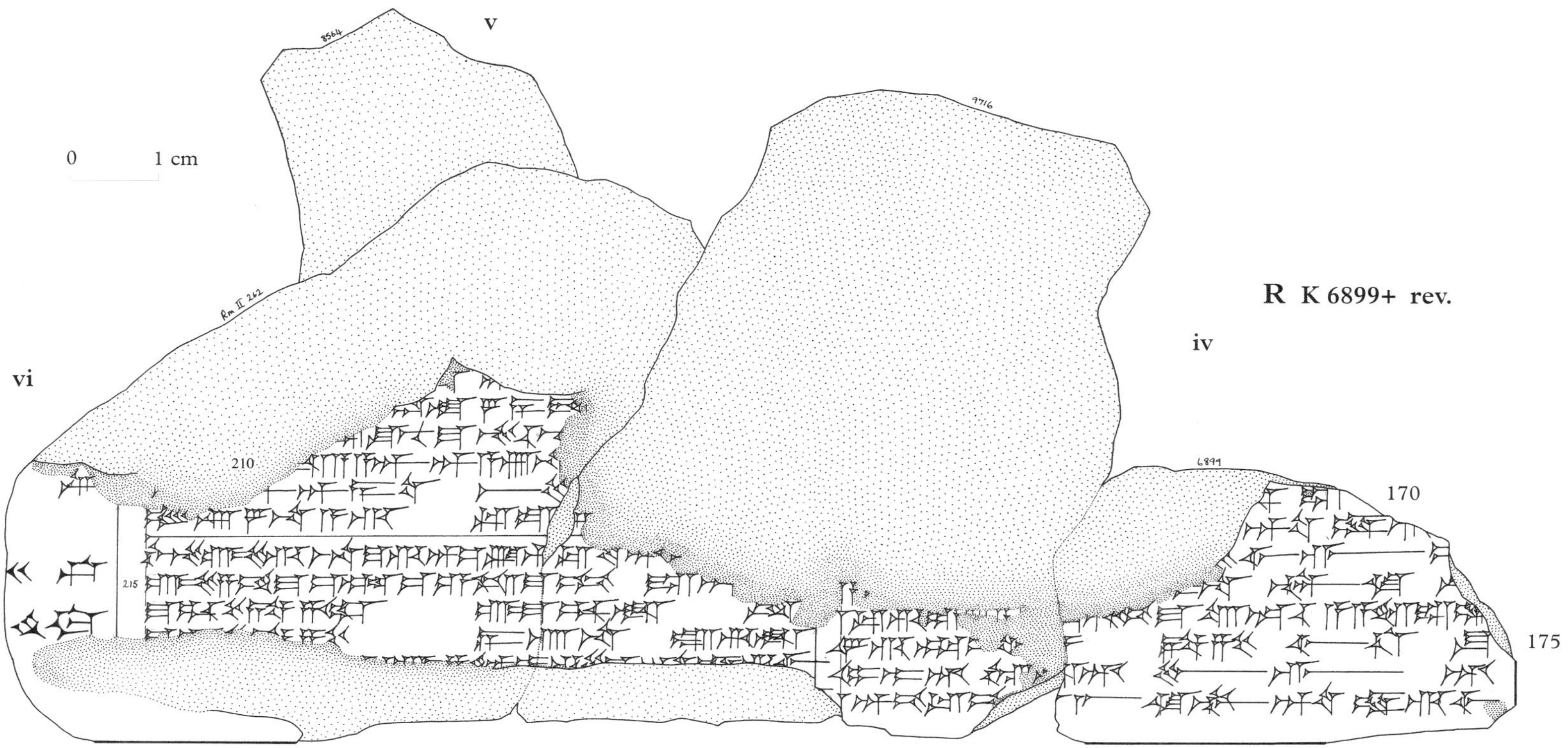

101. SB Tablet VIII. MS R rev.

V$_3$ K 8587 obv.

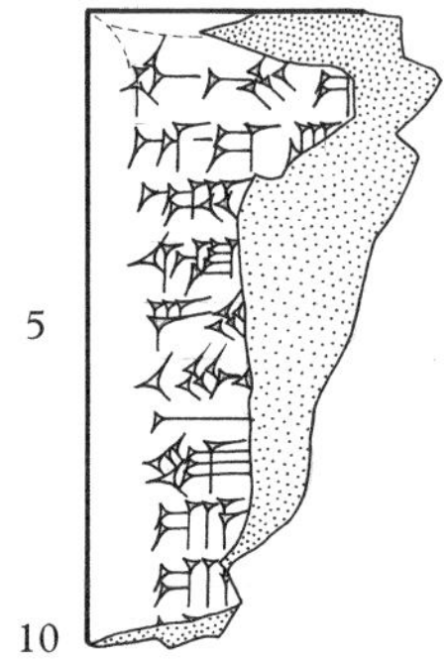

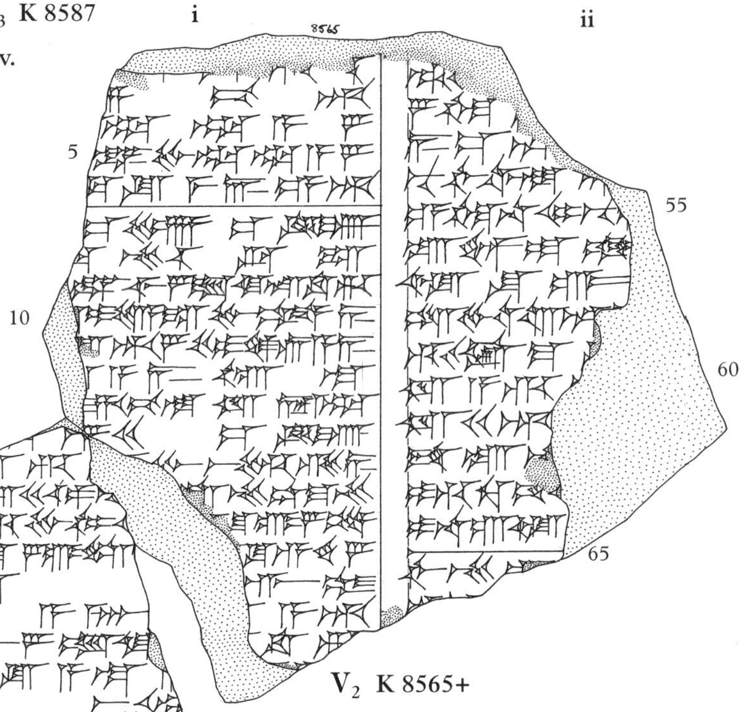

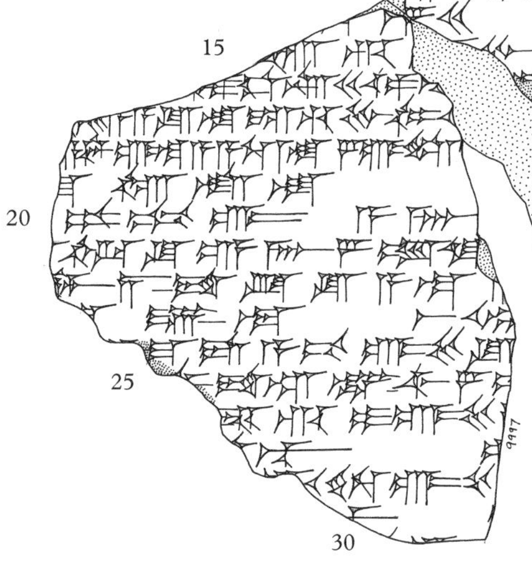

V$_2$ K 8565+

0 1 cm

V$_4$ K 19549 obv.

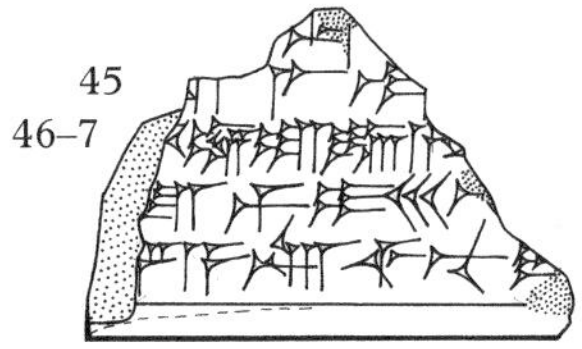

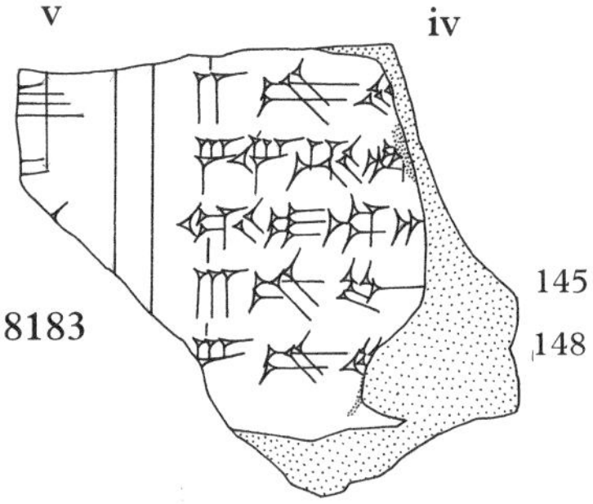

EE K 18183

102. SB Tablet VIII. MS V cols. i and ii.
SB Tablet IX. MS EE

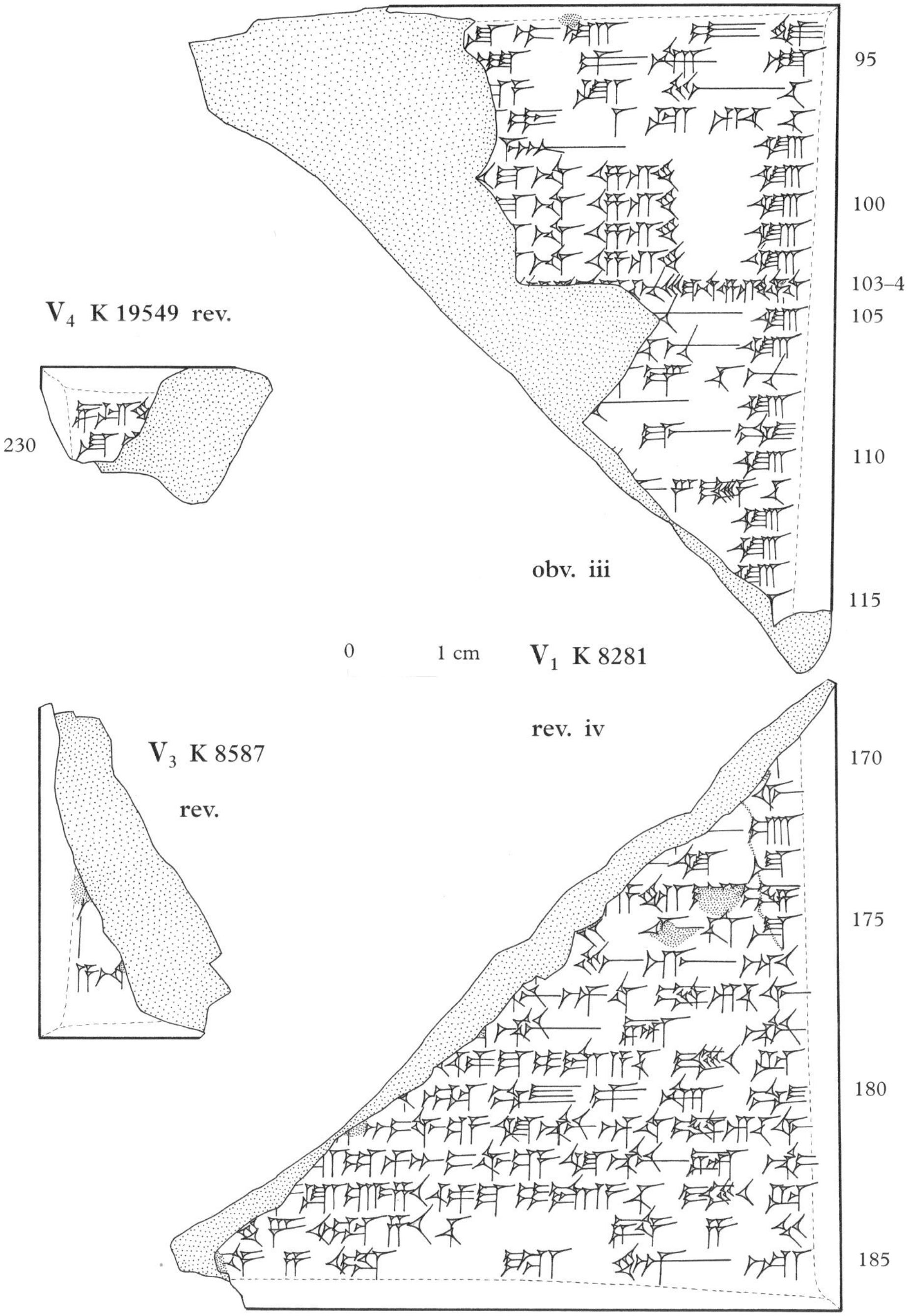

103. SB Tablet VIII. MS V cols. iii, iv and vi

m_2 BM 37189

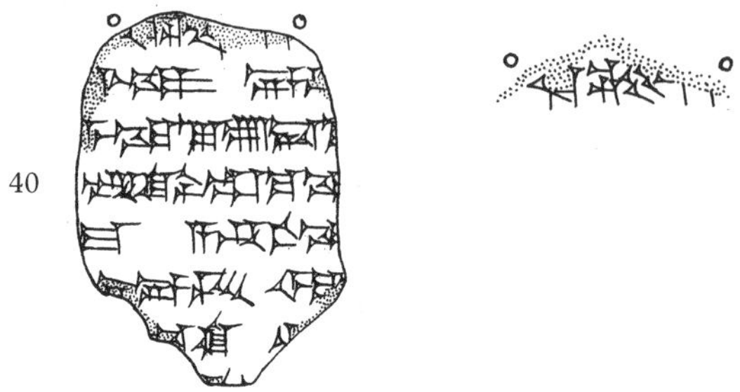

m_1 BM 36909+ obv.

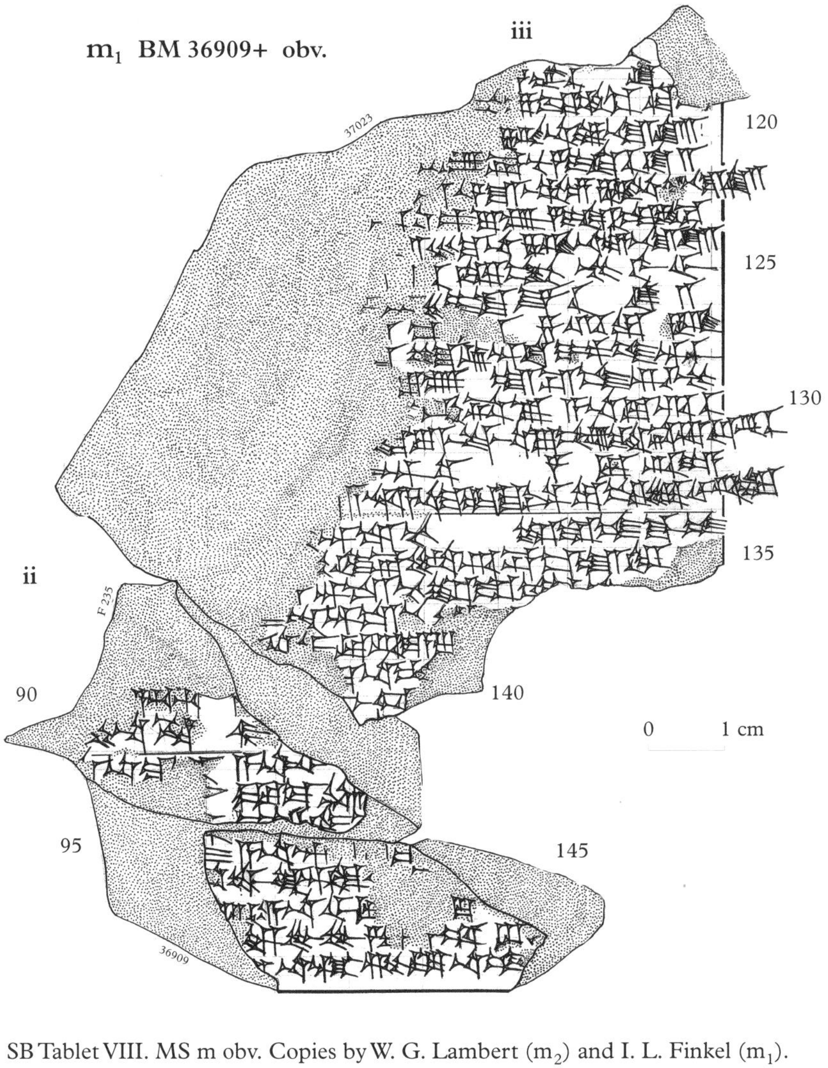

104. SB Tablet VIII. MS m obv. Copies by W. G. Lambert (m_2) and I. L. Finkel (m_1). Collation of m_2 by the author. The scale applies to m_1 only

m$_1$ BM 36909+ rev.

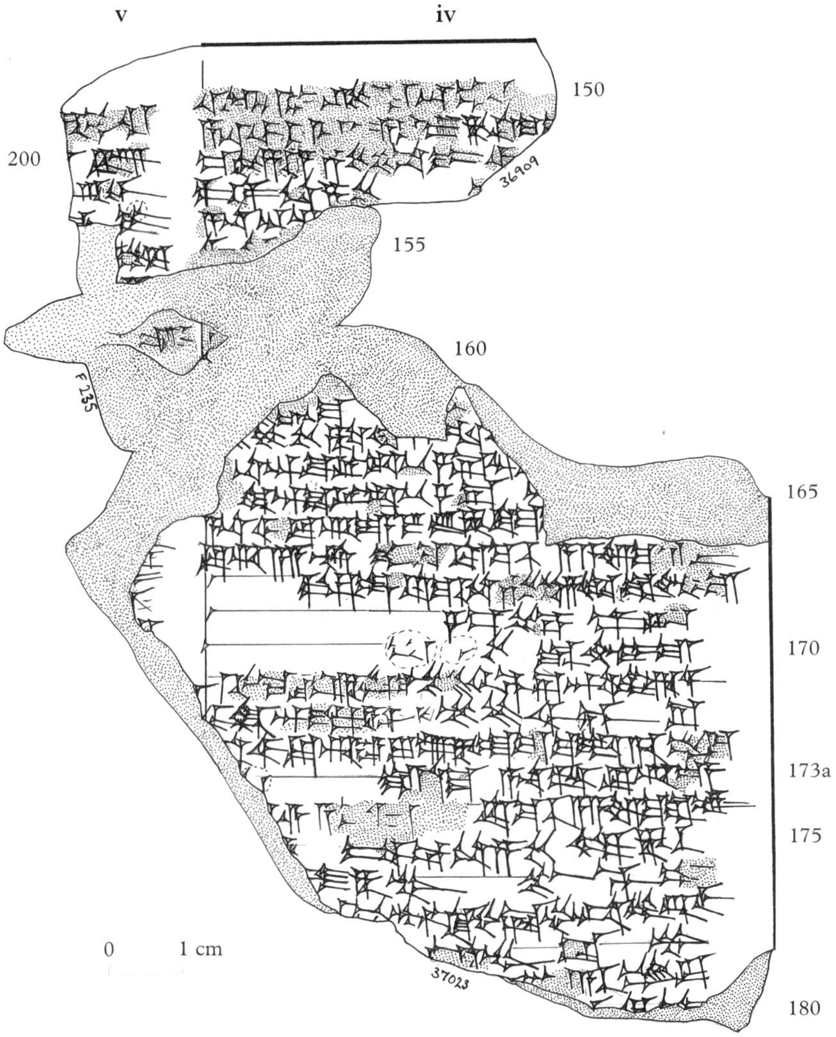

105. SB. Tablet VIII. MS m rev. Copy by I. L. Finkel

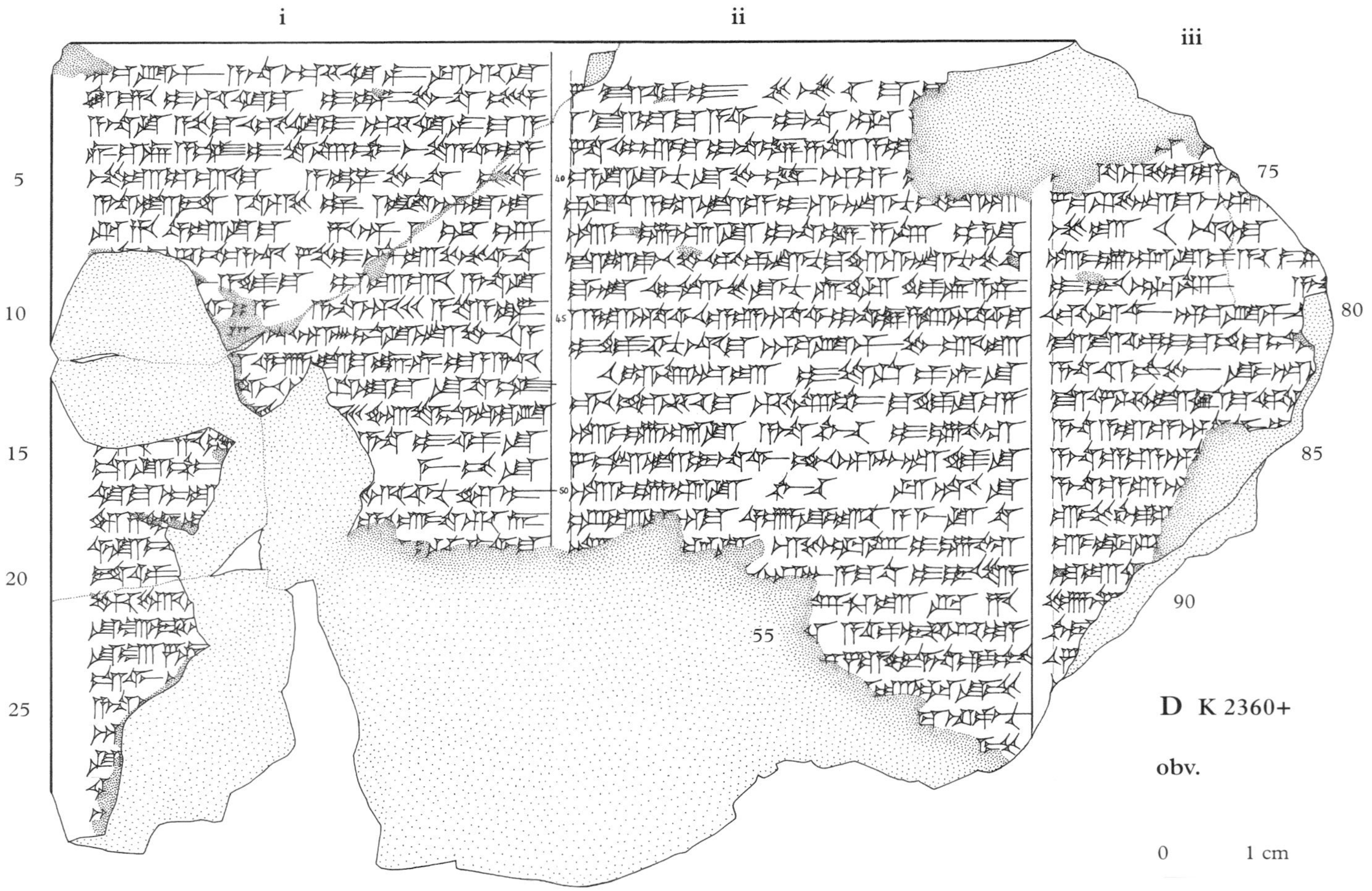

106. SB Tablet IX. MS D obv.

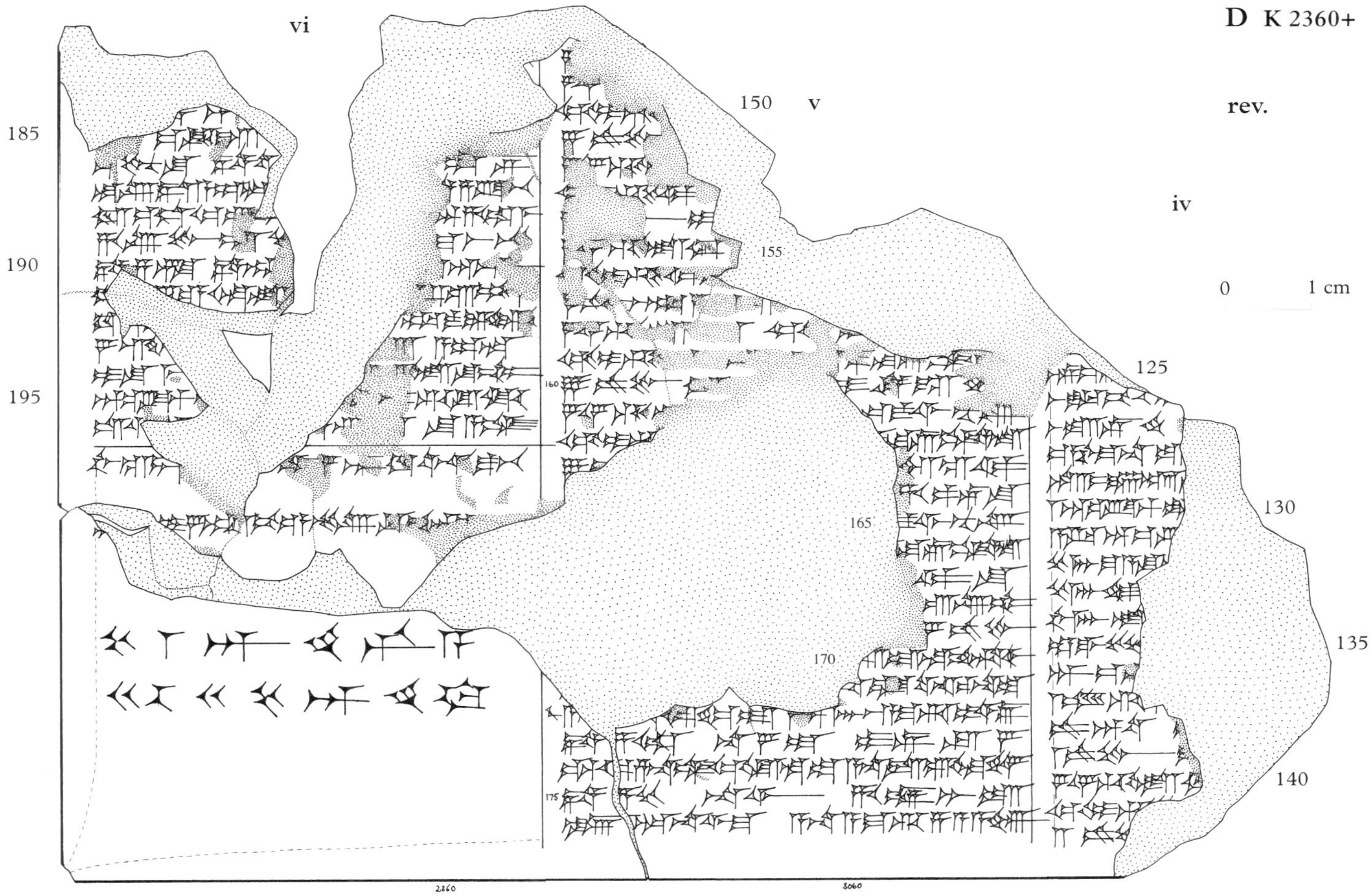

107. SB Tablet IX. MS D rev.

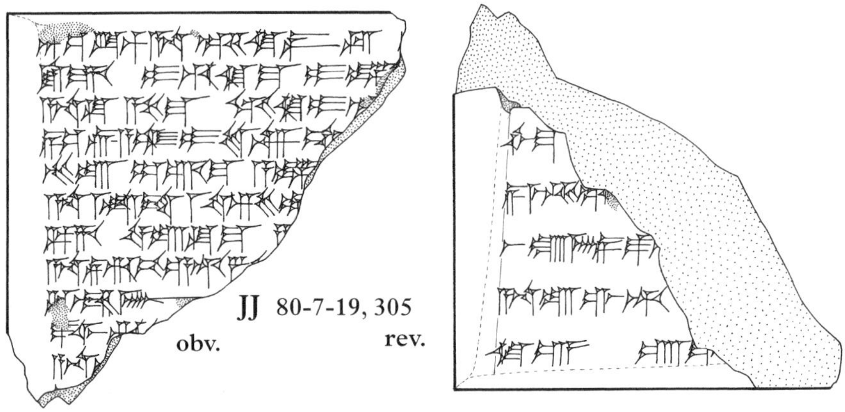

K$_3$ K 8589+ obv.

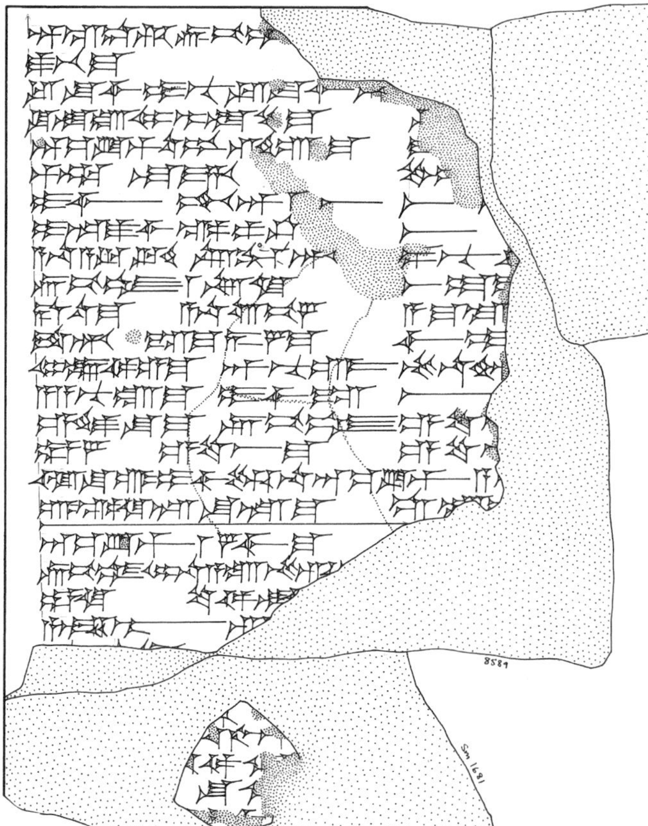

i

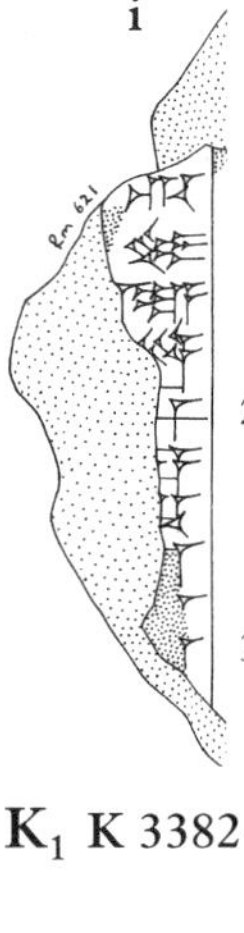

K$_1$ K 3382+

108. SB Tablet IX. MS JJ.
SB Tablet X, MS K col.i

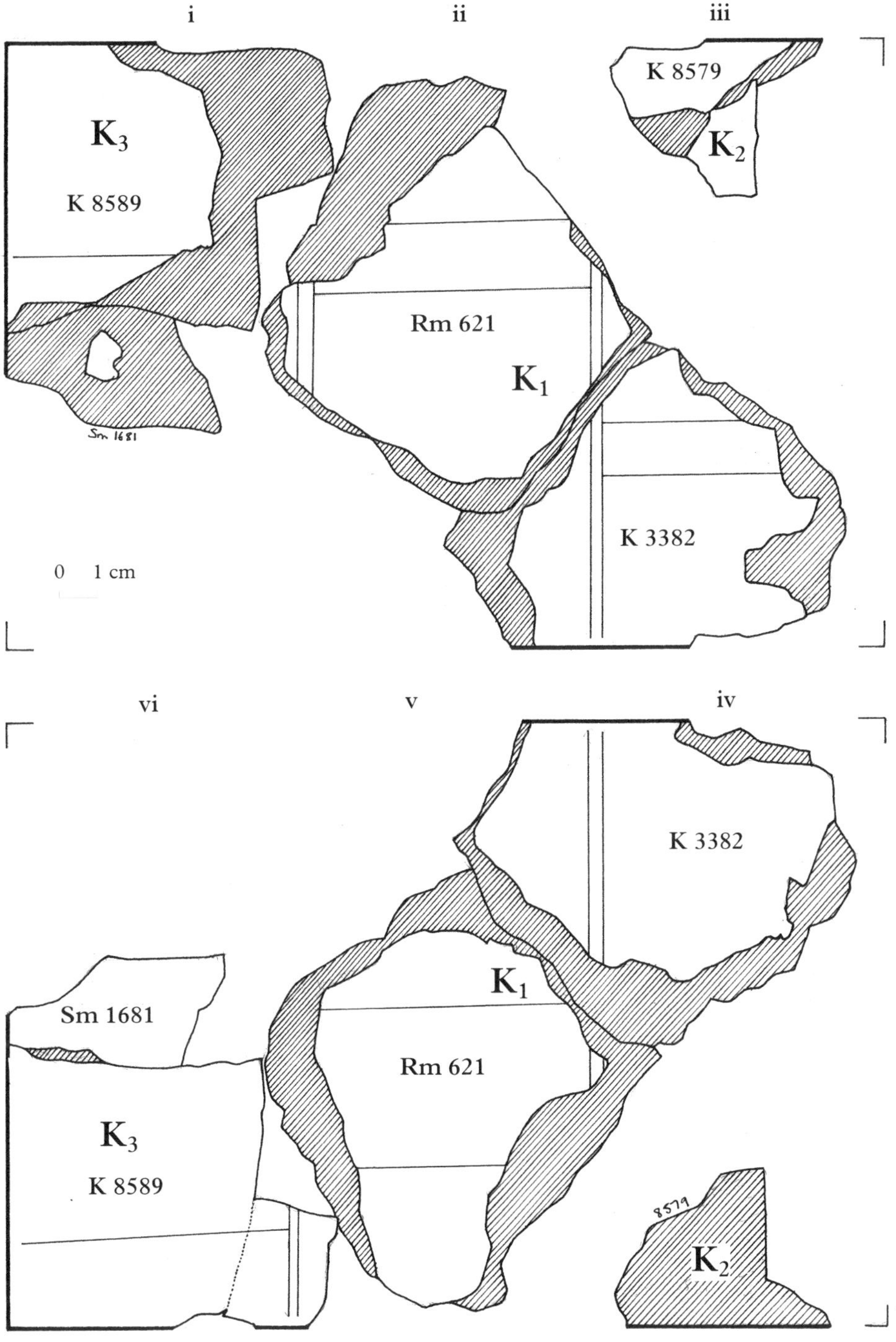

109. SB Tablet X. MS K, outline sketch

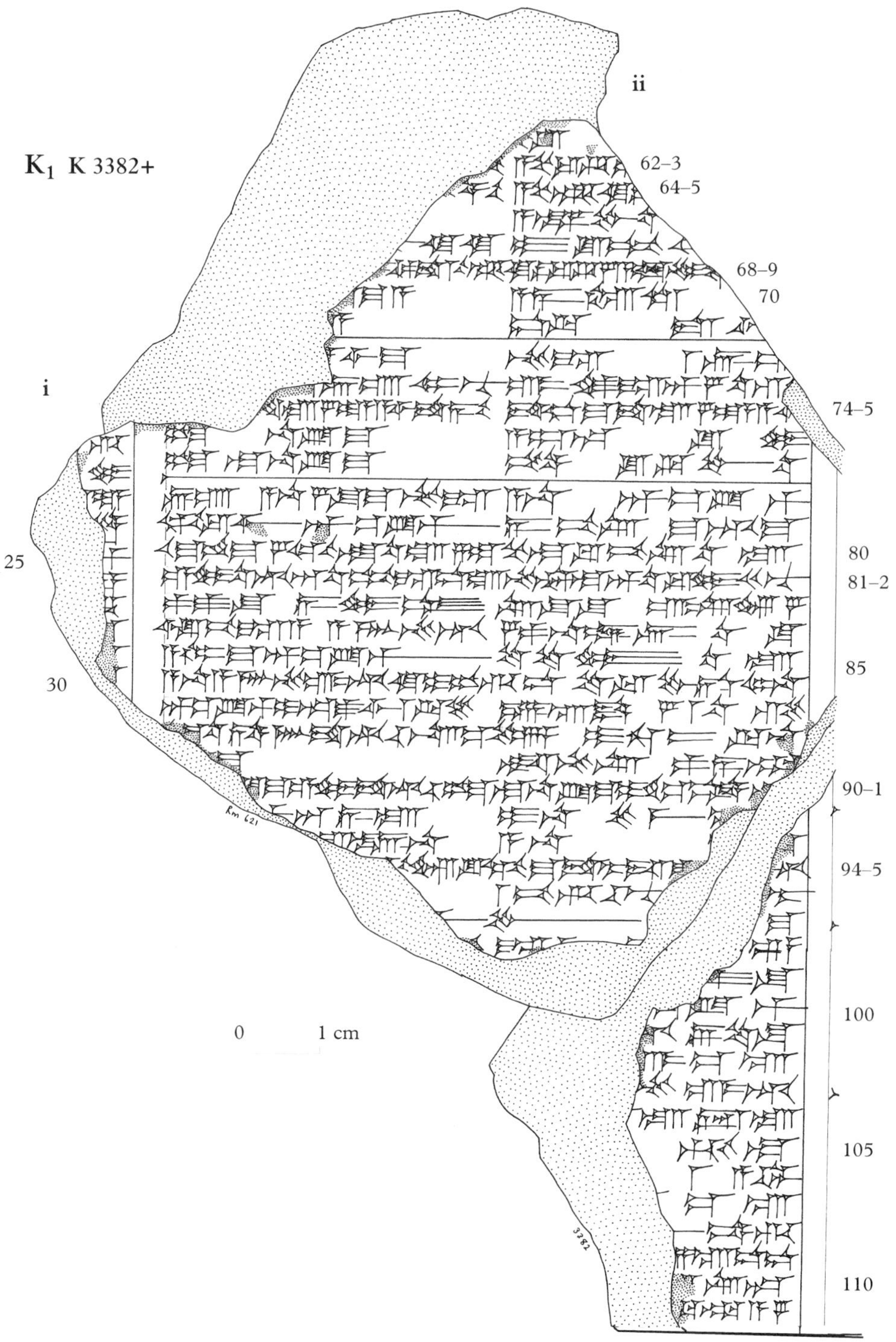

110. SB Tablet X. MS K col. ii

iii

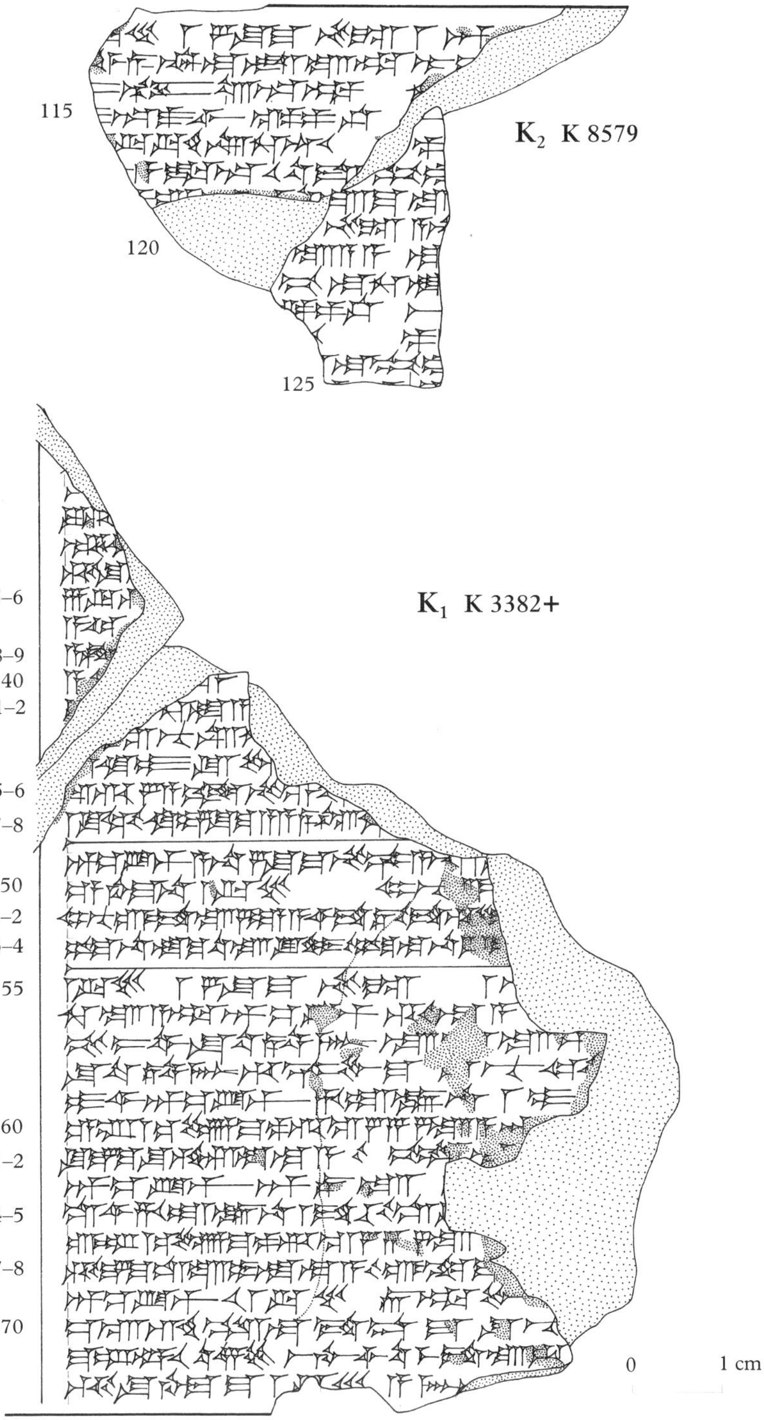

111. SB Tablet X. MS K col. iii

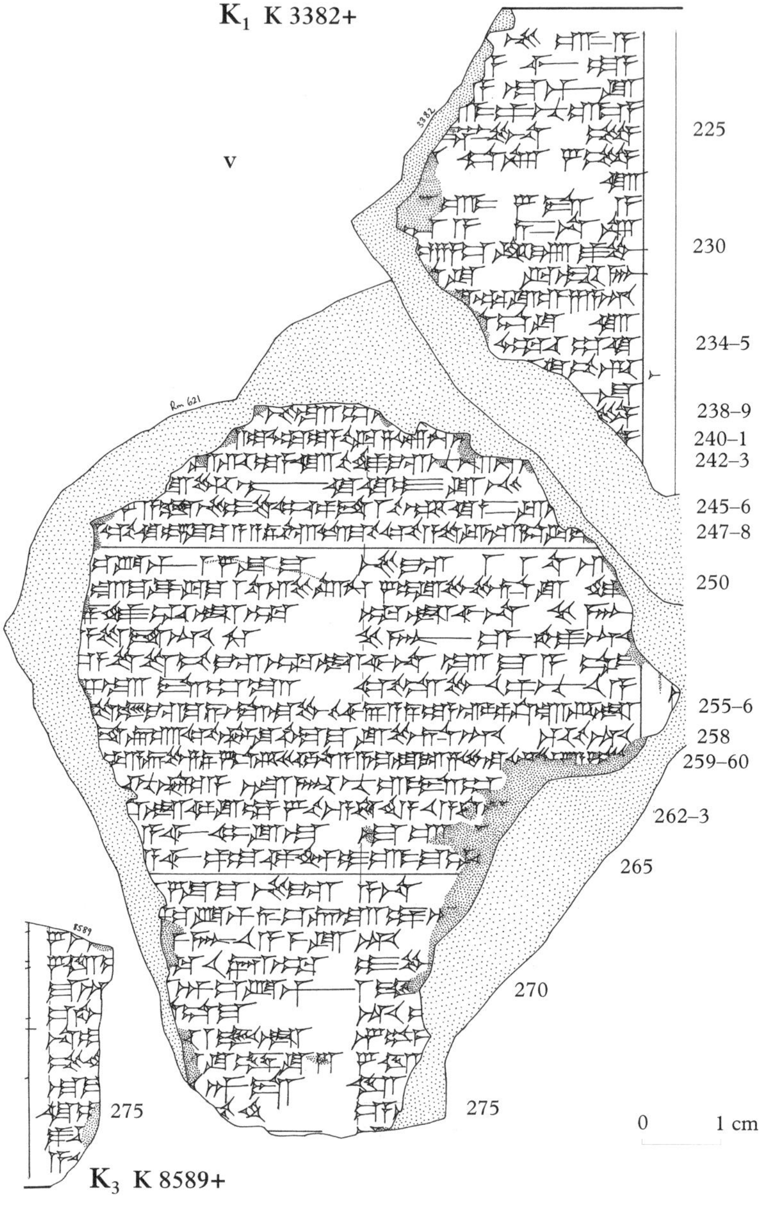

112. SB Tablet X. MS K col. v

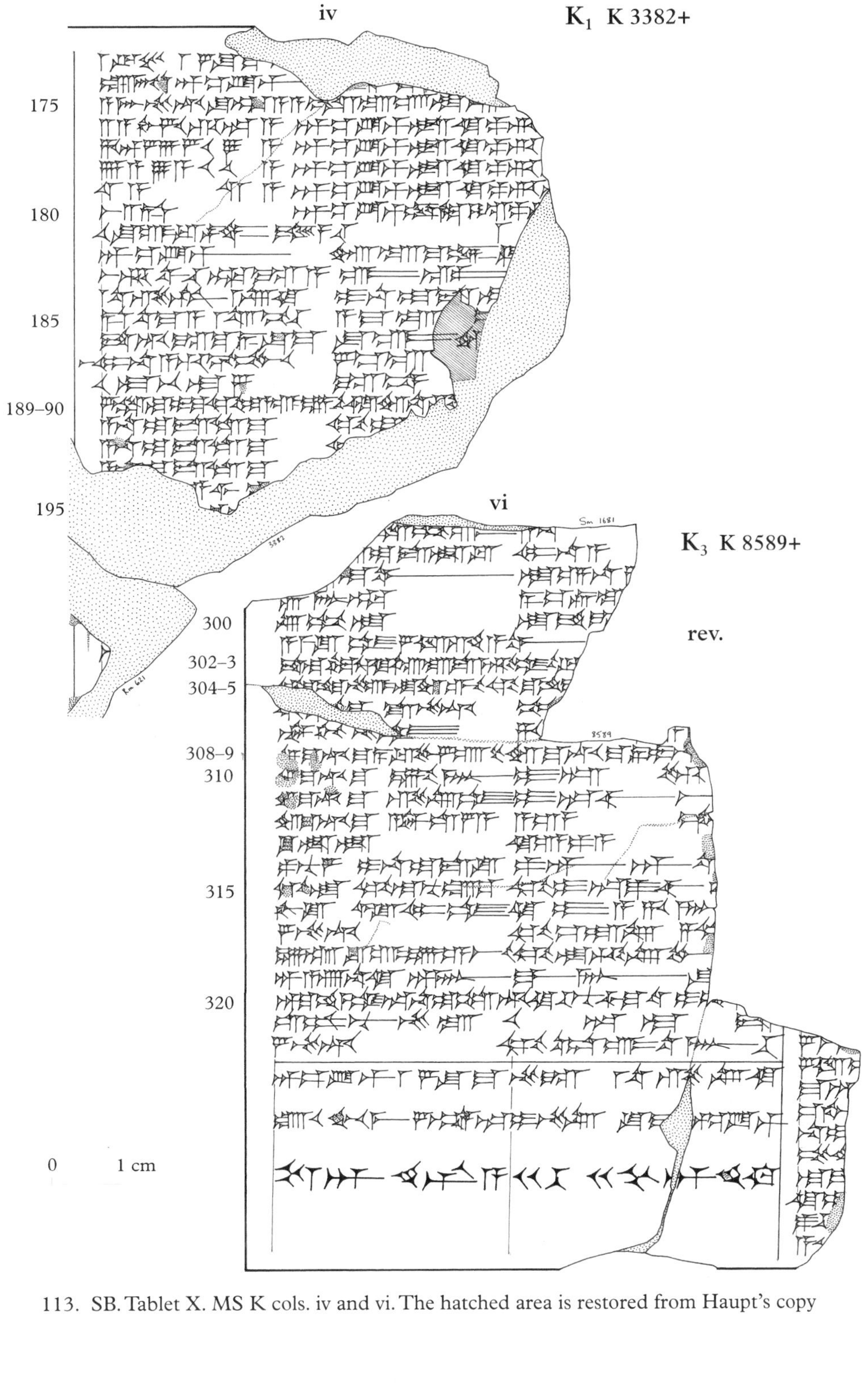

113. SB. Tablet X. MS K cols. iv and vi. The hatched area is restored from Haupt's copy

b BM 34160+

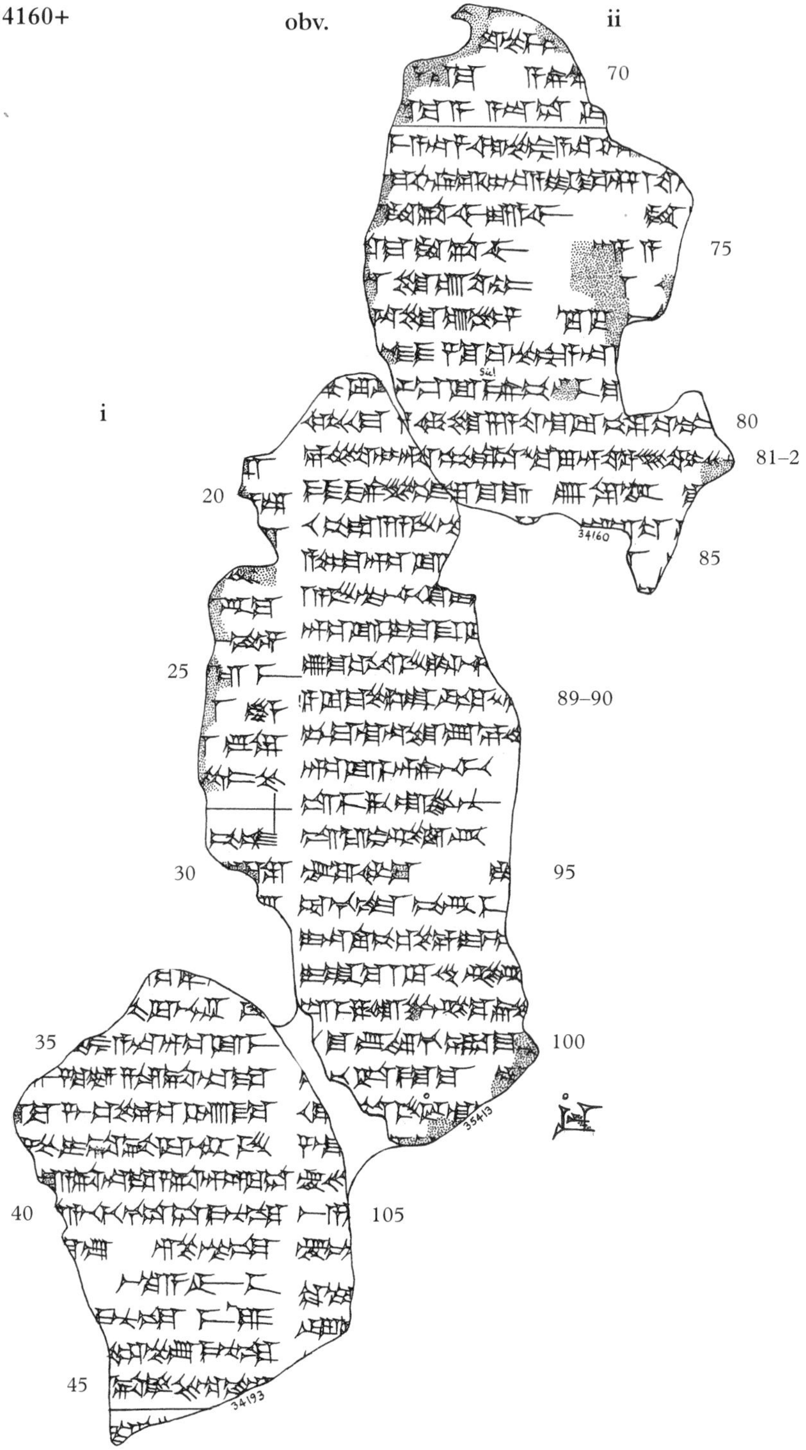

114. SB Tablet X. MS b obv. Copy by W. G. Lambert, collation by the author

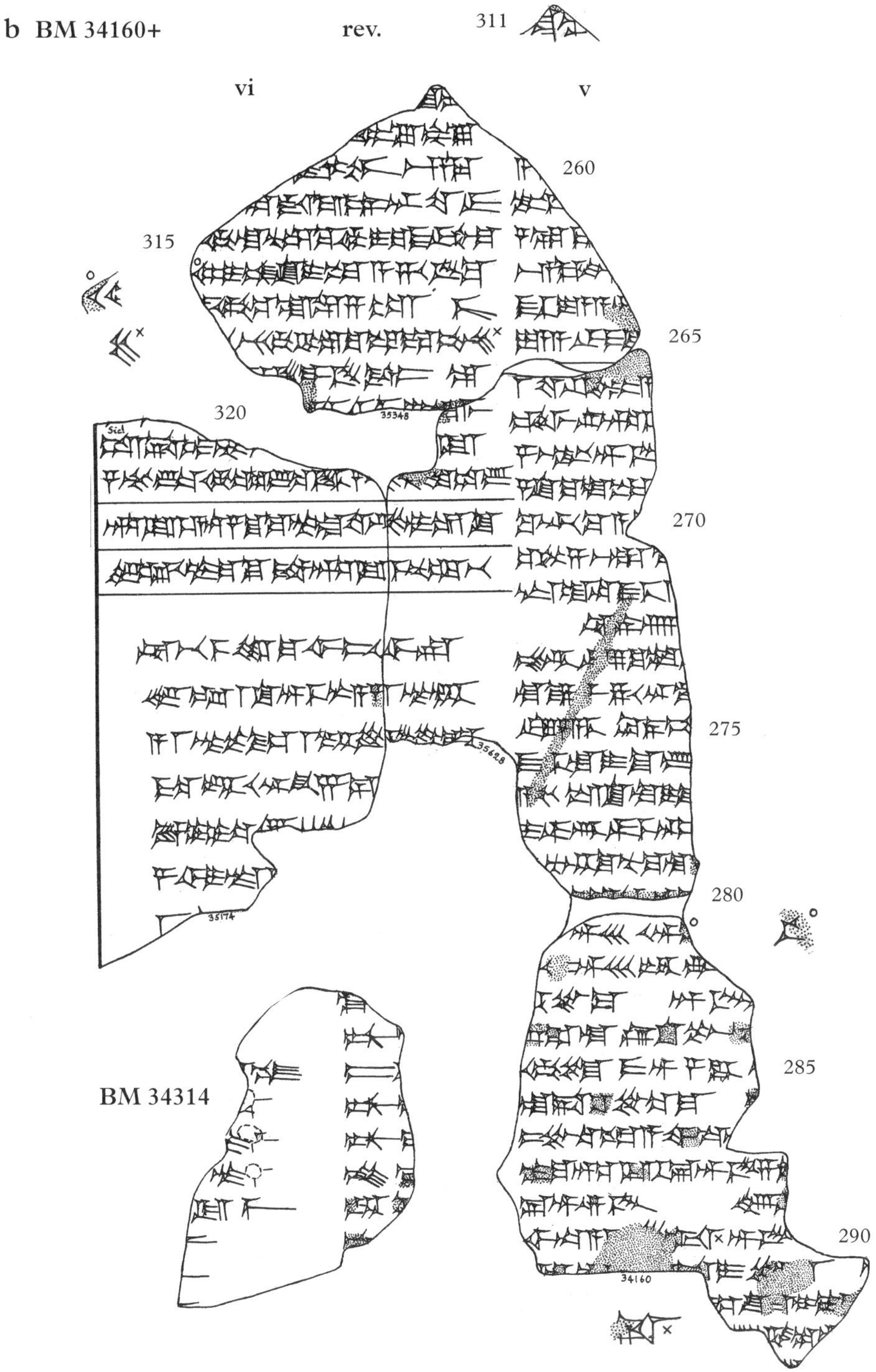

115. SB Tablet X. MS b rev. Unplaced fragment BM 34314. Copies by W. G. Lambert, collations by the author

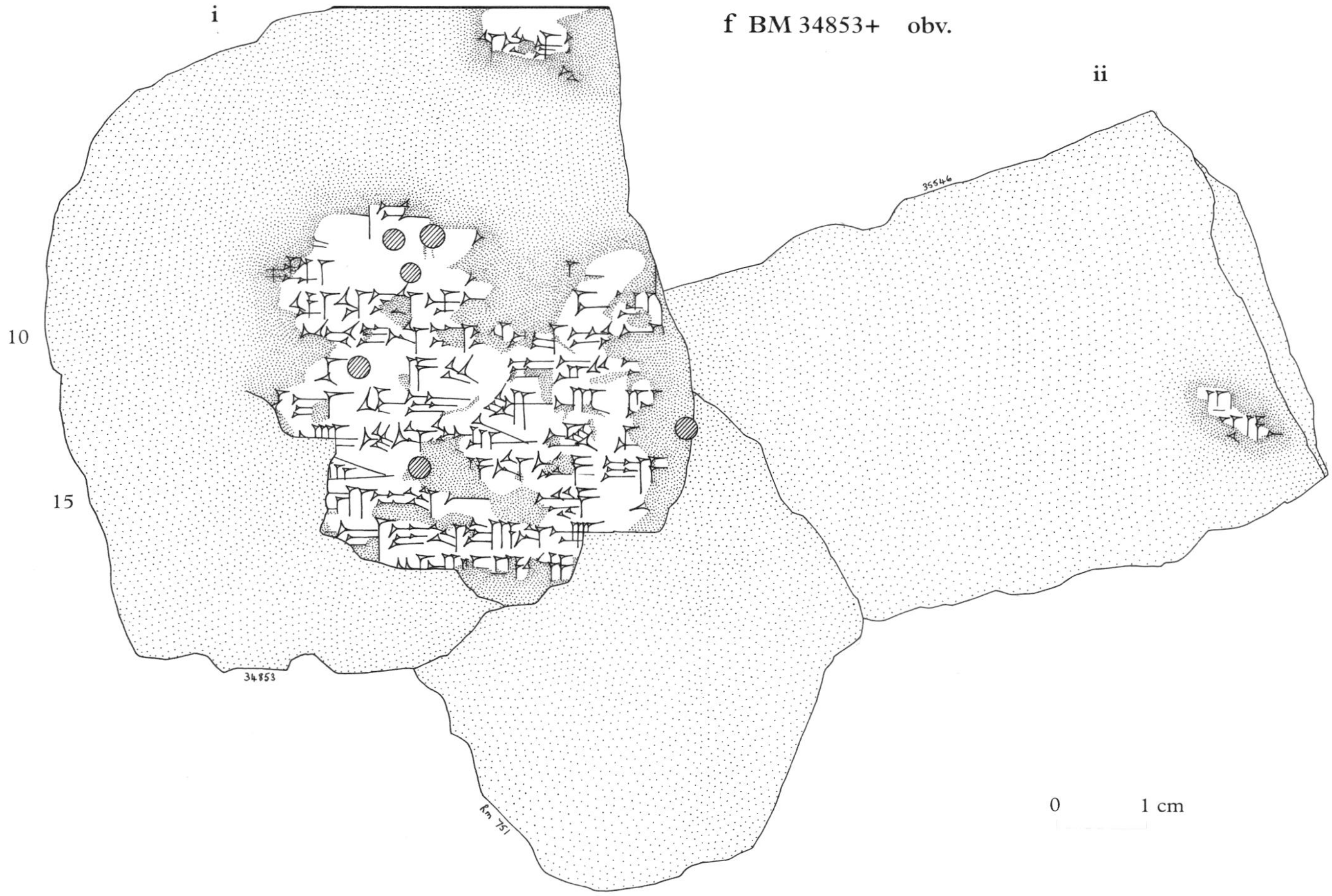

116. SB Tablet X. MS f obv.

f BM 34853+ rev.

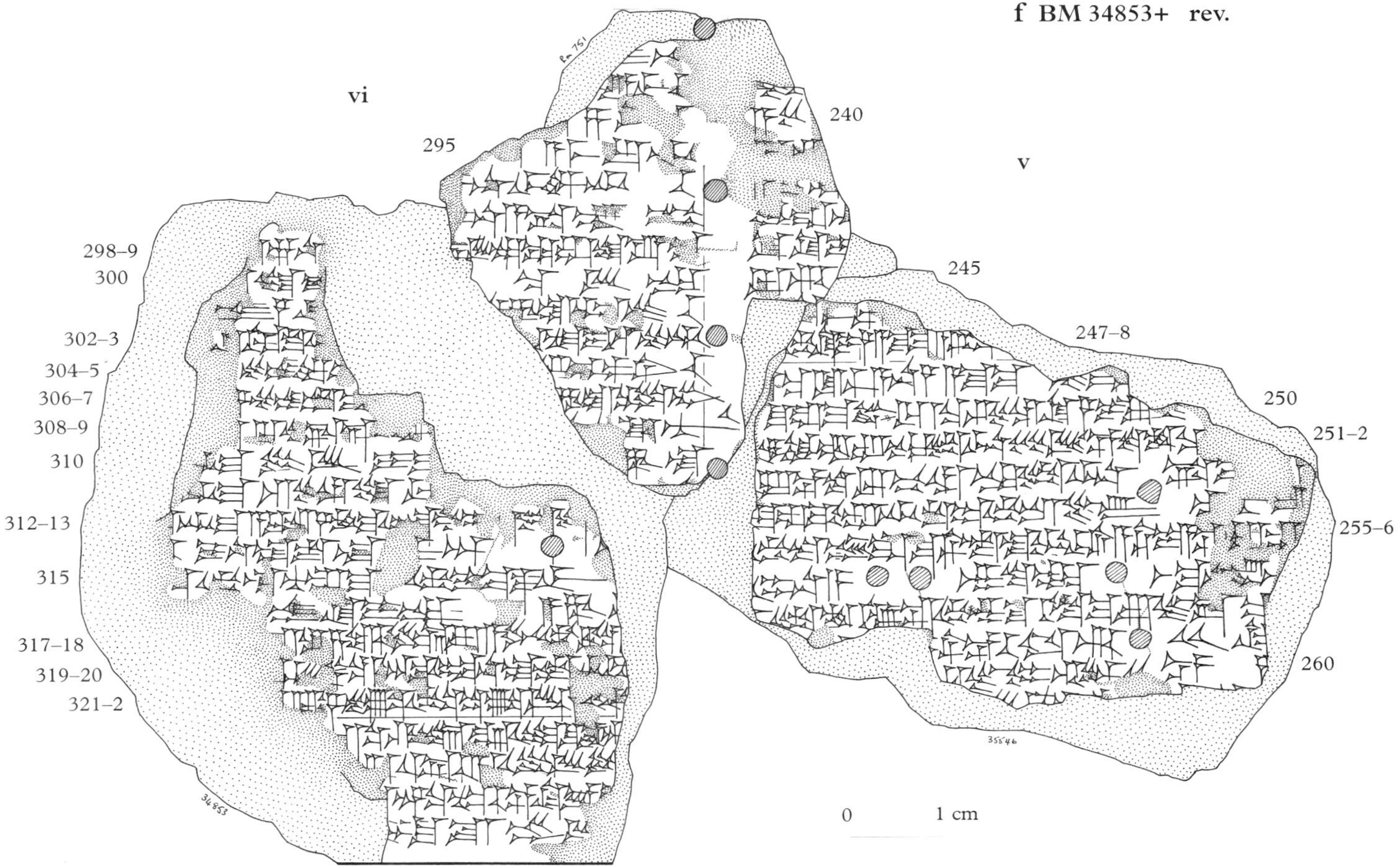

117. SB Tablet X. MS f rev.

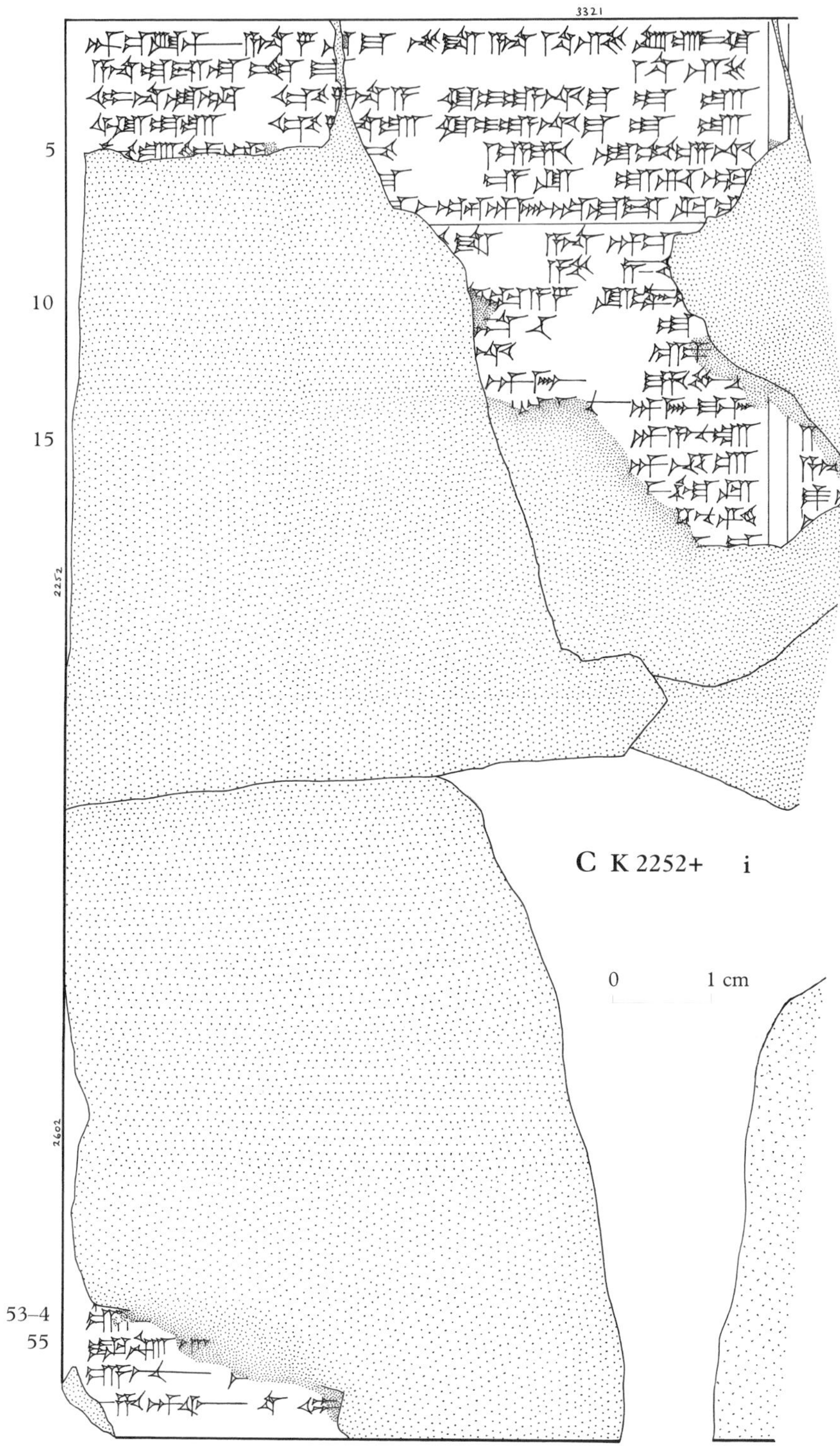

118. SB Tablet XI. MS C col. i

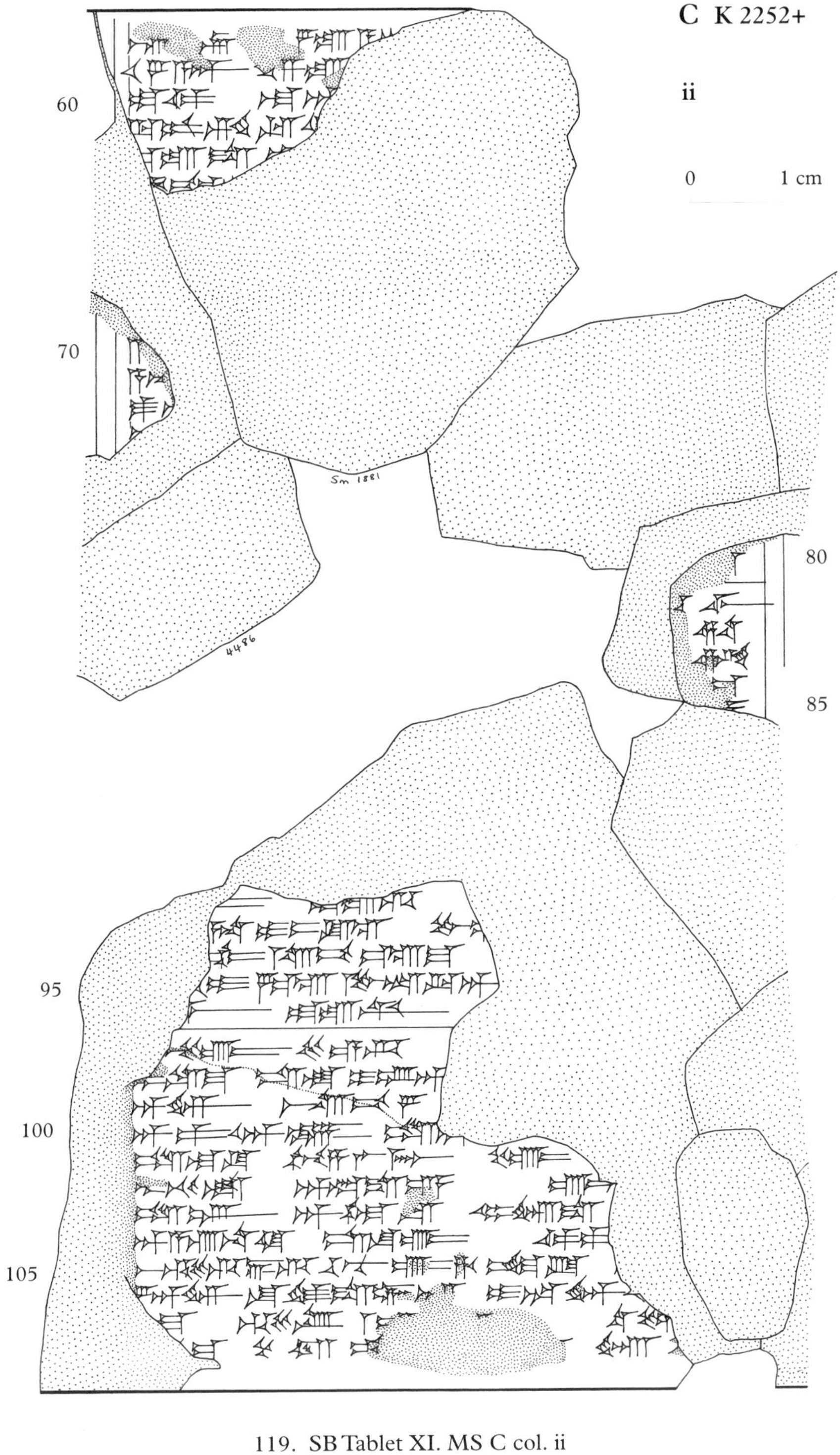

119. SB Tablet XI. MS C col. ii

C K 2252+

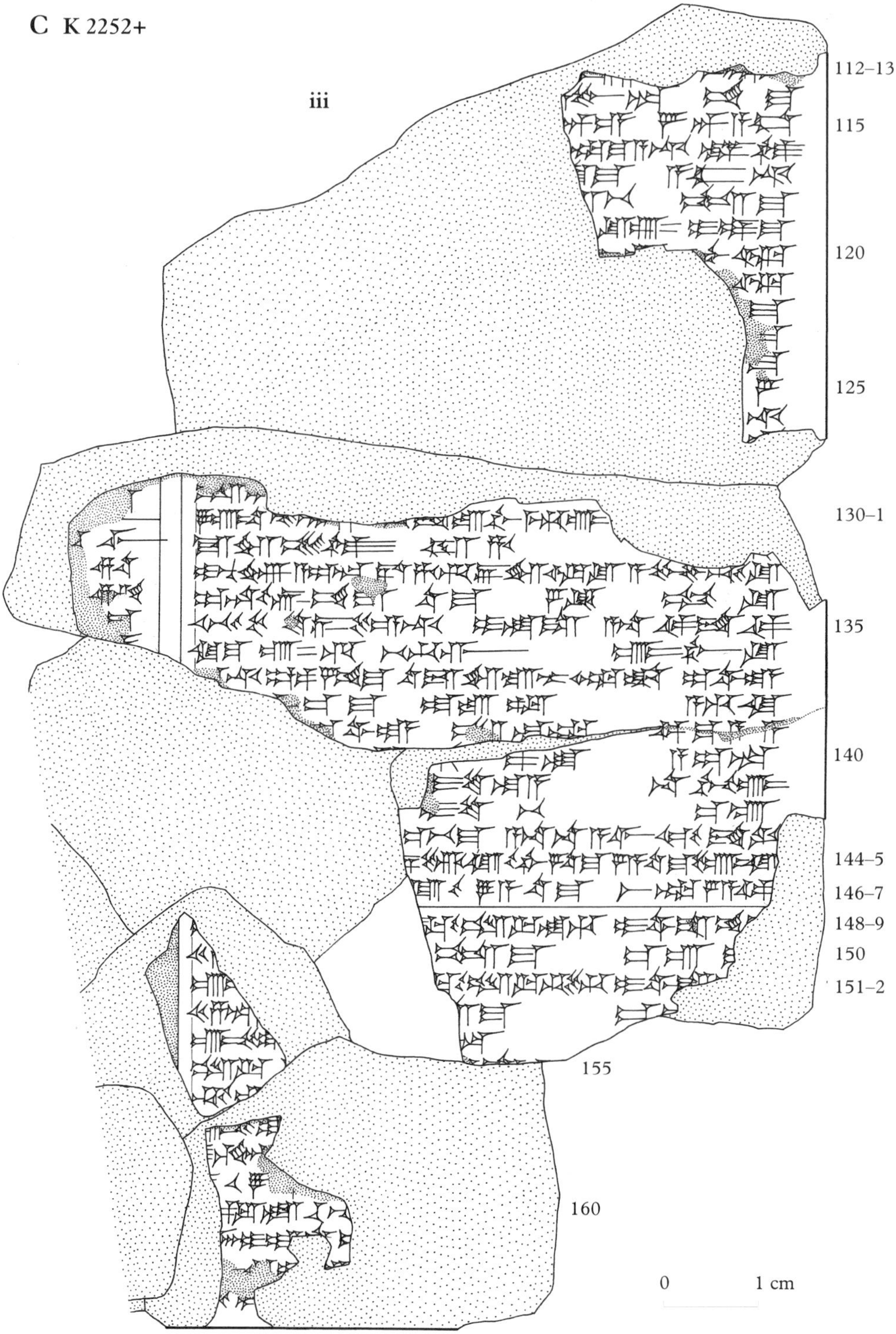

120. SB Tablet XI. MS C col. iii

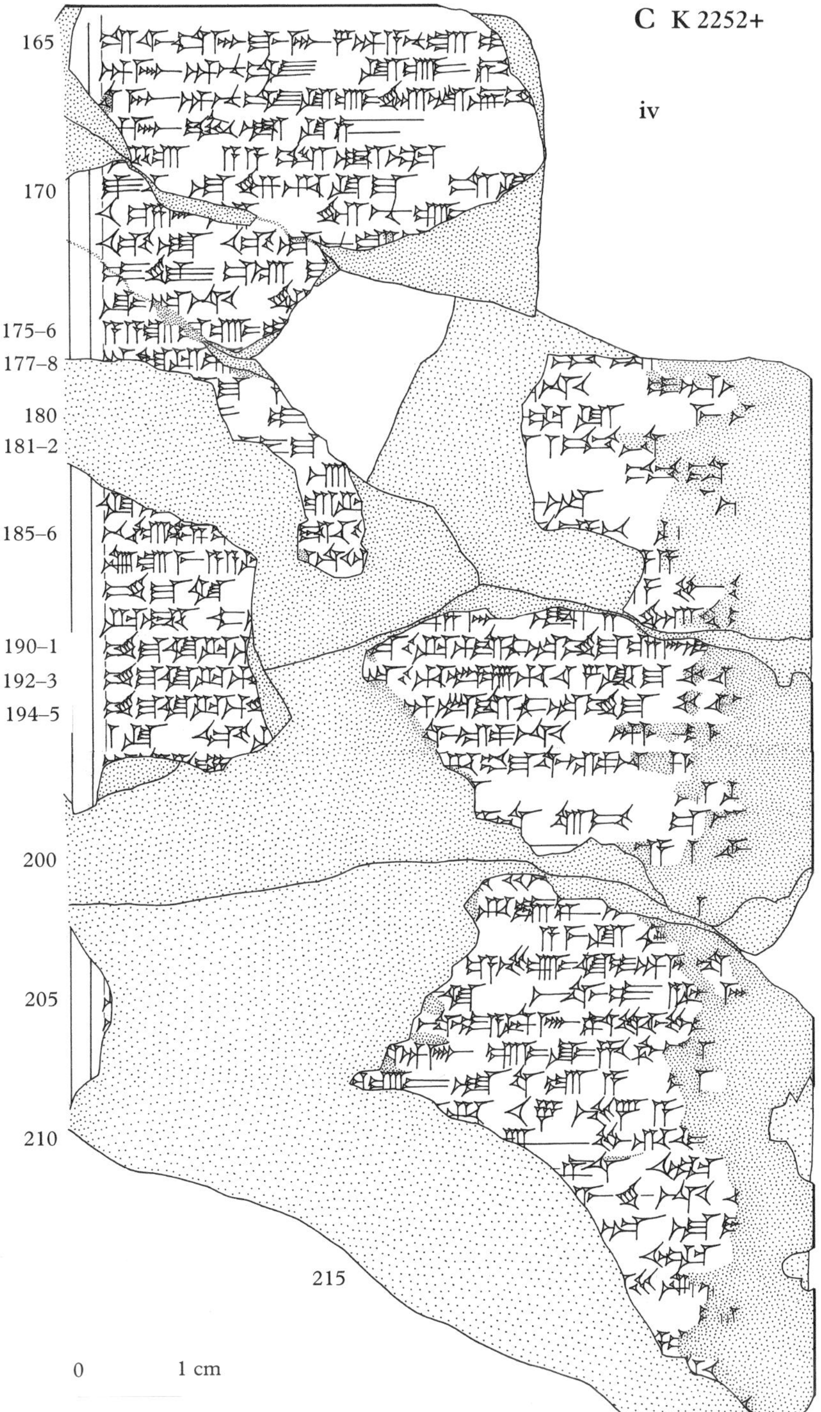

121. SB Tablet XI. MS C col. iv

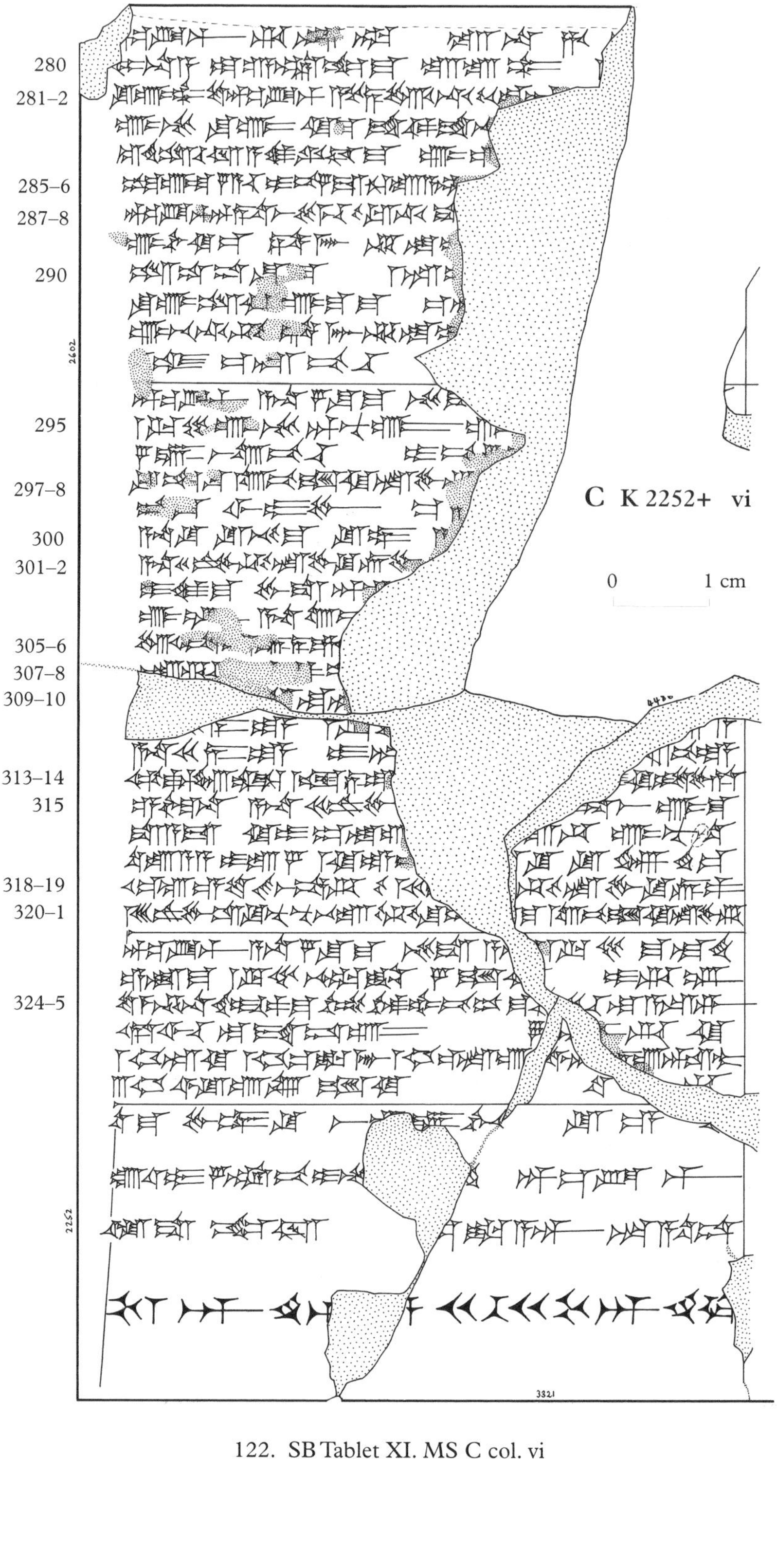

122. SB Tablet XI. MS C col. vi

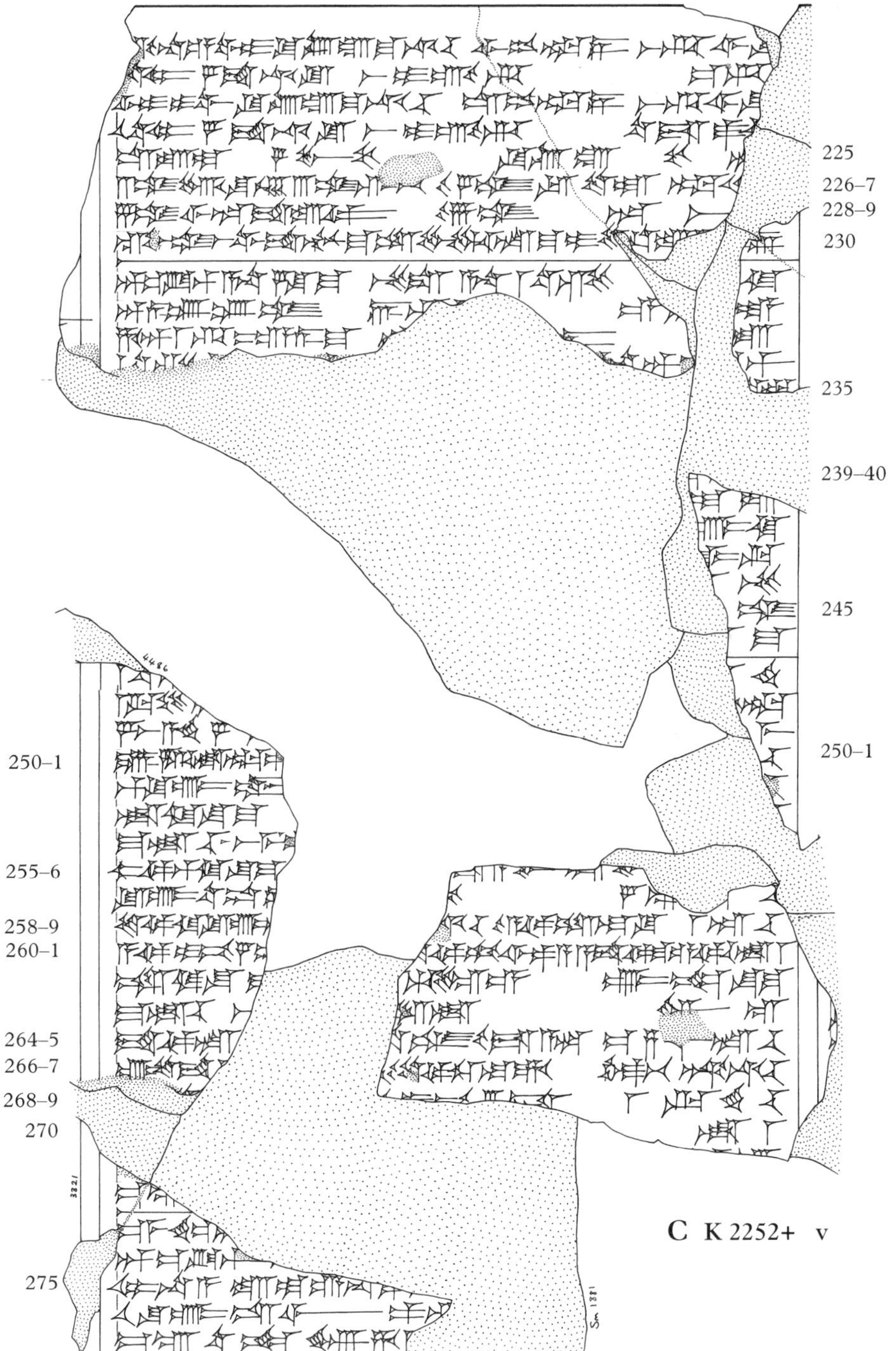

123. SB Tablet XI. MS C col. v

J_1 K 3375

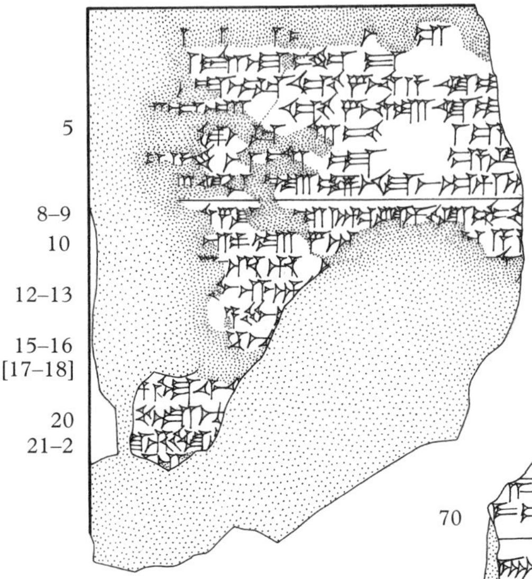

J_2 Rm 616 obv.
[rev. vitrified]

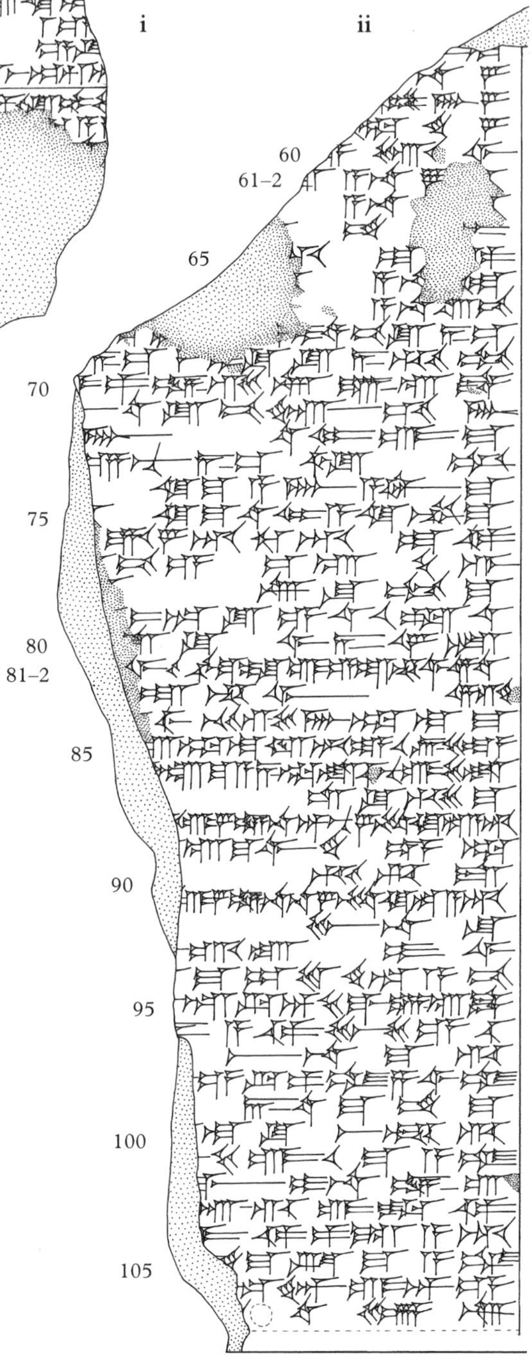

0 1 cm

124. SB Tablet XI. MS J cols. i and ii

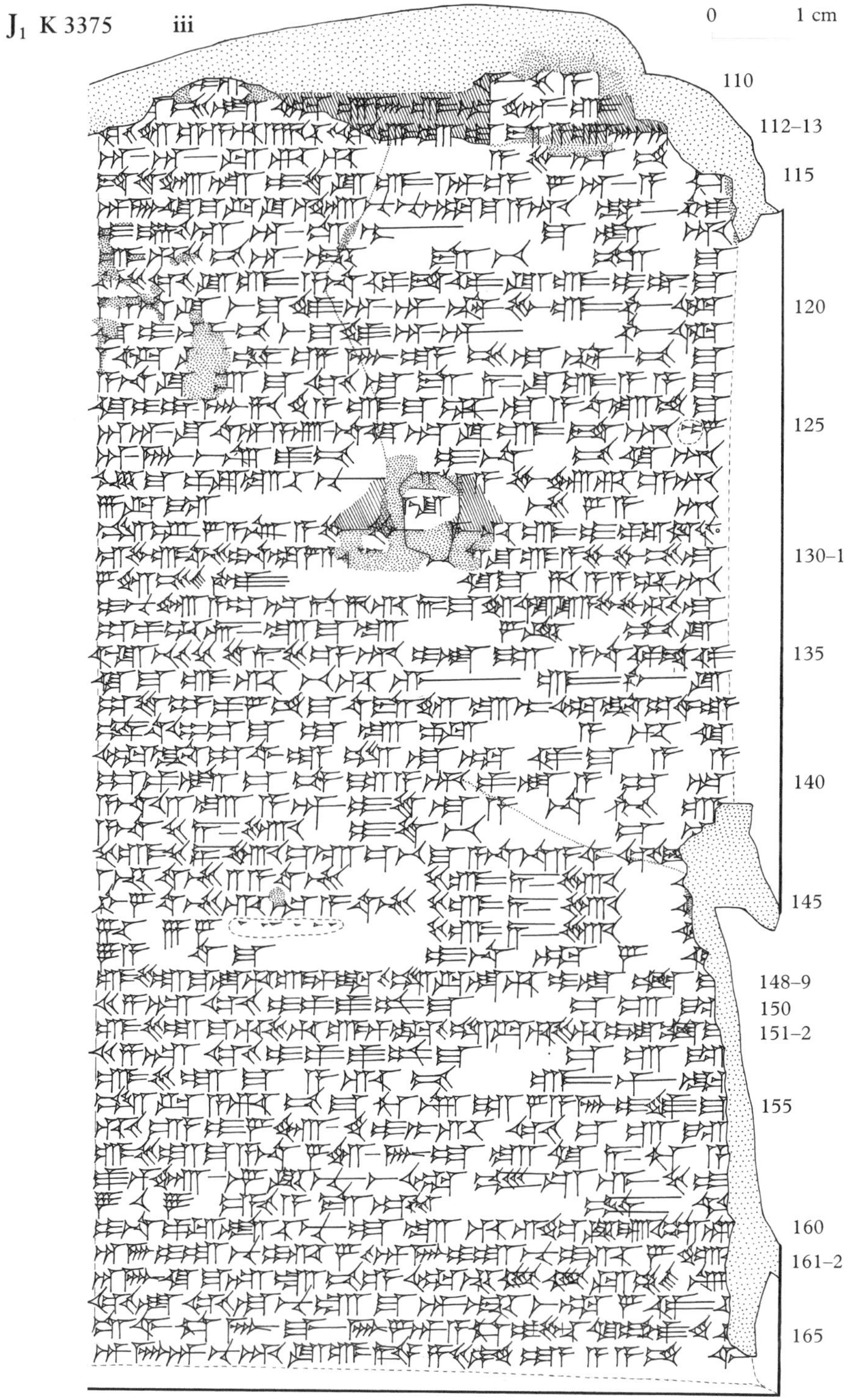

°sup. ras.

125. SB Tablet XI. MS J col. iii. The hatched areas are restored from Smith's copy (*TSBA* 3, pp. 551–2) and the old photograph (Fig. 12)

J_1 K 3375

v

rev.

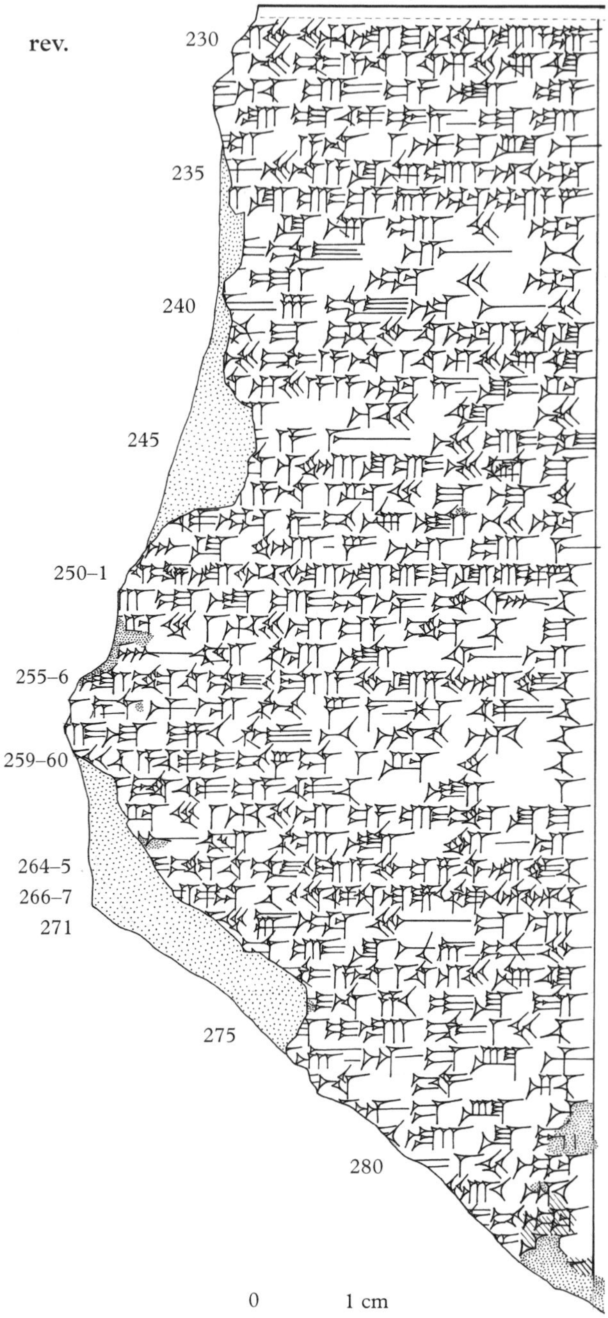

126. SB Tablet XI. MS J col. v. The hatched area is copied from the old photograph (Fig. 13)

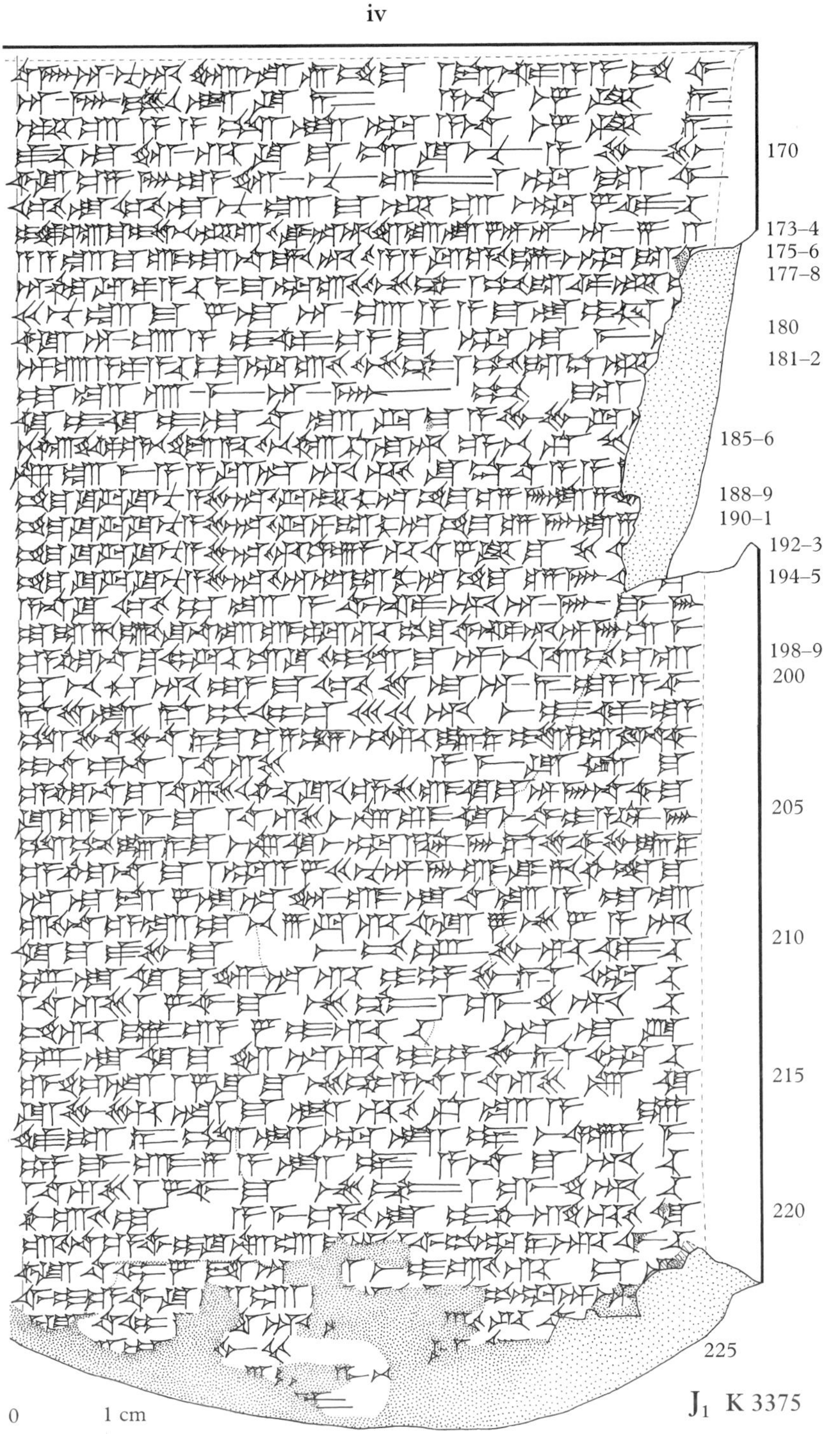

127. SB Tablet XI. MS J col. iv. The hatched area is restored from the old photograph (Fig. 13)

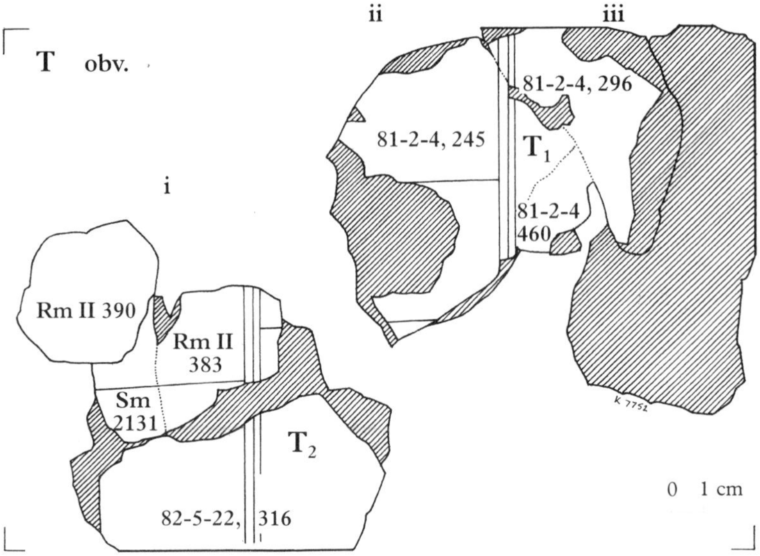

128. SB Tablet XI. MS T obv., outline sketch and col. i

T_1 K 7752+ ii

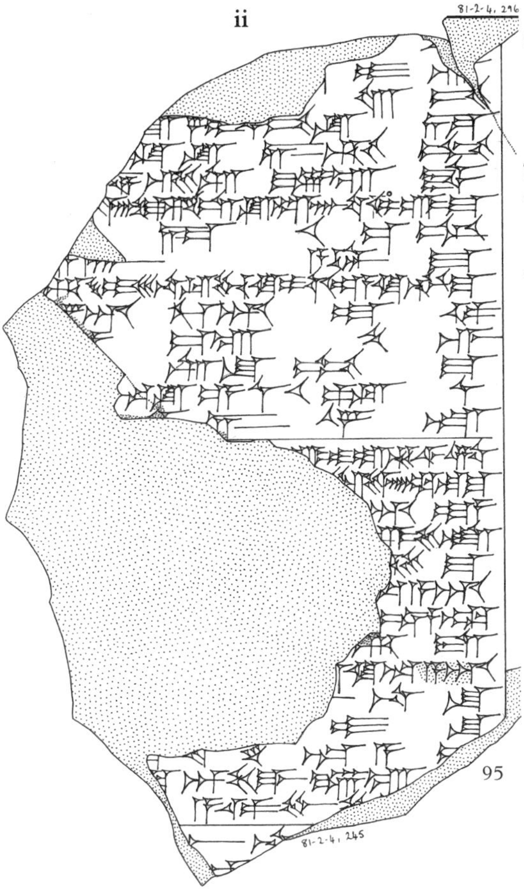

°sup. ras.

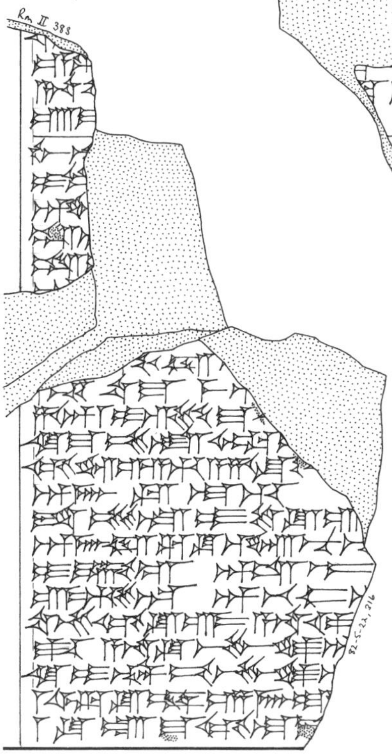

T_2 Sm 2131+

0 1 cm

129. SB Tablet XI. MS T col. ii

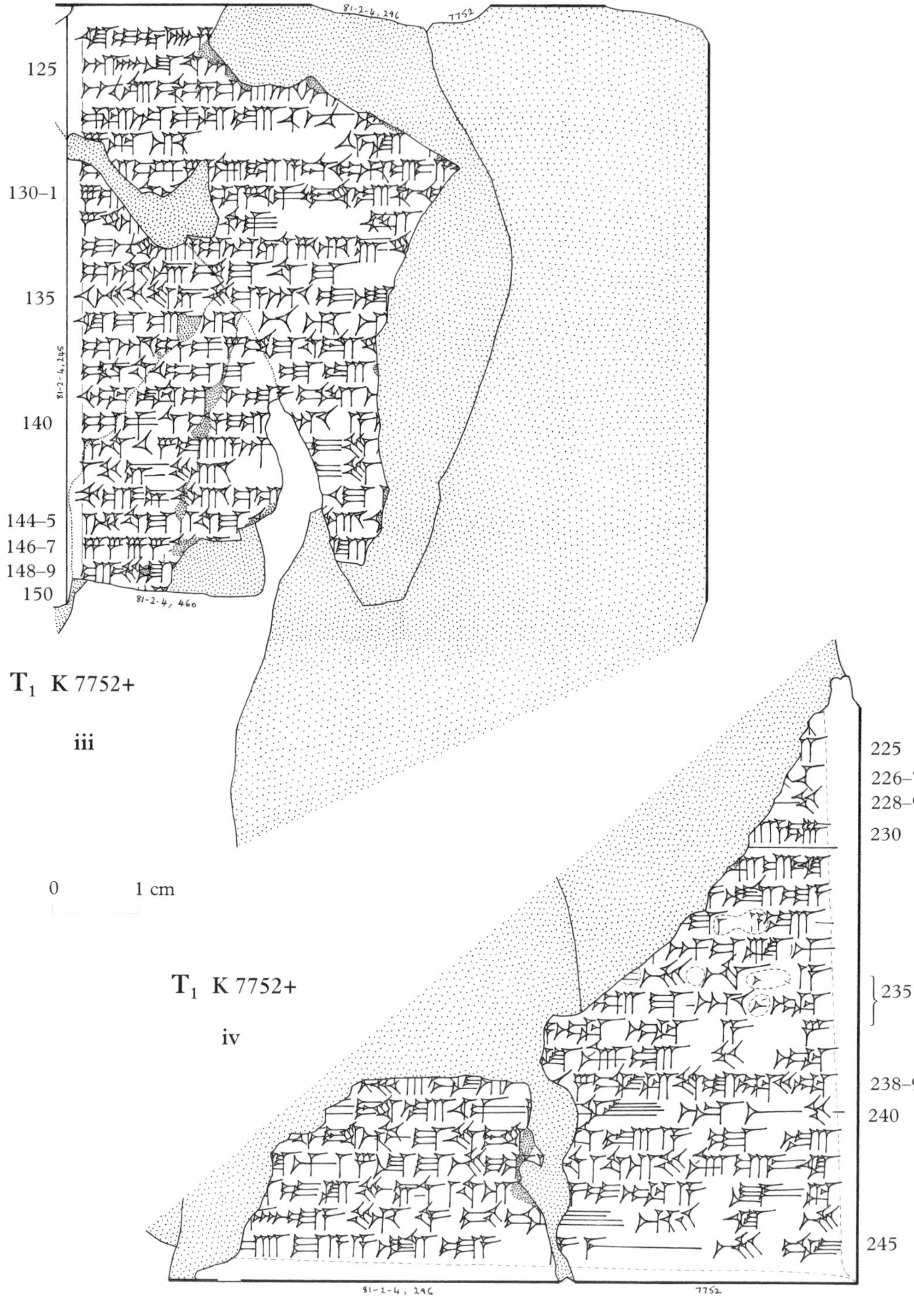

130. SB Tablet XI. MS T cols. iii and iv

T_2 Sm 2131+

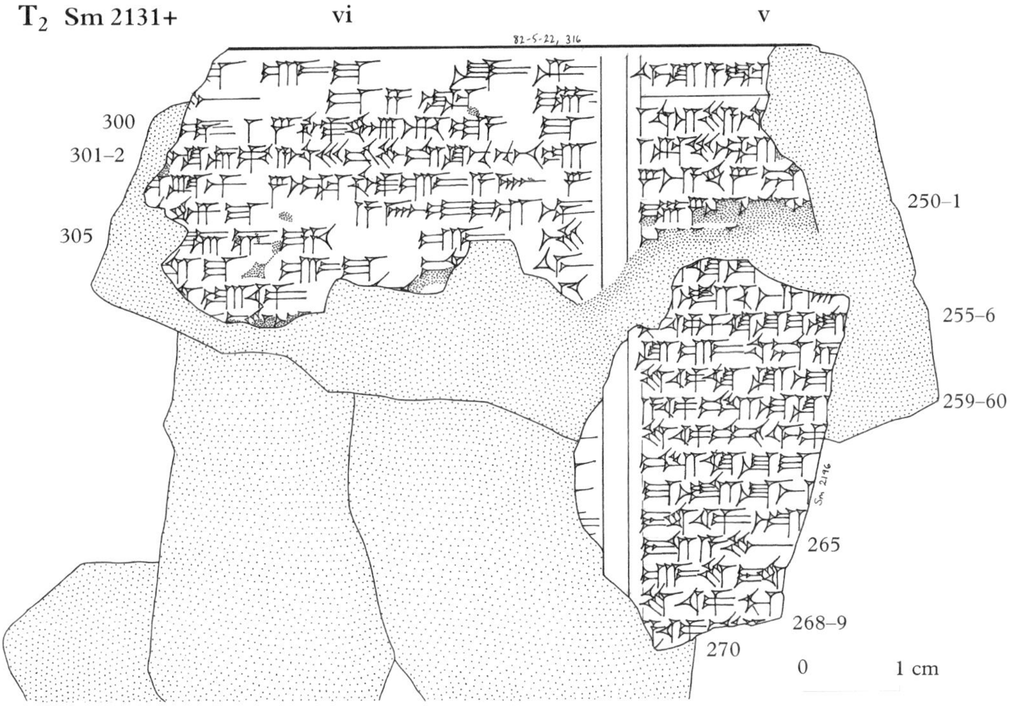

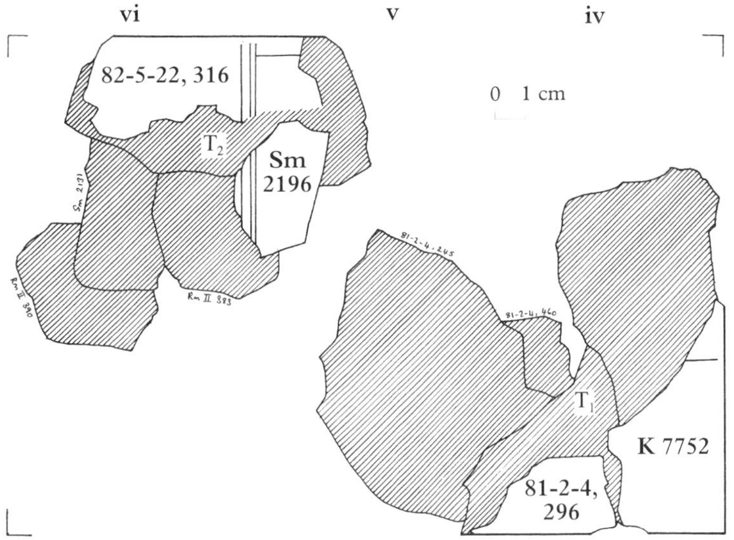

131. SB Tablet XI. MS T cols. v and vi, outline sketch of rev.

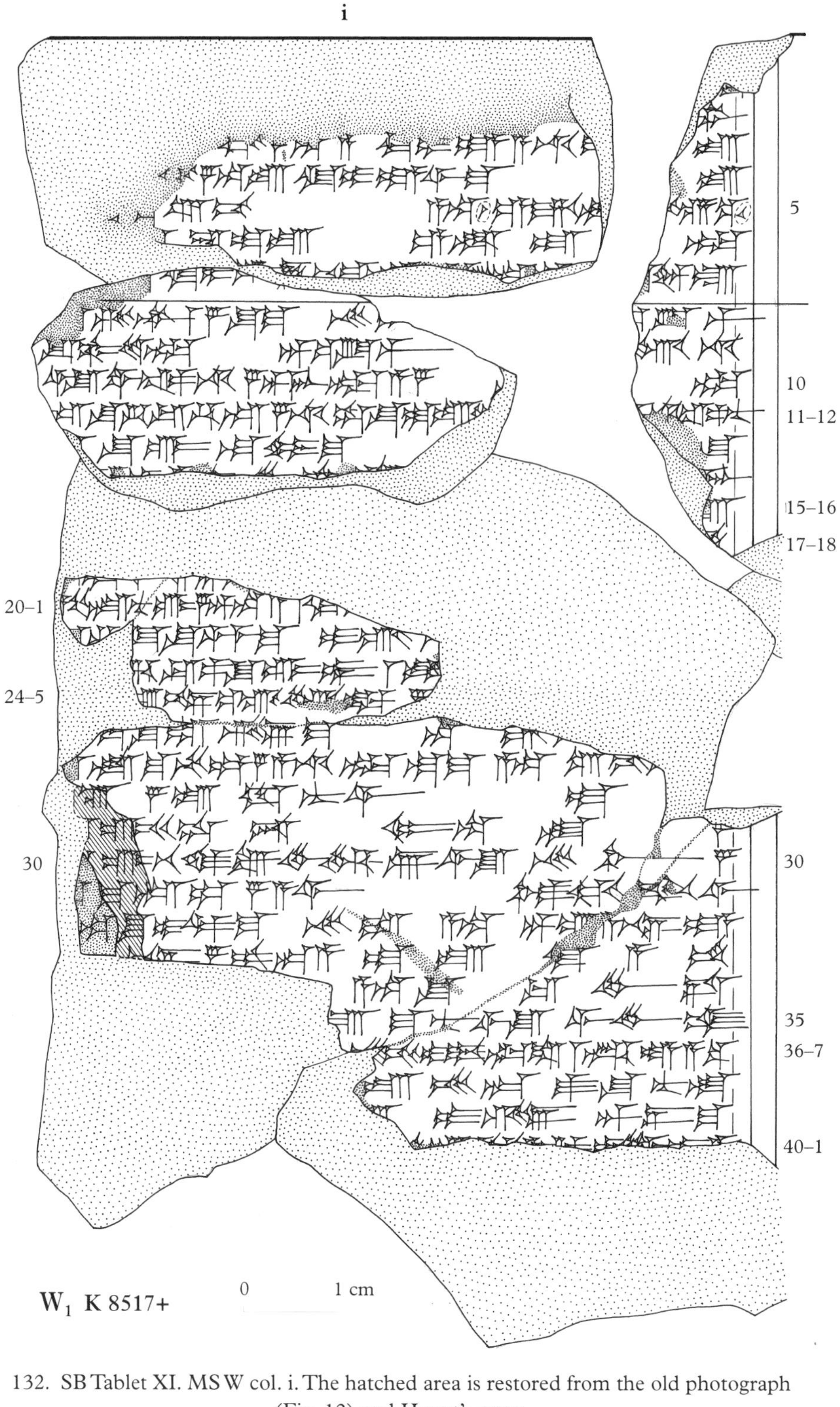

W_1 K 8517+

132. SB Tablet XI. MS W col. i. The hatched area is restored from the old photograph (Fig. 12) and Haupt's copy

W_1 K 8517+

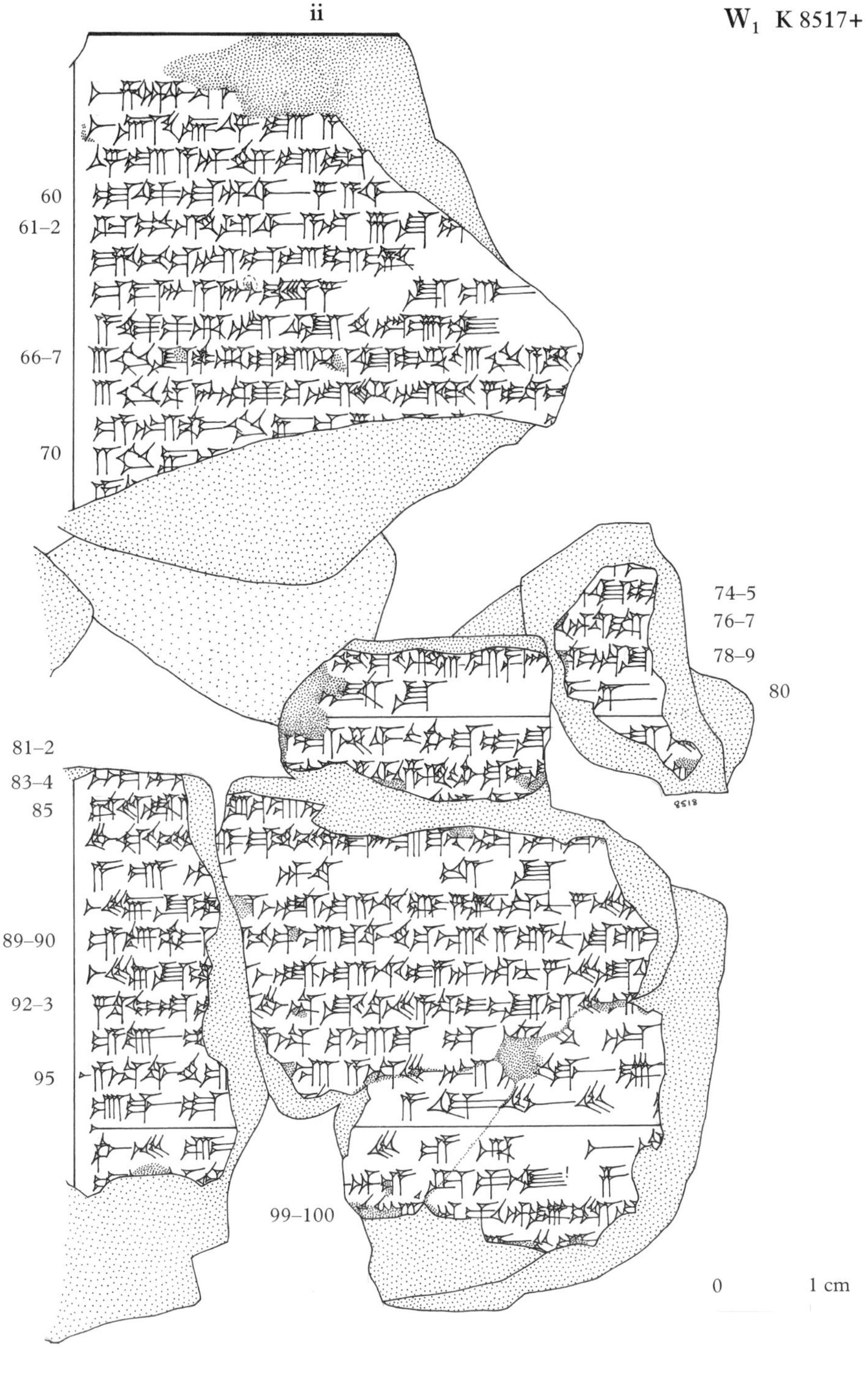

133. SB Tablet XI. MS W col. ii

W_1 K 8517+ vi

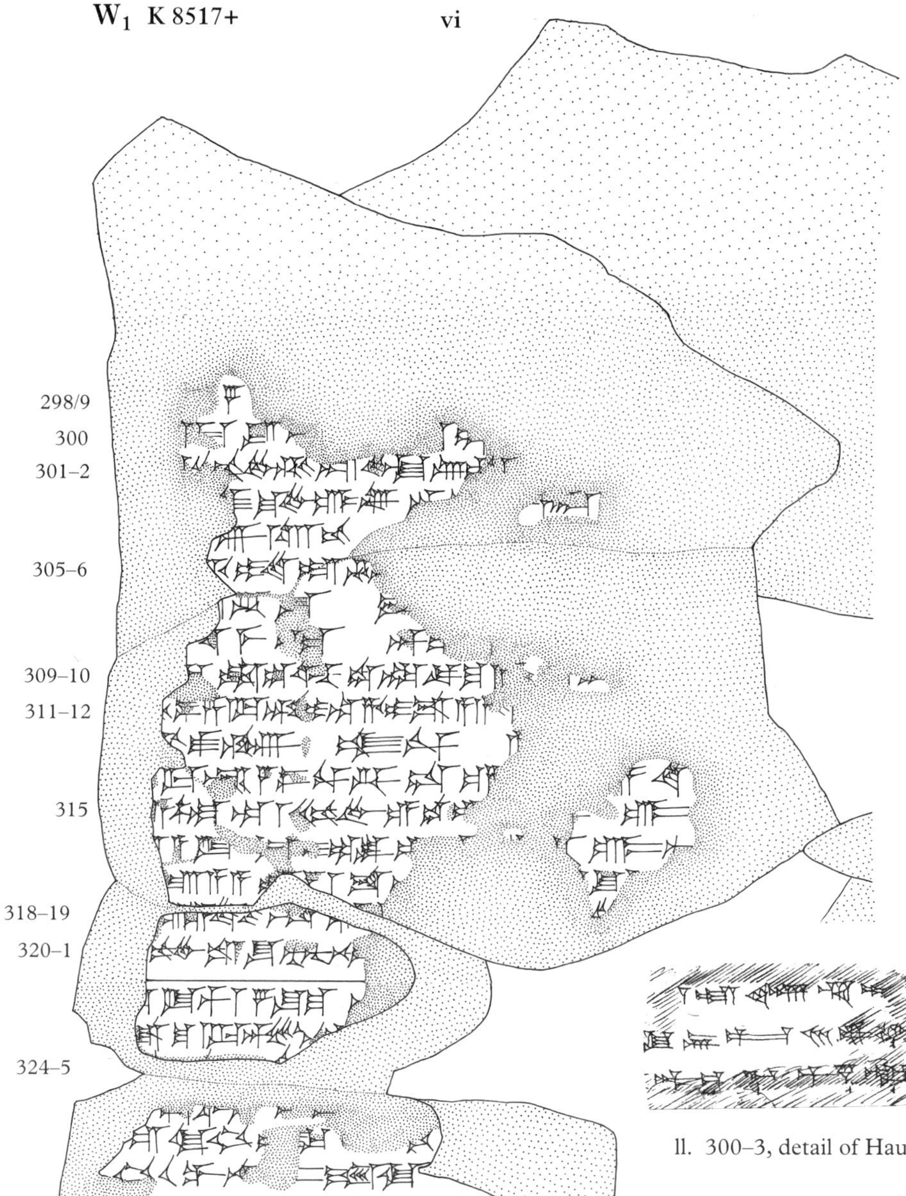

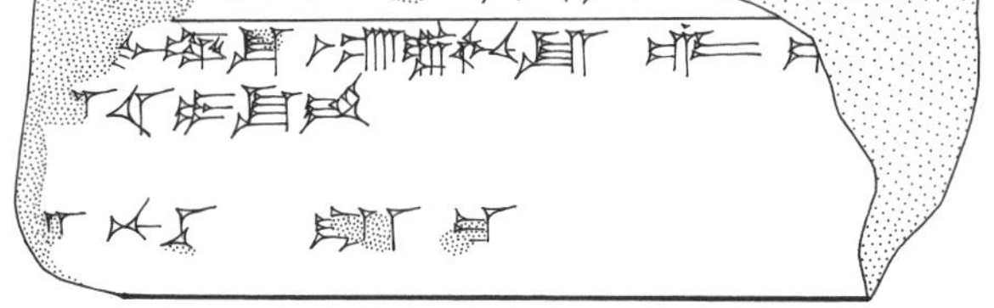

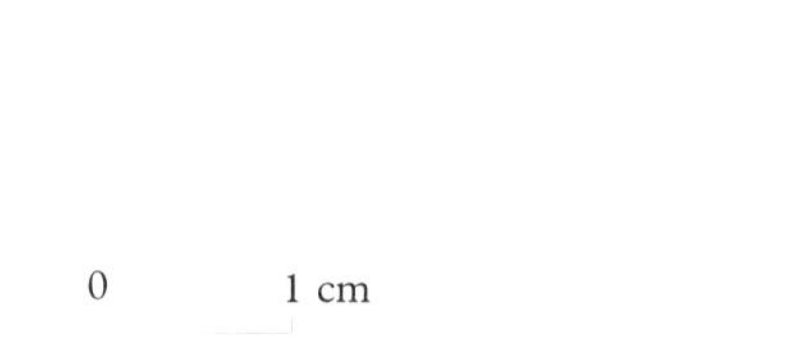

ll. 300–3, detail of Haupt's copy

0 1 cm

134. SB Tablet XI. MS W col. vi, collation from Haupt, *Nimrodepos*, p.119

v

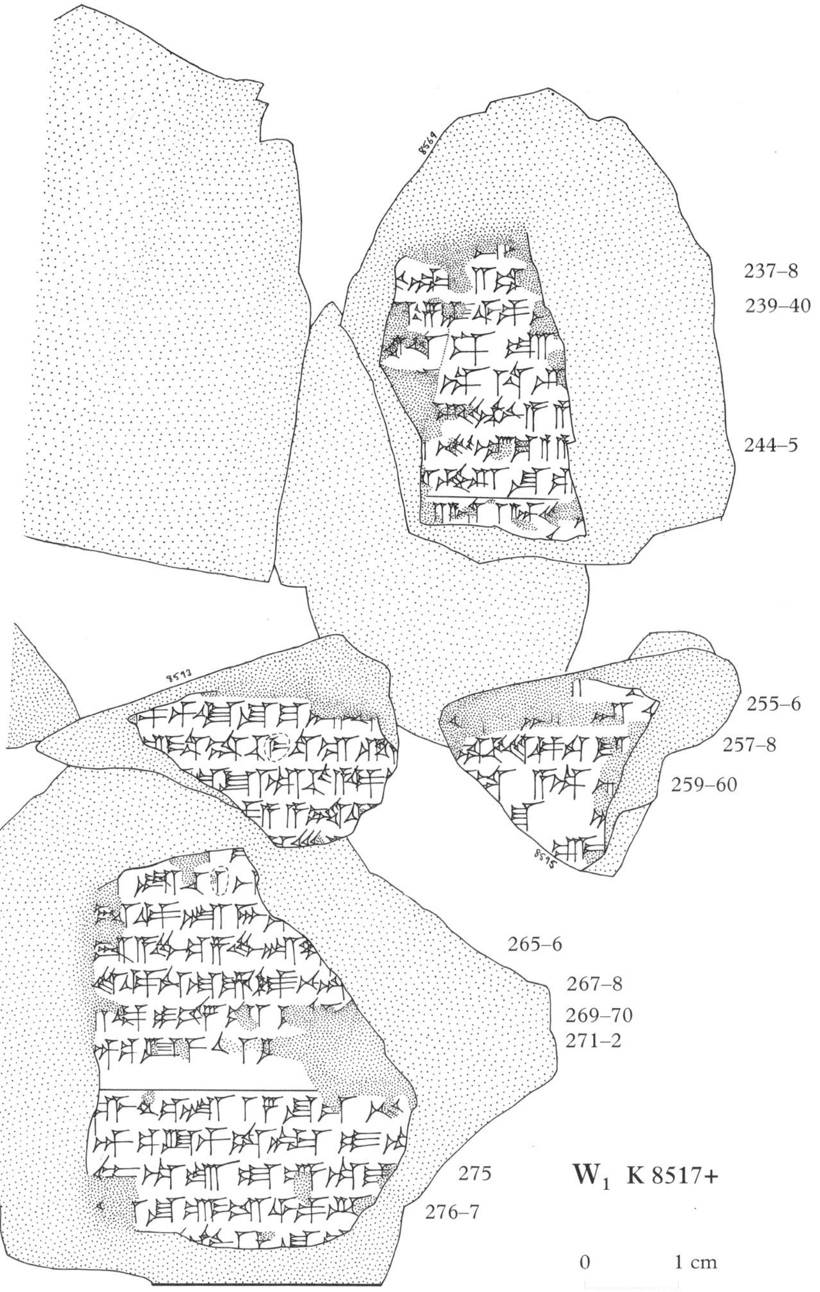

135. SB Tablet XI. MS W col. v

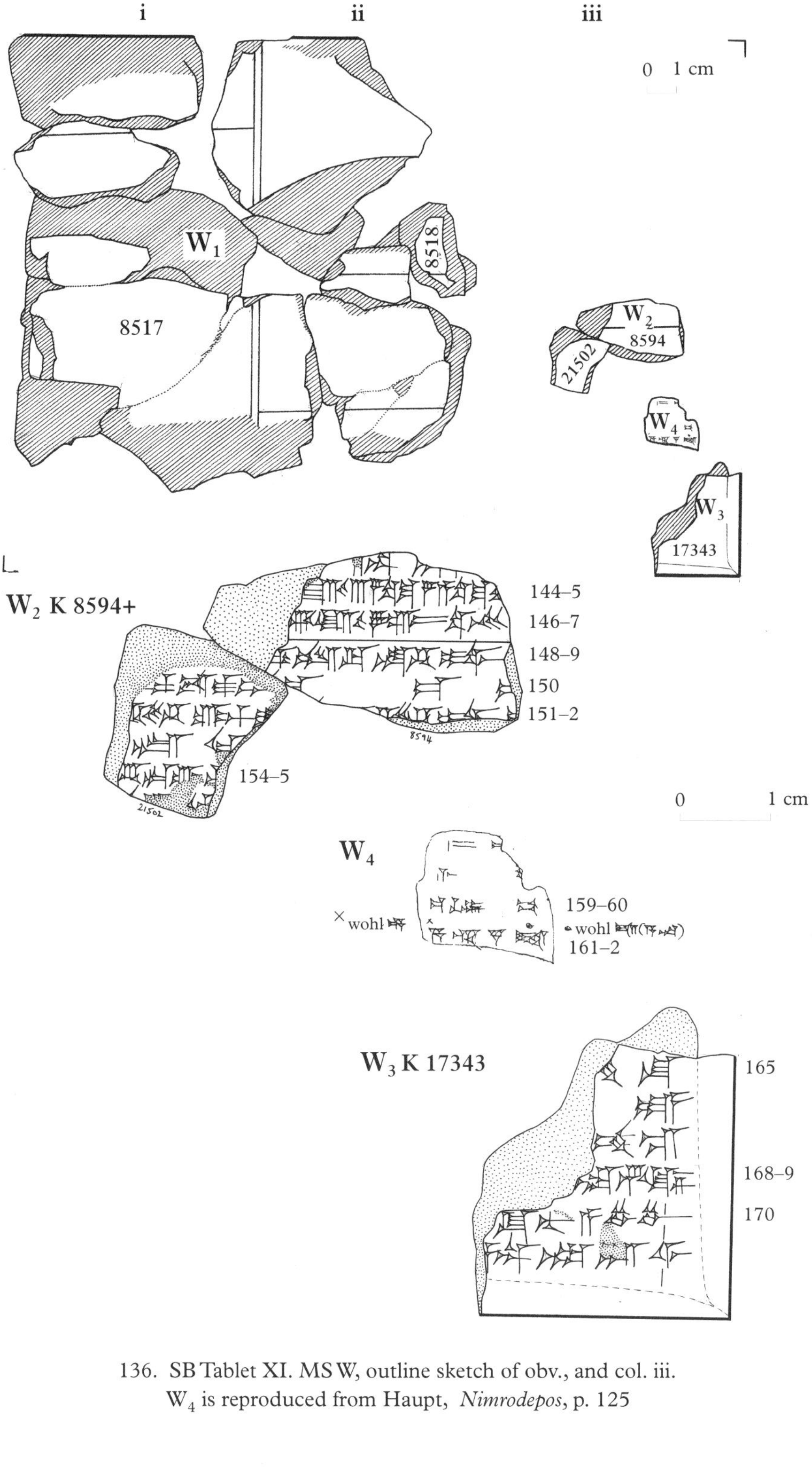

136. SB Tablet XI. MS W, outline sketch of obv., and col. iii.
W_4 is reproduced from Haupt, *Nimrodepos*, p. 125

b **VAT 10586**

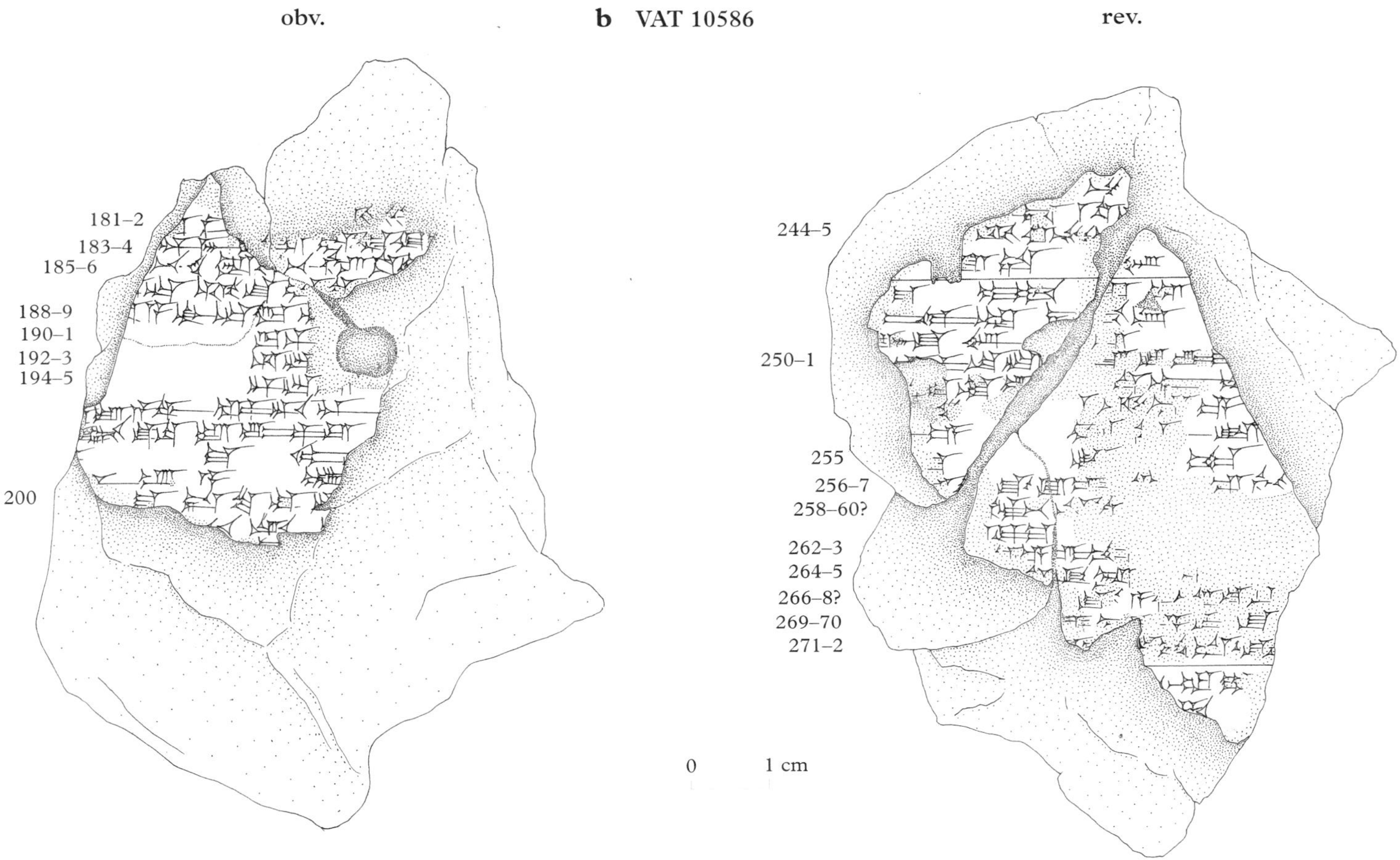

137. SB Tablet XI. MS **b**. Copy by S. M. Maul

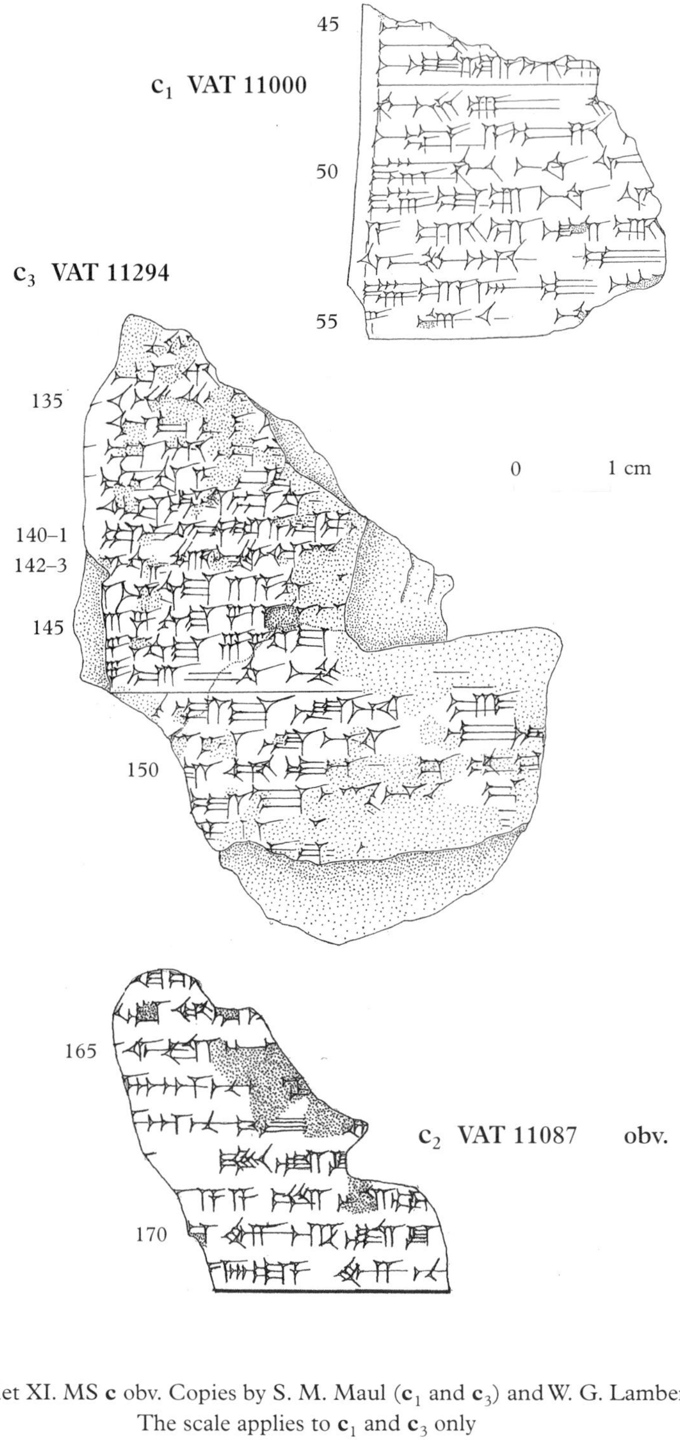

138. SB Tablet XI. MS **c** obv. Copies by S. M. Maul (**c**$_1$ and **c**$_3$) and W. G. Lambert (**c**$_2$). The scale applies to **c**$_1$ and **c**$_3$ only

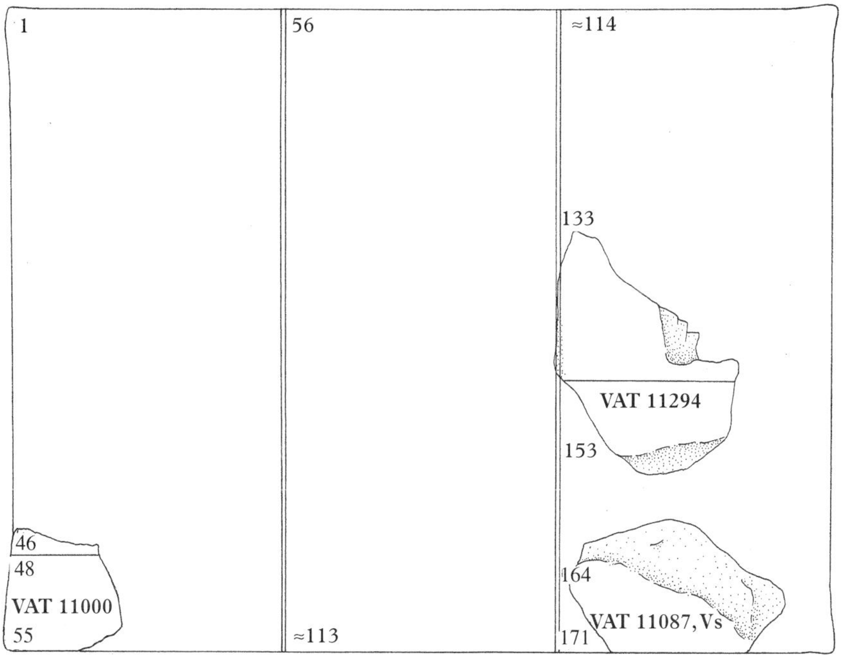

c_2 VAT 11087 rev.

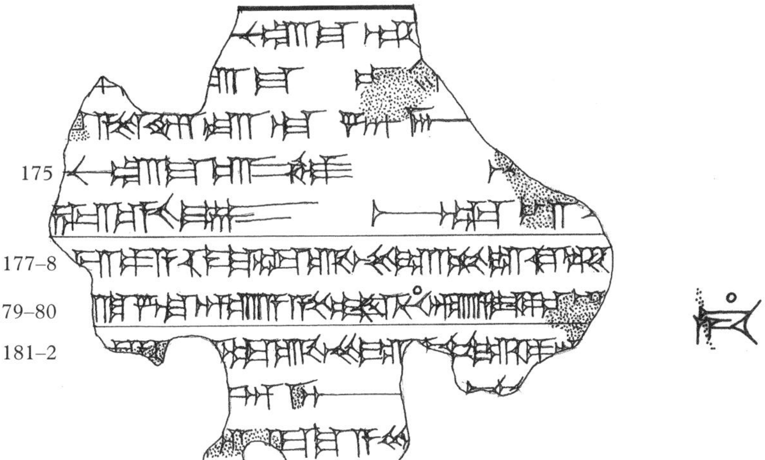

139. SB Tablet XI. MS **c**. Outline sketch of obv. by S. M. Maul, copy of $\mathbf{c}_2$ rev. by W. G. Lambert, collation by the author

j **BM 35380** obv.

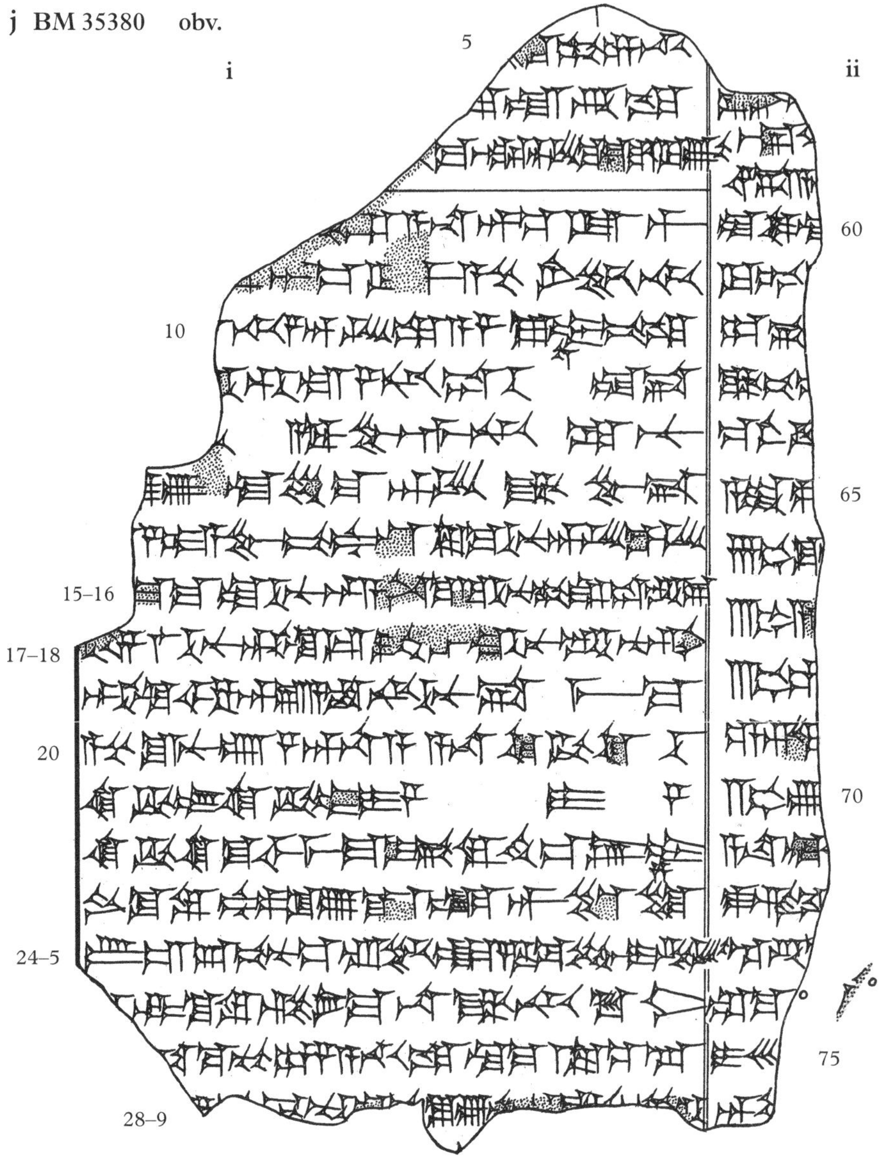

140. SB Tablet XI. MS j obv. Copy by W. G. Lambert, collation by the author

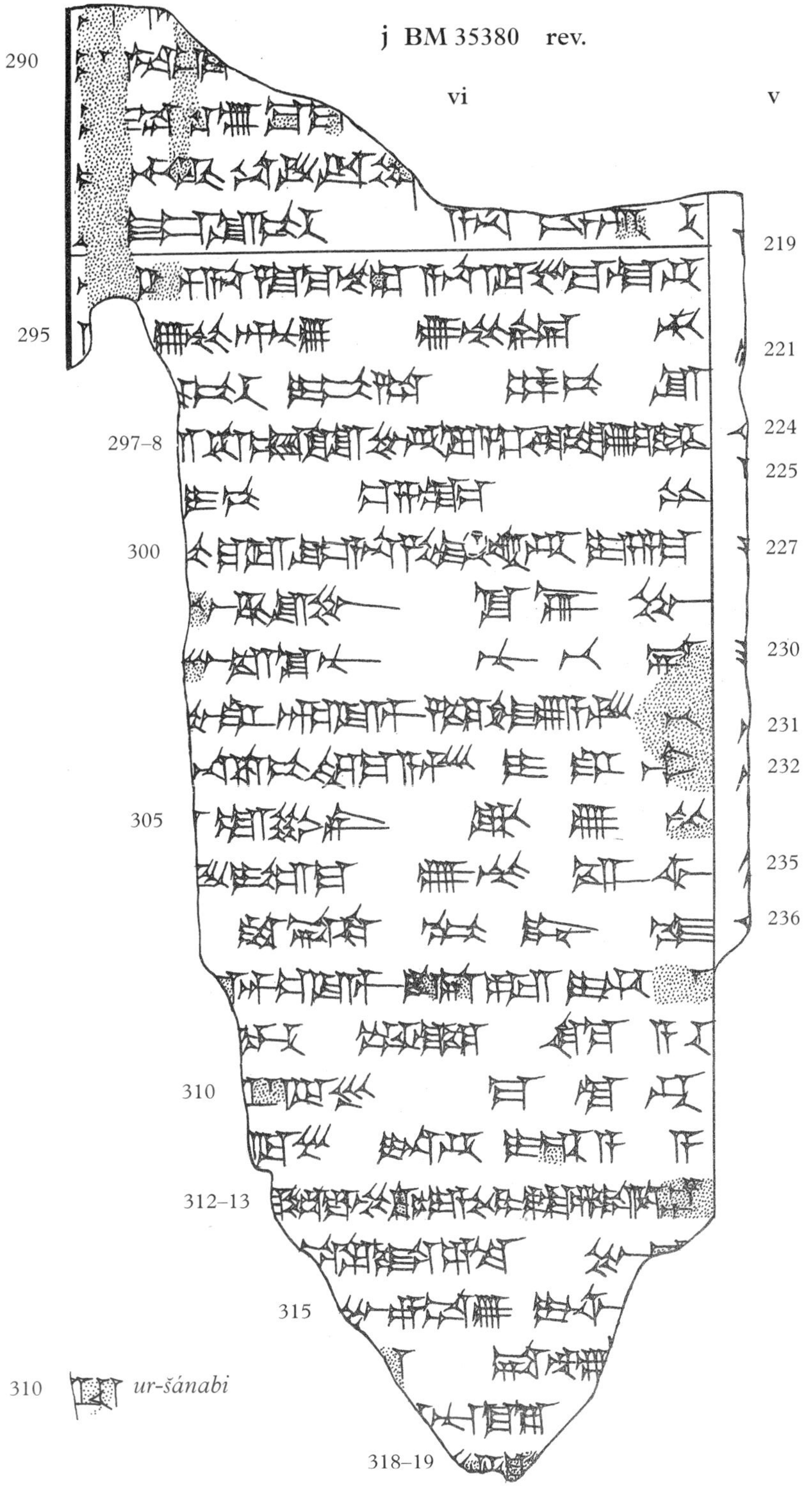

141. SB Tablet XI. MS j rev. Copy by W. G. Lambert, collation by the author

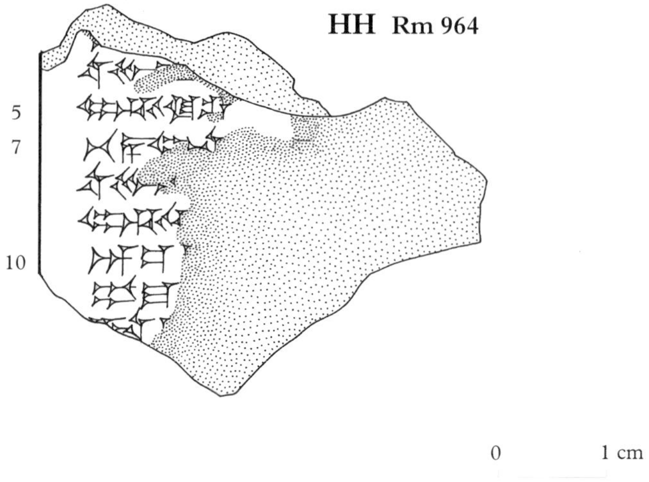

G$_1$ K 2774 i

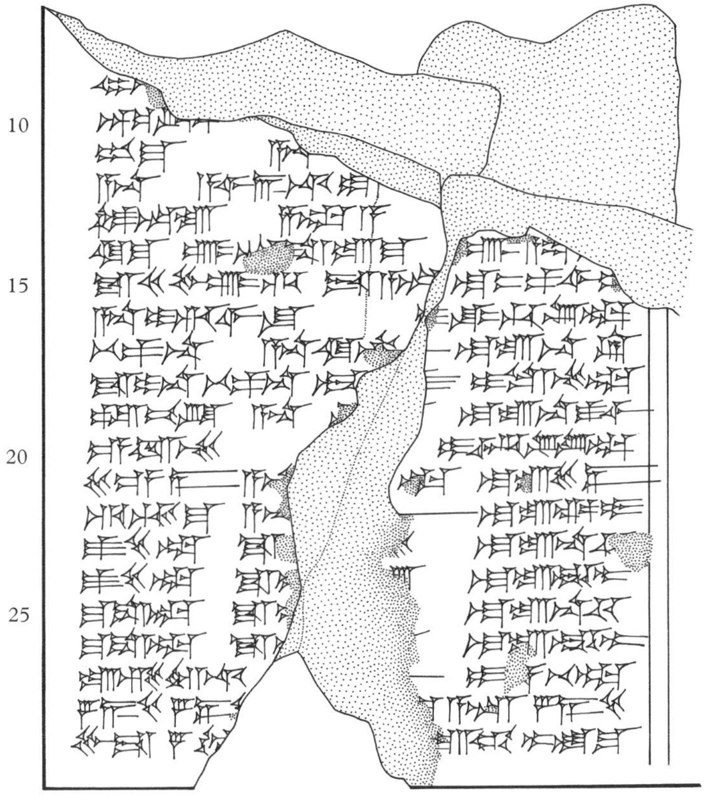

142. SB Tablet XII. MSS HH and G col. i

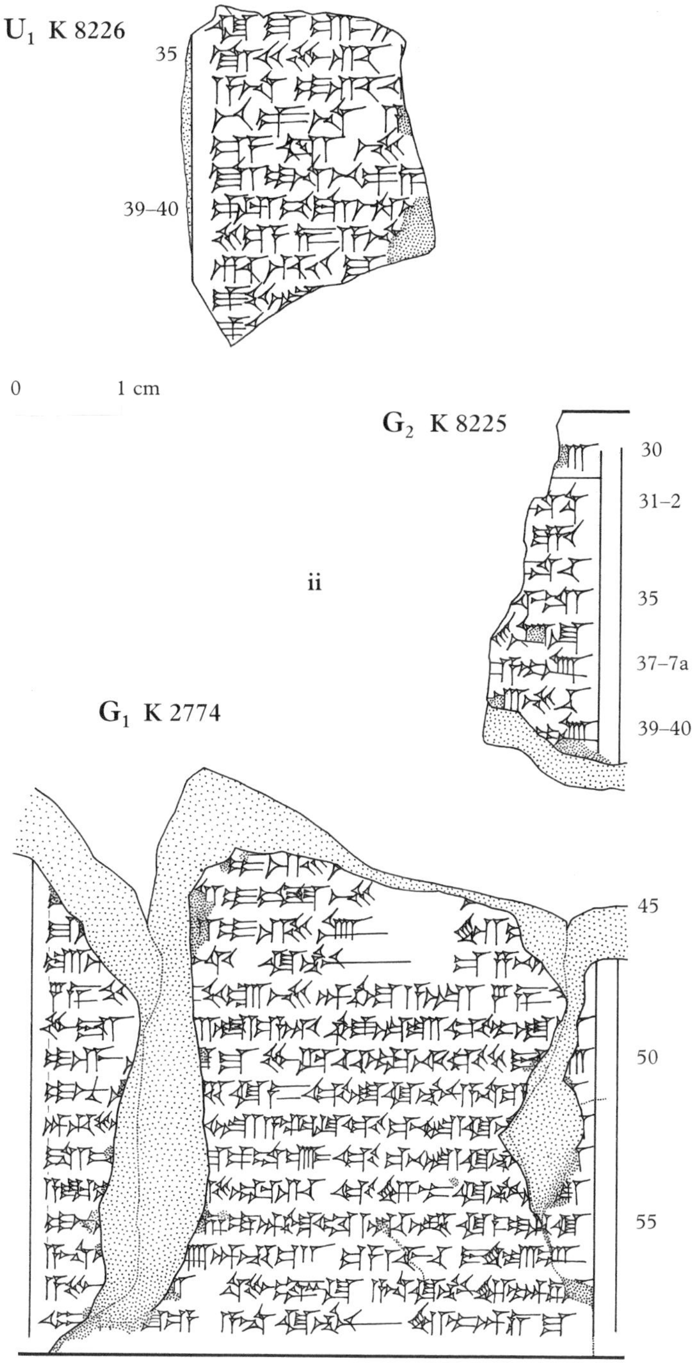

143. SB Tablet XII. MSS U and G col. ii

KK BM 135909

obv.

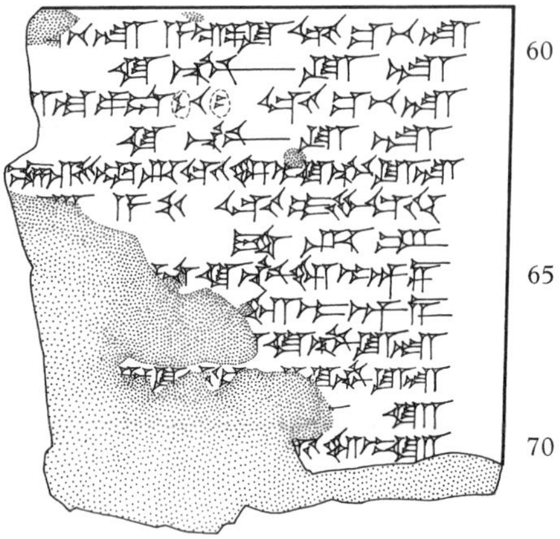

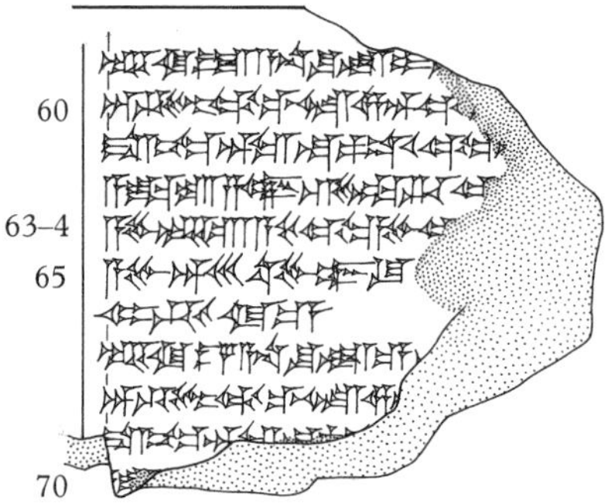

G₂ K 8225

iii

G₁ K 2774

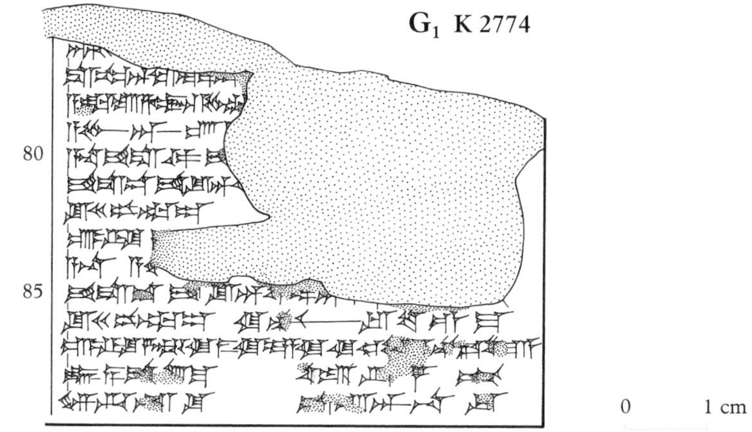

144. SB Tablet XII. MSS KK and G col. iii

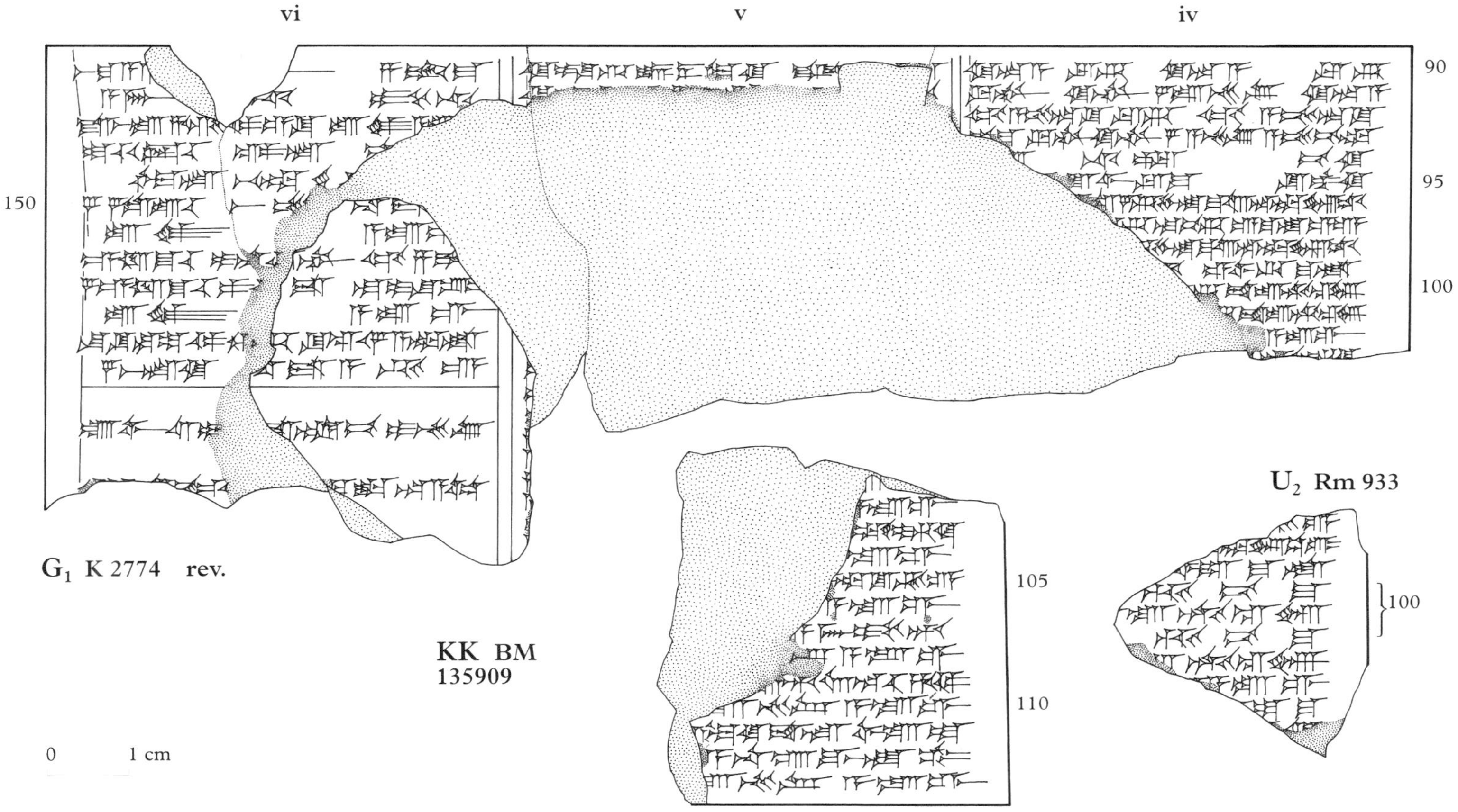

145. SB XII. MSS G, U and KK rev.

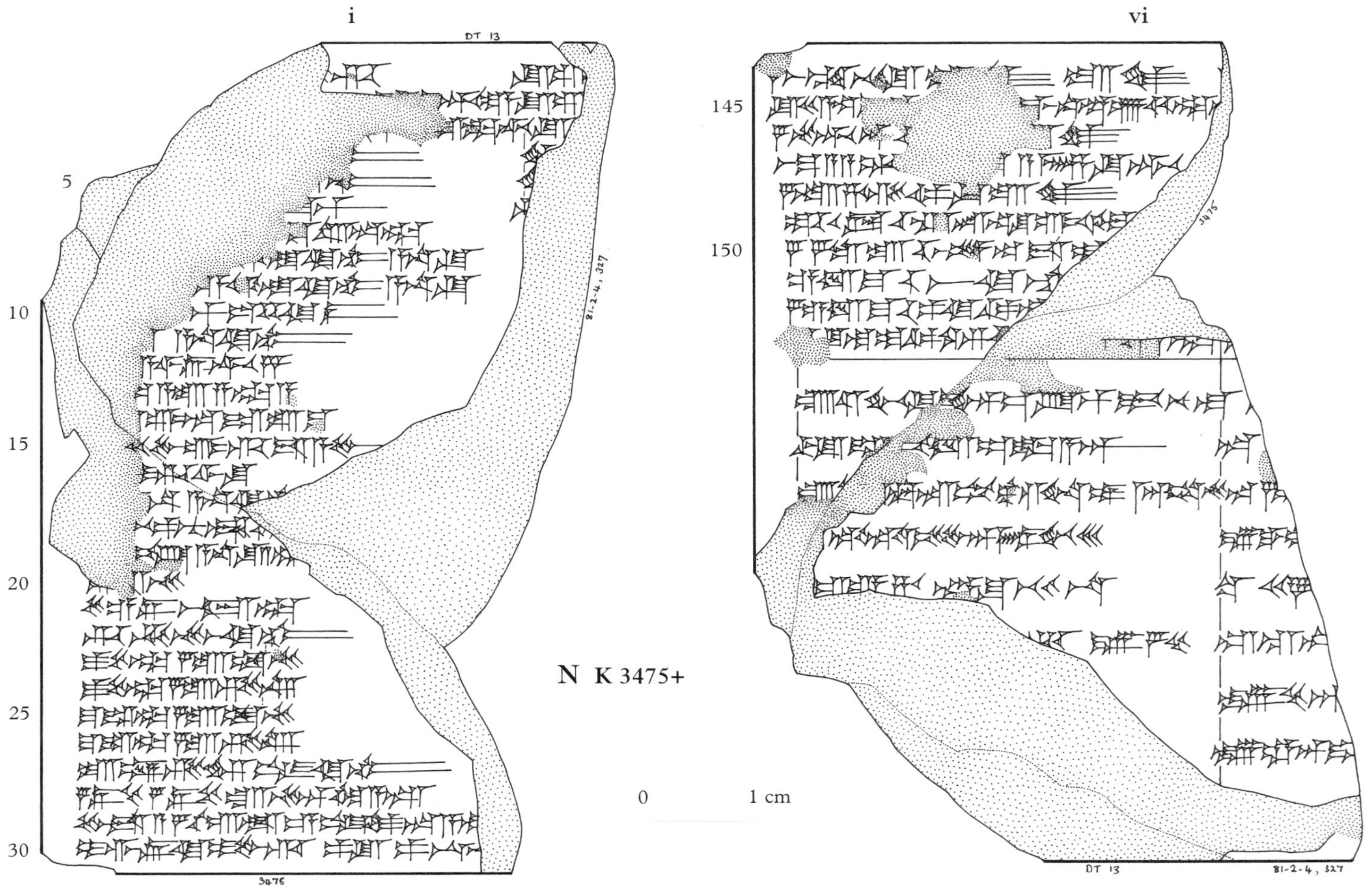

146. SB Tablet XII. MS N

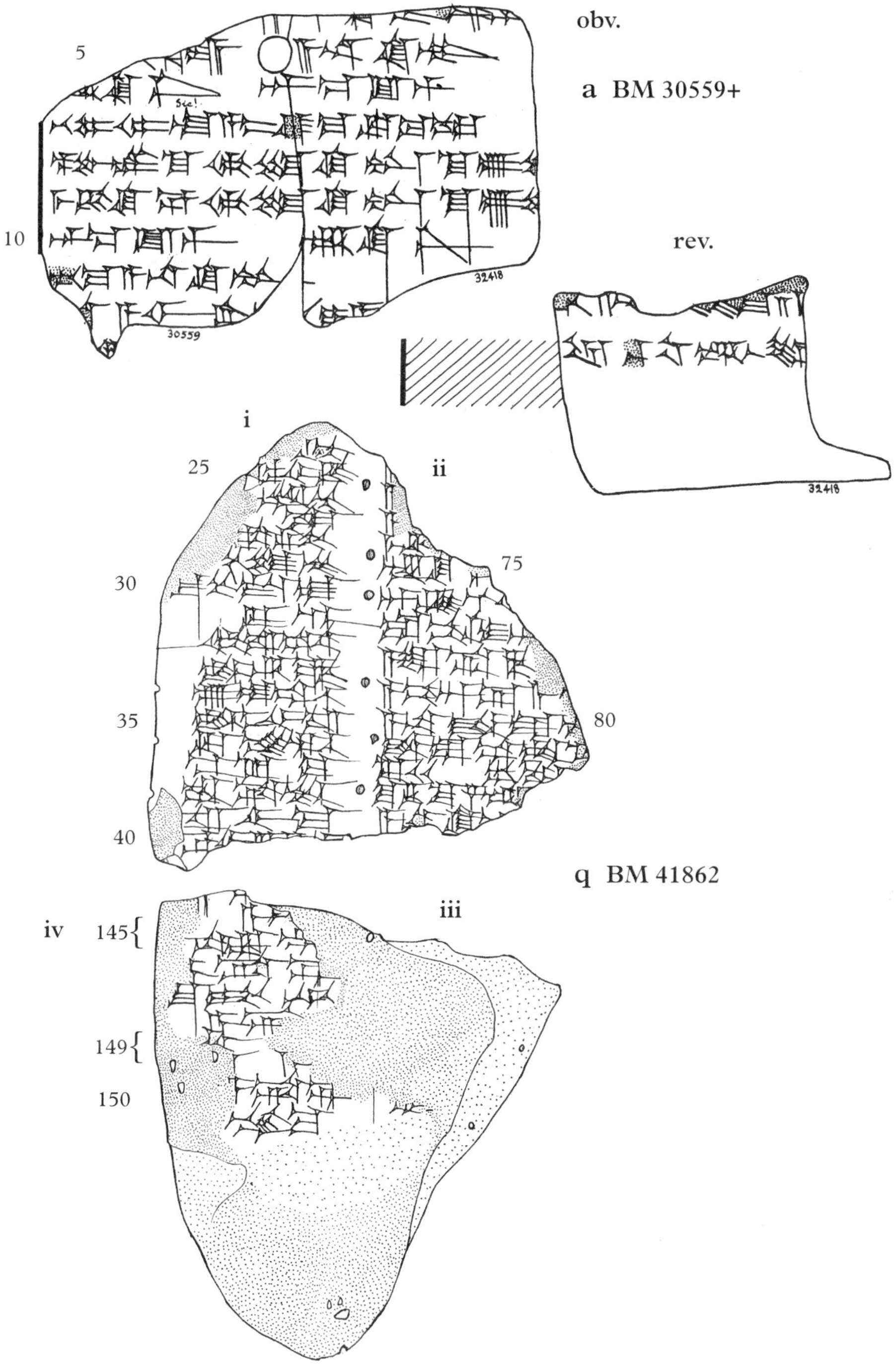

147. SB Tablet XII. MSS a and q. Copies by W. G. Lambert (a) and I. L. Finkel (q)